THE PEOPLE'S HOME?

Studies in Urban and Social Change

Published by Blackwell in association with the *International Journal of Urban and Regional Research*. Series editors: Chris Pickvance, Margit Mayer and John Walton

Published

Forthcoming

THE PEOPLE'S HOME?

SOCIAL RENTED HOUSING IN EUROPE & AMERICA

Michael Harloe

BLACKWELL
Oxford UK & Cambridge USA

First published 1995

Blackwell Publishers, the publishing imprint of
Basil Blackwell Ltd
108 Cowley Road
Oxford OX4 1JF
UK

Basil Blackwell Inc.
238 Main Street
Cambridge, Massachusetts 02142
USA

British Library Cataloguing-in-Publication Data

A CIP catalogue record for this book is available from the British Library.

Library of Congress Cataloging-in-Publication Data

Harloe, Michael.
    The people's home? : social rented housing in Europe and America / Michael Harloe
      p. cm. – (Studies in urban and social change)
    Includes bibliographical references and index.
    ISBN 0–631–18182–2. – ISBN 0–631–18642–5
    1. Public housing–Europe–History. 2. Public housing–United States–History.
  3. Housing policy–Europe–History. 4. Housing policy–United States–History.
  5. Rental housing–Government policy–Europe–History. 6. Rental housing–
Government policy–United States–History. I. Title. II. Series.
HD7288.78.E85H37   1995
363.5'85'094–dc20   94–15837
                                                                CIP

Typeset in 10½ on 12 pt Baskerville by Apex Products, Singapore

This book is printed on acid-free paper

Contents

Preface

As explained in the Introduction, this book has been many years in the making. The number of those who have assisted runs into three figures. They have all contributed to my knowledge of social housing in six countries. None can be blamed for the use which I have made of this knowledge.

My early work on social rented housing was carried out in conjunction with my former colleague at the University of Essex, Maartje Martens (now at the University of Utrecht). It was part of a larger programme of collaborative research on housing in Europe and America, beginning at the start of the 1980s, which also involved Michael Ball (now at South Bank University, London). Jointly and separately the three of us have published the results of this work – on housing and social theory, home ownership, private and social rented housing, housing finance and housing construction – in a series of books and articles over the past decade. This book is one of the last, delayed products of our joint endeavours. Working alongside and arguing with Mike and Maartje has been a productive and intellectually stimulating experience, for which I thank them.

A second debt of gratitude is owed to five people who each worked as consultants, sometimes on more than one occasion, during the course of the research projects on which this book is based. They are Christian Topalov (France), Eberhard Muhlich

(Germany), Hedvig Vestergaard (Denmark), Jan van der Schaar (Netherlands) and Peter Marcuse (USA). Not only did they respond without protest to my endless demands for information but, as leading students of housing in their own countries, their analytical insights also benefited me enormously.

Work of this nature, extending over many years and involving extensive periods spent in each country, interviewing, making documentary searches and working with my consultant colleagues, would not have been possible without major financial support. At one time or another almost all the major sources of social science funding in the UK have given assistance for individual projects. These have resulted in the series of publications noted above as well as this volume. I acknowledge with gratitude the support of the Leverhulme Foundation, the Economic and Social Research Council (formerly the SSRC), the Joseph Rowntree Foundation, the Anglo-German Foundation, the Nuffield Foundation and the Fuller Memorial Fund of the Department of Sociology at the University of Essex. I am also grateful to the Urban Research Program in the Research School of Social Sciences, Australian National University, Canberra, and its Director Professor Pat Troy, for enabling me to spend time there in 1991, as a Visiting Fellow, working on this book. Thanks are also due to Chris Paris (formerly at the University of Canberra, now at Magee College, University of Ulster) for encouraging and assisting me to spend some time at the ANU.

Finally, thanks are due to the many librarians and libraries that have helped me during the course of this work. In particular, I have benefited from the use of my own institution's library and from several periods spent in the Avery Library at Columbia University, as well as numerous electronic visits to the catalogue of the University of California.

It is customary for authors to devote a few words to thanking their spouse, children and secretaries for their support. However, typing this book is one of the few chores that I have not inflicted on my Department's secretaries in recent years. And mere words cannot convey what my wife and family have contributed to my life, although they might be able to contribute some frank remarks about what this book, and its author, have done to them!

Michael Harloe
Colchester

Introduction: Social Housing and Welfare Capitalism

The title of this book – *The People's Home* – appropriates a word – *folkhemmet* – frequently used to characterize the distinctive approach adopted by the Swedish Social Democratic Party to the building of what was seen for many years as the most developed form of welfare capitalist regime in the world. It was first used in 1928 by one of the key figures of Swedish Social Democracy, later Prime Minister, Per Albin Hansson.[1] *Folkhemmet* was a vision of a society with social, economic and political citizenship for all. Social citizenship would be based on the universalistic provision of social services in a decommodified form, that is, on the basis of need, not ability to pay. Such a regime, as Esping-Andersen has pointed out, differs sharply from varieties of welfare capitalism based on conservative ideologies, which seek to preserve and strengthen the divisions of class, status and power arising from the capitalist organization of the economy and society. It also differs from the liberal reform model, which seeks to temper the consequences of capitalism by redistributing some of its output, without challenging the system in any more fundamental way. In contrast, what Hansson and his colleagues had in mind was a welfare regime in which 'social policy became pivotal for the general plan to transform capitalism' (Esping-Andersen, 1987a: 83).

In fact, Swedish social democracy failed to bring about the transformation in its economic system envisaged by the doctrine of *folkhemmet.* [2] However, although Hansson's radical, transformative purpose was not realized, large parts of the Swedish dream home were constructed during the post-war years. [3] In *The Three Worlds of Welfare Capitalism* (1990), Esping-Andersen assembles various statistical indicators to describe the nature of the welfare regimes in 18 advanced capitalist countries. Sweden is notable for having one of the lowest levels of means-tested poor relief (as a proportion of all public social expenditure) and of expenditure on private pensions and health care. It also has one of the highest levels of universality in state benefits for sickness, unemployment and retirement and of the lowest differentials between the maximum and minimum payments provided under these schemes.

Ironically, however, even the Swedish People's Home never fully accommodated and made decommodified provision for one of the most basic of human and social needs – shelter. [4] In a recent analysis, Lundqvist (1992) has examined why 'the peoples' home [became] too expensive for the welfare state', and why, by the 1990s, public involvement in housing was shifting 'from the comprehensive and general to the supplementary and specific' (see also Lundqvist et al., 1990; Elander and Strömberg, 1992). More generally, as Torgerson (1987) vividly remarks, housing has been the 'wobbly pillar under the welfare state' in many countries. The question mark in the title of this book is a perhaps over-economical way of indicating that the history of social rented housing provides evidence for this conclusion. As well as examining some of the evidence, this work seeks to understand why housing, through programmes of social rented housing in particular, has not taken a place alongside other significantly decommodified aspects of social provision, such as health, education and income maintenance, as one of the central pillars of the welfare state. Instead, it has retained an ambiguous and shifting status on the margins of the welfare state, the least decommodified and the most market-determined of the conventionally accepted constituent elements of such states. In some English translations *folkhemmet* becomes 'the house for all the people'. This book explains why social housing has always fallen short of this ideal.

In discussing 'the institutional peculiarity of housing as a welfare state component', Torgerson (1987) points out that the three major domains of welfare capitalist regimes – pensions, schooling and health – have some common characteristics. These include a system and organization of provision which is under state control or regulation, with a universalistic remit to provide for eligible and needy members of the population, and which stands apart from the institutions, operational rationale and allocative rules of the private market. As Torgerson notes, 'in all these respects the domain of housing stands out like a sore thumb'.

In accounting for these differences, Torgerson refers to the permanency of the possession of housing once it has been acquired, which, he contends, means that 'housing as a commodity or good is very different from other goods' (i.e. health care, education and income maintenance). This seems a rather unconvincing explanation of why 'housing stands out like a sore thumb'. However, the suggestion that housing, *as a commodity*, differs from health, education and pensions merits closer inspection. This is because the private market provision of housing for the mass of the population as a capitalist commodity, and the system of private property ownership on which this provision rests, has been a core element in the capitalist organization of society and the economy from the earliest years. Historically, industrial, property and financial capital have been the motive forces driving the system. The production of housing as a commodity involves all these forms of capital. Thus anything more than a limited and partial decommodification of housing is likely to provoke intense resistance. In contrast, although the penetration of capitalist relations into mass provision for pensions, health and education has been significant, especially in recent decades (and for far longer in certain countries), historically, for large sections of the population, the alternative to provision through the welfare state was very little provision at all, rather than commodified provision. In short, housing, like food production, has provided large-scale and profitable opportunities for capitalism in ways that have not been nearly so evident (or took longer to develop) in the other spheres of provision for human needs that we have been discussing.

Even more abstractly, one can suggest that in capitalist societies there tends to be an inverse relationship between the degree to which there are major opportunities for private accumulation in various aspects of human needs provision, and the extent to which such provision may, in certain historical conjunctures, be wholly or partly decommodified. This book, which examines the development of social rented housing in six countries – Britain, (the former West) Germany, France, the Netherlands, Denmark and the United States – provides evidence to support such a proposition. Housing, *just because it is a capitalist commodity* which, in normal times, can be profitably provided to the majority of the population, has never been likely to become as decommodified a form of provision as those other forms for which there has been far less solvable demand (although, in the current era, these services are increasingly being commodified or 'marketized' in various ways).

When viewed from this perspective, the interesting question, which this book explores, does not concern why housing has been such a marginal component of the welfare state but rather why it has sometimes been provided through the agency of the state in a partially decommodified form. More specifically, the examination will centre not on the ways in which the state has supported market forms of housing provision, either private renting or home ownership, but when, how and why the state's housing activities have been directed towards supplanting or making good a lack of these market forms through programmes of social rented housing.[5]

The analysis presented in this book is the end point of an endeavour to understand the nature of housing in capitalist societies which began in the 1970s. An early study with colleagues, *The Organization of Housing. Public and private enterprise in London* (Harloe, Issacharoff and Minns, 1974), concluded that the housing system was disorganized, characterized by competing agencies and contradictory demands and objectives. Conventional social policy analysis, which assumed that there was a fairly direct relationship in welfare state regimes between the existence of housing needs and state policies which responded to them, could provide no satisfactory answer to this problem. By the mid-1970s neo-Marxist analyses were pointing to the necessarily contradictory nature of state urban and social policies in capitalist societies (see, for example, Castells, 1978; Ginsburg, 1979; Gough, 1979). However, while such theories moved the analysis on to an altogether more fruitful level, they also proved defective. In particular, as critics noted, the observation that housing and other urban policies had a certain functionality for capitalism left unanswered why this should be so and how it came about (Harloe, 1979).

In two papers published at the beginning of the 1980s (one with my colleague Maartje Martens), I attempted to develop a more satisfactory meta-theoretical framework for the analysis of housing markets and policies than those adopted by conventional social policy analysts or much of the neo-Marxist work then current, and to sketch out an empirically grounded theorization of the historically varying forms of housing provision in the six countries discussed in this book (Harloe, 1981; Harloe and Martens, 1984). Subsequently, working in collaboration with Michael Ball, who had developed his own critique of conventional neo-classical urban and housing economics, we argued that the changing nature of housing provision can most usefully be conceived in terms of changes in distinctively constituted 'structures of housing provision' (Ball, 1986; Ball, Harloe and Martens, 1988; Ball and Harloe, 1992). Very simply, this recognizes that housing provision is a social construct, that 'there are combinations of social agents involved in housing provision that relate to each other in empirically observable ways' (Ball and Harloe, 1992: 3). Moreover, structures of housing provision are embedded in the wider economic, social and political structures of society. Therefore, any narrowly conceived examination of the agents and social relationships implicated in housing provision and its development only leads to some equally narrow and misleading answers to the 'when, how and why' questions mentioned above. Any account of social housing development which just focuses on the responses of governments and social housing landlords to consumer demands and needs may have a certain descriptive value. However, as this study demonstrates, there are many other agents and sets of social relationships which have helped to determine the history of this form of housing provision. In fact, this approach to the analysis of social housing is merely one example of the more general observation made by Esping-Andersen (1987b: 6), that 'social policy must be viewed as integral to the social and economic order'. This requires 'institutional analyses that analytically situate social policy in relation to its reciprocal political and economic institutions'.

The general concept of a structure of housing provision, it is worth underlining, is meta-theoretic in nature. It is merely a means to an end – the production of theories of housing development, that is, causally based explanations of when, how and why certain developments do or do not occur. The principal objective of this book is to provide just such a theory of the development of social rented housing in a selection of advanced capitalist countries. As already mentioned, a first attempt to do this was published in the early 1980s (Harloe, 1981). This paper, on the 'recommodification of housing', combined some fairly elementary, largely deductive propositions about the class-divided nature of production and consumption in capitalist societies with some of the early results of research in Western Europe and the USA. The general conclusion was that housing provision in these societies had evolved, under the impact of major changes in social, economic and political structures and relationships, through three stages. Under conditions of early capitalist industrialization and urbanization most housing had been provided as a commodity by private landlords. However, for reasons described briefly in this paper, and subsequently analysed in greater depth in Harloe (1985), this form of provision was in long-term decline, especially in the second half of the twentieth century. For ever larger proportions of the population it was being replaced by a separate commodified form of provision, the mass market in home ownership.[6] The third, relatively decommodified form of large-scale provision, social rented housing, was seen as the product of a relatively brief period, notably the years after the Second World War, when the private rental market's inability to provide mass housing was already well advanced (and made worse by the effects of war), but when the necessary economic and other conditions for the growth of mass home ownership were still absent from most of the societies in question. Therefore, the recommodification referred to in the title of the paper denoted both the long-term transition from one form of capitalist housing commodity to another and the more recent displacement of the relatively decommodified form, social rented housing, by the new commodity form, mass home ownership.

There is much that still seems valid in this analysis of capitalist housing provision, its historical transformations and the reasons for the varying fortunes of social rented housing. Most importantly, I have found no reason to reject the paper's proposition that housing will normally be provided in capitalist societies in commodified rather than decommodified forms and that it is only when adequate provision in commodified form is not possible (even with state support) *and* when this situation has some broader significance for the dominant social and economic order, that recourse is made to large-scale, partially decommodified, state-subsidized and politically controlled mass social rented housing (the significance of the reference to 'mass' social housing will be discussed below). The 1981 paper also referred to other aspects of the history of social rented housing which will be considered in detail in these pages, such as the link between mass programmes of social rented housing and economic reconstruction and modernization after the Second World War, the strategic 'targeting' of these programmes on economically and politically significant sections of the population and the failure of social democracy to develop and sustain any radical alternative to the limited forms of decommodified housing which did develop, or to resist their eventual effacement by the new form of commodified mass provision, home ownership.

However, this book describes a more complex history which requires a more developed analysis. First, there has not been one but three broadly defined structures of social housing provision. These I have labelled as the 'residual', 'mass' and 'workers' cooperative' models.[7] They first emerged as ideas and in practice in housing reform discourse, early legislation and pioneering projects in the years around the First World War. For reasons discussed in the book, the workers' cooperative model, which in many cases involved a radical attempt to replace commodified forms of housing provision by a decommodified alternative, was later repressed or absorbed within the structures and practices of state-regulated and financed mass social housing. Consequently, the history of social rented housing divides into several distinctive stages, when one or other of the mass and residualized forms of provision was dominant. Of course, such periodizations offer a clear but oversimplified chronology of transitions in housing systems. These actually take place over many years, with varied national patterns and time-scales. Nevertheless, this study concludes that four periods of unequal length can be identified. In two, a short period after the First World War and a much longer period after the Second World War, the mass model prevailed. In the other two periods, the later 1920s and 1930s and the years since the mid-1970s, the residual model has been dominant. However, this chronology applies only to the five European countries listed earlier. The history of public housing in America has been that of a residualized form of provision for all but the earliest years of its existence.[8]

A further conclusion, developed in this work and missing from the earlier paper, is that, from the interwar period onwards, the residual form of provision has been incorporated within welfare capitalist regimes on a more or less permanent basis. In other words, this is the normal form of social rented housing provision in 'normal' times. The mass model, which cuts across private market provision more significantly than the residual form, gains major significance and state support only in 'abnormal' times, that is, when varying combinations of social, economic and political circumstances limit the scope for private provision *and* when this limitation is of strategic significance for certain aspects of the maintenance and development of the capitalist social and economic system.

The core of the book is structured around these four phases of social housing development, exploring how and why each model became dominant, and was later supplanted, describing and analysing the major social, economic and political dimensions of the two models (plus the third more vestigial workers' cooperative model), providing the empirical evidence for the theory of social rented housing in the welfare capitalist regimes outlined in this Introduction.

Finally, the earlier paper made only very limited references to the changing social, economic and political context to social housing development. This book pays far more attention to relating social housing to changes in what have been called the social structures of accumulation. As Block (1987: 23) explains, this concept refers to the fact that 'each period of capitalist expansion creates a particular set of social arrangements to sustain the dynamics of capitalist accumulation. Particular configurations of urban growth, particular types of financial and governmental mechanisms for structuring demand, and specific ways of organising the relations between workers and employers are constitutive of each phase of capitalist expansion' (for a broadly similar approach see Gourevitch, 1986). Block adds that social structures of accumulation are always time-limited in their effectiveness, there is a process of growth and decay. Eventually, normally after 'dramatic political-economic deterioration ... forces are mobilized to establish new social structures of accumulation' (Block 1987: 23).

As we shall see, each of the four stages of social housing development examined in this book occurred at different stages in the emergence, growth and decline of three identifiable social structures of accumulation. The first was liberal capitalism, the initial form created by the Industrial Revolution which reached its peak in the late nineteenth century. Its dissolution was hastened by the First World War and, despite a concerted attempt to revive the system after 1918, the events of 1929–32 marked its death-knell. The second welfare capitalist (or, as some prefer, Fordist) structure of accumulation began to emerge in the interwar period (earlier in some respects in America than in Europe), came to dominance in the years after 1945 but, from the 1960s, became increasingly unstable and conflict-ridden.[9] The final phase of this regime occurred in the years after the mid-1970s recession. The consequences of its breakdown, in terms of economic instability, industrial and labour market restructuring, political realignments and new patterns of social stratification and social divisions, are still being worked through. How to describe and analyse the emergent social structure of accumulation, and even how to label it, is uncertain. Current attempts are shaped by the varied theoretical perspectives and specific concerns of those who seek to analyse this new era.[10]

In each of these periods the role of the state in relation to the market and civil society has differed. While there were also differences between nations during each period, there have been some broad cross-national similarities. These are well recognized: the growth of state regulation of parts of civil society and the economy under liberal capitalism – but within narrow boundaries; the assumption by the state of far wider responsibilities for steering the economy and shaping civil society (especially through social policies) in the welfare capitalist era; the abandonment of many of these commitments over the past two decades, together with the adoption of a new set of social and economic priorities.

Chapter 1 discusses how most early proposals and projects for housing reform developed out of a more general, elite-led concern about the 'social question' in the late nineteenth and early twentieth centuries and how these were shaped and constrained by the conception of the role of the state in relation to the market and the political and economic structures of the era. However, it also refers to less well-documented struggles by early working-class organizations to provide their own housing during this phase of liberal capitalist development, in which workers were excluded from many of the social, economic and political rights of citizenship.

Chapter 2 deals with the period immediately after the First World War when there was a struggle for survival by the agencies and institutions of liberal capitalism in the face of a new militancy and new demands from the organized working class and sections of the middle class. This produced the circumstance which led, for a brief period, to the large-scale implementation of programmes of mass social housing in most of the countries with which we are concerned (the reasons why this did not occur in two of them, France and the USA, are also discussed). The chapter also describes how, when the challenge posed by this post-war crisis was defused, the commitment to mass social housing provision was rapidly renounced, to be replaced, if at all, by a much smaller scale of residualized provision, targeted on the urban poor and, especially, on the removal of the urban slum.

However, as chapter 2 describes, while liberal capitalism won the battle, it had already lost the war, a fact which only became evident with the final collapse of the post-1918 attempts to turn the economic clock back to the pre-war era, signalled by the Wall Street crash in 1929 and the onset of the Depression in the early 1930s. However, as this chapter demonstrates, this period of societal crisis did not lead in most cases to a reversion to mass social housing programmes. In simple terms, this was because the existence of mass unmet housing needs in the Depression years had less directly destabilizing significance for capitalist economies and social systems than it had had after 1918. Now, in most cases, unemployment was a far more important consideration and developments in social housing provision frequently derived from this circumstance. Again, America provided a partial exception, although even here it was the employment-generating possibilities of the first ever federally subsidized public housing programme which provided a considerable part of the rationale for its implementation. The links between macro-economic developments and state-provided housing which emerged in some countries in this period may be seen as one of the early indicators of the new relationship between the state and the market, and the implications of this for social policy, that developed after 1945. However, an equally significant harbinger of the new order was the development of mass home-owner markets, suburbanization and new patterns of mass consumption linked to the rise of so-called 'Fordist' industries in the USA in the 1920s and in Britain in the 1930s. In the following post-war era the growth of these new forms of mass consumption, together with the economic and political structures that accompanied them, was to spread to all the countries with which we are concerned.

Chapter 3 describes what has been called the 'golden age' of social housing provision, the period which commenced at the end of the Second World War and came to an end around the middle of the 1970s. In Europe these decades saw the provision of mass social housing on a previously unprecedented scale. Again, the chapter argues, this was linked to the functionality of such provision for wider processes of economic, social and urban development. In America, where the new social structure of accumulation was rapidly established with less difficulty than in Europe, public housing became an ever more residualized form of provision. This change only began to occur, at a varying pace, in Europe as the initial rationale for post-war mass social housing was eroded by the very social and economic developments to which it had earlier contributed.

The onset of the first post-war depression, in the mid-1970s, whose underlying causes had been developing over the past decade or more, came just after the high point in most countries for post-war social housing production (and for the expansion of the welfare state more generally). Chapter 4, which deals with the period from the mid-1970s to the early 1990s, examines how these years of recurrent crisis for the social structures of welfare capitalism deepened and intensified the transition to a renewed version of residual social housing provision and the decline of the mass provision. This seems likely to continue in the 1990s, even though the successive economic crises and the consequences of economic restructuring have seriously impeded the ability of the private market to provide decent and affordable housing to considerable sections of the population. A reversion to mass provision is likely to occur only if these unmet needs pose some significant problems for the emergent social structure of accumulation, as they did in the early period after 1918, and again after the Second World War, but not in the 1930s.

In a brief, more speculative passage at the end of this chapter, attention is focused on the emergence in recent years of small-scale, 'bottom-up' initiatives to provide forms of social rented housing which are distinctively different in various respects from the bureaucratized programmes of welfare state mass and residual provision. In some of their objectives, operating principles and forms of ownership and control, they are reminiscent of the long-obscured workers' cooperative model. Like their predecessor, they are appearing during a time when neither the state nor the private market is able or willing to provide adequate and affordable housing for a significant section of the population. In the 1990s, as in the 1890s, these unmet needs are satisfied, after a fashion, in a variety of ways. Some of those in the most dire need, including some who are actually homeless, eventually gain access to the stocks of residualized social housing through the agency of the state, others double up or live in what they can get on the private market, enduring poor conditions and unaffordable housing payments. Only a tiny minority currently find more satisfactory solutions via the innovative forms of non-bureaucratized, 'non-statist' social housing provision referred to above. Even if these projects could expand to far more significant proportions, they might achieve this only at the cost of losing these distinctive characteristics (as the earlier workers' cooperative projects did when they were absorbed within the structures and processes of mass state social housing after 1945). Nevertheless, they could provide some pointers for any attempt to revive and renew a commitment by a major political bloc (presumably social democracy or some fusion of environmental and socialist political philosophies) to a more or less radically decommodified form of housing provision.

Despite the evident links between housing developments and the wider role played by state welfare in the changing social structures of accumulation, housing has indeed been the wobbly pillar of the welfare state, frequently seen, at least in conventional accounts, as being separate from its central concerns and programmes. It is hardly surprising, therefore, that the burgeoning body of literature and theory concerning the emergence and development of welfare regimes has almost entirely ignored the role that state involvement in housing generally, and social rented housing in particular, has played in this history.[11] Most theories concerning the growth of the welfare states (and, in the last decade or so, their 'crises') have centred on comparative studies of income maintenance programmes and the social, economic and political circumstances which gave rise to them and shaped their subsequent growth and decline. Not even health or education have been much considered in the context of general theory building, although there have, of course, been significant cross-national studies of these services.

This seems questionable, at least in so far as such theories do purport to draw conclusions about national welfare regimes as a whole, because, since Titmuss (1958) wrote on the social division of welfare in the 1950s, definitions of the content of the state's role in welfare have been progressively widened, well beyond even a concern with state provided health and education. In addition, as Hage, Hanneman and Gergan (1989: 1) have noted, in one of the few attempts so far to present a broader-based theory of welfare state expansion (incorporating welfare, health and education policies and expenditures), 'little work has been done on attempting to ascertain whether the role of the state in health care and welfare and education' is similarly constituted. In fact, this work suggests that the dynamics of welfare state development do differ according to the nature of provision as 'the interests of different classes are involved'. The last chapter of this book takes up these issues.

NOTES

1   See Tilton (1990) for an account of Hansson's role in the development of Swedish social democracy and his concept of *folkhemmet*.
2   See Korpi (1983); Esping-Andersen (1985); Tilton (1990); Hancock (1993) for analyses of the Swedish case and, for social democracy generally, Przeworski (1985).
3   Whether their foundations will remain solid is now in doubt, with the defeat of social democracy and the installation of a deregulating, privatizing bourgeois coalition government in 1991. This administration immediately abolished the Housing Ministry as a precursor to returning most housing provision to the market. See Elander and Strömberg (1992) and, on retrenchment in the Nordic welfare states more generally, Marklund (1988).
4   Decommodification is a slippery concept. Radical decommodification would involve the removal of any vestige of capitalist market influence over the production, distribution and consumption of goods and services and a fully socialized set of arrangements. But Esping-Andersen uses the term, as it is used here, to denote a much more limited decommodification: the socialization of the distribution of welfare services.

5   The term 'social rented housing' has been opposed on various grounds. Currently, in Britain, some object to the term because of its use in connection with the attempts of Conservative governments since 1979 to end council housing provision and institute a system of 'social' rented housing based on the housing associations and private landlords. No such ideologically biased meaning attaches to its use here. Rather, the intention is to indicate that this housing is provided by various forms of organization, of which the elected local authority (hence 'council housing') is only one.

A second objection is that this label in fact conceals a wide range of nationally specific forms and organization of provision – varied structures of housing provision. However, much of this book is concerned with exploring these variations, so the use of the term social rented housing does not have such a consequence here. In fact, one can provide only an approximate rather than a universally applicable general definition of social rented housing. It is certainly *not* a form of provision that is non-capitalist, either in terms of its immediate production or of its significance for the reproduction of capitalist social relations. But it can be differentiated from other forms of housing in three major respects:

a   It is provided by landlords at a price which is not principally determined by considerations of profit. These landlords are usually formally limited to 'non-profit' or 'limited-profit' status in so far as their social housing activities are concerned. Historically, rents have usually been below the levels charged on the open market for such accommodation, although this may no longer always be so.

b   It is administratively allocated according to some conception of 'need' (although often not to those objectively in the worst housing conditions). Ability to pay can be important but, in contrast to private market provision, is usually not the dominant determinant of allocation.

c   While political decision making has an important influence on all aspects of capitalist housing provision, as do market forces, the quantity, quality and terms of provision of social rented housing are more directly and sharply affected by the former than the latter, relative to other forms of provision. Government control over social rented housing is extensive and increased as it became a central feature of state housing policies.

6   When it is viewed as an abstract tenure form, home ownership is not a creation of the modern capitalist era. What is being referred to here is a specific structure of housing provision: large-scale, capitalist organization of housing for sale as a commodity to housing consumers. Other forms of home ownership, notably those which involve elements of self-provision or petty commodity production, have been common in other eras and still persist today in the Third World and in many

advanced capitalist and former state socialist countries. For an illuminating study of the emergence of mass capitalist home ownership
in France, see Topalov (1987).

7   Note 'broadly defined' – the reference to three models does not
imply that each comprises a uniformly constituted structure of housing provision, invariant cross-nationally and historically. Each model
refers to a range of specific structures of provision, these vary over
time and between countries. Moreover, several structures can coexist
in one country at one time. For example, mass social housing has
been provided in some countries at some times by housing associations and local authorities, each having somewhat differently constituted relations with their tenants and central government. For
parallel examples of multiple structures of housing provision in home
ownership see Martens (1990). The nature of these three models
will be further explored in subsequent chapters.

8   Since the late 1960s the main focus of federal low-income housing
policies – at least in relation to new supply – has been on subsidized
private market provision. See Harloe (1985) for an account of these
developments.

9   The terms 'Fordism' and 'post-Fordism' are now used by different
authors in different ways to refer to different empirically observable
phenomena. In short, the concepts have no commonly agreed theoretical status or empirical foundation. See Sayer and Walker (1992:
194–6); and Sayer (1989).

10 For example, it has been described as 'post- or global Fordist', 'post-
modern', 'post-industrial', 'informational', 'fragmented', 'disorganized',
a 'regime of flexible accumulation', the 'service economy', and so on
(Bell, 1973; Gershuny and Miles, 1983; Lipietz, 1987; Lash and Urry,
1987; Harvey, 1989; Scott, 1988; Castells, 1989; Mingione, 1991).

11 A notable exception is Esping-Andersen (1985), although most of his
subsequent work has focused on income maintenance and employment
policies; see, especially, Esping-Andersen (1990).

1

Social Housing and the 'Social Question': Housing Reform Before 1914

There are several dangers in looking back at the origins of social policies and reform from the vantage point of the late twentieth century. Perhaps the most obvious is a tendency to see the past through a frame of reference which is set by the contemporary vocabulary of concepts, theories and concerns – ignoring the ways in which time and circumstance have altered all of these. A related danger is to misinterpret history by turning it into a teleology, selecting out the evidence to demonstrate an almost inevitable progression of social policy development from its earliest origins to its modern forms. A further problem is to assume too simple and direct a connection between the objective needs to which social reform was purportedly a response, the campaigns of those elites who argued for reforms and the actual development of social policies. Often each of these were related only in limited ways to each of the others.

In reconstructing the history of housing reform, in particular in examining the emergence of social rented housing, we face all these difficulties. Just to illustrate the points made above briefly, first, there are problems of vocabulary. In the past hundred years the meanings and therefore the social significance of words and concepts have changed in ways which are crucially important to note. For example, 'public health' now refers to the control and elimination of physical disease. But in the nineteenth century it carried a far wider burden of meaning encompassing moral and social 'health' too. More precisely still, the concern was with the 'health' of the new working class and this concern was motivated by the actual or presumed consequences of this class's condition for the dominant social and economic order. This concern is re-iterated time and time again in the contemporary writings of social reformers, for example the American reformer Alfred T. White, who, writing in 1879, stated:

> [t]he badly constructed, unventilated, dark and foul tenement houses of New York ... are the nurseries of the epidemics which spread with certain destructiveness into the fairest homes; they are the hiding places of the local banditti; they are the cradles of the insane who fill the asylums and of the paupers who throng the almshouses ... they produce these noxious and unhappy elements of society as surely as the harvest follows the sowing (cited in Lubove, 1974: 35).

Therefore, the nineteenth-century concern with public health in-corporated a whole range of issues lying at the very heart of capitalist society itself.

In fact, the social reformers who campaigned over issues of housing and public health were concerned with a much more fundamental issue, variously described as the 'social question' or, in a telling phrase, 'the dangerous classes'.[1] Their activities were in no simple sense a response to narrowly conceived housing or health needs. These issues were not, as they were later to become, or apparently become, separate fields of social policy, the province of bureaucrats and specialists, divorced from each other and from broader questions of the reproduction and maintenance of the capitalist social formation, with relatively separate sets of issues and debates specific to each policy area. It follows that viewing the early history of, for example, housing reform as if it had a logic and meaning which related purely to a conception of housing needs and policies as they have since become institutionalized within academic and political discourses is inadequate and misleading. Rather, as Niethammer (1981: 31) has suggested, the early debates over housing reform were 'the experimental formulation of a new paradigm of social control'.

Teleological explanations of, for example, the emergence of social housing, seeing it as an inevitable outcome of the failure of other solutions to the 'housing problem' pervade the conventional housing histories. Thus Daunton (1983; 1984) has criticized some of the leading accounts of British housing for their 'Whig' interpretation of history (see also Englander, 1983). Such accounts are defective because, among other reasons, they not only abstract 'housing' from the broader context noted above, but also falsely privilege one often quite minor and highly contentious strand in the arguments of housing reformers in the era before 1914, and suggest that social housing had a much more central role in reformist debates and proposals than in practice it did have. They also tend to perpetuate what Marcuse (1986a) has called the myth of the benevolent state, or at least the myth of a benevolent governing elite, which, once it had recognized that the needs of the working class for housing could be met in no other way, responded accordingly. However, teleology is also to be found in the accounts of those who seek to explain housing developments as some inevitable outcome of working-class struggle or the needs of industry for the reproduction of labour power (for example, Community Development Project (CDP), 1976; Ginsburg, 1979). The problem here is not that class struggle or the interests of industrial capital were wholly irrelevant to the course of history, but that the relationships of these and other factors to this history were far from simple and thus are not matters to be taken for granted by the analyst. What links there were, if any, varied over time and from country to country. So these connections have to be established by research, not just assumed to exist from the outset.

Finally, there is the problematic nature of the relationship between the objective housing conditions of the working class, the slums, squalor and misery so graphically portrayed by the mass of empirical research generated and utilized by the early housing reformers, the reformers' own proposals and the forms taken by the emergent state involvement in housing. The simplistic model which assumes a humanitarian response to perceived needs on the part of the reformers, followed in due time by an inevitable governmental response, bears little resemblance to historical reality. The reformers did not simply respond to need, they had their own perceptions of the housing conditions of the working class, why they existed, and why and how they should – or should not – be addressed by the state. The evidence of these conditions and the language of humanitarianism was often deployed by the reformers but the purposes which lay behind these efforts related to the material and social interests which the reformers sought to sustain, and these were rarely those of the working class. As a German housing reformer noted:

[t]he propertied classes must be shaken from their slumber; they must finally be made to realise that even if they make the greatest sacrifices, that these, as Chamberlain recently said in London, are but a limited and very modest premium with which to buy protection against the epidemics and the social revolution which must surely come, unless we can prevent the lower classes of our great cities being reduced to animal and barbaric existence by the awfulness of their housing conditions (Gustav Schmoller, cited in Bullock and Read, 1985: 52).

Moreover, there are equally problematic connections between the concerns of these reforming elites and the factors which motivated state action. Just to give one example, John Foster (1979) has pointed out that in late Victorian Britain, Parliament tended to pass housing legislation when the London housing market was relatively oversupplied with housing, not when it was in crisis. A similar relationship between the timing of increased tenement house regulation and the state of the property market has been noted by A. Jackson (1976), in his study of New York housing. In such circumstances increased regulation, which had the effect of reducing the supply of slum housing and driving up rents, was in the clear interests of the major property owners. Such developments may have been lent a cloak of respectability by the rhetoric of housing reformers, but were hardly brought about by this means.

Many similar points have been explored in a paper by Topalov (1985), which considers the limitations of many of the 'first-generation' attempts by Marxist analysts in the 1970s to move away from conventional approaches to the study of social policy, and in particular, housing policy. Topalov is concerned to argue for a new approach to the understanding of social policies 'from below', suggesting that the study of social policies in a fragmented and overspecialized way is inadequate. This narrow and abstracted view – already criticized above – began to develop as bourgeois reformers decomposed the 'social question' into a range of specific problems and policies designed to address specific 'needs' and is now entrenched in academic organization and practice. Both conventional and the more recent Marxist studies share an approach which takes for granted as the object of research one of these fragmented fields of enquiry, seeking – without much success – to trace direct causal links between unique sets of policies and their effects on social and economic contradictions. However, there is no neatly compartmentalized relationship between, on the one hand, a specific set of social policies, and, on the other, the practices of the 'working class categories who are the target of social policies'. In reality, 'all these piecemeal state actions act together on the reproduction and transformation of the working class as both a labour force and as a danger to the capitalist order in the production process, as well as on society at large' (Topalov, 1985: 267–8). Faced with this problem, many recent writers have sought a functionalist short cut, assuming a unique connection between specific policies and, for example, the resolution in practice of the problems of labour power reproduction, social integration or whatever is thrown up by the evolution of capitalism. Topalov argues convincingly that the mistake is to start from, and be contained within, the confines of social policy as it is defined by the state itself (a similar point is made by Taylor-Gooby and Dale, 1981). Instead, one must consider the broader field of social practices and their determinations, the real object of concern for social policies.

Although Topalov wishes to direct attention away from a single-minded obsession with state policy as the object for research, he is not suggesting that research into state policies or social reform movements should be abandoned, only that the limitations of such studies will not be overcome until one examines 'from below' how working-class ways of life were actually changed by, and in reaction to, state intervention. However, some progress can be made towards a more adequate analysis even if the focus is on an examination of state policies and social reform movements. This is because the connections between a concern for reform and the broad project of controlling the 'dangerous classes' and sustaining hegemony were often clearly expressed in the reformers' discourses and arguments. By simply reconstructing these discourses not much can be said about their consequences for the working class. However, one can correct the distorted understanding of the housing reform movement that has been produced by a 'reading' of the history of the period which fails to grasp that the *explicit* object of reform was the 'condition of the working class', and that the reasons for the reform proposals had little to do with the simple recognition of 'needs' or humanitarian impulses. This is the mythology that much 'state-centred' social policy research has left unquestioned. In addition, one can also explore some aspects of the response, if any, of the *organized* working class to these reforms. In short, there can be a more adequate account of social policy 'from above' than much recent work which abstracts housing reform from its wider social, economic and political context and thus imposes an oversimplified and misleading set of 'explanations' on the historical record.

REINTERPRETING HOUSING REFORM

In his paper Topalov (1985) sketches in some of the salient issues which those who examine the history of reform, studying the reformers' arguments and the responses to them, soon discover. For example, he notes that organized labour was frequently indifferent or hostile to these reforms in their early stages and that, in so far as claims were made by the exploited working class, they were transformed, reformulated and displaced by state policies. He also notes the strong cross-national similarities between the reformers' proposals in all those countries affected by the Industrial Revolution towards the end of the nineteenth century. He writes:

> [t]hey express the realization that repressing working class revolts is not enough, they have to be prevented ... Everywhere the same kind of tasks are identified as necessary to fulfil this aim. Progressive employers will more effectively enforce their rule within the firm by 'rationalising' production, that is by increasingly depriving producers of any control over the work process. Social reformers and the state will try to reshape workers' habits outside the workplace, especially through far-reaching changes in the urban environment (Topalov, 1985: 259).

Topalov adds that this project led naturally to the multitude of enquiries into the state of the object to be transformed, namely the worker, and the imposition of a framework of analysis on these data. But this analysis had a particular purpose, it 'hardly shed light on workers' actual practices ... [t]hey cannot comprehend the rationality of the latter, which is determined by the reality of and resistance to exploitation and to accompanying discipline outside the workplace. Workers' practices are indeed observed and disguised in ways which fragment social reality in order to yield manageable objects for social policies' (Topalov, 1985: 260).

As Topalov notes, at the centre of this analytical schema lay a classification of workers which linked position in the labour market (or outside it) to an imputed level of morality and what might be described as a 'potential for salvation', i.e. for social integration. He writes that workers are classified as

> skilled, deskilled, or unskilled; permanent or casual; factory, work-shop or home working; native or immigrant; poor to be relieved or outcasts to be locked up [he could have added 'deserving or un-deserving']. The problem at hand is to give some intelligibility to

these various classifications. This can be done by identifying which moral tendencies, or cultural systems ... accompany the material conditions, so as to discriminate between three populations. Standing between adapted workers and undeserving poor are those who may be saved or civilised. Repressive policies deal with outcasts who are to be if possible eliminated, driven into workhouses or ousted through immigration. Reform policies ... are chiefly targeted towards those who might be reshaped so as to comply with the norms of a swiftly changing industrial capitalism (Topalov, 1985: 260).

In a later section of this chapter we note several examples of this type of analysis of the working class by housing reformers, together with the connections that were made between an assessment of 'reformability' and specific proposals for reform. One of the most complete statements of this type of analysis was contained in the first ever US government report on housing, published in 1895. It reads:

differentiation of the great mass ... of working people is a necessary preliminary to the statement of conclusions. In the first place there is the artisan element. Members of this class are in receipt of fair wages. As a rule, they are steady, thrifty and socially ambitious. They are good tenants ... They can pay sufficient rent for good houses, and for them builders, whether private individuals or model companies ... can and usually do make satisfactory provision.

The next step in the gradation is occupied by individuals who have not mounted quite so high in the social scale. One section has been unfortunate, and ... has become discouraged in the effort to maintain a fair standard of existence. The other includes those prone to be lazy or careless, and those who are not particularly intelligent or ambitious or are possessed of bad habits. Both sections ... are not desirable tenants. The first section of this class is generally that which model enterprises of a philanthropic character have attempted to deal with, though the greater number of model agencies have designedly left them out ... They need looking after, and they are the class with which lady rent collectors should establish reciprocal relations of business and sympathetic interest ...

The third section includes the incorrigible, the drunkard, the criminal, the immoral, the lazy, and the shiftless ... as Lord Shaftesbury significantly remarks, they have hardly any domestic or civilized feelings. There must be an entire change of policy on the part of the governing bodies towards this class. Lord Provost Russell of Edinburgh goes so far as to say that they should be driven from their hiding places into municipal lodging houses, where they could be under police control, the sexes separated, and the children placed

in institutions where they might grow up useful members of society
...

The slum must go. Not only is it a menace to public health,
but it is a moral fester wherein character is being continually de-
bauched and the evils which afflict civilization recruited (US Commissioner for Labor, 1895: 439–42).

Topalov also refers to the role that the extended notion of
'public health', already discussed above, played in the reformers'
discourses. He writes: '[a] key word characterized one of the main
ways to reform: cleansing – that is transforming the physical environment of working-class life in order to change its social reality'
(Topalov, 1985: 261). This hygienism gave rise to an urban reform
plan, involving architects, urban planners and housing reformers,
based on environmental determinism. He could have added that
once this movement got under way and became entrenched in the
bureaucracy and in professional organizations, what started out as
means to a broader *end* – environmental reform as a method of
redetermining social reality – soon became, at least for its supporters and those whom it employed, an end in itself, so helping
to fragment and obscure what was originally a unified approach,
not to urban reform *per se* but to social reform and the problem
of the 'dangerous classes'.

Finally, Topalov refers to some of the sources of variation and
conflict in the reform movement. Although there were some common features in reformist programmes, they were neither consistently organized nor did they necessarily achieve their aims.
There were arguments between differing groups and opposition
from industrial and property interests, organized labour and politicians. A key issue was the relative roles of the state and private
initiative. One conclusion that can be drawn from this observation
is that the broader socio-economic and political context within
which reform occurred has to be incorporated in any analysis of
reform in order to make sense of its specific trajectories. A further
consequence is that cross-national studies are invaluable in this
respect, highlighting the nationally specific ways in which a broadly
similar project of social reform, arising in consequence of a broadly
similar process of capitalist industrialization and urbanization and
the creation of a new working class, resulted in nationally specific
institutions and practices. Furthermore, this exploration of cross-
national variations is crucial for the subsequent understanding of
the ways in which policies evolved in the years after the First
World War because, although the later development of policies was

a response to new conditions, the institutions and practices which evolved before 1914, and the social interests which were associated with them, had a continuing influence on how these policies were formulated. And some of these variations continue to have significance almost a century later.

The following sections of this chapter consider some of the salient contours of the housing reform movement and the state's response to it in the Netherlands, Denmark, Britain, France, Germany and the United States. Such an exercise is fraught with difficulties, especially within the limits of a single chapter. But, at the risk of a certain oversimplification and superficiality, some sense of the distinctive ways in which housing reform and housing policies were socially constructed in each nation can be conveyed.

In each case the first requirement is to consider some of the important contextual factors. Although the 'social question' arose in each country in response to broadly similar developments, there are also important differences in these developments and the importance which reforming elites placed on the 'housing question' compared to issues of workplace regulation, the extension of suffrage, education, and so on. Moreover, the scale and pace of capitalist industrialization and urbanization also varied and thus affected the salience of the housing issue. In addition, there were important differences in general social, economic and political structures. These affected matters such as the nature of the political resistance to reform, the extent to which sections of the working class could gain access to adequate housing through the private market without the intervention of the state, and the ways in which such intervention could be made politically acceptable. Such considerations helped in turn to determine the nature and range of acceptable 'solutions' to the housing problem in each country. These solutions will be briefly reviewed. Finally, the question of what role, if any, working-class organization and pressure played in shaping the course of housing reform in its early years will be discussed.

THE NETHERLANDS: SOCIAL HOUSING AS A 'PRIVATE INITIATIVE'

In the first half of the nineteenth century, the Netherlands was still in the long decline which followed its period of political and economic dominance in the seventeenth century.[2] Industrial development was slow, up to about 1850 the rural population was increasing faster than the urban population.[3] In the second half of the century industrialization accelerated but the urban population began to increase rapidly only in the last 30 or so years of the century. This growth was centred on Amsterdam, Rotterdam and the Hague. But even by the end of the century only about one-third of the population lived in cities and towns of any magnitude and it was not until after 1945 that the rural to urban transition was completed. Nevertheless, by the last years of the nineteenth century, the nexus of issues that comprised the 'social question' was evident.

Political development was also slow, for example, in comparison with Britain and France. Purely monarchical rule did not end until 1840, and the rise of the middle class and its liberal ideology and politics was also slower to develop. But in 1848 a new constitution was adopted, based on a limited franchise. There followed a period of Liberal-dominated government which lasted until the end of the century. These years were also marked by the emergence of a key division in Dutch politics, which has been of considerable significance for the structuring of social policy, based on religion rather than class. In the nineteenth century the major division was between the secular Liberals and the Protestant-dominated Confessionals although, in comparison with some other countries (for example Belgium), liberalism took a less extreme form in Holland. Organized party politics in the modern sense began to form only in the late 1870s when the Protestant Anti-Revolutionary Party (ARP) developed the first party programme which included some references to protective legislation for the working class. Labour organization also evolved rather slowly, there was some development of trade unions after 1865 but these tended to be anti-socialist. There was also a Calvinist-based workers' association.

In the Great Depression, which affected all the capitalist economies from the early 1870s into the 1890s, the Dutch economy stagnated. In the 1880s there was some growth in unemployment and social tension and a Social Democratic Workers Party (SDAP) emerged in the 1890s as large-scale industrialization took off. However, it was not until just before the First World War that organized labour became a significant industrial and parliamentary force. Then it chose to reject the opportunity to form a governing alliance with the radical liberal movement which had developed in the preceding decades. Therefore, the impact of organized labour on reform debates and their outcomes in the period up to the First World War was minimal. Instead, the conflict over social reform was fought out between the bourgeois parties which underwent several important transitions from the late 1870s.

As in other countries, following the liberal triumph in the transition from monarchy to parliamentary government, there was a gradual breakup of what was a disparate political grouping. In the 1880s a distinctively radical wing of the liberal movement emerged which was in favour of a universal franchise and various other developments such as the extension of municipal services. It also had some dealings with the still very limited socialist movement as well as having some successes at a local level especially in Amsterdam where the municipality took over and ran the transport system and various other utilities. But, in contrast to some other countries where mainstream liberalism was less open to reform, this political grouping adopted a considerable programme of reform in the early 1890s.

At the same time, there were developments in the Confessional groupings. At first the religious divisions had led to the emergence of two parties, a Roman Catholic (RC) and a Protestant party (the ARP – from which the more conservative Christian Historical Union (CHU) soon split off), but issues soon arose which brought these groups into alliance. Social legislation, in particular education, played a central role in this process. Both religious parties were antagonistic to any proposals for social reform which involved a direct extension of state intervention in social life. They saw this as an attack on their religious freedoms and on the institutions, especially the schools, through which their faiths were sustained. Acceptance of the project of social reform was not in question but the religious parties argued that there should be no subordination of society to the state, that state power should be filtered through intermediary organizations which they would control. So a combination of state aid and 'private initiative' was acceptable, direct 'public initiative' was not. In 1888 the first coalition government of the Protestants and the Catholics occurred, the education issue being the major reason for this alliance. But, in addition, the Catholics were influenced in their attitude to social policy development by the new diffusion of ideas about this topic soon given papal authority in the encyclical *De Rerum Novarum* in 1892. This set out the strategy which subsequently led many Catholic parties to try and coopt and integrate the working class by social policies which stressed the sustenance of family life (and fertility), religious observance, self-discipline and self-help.

As in other countries, such as Britain, concern about the need for social legislation temporarily peaked in the 1880s as working-class protests caused by the adverse economic conditions made the threat of the 'dangerous classes' loom large in the imaginations of the legislators (in fact the legislature was still a very restricted body; in 1887 there had been a small franchise extension, but, even so, only about 14 per cent of the population had the vote). The coalition government passed new legislation to support 'free' schools and an act regulating child and female labour, the first social legislation since a similar measure in 1874. In 1891 the Liberals returned with their programme of reforms and ruled until 1901; the first major Housing Act, passed in this year, was one of the final measures of this last government in which the Liberals ruled alone. There were limited tax reforms, some further extension of the franchise (it now covered about 30 per cent of the adult population, so much of the working class was still excluded), social insurance and health legislation.

In the period between 1901 and 1914 politics remained fragmented and there was often no clear governing majority. The Liberals continued to disintegrate, the Protestant bloc was divided and there were splits among the socialists, although by 1914 the SDAP was firmly in the reformist camp and was not regarded even by its strongest opponents as a revolutionary menace. However, the Confessional parties had the majority of parliamentary seats and it has been this grouping, which attracted support from significant sections of the working class and hence has had a commitment to social reform beyond that normally found in purely class-based bourgeois parties, that has been the dominant force in Dutch politics up to the current era. Its strong adherence to state support for 'private initiative' has also continued to characterize the way in which social policies have been structured, including housing policies – the 'pillarization' of Dutch society which developed from the 1880s onwards, in which the major secular and Confessional groupings developed their own structures of social service, cultural and other organizations, aided by, but retaining a considerable degree of independence from, the state.[4]

As in the other countries, there was a growth of philanthropic housing organizations from the middle of the nineteenth century, although on a very limited scale.[5] Thus one typical housing reform solution, the model dwelling, accompanied by a paternalistic management regime aimed at 'educating' the better-paid and mainly skilled workers who could afford the rents set by '5 per cent philanthropy', was present in the Netherlands. At the same time, a second more working-class-based form of organization began to appear. This was the cooperative building society, arising out of the consumer cooperative movement, supported by small groups of the better-paid and more securely employed working class and (as with some of the philanthropic foundations) often linked to the development of working-class owner occupation. A third 'solution' was also evident – employer housing – although, again, only on a very limited scale. Here the attempt to mould the worker to the newly required regimes of industrial and social discipline was apparent – an objective which will be further discussed below. Many of these 'solutions' to the housing-related aspects of the 'social question' were greatly influenced by foreign experience. For example, in the Netherlands and in many other countries the model housing developed by the Protestant industrialists at Mulhouse in France from the 1850s, which tied the provision of single-family housing to a broader project of social reform and self-help, towards the ultimate aim of owner occupation, inspired similar proposals. A further 'solution' was advocated in the Netherlands, too, inspired by the work of Octavia Hill in Britain, who attempted, by means of a strict management regime which policed the morals and behaviour of working-class tenants, to make commercially run rental housing projects economically viable. An Octavia Hill-influenced 'Association for Dwelling Improvement' was founded in 1893. Finally, another strand in reformist policies first appeared in 1874, when the progressive Liberals in Amsterdam provided some indirect municipal support for workers' housing.

All these developments took place in the context of rising concern about, and investigation of, the 'social question' by governing and intellectual elites. This growth was especially noticeable after 1870 when several investigative and promotional organizations and journals were founded. According to van der Schaar, the 'social question' encompassed not only housing, but child labour, the right to strike, working-class suffrage and poverty/unemployment relief.[6] Statistics were deployed to link bad housing to social and physical pathologies and to workplace conditions. In the 1890s proposals for housing legislation, influenced by knowledge of French, Belgian and British reforms, were developed. Attention focused on slum clearance and increasing the supply of new working-class housing. These were seen as ways in which the environment could be manipulated for the purposes of a broader project of reform. Thus in 1896 a housing report referred directly to the need for more aid to housing in order to, as van der Schaar puts it, 'enable the worker to keep his foothold in the struggle for existence', to keep away from the bar, and from crime, to rehabilitate family life and to increase health and labour force participation.

As in other countries at this time, there were some key issues about how reform should be shaped that concerned the reformers. One was land reform; some reformers (although they had relatively little practical impact at first in the Netherlands) argued that it was the high price of land, the product of rampant speculation in the growing urban centres, that so raised the price of decent private housing as to make its rents unaffordable by the working class. As elsewhere, this concern led to demands for the regulation of land uses via 'extension planning' and the Garden Cities movement. A second issue was whether the regulation of housing and building conditions alone could solve the housing problem (as we shall see, this approach dominated early US housing reform).

A third issue was what type of housing should be built for the working class. Here the debate was between the 'barrack' system or the 'cottage system' – in other words, whether to build rental apartments in the cities or single-family housing which could be owner occupied in rural areas. In Holland, as elsewhere, the dispersal of the urban working class to rural-based home ownership was the preferred solution for many reformers. This promised to inhibit the growth of collectivism and strengthen individualism, self-sufficiency and family life. It would also tie the worker to the dominant social order through giving him or her a stake in the system through petty property ownership. Such a proposal led Engels (1973) to publish his famous attack on German housing reformers, and it was a major objective of conservative housing reform strategies in many countries. The antipathy felt for 'barracks' housing was clearly expressed. For example, the German Wilhelm Riehl wrote in 1854: '[f]amily life ceases ... [i]t would not be surprising if gradually the architecture of the tenement block does not lead us all to the barracks of socialism' (quoted in Bullock and Read, 1985: 76). In contrast, another German reformer, Ludolf Parisius, extolled the virtues of home ownership: 'the knowledge of owning something that the thief cannot carry off, of being master of even a small patch of land, provides the workers with a stake in our whole society' (quoted in Bullock and Read, 1985: 77). However, working-class home ownership was always difficult to achieve, especially in those economies where working-class wages were at a low level and where industrial production remained centralized, as in the Netherlands. Nevertheless, the movement into suburban single-family housing, whether rented or owned, did provide a significant further 'solution' to the housing of the labour aristocracy (plus the rapidly growing clerical labour force) in the two countries with the highest working-class standards of living, the USA and Britain, from this period onwards.

A final and centrally important issue concerned the form and extent of the state's financial involvement in workers' housing. In the Netherlands, as elsewhere, there were strong objections to any use of subsidies to reduce the price of working-class housing below a cost-covering level. Apart from purely ideological concerns, such as a belief that this might foster working-class 'dependency' there was the central issue of avoiding competition with private enterprise. It was argued that subsidized housing with cheap rents would simply drive out private investment which could not compete, thus increasing the subsidy burden and the degree of state intervention. To the bourgeois politicians in power in the Netherlands and their counterparts elsewhere, this degree of intervention in the free market was simply unthinkable.

The 1901 Housing Act, which laid down the basis for much of the framework within which Dutch housing policy has developed ever since, reflected both these general reformist concerns as well as some of the more specific features of the Dutch political and social structure noted earlier.[7] It provided municipalities with powers to regulate housing, building and planning and also provided for loans from the state for working-class housebuilding. But the risks involved were not borne by the central government as the loans had to be guaranteed by the municipalities. Also, the municipalities were not to build; this was too much like state socialism. Instead, any loans would be used by 'private initiative' non-profit housing corporations, approved by government and regulated by the localities but not controlled by them. The corporations could not operate in the direct interest of employers, unions or any other producer/consumer organizations (so the cooperative form of organization was ruled out). This formula, however, allowed the various politico-social groupings to establish corporations linked closely to their own interests, and has been one reason why a polarized 'politics of tenure' has not developed in the Netherlands (Bommer, 1931; Harloe and Martens, 1985). State support for ownership was, interestingly, excluded by the law; apparently this was to prevent working-class housing subsequently becoming a source of speculative profit making by sales to the private market. The act, which is a framework law, laying down widely defined and flexible powers to be spelt out in detail later as and when required, did allow for state subsidies. However, these were to be strictly limited to circumstances in which there was no viable alternative, i.e. in connection with slum clearance and the rehousing of slum dwellers – the poorest sections of the working class, at once a potent source of social danger and yet the least able to pay out of their own pockets for the improved housing so necessary for their social reform. However, it was also envisaged that any subsidies would be purely temporary. With the benefits of better housing the newly fashioned working class would be able to participate more effectively in the labour force, gain higher wages and in time pay an economic rent. In such a manner were the objectives of reformism and the adherence to broadly liberal, free market principles reconciled.

The Housing Act was passed with very little opposition. Other aspects of the 'social question' were more important and caused greater divisions, for example education, the extension of suffrage and labour legislation. But legislation, however wide-ranging, did not automatically lead to a major development in housing policies. Although property interests do not seem in the Netherlands, unlike elsewhere, to have had a major basis within Parliament for opposing the new legislation, they were far more powerful at the local level. Few municipalities were eager to take up their new regulative powers; when they did there was strong resistance from property owners (Prak and Priemus, 1992: 176). There was also resistance to granting applications to establish housing corporations (ibid.: 176–7). Moreover, the Ministry of Finance, which controlled the implementation of the financial provisions of the act, limited its application. The official chiefly concerned tried to impose a regime of economic rents for the new housing rather than historic cost pricing. The latter, he claimed, would be unfair to private enterprise. Cheap rents would favour only a few; the real solution to a shortage of affordable housing was either to raise wages or to increase the private housing supply; subsidies would only be a short-term and inadequate palliative. Against this pure incarnation of liberal market economics, the housing reformers merely argued for some flexibility in rent setting, not for a general regime of below-market rents.

As van der Schaar comments, what becomes apparent from this debate is that both sides accepted that the non-profit housing 'solution' was in practice housing for relatively better-off sections of the working class, however much the rhetoric of reform drew on revelations about the conditions in the slums and among the 'sub-proletariat' to make its case. In fact, another 'solution' was really seen as the answer for the poorer slum-dwelling worker. This was filtering, the movement over time into the somewhat better housing vacated by the skilled artisans. In the Netherlands, as elsewhere, early social housing was definitely not for those in the greatest housing need. It was aimed at the first and, to some extent, the middle group of the threefold classification of the working class to which Topalov referred. To a greater or lesser extent most of the other 'solutions' which involved increasing the supply of housing for the working class, for example by model dwellings, employer housing or suburban development, were also aimed at these sections of the working class. As we shall note later, a far more punitive approach was often adopted towards the treatment of the 'residuum'.

DENMARK: THE COOPERATIVE APPROACH

In terms of their nineteenth-century pattern of urban and economic development, there were some similarities between the Netherlands and Denmark.[8] Throughout the century both remained heavily dependent on agrarian production closely linked to the British market. Both were forced to shift away from grain production as demand patterns shifted. Both retained a substantial rural population at the end of the century and only completed the rural-urban transition after 1945. However, at the end of the nineteenth century, Denmark was even less urbanized than the Netherlands, fewer than 25 per cent of its population living in cities of any size. Urbanization was heavily concentrated in Copenhagen which, together with the adjacent Frederiksberg, contained nearly a quarter of the national population by 1900. Therefore, it was above all in the capital city that the new working class and early housing reform activity were concentrated.

However, industrialization was more widely spread as much of it was associated with the highly successful and distinctive pattern of development of Danish agriculture, especially from the 1870s when the conversion from grain production to dairy and pig production occurred. This had been preceded at the end of the eighteenth century by the transition from feudally based agriculture to a mixture of larger landowners and smaller independent farmers. During the succeeding century a strong tradition of rural-based producer cooperatives developed – a form of organization which was later copied in the cities and had a particular influence on the institutional structures through which housing reform came about.

The development of a large sector of small-scale farming also had a major impact on the form which party politics took when it emerged after the ending of the absolute monarchy in 1849. As in the Netherlands, liberalism began to develop within the rising middle class in the first half of the century and this group, pressing for constitutional reform, allied itself with the small farmers.[9] The 1849 Constitution contained only limited reforms, however. The monarch continued to rule in association with Conservative ministers (representing large-scale landowning and capitalist interests) until the end of the century, using his constitutional power to appoint the executive even after the Liberals and their allies had taken control of a somewhat more widely elected Lower House of the legislature (about 15 per cent of the population was enfranchised). This was the central conflict which dominated Danish politics until 1901 when the king was at last forced to recognize the changed balance of power and appoint the first Liberal (Venstre) government. As Baldwin (1990) explains, early Danish welfare reform, initiated by the Liberals, was a by-product of the struggle between the monarchical party and the agrarian interests in the years before Venstre finally gained power.

As elsewhere, once it had achieved this objective the Liberal bloc began to disintegrate. A Radical Liberal (RV) party, supported by the intelligentsia and professionals, split away from the main grouping in 1905. RV has never been a large party but has acted as a key power broker in the political system for much of the twentieth century. Venstre became a more right-wing agrarian party after the break and in time was to look to the formation of governing alliances with the old right-wing grouping which, by the time of the First World War, accepted the transition to parliamentary democracy and had become a recognizably modern Conservative party (KF), although, given the continuing existence of the agrarian party, it long remained a largely urban-based grouping. In contrast with the Dutch case, the fragmentation of the non-socialist parties in Denmark has, therefore, not been based on religion but on the rural/urban division.

The transition to a modern system of industrial organization was retarded, not only by the country's lack of natural resources, which limited the growth of large-scale industry, but also by the guild system, a relic of the pre-industrial era, which inhibited the growth of trade. After this ended in the 1860s there was considerable industrial growth, rural to urban migration and the start of the labour movement. The Social Democratic Party (Socialdemokratiet – S) was founded in 1871. It soon moved away from Marxism towards reformism and the relations between this party and the trade union movement on the one hand, and industrial capital and its political representatives on the other, rapidly became accommodative rather than conflictual. Remarkably, by 1899 the employers and the unions had agreed on a system of collective bargaining which has been in place ever since and has limited – though not, of course, eliminated – industrial conflict. The reformism of the labour movement was encouraged by the fact that the size of the industrial workforce, within which it rapidly built up a strong basis of support, remained restricted (RV attracted a significant proportion of rural working-class votes). [10] More generally, the structure of the Danish economy and society has prevented the absolute domination of any of the main political/economic blocs and has contributed to the lack of sharp conflict and the growth of a politics based on coalition building (a feature which the institution of proportional representation, together with universal suffrage in 1915, reflected as well as encouraged).

By 1905 the pattern of political alliances which was to dominate Danish politics for the next 50 years had emerged, as the Radical Liberals formed their first government with support from the Social Democrats who had rapidly gained parliamentary seats following their first electoral victory in 1884. In fact, by 1913 S could have taken power with support from RV, but the party chose to wait until, it hoped, it could gain an absolute majority (Socialist ministers joined the wartime government and the party formed its first minority administration in 1924).

Given its distinctive pattern of economic development, the growth of the new working class seems to have created rather less of a disturbance than elsewhere and the 'social question' took a less acute form, even in Copenhagen, where the housing of the working class was notably less squalid than, for example, in German, British or, above all perhaps, French cities at the same period (Boldsen, 1935). Certainly, at the beginning of the century, the private market provided a quite substantial supply of working-class housing in Copenhagen at comparatively low rents, although after 1907, when the market collapsed following a financial crisis, the situation became increasingly stressed and there were demands for state intervention to meet the rising needs caused by the continued migration to the city and to deal with the slums. Philanthropic efforts had begun on a small scale, as in most of the other countries discussed here, in the 1850s (Hyldtoft, 1992: 46). By the 1880s they had begun to be eclipsed by various forms of self-build associations. However, these efforts were not aimed at increasing the supply of housing for the poorest sections of the working class but, as elsewhere, were for the 'respectable' working class and were usually for ownership rather than rental (ultimately, many of the dwellings were sold to housing speculators) (Greve, 1971). In 1886 the first Social Democratic Members of Parliament introduced a bill which led, in 1887, to the first state loans becoming available for the building of working-class dwellings by the associations or by local authorities, although the results of this legislation were minimal (Hyldtoft, 1992: 50–1). From the 1890s there was an upsurge in cooperative building organizations, especially after a building strike. In Copenhagen the cooperative sector later had a considerable significance in the provision of social housing (Umrath, 1950). However, up to the First World War and beyond cooperative housing, like the self-build associations, mainly housed the highest-paid and most securely employed workers (Hyldtoft, 1992: 51, 53). The Garden City 'solution' also had some influence before 1914; a 'Garden City Association' was founded in 1911.

Pressure for the extension of state intervention occurred only after the housing market collapsed in around 1907/8 (Madsen and Devisscher, 1934). The 1887 law, which provided loans mainly linked to slum clearance and rehousing, had not been used at all by the local authorities and by only a few cooperatives (Department B, School of Architecture, 1971). In 1897 loans were provided for local authorities and cooperatives to build for working-class owner occupation (and, unlike the earlier act, the state assumed some risk, as the local authorities no longer had to guarantee the loans). This led to some building activity, and from 1900 there were also loans for buying rural smallholdings. After 1907 a more regulated system of state loans for building societies and local authorities began to emerge; there were set standards and central government supervision. The loans were now for housing people of 'moderate means'. In fact, the local authorities mainly passed the loans on to the societies. Although the problem of the slums played an important role in the arguments for housing reform, as in other countries, problems of compensation were considerable. Much of the building activity of the societies was linked to home ownership and white-collar and better-paid working-class-occupied single-family housing began to develop around Copenhagen before the First World War. However, cooperative housing built for rental by organizations linked to the labour movement, which were to become very active in the interwar period, was built in the capital from 1912 (Hyldtoft, 1992: 58).

BRITAIN: THE DEBATE OVER REFORM

While the Netherlands and Denmark were small countries with a relatively slow rate of urbanization, in which the new working class was limited in scale and located in only a few large cities, Britain was very different. It was the first industrial nation, 80 per cent urbanized by 1900, with a mass working class, the skilled sections of which were strongly organized in craft unions (Mathias and Postan, 1978). Unlike any of the other countries with which we are concerned, the fastest period of urban concentration had occurred in the first half of the century.

By the turn of the century all of the distinctive 'solutions' to the housing problem had been discussed and, in some cases, implemented.[11] Indeed, British debates and experiments were often followed with great interest by reformers in other countries. As elsewhere, the regulation of housing conditions on public health grounds could most easily be reconciled with the liberal state, although the record of resistance to regulation by property interests, strongly represented in the fragmented local government organization which persisted until the last decade or so of the century, was evident. Model housing first began to be built in London in the 1840s. In the second half of the century the model dwelling companies obtained some public capital and land at reduced costs. The need for slum clearance, justified in terms of the factors already discussed in this chapter, was the main argument used by housing reformers (English and Norman, 1974). Employer housing was limited in extent although a few model projects were built. Very little of the model housing was affordable by less-skilled workers. By the latter part of the century it seems to have been accepted that filtering was the main possibility for this group, although Octavia Hill – as already described – attempted to 'educate' poorer workers in the virtues of thrift, sobriety and good rent-paying habits, thus making minimal quality housing financially viable.

In fact, the scope for private market housing for the better-paid working class was considerable because, despite extensive poverty in the major city centres, by the 1880s there was a growing number of workers with reasonably secure and high wages. There was a long history of limited working-class owner occupation, based on the activities of cooperative building societies. By the end of the nineteenth century these were becoming large-scale organizations, no longer with any real cooperative basis and certainly not with any strong links to the organized working class, collecting working- and lower-middle-class savings and providing loans for home ownership. Aided by cheap transport legislation, suburbanization offered a way out of the city for such groups and, as Offer (1981) has pointed out, Conservative politicians sought to encourage such developments, seeing the creation of a mass of small property owners as a sort of 'outer defence' against attacks on landed property. In this context it is interesting to note that Howard's proposal for Garden Cities, first published in 1898, which linked a new form of urban development to cooperative and public ownership of property and industry, was soon taken up by Conservative and business interests. This resulted in some practical experiments which ignored Howard's wider reform objectives (Fishman, 1977).

Housing reform was almost entirely a matter of debate between Conservatives and Liberals, the two main parties which had emerged in a recognizably modern form by the last quarter of the nineteenth century. However, the extension of the franchise in 1867 and, more significantly, in 1885, did mean that the artisan and lower middle class gained a potential political voice. Also the wish to coopt these workers, and to provide a measure of paternalist reform rather than concede full political rights, played a part in the Conservative social reform strategies adopted by Disraeli in the 1860s and 1870s. Traditionally, the Conservatives were the party of the rural land-owners, whose main priority was to defend these interests. They had no strongly doctrinaire resistance to some measure of state intervention if this was necessary to ensure such protection. As in other countries, the Liberal Party represented the new forces of industrial capitalism and the middle classes, strongly committed to *laissez-faire* and the 'night watchman state'. But by the 1880s not only was there competition for the political allegiance of the new working class, there was also – especially in this decade of economic depression – a concern across the political and social system about social unrest. In fact, it was an article by the Conservative leader Lord Salisbury in 1883 which led to a Royal Commission on the Housing of the Working Classes in 1885. This demonstrated that none of the so far canvassed 'solutions' to the housing problem could provide affordable accommodation for the mass of the working class.

However, subsidized housing was unacceptable, not just on economic but also on moral grounds. As the Earl of Shaftesbury (a noted reformer) stated: 'if the state is to be summoned not only to provide houses for the labouring classes, but also to supply such dwellings at nominal rents, it will, while doing something on behalf of their physical condition, utterly destroy their moral senses'

(Earl of Shaftesbury, 1883). So little occurred as a result of the Royal Commission except a consolidating Housing Act in 1890. This re-enacted powers which had existed since the 1870s for local authorities to build housing in connection with slum clearance, but at economic rents, as well as earlier and largely unused powers which enabled local authorities to provide 'working-class lodging houses', defining these in ways which allowed the construction of single-family houses and apartments. However, it was not envisaged that these powers would be used to provide a major source of new housing. Moreover, any public intervention was to be a temporary expedient because the local authorities were required to dispose of the housing after ten years.

Two factors probably lay behind the impetus to housing reform in this period. As Foster (1979) noted, Parliament often passed regulatory reforms when the housing market was slack and rents were stagnating. Also, as Stedman Jones (1971) shows in his study of London, the social unrest of the period led to a fear that the 'respectable working' class might find common cause with the 'residuum' – the old spectre of the destabilizing 'dangerous classes'. In the 1890s when this fear faded the discussion about reform also diminished (Stedman Jones, 1971; Sutcliffe, 1981: 55). In fact, Stedman Jones notes that the expansion of cheap transport and working-class suburbanization in the 1890s reduced the risks of close links between the two sections of the working class. But the problems of casual, ill-paid labour, which were the root causes of the social conflict in the previous decade, were not solved. What changed was the way in which the poor were viewed. Now, he argues, the poor increasingly became seen, partly under the influence of Social Darwinism and imperialism, as a problem which weakened the British Empire and which ought to be eliminated (see also Semmel, 1960). Punitive attitudes to the poor were increasingly evident – slums and overcrowding should be solved by the clearance of the urban centres and the dispersal of their populations. It was even argued that cheap housing in London would inhibit the outward movement of industry then occurring. This would be a mistake as it would reduce industrial efficiency. Those workers who were fit to work could migrate outwards too, leaving only the remaining poor whose plight was a product of their individual criminality, fecklessness, etc. Punitive attitudes to the poor were widespread well into the 1900s (including within the Fabian Society, which tried to impress its ideas on Conservatives and Liberals before it came to be involved with the new Labour Party). The advocacy of repressive 'solutions' to the problem of the residual poor, such as deprival of citizen and parental rights and incarceration in labour 'colonies', was shared by many welfare reformers, including Beveridge, the Liberal who was the architect of the post-1945 welfare reforms. The celebrated economist Alfred Marshall, writing in 1884, clearly conveys the attitude of contemporary elites to the residual poor:

> [d]oubtless many of the poor things that crouch for hire at the doors of London workshops are descended from vigorous ancestors ... [b]ut a great many more of them have a taint of vice in their history ... [o]f these immigrants a great part do no good to themselves or others by coming to London; and there would be no hardship in deterring the worst of them from coming by insisting on strict regulations as to their manner of living here (A. Marshall, 1884).

Such attitudes were shared by many labour leaders (Englander, 1983). The skilled trade union leaders were socially and politically conservative and by the 1890s a few working-class representatives had been elected to Parliament as Liberals, starting a period of collaboration between the Liberals and organized labour which lasted until 1914. An Independent Labour Party (ILP) was formed in 1892 but it was dominated by trade union interests, rejected Marxism and had only very limited support. The modern Labour Party was formed by the trade unions, the ILP, the Marxist Social Democratic Federation and the Fabians in 1900, and elected its first Member of Parliament (MP) in 1903. In the last election before the war, in 1910, the party gained 42 seats. From the start the party mainly reflected the respectable and patriotic face of labour which offered little threat to the established social and political interests, provided, in particular, that trade union rights to organize their members were protected (Halévy, 1961). In fact, up to 1914 it was possible that Labour would be incorporated in the radical wing of the Liberal Party (which, as elsewhere, had emerged towards the end of the previous century) rather than developing as a separate mass party. Unlike the situation in Germany or France, the respectable face of organized labour in Britain was rarely regarded as a serious threat to the social order. The integration rather than the exclusion of this sector of the working class, through modest social reforms and, above all, a conciliatory approach to industrial relations, was clearly evident.

In fact, it was not until the 1900s, when a series of key events put trade union rights under threat, that trade unions increasingly came to see a need to support the new party, in order to defend themselves. However, the Labour Party remained just that: a party to defend labour, not a socialist party, and it had no clear social reform programme. The party leaders, like the Liberals with which they formed electoral pacts, were Free Traders who wanted increased trade union protection and some very limited industrial and social reforms – housing was not very significant among these. Halévy (1961: 445) acidly remarks that the Labour Members of Parliament in the years before 1914 were like the bourgeois radicals, only more conservative. He adds that this group had no interest in the lumpenproletariat and did not campaign for the extension of the franchise to it. There were, in fact, a few local authorities which built unsubsidized housing for rental for the 'respectable' working class, but this was not a socialist programme; rather, it was an expansion of so-called 'municipal socialism' and a range of Conservative, Liberal and Labour local political groupings supported such small-scale experiments. The most notable pre-war development of council-built housing occurred in London, where the London County Council, formed in 1888, began in the 1890s to build inner-city apartment blocks on slum-cleared sites and a little later some suburban single-family rental housing (Greater London Council, 1980).

In these years the politics of urban reform was dominated by a conflict between the two major parties over who should pay for the costs of urbanization (Offer, 1981). The main source of revenue for the rapidly rising expenditures of the local authorities, who were responsible for much of the infrastructure and public service provision, was the local property tax (the 'rates'). The Conservatives, who were not ideologically hostile to state involvement when it served their interests, argued for an extension of central government grants to aid local expenditure. This would relieve the rate burden on the larger urban property interests, which they tended to represent, as well as on the rural landowners – still the core of the party. The Liberals were ideologically opposed to increased central spending which would also, of course, raise taxes borne by the industrial interests which they represented. But in the years just before the First World War Lloyd George, the leader of radical Liberalism, developed a distinctive programme aimed at attracting rural votes (Swenarton, 1981). This combined land taxation, minimum income legislation and other social reforms. The claim was that high land prices were the fundamental reason for high rents. So land reform would enable the problem of working-class housing affordability and the other issues of urban finance to be solved.

Interestingly, it was the Conservatives who pressed, unsuccessfully, for some very limited state subsidies for urban and rural workers' housing before 1914 (Wilding, 1972). Their motives were clear. First, some housing would be built in rural areas, reducing the pressure on landowners to raise rural wages. Second, the urban housing would aid slum clearance and the more profitable reuse of city centre land. In contrast, the Liberal government – in power from 1906 until the war – was resistant to pressure for housing subsidies. Instead, it passed the first weak town planning legislation in 1909.[12] The strategy for housing was to control land use and tax land profits so as to further open up the 'suburban solution'. Liberals also looked to an extension of cheap suburban transport and supported Garden Cities.

To summarize, in Britain there was a variety of 'solutions' to the working-class housing problem canvassed before 1914. State-subsidized social housing was advocated only by relatively few and uninfluential voices. The Conservatives, representing major property interests, looked to a strategy which would protect those interests, favouring the development of the 'ramparts of property' – an extension of petty property ownership to the 'respectable working class' who, it was assumed, would then support the general interests of property. The Liberals looked to solve the solution by land reform and planning which would make the private market solution open to more of the working class. Organized labour tended to support Liberal policies, although with increasing criticism in the period just before 1914. Meanwhile, no version of the housing reform argument had much more to offer unskilled labour than the possibility of upward filtering into the housing left by the better-off workers *en route* to the suburbs or, for the 'undeserving poor', a variety of punitive solutions. Finally, the relatively high wages of the labour aristocracy plus cheap transport did, in practice, lead to a considerable growth of working-class suburbs from the 1890s onwards.

France: liberalism and repression

Both the political and the economic context to French housing reform differed in some significant ways from those of the countries so far reviewed in this chapter.[13] Large-scale industrialization and urbanization did occur in France in the nineteenth century. However, the level of urbanization remained only a little higher than that of Denmark and below Britain and the Netherlands. It

was particularly concentrated in Paris. Population increase was
slow, with a decline in the 1890s. To some extent this may have
moderated the urgency with which the housing question was viewed.
With some notable exceptions, industry remained small scale and
there was a large and politically important peasant-based agriculture. In practice, the politics of housing reform and perceptions of
the housing problem centred on the situation in Paris. There was
a large petty bourgeoisie based on small-scale property and industrial interests which was strongly resistant to extensions of state
intervention – a rather different situation from that occurring in
Britain where, for example, small-scale landlordism had a much
less powerful national political voice.

Housing conditions for the working class, especially in the big
cities, above all in Paris, were probably worse in the period up
to 1914 (and later) than in any of the other countries reviewed
here. [14] In 1909 the British Board of Trade published a report
on the working-class cost of living in France and noted that, in
comparison with Britain, there were higher death rates and much
poorer sanitation in France, that French workers worked longer
hours for less wages than their British counterparts and yet paid
rather similar levels of rent. Levels of overcrowding were also very
high (Board of Trade, 1909).

The development of French politics in the nineteenth century
was marked by great conflict and, so far as the emergent working
class was concerned, severe repression. Magraw (1983) notes that,
in contrast with Britain, there was little sign of the aristocratic
landowning elite merging with the new bourgeois interests in the
first part of the century. There was a series of conflicts between
royalists and republicans, between secular and religious interests
and large-scale repression of the working class in 1848 and after
the Paris Commune. Republican government was not firmly established until the Third Republic in 1875, by which time the royalist
threat was largely ended, although the anticlerical struggle remained significant. The dominant forces in the Third Republic
were industrial capital and the professional middle class in uneasy, often conflict-ridden alliance with a large part of the petty
bourgeoisie and the peasant sector. But the situation was complex;
historical and religious divisions cut across class divisions and there
was no unified ruling party. So governments consisted of a series
of unstable coalitions. However, for all these differences the bourgeoisie was characterized by a strong adherence to liberal principles and by opposition to extensions of state intervention. In fact,
attempts in the 1890s to develop 'municipal socialism', promoted

and accepted widely in Britain and Germany, were strongly opposed in France.

Although fear of the 'dangerous classes' was a significant feature of the impetus for limited social reform in each of the countries discussed here, it was particularly strongly felt and expressed by the French bourgeoisie (Rimlinger, 1971; Köhler and Zacher, 1982). But repression rather than an integrative strategy was the dominant response. Certainly, working-class organizations were regularly repressed, industrial relations were extremely exploitative – or at best paternalistic – and property interests were very resistant to any effective extension of state regulation of housing and public health. At the same time, social reformers were, perhaps more unequivocally than in some other countries, defenders of the status quo and unwilling to consider more than the most limited incursions on liberal principles, either in the workplace or in the urban arena. The British model of rapid industrialization and urbanization and the extension of state regulation of industry and social life was regarded by many of the French governing elite as an example to be avoided rather than emulated. In fact, the significance in the French economy and political system of small-scale property and industry and the large peasant sector meant that large-scale industrialization on the German, British or American pattern was much more limited in France. This continued after the First World War and the completion of France's transition to a modern urban-based economy occurred only after 1945.

So, unlike the situation in the countries reviewed earlier in this chapter, there was little attempt to integrate or coopt the working class (except, as discussed below, for a period in the 1850s and in a sense also by the use of appeals by key sectors of the bourgeoisie to anticlerical and republican sentiments among the workers). In any case, the slow pace of industrialization limited the size of the industrial workforce compared to the other large industrializing economies discussed here. Also the predominance of small-scale enterprises and the strong tradition of employer-dominated industrial relations hardly encouraged collective organization. Various historians refer to the prevalence of extreme expressions of antipathy towards the working class on the part of the bourgeoisie. For example, Guerrand (1967: 17–21), in his history of early housing reform, suggests that the working class was widely regarded as barbaric, a dangerous, immoral and inferior race (see also Butler and Noisette, 1983). There was also a great sensitivity to the dangers which were presumed to lurk in the slums where immorality and revolution were thought to breed. One illustration of

this concerns the debate about the merits and demerits of apartment housing and single-family housing. Such discussions occurred
in many countries and many housing reformers believed that the
latter would foster working-class 'respectability'. But in France the
preference for encouraging working-class owner occupation and
opposition to 'collective solutions' was especially evident. In this
country, too, the Catholic doctrines on social reform also pointed
to the encouragement of petty property ownership as a means of
protecting existing society and were a strong influence on some
reform thinking.

In contrast to the situation in the countries already discussed,
where the trade unions and the main working-class political organizations soon developed a reformist character, there were deep
divisions and a much stronger revolutionary current in France
(in addition, religion, and its converse, anticlericalism, was a source
of division). It took working-class organization about a decade to
recover from the Communard repression and then there was a split
between the Marxists and the reformist socialists. Apart from some
support for municipal socialism in the 1890s, most socialists were
opposed to most of the social reformers' proposals, including the
first cheap housing legislation. Given the history of state repression and the hardly disguised motives of most social reform, such
suspicion and hostility is not surprising.

As in other countries liberalism developed a radical wing towards
the end of the century. But this was a very narrow radicalism;
certainly it could not conceive of any alliance with working-class
politics, as occurred, for example, in Britain and Denmark. This
political grouping – the Radicals – was dominated by the petty
bourgeois professions (teachers, lower-status officials and so on)
and sections of the peasantry and the working class. It was anti-
big business and was strongly individualistic. By 1900 it was a
central party of government but was quite conservative in practice.
Magraw (1983) notes that the Radicals used anticlericalism as a
weapon to sustain their hold on working class support but that
when this ran out they had to choose between immobilism or social
reform. They chose the former. In general, as Kuisel (1981) notes,
the liberals, however internally divided they were, tended to be
united in opposition to Catholicism and socialism, as well as to
any more than a very limited state intervention in the freedoms
of contract and the marketplace.

As might be expected in such a society, opposition from property
owners to any extension of regulatory housing and public health
legislation effectively prevented much improvement in housing con-

ditions. A very weak and ineffective public health law was passed in 1852, and no further legislation occurred until 1902 (Dennery, 1935). Even then, communal powers to deal with slum housing were much more limited, in law and in practice, than in Britain, for example. To illustrate the general point, not until 1894 was there legal compulsion in Paris to connect houses to the sewers, but even by 1925 it was estimated that one-third were unconnected owing to strong landlord resistance (Bullock and Read, 1985: 356).

There had been some abortive experiments in model housing in the 1850s. This was a by-product of the attempt by Louis-Philippe to build a political and social base by supporting large-scale industrial and urban capital and coopting working-class support. The latter element of this project soon faded, however. There were also several experiments in employer-provided housing from mid-century, although this solution never seems to have been seen as viable except in rather isolated locations. As the reformer Emile Cheysson wrote in 1886: 'while, in the country, the employer is forced to resolve the question of cheap housing, he has no interest in the question within towns' (quoted in Bullock and Read, 1985: 430). The reason for this was that the major urban labour markets were fed by a stream of immigrant workers who could be employed cheaply and easily replaced. But the development at Mulhouse had a considerable influence on subsequent reform debates and proposals. This emphasis on the encouragement of working-class owner occupation was reinforced by the influence of Le Play, whose work stressed the need to encourage family-centred life and small-scale property ownership as a means of ensuring social integration and to counter the spread of socialism (Lescure, 1992: 229).

There were also some developments in cooperative and limited-dividend housing. The cooperative movement (made legal in limited-liability form in 1867) began to grow in the 1880s, but there was soon a split between those cooperators who wanted to ally with the socialists and those – supported by the housing reformers – who relied on elite patronage and working-class self-help to develop home ownership. Limited-dividend housing began in the 1850s and increased in the 1860s. But, as elsewhere, the availability of capital for such ventures was limited. In addition, many housing reformers were highly critical, for the reasons which have already been noted, of the blocks of apartments which many of these organizations built. However, the solution of suburban working-class single-family housing was hardly significant in France, compared to Britain or the USA. Lower wages and the lack of cheap transport were important here (and probably the lack of industrial decentralization too). But especially in Paris there was a considerable suburbanization of the poorer working class, driven out of the centre by rising rents as other land uses, including middle-class housing, expanded. Many of these expelled workers lived in self-built shacks without any urban infrastructure and faced great difficulty in commuting to their low-paid jobs in the city. The problems of this ring of *lotissements* – suburban shanty towns which were the eventual basis for the so-called 'red belt' after 1918 – were simply ignored.

The key French housing reformers, responsible for forming the Société Française des Habitations à Bon Marché (SFHBM) in 1890, which led to the first cheap housing law (Loi Siegfried), were strongly in favour of strictly limiting the role of the state and were deeply suspicious of anything which smacked of collectivism, such as apartment blocks and the more genuine elements of the cooperative movement. Siegfried regarded the British 1890 Housing Act – as we saw, a very limited measure – as nothing less than state socialism. It is not surprising, then, that the law which was passed in 1894, after much dispute, was of a minimalist nature and was based on the strategy of fostering working-class cooption through petty property ownership. The law aimed to encourage limited-dividend housing societies and cooperatives by providing cheap loans and limited tax privileges. Rental housing was not ruled out but there was a strong preference for owner occupation. The law provided no role for the local authorities in housing provision: this was absolutely unacceptable. An indirect role was conceded only later, under considerable pressure, especially for an increased housing supply in Paris, in the years just before the war.

In fact, the law achieved little as the state organism which was supposed to provide the loans was reluctant to do so. By 1905 the largest cooperative to benefit from the act had built only 170 units and the largest association only 200. In all, not much more than 7000–8000 units had been built with some form of cheap capital by this date and other aspects of the law, such as the establishment of local cheap-housing promotion committees, had also been very unsuccessful (some Prefects prevented their formation and the Ministry of Finance was hostile to loan financing) (Bullock and Read, 1985: 485–7; Lescure, 1992: 231). In 1906 communes and *départements* were allowed to give some limited assistance to the housing societies and cooperatives but not to take them over. The housing built under the 1894 Act had to be let or sold at economic prices/rents so it did not compete with private enterprise.

As elsewhere, there was little attempt to pretend that this was housing which would be affordable by other than the better-off working class (in fact, much of it was probably occupied by the lower middle class).

In so far as there was pressure for a greater degree of state and communal intervention in housing, this mainly centred on Paris. Here socialist councillors pressed for municipal building, citing examples of council housing in Britain. Interestingly, the mainstream of housing reform, represented by the SFHBM, was strongly opposed to this policy, as were the major political parties. Unlike the British situation, where in some localities Conservatives and Liberals supported limited council housing activity, there was no possibility of such support in France. After 1910 the share of working-class housing in new building fell sharply and rents rose rapidly in relation to incomes; middle-class housing was a much more profitable investment (Topalov, 1987: 107–228; Lescure, 1992: 223–8). Intense overcrowding continued and evictions and homelessness were rising. There was an increase in agitation and demonstrations about evictions and high rent levels and an atmosphere of crisis among governing elites. But the resistance from the SFHBM and the government to publicly built housing remained strong.

In 1912 a new law compromised between the necessity to make some response to the crisis and the desire to limit state intervention and its encroachment on the private housing market. This law allowed local authorities to promote the establishment of independent public housing agencies (the model was drawn from the recently formed Italian housing institutes). These were nationally regulated and governed by committees, one-third of whose members were nominated by the Prefect, one-third by local organizations which had housing interests, and one-third by the local communes or *départements*. In this way, the possibility that the local authorities would be able to control rent levels, competing unfairly with private enterprise or buying the voters' favours, was prevented. In addition, the public housing offices had to build on the same terms as the private limited-profit groups which had used the 1894 act, so that there would be no unfair state competition. An interesting addition to the law was that large families could obtain subsidies to reduce their rents in both sectors of HBM housing (the concern to foster and sustain family life being a common thread in much French social policy, the product of Catholic social philosophy and a more general concern about the country's low fertility rate – seen as one of the elements which weakened the country in the age of imperialist expansion).[15]

To summarize, housing reform remained narrowly conceived in theory and very limited in practice in France before 1914. To some extent the rather slow rate of industrialization and urbanization and the limited size of the urban working class may have contributed to this. But the nature of class relations and ideologies meant that the widespread fear of the 'dangerous classes' encouraged repressive rather than integrative policies. In any event, the organized working class was deeply divided and was manipulated by appeals to its anticlericalism and republicanism. State intervention that might have threatened the freedom of the *patron*, the landlord or the landowner was strongly opposed. At the same time, even the better-paid and more securely employed French working class, unlike its British and American counterparts, was not able to move out from the central slums to improved suburban housing and the feebly developed regulative machinery meant that conditions in these areas – most notably in Paris – remained, up to 1914 and beyond, at a level whose inadequacy had by then all but disappeared in London or New York.

GERMANY: NEGATIVE INTEGRATION AND SELF-HELP HOUSING

While in France the transition from a rural to an urban society occurred relatively slowly, under the political control of the bourgeoisie and with strong adherence to liberal principles, the situation in each of these respects in Germany was very different.[16] For a variety of reasons, including the lack of a unified state before 1870, industrialization was retarded. But it then took off very rapidly and was on a large scale (the interpenetration of large-scale financial and industrial capital in Germany had no real parallel in any of the other major economies reviewed here). Moreover, German modernization occurred in a monarchical and authoritarian political system, in which the Prussian landed aristocracy allied itself with industrial capital and, especially under Bismarck, an explicit strategy of excluding from power the rising liberal middle class and the working class was pursued.

In his classic study of the growth of cities, Weber (1969: 88) shows that there was almost no tendency for an increase in the urban population in Prussia – the dominant state in the German Reich – in the first half of the nineteenth century, but there was then a very rapid acceleration in the growth of the large cities, especially of Berlin. Weber also notes that there then came 'all those fundamental changes in the organisation of industry which had been made in England earlier in the century', including large-scale production and the growth of a developed financial system. He adds that since the 1880s Germany had rapidly increased its commerce and industry, 'her city populations have increased amazingly', and that there had been a particularly strong concentration of the population in the largest cities – some of which were by now superseding even Berlin in their rate of population growth. By 1900 Germany was somewhat more urbanized than France, while 50 years earlier the reverse had been the case.

This exceptionally rapid concentration of the population took place not only in the established cities such as Berlin, but also in formerly rural areas, most notably the Ruhr, where the natural resources required by industry were located. The problem of housing supply for the new mass labour force was acute and in Germany, more than any other country discussed here, there was a major development of employer housing, especially in locations such as the Ruhr where there was little pre-existing housing. Therefore, in Germany, the direct links between industrial needs and housing policies were especially strong. The early accounts of this employer housing show that the provision was seen as an effective means of reducing labour turnover and enforcing labour discipline especially among the more skilled sections of the workforce whose opportunity for mobility in a rapidly expanding economy was considerable. As Fritz Kalle, a reform-minded industrialist, wrote in 1892: '[t]he aims of the employer in providing for the welfare of his employees must be to ensure that they remain contented and efficient at their work ... above all the employer must attempt to create a healthy setting for family life' (quoted in Bullock and Read, 1985: 213). The situation was rather different in the existing urban centres, especially Berlin, where massive speculation in land and property occurred supported, by the banking system, and where rents rapidly reached very high levels and overcrowded *Mietkasernen* ('rent barracks') became the main form of working-class housing.

As already mentioned, the German industrial revolution initially took place in a society which was dominated by the Prussian aristocracy. This aristocracy ruled through a strong and interventionist state bureaucracy. Certainly there was no principled objection to state involvement in the control of social development and a variety of authoritarian and paternalist methods were freely employed. The governing elite remained narrow and closed, and while a substantial liberal middle class also developed, it tended to rely on the power of the state as a bulwark against the threat posed by the emergent working class, rather than being able, as elsewhere, to capture the state apparatus for itself, establish a liberal parliamentary system and limit state intervention. The Prussian parliament, which dominated the national political institutions, was elected on a basis which gave the property interests a dominant role. Moreover the parliamentary institutions had only weak powers *vis-à-vis* the Kaiser and his ministers, so the real government of Germany remained in the hands of a powerful coalition of landowners and major industrialists up to the collapse of the Reich at the end of the First World War. As in Britain, although to an even greater degree, policy was marked by an aggressive imperialism and nationalism, especially from the turn of the century. One function of this policy was to provide a means by which the ruling elites could manipulate mass opinion and stifle discontent (and the 'threat' and subsequent repression of the workers' movement, described below, was also a means of ensuring middle-class acquiescence).

While several of the countries already discussed in this chapter had social, economic and political structures which encouraged various sections of the bourgeoisie into an accommodation with the reformist wing of the workers' movement, this was not so in Germany where the bourgeois parties were fragmented, being divided by religion (Catholic/Protestant), by location (rural/urban) and by occupation (professional/commercial-industrial), and were competing for what little power was available to most of them through the authoritarian political system. Overall, as Berghahn (1982) notes, the German ruling elite was a quasi-autocracy with little taste for compromise up until 1918.

The German workers' movement was of major importance in terms of its size and rapidly developing organization. But it was also heavily repressed and excluded from any access to political power nationally. Socialist ideas and organizations took root in Germany earlier than in Britain, for example, and a Socialist Party, linked to the First International, was founded in 1869. In 1875 a unified Social Democratic Party (SPD) was founded in which Marxist influence remained strong, although there were important internal struggles between Marxists and reformists (Fletcher, 1987). By 1914 this had become the first and greatest mass socialist party and the largest German party, but, in its early years in particular, it was based on the artisan workforce and its penetration of the unskilled workforce, let alone the lumpenproletariat, remained very limited. The rise of the party and strong trade union organization was perceived by the ruling elites and the middle class as a considerable threat, but Bismarck also sought to manipulate this factor to discredit liberalism. Between 1878 and 1890 anti-socialist laws led to the repression of the workers' movement and its organizations. To some extent this radicalized the SPD and its electoral vote rose during this period (it was not banned from electoral politics). This attempt to marginalize the socialist and trade union movement was mirrored in the workplace where repression was also the norm. One consequence was that the workers' movements developed an enclosed subculture, with an impressive array of social, cultural and community organizations. This aspect of the German workers' movement was on a larger scale than anything to be seen in the other countries discussed here, although, as Topalov (1985) notes, it was a general feature of working-class organization at this time. Various historians, noting the unwillingness of the dominant groups to come to any accommodation with the new working class, have described this as a form of 'negative integration'.

The history of social reform in Germany is well known.[17] Essentially, Bismarck promoted social insurance legislation in an attempt to coopt and bind the skilled working class and the lower middle class to the existing social and political order. This was, however, an attempt which he soon abandoned and it was viewed with suspicion and hostility by the liberal middle class and the workers' movement. In addition, the industrialists, some of whom had supported the effort to coopt the working class, became increasingly opposed to further social or industrial reform, as the failure of the policy to achieve its ends became apparent. Ironically, the legislation did lead to some degree of integration, as trade union leaders and other working-class representatives became involved in the rapidly expanding social insurance apparatus, seeing this as a useful basis for working-class mobilization. This in turn helped to strengthen the drift to reformism in the socialist and trade union movements from the latter years of the nineteenth century. However, the belief that only the inevitable revolution would really set the workers free remained strong and there was neither the opportunity nor the inclination in Germany, unlike Britain, to adopt a thoroughgoing reformism and collaboration with bourgeois political groupings.

Social reform movements began to develop from the 1870s, involving a mixture of conservative, liberal and Catholic ideologists. At first Bismarck showed some signs of being responsive to their influence but, as described above, he later shifted away from using social reform as a means of social control and argued that working-class conditions could be improved only by industrial expansion, leading to an increase in workers' standards of living. Meanwhile, discontent must be repressed.

As in other countries, the earliest experiments in housing reform date from the middle of the century, when the conservative writer Huber was involved in the formation of a building society in Berlin.[18] It was a straightforward attempt to foster a form of cooperative owner occupation for skilled workers, for the same reasons that conservatives supported the extension of petty property ownership elsewhere. This was an isolated experiment and a revival of interest in housing reform took place only when the liberal social reform movement began to appear in the 1870s. The value of social reform as a protection against revolution ('to prevent a Paris Commune in Germany') was at the forefront of the reformers' concerns (Bullock and Read, 1985: 52, 68). However, they were deeply split; for example, the conservatives tended to support cooperative housing but liberals opposed such collectivist solutions.

As elsewhere, the ebb and flow of the reform debate often coincided with the perceived level of threat emanating from the 'dangerous classes' and Bullock and Read (1985) suggest that the revival of social reform in Germany in the 1880s may well have been influenced by the concurrent social unrest and the reform debate in Britain. All the familiar elements of this discourse were present in Germany. There were calls for the increased state regulation of housing conditions, the need to educate the working class to want better housing (influenced by Octavia Hill), the desire to promote working-class owner occupation and the reluctance to accept tenement housing. There was, however, rather less opposition from some reformers in Germany than in France to a measure of state and local government involvement in housing supply. This reflected the difference in attitudes to the state–civil society relationship in Germany, as well as a long tradition of civic involvement in certain urban service functions seen as essential for the general public good (Dawson, 1914). Hardly surprisingly, given the extreme speculative pressures in the major urban centres, the question of land reform and its relationship to working-class housing supply was an important topic. Liberal economists here, as elsewhere, strongly opposed any intervention, but those who argued for the development of municipal land policies had greater influence in practice and, from the 1890s, many cities began to purchase land and seek to control its development in other ways.

Sanitary reforms and building and housing inspection powers began to develop from the late 1860s and 1870s. Compulsory purchase was possible in Prussia from 1874. There was also a slow development of limited-profit and cooperative housing, although, as in France, there was a split between what might be described as genuine cooperative self-help building and Huberist exercises in paternalist control from above. In general, the fluctuations of political interest in housing reform were rather similar to those which occurred elsewhere. Opposition from property interests – strongly entrenched in the electoral system in local and central government – tended to peak at times of housing crisis when the shortage of supply and profits were greatest. There was more support for regulation when market conditions were slack. By 1914 a few cities had built a little housing and there had been a modest expansion of non-profit and limited-profit housing for the better-off working class (Local Government Board, 1919). But opposition to state-supported building for general working-class needs, because it might compete with the private market, remained strong. In fact, as will be argued below, most assistance was used to support forms of 'tied' housing provision, which can be seen as an extension of the tradition of employer housing.

From the late 1880s housing reformers began to press for national regulatory legislation and a few years later for a state role in the provision of housing. Action by the Imperial government was seen as the only way to circumvent the strength of property interests at local and Land (state) levels. But such interests were also strongly represented in the Imperial political system and there was no disposition on the part of the powerful state bureaucracy to make more than token concessions to reform pressures. The SPD was, on the whole, inimical to the extension of state intervention, because of the influence of revolutionary theories and because the cooptative nature of state welfare policy was evident. However, by the 1900s some elements in the SPD were beginning to support reform, especially in the south, where the Prussian electoral system did not apply and where they had had local electoral victories, and so had some local power.[19] In 1900 some local SPD candidates advocated a reform programme and the national party was thinking about voting in the Reichstag with the centre parties on housing reform. But an added complication was resistance from city and state governments to Imperial intervention – this was seen as an interference with their autonomy.

Between 1903 and 1907, a time of relative prosperity, interest in national housing reform languished. This revived in the years before 1914 as the housing crisis returned. As it had done in the previous crisis in 1904, the government attempted to deflect the pressure by proposing a Prussian Housing Bill. This concentrated on extending regulative powers and avoided any direct intervention through subsidies. But the new Prussian Bill was even weaker than the 1904 measure and sought to protect property interests. In general, attempts at national reform were thwarted, both by the steadfast opposition of property interests and by the split in the reformers' ranks between the centralizers and the localists. In the event, the Prussian Bill was not passed until 1918, under very different social and political circumstances.

This minimal progress towards national housing legislation meant that in this respect less had been achieved in Germany by 1914 than in most of the other countries discussed in this chapter. However, this was not the whole story for, apart from the local developments in land and planning policies which were noted earlier, there was a considerable amount lent by the social insurance funds for various forms of cooperative and limited-profit housing. This development seems to be in sharp contrast to the general history of minimal state housing legislation and requires some explanation. Cooperative housing activity had expanded after 1889 when a new law made it viable (Umrath, 1950). However, it was a possibility only for the skilled working class and for the rapidly growing mass of white-collar workers. There were three main types of cooperative housing. The first was the traditional type, building for ownership. The second built for renting, mainly to the skilled working class; many of these cooperatives had strong links with the trade unions and the socialist movement. The third type of cooperative was founded by white-collar workers and expanded rapidly up to 1914. Direct government support for these ventures was on an extremely small scale, although cheap land was frequently made available by city governments. What made their growth possible was the availability from the 1890s of loan capital from the social insurance funds.

There were two main factors which lay behind this development (US Bureau of Labor Statistics, 1914; Local Government Board, 1919). The first was that, in their early years, the insurance funds had to pay out few benefits and were accumulating considerable reserves. So housing built for reasonably securely employed and better-off sections of the working class and the middle class provided an opportunity to invest the funds and earn a modest but steady return. Interestingly, this situation would not have continued as the demands on the insurance funds grew. So just before the First

World War the government increased the interest payable on the loans and restricted their availability. Second, in the majority of cases the housing built with these loans had to be occupied by the workers who were contributors to the social insurance schemes (i.e. the better-off working and lower middle class). The rationale was that better housing conditions would improve the health of these workers and limit their need to claim insurance benefits. A further feature was that most of this housing was linked to individual industries and occupations. For example, central, state and local governments encouraged and supported the formation of building societies to provide housing for their own workers. There were very few examples of building which were not tied to specific sources of employment in this way. Therefore, to a considerable extent this housing may be seen as a form of employer housing, although of a less directly controlled nature than the type of housing provided in the first phase of German industrialization in the isolated, formerly rural locations, where no other source of supply existed.

To summarize, housing reform remained a fairly marginalized cause in Germany up until 1914. In this respect housing mirrored the wider constellation of political and economic forces in the country. The exclusion of reform was not, however, the product of any deep-rooted and ideologically determined resistance to state intervention, but of a distinctively constituted balance of political and economic forces and an approach to the 'social question' which relied on repressing and isolating the working class rather than any very sustained attempt to integrate even the skilled worker into the system. This in turn encouraged the development of a 'negatively integrated' working-class movement, in which self-help housing cooperatives took their place alongside a range of other cultural and social institutions. A distinctive feature of the German experience was the use of social insurance funding to support workers' housing but, as has been argued above, access to this was restricted on the basis of employment and participation in the social insurance schemes.

All this is put in perspective by a 1908 report in which the British Board of Trade reviewed German housing conditions (Board of Trade, 1908). The report notes that rent levels were very high and overcrowding extreme; compared to Britain, rents were about 25 per cent higher in Germany but wages 20 per cent less, while food costs were also higher in Germany and hours of work longer. In short, the majority of the German working class remained in poor housing and was heavily exploited. As far as the cooperative and other building societies were concerned, the report suggested that this was largely 'middle-class housing', being far too costly for most workers. There was some limited attempt at Octavia Hill-type solutions by the 'improvement' of one- and two-roomed apartments, but no reference is made in the report at all to the suburban housing solution. In fact, there is little evidence that this was, to any degree, a feature of working-class housing in Germany at this time. Perhaps the only lighter note in this report comes when reference is made to a housing society formed by the Social Democrats, hopefully named 'Paradise' but, the report adds, 'its operations are limited'.

THE UNITED STATES: REGULATING THE TENEMENTS

While the possibility of national housing reform at least existed in Germany before 1914, it was entirely absent in the USA, where any public responsibility for housing matters was reserved for state and local governments.[20] Therefore, there is simply no national history to examine before the First World War and, apart from a brief period then, not in fact until the Roosevelt New Deal in the 1930s. Moreover, to a very considerable extent the early history of reform centres on developments in one city, New York. The approach to housing and planning issues which evolved there had a major influence on many other cities. So, in this chapter, the history of housing and social reform in New York will be the major focus of discussion.[21]

New York was of course a major urban centre in the first half of the nineteenth century, along with a few other ports. But urbanization linked to industrial growth did not take off until the 1860s, after the Civil War especially (Warner, 1972). It then proceeded very rapidly as the American economy boomed and the large industrial agglomerations expanded, especially in the north-east.[22] A distinctive feature of this growth was that its ever expanding labour force requirements were met, not as in Europe from rural to urban migration within the country, but by successive waves of immigrants from Europe, especially from rural areas. One consequence, of particular significance to social reformers, was that the problem of the 'dangerous classes' involved a concern that immigrants, with their 'alien' cultures and patterns of life, be assimilated as citizens to the 'American way of life' and to the values which, it was presumed, were therein enshrined. As is well known, these values were said to include self-reliance, sobriety, individualism and so on, and the somewhat mythical model of a 'golden age' of rural and small town independence was drawn upon in this context. Developments in Europe were often viewed with distaste, especially when these involved anything which smacked of collectivism or 'state socialism'.

Weber's (1969) study shows just how explosive the growth of the urban population was in the second half of the nineteenth century. Over the whole century to 1890 the population of the major cities increased from about 300,000 to over 18 million and the number of such cities from six to about 450. There was a particularly rapid increase in industrially related urbanization in the decade from 1860 and in the 1880s. In the latter period the growth of manufacturing employment was very significant. This urban population was concentrated in the North Atlantic and North Central states. Weber calculates that 80 per cent of it lived in these two regions in 1890 and five states, ranging from Massachusetts in the north to the District of Columbia in the south, had over 50 per cent of their population living in cities. New York had grown from about 60,000 in 1800 – smaller than Philadelphia and minuscule compared to the major European centres – to 2.7 million in 1890, second only to London in size.

By the 1860s all the familiar features of the 'social question' which so concerned European social reformers were present in New York. There was a complete lack of public health and housing regulation and a growing slum population which was viewed with extreme anxiety by the middle class, both because of the threat of disease – there was, for example, a panic in the 1860s that cholera might be about to arrive with the foreign immigrants from Europe – and also because of the threat of social unrest, which at times became a reality. The first reform movements saw the slums as leading inevitably to a degradation of the moral character of the poor. Their control was also necessary as a means of ensuring that the alien mass of immigrants was integrated into the American way of life. At the same time these reformers, who tended to get support from larger-scale business interests, were opposed to the corrupt machine politics which dominated city government and which was seen as an obstacle to any effective reform. But, as elsewhere, the pressure for reform tended to ebb and flow. The Draft Riots of 1866 helped bring about the first measure of tenement house regulation but the law was minimal and was not enforced. Moreover, as the perceived threat from the 'alien masses' receded in subsequent years, so did the prospects for reform.

There was some interest in European experiments, especially the British development of '5 per cent philanthropy' and from the 1870s a few 'model dwellings' were built. Alfred White, who was responsible for the best known of these, made it clear, however, that such housing was not to be regarded as 'charity': this would only weaken self-reliance and lead to an unhealthy dependence. Rather, the model projects had to be based on sound business principles, charging market-level rents but providing better quality than the private landlord. But, at a time when capital could obtain high returns by investing in private housing, there was very little interest in supplying cheap capital for model dwellings, although this 'solution' continued to dazzle the reformers for many years, according to Lubove (1974). As the French reformer Emile Cacheux noted sadly in 1880, '[i]t is easy to obtain the plans for healthy, comfortable houses from an architect, but it is less easy to persuade investors to make them a reality' (quoted in Bullock and Read, 1985: 413).

The rapid growth of the economy in the 1880s, together with renewed migration from abroad, followed by an agricultural depression in the 1890s, all contributed to an increase in industrial and social unrest and unemployment. In these years there was again a sense of heightened social and urban crisis. This found various expressions, for example there was a growth in pressure for anti-immigrant legislation. Racist and nativist sentiments cut across class divisions and served as a means of dividing the working class. On the one hand, there was the (often) skilled 'American' worker and, on the other, the 'un-American' alien masses.

The role of social reform as a means of integrating this alien threat became central to the Progressive reform movement and its proposals not only for housing but for education, social work, the provision of parks and so on. This integrative social engineering was based on a strong belief in the ability of the environment to modify behaviour. It was also profoundly conservative, seeking to sustain the existing economy and society and showing great distaste for anything that would involve more than a very limited regulative role for the state. An interesting example of these views was contained in a report of the US Commissioner for Labor (1895) on European housing. He concluded that the early experiments in municipal housing, especially those in Britain, were a mistake. Decent housing for the majority of the working class could be provided on a sound commercial basis, some of it through model dwellings, and for those who could not afford such housing the Octavia Hill solution was the answer. Government should do no

more than regulate private market conditions; state-supported
building would only interfere destructively with the private market.
In the longer term the Commissioner looked to the development
of cheaper suburban housing, aided by improved transport links,
as an important solution, at least for the better-off working class.

This deep conservatism may also be seen, for example, in the
writings of Jacob Riis, who drew attention to the plight of the
New York slum dwellers in 1890 (Lubove, 1974: 49–80). For all
his concern, Riis drew a line between the 'deserving' and the 'undeserving' poor and was harsh in his condemnation of the latter.
As far as any positive suggestions for relieving the problem were
concerned, he kept within the common framework of assumptions
and values that characterized most of the reform movement. There
was an appeal to the Christian ethic, a belief that a return to the
rural and small town Utopia of the now vanished 'golden age'
of early settlement was desirable, a strong assertion of individualism and hostility to any form of collectivist solution which might
inhibit private enterprise. As the leading housing reformer of the
period, Lawrence Veiller, wrote:

> [t]he assumption that thousands of people live under conditions
> such as are found in our large cities throughout America because
> there are no other places in which they can live is wholly un-
> warranted and not borne out by the facts ... We may as well frankly
> admit that there is a considerable proportion of our population who
> will live in any kind of abode that they can get irrespective of how
> unhygienic it may be (Veiller, 1914: 71).

In 1900, partly in response to the perception of social and
urban crisis in the city (where population densities in some parts
of Manhattan were the highest in the world and typical working-
class rents took 25 per cent or more of income), a Tenement
House Commission was established, under the control of the Progressives. This provided the basis for the approach to housing
reform which was to dominate not just New York, but the other major
cities for the next 20 years, a movement in which Veiller, the
secretary to the Commission, played a central role as an organizer
and propagandist. Three possible approaches to practical housing
reform were promoted by various reformers: model dwellings,
Octavia Hill 'improvement' and increased tenement house regulation. Veiller regarded the first two as limited in applicability and
opted strongly for regulation. According to Lubove (1974), in some
of his writing he indicated that, in the long term, the removal of

the working class to smaller rural settlements and the encouragement of home ownership would be desirable. But he was a practical man who concentrated on what was immediately possible.
This was regulation (Robbins, 1966).

The report of the Tenement House Commission reflected these
priorities, rejecting municipal housing as benefiting a 'favoured few'
only and at the 'sacrifice of self-dependence'. Such housing would
also not be efficient 'under the necessarily cumbrous and mechan-
ical methods of the government system', and could also be used
by political parties to retain their control 'if tenanted with a view
to votes' (quoted in Lubove, 1974: 180). But above all it would
compete unfairly with private enterprise. In fact, the Commission
opposed anything which would be 'unfair' competition, such as tax
concessions for cheap housing. Assisted by Theodore Roosevelt, the
state governor, a revised tenement house law was passed in 1901.
This became the centrepiece of the housing reform effort in New
York City and the many other cities where Veiller spread his
gospel over the next 20 or so years. Although by 1914 a few other
reformers were beginning to question this regulative solution, some
of whom campaigned for public housing in the interwar period,
their proposals had no practical impact. A more significant development in the regulative tradition was the spread of land use zoning,
first instituted in New York City in 1916, which according to its
first advocates would improve housing affordability by controlling
land values. In practice it was taken up by business and the middle
class as a way of preserving high land values and protecting their
own residential and commercial areas from possible incursion by
undesirable uses, including housing for the poor.

A notable feature of this history is the lack of any reference to
the role of working-class organizations in relation to housing reform. Of course the failure of a mass socialist party to develop
in the USA and the conservative attitudes of the craft unions to
social reform have been widely analysed, but it is interesting to
note that, according to Marcuse, there was no housing element in
the reform programmes of the populist movement which gained
significant working-class support around the turn of the century.
Neither was housing an issue in the successive presidential campaigns of the Socialist Party candidate, Debs (Marcuse, 1980, and
personal communication, 1985). One reason for the lack of pressure
for reform from the section of the working class which was at the
core of the organized labour movement in Europe, the skilled
worker, may have been that, compared to his or her European
counterpart, the American worker was considerably better off and

therefore able to obtain private market housing. An additional
factor was the availability of cheap suburban land and the rapid
development of suburban transport systems (and some decentralization of manufacturing from the 1890s onwards) (Warner, 1972).
Furthermore, although the housing conditions among the immigrant
population in the notorious slums of New York's Lower East Side
were as bad as anything in comparable European neighbourhoods,
there was more mobility out of this situation into better working
and living conditions in an economy which was rapidly expanding.
So the duration if not the intensity of housing deprivation for
much of the working class may have been less than in Europe.

Some of these suggestions are confirmed by the British Board
of Trade (1911) survey of the living conditions and wages of the
US working class. The report refers to a degree of material prosperity among many workers which was tending to increase housing
standards. It also refers to the importance of rapid transit systems
in encouraging suburbanization. The survey found that the rental
per room demanded tended to increase for larger-sized dwellings,
the reverse of the European experience (i.e. there was a strong
demand at the time for better-quality working-class housing) and
that there was a considerable amount of working-class owner occupation, again a rare feature of European cities at this time. The
report also suggests, however, that some sections of the population
were in very poor housing, namely recent migrants and blacks
(who had begun to migrate to the cities in search of work in increasing numbers around 1900). In fact, a parallel is drawn between
the housing and living conditions of two main sectors of the working class in the USA and Europe. In the USA the 'American' workers
were doing well compared to 'negroes and immigrants'; in Europe
the key distinction was between 'organized and efficient labour'
and 'unorganized and inefficient labour'. But, it was suggested, in
the USA the standards of the immigrant group in most cases soon
began to improve. Above all, the Board of Trade Report provides
some hard evidence for the greater ability of many American
workers to afford private housing. Comparing the wages and
standards of living of skilled American and British workers (the
latter being notably better paid than their counterparts in France
or Germany), the former earned about 2.3 times as much as the
latter for a very similar number of hours worked. The cost of
housing was about twice as much in the United States as in Britain
but the quality and size of the accommodation in America was
clearly superior. At the same time the cost of food was about 25
per cent more in the USA but, the report noted, the larger absolute

incomes of the US workers left them with more to spend on other items, including housing. The cost of food and rents together was about 50 per cent greater in the USA but, as noted above, the wage differential was far greater.

To conclude, US housing reform in the pre-1914 era (and subsequently) was much more limited than in the industrializing European nations. It amounted to little more than tenement house regulation which began to spread from New York to other major centres from the 1900s. As in Europe, the pressure for housing reform mainly came from a bourgeoisie which was, from time to time, fearful of the destabilizing consequences of the new, alien mass working class. But ultimately such pressures were relieved by economic rather than social or political means, by upward mobility in an expanding urban and industrial system. Tenement house reform was at best a marginal aspect of the improvement in working-class housing conditions that was occurring at this time, but it was a method of state intervention that fitted in with the strong desire to support what were seen as the core values of this, the 'first new nation'. As Lubove (1974) points out, there were also three more prosaic reasons why Veiller's proposals for tenement house reform may have been particularly attractive to the Progressives at the turn of the century. First, in an era of rapid immigration and urbanization, any alternative would probably have involved large-scale public expenditure commitments. Second, commercial landlords did provide some form of potentially acceptable housing for large sections of the working class. Finally, restrictive legislation held out the promise of a cheap solution to the problems of slums and urban blight.

THE SOCIAL CONSTRUCTION OF HOUSING REFORM

It has not been possible in a single chapter, dealing with six countries, to do more than skate, sometimes precariously, across the surface of the early history of housing reform. Much detail has had to be omitted and complexity cut through in a search for the general contours of reform in each country. However, the main purpose of this chapter is to provide the necessary context and orientation for the analysis of social housing which follows. Several broad conclusions can be derived from these accounts of housing reform before the First World War.

The first point is that there was no inevitable progression towards greater state involvement in housing supply and no general recognition, as other 'solutions' failed, that directly subsidized provision was necessary. Housing reform must be viewed in a much wider context than that provided by many conventional accounts. At the same time, 'radical' accounts which stress, for example, the role of organized labour or the centrality of capitalist requirements for labour force reproduction are, at best, oversimplistic in their understanding of precisely what these involved.

There are two important aspects to the re-examination of the historical record. The first is to place the concern with housing reform in the context of the real object of the reformers' concern – this was the defence and maintenance of property and class privilege from the threat which the emergence of a mass, urban-based proletariat *seemed* to present. Better housing was seen as a means to a wider societal objective, as an English local government official stated in 1895: '[t]he education of the poorest classes to fully appreciate the benefits accruing from their being housed in healthy dwellings, provided with all the requisite sanitary arrangements and appliances tending to promote cleanly and tidy habits ... must precede their intellectual and moral elevation' (quoted in US Commissioner for Labor, 1895, 171). But, second, the actual nature of this threat also has to be examined because it was the *realities* of the situation that largely determined policy formation, not the frequently exaggerated arguments and the appeal to bourgeois fears deployed by the reformers, who were often not the real holders of political and economic power.

This brings us to what lies at the heart of any attempt to understand the early history of reform, the issue of how the new working class was to be controlled, disciplined and integrated into the social and economic order. Here there are several key considerations. First, there was the sheer size of the problem and, more particularly, the potential or actual ability of the working class to mobilize against its exploitation in the economy and in urban life. On the whole, we have seen that this ability was rather limited and the contribution of even the organized working class to housing reform was marginal – although the development of prototypical housing institutions based on working-class self-help was notable in some European countries, where they continued to be significant in the interwar period, when state subsidies were sometimes available. Second, we have to examine the strategies adopted by the dominant groups regarding the 'social question'. In each country political and economic relations were differently constituted and the importance of industrial versus property interests, rural versus urban interests, secular versus religious interests, and so on, varied. These differences influenced the extent to which repression rather than reform was employed and determined the ruling ideology regarding the perceived scope for state intervention and the form which that might take. A third issue concerns the necessity for housing reform directly linked to labour force supply. This was important in Germany but less apparent elsewhere (although some support from industrial capital for the improvement of worker housing was present in other countries).

A further aspect of history has often been underemphasized – the extent to which the problem of working-class housing could be left to the private market. It tends to be assumed that the private market always failed. But this was not so as, for example, the comparison of the American and the European situation showed. In some countries, even before 1914, the 'suburban solution' was a means by which a part of the better-paid and more securely employed working class and the growing lower middle class could move out from the urban slums to better housing and living conditions. Even in France working-class suburbanization occurred, notably round Paris. But here low wages resulted in the growth of suburban *lotissements*, self-built shanty towns, a form of settlement which persisted even after 1945.

This raises the more general need to consider the whole range of solutions to the housing problem which were espoused by reformers and to link these differing strategies to the perceptions that the reformers had of the segmentation of the working class and the way in which each of these segments related to the proposed reforms. As we have noted, many reformers divided the working class into three sections (see, for example, US Commissioner for Labor, 1895: 439–41). First, the skilled and 'responsible' workers – these were a key target for many reform proposals, because it was seen as essential to ensure that this group was securely integrated within the existing social and economic order. Its potential for assuming the leadership of oppositional movements – in the workplace or in civil society – was frequently noted and it was from this group that the leadership and membership of most working-class industrial and political organizations were drawn. In many countries conservative forces looked to the promotion of single-family owner-occupied housing as a major means of binding the 'aristocracy of labour' to the existing social order and of separating it from possible contagion, morally or politically, by those who lay below it in the social order. A second reason why this group featured largely in the projects, such as model housing, that were developed before 1914 was more narrowly economic. It was only this sector of the labour force that could afford the levels of un-subsidized housing costs that had to be met.

A second section of the working class was the 'deserving poor'. Solutions to the plight of this group were rather less apparent, although there are frequent references to the use of 'Octavia Hill' methods, in other words the imposition of a regime of paternal control aimed at encouraging thrift, sobriety and other virtues which, it was believed, would make minimal commercially run housing available to this group. But, as the following quotation from Hill implies, the deeper purpose again concerned social integration, not just housing provision:

> [o]n what principles was I to rule these people? On the same that I had already tried ... firstly, to demand a strict fulfilment of their duties to me, one of the chief of which would be the punctual payment of rent; and, secondly, to endeavour to be so unfailingly just and patient, that they should learn to trust the rule that was over them (Hill, 1871, 456–9).

In addition, some faith was placed in the regulation of housing and public health conditions as a means of enabling this group to improve its housing conditions. Also there was an expectation that, as the working-class elite moved into better housing, the accommodation which it left would filter down to the deserving poor.

Finally there was the 'undeserving poor', the dangerous and unstable residuum for which repressive and punitive solutions were frequently advocated. On the whole, this group was regarded, with a greater or lesser degree of frankness, as a hopeless category for which no solution other than their eventual elimination from the urban scene could be expected. This brutal attitude was widespread, even among the more socially progressive housing reformers (and was probably shared by many representatives of the skilled working class). A good example of this is to be found in an article by Carol Aronovici (1914), a critic of the Veiller approach to housing reform and an advocate of more broadly based governmental intervention. He divided the population for which housing needed to be provided into seven classes, the top three of which covered the middle and upper classes. The bottom four ranged from the 'skilled wage earners' and the 'well-paid unskilled wage earners' – for which, he noted, the private market could largely cater – down to the 'wage earners capable of paying rentals on the basis of a minimum standard of housing' (i.e. the 'deserving poor' who could be served by filtering and 'Octavia Hill methods') and the final group which was described as 'the *subnormal* [my emphasis] who are unable to pay a rental that would yield a reasonable return on a home of a minimum standard of sanitation'. Although Aronovici does not offer any solution to the housing problems of this group, the implications of the language he uses are clear and other, less liberal minds did not hesitate to suggest how this group should be treated. For example, Veiller referred both to the forced relocation of ex-peasant migrants back to rural settlements and the creation of racially segregated dormitories where the alien masses could be kept under close control (see Lubove, 1974, for an account of Veiller's views). We also saw, in Stedman Jones's (1971) account of London in the 1890s, how a variety of punitive solutions to the problem of housing and controlling the 'residuum' were advocated in this city.

Of course, there were deep divisions between the housing reformers. There was no neat, universally agreed and comprehensive matching of this classification of the working class and the available reformist solutions. Some reformers regarded model housing as the key to reform, others dismissed it as insignificant and stressed regulation or 'Octavia Hill' methods. Some reformers believed that the control of land prices and development was the solution, others argued that state assistance was required. To some extent these contending proposals reflected different perceptions about which sections of the working class should be targeted for reform. Thus the proponents of model housing were frequently forced to recognize that their solution could be applied only to better-off workers. But the differences and conflicts also reflected the broader social and economic interests which these reformers represented, a good example being the distinctive proposals for housing-related reform advanced by Liberals and Conservatives in Britain. Also wider national differences were significant, for example an emphasis on land reform was more relevant in the high-density European cities than in America, where land was plentiful and cheap.

But what role did the case for state-subsidized rental housing play in all of this? A limited one in many cases as few housing reformers clearly prioritized this solution, although there were some exceptions. There were several reasons why subsidized housing was not supported. A first point is that there was stronger support in Europe than in America, at least for initiatives to increase the supply of long-term and reasonably cheap loan capital for housing (and, in some cases, of cheap land). Essentially, this was a response to the problem which model housing had encountered, the lack of investors willing to accept a limited but still profitable return on housing capital when better opportunities existed elsewhere, including in the private housing market. But the provision of cheap loans was not seen as marking an essential break with the principles of liberal political economy, at least if this doctrine was interpreted reasonably flexibly. Some degree of intervention to correct the worst abuses of speculation and profiteering ('market imperfections') could be advocated. However, there was a strong reluctance to set rents at much below what they would be in a reasonably functioning private market by extensive direct subsidization. And, in practice, 'cheap' capital usually meant borrowing at interest rates similar to those which governments paid for their funds, i.e. the lowest possible commercial rate. However, these loans did solve the other main problem, which was that private housing loans usually covered only some of the capital costs, not the whole or even a large proportion necessarily.

Objections to state subsidies were expressed in various ways. For example, it was claimed that they would privilege only a few unfairly; that they would breed dependence and inhibit thrift and self-reliance; that they would be open to political and other abuse; that they would encourage bureaucratic and inefficient state provision (all arguments still familiar today). In America the opposition was especially vociferous. This quotation from Veiller (1920: 127) is typical: 'any government housing [is] unsound and against public policy. For, it is class legislation which takes from some of the people the burdens that belong on their own shoulders and puts them on the shoulders of other people where they do not belong'. In addition, some claimed that with reforms – regulation, land reform and planning – the private housing market (for renting or home ownership) could meet working-class housing needs. Others even argued – perhaps seriously – that the real answer was to raise working-class wages, not to subsidize housing supply. However a common thread in all these arguments was the wish to do nothing which would provide serious competition for the private market as the main source of working-class housing.

All this resulted in a general reluctance to advocate state subsidies for housing, except in special circumstances. In France, for example, subsidies were first provided for large families in HBM housing. This was justifiable in terms of the general national interest in increasing the birth-rate and sustaining family life. In Germany, in so far as assistance was provided, it was mainly tied to the needs of governmental and private employers to house their labour forces and the interest that the social insurance funds had in minimizing claims upon them. But the most widespread basis for legitimizing some demands for state subsidies related to slum clearance.

On the one hand, the inability of slum dwellers to afford the rents of minimal standard replacement housing was apparent. Yet without such replacement housing, when displaced they would only recreate slum conditions elsewhere in the city, it was argued. On the other hand, the clearance of the worst inner-city slums could be seen as necessarily in the public interest, especially when slums were viewed not just as sources of physical disease and squalor but as socially and morally dangerous. In addition, there was some interest in clearing potentially valuable sites for commercial and other forms of more profitable development and, especially when the housing market was slack, in reducing the supply of cheap housing (mostly owned by the smaller and less politically influential landlords in all probability).

So the case put for subsidized housing was as a limited supplement to other methods of housing reform and to the continued centrality of private market provision. As we shall see, it was this case that has subsequently provided the most widely accepted rationale for state-subsidized social rented housing. Before 1914 state-subsidized social rented housing was not seen, except by a few socialists, as a solution to the mass housing of the working class. Ironically, however, the same reluctance to interfere too greatly with the private market meant that most of the assisted housing built before 1914 was too expensive for those in whose name and for whose needs its construction was justified. Instead, it was occupied by better-off sections of the working class and the lower middle class, who also became the main beneficiaries of social housing in the immediate period after 1918. This contradiction between the *social* arguments for subsidized housing and the *economic* realities which govern its actual provision is one which, in various and changing forms, has been central to understanding its evolution throughout the twentieth century.

CONCLUSION: THE LEGACIES OF EARLY HOUSING REFORM

By 1918 profound changes had come about in the social, economic and political context within which the early movements for social reform had operated. In the next chapter we shall discuss some of these changes and their consequences for social housing in detail. Before 1914, state-subsidized social rented housing was just one of several competing answers to the housing question. After 1918 in Europe it became much more important than that, at least for a period. The war also rendered obsolete, or at least suppressed, many aspects of the discourse which surrounded housing reform before the war. As we shall see, after 1918 housing policies were still driven, in part, by a fear of the 'dangerous classes'. But now there was a more substantial basis for this fear, and it centred not on the slum dweller and the lumpenproletariat but on the group which the pre-war reformers had sought to separate from moral and political contagion, the 'respectable' working class and even some sections of the middle class. The post-war shortages of housing for these groups contributed to a wider and larger-scale discontent whose destabilizing possibilities were far greater than anything experienced in the years before 1914. These groups had won the right, on the battlefields and through the completion of virtually universal (male) suffrage, to a far greater access to constitutional political power than hitherto. For this and other reasons, their demands for at least a modicum of social protection from the state could be denied, in the immediate aftermath of war, only at a potentially disastrous cost to the dominant social and economic order.

Even though the revolutionary movement soon failed in most countries, and organized labour experienced many reversals and defeats in the years to come, social democracy had moved from the margins of the pre-war political system to a position of major influence and, in some cases, real power after the war. In the post-war world the huge social distance which separated the reformist elites and the working class, in which the former viewed the latter almost as alien beings, to be openly controlled, disciplined and repressed, could not be recreated. The balance of power between labour and capital, and between their political representatives, was altered significantly. So, while revolutionary demands disappeared from the agenda of mainstream politics, reformist demands became far more firmly established than they were before the war (at least in Europe). Central to these demands was the extension of state-subsidized welfare provision, including social housing.

The war also brought about, or accelerated, other important changes. Among the most significant was the extension of state regulation and control into many areas of the economy and society where its presence would have been hitherto unthinkable. Although, as we shall see, most post-war regimes sought to reverse these changes and return to 'business as usual' after 1918, for the reasons stated above it was never possible fully to renounce the enhanced responsibilities that the state had exercised in the economy and in civil society in wartime. In relation to social policy, this involved a broader and deeper commitment to providing a degree of security in poverty, sickness, unemployment and old age than had existed before 1914.

A further important set of changes occurred in the capitalist economic system. Britain finally lost its role as the leading world economic power, to be replaced by America, whose whole economy was strengthened by the conflict. Within industry, war accelerated the growth of mass production and new patterns of organization and management. At the same time, older industries entered a long-drawn-out process of decline while the new 'Fordist' industries began to emerge. Such changes had profound effects on the class structure and on the distribution of economic opportunities. As we shall discuss later, the war also left national and the international economies in a precarious state, not just in the years immediately after 1918 but in the longer run too. These changes had consequences for the varying fortunes of social rented housing.

In short, these and many other changes meant that the social, economic and political context to post-war social housing was radically altered from that which had existed before the war. However, there were also some important legacies from the period before 1914. During this period foundations were laid that were of lasting significance. The first, most obvious, but also most profound, legacy was a conception of social housing which limited its scope, more broadly or more narrowly, to that of a *supplementary* form of provision, rather than as an *alternative* to the private market. The second legacy concerns the rationale for social housing provision. Neither before 1914 nor later could this be simply understood as a response to the mass of unmet housing needs. Rather, it was a selective and limited response to unmet needs which were perceived, whether accurately or not, as of wider significance for aspects of social development. What changed after the First World War, and again in subsequent periods, was the content and nature of this rationale. However, the ways in which social housing has been shaped over time by these two factors provides the essential basis for understanding its nature, evolution and varying fortunes. Thus, social housing provision has been socially constructed and reconstructed several times in its history. Accounts which fail to recognize this reality, which focus narrowly on the content of, and changes within, systems of housing provision, are bound to prove superficial and misleading.[23]

A third significant legacy of the period before 1914 concerns the organizational and institutional aspects of social rented housing provision. To a considerable extent, major decisions and choices about how such housing, if provided at all, would be organized and delivered had already been settled by the time of the First World War. The cross-nationally varied patterns of social housing land-lords in place before the war, even in the most embryonic form, persisted in the post-war world. For example, the choice of direct state provision, through the local authorities, was well advanced in Britain by 1914. In France, the distinctive organization of HBM housing was in place. In Germany, the Netherlands and Denmark similar developments had occurred. Embedded in these alternative institutional structures were varying conceptions of the detailed relationships that were acceptable between the state and 'private initiative', to use the Dutch phrase. In many cases, too, cross-nationally varied arrangements over matters such as state regulation of the sector, subsidy forms and so on had begun to take enduring shape. After 1918, when governments urgently needed to launch mass programmes of social rented housing, these pre-war develop-ments provided ready-made foundations on which to build rapidly.

A fourth important legacy concerns the politics of social rented housing, in particular the conceptions of such housing and its role held, on the one hand, by the representatives of organized labour and, on the other, by the bourgeois political groupings (some of which incorporated considerable sections of the working class). Here, too, patterns which first became evident before 1914 frequently had a long life. Thus, the insistent American rejection of state-subsidized housing before 1914, maintained even by re-presentatives of organized labour and first breached, in a limited and grudging way, only in the Depression, has had profound con-sequences for the politics of public and other low-income assisted housing ever since. And the incorporation of a limited acceptance of social rented housing, and of social rented housing tenants, within the programmes and the social bases, respectively, of bour-geois political parties in some of the European countries with which we are concerned (especially, but not only, through the labour wing of the Catholic parties), has been equally significant.

A final legacy of the pre-war years, which incorporates these other legacies, concerns what might best be described as the dif-fering models, structures or forms of social housing provision. These refer to the differences in the *social meaning and content* of social housing provision, in different societies, at different times, between differing socio-political groupings and so on. They are the various sociologically significant sets of meanings, relationships, forms of social organization, and forms of inclusion or exclusion from provi-sion. These variations tend to be obscured by the reified language of tenure which attaches a single label, 'social rented housing', to distinctively constituted structures of provision. Different models of social housing provision embody, among other features, differing rationales for that provision, differing conceptions of the scope for social rather than market provision, differing decisions about which sections of the population are 'targeted' for accommodation, and differing social relations between landlords and tenants, with a varying distribution of power and control between the two parties.

As already noted in the Introduction, such models are analytical constructs of a meta-theoretical nature. They are aids to the analysis of, and theorizing about, social housing development, not a substitute for empirically grounded analysis and explanation (see the discussion in Ball and Harloe, 1992). It follows that there can be no 'correct' specification of such models, only ones which are more or less useful for advancing our understanding of the phenomena under investigation. In this book, which seeks to theorize about the broad sweep of social rented housing development in six countries across the best part of a century, it will be argued that the history and development of this form of provision can be most usefully analysed in terms of three models of provision, each of which has had a differing degree of significance during the various stages in the broader development of these advanced capitalist economies and societies. This threefold classification, applied across six countries, does not, however, imply that each model had the same detailed format in every country. Cross-national differences resulted in their being somewhat differently constituted in each case, as we shall describe. In other words, it is necessary to grasp both the generality and the specificity of the varying structures of provision.

As we have noted in the Introduction, these models, whose content will be further developed and given an empirical grounding in the following chapters, can be labelled as 'residual', the 'mass' and 'workers' cooperative' respectively. The three models are empirically grounded in the history of social housing in the countries with which we are concerned. They are not the only possible models, in theory or in practice. Indeed, the twentieth century has seen at least one other major model of social rented provision, now in dissolution, that of state housing in the former state socialist countries. More important in relation to two of our selected countries – Germany and France – has been the social home-ownership model. As we have seen, this model, as well as the residual and the workers' cooperative models, originated in the years before 1914. The residualist conception provided the basic rationale for the 'top-down' proposals for state-subsidized social rented housing reform in this period, although the conflict between economic and social ideologies frequently resulted in schemes which could not be afforded by those in whose name they were justified. In the course of the following chapters we shall show that this minimalist form of provision has been the dominant model in 'normal' times. The second, mass model, which first became realized in some countries for a brief period after 1918, arose in response to broader social, economic and political circumstances, as well as specific housing market developments, which legitimated and made necessary its implementation. When such circumstances no longer held, the residualist model re-emerged. The choice of the term 'mass' to signify this model indicates that it was targeted at what British housing legislators have called 'general needs', that is, a broad range of lower- and middle-income groups, not just or even mainly the poor.

The third, workers' cooperative model, unlike the other two, originated neither in the 'top-down' prescriptions of housing reformers before 1914 nor through government action after the First World War, but in the 'bottom-up', grassroots efforts of working- and middle-class organizations, evident both before the First World War and in the interwar years. These projects were constituent elements in the wide range of self-help and mutual organizations developed by groups that to a greater or lesser degree suffered from economic insecurity and political marginalization in nineteenth- and early twentieth-century capitalism. Such organizations arose during a period when state organized and provided welfare was minimal. They provided the basis for what Esping-Andersen (1987: 81) has called the 'ghetto strategy' of early social democracy, 'a proto-socialist haven ... that stood in glaring contrast to the outside bourgeois world'. However, as De Swaan (1988: 143–51) has argued, 'workers' mutualism' was a fragile construction which, with few exceptions, did not survive in the face of the modern welfare state. As we shall see, this third model of social housing provision fared no better in the longer term than the other mutual social welfare institutions, although some of its forms persisted, emptied of their original content, meaning and purpose.

However, despite its relatively limited development and historical significance, the workers' cooperative model did, in many instances, embody a radically different conception of housing provision to those shared by the first two models described above. Both these conceived social housing as a partly decommodified form of provision within a housing system based in the main (certainly in 'normal' times) on the production and distribution of housing for the mass of the population as a capitalist commodity. In contrast, despite many ambiguities and contradictions between theory and practice, the workers' cooperative model embodied a radically different concept of housing as a decommodified form of provision in which the distinctions between landlord and tenant, and consumer and producer, inherent in capitalist forms of housing provision were non-existent. In embryonic form at least, this could be seen as a distinctly *socialist*, or at least *socialized*, conception of social housing provision, in contrast to the capitalist conceptions which predominated. The failure of social democratic parties to incorporate demands for radically decommodified housing provision in their programmes, let alone implement any such programmes when they came to power, reflects the more general incorporation of social democracy within the structures, processes and limits of welfare capitalism. It also provokes some interesting speculation, indulged in briefly towards the end of this book, about whether, in the contemporary era of crisis for the social democratic programme and profound changes in the economic and social order, the workers' cooperative model, or a modern variant thereof, might again have some significance.

NOTES

1 The phrase first appeared in a book on slum dwellers in New York in 1880 (Lubove, 1974: 44–5).
2 The following discussion draws on Daalder (1987); Kossmann (1978); and Gladdish (1991).
3 Data on population growth and urbanization in each of the six countries are taken from Weber (1969).
4 Pillarization (*verzuiling* in Dutch) refers to a vertical (i.e. cross-class) division of society into semi-separate subcultures based in particular on religious factors. There is an enormous literature on this topic, exploring how such a divided society and political system survives and develops. In a seminal analysis Lijphard (1975) proposed that a 'consociational' democracy had developed in the Netherlands, from the time of the First World War, which involved negotiated agreements between the leaders of the various pillars. Much debate has surrounded this concept, as well as questions of just how the pillars were constituted in the Netherlands and whether 'depillarization' effectively ended this system from the 1960s onwards. See Lijphard (1975); Gladdish (1991); Middendorp (1991); Andeweg and Irwin (1993).
5 Useful discussions of early housing developments can be found in Bauer (1934), who also reviews other Western European countries; US Commissioner for Labor (1895), on Britain, France, Denmark and

the USA; Searing (1971); Grinberg (1982); and Prak and Priemus (1992).

6 I am grateful to Jan van der Schaar for providing me with translated versions of his published papers from which these and the following details of the early housing reform movement are taken.

7 For detailed accounts of the act see van der Kaa (1935); Ministry of Reconstruction and Housing (1948); Hetzel (1983); and Prak and Priemus (1992).

8 On Danish social and economic development generally see Hildebrand (1978); and Rying (1988).

9 The following discussion draws on Miller (1968); Fitzmaurice (1981); Elder, Thomas and Arter (1982); Glyn Jones (1986); and Daalder (1987).

10 For discussion of Danish social democracy see Esping-Andersen (1985); and Einhorn and Logue (1989).

11 See Tarn (1973); Gauldie (1974); Wohl (1977); Burnett (1978); Englander (1983); Daunton (1983); and Holmans (1987).

12 For a history of town planning in this period see Ashworth (1954); Sutcliffe (1981); and Hall (1988).

13 On French political and economic development see Landes (1969); Kemp (1972) and (1989); Mathias and Postan (1978: 231–381); Kuisel (1981); Magraw (1983); and Rimlinger (1989).

14 See Dennery (1935); Guerrand (1967) and (1992); Sutcliffe (1981); Butler and Noisette (1983); Bullock and Read (1985); and Shapiro (1985).

15 On Catholicism and French social policy see Ashford (1986).

16 On German economic and political development see Landes (1969); Rimlinger (1971); Lee (1978); Mathias and Postan (1978: 381–589); Berghahn (1982); Ritter (1986); and Hentschel (1989).

17 See for example Rimlinger (1971); Mommsen (1981); Flora and Heidenheimer (1981); Köhler and Zacher (1982); and Ritter (1986).

18 The following account of housing reforms draws on US Bureau of Labor Statistics (1914); Dawson (1914); Local Government Board (1919); Sutcliffe (1981); and Bullock and Read (1985).

19 For a discussion of the SPD's attitudes to housing reform see Teuteberg and Wischermann (1992: 253, 255).

20 On social policy in this period generally see Rimlinger (1971).

21 The following account draws especially on Lubove (1974); Friedman (1968); A. Jackson (1976); Fish (1979); Marcuse (1980); and Boyer (1983).

22 On US economic and political development see A. Chandler (1978); Morison, Commager and Leuchtenberg (1980); Blum et al. (1985); and Letwin (1989).

23 For additional discussion of this point see Harloe and Martens (1984); Ball, Harloe and Martens (1988); and Ball and Harloe (1992).

2

The Temporary Solution: Social Housing after the Great War

As we have seen, before 1914 social housing was only one of several competing solutions to an aspect of the 'social question'. Working-class demands for such housing were muted, housing-related interests were hostile and industrial capital – if concerned at all – frequently preferred the greater control exercised through its own provision. Relatively few saw a legitimate role for significant state involvement in the provision of new housing. Reformist elites promoted a variety of schemes, most involving no more than marginal incursions into private property rights and the private housing market. In these respects the early history of social housing reflected the distinctive social structures and policy regimes which typified pre-war liberal capitalism.

The Great War and its aftermath destroyed or radically refashioned many of the institutions and social relations which shaped and confined early housing reform. War redefined the state/economy relationship, accelerated changes in the organization of production, altered political and social relationships between classes, and dramatically changed the politico-economic status of nations (see, for example, Marwick, 1974). The growing crisis of housing supply and affordability, which rapidly became evident after 1914, threatened the ability of the belligerents to wage war and fuelled social and industrial unrest in these countries and elsewhere. State action ensued. After the war ended, for a brief period, the combination of private market collapse and social unrest provided further stimulus to state action.

However, these social and economic changes, and their consequences for housing markets, were rarely seen, except by some socialists, as more than a temporary interruption of the pre-war situation. The growth of the state's role in the economy and society after 1914 was only reluctantly accepted and remained severely limited by the interests of private capital. While some envisaged a new era of radically altered social and economic relations after the war, either a modernized capitalism or socialism, most believed that a rapid return to 'business as usual' was desirable and achievable after a few years of reconstruction and readjustment (see Maier, 1975). In the event, these hopes were only partly realized. By the mid-1920s, earlier in some cases and later in others, the post-war social and economic crisis had passed, along with many aspects of the enlarged state role which had accompanied it. The changing fortunes of social housing in this period reflect this fact. However, a complete return to the *status quo ante* was not possible in the vastly altered circumstances of the post-war world. The new links between labour, capital and the state forged in wartime, the new social structures of accumulation and policy regimes persisted to a degree. Above all, they provided a legacy for developments in later periods of economic and social crisis, in the Depression years of the 1930s and during and after the Second World War. In the case of social housing, the methods and the institutional structures of provision, which emerged in embryonic form before 1914, were built upon during the Great War and its aftermath. Social housing became a matter for professional and bureaucratic organization, along with many other aspects of social and urban reform. When governments returned to mass programmes of social housing in the 1930s and 1940s, driven by different concerns on each occasion, the ways in which these programmes were implemented were strongly influenced by the assumptions, structures and practices of the earlier period.

THE EXIGENCIES OF WAR

When France, Germany and Britain went to war in August 1914 there was a widespread belief that the conflict would be over in a matter of months. State control of the factors of production and consumption, including housing, was minimal. The subsequent developments are well known so need only to be summarized here.[1]

By 1915 the need for central direction of armaments production and related activities, notably transport and energy production, was pressing. This led, for example, to the appointment of Lloyd George as Minister of Munitions in Britain in 1915 and the socialist minister Albert Thomas in France in 1916. There were important changes in the nature of production too, with the development of standardization and techniques of mass production (thus pioneering the methods that were adopted in the boom industries of the 1920s and 1930s, notably, of course, in car production).

In turn, these new methods, together with the rapid influx of less-skilled, often female labour into the workforce ('dilution', as it was called) created conflicts with the entrenched, mainly skilled male manual trade unions. In addition, state direction of production was possible only with the acquiescence of the major private industrial interests. In Britain and France (and later in the USA), a new set of relationships between labour, capital and the state emerged – a form of corporatism but an unequal partnership. In broad terms the unions, or at least their industrial and political leaders, accepted the need for an industrial truce in exchange for a degree of recognition by both the state and the industrialists and for some involvement in social and economic development. Earnings guarantees and some state control of the rapidly inflating cost of living formed a part of this bargain. The relationship between the state and industry was far closer, however. Indeed, many parts of the new state organs of economic direction were staffed by representatives of large-scale industry (which gained greatly by the requirement for large-scale production). In exchange for this assistance, very little control was exerted over the level of profits obtained from war production. As a consequence of this, while unemployment and the extreme poverty which had existed prior to the war rapidly diminished, inequalities of income were exacerbated. In every country, including Denmark and the Netherlands – the two neutral countries – there was growing unrest and popular opposition to wartime 'profiteering'.

The modalities of this new corporatism varied from country to country. In Britain and France moderate socialists joined the wartime governments and in the former country the interests of labour probably had more influence than elsewhere. It has been suggested, for example, that the standard of nutrition of the British working class was sustained far more successfully during the war than that of the German or even the Dutch working class (Hardach, 1987: 130). In France the major industrialists rather than the state took

the lead in working out the new methods of industrial organization. In Germany civilian government, reflecting its historic weakness, played second fiddle to a dominant coalition of big industry
and the generals. Collaboration with the unions was limited and
grudgingly conceded. In consequence, the German working class
suffered far higher levels of deprivation than their counterparts
elsewhere. Incompetence, the greed for profits and incoherent
economic organization led, for example, to a virtual collapse of
the food distribution system in winter 1916/17, and starvation and
strikes for 'bread and peace' in 1917. One reason for this, and for
the spread of food adulteration and black markets, was the opposition of Junker landowners to a more consumer-oriented food policy
(Hardach, 1987: 120).

War led to a huge increase in public expenditure. It also created
massive inflation, rapid currency depreciation and undermined the
basis of fixed parities and the mechanism of the gold standard
which supported the pre-war liberal economic order. The competition for raw materials, manufactures and transportation inflated
prices worldwide – transmitting the economic consequences of war
well beyond the belligerent nations. The liquidation of foreign investments to pay for war, import demands and the reduction of exports
(at least those for which payment was made) created or increased
balance of payments deficits. Before 1914 Britain was a net creditor
nation; afterwards it was a net debtor. The inflationary trends were
greatly accentuated by the means which the nations used to pay
for the war – by massive borrowing at interest rates well above
those current before the war and by the printing of money to pay
for these loans. Of course, given the scale of expenditure, such
borrowing was inevitable, but it was augmented by the reluctance
to increase taxation sufficiently. On the one hand, industry successfully opposed effective taxes on its inflated profits; on the other,
oppressive taxation on consumption and wages was politically and
socially too dangerous to contemplate, especially if it was not also
imposed on industry. [2]

Denmark and the Netherlands, as neutrals, were on the periphery of these changes. But their economies were also profoundly
affected by the war and its social and political consequences. Both
countries had important trading links with Britain and Germany.
For example, a major trading route into Germany ran through
the Netherlands. Both countries exported food to Britain and
Germany in exchange for manufactured goods. These links were
disrupted by war and particularly by the allied economic blockade
of Germany. At the same time, their price levels were affected by

inflation and domestic consumers suffered greatly. So, here too, there was an increased role for the state in the direction of the economy through controls, rationing and so on. There was also a growth of the tripartite relationship between capital, labour and the state that occurred elsewhere. Danish socialists, for example, entered their wartime government, although the Dutch Social Democrats refused a similar opportunity.

Although it did not become a belligerent until 1917, the war's effects on the American economy began much earlier. European demands for food and war *matériel* provided an enormous boost to agriculture and manufacturing industry, and the large-scale US munitions industry dates from this time. The demand for loans benefited the financial sector. Nothing symbolizes more clearly the shift of world economic leadership from Britain to the USA at this time than the fact that, while Britain moved from creditor to debtor status, the USA travelled the reverse course. But patterns of wartime industrial and economic organization mirrored those in Europe: the creation of state agencies to control food, finance, labour relations, trade and war production, staffed by industrialists (with protected and high profit margins), plus a measure of collaboration with labour including price controls and regulation, although these were less far reaching than in Europe. Of particular significance for housing was the establishment of an organization to control shipping production (and to extend the techniques of mass production in this sector) – the US Shipping Board (Topalov, 1988).

As the war continued, with massive loss of life on both sides, losses in real incomes as a result of inflation running ahead of wages, and consumer shortages, notably of housing and food, the strains in the temporary *rapprochement* between labour, capital and the state became ever more apparent. Strikes, mass demonstrations and other symptoms of social unrest multiplied. Revolutionary socialist movements and ideas were given an additional stimulus by the 1917 Bolshevik revolution and Russia's withdrawal from the war. Reference has already been made to the strikes for bread and peace in Germany and there was a wave of strikes and food riots in the Ruhr and elsewhere throughout 1917 and beyond (Marwick, 1974: 30–1; Berghahn, 1982; Fletcher, 1987). Workers' committees, which had been established under the agreement with the state and industry earlier in the war, became bases for revolutionary agitation, to the chagrin of the trade union and Social Democrat leadership. The forcible suppression of strikes and demonstrations intensified the radicalization of the working class and opened up splits on both the left and the right. Similar divisions, although less intense, radical and destabilizing, occurred in Britain where, despite the collaboration between the leaders of labour, capital and the state, revolutionary activity and strike action developed through factory-floor-level shop stewards' organizations (Taylor, 1965; Hardach, 1987: 185–96; Marwick, 1991: 108–16). One such movement, on the Clyde, played a notable role in the development of housing policies. On the whole, though, the British government reacted to unrest with concessions rather than repression, in contrast to the German response. In France there were mass strikes in 1917, in the munitions industry especially, and anti-war sentiment grew. In the USA worker militancy and strikes rose rapidly, reaching a peak in 1919 which was not achieved again until the mid-1930s (Topalov, 1988).

In all six countries the war radicalized large sections of the working class and, equally importantly for the subsequent course of social reform, this seemed to threaten the social order. Revolutionary ideas, the preserve of a tiny minority before 1914, became accepted by far wider sections of the working class. However, what really fuelled this radicalization was the (correct) perception that, while some (the 'profiteers') were benefiting enormously from war, the masses were bearing most of the costs. In Britain, Germany and France real wages fell sharply, as they did for the American working class, despite that country's economic boom. In the two neutral countries real wages fell until 1917, after which a combination of trade union pressure and controls stabilized the development (Hardach, 1987: 196–209, 256–7). An important feature of these economic changes was that they affected not only the working class, but also substantial sections of the middle class, whose salaries fell in real terms but whose investment income was also hit by inflation and currency depreciation. Much of the German middle class, in particular, was impoverished as a consequence. So those in power faced not only a growing working-class revolt but the disaffection of sections of their own social base as well.

HOUSING AND THE WAR

These social, economic and political changes provide the essential context within which housing developments can be understood. The exigencies of war led, in all five European countries, to some common developments, although their scale and severity varied (American developments will be discussed later). These were:

1   The virtual cessation of housing investment.
2   The collapse of housing finance. The supply of new finance was cut off and existing lenders lost massively as inflation destroyed the value of their loans and of debt repayments.
3   Rapidly inflating rent levels, together with evictions of tenants unable or unwilling to pay more, and resentment at landlord profiteering.
4   These developments were particularly acute in the large urban industrial centres where the demand for housing was swollen by the in-migration of war workers. Problems of security, affordability and access had immediate effects on the ability to sustain war production, as well as the socially and politically disruptive effects noted above. In mainland Europe refugees from the war zones added to such pressures.
5   An even more acute housing problem occurred in rural areas and in smaller cities where war industries were located and where there was no pre-existing stock of working-class housing.

In 1924 the International Labour Office (ILO) published a comprehensive study of European housing developments in the years from 1914 to 1923. This documented the common developments referred to above. Noting that the housing system before the war was ruled by the 'liberal economic theories prevailing in the nineteenth century' and that these had already created a housing problem immediately before 1914, the ILO stated that the war had 'precipitated the [housing] crisis, increased its intensity, and gave it the specific form which make it one of the most serious social and economic problems of the present day' (International Labour Office, 1924: 3). By the second and third year of the war this situation was so serious that, in country after country, rent and security controls were imposed: by France in 1914, by Britain in 1915, by Denmark in 1916, and by the Netherlands and Germany in 1917. These controls were effective in restricting rents; ILO data for Denmark, Britain and France suggest that rents rose far slower than the cost of living in the war years. The consequences for the private rental market were, however, severe (Harloe, 1985). Landlords' returns were decimated. However, the real value of their mortgage debts was similarly decimated by inflation, so the private housing finance market also suffered.

In France, Germany, Britain and Denmark new building slowed to a trickle, although there was far less reduction in the Netherlands. The diminished supply of housing was particularly acute in Germany. Here the compulsory rationing of housing was adopted, although this was not the case in the other five countries with which we are concerned. As we describe below, this situation and its continuance into the immediate post-war years led, in all the European countries, to major programmes of subsidized social housing. Precursors of these programmes were the schemes of state housing construction for key war workers in two of the belligerent nations, Britain and the USA, which were the main providers of armaments for the allied powers. In Germany, as a report of the British Local Government Board (1919) revealed, there was powerful resistance from landlord and property interests to the government's housing controls and, although the Reich government provided the equivalent of £25 million in loans, guarantees and subsidies (to match funds from the Länder and local authorities), there was no equivalent programme. The Local Government Board noted that the German housing shortage was far more acute than that in Britain by the end of the war, being, with the exception of Russia, the worst in Europe (see also International Labour Office, 1924). In France too, there was no significant alteration in the pre-war hostility to state-subsidized housing. One housing solution which expanded from now on was the housing of the urban workers in the suburban *lotissements*. Some of these, notably in the Paris 'red belt', became centres of socialist and communist strength.

In Britain there has been much literature examining the war housing programme (P. Johnson, 1968; Gilbert, 1970; Swenarton, 1981; Englander, 1983). Essential details are also found in the official History of the Ministry of Munitions (1976), for whom most of this housing was constructed. The first housing units for war workers were provided for the Woolwich Arsenal in 1915. State housing loans were also provided for the major armaments producer, Vickers, for three schemes. As the official history succinctly remarks, the Ministry's 'primary interest was to secure increased output . . . .the welfare or social side of the question was but a means to an end' (History of the Ministry of Munitions, 1976: 3). At every turn the Ministry found itself up against Treasury opposition; there was an insistence on minimal provision, temporary building wherever possible, and a fruitless attempt to extract economic rents. In so far as permanent housing was built, the Treasury expected the local authorities to be responsible, using powers contained in the 1890 Housing of the Working Classes Act. However, the local authorities were not cooperative. By 1917 the Ministry was building more permanent than temporary housing, with financial contributions from the firms thus aided (£20 per unit in exchange for tenant nomination rights). About 10,000 permanent units on 38 estates and 2800 temporary ones were built by 1919, as well as 20,000 hostel units (mainly for women workers) (Swenarton, 1981: 51). Despite the protests of the Treasury, the estates were constructed on 'Garden City lines', setting new standards for working-class housing which were later incorporated in post-war mass social housing. In this respect the intention of pre-war housing reformers, to improve the environment of working-class life, was incorporated in wartime housing policy. Many architects and planners who had championed the cause of improved working-class housing before the war left their private practices and staffed the new state housing bureaucracy which expanded in the post-war era.

The government tried to get a promise from the local authorities to buy the housing at the end of the war but Treasury attempts to impose unrealistically high rents (and therefore unrealistically high purchase prices – as a multiple of rents) met with resistance. The greatest conflicts, however, were with the tenants over the high levels of rents, imposed by the reluctant Ministry of Munitions at the bidding of the Treasury. The Ministry history states bluntly that the rents were too high. For instance, in Coventry they were between 50 and 100 per cent above market comparables, and as rent controls led to a rapid diminution of real rents in the private sector, these differentials became an ever more potent cause of tenant militancy. In this city a rent strike produced some reductions and in mid-Lanark, in the Scottish industrial belt, there was agitation by tenant defence associations and trades councils and a serious threat of strike action in 1917 (after the armistice labour unrest increased and there were strikes). There were also labour troubles relating to rent levels in the workers' 'colonies' (hostels) which the Ministry provided (Englander, 1983).

The Ministry history reveals that this small-scale programme, important though it was in helping prepare the way for social housing 'proper' after the war, must not be viewed as just, or even perhaps mainly, a simple response to the acute housing needs of war workers. Of course, the permanent houses and the hostels did provide housing for key workers, but in relation to the size of the need, this was a modest effort. In some cases, notably the housing for explosives industries at isolated locations, such as Gretna in Scotland, state housing was essential as no other stock existed. Gretna was a complete township, managed by the Ministry, which provided education, health and other social services. It was notable for being planned by Raymond Unwin, one of the dominant influences on the design of social housing and on urban planning after the war. In other cases in established industrial areas, calculations of the impact that even a modest supply of new housing might have on damping down worker militancy and threats to production played a role in determining where the units were built. For example, in the Vickers company town of Barrow in northern England, the flood of war workers into the town led to 'box and cox' sleeping arrangements, cases of up to nine people living in a single room were reported, and in 1917 an official Commission on Industrial Unrest reported on the turbulent situation there. Construction of a thousand Ministry houses was started, although, interestingly, the project was aborted after opposition by trade unions to 'bungalow-style' construction, by the council and by working-class home owners who were subletting – both of the latter complaining about unfair competition with the private market. In Coventry complaints of overcrowding and profiteering led to a 250-unit scheme in 1917. But by far the most serious centre of worker militancy which related, in part, to housing conditions, was on the Clyde. Here the Ministry built a thousand houses, the city council also built houses – after interminable wrangles with the Treasury about the financial and other aspects of this programme. One of the oddest developments was the industrial village of Elizabethville (near Elswick, Newcastle), linked to the Armstrong Whitworth armaments works. This was entirely inhabited by Belgian war workers, managed under a military administration by the Belgian government (a fact which caused a riot in 1916).

There are many similarities between these developments and those which occurred in the USA (International Labour Office, 1925: 8–9; Topalov, 1988: 1990a). Generally, as the ILO reported later, in America 'the housing shortage never approached in intensity the situation ... in many European countries'. So the 'drastic measures utilised in Europe to meet an acute crisis would have seemed wholly disproportionate to American needs ... [in addition] measures of a restrictive housing policy which interfere with established property rights ... are foreign to the American habit of mind'. Nevertheless, 'the situation in the munition centres during the war did lead the United States to adopt, for a short time, the policy of government housing'.

As in Europe, the diversion of resources from housing to war production and the flow of workers into such production (including many black workers from the rural South) led to acute shortages in some industrial centres. Overall, new building fell from around 400,000 per annum in the early years of the war to barely a quarter of this figure by the end. As in Europe, there were protests about rent profiteering from tenants' organizations and trade unions, especially in the large industrial centres, leading in 1917–18 to the imposition of rent controls in five states and Washington, DC. A government committee reported in October 1917 'that the lack of housing facilities is sufficiently extensive to menace the quick preparing of ships and war materials, that therefore financial aid for house construction should be afforded by the Federal Government and that an appropriate administrative agency should be created' (quoted in International Labour Office, 1925: 12). By mid-1918, almost at the end of the war, this effort was getting under way as Congress voted $100 million for war housing and established the United States Housing Corporation (USHC). In addition, the United States Shipping Board was allocated $75 million for housing shipping workers which it provided through the Emergency Fleet Corporation (EFC). USHC and EFC did not merely build houses, however; they were also given powers of requisition and rent control over the existing housing stock in those localities where the need for war worker housing was most acute. They were empowered to improve transportation between home and work and aid private enterprise building. In short, the aim was, wherever possible, not to build directly, but to take this step only as a last resort.

This last-resort housing effort was abandoned at the war's end. Most USHC projects were stopped by mid-November 1918, only 27 schemes having been carried out. A total of 6000 houses were built and 7200 hostel places provided (Topalov, 1988: 101). In all, 17,500 workers and their families were housed. The EFC completed 28 projects, amounting to 9500 houses and 7500 hostel places, housing 30,500 workers. In 1919 Congress, where there had been strong opposition to the programme, required all the projects to be sold to industry, real estate investors or the tenants at bargain prices.

According to Topalov (1988), the projects were located, as in Britain, in areas of housing shortage where there was also considerable worker militancy. As before the war, the housing solutions adopted reflected the distinctive division which was made between the 'respectable' working class and the residuum, the latter having been drawn into the war industries as a result of the demand for labour. Unskilled and black workers, including women, were mainly housed singly in the temporary hostels located near the factories and were subjected to a high degree of supervision (especially the women) by housing managers; projects were strictly segregated by race and gender. Skilled men and their families were housed on suburban estates of permanent housing which were planned according to the Garden City-influenced principles of reform-minded architects. These professionals saw the projects as an opportunity to test out their ideas and to set new standards for post-war working-class housing. As in Britain, the design and planning of the permanent houses pioneered new techniques and assumptions. A limited series of house types and plans was used and materials procurement and building organization were rationalized on a large scale. Middle-class conceptions of how working-class life ought to be socially engineered were incorporated in the schemes, for instance in relation to the internal segregation of space, the prohibition of subletting and doubling up, the exclusion of work-related activities from the home and the provision of small gardens, suitable only for recreation. Through-traffic was excluded from internal estate roads. These estates were planned as autonomous suburban communities, not company housing. In this they also reflected assumptions about what was appropriate in relation to skilled workers and their families.

As in Britain, some of the leading figures in the newly emerging urban and housing professions were drawn into the state housing organizations. However, they returned to private practice at the end of the war, unlike many of their counterparts in Europe, who became engaged in the mass social housing programmes. As in Britain too, there was considerable conflict over the rents which were charged for this housing. Should it be let at full market rents, as majority opinion demanded, or substantially subsidized? Eventually the rents charged were somewhere between market levels and the levels which would have been readily affordable by the workers.

Although these programmes of war housing were on a small scale, they provided the first opportunity for housing reformers and professionals to try out their ideas, and marked the first steps in the development of state policies regarding the design, financing and administration of social housing and of the conversion of the essentially private projects for working-class reform which had developed before the war to an institutionalized, bureaucratized and professionalized arm of state social policies. In all these respects, they prefigured and provided a base for the subsequent programmes of social housing.

POST-WAR RECONSTRUCTION AND THE RETURN TO 'BUSINESS AS USUAL'

While the war housing was being built the first steps were being taken in Britain, the Netherlands and Denmark towards these social housing programmes. However, these developments must be viewed in the context of the post-war history. The period from the end of the war to the late 1920s divides into three phases; first, from 1919 to 1921, when there was a short but intense post-war boom, high levels of working-class militancy and political radicalism, and a notable growth of social policy; second, from 1921 to mid-decade, when the boom collapsed, there was rising unemployment and worker militancy declined or was defeated; finally, from mid-decade most countries appeared to have achieved the return to 'business as usual', symbolized by the return to the gold standard.

By the armistice in November 1918, most governments faced large budget deficits, high levels of inflation and currency depreciation, the collapse of capital markets, severe shortages of raw materials and, in some cases, food, owing to wartime depletions and the disruption of production and trading links with the primary producers. It has been estimated that by 1918, aggregate national debts were 6.5 times the level to which they had risen in the period from the end of the eighteenth century to 1914 (Aldcroft, 1987: 30). The major war expenditures had been made by Britain, the USA, Germany and France (in this order). Real income and industrial output had fallen, to below pre-war levels in France and Germany, and to about these levels in the other European nations with which we are concerned. In contrast, output, though not real wages, had boomed in the USA, the major economic beneficiary from the war, as a result of its role as a war exporter and because of the stimulus to domestic industries created by the loss of European imports. Among the European belligerents there were serious losses of the economically active population and of physical capital, including housing, especially in the front line areas of France, which included much of its industrial heartland. In countries which had been on the losing side famine and disease (notably a devastating influenza epidemic) threatened their very existence.

Developments in the immediate post-war period accentuated many of the economic problems caused by war (Aldcroft, 1987; Kindelberger, 1987: 14–41). In sharp contrast with the post-1945 period of reconstruction, there was no coordinated international action to restore the economic system. Each country pursued its own narrow interests. Britain had lost its pre-war role as the international leader in trade and finance. America, now the economically strongest nation, refused to accept this role (it did so only from the late 1930s and especially after the Second World War) and to provide the necessary help to restore the European economies in a relatively ordered way. About the only semi-coordinated, though conflict-ridden, international action was the attempt to extract massive reparations from Germany, the self-defeating and destructive consequences of which were sharply exposed by Keynes (1919) and which contributed to the fatal instability of the Weimar Republic.

Industrial production not only declined during war, but its structure had also been distorted. There had been an overdevelopment of older basic industries that were required for war production but which were, in some cases, already in long-term decline before the 1914. Some economies, notably the American one, moved rapidly into the new areas of technology and production which had also emerged in wartime, such as electricals, oil, vehicle production and rayon, adapting and developing the modern methods of work organization, standardization and deskilling which had been used to boost wartime output. Other economies, notably Britain, were weighed down throughout the 1920s and beyond by the problems of declining older industries and the structural unemployment which resulted. The virtually universal desire to return to pre-war normality as soon as possible led to the wholesale scrapping of state controls over industry, commerce and finance, and hence the only means by which the subsequent period of inflationary, debt-financed reconstruction could have been avoided. As soon as the Peace Conference was concluded in 1919 American food aid to Europe was ended. With the Congressional rejection of American entry to the League of Nations, the USA also rejected any continuing obligation to contribute to European stabilization.[3] Contrary to many expectations, the end of the war and demobilization did not immediately lead to an economic depression but to a short and intense boom from spring 1919 and a further acceleration of inflation and economic chaos. Investment and consumption which had been restrained during the war years were now released and there was a scramble for limited supplies of raw materials. Prices and profits rose rapidly, driven further upwards by speculation (notably in construction and real estate). Easy credit fuelled the boom. Rising balance of payments deficits were financed by borrowing, much of it from the USA, and by the printing of money, so currency depreciation continued. By early 1920 this boom began to collapse and by 1921 there was an intense depression, with rapidly falling prices and rising unemployment. Subsequently there was a slow recovery. At this time most governments moved towards their central objective, the restoration of the gold standard, with the adoption of deflationary economic policies and the withdrawal or curtailment of housing and other state programmes.

Within this broad pattern of development, the various countries with which we are concerned followed distinctive paths.[4] Taking the post-war period up to the mid-1920s as a whole, US production rose to well above its pre-war levels. In Europe aggregate production levels were reaching these former levels, with the Netherlands especially and Denmark achieving better than average levels. Britain struggled to recover and France did rather better than this. German production was still depressed by the war and the economic chaos which followed.

France emerged from the war with massive debts, huge losses of productive capacity and urban infrastructure, and industrial and agricultural production 30 to 40 per cent below pre-war levels. It embarked on massive reconstruction in the war territories, funded with short-term loans, in the belief that German reparations would eventually meet the bill. This inflationary programme led to a rapid depreciation of the franc which aided an export-led industrial boom – the period was notable for the modernization of sections of large-scale industry with the introduction of new techniques learnt in wartime. Eventually, when the bill for reconstruction was not met by reparations, amid political instability and general panic, the franc's value plummeted. This eventually brought the conservative Poincaré to power. He stabilized the franc by 1926 (1928 *de jure*), with the aid of deflationary policies, at a level against the dollar which was only one-fifth of its pre-war value (this undervaluation continued to aid French exports).

The British economy boomed until 1920. Then there was an exceptionally sharp collapse of production, prices and wages, together with rising unemployment. Between the beginning of 1921 and the end of 1922 average wages fell by 38 per cent and prices by 50 per cent. Kindelberger (1987: 16) remarks that this depression was the last time when wages fell so far and so fast. In the emergent regime of accumulation, with the changed relationship between capital and labour, future depressions were marked by resistance to wages fully following the downward trend in the economy. Instead, there were compensatory rises in unemployment. The British economy began to recover slowly from 1922, though real wages still fell and unemployment remained high, in part due to the policies adopted in order to return the currency to the gold standard in 1925 (and because the insistence on returning at the pre-war parity overvalued the pound), but more fundamentally because of the growing problem of Britain's obsolete heavy industries. This structural problem continued throughout the decade and resulted in a far weaker economic performance than those of many other countries in Europe or the USA.

Denmark and the Netherlands did not face the same weight of economic burdens as a result of the war. But their economic systems were affected by inflation and their export markets were severely damaged. Denmark suffered more than the Netherlands from the collapse of the post-war boom, but by 1920 the level of production was above that of 1913. Deflation after the collapse of the boom was more severe in Denmark than in the Netherlands, but the former country recovered quite quickly as deflationary policies were not taken as far as elsewhere in Europe. However, after 1925, this changed as the government imposed more severe deflation up to 1928 in order to return the krone to the gold standard at its pre-war parity in 1927. Danish growth suffered for the rest of the decade. Only the Netherlands managed to avoid deflationary policies throughout the 1920s, returning to gold at the pre-war parity in 1925 and experiencing an export-led boom.

Given its wartime performance, it is hardly surprising that the United States was the first country to return in 1919, with no great difficulty, to the gold standard at the pre-war level. It went through the same cycle of boom and slump as the other countries, but from mid-1921 production began to rise again. Despite minor recessions, this upturn continued throughout most of the 1920s, with housing a leader in the earlier years, later to be superseded by consumer durables – the products of the new, mass production industries and new technologies, such as electricity and the internal combustion engine. Speculation in real estate and on the stock market as well as massive lending abroad, especially to Germany, fuelled this boom and helped bring about the disastrous collapse of the American and world economy in the early 1930s.

In Germany the course of events was far more turbulent during these years and the outcome can hardly be described as involving a return to 'normality', even in the far from accurate terms in which this was interpreted in other countries (Maier, 1975; Berghahn, 1982; Fletcher, 1987; Hentschel, 1989). The devastation of the economy in wartime was accentuated by the loss of territory and productive capacity to the allies at the Peace Conference, and by the French-led attempts to exact reparations. The early Weimar governments, in which the Social Democrats played a leading role with the Catholic Centre Party, failed in their attempts to raise taxes rather than print money in order to keep the economy afloat in conditions of accelerating inflation. On the one hand, it has been argued that this policy of allowing inflation to grow unchecked may have been implicitly regarded by government as essential to preserve social order and prevent the working-class revolution which had been narrowly avoided at the end of the war (Hentschel, 1989: 84). On the other hand, there was strong opposition from conservative big business (which rapidly recovered its power during this period) to increased taxation and, for a time, the depreciating currency and inflation which outstripped wage rises increased export and profit levels (Aldcroft, 1987: 137). The subsequent hyperinflation ended only in 1922 with the introduction of a new currency, the *Rentenmark*, limited in issue and backed by the nation's real property assets and the Dawes Plan, reorganizing reparations payments with the aid of a large US loan. By 1923 real national income and industrial production were around one half their 1913 levels, real wages were about two-thirds of this level, and there was mass poverty and starvation. Production regained pre-war levels only by 1927 and wages by 1928 (Aldcroft, 1987: 142). This recovery was largely financed by massive borrowing from abroad, especially from the USA, attracted by high interest rates (required to sustain bankers' 'confidence' in the stabilized currency). A significant proportion of the money was lent to municipalities and other public bodies for housing, infrastructure and urban amenities (Kindelberger, 1987: 27). An important consequence of the hyperinflation had been to wipe out the financial assets of the middle class, which had invested in housing and urban development before the war.

The politics of the period closely reflects this economic periodization (see, for example, Maier, 1975). Levels of working-class militancy, rising during the war, exploded at its end and while the post-war boom persisted. There is little doubt that the capitalist system came closer to being toppled by revolution at this period than either before or since, although estimates vary as to how close this was. More to the point, most governments and ruling elites felt that a social revolution was imminent and made substantial concessions to working-class demands in order to contain the situation. One change was the virtual completion of universal suffrage (although only for men in Britain) during and immediately after the war. This development, together with the role that many of them had played in the wartime coalitions, marked the start of the full incorporation of social democratic parties into established political institutions. However, there was also a split in the socialist movement between the revolutionaries, who, under Soviet tutelage, formed the Third International in 1919, and the reformists of the

Second International. The divisions between social democratic and communist parties seriously weakened the left in several countries, especially in France and Germany (Maier, 1975; J. Roberts, 1978: 378–86, 436–52).

The collapse of the post-war boom marked the end of this period of militancy and the reversal of some of the advances which the labour movement had made in terms of industrial recognition and social welfare policies. However, as in the economic sphere, there was no simple return to the *status quo ante*. The gains in working-class enfranchisement could not be reversed, for example. Extensions in social insurance benefits and, more generally, the wider role for the state in regulating economic and social conditions, could not be altogether abandoned, given the growing role and strength of the political representatives of labour, which persisted even after strikes and demonstrations no longer posed an immediate threat.[5] The growth of social democratic control and influence over subnational, regional and city governments was also relevant, especially in relation to social housing and urban development.

Many of these developments were far more muted in the USA (McCoy, 1977; Morison, Commager and Leuchtenberg, 1980; Blum et al., 1985). This was a consequence of the limited development of working-class political and union organizations before the war (and the anti-socialist ideology of all but a small minority of these), and the extent to which American capitalism emerged stronger rather than weaker from the war, making a rapid return to 'normality' possible, as well as the long boom of the 1920s. Nevertheless, there was a brief period of labour militancy in the last stages of the war and immediately afterwards. In 1919 over 4 million workers went on strike, but as the post-war boom collapsed and unemployment began to rise, employers struck back, defeating union actions, frequently by repressive methods. The state also played a role, with the initiation of a 'red scare' and events such as the notorious 1919 Palmer raids, when 6000 'reds' were arrested, and the executions of Sacco and Vanzetti. Membership of the American Federation of Labor (AFL) plummeted and many employers adopted the so-called 'American plan', refusing to recognize worker unions and establishing 'yellow dog' company unions. In the pre-war years the Progressive Movement had campaigned for urban and social reform, uniting a coalition of large-scale industrial and financial interests, which wanted efficient government in its interests, with other urban reform elites (Lubove, 1974). This era ended with the election of Republican majorities in both Houses of Congress in

1919 and the succession of Republican Presidents in the 1920s (Harding, 1921–3, Coolidge, 1924–8, and Hoover, 1928–33) confirmed and reinforced these reversals.

In Britain Lloyd George campaigned in late 1918 for the re-election of his Conservative-dominated coalition (which Labour had left at the war's end to form the opposition, along with that part of the Liberal Party which had split from Lloyd George in the war) (Taylor, 1965; J. Roberts, 1978). Benefiting from his war achievements, and with a programme which promised social reform (making 'a country fit for heroes to live in') as well as punitive measures against Germany, the coalition won a massive majority in the notorious 'coupon election'. Whatever Lloyd George's personal commitment to social reform may have been, the new coalition as a whole was deeply conservative, wishing to return as soon as possible to pre-war conditions. These were, in the memorable phrase retailed by Keynes (but which, interestingly, was originally used by Baldwin, soon to become the Conservative Party leader), 'the hard faced men who had done well from the war'. However, this restoration took some time. Early in 1919 the miners, railwaymen and transport workers re-formed a pre-war alliance. Demands for nationalization of the coal mines were deflected by a combination of some concessions and evasionary tactics and there were also concessions to railwaymen and other transport workers. Labour militancy in 1920 stopped munitions being sent to support the Polish campaign against Soviet Russia. However, as soon as the economic boom broke, in the winter of 1920–1, the government went on the offensive. Trade union militancy began to collapse, culminating in 1921 in the failure of an attempt by the miners to prevent the return of their industry to private control and the imposition of severe wage cuts.

This period saw the end of Lloyd George. His skills, as someone who could manage labour and trade union militancy by a combination of guile and concessions, were no longer necessary. In 1922 he was replaced by a Conservative administration under Bonar Law. In three successive elections (1922, 1923 and 1924), the destruction of the Liberals and their replacement by Labour as the main opposition to the Conservative Party was virtually completed. As Taylor (1965: 199) notes, however, many of the new Labour Members of Parliament came from the middle class (even though their electors were mainly working class) and 'even the most assertive socialists had little in the way of a socialist policy. They tended to think that social reform, if pushed hard enough would turn to socialism of itself'; they believed that things could be changed 'simply by administering the existing machine in a different spirit'. From this time onwards Labour's moderate reformism was firmly fixed within the orbit of established British politics and the growth across the political system of a broad measure of consensus on *some* continuing role for the state in meeting social needs, especially in the key areas of social insurance and assistance. After the 1924 election Labour formed its first minority government. It lasted less than a year, and among its few achievements was a major housing act, which will be discussed later.

Perhaps this outcome, the emergence of moderate, parliamentary social democracy in a time of defeat for militant labour, was always likely, given the pre-war development of the labour movement and its party in Britain. But, in a study of the 'recasting of bourgeois Europe', based on Germany, France and Italy, Maier (1975) has argued that, more generally, this was a period of 'transformation and redirection' on the left, with the development of the communist parties and trade union organizations on the one hand, and the incorporation of social democracy within the mechanisms of the established political and economic system on the other.

In France the conservative nationalist Prime Minister Clemenceau had virtually become a dictator in the latter stages of the war (Maier, 1975; Kuisel, 1981). The left, which, broadly defined, included the socialists and the left-leaning Radicals, was fragmented. Before the elections in 1919, and into 1920, there was a wave of strikes and other manifestations of working-class militancy. However, as in Britain, the movement was fatally disrupted by the failure of the trade unions to take concerted action, union membership went into decline and labour militancy did not revive until the Popular Front period in the mid-1930s. Meanwhile, the ruling centre–right Bloc National prepared for the elections with a combination of the appeal to national vengeance on Germany used by Lloyd George in 1919, and the red scare tactics employed in the USA. The fragmentation and complexities of the French political system defy any simple summary here, but, as in the pre-war period, the Radical grouping held a pivotal position between the left and the right. In some ways, the outcome of the 1919 election was rather similar to that which had occurred earlier in Britain. The conservative, centre–right parties made gains and the Radical–left grouping lost out, even though the popular vote for the socialist party, the SFIO, rose slightly. The ensuing moderate Briand government, weakened among other things by the complex politics which surrounded reparations, lasted only until early 1922, when the conservative Poincaré took over. While the Briand government did not adopt the strongly anti-socialist and anti-labour policies which the far right supported, there were fewer concessions to working-class demands than in Britain. Among the reasons for this were the fragmentation and disorganization on the left (including a split between the SFIO and a new Communist Party), the persistence of pre-war bourgeois attitudes to state intervention (and, indeed, working-class suspicion), and the persistence of fragmented, small-scale and paternalistic firms. In any event, the major state effort and expenditure in this period concerned the reconstruction of the devastated regions.

By 1924, with the franc depreciating rapidly and a state of near panic developing, Poincaré could find no majority for proposed deflationary policies. A new election resulted in significant gains by the left, including the election of 26 communist deputies. But the centre–left bloc soon began to disintegrate in the face of the growing currency crisis. There was a rapid succession of unstable administrations before the return of Poincaré in 1926 to rescue the franc with deflation and retrenchment.

The political history of Germany during this period divides into three stages (Maier, 1975; J. Roberts, 1978: 436–52; Berghahn, 1982; Fletcher, 1987). The first, from late 1918 to early 1919, covers the immediate post-war proto-revolutionary period, the fall of the *ancien régime* and the temporary eclipse of the conservatives, the accession to power of the first republican President (Ebert) and a socialist government which reunited the SPD and the independent socialist USPD (a left-wing split from the SPD which had occurred in 1917), a developing divide between the reformist and the revolutionary left and the formation of the German Communist Party (KPD). This led, in the first few months of 1919, to a form of civil war, as the government relied on the regular army and right-wing volunteers to repress the revolutionary left challenge, in the course of which its leaders, Rosa Luxemburg and Karl Leibknecht, were murdered.

The second stage opened with the 1919 elections, in which the three 'Weimar parties', the SPD, the Catholic Centre Party (which had strong links with the Catholic trade unions) and the DDP (a centre–left non-socialist grouping formed from former liberals) won three-quarters of the seats in the Reichstag. The Weimar Constitution formally incorporated the central social and economic rights which had been set out in the largely reformist socialist Erfurt programme in 1891. This involved employer recognition of the unions, with rights to collective bargaining and state-provided social security. However, the conservative forces, centring on the large-scale industrial sector, soon began to reassert themselves, with an attack on the new worker rights, especially the eight-hour day and compulsory arbitration of industrial disputes (these lasted only until 1923 and 1924, respectively). The accelerating breakdown of the economic system and the failure of the government's moderate reformism to satisfy either the right or the left began the erosion of Weimar democracy, with a growth of right- and left-wing anti-republican parties. In the 1920 election the three Weimar parties received only minority support, the nationalist right gained one-third of the votes and the revolutionary left one-fifth. By 1924 the SPD was out of office, and only returned to the Reich government in 1928. However, it remained the dominant party in the Prussian Land government and in many local jurisdictions. In this period the SPD, in a well-known phrase, 'exchanged socialism for social policy'. Its role in subnational governments in the 1920s gave it considerable scope for the exercise of this option (Maier, 1975: 514–15). For the rest of the period with which we are concerned the governing coalition was based on a centre–right grouping of the Catholic Centre Party, the formerly anti-republican DVP (right-wing liberals) which became a Weimar party after 1923, and the DDP. At times this coalition also included the right-wing, anti-republican and nationalist DNVP, or was dependent on its political support.

Thus by 1924 the German economy had reached a degree of stability, the workers' challenge of the immediate post-war period had been dissipated and many of the reformist gains made by the Weimar socialists had been reversed. However, this did not mean that the reformist programme ceased to have any significance, particularly in regard to social rights. Apart from the still power-ful role of the SPD in the Prussian Land, which contained about 60 per cent of the national population, there was continuing un-employment and poverty, social and political turbulence and the persistence of the revolutionary left. This mix of circumstances, which provided the rationale for post-war concessions to labour elsewhere in Europe, persisted in Germany after it had faded else-where. In addition, the interests of labour, as expressed through the Catholic trade union movement and the Centre Party, continued to be represented in the government. In fact, the Catholic trade union leader Brauns held the Ministry of Labour from 1924 to 1928 and bargained to restore the eight-hour day, reaching a compromise solution in 1927 (this government also passed an unemployment insurance bill) (Maier, 1975: 512).

In comparison with these complexities, post-war politics in the Netherlands and Denmark was rather simpler. The Dutch Social Democrats supported the wartime Liberal government which enacted some reforms, including universal suffrage in 1918.[6] By the end of the war the Netherlands shared many of the same symptoms of economic disorganization and social unrest as other countries (Kossmann, 1978: 553ff.). In the 1918 election the Liberal vote collapsed, Social Democrats made gains to become the second largest party but the Confessional parties held half the seats and formed a government. They dominated Dutch politics throughout the interwar period. The new Communist Party failed to make an impact, except in Amsterdam.

Later that year soldiers rioted and, amid fears of an incipient revolution (which had little material basis), the Social Democrat leader Troelstra pronounced that the bourgeoisie was about to lose power. Troops were dispatched to Rotterdam, Amsterdam and the Hague and the scare fizzled out. Other Social Democrat leaders and the trade unions failed to support any action, but it took the party years to recover the prestige which it had lost. In any case, only a minority of the new working-class electorate was linked to the socialist trade union federation and party; others were in the Catholic and Protestant federations and the majority of union members were not linked to any of these pillarized organizations.

The new government pushed through social reforms following the revolutionary scare; according to Kossmann (1978: 560), 'in the eyes of the frightened masses and of the higher classes this social policy was a guarantee against a repetition of what had seemed for one tense week the start of revolution'. As in Germany, working-class interests had some representation in this government through the Catholic trade unions and a new Ministry of Labour, which took over responsibility for housing from the Interior Ministry, was directed by a member of the Roman Catholic State Party (Searing, 1971: 263).[7] A key Catholic objective was to ensure that the new reforms did not result in state-provided services but rather state support for the 'private initiative' organizations adhering to the major power blocs. This was seen as a way of inhibiting the secularization of society and the growth of socialism.

The social reform era ended, as elsewhere, when social unrest declined and 'business as usual' was achieved with the return to gold in 1925. There were sharp reductions in government expenditure from 1922 to 1926 in order to deal with the problem of war debts, initiated by the dominant politician throughout the interwar period, the ARP leader Colijn, with cuts in education, defence, public service salaries and housing and tax increases. Nevertheless, this deflation was less extreme than that which occurred elsewhere (Aldcroft, 1987: 112). Moreover, economic growth after 1925 brought some improvements in the position of sections of the working class.[8] As in France, this was an era of industrial rationalization and growing export markets (Kossmann, 1978: 661). The Social Democrats never achieved more than a quarter of the vote in the interwar period, in part a consequence of the divided loyalties of the working class, many of whom voted along religious rather than class lines (Daalder, 1989). Also, the party kept its publicly pronounced commitment to the class struggle longer than others elsewhere. It did not enter government until 1939 and, unlike its Danish counterpart for example, had little direct influence on government policies. Its relative isolation from government resulted in the development of many ancillary organizations in this period, characteristics of the 'negative integration' which was earlier referred to with respect to the German SPD (Daalder, 1989: 11). Nevertheless, Kossmann suggests that the period also saw a growth in the private consultations and compromises between the major political blocs that lay at the heart of the pillarized political system and of consociational democracy and became institutionalized after 1945.

In Denmark the war saw the formation of a coalition government, including Social Democrats, with a Radical Liberal Prime Minister. The Social Democrats' progression towards moderate, reformist socialism continued.[9] In 1915 there was a constitutional reform, including universal suffrage. By the last years of the war, inflation, problems of food and housing supply, and resentment at war profiteering led to unofficial strikes and rioting. The government, fearing the growth of revolutionary movements inspired by the Russian example, repressed these events sharply. Stauning, the Social Democrat leader, who had joined the government in 1916, and the moderate trade union leaders, supported this policy, which was accompanied by some concessions such as the introduction of the eight-hour day and new social programmes. In 1920 there was a further political crisis, over the post-war partition of Slesvig between Denmark and Germany, but which ultimately involved the powers of the king to dismiss a government. As in the Netherlands, but for different reasons, there was a brief period, over Easter 1920, when fear of revolution was widespread as a general strike to resolve the political crisis was threatened. Unlike his Dutch counterpart, Stauning was a determined moderate and the moment passed. However, as in the Netherlands too, there was a political reaction and an election led to a right-wing Liberal minority government which, with Conservative support, abolished most economic controls (but not rent controls) in 1921, a move that industry had been pressing for.

By 1922, after the collapse of the post-war boom, unemployment reached almost 20 per cent and the krone was depreciating. The Liberals and Conservatives could not agree on a policy, so an election took place in 1924. The Social Democrats became the largest party (a position which they have subsequently maintained) and formed their first minority government under Stauning. It lasted until 1926 and was mainly concerned to establish the respectability of the Social Democrats as a party of government. The key economic issue was the restoration of the krone to the gold standard. The government agreed a package of deflationary policies with the Liberals to achieve this. The resultant unemployment destroyed the government when it then tried to get Parliamentary approval for tax cuts and an increase in public expenditure. It was replaced by a Liberal minority government which instead imposed expenditure cuts. As already noted, these policies impeded economic growth for the rest of the decade.

SOCIAL HOUSING AND THE 'GUARANTEE AGAINST REVOLUTION'

The housing history of this period, especially that of the first mass programmes of state-subsidized social housing, was shaped by the changing relationships between the state, labour and capital – the social structure of accumulation and the accompanying policy regime – which have been discussed in the previous sections of this chapter. As already noted, the acute problems of housing supply, affordability and security of tenure were among the principal causes of social unrest from the war years onwards. In these circumstances, governments could not avoid some intervention which, in the case of Europe, although not the USA, lasted beyond the early 1920s. However, the programmes of state-subsidized social housing were costly and seen as a more controversial or a less essential infringement on the private housing market than rent and security controls. One reason for this may relate to the nature of those accommodated by the new social housing. The development and curtailment of social housing more clearly coincides with the shift from the post-war social crisis to the 'normality' of the mid-1920s than does the history of rent controls.

As the war ended the housing crisis intensified. Demobilization, followed by a rapid increase in the rate of household formation as marriages which had been postponed by the war took place, major refugee movements and the needs of those whose homes had been destroyed or damaged by warfare, added to the wartime shortages. A lack of capital and materials disrupted new building. Inflation and currency depreciation had wiped out the value of housing loans and, while these trends continued, it was unlikely that the private housing finance market would revive. Moreover, the combination of rent controls and inflation meant that the real value of landlords' returns had fallen sharply. Until 'normality' was restored and economic controls were lifted or at least relaxed, there would be no major revival of private rental supply. However, given the tense social and political situation, it was not immediately possible to end housing controls (in some cases they were tightened after the war). Indeed, a potent indicator of the extent to which housing was seen as a central cause of social unrest is that rent controls were maintained long after other forms of state economic controls were scrapped. In the early post-war years there seems to have been very little dissent about this from any part of the political spectrum, at least in Europe.

A second necessity was to expand the supply of housing in order to alleviate the conditions which gave rise to the need for controls, and which therefore prevented the reversion to a functioning private market. State subsidies, it was argued, were required to meet that proportion of the cost of new housing that was 'non-recoverable' (International Labour Office, 1924: 47–8). This comprised the difference between the very high costs incurred because of post-war inflation and the levels of controlled rents. In short, subsidies would reduce the housing price to a level that would be economic in a normally functioning free private market. When this normality was restored, the need for such subsidies would disappear.

In the previous chapter we noted that the arguments for state-assisted housing advanced before 1914 were couched in terms that were compatible with the maintenance of the private housing market and liberal economic principles. In line with the general theme of a 'return to normality' after the war, it may be seen that the rationale which was constructed for *temporary* state subsidies during and immediately after the conflict maintained these principles. We also saw in the previous chapter that what such reasoning ignored was the fact that the private housing market, even in 'normal' times, was unable to provide an adequate supply of affordable housing for the poorer sections of the working class and that most pre-war experiments in state-assisted housing had rents which were too costly for these groups. Instead, although they were legitimated by reference to the housing conditions of the poorest slum dwellers, most schemes were targeted at the 'respectable' working class, who were regarded by the housing reformers as of crucial political and social importance. The terms in which the argument for state subsidies was set out after the war indicate that this section of the population was again the main focus of concern, but now with parts of the lower middle class, whom the housing crisis had also affected severely. The first mass programmes of social rented housing were, therefore, not a simple response to housing needs but a response to *strategically important* housing needs, in brief the needs of those sections of the population – the skilled, organized working class and part of the middle class – whose continuing disaffection posed the greatest threat to the re-establishment of the capitalist social order.

Having decided that state subsidies were an inevitable if temporary necessity, governments then had to decide who would build the new housing. Although some workers' and tenants' movements and the revolutionary left advocated the socialization of the housing sector, along with the rest of the capitalist economy, this demand was no serious part of the programme of any of the major emergent social democratic parties.[10] Writing later Catherine Bauer (1934: 122, 129) commented:

> [t]he various post-war governments of a 'Labor' or 'Social Democrat' flavor had, as subsequent events have proved, little greater desire or power to 'socialize' anything ... than had the Liberals or Conservatives ... Except in Russia and possibly on occasion in Vienna, it has never been the conscious vocal purpose of either the city fathers or the State officials to 'socialize' housing.

Given the lack of powerful demands for the socialization of housing, one option was to allocate the new subsidies to private builders and landlords. As we shall see, this did occur. However, the adverse consequences of the war on the private housing market, the building industry and the financial sector limited the extent to which this was feasible. Even with subsidies, private enterprise was unable to supply all the new housing required. The obvious alternative or complementary strategy was to rely on an expansion of the activities of the embryonic institutions which had emerged before 1914 – the housing associations, cooperatives and local authorities. In most European countries, for reasons discussed in the previous chapter, the most acceptable institutions, on political and ideological grounds, were the associations and cooperatives. However, in several countries the crisis was sufficiently severe and the capacities of these institutions too limited to avoid, for a time, some direct local authority provision. Only in Britain was there a clear acceptance that the local authorities were the bodies to use the new subsidies, and even here there was a wartime debate about the possibility of using the 'public utility societies'. However, for pragmatic reasons – they were few in number and could not be expanded rapidly – this was never a serious alternative (Swenarton, 1981: 68–9).

The post-war ILO reports on housing in Europe and America provide a useful overview of developments in the countries with which we are concerned (International Labour Office, 1924, 1925, 1930). The report on French conditions after 1918 focuses on Paris. It notes the impact on the housing shortage of foreign migration, the return of demobilized soldiers and the increased rate of household formation (there were twice as many marriages in 1920 as in 1913). Interestingly, it also refers to the effects of the short post-war boom which 'resulted in a crop of new banks, industrial combines, nouveaux riches, and speculators, who took over buildings previously used for residential purposes' (International Labour Office, 1924: 113). As a result the official vacancy rate in Paris fell from a low 2.6 per cent in 1918 to zero by 1921. The ILO (1924: 114) comments '[t]he above figures indicate the critical situation, which some have in fact regarded as a serious social danger threatening the very foundations of national life. The French Government and the various organisations concerned therefore devoted constant and serious attention to the question'.

However, the socio-political factors described earlier in this chapter shaped and limited the resultant policies. The intention of returning to normality in the private rental market was clear. According to the ILO, there were three elements in the changes in rent control which occurred between 1918 and early 1922; while the tenant's right to a continuing lease was extended (presumably to restrain the social turmoil caused by mass evictions), landlords were allowed to begin raising rents and the operations of tribunals which had arbitrated between tenants and landlords in wartime were restricted. However, when in 1923 the Senate proposed a rent rise of up to 100 per cent over the 1914 levels, '[t]here were protests from the Municipal Council of Paris, proposals for the requisitioning of vacant dwellings were again put forward, and a general strike of tenants was threatened' (International Labour Office, 1924: 125). Faced with this revolt, the politicians backed down, extended controls to 1926, strictly limited the grounds for rent increases and the maximum increase allowable and established landlord/tenant committees to determine increases. In short, the return to a free market was blocked by the recognition that this was a social and political impossibility. It remained so throughout the interwar period.

As we have noted, there was less effective pressure for social concessions in France after 1918 than in some other countries. However, the failure to remove rent controls shows that such pressure was not negligible. But there was another factor, too, for, as Butler and Noisette (1983) conclude, rent control was imposed by and in the interests of industrial capital at the expense of property capital. However, the limits of such impositions are illustrated by the post-war history of social housing. In chapter 1 we examined why there was such vehement resistance to state intervention in the supply of new housing in France. The social forces and ideology which sustained this position continued to be influential after the war. It was reinforced by economic exigencies; as Lescure (1992: 234) points out, until the franc was stabilized the state was paralysed by crippling debt repayments, resulting in deep cuts in social and economic expenditure, which fell to below their pre-war levels.

As in Britain, concern about post-war housing, in this case the reconstruction of the war-devastated zones, arose from 1916 onwards. Immediately after the war the main focus was on reconstruction. Over 400,000 units were repaired or rebuilt, incurring massive state expenditure (International Labour Office, 1930: 202). This was acceptable expenditure because it restored private property. However, in 1919 new legislation provided state subsidies for communes and HBMs to support new housing. These involved below-market interest loans from the Caisse des Dépôts, which received national savings deposits (on which it paid a very low rate of interest). There was also additional assistance for large families, indicating yet again the significance of Catholic and pro-natalist ideology in French policy formation. However, as before the war, there was stiff resistance to the subsidies from the Caisse, a guardian of economic orthodoxy, and it refused to lend. So, in 1921, direct state loans were, in·theory at least, made available.

In 1920 an official commission reported on the housing problem. It was chaired by Loucheur, a former Minister of Armaments and Reconstruction and a corporate financier who had been active in industrial reorganization and rationalization (Maier, 1975: 73). Subsequently, Loucheur and Bonnevay drew up a programme based on this report. They estimated that to relieve the shortage and restore normal market conditions, 500,000 houses should be built over a period of ten years, funded by private sector loans with a state-subsidized interest rate. Controls, similar to those imposed on the war industries, would ensure that the necessary labour and materials were available, not just for this programme but for housing generally.

These proposals reflected a more wide-ranging coalition of interests between moderate liberal politicians, the modernizing sector of big industry, reform experts and moderate sections of the workers' movement (Magri and Topalov, 1988). They were not acceptable to property interests or to the more radical left (who regarded them as a means of restoring the private housing market). The programme was targeted at those sections of the population which were of key concern, skilled workers and sections of the middle class. The concern with middle-class needs – as the ILO (1924: 129) put it, 'the movement for the provision of houses at moderate rents, but nevertheless reaching a certain standard of comfort, for the classes generally referred to as intellectual workers' – was clearly expressed at the time. For example, a leading Deputy wrote in 1922: '[t]he housing shortage does not only affect ... the working classes; it presses just as hard, if not more so, on ... all the members of the middle class which is so numerous in France, and which in many respects is the backbone of the state and of society' (International Labour Office, 1924: 159–60; see also Topalov and Magri, 1988).

The Loucheur/Bonnevay programme envisaged considerable participation from industry in the organization, management and financing of regionally based HBM organizations which would provide the bulk of the new housing and a smaller programme of subsidized construction for the middle class by private enterprise outside the HBM regulations. It also built on wartime developments in production techniques by suggesting the increased use of mechanization in building, standardization and a smaller range of house types, attempting by these means to lower costs and accelerate output.

However, the programme was stillborn, as were many other proposals at this time, some of which are listed in the ILO (1924) report. But the HBM legislation, which had been amended seven times between 1919 and 1921, was codified in a single act in 1922. All this post-war legislation still continued to favour home ownership, as it had done before the war. With the collapse of the boom and of worker militancy the credits for workers' housing were rapidly cut back. Throughout the 1920s various attempts were made to institute a new programme, but no legislation got through the Senate until 1928, when the Loi Loucheur authorized the first, short-lived programme of mass social housing. This will be discussed in the next chapter.

Reporting on the situation up to 1923, the ILO (1924) showed just how limited the post-war activities had been. By this date there were about 560 private sector and cooperative HBM landlords. But the main providers of social rented housing for the less well-off working class were the public HBM offices, first authorized in 1912. Despite an order in 1918 from the Minister of Labour to Prefects instructing them to establish such offices, only 139 had been created. Only one loan for cheap housing had been made in wartime by the Caisse des Dépôts; lending resumed in 1920 but was cut back in 1921. The results were unimpressive: according to the Minister of Health, reporting to the Chamber of Deputies in June 1922, only 3393 new dwellings were aided by the HBM legislation between 1918 and 1921. Outside Paris, which had obtained special permission to raise a housing loan, there was virtually no new building. Data on cheap housing which had also received property tax exemptions for the first time between 1920 and 1927 suggest that no more than about 14,000 new units were provided in this period (International Labour Office, 1930: 225). However, a later account states that by 1931: 68,500 units were 'erected with public means on the basis of the various acts previous to the act of 1928' (Schwan, 1935: 202). Bauer (1934) suggested that the legislation supported about 58,000 new dwellings between 1920 and 1927, but less than half of these were for rented accommodation; the rest were for individual owners. As one legislator had earlier remarked: 'the legislation ... has produced comparatively small results ... even in the special sphere to which it is limited it cannot contribute to a really appreciable extent to the solution of the present crisis' (quoted in International Labour Office, 1924: 151).

In France, therefore, despite the early housing-related social unrest and the campaigning of reform-minded elites, the forces supporting social housing were weaker than elsewhere.[11] The main outcome of this period was the continuation of rent controls. There was also a further rapid development of a private solution to working-class housing needs – the *lotissement* – also a source of profits for landowners on the suburban fringes. As Read (1976: 304) has commented, '[t]he dream [of workers' housing] was fed by developers' publicity, but it also had the support of the government. Poincaré, the leader of the government in 1922, was actually photographed digging potatoes on his suburban lotissement – what better publicity for the developer?'. In fact, over half the net interwar increase in the number of dwellings in the Paris region was in *lotissements*, mainly appalling, ramshackle, overcrowded and unhealthy semi-rural slums (Read, 1976: 304–5).

According to Bowley (1944: 12), at the armistice there was a housing shortage of about 600,000 units in England and Wales alone. Following the imposition of rent controls in 1915 (which were frequently evaded and had to be extended in coverage up to 1920 in response to continuing pressures), agitation and unrest over housing conditions had continued (Englander, 1983: 234–97). The introduction of compulsory billeting of war workers in 1917 aroused open, class-based antagonism (with middle-class horror at the prospect of working-class lodgers and working-class resentment at the evasion of their duties by the middle class). This coincided with the more general wave of strikes and industrial unrest in 1917.

These events gave added urgency to government discussions on post-war housing, which had begun in mid-1916. The first real proposals for council housing were set out by Seebohm Rowntree, the Quaker social reformer whose poverty studies had a formative influence on British social policy, and who was an influential government adviser. Swenarton (1981) has published the definitive account of the subsequent evolution of policy. At an early stage it was recognized that private enterprise would not immediately be able to supply the necessary housing, state aid to individuals was apparently unthinkable and the public utility societies were too small to respond adequately. This left a choice between the local authorities and central government. Conservative officials at the Local Government Board favoured the former option, more radical official advisers and politicians the latter.

Government reports on the 1917 unrest highlighted food prices and shortages and housing problems as of major importance. The War Cabinet noted that: 'for the vigorous prosecution of the war a contented working class was indispensable' (Swenarton, 1981: 71). This led to a morale-raising but unspecific public promise of financial assistance to local authorities to build 'a programme of housing for the working classes' after the war. As in the case of war housing, the Treasury fought a tenacious rearguard action against any clarification of just what the financial assistance would be, but by the end of 1917 a new political crisis arose over enlistment for military service. This led Lloyd George to make a famous speech setting out his war aims, while on the same day the Treasury began to give ground on housing subsidies. Further unrest in early 1918 moved the process a stage further. Now the fear of revolution was widespread within political circles, a general strike was thought possible and the moderate Labour leader Henderson wrote to *The Times*: 'the temper of the workmen is dangerous and the unyielding attitude of the government is bringing the country to the verge of industrial revolution'. By this stage the arguments in government were about how radical the new housing policy would be – whether the government would just assist local authority building or whether there would be a centrally directed local authority programme, led by the reform-minded architects and planners that had been involved in the war housing schemes.

This conflict was resolved by a further upsurge of social unrest. Demobilization, which began very quickly after the armistice, led to a new flood of reports to the government which noted the 'very general talk of revolution in the country' (Swenarton, 1981: 77). A strike on Clydeside in early 1919 was referred to by the Secretary of State for Scotland as a 'Bolshevist rising'. More generally, the growth of strikes and threats of strikes by the three core unions, miners, railwaymen and transport workers, and the fear that demobilized soldiers might form a revolutionary vanguard, were alarming, Lloyd George referred to the threat of a miners' strike as 'a menace to the whole foundation of democratic government' (quoted in Swenarton, 1981: 78). As Swenarton notes, whether Britain was in a pre-revolutionary state in early 1919 is beside the point; the fact is that the ruling elites believed it to be so and, as documents of the period indicate, recognized that concession rather than repression was the only feasible response.

The outcome was a series of social reforms (Gilbert, 1970). But the central proposal was the council housing programme, in Lloyd George's famous phrase the 'homes for heroes', whose real purpose was expressed by a junior minister thus: 'the money we are going to spend on housing is an insurance against Bolshevism and Revolution'. In these crisis circumstances, a fairly radical approach was adopted, with considerable central direction and large subsidies. In fact, local authorities had refused to promise that they would build enough houses under the more voluntaristic scheme initially put to them unless more generous financial assistance was provided. What emerged, in the 1919 Housing and Town Planning Act (the 'Addison Act'), was a three-year programme to build 500,000 houses.[12] The annual deficits (the difference between cost and actual rents) for the first seven years would be met by the

Treasury, after which it was envisaged that the housing market would have returned to normal levels of costs and rents.[13] Because of the high costs of building and finance, this 1919 programme was more heavily subsidized by government than any of its successors in the interwar period (see Bowley, 1944).[14]

At the end of the seven-year period the rents charged for the new houses were to be the same as those on the private market. The aim was to encourage the private sector back into the provision of working-class housing; if public housing rents remained low this would not occur and the government would be left with a long-term requirement to subsidize working-class housing (as we shall see, to a degree this is just what happened, at least up to the early 1930s). In fact, even with the substantial subsidies, the inflated costs of finance and construction led, in the words of a Member of Parliament, only to those who were 'the aristocrat of the working classes, the skilled and highly paid artisan' (quoted in Swenarton, 1981: 83) being able to afford the new houses. After the collapse of the post-war boom, with falling wages, these units became even less affordable by much of the working class.

The new housing programme marked a further step in the incorporation of some of the aims of the housing reformers and professionals in the operations and organization of state housing. Swenarton (1981) describes the role played by these people in the 1918 report of the Tudor Walters Committee on housing planning, organization and design, which set the standards for the new programme. However, this report also marks the point at which the explicit links made before the war between better housing and working-class 'improvement' became less overt and the standards and methods of implementation of housing policy began to be seen as a technical matter, a topic of concern for the various urban professions working within the bureaucratic procedures and organization of the state. These new plans for working-class housing incorporated the 'Garden City' principles of low density, 'cottage'-style development (Evans, 1976). In the process they also ignored, as did 'Garden City' planners elsewhere, various aspects of working-class living arrangements which seemed less than appropriate or necessary to middle-class professionals. Another key input to the report derived from the lessons of wartime production. Thus the new housing schemes were to use a rationalized and restricted series of house types and methods of construction, with an emphasis on the use of new materials and technologies (Hawkes, 1976).

Although the housing reformers had a major influence on the nature of the new housing programme, there were limits to what they could achieve. In pressing for the controls over raw material and building to be maintained, to ensure that the houses got built at an affordable cost, they challenged core economic and political interests who were determined to scrap all economic controls. As we have seen, this did indeed happen. The subsequent inflationary boom, fuelled by speculation, robbed the infant programme of the means by which it could be carried out. By late 1919 the programme was in crisis with very little construction occurring. At the same time the financial sectors' concern to reorient the economy, in order to make possible the return to gold and the re-establishment of the City of London as the world's financial centre, began to take effect (Gilbert, 1970; Swenarton, 1981). The first step involved ending debt-financed government budgets and deep cuts in public expenditure. The intention was to make a budget surplus and repay the national debt. While this degree of deflation was a political impossibility for the time being, the Treasury insisted that the new housing be funded from private capital borrowed by the local authorities, not from direct state loans. In the boom conditions, and lacking the relevant financial expertise, the local authorities were unable to attract much private finance.

Throughout this period there was a steadfast refusal to adopt any radical measures to deal with these resource problems which might cut across the return to free market conditions. Instead, there were some limited and fairly ineffective 'fudges' which enabled some very costly housing to be built. However, a more important change was the decision, in late 1919, to provide lump sum subsidies for private builders, in order to boost output and support the re-establishment of the industry. Another was concessions made to the building trade unions in exchange for labour force 'dilution', the recruitment of unskilled workers and the use of councils' own building forces ('direct labour').

By 1921, with the recession gathering pace, the price of the new housing was rapidly falling but, as Swenarton (1981: 129) remarks, 'the irony was that the end of the boom, while making house-building possible, also removed the political imperative operating on the government to proceed with the programme. As the numbers out of work increased, the power of labour ... visibly weakened, and the "insurance against revolution" appeared no longer necessary'. This was the cue for the guardians of financial orthodoxy to mount a final attack on the housing programme. In 1921 the senior Treasury official responsible for housing argued for a greater reliance on subsidized private enterprise and the ending of expensive local authority construction which, he felt, was being built to far too high a standard for the working class. Documents from the period show just how closely the Cabinet's decisions regarding the future of the programme were linked to its estimation of the level of working-class unrest and trade union militancy. Soon after the failure, in spring 1920, of the triple alliance of miners, railwaymen and transport workers to call a general strike (the turning-point for working-class mobilization in this period), the first cuts in the housing programme were agreed. Addison, who fought for the programme, was eventually a victim of a sustained campaign that was waged in the Conservative press and in government against this 'wasteful' programme, being moved from the Ministry of Health and then dismissed by Lloyd George, whose own power was now slipping, in a notable act of disloyalty (see Gilbert's (1970) account of this episode; see also Merrett, 1979: 40–1). In mid-1921 the programme was ended, with only 176,000 houses completed or under construction. The only promise that remained, reflecting the recognition that working-class pressure over housing would continue while the private market failed to supply its needs, was the classic British ministerial statement that the housing problem would be kept 'closely under review'.

As we have seen, the British economy remained in the doldrums throughout the 1920s, with slow economic growth and a high level of unemployment. The hope that the private market would be able to cope with working-class housing needs after a fairly rapid reversion to 'normality' proved a chimera. Successive governments, despite making several attempts, were unable to extricate themselves from keeping controls on working-class rents. Various official committees throughout the interwar years agonized not only over the harm that controls were doing to the prospects for a functioning private market, but also over the social unrest that would occur if controls were completely abolished. Some decontrol of the rents of higher-value housing did occur, but blanket controls were reimposed on the outbreak of the Second World War (Jarmain, 1948: 10–18; Englander, 1983: 298–317; Holmans, 1987: 386–407).

It also proved impossible to avoid commitments to subsidized housing. Not until the 1930s, with new sources of economic growth in some parts of the country and falling construction costs, could the claim that 'normality' had been re-established in the bulk of the working-class housing market be credibly asserted by politicians. By 1923 the last houses in the truncated Addison programme were nearing completion, private building had not revived and political pressure built up for a new initiative.[15] So the Conservative government aimed to aid private sector revival by providing a lump sum subsidy or annual contributions over 20 years. Local authority building was banned unless a council could show the Minister that private enterprise would not build in its area. Even more clearly than the Addison programme, this subsidy was not targeted on those in the greatest need but on the lower middle class and upper working class, providing housing for rental or for sale. As Holmans (1987: 305) notes, the subsidies were to be available only for two years, after which the government believed it would be possible to effect a 'rapid transition to conditions in which the state would do no more in housing than it had done in 1914'.

However, the advent of the first Labour government in early 1924 resulted in a significant shift of policy. Wheatley, the Labour Minister responsible for housing, came from the Clyde, the prime centre of working-class militancy over housing and industrial conditions in the First World War (events here in 1915 were the immediate cause of the first rent controls), although he was, in fact, an industrialist. His 1924 Housing Act was a determined attempt to establish council housing as a major and permanent alternative to the private sector (for details, see Bowley, 1944). Interestingly, Taylor (1965: 210) suggests that this was very much Wheatley's own initiative, as 'it had no background in party discussion or programme'. Again, local authorities were given the main responsibility for meeting working-class housing needs. The subsidies were higher than those provided by the 1923 scheme for private enterprise (which continued) and they were only for rental housing. In his short term in office Wheatley also tried to persuade the building industry to cooperate in enabling the houses to be built. His act was one of the few achievements of the first, minority Labour government, which lasted less than a year.

The new Conservative Prime Minister was Baldwin, soon to be victorious over the unions in the 1926 General Strike. His reforming Minister of Health was Neville Chamberlain (the architect of the 1923 Act). Both men shared in the long tradition of Tory reformism that stretches back to Disraeli and the nineteenth century housing legislation. They recognized that 'normality' was still to be achieved in housing and that some government role remained necessary. So the Wheatley subsidies were continued, although at reduced levels, to the end of the decade and beyond. According to Holmans (1987: 308), this decision in 1925 marks the point at which local authority housing really became an established part of British society.[16] It certainly marks a recognition that the return to the pre-1914 system had not been fully achieved in housing.

However, it did not mark a final abandonment of something close to this aspiration, as developments in the 1930s demonstrated.

Throughout the 1920s, as Britain made a weak recovery from the post-war recession, with persistent unemployment, low wages and an enfeebled private housing market, state subsidies continued to underpin new building. The crude housing shortage, estimated at 1.3 million in the 1921 census, fell only to about 1.18 million by 1931 (it had been 450,000 in 1911) (Holmans, 1987: 74). Between 1919/20 and 1929/30 almost 1.5 million houses were completed, of which just over one-third were local authority units, and somewhat less than one-third were private but subsidized. In the first post-war years of crisis (allowing a little for the lag in completions), the key role was taken by the local authority sector, which accounted for over 60 per cent of all units built from 1919 to 1922/3 and aided private enterprise another 17 per cent. By 1929/30 the picture was very different, with council housing accounting for about 30 per cent, aided private enterprise 25 per cent, and the reviving private market the largest share at 45 per cent (Holmans, 1987: 66).

Major working-class housing shortages remained, but now they did not pose a political challenge as they had a decade earlier. Here, a contributing factor may have been the extent to which the subsidies had provided housing for politically significant sections of the population, the lower middle and skilled working classes, thus easing their situation and their discontent about it. In the first authoritative study of interwar social housing policies, Bowley (1944: 51ff.) considered the empirical evidence concerning this question. Her conclusion, also shared by others (Gilbert, 1970; Jarmain, 1948; Malpass, 1990), was that most of the subsidized private housing benefited 'intermediate' rather than 'ordinary working-class' households and that most of these units were sold, not rented. Moreover, council rent policies were such that 'the market for local authority houses was largely confined to a limited range of income groups ... the better-off families, the small clerks, the artisans, the better-off semi-skilled workers with small families and fairly safe jobs' (Bowley, 1944: 129). Bowley's detailed local studies and other evidence since, show that to a considerable extent, this outcome was neither accidental nor a product of central government regulation.[17] Rather, it seems that many local authorities, if they wanted to build at all, were concerned to build for this group – the core working class and lower middle class – who would be 'respectable' tenants and many of whom were of course (paraphrasing the French description quoted earlier) the 'backbone' of the labour movement.

Bad though post-war housing conditions in France and Britain were, those in Germany were worse. Immediately after the war the British Local Government Board (1919) reported on German housing. The housing shortage was estimated at up to 800,000 units and output in the major towns had fallen from over 60,000 in 1912 to around 1700 in 1917 (see also Denby, 1938). Despite this situation, there was fierce resistance from the house and property owners' associations to admitting that there was scarcity. One reason for their opposition, especially to building by the housing associations, was that schemes for providing cheap building land threatened the large speculative gains that were being made by local landowners before and during the war (Local Government Board, 1919: 51) In fact, the associations that had been developed before the war were now inactive and private investment was non-existent. In wartime there had been pressure on the government to make some resources available for housing, so in 1916–17 very small sums were provided, and permission was given to allocate some of the housing produced to disabled soldiers and war widows. The Local Government Board (1919: 37) reported, perhaps accurately, 'much satisfaction was expressed at this concession by the Social Democratic Party'. In May 1918, with rising social tension, the first significant policy initiative was taken when the Reichstag voted a credit of £25 million, to be matched by local and Land funds. This was the first state housing finance for the general population. It was for use by the associations and private enterprise to provide houses for the working and middle classes, especially those with large families, war widows and disabled soldiers. At the same time, several Länder, notably Prussia, also voted to provide financial support.

By 1917 local rent and security controls were proving ineffective against rising rents and evictions. So a nationwide system of controls was imposed. These were also not very effective and tenant protests continued into 1918 and beyond. In 1920 direct controls were imposed on the use of accommodation, empowering local authorities to allocate vacant accommodation and requisition units kept empty. This led to the development of municipal housing offices which also administered state subsidies. However, the social, political and economic turmoil of the immediate post-war years inhibited the response to the dire housing situation in this period. The International Labour Office (1924: 316) later noted:

> the acuteness of the housing problem in Germany during and after the war places that country in a separate class in an international

comparative study ... while signs of improvement are to be found in almost all other countries, Germany is the only country in which the crisis has latterly been aggravated, owing to general economic and political developments.

The ILO (1924: 317–23) reckoned that by 1921 there was a deficit of 1.4 million units. Other estimates put it at almost 600,000 in Prussia in early 1921 and over 200,000 in Berlin in late 1922.

As in Britain, the accelerating housing crisis led to a strengthening of rent controls and in 1922/3 their prolongation to at least 1926. In the era of hyperinflation the increases allowed under this legislation fell further and further behind the rate of price increases, even though by 1923 a pre-war rent of 20 marks a month had become a staggering 25 billion marks.[18] In these circumstances, any revival of unaided private building was inconceivable. Apart from the impact that inflation had on landlords' real returns and on the market for loan capital and the devastation of the building industry, real wages for skilled workers in August 1923 stood only at about 78 per cent of their 1913 level, according to the ILO. By the autumn they had fallen to about half or less of this level, and working-class immiseration was on a scale which did not exist in any of the other five countries under discussion.

This level of poverty, in the political and social circumstances after 1918, meant that there was little option but for state subsidies to be provided. The 1918 subsidies provided lump sum grants to any builder prepared to construct small and medium-sized dwellings for sale or rental, the sales prices and rent levels being fixed by the municipalities in order to avoid speculation. Half the subsidy came from the federal government, the other half from the Land and municipality. As in Britain, the subsidies were originally intended to cover the 'unrecoverable costs' created by inflation – 'the difference between the actual cost and either the cost of a new building of the same kind after the return of "more lasting conditions", or the sum obtained by capitalising the rent to be charged for similar buildings in the municipality concerned' (International Labour Office, 1924: 343).

However, by 1919 it was realized that 'more lasting conditions' were not an immediate prospect and that deeper subsidies were required to produce cheaper housing. In 1920 a new system of state loans was provided, with matching municipal contributions. Loans were calculated at a fixed rate per square metre of housing with an overall limit of 70 square metres and rents were to be set by the municipality, revisable every five years. In what was probably

the first example of a 'degressive' subsidy system (an idea returned
to in Germany and elsewhere in the 1960s), the loans were interest
free at first and there was no amortization. But if the rent yield
increased above a set level some of the loan would become repayable at a low rate of interest and amortization. If the building
was sold at a profit up to two-thirds of the loan was repayable.
Reflecting the now pessimistic prospects for the return to housing
market normality, the value of the houses was to be finally fixed
after 20 years (note that in the parallel British situation this period
was set at seven years). If this value fell below the building cost
the deficit would be written off.

Setting a pattern which has endured in Germany ever since,
the subsidies could be used by commercial, non- or limited-profit
builders and by individuals, although there was a preference for
the cooperatives and other non- or limited-profit building societies
that had developed in the pre-war period. In the years up to
1921, about 315,000 subsidized units were constructed and another
105,000 by unaided private enterprise (International Labour Office,
1924: 345). The economic collapse in 1922 cut total output to
30,000 and in 1923 subsidized construction collapsed completely.

One source of funding for the state loans was the *Hauszinssteuer*,
a rent tax which was first imposed in 1921, and was mainly to
support public and non-profit building. Hyperinflation wrecked the
first scheme, and by October 1923 it was estimated that the sum
collected would not support the building of more than ten units
(International Labour Office, 1924: 346-7). The idea was to raise
rents closer to 1914 levels in real terms, with half the increases
going to the landlords and half diverted by taxation to a new
building fund. The rationale for this was that landlords had benefited from inflation which had decimated the value of their mortgages and debt repayments.

The 1922-3 crisis completed the collapse of confidence in the
private capital market for housing. However, as we have noted,
after stabilization foreign capital began to flow into the country,
attracted by the high interest rates. Nevertheless, housing capital
remained in short supply and was very expensive (International
Labour Office, 1930: 351). First mortgage rates of 8-10 per cent
and second mortgage rates of 14-16 per cent were common. At
the same time, building costs rose about twice as fast as general
wholesale prices. Rents of existing houses, whose real value had
fallen virtually to zero during the hyperinflation, were only slowly
increased. In these circumstances any 'return to normality' in the
housing market for the working class and a large proportion of the

middle class was still a distant prospect. As the ILO (1930: 352) noted, the government's plans to build 200,000 houses a year after 1925 would absorb around a quarter of the new capital available 'including foreign capital' and 'when industry as a whole suffered from a want of capital and favourable openings for investment abounded, the authorities were forced to intervene on a large scale and themselves furnish a considerable proportion of the funds required'.

The revived rent tax now became a crucial source of capital for housing, and remained important up to 1931, when its revenue was diverted to other budgetary purposes. When the currency reform took place in late 1923, mortgage charges outstanding on pre-war housing debt were assessed at only 25 per cent of their pre-war rate (thus confirming the economic ruin which the war and its aftermath had imposed on many thousands of middle-class investors), and this windfall benefit to the (none the less suffering) landlords provided a justification for the taxation of rent increases. Throughout the 1920s the level of authorized rent increases continued to lag behind inflation and around 40–50 per cent of these increases was taken in the new tax. While this provided capital for new housing and was necessary for socio-political reasons, it helped to postpone the return to housing 'normality' still further. Various forms of publicly provided capital therefore remained an essential feature of German housing production, not just for the working class but for much of the middle class too, throughout the decade. Such capital amounted to about half of all investment between 1924 and 1928 and, by 1926, the rent tax contributed about half of this latter sum. Moreover, much of the private capital came from state savings banks, public credit and insurance institutions, while probably only 10–15 per cent of all building capital came from private mortgage banks, private builders' own capital and individuals – the main sources of housing investment before the war. Even after some recovery in the economy, state aid remained essential. In 1928 and 1929 it was estimated that 87 per cent of all new housing received some form of support. Indeed, data for Prussia, covering about 60 per cent of national output, show that the increased building production of the later 1920s was entirely dependent on increased state aid, mainly from the proceeds of the rent tax (International Labour Office, 1930: 332–4). Most of the assistance consisted of cheap second mortgage loans, available to any type of builder who was prepared to accept minimum and maximum building standards. As has remained the case in the German federal system, the detailed nature of the subsidy schemes varied according to the policies and resources of the individual Länder. In Prussia, for example, the rate of interest charged in the late 1920s was 3 per cent (compared with commercial rates of around 15 per cent), with amortization postponed until 1930 and then set at 1 per cent for ten years and 2 per cent thereafter (International Labour Office, 1930: 356).

In these circumstances, private building remained far below pre-war levels. Annual housebuilding totals did not reach pre-war levels until 1927, at which date the government estimated that there was still a shortage of 600,000 units, although the trade unions put the figure at twice this level. As in other countries demographic factors, with rising headship rates, had added to the deficit. The major share of building was done by public bodies, the cooperatives and other social housing agencies. Before 1914 their output probably amounted to no more than 5 per cent of all housebuilding. In contrast, data for 1919 to 1926/7 show that around 60 per cent of all building in larger towns (over 50,000 population) came from these sources. Most private building occurred in smaller towns and rural areas, so that the overall share of the social builders was around 40 per cent (International Labour Office, 1930: 370). As in other countries, the social housing institutions produced most of the social housing output (around 75 per cent), rather than the public authorities directly, although the post-war crisis did lead to much more direct building than would have occurred under more normal circumstances, as well as the formation of 'public interest' institutions in which the local authorities were the only or main shareholder (Brahl, 1931). There was also a major need, which the local authorities met, to house the homeless, a high proportion of whom were unemployed. Such people were housed in very different circumstances to those of the 'respectable' working and middle classes, as the following account illustrates:

> [i]n the majority of cases large buildings of the barrack type have been erected at great expense, and sometimes discarded railway carriages and wagons have been used. Former military depots, munition and rolling stock sheds have also been adapted for the purpose. In large cities special homes are built for the homeless, in which there are large mens' and womens' dormitories ... this kind of accommodation is a temporary measure and it is intended to abolish this as soon as possible and provide the usual type of dwelling instead, although this will of necessity be of a primitive kind (Brahl, 1931: 193; see also Denby, 1938).

The number of social housing institutions expanded rapidly, especially the cooperatives, which increased from around 1300 before the war to over 4000 by 1927 (International Labour Office, 1930: 324). There was also a growth of regionally based organizations to provide technical support and to pool materials supply (Schwan, 1935). Most cooperatives built for renting only to their members, although some sold units to them with restrictions on resale to prevent profiteering and their loss to the private market. Many employers shifted from building their own housing for workers to supporting social housing institutions. Frequently these organizations had close links with the major political groupings, notably the trade unions and Social Democrats, and the Christian trade unions and the Centre Party (each of which formed federal associations of 'their' social housing organizations) (Neue Heimat, 1972; Umrath, 1950). As before the war, many cooperatives were formed by groups of employees, including the professional middle classes (Blumenthal, 1934). Like their counterparts elsewhere, the social housing institutions 'made it their aim to apply the principles characterising the movement in favour of housing reform' in relation to the planning and design of their housing, and German social housing, for example in Frankfurt under the direction of Ernst May, produced some of what are still the best examples of social housing design influenced by the earlier currents of housing reform and the Modern Movement in architecture (Bauer, 1934; Denby, 1938: 126–35; Benevolo, 1971: 507–39). Particularly in the case of those organizations linked to the labour movement in towns such as Frankfurt, the new social housing schemes carried a social meaning for their inhabitants which went beyond the purely individual satisfaction of housing need. They were a central element in the cultural reproduction of social democracy, alongside, in those localities under SPD control, considerable investment in public social amenities and other forms of collective consumption, frequently financed by loan capital from the USA (Maier, 1975; Fletcher, 1987).

However, social housing institutions were also exploited for private and speculative ends, in a situation where the need for crisis solutions had, as yet, ruled out any considered legal framework for social housing (this was first provided in 1930 and reformulated under the Nazi regime in 1940; Wollmann, 1986). As the ILO (1930: 371) reported,

> builders and architects who wish to construct houses for professional
> reasons and landlords who desire to increase the value of their land,

have for some years past formed so-called public utility societies in order to benefit by the special advantages of these. It is proposed to put a stop to such practices by legislation to define strictly the term "public utility house building", and to limit it to organizations officially recognised by the authorities, and thus provide the necessary safeguards to ensure that private persons or societies working for a profit will not be able to build under cover of that name.

As in other countries, there was also a growth of self-regulation with the formation of a 'Central Union of Building Societies' and regionally based federations to control the auditing of accounts (Schwan, 1935).

Germany's continuing economic weakness and its political and social instability both contributed to the failure of any 'return to normality' in housing in the 1920s and made the continuing state commitment to housing an imperative. Nevertheless, even this commitment had its limits; it did not encompass the wholesale socialization of the production and distribution of housing although, according to Wollmann (1986: 135), this was briefly discussed in the early 1920s. Even if such a course had been a political possibility, and resistance to it from capital would have been intense, reformist social democracy had no real place for such an option. In practice, the only manifestations of a more radical impulse to socialization were the building guilds, which also appeared briefly in several other countries, such as Britain and, more substantially, in Denmark. These were producer cooperatives formed by building workers. By the late 1920s there were two federations of building guilds. The largest, linked to the labour movement (the Verband Sozialer Baubetriebe) involved around 18,000 workers in 1928, organized in 127 guilds. These mainly built for the social housing organizations and completed about 53,000 houses between 1921 and 1928. The smaller federation, with no political links, involved just over 6000 workers in 1926 in 27 guilds and had built around 6000 houses between 1921 and this date (International Labour Office, 1930: 374–5). But in general, as Rusch (1931) noted, '[t]he promotion of dwelling house building in Germany by the use of public funds does not constitute a measure for the support of poorer sections of the population, but rather an economic step in a general sense towards facilitating house building activity as a whole' (see also Bauer, 1934, and Denby, 1938: 136–7 on the continuing shortage of low-income housing).

As we have seen, the economic and social consequences of the war were slower to develop in neutral Netherlands and Denmark than in the belligerent nations. Nevertheless, by 1916 there was a housing shortage in the Netherlands and the 1919 housing census found a vacancy rate of only 0.6 per cent (International Labour Office, 1924: 237). In Amsterdam in 1918 there were reported to be only 32 unoccupied dwellings. The overall shortage was estimated at 60,000 units in 1918 and at 75,000 to 100,000 in 1920 (International Labour Office, 1930: 103ff. for these and subsequent figures). These figures were inflated by rapid population growth. While some building continued in the early stages of the war, from 1916 it fell away as inflation made purely private building an economic impossibility. As elsewhere, inflation accelerated after the war and building costs did not fall until the post-war boom was over in 1922. Rent controls were introduced in 1917, although these were enforced at the discretion of the local authorities, except in the case of smaller houses where controls were compulsory. Tighter controls and security measures followed in 1918. A notable feature of these controls, reflecting the less severe impact that war made on the Dutch economy than on those of the European belligerents, was the early imposition of substantial rent increases. Far sooner than the other countries which we have so far discussed, the Netherlands began to move back to a regime of freely set rents. From 1923 rent controls began to be lifted area by area, and ended completely in 1927. As a result of the controls rents were held far below the rate of inflation in the early 1920s (in 1920 rents had increased only some 14 per cent above their 1911–13 level, while wholesale prices had virtually trebled), but by 1923 the combination of the sharp economic downturn and the statutory rent increases resulted in rents which were 60 per cent above pre-war levels, compared with a price index rise of 50 per cent. During the rest of the 1920s prices drifted down while rents continued to increase, so that by 1929 the rent index stood at 183 while the price index was 142. In these circumstances, and in sharp contrast to most other countries, private renting soon became profitable again. As the ILO (1930: 101–2) reported, 'when normal conditions were restored, private enterprise developed rapidly and the authorities were able by degrees to abandon a policy which had been forced on them by the abnormal situation due to the housing shortage'.

Both the relatively less severe economic situation and the political composition of the wartime government seem to have resulted in a rather limited response to the wartime housing shortages (which were much worse than national statistics suggest in the big cities such as Amsterdam and Rotterdam). The 1901 Housing

Act allowed but did not require state loans for social housing to be provided. By 1914 there were also some shallow subsidies available to reduce the rents of housing, provided, for example, in connection with slum clearance schemes, and about 9900 Housing Act houses had been built. The act also allowed the state to provide larger-scale and more generous subsidies. In the war the government had eventually agreed to provide such subsidies to compensate the builders for the extra costs incurred because of the war inflation. Rents were set at between one-sixth and one-seventh of tenants' income, and the state agreed to pay 75 per cent of any deficit, while the local authorities had to find the other 25 per cent. As before the war, considerations of financial orthodoxy limited the terms of the scheme, although the Social Democrats – more radical than some of their counterparts elsewhere – and some housing reformers argued for the socialization of housing production and distribution (Searing, 1971: 264).

However, by 1918, the social and political situation forced the government to recognize that the scheme was ineffective because, like the rent control legislation, it permitted rather than required local authority action. Local authorities had to guarantee all repayments on state loans, including those made to the non-profit corporations. This made Housing Act housing risk free for the central government, but it also made many local authorities reluctant either to build or to allow the corporations to build in their areas. Also, the subsidy formula meant that the government benefited from 75 per cent of any rent increases and the local authorities gained only 25 per cent. So, in 1918, an emergency act gave the government powers to compel localities either to build houses or to support building by the non-profit social housing corporations. As in the case of rent control, the imperative of returning rapidly to a free market situation affected rent policy for the new dwellings. By 1920 rents had to be set at between 50 per cent and 70 per cent of economic levels, by 1921 at 70 per cent and soon after at 75 per cent.

The increased state aid now available led in 1919/20 to the first state regulation of the standards and rent levels of the new housing. However, the regulation of standards was fairly limited compared, for example, to what occurred in Britain. But in some localities, as in Germany, the proponents of working-class housing reform and the Modern Movement in architecture had a notable impact on the planning, design and construction of the new housing. Searing (1971) describes such developments in Amsterdam, for example, and Oud's work as chief architect of Rotterdam from 1918 to 1933 is renowned (Benevolo, 1971: 410ff.).

The post-war housing shortage affected not just the working class, but also considerable sections of the middle class. Therefore, in 1918, subsidies were provided (through the local authorities) for private enterprise to construct middle-class rental housing. These could also be used by the corporations and local authorities. They comprised a lump sum grant or premium, intended, in principle at least, to compensate the builders for the effects of excessive inflation on building costs. State loans, guaranteed by the local authorities, were also made available. As prices fell after the boom these guarantees cost some local authorities a considerable amount of money, as many properties sold for less than their initial cost.

The subsidies to social builders and to private enterprise were cut back from the end of 1921, as the return to economic 'normality' occurred (Prak and Priemus, 1992: 177–8). In 1923 the private sector premiums and loans ended, although a very small-scale programme of state loans for second mortgages remained for some years. In 1924 the social subsidies were ended, leaving only the state loans plus the minimal provision of subsidies in special cases as had existed before the war for 'the cheapest class of dwellings such as could not be provided by private enterprise in sufficient numbers', and for housing to replace cleared slums (International Labour Office, 1930: 107). In fact, the cost limits for such housing were so low and the subsidies so small (50 guilders per unit) that very little subsidized building at all was possible in the larger towns where the main shortages were, although state loans continued to be available. Between 1918 and 1928 about 74,000 units were built with state loans by the housing corporations and another 20,000 by the local authorities. Between 1917 and 1923 (after which they virtually ceased), almost all these dwellings also received subsidies (85,000 units). About 33,000 privately built units for the middle class were also constructed. For reasons which we discussed in chapter 1, the normal expectation was that the builders and owners of social housing would be the 'private initiative' housing corporations, not the local authorities, whose more active role immediately after the war was a short-term emergency response. As 'normality' returned and the subsidies were cut back, the level of non-private building fell sharply, from a peak of just under 23,000 in 1921 (about 60 per cent of all output) to 6500 in 1922. In the late 1920s the level fluctuated between around 1000 and 3000 per annum.

There were 389 housing corporations at the end of 1914, but new ones were formed at an increasingly rapid rate from 1915, peaking in 1920 when 379 were formed, making 1294 in all. Later their numbers contracted, and there were 1118 in 1930 (Bommer, 1931). As in Germany, some of the associations were cooperatives and some were linked to specific groups of middle- and working-class employees.[19] The religious denominations also formed many corporations in this period (Hetzel, 1983). The cooperatives normally had management boards elected by the tenants, but 'in larger associations of a philanthropic character this task is generally entrusted to a lady inspector trained in social matters' (Bommer, 1931: 336). In other words, there was recourse to 'Octavia Hill' methods of paternalistic supervision and tutelage of tenants (see also Denby, 1938). At first there were few controls on the corporations' operations; there was some speculative selling of Housing Act properties in wartime and in the short post-war boom, for example. Up to 1921 the state had no power to refuse to register new corporations. But a restrictive regime was then imposed, so that only 37 were founded in 1921 and three in 1923. As Hetzel (1983: 14) notes, the new requirements allowed the municipalities to control the use of any surplus arising from the operations of the corporations, and the possibility that such surpluses would no longer be available to finance new development 'meant an end to the concept (which had been accepted previously) that the associations would become financially healthy and autonomous private institutions; instead, they became much more dependent on future government funding'. Most continued to operate only in a single local authority area and were small-scale. Many that were formed in and after the war built very little and half of the corporations founded at this time later ceased to exist.[20] One reason for this attrition was that after the subsidies were withdrawn, as prices, market rents and real wages fell, the corporations were left with housing that had been very expensive to build, so they soon experienced severe financial difficulties with rising rent arrears and vacancies. Demands that the government write off the unprofitable portion of these investments continued until a Commission investigated the financial circumstances of the corporations in the late 1920s. When it reported in 1932 the country was in the grip of the Depression and was following orthodox deflationary policies. Accordingly, assistance was refused.

Partly because of these difficulties, but also because of the haphazard way in which corporations had been formed in the post-war emergency, in the 1920s social housing had a reputation for being costly, inefficient and badly managed. Tenants frequently resisted the higher rents which they were being forced to pay because of the financial circumstances of the corporations. All this reinforced the view that they were a poor alternative to private enterprise. However, it is also important to note that the corporations frequently built to higher standards than the private sector. It had been a central theme of the housing reformers in the Netherlands, as elsewhere, that one function of Housing Act dwellings must be to raise the standards of working-class housing and, by influencing the whole market, force improvements in private building as well. This was one ground for the strong opposition to private sector subsidies which existed, and to government cut-backs, and the reversion to the private market plus cheaper, smaller units and much reduced scale of Housing Act production from the early 1920s (Searing, 1971: 269).

The composition of the corporations reflected the pillarized nature of Dutch society. Two federations developed, one linked to the Social Democratic Party and the trade unions, the NWR (Nationale Woningraad) founded in 1913; the other, founded in 1911, linked to the Catholic associations and the Catholic wing of the Confessional political bloc, originating in housing activism in the mining area of Limburg (Hetzel, 1983; Jurriens, 1981). By 1930 the NWR had 325 members, owning 68,000 dwellings, and the Catholic federation had 125 members (Bommer, 1931). However, there were strict rules preventing the direct ownership of the corporations by employers, unions or other consumer or producer organizations, in contrast, for example, to the situation in Germany or France. But this integration of social housing within the pillarized system meant that it never became wholly or mainly associated with the interests of only one section of the political system, as it did in Britain. It is significant, for example, that both federations opposed the scrapping of subsidies and the reversion to economic rents in the 1920s, although even the Social Democrats agreed that some rent increases were necessary (but they wanted a proportion of the increases to be taxed to provide a fund for new building, as in Germany). The corporations linked to these political blocs were particularly active in the big cities.[21]

The history of Dutch housing in this period reflects the relatively rapid return to economic stability after the war. Price inflation peaked in 1918, and by 1922 the currency had almost returned to its pre-war parity and interest rates were falling. Building costs stabilized by 1923 at about 60 per cent above their pre-war levels, having peaked at three times the pre-war level in 1919. By 1926 private housing output had reached 40,000 per annum, well above the pre-war average of around 25,000. Between 1921 and 1929 about 420,000 houses were built, just over 70 per cent by private enterprise. This share had grown from only 36 per cent in 1921 to around 85 per cent by 1929 (International Labour Office, 1930: 114). However, while this return to a semblance of pre-war normality in the housing market was more complete in the Netherlands than elsewhere in Europe, it was also accompanied by the pre-war limitations of this market in relation to lower-income housing. As the ILO (1930: 116) noted, 'most of the houses built after the war by private enterprise are hardly within the reach of the working classes ... [but] the tremendous development of private enterprise has caused a large increase in the number of middle class dwellings: in some towns there is even said to exist a surplus of such dwellings'. Data for Amsterdam show that about half the dwellings built in 1921 in that city were affordable by skilled manual workers, but only 7.5 per cent by 1927. For unskilled workers the position was far worse, because even the lower rents of the Housing Act dwellings were rarely within their means (Denby, 1938). Given this situation, it is not surprising that by the end of the 1920s the ILO (1930: 117) reported: 'demands are being made in many quarters for the resumption of State housing programmes'. However, these did not meet with a ready response from government.

The relative weakness of social democracy and relatively low level of worker militancy in this period seems to have resulted in little effective resistance to the abandonment of state housing subsidies, despite the continuing shortage of working-class housing and the fact that there were considerable protests inside and outside Parliament in the immediate post-war period concerning the government's objective of returning to the free market in housing. As elsewhere, most of the social housing which was built in the early 1920s was occupied by skilled workers and was beyond the financial resources of the less-skilled workers. But after 1923 state support for social housing reverted to the role which had been conceived for it before 1914, as an aid to slum clearance and rehousing – in other words, an extension of sanitary policy. In fact, even this new social housing was too costly for the rehousing of low-income households directly from the slums. The assumption was that some filtering would take place. In so far as cheaper replacement housing for slum clearance was built, it tended to be provided by the local authorities rather than the corporations (van der Kaa, 1935; Denby, 1938). There are many references in the literature of the period to the sort of repressive housing management of the tenants in this housing that recall the disciplinary approach to the working-class residuum advocated by social reformers before 1914 (Central Housing Committee, 1935a; Denby, 1938).

Following the collapse of private building in Denmark from 1908, there had been a growing shortage of working-class housing in the period up to 1914 (Madsen and Devisscher, 1934). Data for Copenhagen show a vacancy rate of only 1.4 per cent in 1913; by 1916 it had fallen to 0.3 per cent and remained negligible up to the early 1920s. Provincial towns fared little better and by 1916 there was an acute housing crisis. As elsewhere, the level of demand was accentuated by an increased rate of household formation. By 1920 there was an estimated shortage of 10,000 dwellings in Copenhagen and 2000 in the provincial towns (International Labour Office, 1924: 251–3). This was a very conservative estimate which took little account of the very high levels of doubling up and overcrowding that existed, especially in the capital city, even before the war. Many households had no proper housing and were accommodated in barracks, school buildings and other such structures. This homeless population expanded very rapidly, from under 2000 in 1916 to almost 20,000 by 1923 (of whom just over half were in Copenhagen), and rose even higher by 1925. The number of households sharing accommodation in Copenhagen doubled between 1917 and 1920 and doubled again to 1923. The number of sub-tenants in this city rose by 74 per cent between 1916 and 1920 (International Labour Office, 1930: 139–40). The building industry declined even further than it had before the war in the inflationary conditions. In 1914/15 about 13,500 dwellings were built in Greater Copenhagen; by 1916/17 new output was only just above 1300, although it recovered to around 3000 per annum in 1920–2. Building costs rose by about 350 per cent between 1914 and 1920, the peak year for the post-war inflation, and inflation also produced the same effects on the mortgage market as elsewhere – finance became very expensive and in short supply (International Labour Office, 1924: 253–4).

By 1916 conditions, especially in Copenhagen, made the imposition of rent and security controls inevitable. At first, controls were extended for a year at a time. They were widened as the crisis worsened, but they also allowed the landlords some rent increases after 1918, although these fell far short of the rate of inflation. In 1923 controls were lifted in some areas, elsewhere they were extended until 1925 (1926 in Copenhagen), by which point it was assumed the housing market would be restored and they could be abolished. Later they were extended in the capital until 1935 (Boldsen, 1931). Far weaker legal sanctions against rent profiteering were extended to 1930. The effects of these controls on landlords' profitability were similar to their effects in the Netherlands.

As the post-war boom accelerated to the end of 1920, rents, which had been held near 1914 levels because of controls, rose by about 30 per cent while the cost of living, already 80 per cent above pre-war levels in 1918, rose to 160 per cent above the 1914 level. However, the combination of falling prices and wages after the boom burst, together with the liberalization of controls, meant that by the end of 1923 rents had increased by 160 per cent since 1914 and the cost of living by just over 200 per cent (International Labour Office, 1924: 261).

The act which introduced rent controls in 1916 also contained measures to stimulate building. Municipalities were allowed to grant complete or partial tax exemptions to all new property for ten years, a measure which remained in force up to 1925. In 1917 a further step was taken with the first state loans for the cooperative housing associations (90 per cent loans at an interest rate of 4 per cent), further legislation up to 1920 increased the amounts available. As in the Netherlands, the crisis situation also led to state assistance for local authority building from 1917 onwards, taking the form of second mortgage loans (up to 40 per cent at 5 per cent). They could be used by the authorities or passed on to the housing associations or private builders. Finally, as these state loans provided insufficient support, there was resort, as elsewhere, to direct subsidies from 1918 onwards (some measure of the emergency is conveyed by the fact that three separate appropriation acts were passed in 1918 and two more in 1919–20). Subsidies went to the local authorities, housing associations and, from 1919, to private builders. Subsidized building was subject to state controls to restrict costs, rents (which had to be set at cost-covering levels, net of subsidies) and dwelling allocation. Subsidies for local authority building were payable over eight years (after 1920 they were paid as a lump sum grant on completion) and covered not more than 20 per cent (24 per cent between 1918 and 1920) of the cost of local authority building. Subsidies for the housing associations were originally limited to 10 per cent of the cost with a matching grant of 10 per cent from the municipalities, though the figures were soon raised to 15 per cent from each and in 1920 to 20 per cent each. Private builders also received 20 per cent state grants if they agreed to permanent controls, similar to those on housing association property, 15 per cent if they agreed to controls for 12 years and 10 per cent with no controls. After 1920/1 the requirements for a matching contribution from the municipalities was abolished (International Labour Office, 1930: 141–2).

As the post-war boom collapsed in 1922 subsidies were ended; according to the ILO (1924: 264), 'all these funds were exhausted, and the Government found it impossible to continue the policy of state aid on as large a scale as before'. However, there was still an acute housing shortage and little sign of a real recovery of private sector output. So, as an intermediate stage in the reversion to the private market, a State Housing Fund to provide second mortgage loans was created, although this was to end in 1924 (in fact, it lasted until 1927). The loans could cover up to 40 per cent of costs, provided that all loans on the property did not exceed 85–90 per cent. The municipalities had to guarantee half the state loans which were at an effective interest rate of around 5–6 per cent (similar interest rates were charged for first mortgage loans at this time, obtained from Denmark's unique system of mortgage credit institutions).[22] As in the Netherlands, there were repayment problems later in the decade in relation to properties built with these loans at the time when building costs were still highly inflated. Landlords had to lower their rents as the cost of building and market rents fell. In 1928 the government agreed to the deferral of payments on some property built between 1923 and 1925.

About 30,000 dwellings, two-thirds of total output, were built with these loans between 1923 and 1927. According to the ILO (1930: 143), 'the persons who benefited by these advances for the most part belonged to the more highly paid workers, the salaried employees, the official class and to some extent the middle class'. In so far as low-income households were housed, as in the Netherlands, these came from slum clearance areas or from the homeless accommodation provided after the war and were rehoused by the local authorities (Madsen and Devisscher, 1934: 32–3; Heiferman, 1939: 31).

The State Housing Fund was accompanied by the establishment of a Board to control building and the price of materials. The Board soon concluded that output during the two years that the legislation was expected to be in force would be quite insufficient, and it tried to use its powers to encourage more winter building. This was also a means of combating high levels of seasonal unemployment and of restraining costs by utilizing labour when the demand for it elsewhere in the industry was at a low point. In addition, the Board encouraged similar developments in rationalized construction, design and planning to those which occurred elsewhere.

Despite the fall in prices after the post-war boom collapsed, the Danish economy continued to be weak until stabilization in 1926. Capital remained in short supply and was expensive, prices stabilized only at about 50 per cent above their pre-war levels from 1927 (International Labour Office, 1930: 135–7). As elsewhere, it proved impossible to remove all controls by the planned dates; some remained in provincial areas and in Copenhagen throughout the decade. In consequence, there was a growing gap between the rents of decontrolled houses (including the unsubsidized post-war building) and those which remained under control. Controlled rents rose at about the same rate as wholesale prices generally, whereas the overall rent index rose far more rapidly. As elsewhere too, new private rental housing was targeted mainly at middle- and upper-income groups, not the bulk of the working class, although the ILO suggests that 'normal conditions' were restored by 1927. After this date the only assistance available for housing was the power that municipalities had to exempt new building from property taxes for ten years. In 1928 this provision was extended until 1943. However, it was used only in Copenhagen and about ten other municipalities. Several attempts were made to introduce a German-style rent tax to finance new building, but these were not successful (Boldsen, 1931: 101).

The programmes of state assistance resulted in a substantial rise in building output, from almost 4300 in 1917 to a peak of just over 7700 in 1921. The withdrawal of state support and the difficult economic conditions resulted in a fall in output from 1922 to 1924, but then there was a further revival. Output reached almost 9500 by 1929, still below the pre-war level in good years, however. As in the Netherlands, the share of private building increased as the market recovered and subsidies and loans were cut back. In 1920 42 per cent of completions were by the local authorities and 33 per cent by the associations. However, after 1921 the local authority share was sharply reduced and the share of private building began to increase. By 1925 about half of all building was in the private sector and 38 per cent was by the associations. By 1929 83 per cent of all building was in the private sector, 9 per cent was by the associations and 8 per cent was by the local authorities. Of the social housing built between 1920 and 1929, 80 per cent was in Copenhagen, about one-third built by the local authorities and two-thirds by the associations. After 1927 virtually the only social housebuilding to occur was in the capital with the aid of financial support from the local authorities alone (International Labour Office, 1930: 147; Heiferman, 1939).

As elsewhere, the post-war emergency led to the rapid formation of new housing associations, not all of which survived. As Boldsen (1931: 104) commented,

[f]rom 1918 to 1927 the Authorities operated on a larger scale with the so-called "pirate" building organisations than with those of genuine character, so that the latter had to carry on under most unfavourable circumstances and without the essential capital reserves. Owing to the frequent collapse of these "pirate" associations and to the unsatisfactory administration of the older organisations public opinion was anything but favourably impressed ... if these societies are to be of real public service in the performance of these tasks it is absolutely essential that they should be managed by persons well versed in technical, financial and administrative matters.

There were various forms of housing associations which built in this period. They included partnership associations, particularly active in provincial areas, which were self-governing tenant associations whose members paid a 3 per cent deposit to obtain their units. In effect these were (and were later renamed) cooperatives (Greve, 1971: 32). Cooperative building associations were joint stock companies paying limited dividends, founded, owned and managed by the building unions. Finally, there were self-governing associations, often closely linked to the local authorities, especially in Copenhagen, and later called public benefit or social housing associations (Boligselskabernes Landsforening, 1973).[23] In 1919 a Federation of Non-profit Housing Societies was founded in response to the fact that a number of the early associations had allowed their members to put properties on the open market and make substantial capital gains (Greve, 1971: 28). The Federation was formed by cooperatives opposed to the use of social housing for speculative purposes. It gradually came to include almost all the associations which have survived into the current era.

Most associations required deposits of between 5 and 10 per cent from their members, which helped limit their membership to those groups who had sufficiently high and stable earnings to save this amount. At the height of the housing crisis many of the new units constructed by the local authorities were centrally sited apartments. However, the associations pioneered the development of garden suburbs, especially around Copenhagen (Madsen and Devisscher, 1934). One of the largest associations, the Workmen's Cooperative Building Society (Arbejdernes Anndels-Boligforening), founded in 1912, was later described in detail by Graham (1940). He reports that membership was open to 'reputable people' who could afford the 5 per cent deposit and the nominal cost of a share in the cooperative, and describes the means by which tenants participated in the management of their own buildings and in the society as a whole. This form of management contrasts sharply with the treatment of lower-income households in the local authority stock, where a more traditional pattern of landlord/tenant relations existed. According to Heiferman (1939), here 'the relations between the Municipal Administrative Authorities and their tenants are not always harmonious. A number of complaints were reported that tenants make claims in respect to rents, renovation, etc. which they never would have made if the dwellings were privately owned'. In addition, the supervisory and disciplinary role of management was clearly important: 'Everywhere ... the most rigorous measures are adopted for the collection of rents. In the event of illness, unemployment etc., each case is carefully investigated'. However, despite the rather high degree of tenant influence on the management of many associations, there was already evidence at the end of the decade that this might be in decline. Thus Boldsen (1931: 103) commented: '[t]here is a noticeable tendency amongst the building societies to consolidate management in a form reactionary to exaggerated parliamentarism, which latter has not always produced satisfactory results'. This shift away from grassroots, tenant-based management and administration of the associations was probably in part a response to the problem of the 'pirate' associations mentioned earlier, but it also accompanied the increasing scale of the organizations and the advent of government subsidies and regulation. It was also encouraged by the manner in which many of the associations grew in Denmark as conglomerate (or vertically and horizontally integrated) organizations, with a central administration and a number of subsidiaries, individual housing projects plus enterprises, such as those supplying building materials discussed below.

The Workmen's Cooperative Building Society (AAB) had strong links with cooperative building materials supply organizations and with the Danish Cooperative Bank. It used its own plants for the production of some building materials. Such developments, which also characterized other of the larger associations, went considerably beyond the limited development of building guilds in Germany and Britain. However, they were less the products of a radical socialist approach than a development which was linked to the strong, non-socialist traditions of rural and consumer cooperatives in Denmark and to the post-war unemployment of building workers, although, as Hyldtoft (1992: 58) notes, social democratic influence in the consumer cooperative movement was considerable by the post-war period.

Thus the familiar pattern of housing development also occurred in Denmark. In the post-war crisis there was a resort to subsidized social and private building. Once the immediate post-war turbulence had ended and the economic boom had collapsed these subsidies were sharply cut back and then eliminated. Some limited support, which especially aided middle-income groups and the revival of private building, was kept for a longer period. But by 1927 even this support was ended. Although the immediate crisis was over, much of the new housing created did little or nothing to improve the housing conditions of low-income households. At the end of the decade, for example, almost 40 per cent of the population of Copenhagen still lived in old, poor-quality and cramped two-room flats (Boldsen, 1931: 102). In these circumstances, rent controls proved rather more difficult to dispense with, especially in the capital city. But even these were lifted in many areas and were within sight of ending completely by the end of the decade. There is very little evidence that the policies followed in Denmark, with Social Democratic participation in the war coalition government and the first minority socialist government from 1924 to 1926, resulted in the concession of a greater or more permanent role for social housing than in the Netherlands, where the Social Democrats were excluded from power throughout the interwar period. The first Social Democratic government was unable to pursue expansionary policies in order to deal with rising unemployment in the run-up to currency stabilization in 1927 and, as we noted before, fell on this issue. It did not reverse the earlier cuts in state support for housing which had been imposed by the Liberal-led government, in office from 1920 to 1924, although the existence of the State Housing Fund was extended while it continued in office (the Fund was ended by the Liberal-led 1926–9 government). The relative powerlessness of the Social Democrats, who became the largest party in 1924 and retained that position, partly derived from the fact that they never managed to form a majority government by themselves. Only in the altered circumstances of the 1930s, and in coalition with the Radical Liberals, were they able to achieve some major social reforms.

As we saw in the last chapter, opposition to state-subsidized social housing was more complete in the United States than in any of the European countries with which we are concerned. The need in wartime for the state to support a limited quantity of housing to meet urgent industrial needs and to contain unrest was very grudgingly conceded, and the programme was ended almost as the armistice was signed. The repressive measures taken in the early post-war period to deal with worker militancy, the use of 'red scare' tactics, mass arrests and strike breaking, hardly encouraged the advocacy of what was generally regarded as a socialist policy. In the 1920s the dynamism of the American economy, with a housing-led boom, meant that even most lower-middle-class and skilled, better-paid working-class households could look to the private market for accommodation. In contrast, as we have seen, it was precisely towards such groups that state-subsidized social housing was mainly directed in Europe. So the economic and political context to housing provision in America was radically different from that which existed in Europe.

Despite these differences, housebuilding failed to recover immediately from the controls which had been imposed in the last months of the war. In 1920 the housing shortage was estimated at 1 million dwellings (Andracheck, 1979: 137). As in Britain, the post-war boom, which first stimulated housebuilding, then directed investment into more profitable commercial and industrial construction. Housing output, which had fluctuated between 400,000 and 500,000 per annum in the years up to 1916, fell to only 118,000 in 1918. It then rose rapidly to 315,000 in 1919, only to fall back to 217,000 in 1920. But in 1921 the recovery to 449,000 indicated the start of a suburban building boom which continued up to mid-decade. Output peaked in 1925 at a record interwar level of 937,000, then declined, in part because the middle-income demand for housing was saturated (Jacobs, 1976: 24; Kindelberger, 1987: 104). By 1928, according to Wood (writing in 1931), the crude housing shortage was eliminated (cited in Andracheck, 1979: 175). As elsewhere, the upturns were fuelled by speculative pressures and the cost inflation, which had occurred in and immediately after the war, resulted in new housing which was affordable at first only by the well-off, and subsequently by a broader section of middle- and upper-income demand (International Labour Office, 1925).

Despite the fierce resistance to any continuing federal role in housing, the Senate was moved by the immediate post-war housing crisis to appoint an investigatory committee. This reported in early 1921. It rejected federal subsidies, commenting critically on the European examples:

[i]f society takes the line of least resistance and attempts to absorb the increased cost as England is attempting to do, through bonuses and subsidies ... the moral and economic standards of the country will be lowered ... It is an insult to the ingenuity and enterprise of the American people to assume that structural and material costs cannot be satisfactorily reduced. If there is anything in which the

American people have confidence, it is in their own ingenuity and low-cost production (quoted in International Labour Office, 1925: 19–20).

The proposed solution was to apply to housing those methods of rationalization, scientific management and mass production whose development had been accelerated by the needs of war production and which were now being applied in manufacturing industry with increasing success. With the exception of some proposals (which were rejected) for a federal role in the easing of the supply of housing credit, all that could be done was to disseminate information and exhort the private sector to do better. This remained the stance of the federal government throughout the 1920s, with a particular emphasis on the promotion of home ownership through a government-supported organization, Better Homes in America Inc., founded in 1923. In 1921 the first permanent federal agency with a housing remit, the Division of Building and Housing, was set up in the National Bureau of Standards of the Department of Commerce under Secretary Hoover. Hoover, a mining engineer by profession, was a leading exponent of industrial rationalization and an enthusiastic supporter of home ownership, both then and when he succeeded to the presidency in 1928 (A. Jackson, 1976: 168).

So, very little of the new building helped those groups of the population which suffered the greatest shortages. Interestingly, however, as in Europe, in the immediate post-war period the housing shortage affected middle-class as well as working-class households (Topalov, 1988: 161). The situation was particularly serious in the bigger cities and the ILO (1925: 37) commented that in New York the housing crisis was as severe as in European cities (see also A. Jackson, 1976). Before the war, around 30,000 apartments a year were constructed in the city; by 1918, only 2706 were built, and after the brief building boom, about 5000 were constructed in 1920 and 5500 in 1921. The apartment vacancy rate fell to 0.15 per cent in early 1921. This led to widespread speculation in rental housing. By late 1919 there was a wave of evictions, as landlords raised rents and tried to force tenants out. Nationally, while real rents fell by 36 per cent between 1913 and 1919 and real wages rose by 5 per cent, between 1919 and 1923 real rents rose by 4 per cent and salaries by 1 per cent (Topalov, 1988: 136). Already in 1918 there had been protests about landlord profiteering by trade unions and tenants' organizations. In 1918 there was a limited federal law to inhibit the eviction of armed forces' families. By 1920 the tenant protests were spreading rapidly.

There were rent strikes in New York in 1919/20, and eventually a general strike involving tenants and the trade unions was threatened. The leaders of these movements became some of the targets of the red scare propaganda and repressive actions of the authorities which occurred during this period (Topalov, 1988: 136–49).

As a result of this crisis rent controls were imposed in New York (and in Buffalo for a short period), originally as a short-term measure, but the controls had to be extended and were eventually abolished in 1929. Similar conditions in Washington, DC led to controls in 1919, and a fierce battle ensued to maintain them between tenants and labour organizations, led by the AFL, on the one hand, and property owners, on the other. Controls were abolished in 1925.[24] From 1921 tenant militancy faded as unemployment rose, to 19.5 per cent in this year. However, by 1923, it was back down to 4.1 per cent and after 1924 it remained below 7 per cent for the rest of the decade. Trade union membership slumped and many employers adopted the so-called 'American plan', setting up docile house unions. Many workers had substantial rises in real income, housing market conditions (aided by booming output) became less tight and, between 1924 and 1929, real rents fell by 7 per cent while real incomes rose by 13.4 per cent (Topalov, 1988: 165–70).

Increasingly, large sections of the middle class and better-paid working class whose pressure for government action had had at least a limited impact after the war, and especially those working in the growth industries, were able to afford better-quality private housing than before the war. Many of them became suburban home owners, only to lose their houses a few years later as the Depression struck America. The non-farm home-ownership rate rose sharply in the 1920s, from 40.9 per cent in 1920 to 46 per cent ten years later (Andracheck, 1979: 135). However, income inequality grew in the 1920s and large scale concentrations of slum housing in the centres of the older cities remained (as well as an acute rural housing problem) (Jacobs, 1976: 23; Andracheck, 1979: 167). Now, too, the pattern of racially divided inner-city neighbourhoods became clear – a development accelerated by the large-scale migration of southern blacks northwards, pushed by the mechanization of plantations and pulled by the demands of booming war and post-war industry. The building boom and the decentralization of better-off households to the suburbs probably did provide some opportunity for filtering of lower-income households out of the worst inner-city properties, but this was all (see A. Jackson, 1976: 169 on New York City). The sharp curtailment of new immigration to the USA from 1914 also aided this process by reducing the level of demand at the bottom end of the housing market.

In these years New York was about the only city where some attempts were made to respond to the housing shortage. Thus, in an effort to increase private building, as a temporary measure new units were exempted from property tax on part of their value. This aid to private enterprise was advocated and pushed through the state legislature by influential reform elites, many of whom had construction-related interests (A. Jackson, 1976: 169). It may have slightly stimulated the production of middle- and upper-income housing, including for home ownership. It did nothing for those in the greatest housing need (International Labour Office, 1925: 39). In 1923 restrictions were introduced to target the tax reliefs on lower-cost apartment building. In 1925 the city's Tenement House Commissioner reported that builders remained uninterested in providing low- or even moderate-income dwellings; the savings from tax exemptions, which were anyway not needed by the upper-income tenants of new housing, were not passed on to them but were retained by the investors. Most tax-exempt dwellings were built for home ownership in suburban Brooklyn and Queens (A. Jackson, 1976: 174–5). In 1926 a state housing law aimed to encourage cooperatives and limited-dividend corporations, in effect a modernized form of 5 per cent philanthropy. It too achieved very little (A. Jackson, 1976: 186ff.). Topalov (1988: 156–61) gives an account of the handful of initiatives which existed at this time in other states to provide assistance to housebuilding. None of them achieved any significant results in the few years of their operation (see also Wood, 1934).

In the war years there had been a growth in support for state-subsidized housing among a minority of housing reformers, although Veiller and his supporters continued to fulminate against this socialistic excess throughout the 1920s (Veiller, 1920; Murphy, 1929). However, the most important development in these years was the spread of the regulative approach to housing, involving tenement controls and zoning, that the Veiller school had promoted before the war. This was strongly supported by real estate interests as a means of sustaining property values. In 1914 the AFL had endorsed a government role in supporting housing construction but did not campaign on this issue and dropped it as a demand in 1921. New York remained the intellectual centre of the housing reform movement in the war years and support for municipal housing was stronger here than elsewhere (A. Jackson, 1976: 172).

In 1919 one of the prominent people in this movement, Edith Elmer Wood, published a book reviewing US and European experience with state support for housing and arguing for governmental action (Wood, 1919). It was endorsed by the Democrat Al Smith, who became state governor in 1919. However, the state legislature rejected a proposal for municipal housing, and instead instituted the tax exemptions to aid private building which have already been described. As A. Jackson (1976: 173) comments, '[t]he first major attempt to introduce housing as a public service had foundered against a set of beliefs that considered any such act to savor of bolshevism'. Smith lost the governorship in the national Republican landslide in 1920 and when he returned to office in 1923, the housing unrest had died away and a Republican state legislature anyway made municipal housing an impossibility.

The changing times also led to a decline in the housing reform movement (on housing reform in the 1920s generally see Andracheck, 1979). There had been a growing split between a younger, more radically minded generation of reformers, such as Edith Wood and the older, conservative forces (reactionary, in fact – see Robbins, 1966), led by Veiller. Veiller's creation, the National Housing Association (NHA), founded in 1911, began to fade away after the early 1920s, by which time most contributors to its annual conferences accepted the view that rationalizing private construction would solve the housing problem. It eventually petered out at the end of the decade, at which point even Edith Wood, who become a key activist for public housing in the 1930s, accepted that the state ought to do no more than aid the financing of private housing; government-built housing was a socialistic European expedient to which America would never submit. Robbins (1966: 11), narrating the death of the housing reform movement in this period, notes sarcastically that, at the NHA's last conference in 1929, papers dealing with the major issues of slum clearance and poor housing 'did not arouse as much interest as those which advocated glass for windows permitting ultra-violet rays to enter houses and cure the ills of the slum dwellers'.

Neither the politics nor the economics of the United States in the 1920s allowed any room for state-subsidized social housing. Early pressure for action was headed off by a combination of repression and the sharp collapse of worker and tenant militancy after the immediate post-war period. From the early 1920s economic growth resulted in rising real wages and housing output, enabling many of those who had been in acute housing need towards the end of the war to find private market solutions to their housing needs. In a recent paper, Marcuse (1988) has referred to the way in which American housing policy tends to siphon off those sections of demand which have some economic and political power, leaving the poor isolated and in continuing need. This is what the private sector boom of the 1920s appears to have achieved, without, in fact, much government intervention. Writing in 1931, Edith Wood suggested that, in 1917, one-third of Americans lived in good housing, another third in adequate housing and the final third in 'the oldest and worst castoff houses which no one else wanted'. The post-war crisis made the conditions of this last group worse and enlarged its size. However, 'the subsequent period of intensive building brought it back to normal. We are now approximately where we were fourteen years ago' (quoted in Andracheck, 1979: 175).

CONCLUSION: FROM IDEOLOGY TO PRACTICE

The exigencies of war accelerated existing trends and brought about new changes in the relationship between labour, capital and the state. The return to 'normality' desired by so many in 1918 was, in truth, an appeal to a past that was already dissolving before 1918. After the war ended, for the briefest of periods it seemed to many contemporary witnesses as if a revolutionary break with this past was imminent. What transpired, however, was social reform, not revolution. Nevertheless, while capitalism survived, on shaky foundations, as Maier (1975: 580) has noted, 'just restoring the facade of stability required significant institutional change'.

As we have seen, the development of social housing, and, more broadly, the state's role in housing in this period, reflect the more general development of the social structures of accumulation and related policy regimes. The first mass programmes of social housing were a direct response to the social and economic crisis of the later war and early post-war years. They were a response to the needs of particular groups of the population, mainly the skilled workers and lower middle class, whose discontent over housing affordability and supply contributed to more broadly based social unrest. Rent controls and, when these proved inadequate, large-scale housing subsidies, were explicitly timed and designed to be temporary, crisis-abating measures. Accordingly, it is not surprising that there is a close parallel, because there is an intimate connection, between the historical rhythms of housing policy, political and economic development and social conflict in this period. The most striking evidence for these interrelationships was the concurrent downturn in social tension and in the fortunes of social housing when the post-war boom turned to depression in the early 1920s. However, while retreat from state intervention in housing and reversion to the private market was the dominant strategy, it hardly suffices to make this the conclusion of the chapter. The extent to which this transition was achieved and the legacy of the crisis years must also be considered.

First, however, it is worth looking back to the pre-war era, to consider what happened to the aspirations and plans of the early housing reformers. We have already described the extent to which the post-war programmes of social housing were built on the institutional foundations which began to emerge before 1914. In the crisis conditions of wartime and beyond there was neither time nor inclination by governments to invent new institutions to build and manage social housing. Instead, all governments looked to adapt and expand institutional solutions which already existed. In most European countries, for reasons which we discussed in the last chapter, direct state provision of social housing was not the preferred solution. Only in Britain had the local authorities been the more or less acceptable providers of social housing (if any was to be provided at all) before 1914. Here too, then, post-war developments drew on this legacy. Nevertheless, the large scale and speed of implementation of the new programmes did require some resort, at the height of the emergency, to direct state provision by the local authorities. In addition, the special circumstances which surrounded war workers' housing led to a brief involvement of central government in direct provision in the USA and Britain.

However, the incorporation of the social housing institutions as the executive arm of a new state policy also changed them. They grew rapidly in numbers and began to evolve their own forms of federative organization to represent their collective interests in dealings with the state and to regulate and develop their own procedures and standards. At the same time, governments discovered that merely making subsidies available was not enough. The widespread experience of 'pirate' social housing institutions, inefficiency, failure and public criticism, led to the beginning of the apparatus of state supervision, advice and regulation that accompanies the dependency of these institutions on state support. In response to the same imperatives, the internal constitution of the social housing agencies began to change, away from amateur administration by middle-class elites or the tenants themselves, towards more bureaucratized, larger-scale and professionalized management. In the interwar period housing management began to move beyond, or rather, build on, its Victorian origins.

A second but mutating legacy concerns the ideological foundations of social housing. In a series of important publications, Topalov and Magri have discussed the changes which occurred in the ideology and methods of the housing reformers in the war years and beyond and how these perspectives, and those who expounded them, were incorporated in the new structures and practices of the state housing apparatus (apart from the works already cited, see Magri, 1988; Topalov, 1990b). They have shown how the holistic project of the pre-war urban reformers – the socially engineered alterations in working-class practices by means of changes in the urban environment – developed a new scientific basis for its legitimacy under the influence of the changes in productive organization which had occurred in wartime. In some respects the openly moralizing stance of pre-war reformers gave way to a quasi-scientific rationalism. The dominant image was that of the city as a factory, organized on the best Taylorist principles, with planning guided by the all-pervasive organic metaphor. Hence the evolution of standards and methods of housing design, production and planning based on the (supposedly) scientific calculation of needs and examinations of how these could be met, in ways which maximized the efficient operation of urban systems and their inhabitants (Denby, 1938, contains some useful details). In their papers, Topalov and Magri trace the links between this new vision of urban reform and the new vision of reorganized, mass production which emerged in the same period.

However, the broader objectives of this reformulated reform project were not realized. The corporatist dream of a new capitalist order based on the efficient, harmonious and scientific cooperation of the state, capital and labour in the workplace and in the city could not survive in the real world. Nevertheless, its more fragmentary impact on the new housing programmes was considerable. As we have described, these programmes resulted in major and persisting changes in housing design, planning and construction, with the adoption of rationalization, larger-scale organization and new standards of provision. Henceforth, housing needs and provision became a matter for scientific study and technical expertise, carried out by the rapidly growing ranks of the urban professionals. And just as the Taylorist organization of industry required a new and more complex division of labour, so did the new housing schemes. From this time forward, the search for housing solutions became led not by the amateur exponents of urban reform with their holistic visions, but by the technically advanced though compartmentalized and specialized competencies of the professionals. In time, these interests formed a powerful element in the social housing lobby which developed in all the countries under discussion and which, at times, was a significant source of resistance to government policies which threatened their position.

Therefore, the shift of housing reform from ideology to practice resulted in some profound changes. Social housing began to become routinized, bureaucratized and professionalized. The state and the major political parties, rather than self-organized groups of tenants or middle-class patronage, took increasing control over the fortunes of the tenure. In the process the manifest connections which were made between forms of social housing provision and the requirements of wider social reform became less apparent. This is not to say, however, that these disappeared. In various ways the location, planning and internal design of the new houses continually sought to engineer a break with working-class practices, remoulding them according to the by now scientifically legitimated preferences of the new urban technocracy. Moreover, the targeting of these programmes not at the totality of those in housing need but at groups which were of strategic socio-political and economic importance, provides the most important example of pre- and post-war continuity.

If the more grandiose aspirations of those who argued for a Taylorized urban order in a modernized capitalist society were disappointed, so too were the more dimly glimpsed hopes of those who wished to transcend capitalist urbanization and the housing market. The revolutionary left hardly had time to make any impact on these matters in the countries with which we are concerned before it fell victim to political repression and economic depression. Social democracy occasionally flirted with radical schemes for the socialization of housing production and distribution, but the acceptance of social reform and a measure of recognition by the state and industry entailed an acceptance in practice (whatever the rhetoric may have been) of social housing as a complement to market provision, rather than as an alternative to it. One consequence of the endorsement of this limited role was that, in some countries, social democratic pressure for social housing was able to make common cause with demands originating from non-socialist workers' movements, expressed through non-socialist political parties that were central participants in government. This was an important foundation for future developments.

Another important development was the growth of socialist and 'workerist' subnational governments, eager to make use of the new subsidies to build social housing. Within limits, some of these new developments contributed to a broad-ranging attempt to maintain and extend distinctive types of working-class community, based on political or religious allegiances, within the interstices of capitalist society and the oversight of the state. With the benefit of historical hindsight, we can see that this project, whose features were really moulded by class relations and conditions as they existed before 1914, was doomed to failure. The emergent relations between capital, organized labour and the state, and the selective incorporation of the newly enfranchised working class's demands and organizations into the mainstream political agenda and into the machinery of professionalized government, left little room for the construction of alternative forms of local and grassroots social organization. Recourse to the strategy of negative integration, while still evident in the 1920s, became less an imperative response to poverty and oppression and more a Utopian aspiration for the future, held by a declining minority of activists.

So far we have set out some general conclusions concerning the changes which occurred as social housing became a reality after the First World War. But it is important to return to the central supposition and intention of those who legislated for the new programmes, namely that they would be temporary expedients, rather than the start of a permanent state role in housing provision. As we have seen, this motive, the 'return to normality' in housing, is an important key to understanding the history and nature of these programmes, as is their role as a 'guarantee against revolution'. The reason why, in some countries, a commitment to social housing survived the immediate post-war era is not simply because housing needs remained unmet, but because underlying social and economic conditions prevented a politically convincing, legitimized return to the 'solution' of private market provision. The accounts of developments in each country show how the 'space' for state-subsidized social housing, its role and the temporalities of its provision were determined not by any simple calculation of housing needs, but by the existence of needs that were regarded as strategically important to meet, or at least to make some gestures towards meeting. And what determined this strategic importance were the varying economic conditions in each country, the relations between labour and capital, the state of internal organization or disorganization of social classes and their perceived interests, and, of course, the ability of the private housing market to recover from the war-induced collapse.

As all these factors varied cross-nationally, so too did the fortunes of social housing. At one extreme, there was no basis for the acceptance of state-subsidized housing in the USA after the war. At the other extreme, state support proved indispensable in Germany throughout the 1920s. In Britain, too, the continuing economic weakness and high levels of unemployment and low wages, together with the limited but significant influence of the labour movement, combined to prolong the subsidy commitment. Of the European countries, Denmark and the Netherlands achieved the return to housing 'normality' most completely, and not even the incorporation of the Social Democrats as a governing party in the former country, or the influence of the pillarized organizations in the latter, significantly impeded this transition.

All these European countries, whatever their subsequent trajectories, responded to the post-war housing crisis in a similar way. France did not, despite the existence of similar housing needs and similar social and political pressures for state action. Instead, significant state subsidies for social housing were delayed for a decade. Many of the factors which severely inhibited social reform in the pre-war period continued after the war and their persistence delayed not only housing reform, but other social policies too (Flora and Heidenheimer, 1981). The nature of French industry and industrial relations, the weak and divided trade union and political representation of the working class, the political and social importance of a property-owning petty bourgeoisie and of liberal ideology were just some of the key determinants of the limited state response to housing needs after the war. Demographic factors may also have made a contribution to the failure of the state, or the private market for that matter, to build much housing throughout the interwar period. However, whether by compulsion or by choice (as some argued), the housing conditions of the French working class remained exceptionally poor. The main concession to housing needs was the continuance of rent controls. In addition, the lack of state regulation of land uses allowed *lotissement* development, a sort of private market housing 'solution' to some lower-income housing needs, to continue and grow.

That the mass social housing programmes of the 1920s did not in fact do very much to meet the housing needs of large sections of the less well-paid, unemployed or economically inactive working class was clearly recognized and frequently discussed at this time. Some commentators were highly critical of this failure. Others, including many of the growing number of those involved in the development and management of social housing, had no real desire to extend its role, and their management responsibilities, beyond the 'respectable' working and middle classes. And yet the manifest inability of the private rental market to house these populations in other than slum conditions, with all the external diswelfares that this entailed, and the failure of private investors in the 1920s, even with state subsidies, to build for low-income groups, left a problem. No longer could a state which had intervened to such an extent in housing provision in wartime and after simply revert to the *status quo ante*. Demands for some state action, and even the acceptance of a limited responsibility, had been legitimized by these events and this process was not wholly reversible.

The most widespread response, as we have seen, was the maintenance of some rent and security controls (although, in the USA, hardly even this) well beyond the date at which they were originally to be terminated. In addition, the notion of filtering as a solution for low-income housing needs began to become popular (see, for example, the critical discussion in Fisher and Ratcliff, 1936). The new higher-rented social housing would create a chain of vacancies in lower-quality but still adequate private rented housing into which the slum dweller could filter. This formula suited most key interests, preserving social housing for the 'respectable working class' and the professionalizing housing managers, requiring no additional public expenditure and preventing the large-scale replacement of the private by the social landlord. However, as the figures for housing shortages at the end of the decade illustrate, it did very little for the urban poor. New social housing production was too limited, especially when combined with accelerating rates of household formation, to raise vacancy rates to the level where filtering might have occurred. Only in America, where private housing boomed, is it arguable that there may have been some emptying out of the very worst pre-1914 slums by this process.

However, despite the exclusion of the poor from much of the social housing built in the early 1920s, by the latter years of the decade, one can also discern the emergence of a residual rather than a mass role for social housing, not as the houser of skilled manual and white-collar workers, but as a houser of the poor and as an adjunct to slum clearance. As we noted in chapter 1, the model of state-subsidized housing advanced before 1914 by housing reformers was one which implied residual rather than mass provision, although in practice such state assistance as was provided helped house better-off workers. Later the strategic importance of these latter's needs was what converted earlier resistance to subsidies to a grudging and limited acceptance of their necessity. However, as the dominant rationale for mass social housing receded in the 1920s, the maintenance of a much more limited role for state assistance in meeting the costs of housing the homeless and enabling slum clearance and modernization of the urban infrastructure to occur, re-emerged as the main justification for some social housing provision, in theory and in practice. This residual role entailed a distinctively different conception of the scope and functions of social housing to that of the regimes which provided for 'mass needs' in the early post-war period. As Marian Bowley (1944) described it, it amounted to an extension of 'sanitary policy'.

The new or revived residual social housing model was tied to and evolved out of, the responsibilities of the local authorities for the regulation of public health, hygiene and housing conditions which had built up before 1914. These responsibilities were widened, with the addition of rent and security matters especially, in the course of the war. After the war the local authority involvement continued and a more comprehensive conception emerged of its duties in relation to local housing conditions. For a time, when the new subsidy programmes were in full swing and the social housing institutions inadequate in number and scale, substantial local authority building occurred. At the same time, local authorities provided very poor quality, makeshift accommodation for some of those in the most desperate housing needs, including those without any home at all. However, in most cases the local authority role contracted as programmes shrunk and as the social housing institutions and/or subsidized private enterprise developed. With the exception of Britain, where only subsidized private enterprise was available and a major local authority role thereby remained, a clear division of labour began to emerge between, on the one hand, the social housing provided by the cooperatives, housing associations and other institutions and, on the other, the diminished building activities of the local authorities.

By the late 1920s the trickle of local authority housing which continued in some of the European countries was increasingly targeted at the urban poor and was frequently very different from that being produced and managed by the other social landlords. Typically, it was built at higher densities, to lower standards, quality and price. It was located not on well-planned, low-density suburban estates but on high-density inner-city sites close to the sources of its inhabitants' low-wage employment. Its management reflected the repressive and disciplinary impulses which, as we saw in chapter 1, underlay pre-war prescriptions for the reform of the 'undeserving poor'. In short, and to anticipate the later history of social housing, it provided the first clear evidence of the

moulding of social housing into its dominant contemporary role
as residual housing for a marginalized section of the population –
the urban poor. In effect, this conception of social housing views
it as a sort of functional equivalent of, or replacement for, the
nineteenth-century slum landlord, a parallel which has not been
without its practical consequences for the state and fortunes of this
tenure in the late twentieth century.

In conclusion, the history of social housing in the period from
1914 to the late 1920s may be read in two different ways, both
of which describe a certain reality. From one perspective, we see
the rise and decline of social housebuilding for mass needs, more
accurately for the needs of core sections of the labour market
whose interests were more or less incorporated in the established
political system. Many developments occurred as a result of this
experience in relation to the organization and practices of social
housing provision which were to outlast the demise of the first
mass building programmes. But they would not by themselves have
sustained any continuing state role in social housing provision for
mass needs on the scale which occurred in the early post-war years.
Only when such social housing provision became, for a longer or
shorter period, an essential element in the resolution of wider
processes of social and economic crisis and restructuring was the
need for its major expansion again accepted. As we shall see,
these conditions recurred, although in very different ways, in some
countries in the Depression years of the 1930s and, more generally,
after 1945.

From a somewhat different perspective, we can see the more
permanent emergence in the 1920s of a restricted, residual role
for social housing. Here, it does seem valid to stress the historical
continuities connecting the 1920s with the modern era because,
while the rationale for mass social housing has waxed and waned,
for the reasons already described, the residual definition of its role
has persisted and, as the first rationale has faded, has become the
dominant one, notably in the late 1920s and 1930s and again in
the 1990s.

Half a century ago Marian Bowley (1944) recognized, in her
study of interwar British housing policies, the differing nature and
consequences of these two rationales for state-subsidized social
housing and showed that the history of policy is marked by their
varying significance over time. On the one hand, Bowley (1944:
183) noted that there were two sets of ideas and interests which
sustained the early policy of mass building – the coming together of
the requirement for mass social housing as a temporary expedient

pending the return to health of the private market with 'the rather vague idea, held by an important section of the community, that standards of working class housing must be improved by state intervention'. On the other hand, there was the 'matter of the slums and the worst types of overcrowding; it was suddenly remembered that this old-fashioned type of housing problem had continued to flourish unchecked since the Great War'. The mass policy had provided little for 'those families whose housing conditions were undoubtedly deplorable socially, morally and on grounds of public health'. Hence the emergence in Britain in the 1930s of a role for social housing as a 'new sanitary policy', but one which, like the mass policy, in fact provided new housing only for 'the limited number' and 'had no concern with achieving this standard for all'. Subsequent social housing programmes which have been cast in this residual mode have continued to have this minimal characteristic. In this they reflect, as do the phases when mass building policies have been uppermost, the manner in which social housing is confined and shaped by its wider social and economic functions, as an adjunct, for example, to private sector-led slum clearance and urban renewal, or in a less sharply defined contemporary role as accommodation for the economically marginalized urban poor, shut out of even heavily subsidized home ownership and excluded from that part of the private rental market which has survived slum clearance and gentrification. As we shall describe, by the 1990s, the role of social housing as housing of last resort for the homeless and the urban poor, which began to emerge as a minor theme in the 1920s, had increasingly become the central justification for its continued (if limited) existence.

NOTES

1　In addition to the general sources of social and economic history cited in chapter 1, see van der Flier (1923); Renouvin (1927) and (1969); Westergaard (1930); Clark (1931); Hirst (1934); Grebler and Winckler (1940); Marwick (1974); J. Winter (1986); and Hardach (1987).

2　For surveys of the economic effects of the war see Hardach (1987: 283–94); and Aldcroft (1987: 11–54).

3　At least in political terms – although American bankers lent a great deal of money, at high rates of interest, to debt-ridden European governments and the private sector in the 1920s, not always, as we shall see, with the most positive results.

4　See the sources already cited and Cipolla (1978) for country studies.

5   And the reversals of the working-class gains occurred differently, and
     to varying degrees, in the six countries. As Maier (1975: 154) notes,

     [b]usinessmen, and elites in general wanted to go back even as they
     reorganized for new competition, hence they found labour's claims
     . . . whether the demands of the conference table for nationalization
     schemes, or the demands of strikers for organization and power
     in the workplace – radical and unacceptable. But the tactics chosen
     for the workplace or the conference table differed according to the
     strength of the challenges, the underlying sense of bourgeois security
     or anxiety, and the political temperaments of the men in power.

6   The government was headed by Cort van der Linden, who had been
     Minister of Justice when the 1901 Housing Act was passed and had
     had a major role in its formulation (Searing, 1971: 263).

7   Jurriens (1981) discusses the relationship between the Catholic social
     movement and the trade unions at this time.

8   Industrial wages remained fairly level in the late 1920s and there was
     a decline in prices (Mitchell, 1978: 74; de Vries, 1978: 33).

9   On Danish politics in this period see Miller (1968); Fitzmaurice (1981);
     Logue (1982); Elder, Thomas and Arter (1982); Glyn Jones (1986);
     and Rying (1988).

10   See, for example, Butler and Noisette (1983), Wollmann (1986), and
     Searing (1971) on France, Germany and the Netherlands, respectively.

11   But one achievement was the much publicized *cité-jardins* round Paris
     directed by the socialist politician Sellier (see Magri and Topalov,
     1987).

·12   Addison, the Minister responsible, had succeeded Lloyd George as the
     Minister for Munitions, then became Minister for Reconstruction
     and, finally, the first Minister of Health – he might be called the
     British Loucheur.

13   There was also a small amount of local authority subsidy, based on
     the taxable value of property in individual local authority areas.

14   The legislation also contained some assistance for public utility societies
     to build social housing. However, it was expected that most of these
     societies would be promoted by industrialists, in effect a form of
     employer housing. This meant that the labour movement was hostile
     to the provision. In any event, little resulted. An official report
     published in 1939 indicated that the societies (now known as housing
     associations) had built under 30,000 units, under all the main post-
     war Housing Acts, and were playing an even smaller role in the
     new slum clearance programmes (for details of these see later in this
     chapter) (Ministry of Health, 1939: 6). In the 1930s minor changes
     were made to provide slight encouragement to the associations but
     the 1939 report reasserted the prime role of the local authorities and
     rejected proposals put forward by the associations for a central state
     authority to finance their operations. Such ideas finally bore fruit

over 30 years later, with the establishment of the Housing Corporation as a major funder and regulator of housing associations.

15 In early 1923 a newly appointed Minister of Health failed to gain election to Parliament; apparently, discontent at the government's abandonment of subsidized housing programmes was a significant factor (Gilbert, 1970: 197).

16 Interestingly, Bowley (1944: 40) makes a similar observation with respect to the resumption of local authority subsidies by Wheatley.

17 See Jarmain (1948); Daunton (1984); and Malpass (1986).

18 The cost of living index went from a value of 1 in 1914 to 26 in March 1922: 685 by the end of this year and 15 million by September 1923. By the following month the average weekly wage for a brick-layer was 204 billion marks – it had been 695 million the previous month! (International Labour Office, 1924: 329, 337).

19 However, cooperatives were discouraged and were difficult to form, see van der Kaa (1935).

20 I am grateful to Jan van der Schaar for supplying these and subsequent details about the housing corporations.

21 Before the war the corporations only had any major role in Amsterdam, where they accounted for about 25 per cent of output in 1914, but less than 5 per cent in Rotterdam and none in the Hague. By 1918/19 virtually no private housing was being built in Amsterdam and Rotterdam, the two main working-class cities, and even in the more middle-class Hague less than half the output came from the private sector. By 1921 there was a considerable recovery in private building; nevertheless, its share amounted only to about one-third in Amsterdam, 45 per cent in Rotterdam and 50 per cent in the Hague (International Labour Office, 1924: 248).

22 For a description of the mortgage credit institution see Ball, Harloe and Martens (1988: 137–41).

23 There were also a small number of charitable or philanthropic societies which had been founded in the late nineteenth century.

24 Some cities in Maine, Massachusetts, Illinois and Wisconsin also had controls during this period.

3

Social Housing in the Depression

At the end of the First World War Keynes (1919: 238) wrote: '[t]he forces of the nineteenth century have run their course and are exhausted. The economic motives and ideals of that generation no longer satisfy us: we must find a new way and must suffer again the malaise, and finally the pangs, of a new industrial birth'. However, this message fell on deaf ears, for, as we have described, the fondest hope in the 1920s was that the clock could be turned back to the supposed 'normality' of the pre-war era. The aims of state housing policies reflected this objective, although 'normality' frequently proved an elusive quarry.

At first inspection, the history of social housing in the 1930s may seem less dramatic or significant than that of the previous decade, although not in the United States. Nevertheless, this new period of social crisis and recovery had specific consequences for social housing. However, on this occasion the cross-national variance in outcomes was considerable and is a major topic for discussion in this chapter.

ECONOMIC CHAOS AND RECOVERY

Most economists and historians date the start of the Depression from the collapse of the New York Stock Market in autumn 1929, although the real economic devastation began in the crisis year of 1931. Beyond the chronology, there is little agreement about the causes of the Depression – monetarists, Keynesians and Marxists tell different stories and, within these broad schools of thought, there are further arguments (see, for example, Kindelberger, 1987: 1–12; Devine, 1992). Thankfully, our concern is with the consequences rather than the causes of the global collapse of production, prices and employment in the early 1930s.[1]

Even in the period of economic growth which most countries experienced in the second half of the 1920s, unemployment had stayed at higher levels than before the war and real wage growth had been very limited. These limitations on consumer purchasing power were particularly significant in the dominant US economy where, as Aldcroft (1987: 199) notes, investment opportunities began to dry up as a result of declining demand after mid-decade for housing and in the linked market for the new consumer durable industries. This downturn had a wide impact, affecting the demand for urban infrastructure, consumer and mortgage credit, electricity, chemicals and steel. Meanwhile, the older industries were still declining, agricultural prices were falling rapidly and wholesale stocks rose (see also McCoy, 1977: 168–92).

That this fragile situation was converted into disaster by 1931 was largely due to the failure of the USA, Britain and France to take concerted and appropriate action. They pursued conflicting, inadequate and uncoordinated policies which intensified rather than alleviated the growing crisis. The US stock market boom of the late 1920s was fed by a liberal supply of bank credit, much of it from abroad. This export of funds began to threaten the central bank reserves of those countries which had returned to the gold standard in the 1920s. Eventually, US interest rates were raised to choke off the flow of funds, despite the underlying weakness in the economy. By this stage production had begun to fall in most other major economies. Conditions were especially bad in Germany, where unemployment rose near to 2 million in the summer of 1929.

There ensued an abrupt collapse of confidence on the New York Stock Market. Between September and early November the Dow-Jones index fell from around 380 to just under 200. The other stock markets followed suit. This led to retrenchment by firms which had relied on access to the stock market for finance. Production fell sharply. The liquidity shortage fed through to the US home mortgage market. At this time most mortgages were three-year unamortized loans, so frequent refinancing was a necessity

(Kindelberger, 1987: 112). New loans became hard to get and the rate of mortgage foreclosure began to rise.

Fairly soon, however, conditions in the US economy stabilized, credit markets eased and the stock market rose a little. However, the production cuts resulted in a fall in US commodity imports and their prices. The primary producers therefore had to reduce their levels of US imports. The downturn in world investment and trade was increased by the spread of protectionism as nations sought to sustain their domestic industries. In 1930 the US legislature passed the Smoot–Hawley Tariff Act, which resulted in a wave of retaliatory action by the other major economies. The downturn in production also affected the US banking system, which consisted of a myriad of small local banks; as local industries declined the banks which had supported them began to fail. By 1930 European banks were in increasing difficulties. In Germany, where unemployment, political and social conflict were rising rapidly (see below), the foreign capital which had sustained economic recovery in the 1920s (and which, as we noted, supported housing and urban investment) began to be withdrawn. Bank deposits fell and the central bank lost a major part of its holdings of gold. In addition, the main German, Austrian and other Continental banks had major industrial shareholdings, whose value was severely affected by the recession.

In 1931 the combination of deflation, falling prices for manufactures, commodities and securities, falling profits and the consequential rise in loan defaults resulted in a global banking crisis and the collapse in world trade and employment. The immediate event which touched off the crisis was the failure of the main Austrian bank, which then caused a crisis in the German system. By the summer sterling was under pressure as foreign funds were withdrawn to compensate for the loss of access to blocked funds in Germany. At the same time, there was concern by foreign investors about the British budget deficit. In August the Cabinet of the Labour minority government, which had been in office since 1929, split over the demand, strongly pressed by the financial community and the Bank of England, that unemployment benefit be cut as part of a deflationary package. The new coalition National government imposed the cuts, but the withdrawal of foreign funds continued and in late September Britain left the gold standard.

From this point, with the collapse of the international mechanism of the gold standard, the various countries took different paths. Twenty-five countries followed Britain and left the gold standard, but, of the countries under discussion here, only Denmark was in this group. In Germany, despite the desperate situation, the experience of the early 1920s reinforced the reluctance to allow a devaluation, thus intensifying the recourse to further deflation and unemployment, assisting the Nazi rise to power. The Netherlands and France formed part of a new gold bloc of countries that were determined to stay at the set parities, whatever the deflationary costs might be.

The final stage of the collapse occurred early in 1933. It was produced by the interaction of the various international developments and domestic conflict over reflationary versus further deflationary policies at the time of transition to the Roosevelt presidency. Widespread panic withdrawals occurred from US banks which then failed in large numbers. In April the US left the gold standard, returning to it in early 1934 after a major devaluation. The reflationary programmes of the first New Deal administration were enacted in rapid succession during 1933, the control of agricultural output, industrial agreements on production, prices and labour rights, and large-scale federally funded public works programmes. The institution of bank deposit insurance was of particular importance to the private housing market.

Most countries which left gold and adopted less deflationary policies began to recover slowly. Britain imposed a protective tariff on imports and controlled the exchange rate. Interest rates were sharply lowered, the discount rate was cut from 6 per cent to 2 per cent in the first half of 1932. This monetary policy was maintained throughout the decade; as Kindelberger (1987: 178) notes, it made a major contribution to British economic growth through its stimulation of the housing market. Private building rose 70 per cent between 1931 and 1933, building costs and prices fell, so real incomes and consumption (notably of housing) rose for those sections of the population in the growth areas of southern England. A new subsidy programme for slum clearance, discussed below, also aided the upturn in housing output and the consequential rise in consumption-related production. In many ways the pattern of expansion and urban growth in these years mirrors the similar process which occurred in the USA in the 1920s.

US recovery was more faltering and unemployment declined only slowly to mid-decade. The administration remained committed to balanced budgets, so programmes to expand activity and output were restrained. In Germany Hitler's accession to power led to a controlled economy with large-scale rearmament and public works programmes which reduced unemployment. Denmark's mainly agricultural exports had been severely hit by the crisis years, falling by 55–60 per cent between 1928/9 and 1932/3. The Netherlands had suffered a slightly greater fall. However, their subsequent economic policies diverged radically, as the Netherlands joined the new gold bloc but Denmark, having abandoned the gold standard, devalued its currency, while a Social Democrat/Radical Liberal government adopted measures to support agriculture and reduce unemployment.

France became the leader of the gold bloc, while Kindelberger (1987: 246) comments that the Dutch 'clung . . . to gold at the old parity as an act of faith'; the French, having devalued in the 1920s, 'at substantial costs to the rentier classes', were determined not to repeat the process. French policy was still dominated by the political and economic interests of this group. However, according to Kemp (1972), even the Communist Party supported the fixed parity of the franc in the early 1930s. Both countries subsequently suffered from overvalued currencies, falling exports, continuing unemployment and low wages. In both cases deflationary budgets reduced the wages of government employees and pension payments (Abma, 1981). In France and the Netherlands a policy of economic Malthusianism was followed, as production fell in line with reduced demand.

Workers were forced out of French cities in search of a means of subsistence in the countryside. Opposition to government policies grew, with mass strikes and demonstrations, leading to the Popular Front government in 1936 (Larkin, 1988: 34–62). This administration forced employers to increase wages, cut working hours and provide paid holidays. There ensued an increase in the outflow of capital from the country and France was forced off the gold standard. The Netherlands followed. Here the devaluation stimulated some recovery as export prices fell, and exports rose between 1936 and 1937. In France 'it proved impossible to restore the trading position or confidence of the rentier with the forty hour week, or to quiet the worker without it' (Kindelberger, 1987: 253). The government was defeated, there was further devaluation and a reversal of most of the workers' gains of the Popular Front period. In late 1938 French production began to recover. However, taking the decade as a whole, the picture was one of economic stagnation, with the perpetuation of France's backward industrial structure and limited urbanization. In the Netherlands there was actually a reversion to a more agriculturally based economy.

One further economic episode was of particular significance for social housing in the USA. In 1937 the slow US recovery was interrupted by another stock market slump and sharp falls in production and prices. This led the administration to adopt new public works policies, including the first public housing programme, and to accept, reluctantly, a temporary budget deficit. Recovery followed in 1938 and 1939.

POLITICAL RESPONSES TO THE CRISIS

The varying economic fortunes of the countries with which we are concerned were accompanied by an equally wide range of political outcomes.[2] Social democracy was defeated in Britain in 1931 and later in France, and remained excluded from power in the Netherlands while it secured power in Denmark in a coalition with the Radical Liberals. Democracy itself was annihilated in Germany, while America moved through the reform years of the New Deal. In each country there was rising unemployment and renewed social tension. However, the responses to this new crisis, and the role of state policies in its resolution, varied greatly.

In Britain the Conservatives and their allies obtained a crushing victory in the election which followed the 1931 crisis. The Labour Party only re-entered government in the wartime Churchill coalition. With economic recovery under way and the gold standard no longer a constraint, deflationary policies were not as severe as they remained in other countries. However, there was resistance to the adoption of Keynesian policies of deficit spending, including public works programmes to relieve unemployment. But subsidies were provided to support agriculture and state-directed rationalization began to occur in some of the older industries. Once the conditions for recovery had been set by devaluation, protective tariffs and low interest rates, private consumption started to rise, aided by increasing real wages due to falling prices. Investment flowed into the domestic market, notably into housing and the related industries. However, as we have already noted, the recovery benefited mainly the southern part of the country, where the new industries and their consumers were located. Elsewhere high unemployment persisted as the older basic industries continued to decline. According to Taylor (1965: 346), class antagonisms sharpened in this period and the Labour Party adopted a more radical programme. As the decade progressed the left generally, and the Communist Party in particular, gained more support, although this was much influenced by foreign rather than domestic developments. However, the experience of unemployment and government inaction was a potent factor leading to the return of a Labour government in

1945. Meanwhile, Labour had no opportunity at national level to obtain social and economic reforms, although it remained a considerable force in local government, notably through its control of the London County Council and other big city administrations.

In France the split between the Socialists and Communists in 1920–1 weakened the left throughout the 1920s. The economic crisis and deflation of the 1930s led to a growing political polarization, with the rise of an anti-democratic right. There was no agreement on economic policies between the Radicals and the Socialists (which together had a parliamentary majority after the 1932 elections), and there was a succession of weak governments. In Paris in 1934 a battle took place between security forces and right-wing demonstrators who aimed to remove the Radical-led government. Fourteen people were killed when the police opened fire. This may have encouraged the subsequent *rapprochement* between the Communists and the Socialists, although the key factor was the Comintern's reversal of its disastrous policy of opposition to 'social fascism' (i.e. social democracy), which had contributed to the Nazi rise to power and the crushing of the left in Germany. The Popular Front of Socialists, Communists and Radicals which was then formed campaigned on an anti-fascist programme for a reduction in the hours of work, paid holidays, national pensions and nationalization of the banking and finance system. Between 1934 and 1937 trade union membership rose fivefold and the Popular Front came to power in 1936. However, as Zeldin (1975: 280) has pointed out, mass factory occupations which occurred in that year were uncoordinated by the Communist-led trade union federation and '[a]lmost none seem to have envisaged any destruction of the capitalist system'.

The Popular Front was a fragile affair: the Radicals had lost seats in the 1936 elections, and the Communists refused to participate in the government, which was led by the Socialist Blum. The devaluation, in October 1936, came far too late for France to reap much benefit, industrial production remained depressed and unemployment did not fall. The government came under increasing attack from both the right and the left. In early 1937 Blum announced a pause in the Front's programme of social and economic reforms. Eventually the Radicals overthrew the administration. There followed a series of weak Radical-led governments of an increasingly conservative disposition, especially in relation to economic and financial policies. The remaining period leading up to the war was marked by continuing political polarization and disintegration of the established system of republican politics.

In the Netherlands the succession of Confessional governments continued throughout the decade, dominated by the austere Anti-Revolutionary Party leader Colijn. As Kossmann (1978: 604) notes, 'the Protestant parties remained in general profoundly sceptical about all projects of systematic social reform', despite the presence of the Christian trade unions in the ruling bloc. Colijn, whose small party had a lower-middle-class base, wanted to protect the gains made by this group in the past and, coming from a strict Calvinist background, believed that 'it was the statesman's task to teach society how to come to terms with a permanently reduced standard of living' (Kossmann, 1978: 606). The Liberals also wanted to preserve the status quo, once the reforms of the early 1920s had restored a degree of social and political normality. So little was done to alleviate the effects of the Depression, beyond some very limited public works programmes. However, major powers were taken to regulate and reorganize agriculture in 1933.

But generally, as Kossmann (1978: 665) comments, '[i]n the Netherlands there was no social unrest and no digression from the principle of deflation'.[3] Uniquely, perhaps, the return to 'normality' persisted, unchallenged by communism or social democracy on the left, or by the anti-democratic right. The Social Democratic Worker Party (SDAP), which had remained, according to Abma (1981), a rather dogmatic, Marxist-influenced party, saw its vote decline in the 1933 election and had its first cabinet ministers only in the wartime coalition formed in 1939. Union membership rose in the interwar period, but many of these members were in the Christian unions and the proportion of workers who were unionized remained lower than many other European countries. In the early 1930s the SDAP struggled to make any coherent response to the economic crisis. However, events such as the demise of the German SDP (which had close links with the SDAP) reinforced the position of those who wanted to transform the party from a workers' to a 'people's' party, appealing to voters beyond the limited manual working-class section of the electorate.

In this climate, with growing concern about the spread of fascism, the SDAP produced its 1935 Labour Plan for economic and social reform (Abma, 1981). This involved large-scale public works, to reduce unemployment and stimulate demand, and the rationalization and reorganization of key branches of the economy. The plan envisaged a corporatist planning mechanism, involving capital, labour and the state, prefiguring developments which occurred after 1945. It proposed an annual housing programme of 50,000 units, with a tripartite industry-level body allocating resources among building firms; again, such ideas were influential after the war. However, this plan also marked the final acceptance by the Dutch socialists of a moderate, reformist approach. Interestingly, it also assumed that balanced budgets should be maintained and the SDAP did not support devaluation (Klein, 1975; Kossmann, 1978: 663). The Communist Party grew very slowly but never achieved more than four seats in Parliament in this period. The Dutch National Socialists had some electoral successes in mid-decade, gaining almost 8 per cent of the vote in provincial elections in 1935, but they then declined, being opposed by all other parties.

Denmark had a very different history. After the fall of the first Social Democratic government at the end of 1926, there had been a period of Liberal administration, with support from the Conservatives. However, there were major differences of interest between the urban-based Conservatives and the agrarian Liberals. As Andersen (1980) notes, it was this division between the industrial bourgeoisie and the agrarian classes which created the opportunity for what he calls 'the intervention state' to emerge. In the 1929 elections the Social Democrats made gains and Stauning formed a coalition government with the Radical Liberals which lasted throughout the 1930s. By 1933 around 40 per cent of the working population was unemployed. With world prices plummeting, the farming sector was in crisis, and there were large-scale bankruptcies. Falling agricultural earnings reduced consumption and hence affected manufacturing industry. In these circumstances, it was possible to form a compact between the Socialists and the agrarian/Liberal parties, the first of the so-called Red–Green coalitions that have been a distinctive feature of growth of the Scandinavian welfare states. This left the Conservatives isolated (Andersen, 1980; Esping-Andersen, 1985). The krone was devalued, aiding farm exports. Strikes and lockouts were banned, wage cuts were prohibited and, to relieve unemployment, credits were made available for housebuilding and public works. Sectors of agricultural production were regulated to raise prices and imports were restricted to boost employment. In addition, there was a major reform of social security which abolished the old poor law and raised unemployment benefits.

These changes lay the foundations of the modern Danish welfare state and they prefigured the model of welfare capitalism which characterised the Western European democracies after 1945. Nevertheless, financial orthodoxy still had a firm hold on the government budget. The expansion of public works was financed by raising taxes rather than by running a deficit, so their impact on reducing unemployment was limited. In addition, the farm crisis continued and angry farmers staged large demonstrations; the small Danish Nazi party was later able to draw on some of these disaffected farming interests. However, in 1935 the Social Democrats, campaigning under the slogan of 'Stauning or chaos', won 46 per cent of the votes, a proportion which they have never again been able to achieve (P. Svensson, 1974). They also finally won a majority in the upper house of the Folketing, so the government was now able to rule without having to seek support from the opposition parties for particular measures.

In Germany the economic collapse destroyed the Weimar Republic. J. Roberts (1978) summarises the background to this transition: the power of the reactionary forces which had not been destroyed by the institution of democracy in 1918; the persistence of anti-democratic and anti-individualist ideas of the *volkisch* community, of anti-Semitism and nationalism; resentment over the Peace Treaty and reparations; and the economic ruin of the middle class in the immediate post-war years. During the 1920s, under the influence of these factors, the Centre Party shifted to the right and the SPD was unable to mobilize an effective opposition. As elsewhere, the Social Democrats failed to break through electorally to sections of the middle class. At the same time, the SPD and the trade unions became increasingly bureaucratized and entrenched in the existing political and economic institutions. Neumann (1942: 336) refers, for example, to the mass of jobs that the unions created, not only in their own organizations, but in the Labour Bank, the housing associations and construction enterprises, printing houses, insurance companies – and even a trade union bicycle factory! Housing provided a key part of these emergent economic empires; thus Umrath (1950) refers to the VSB (Verband Sozialer Baubetriebe – Federation of Social Building Enterprises) owned by the building workers' union. By 1922 the VSB presided, as the 'mother society', over 207 'daughter societies' which had 21,000 employees. By 1929 it had installed professional management and also controlled 12 brickyards, two sawmills, four quarries, three joineries and three cementware factories. The process of bureaucratization which Michels (1911) had analysed earlier advanced rapidly in the 1920s and left the SPD and trade union leadership quite unable to respond adequately to the social crisis. Instead, outside the established parties, the Communists and the Nazis attracted support from those groups of workers and *petits bourgeois* who had suffered most from the wartime defeat and the economic collapse.

The Nazis were, however, of limited significance until the new economic crisis in 1929. Rather as occurred in Britain, the SPD, back in government from 1928, left it in 1930, refusing to agree to cuts in welfare benefits (it only returned to government in 1969). As unemployment rose, Nazi and Communist support increased. The Centre Party leader Bruning, lacking a parliamentary majority, governed by decree. Continual attempts to solve the economic problem by additional deflation and public expenditure cuts only fed the crisis. Eventually, acting through the President, Hindenburg, the conservative coalition of landed property, the military and big industry forced Bruning to resign and replaced him with the reactionary von Papen, intending also to use the Nazis to crush the left. The SPD, offering no resistance, was removed from power in Prussia. In July 1932 the Nazis became the largest party in the Reichstag, although the SPD and the KPD together were almost as large. However, the left was completely divided: the KPD, for example, approved of the coup that had removed the Prussian government. Violence between the Nazis and the left grew rapidly in this period.

After many manoeuvres, Hitler came to power legally as the German Chancellor in January 1933 with no real opposition. He soon obtained, with the aid of the nationalists and the Centre Party, a parliamentary vote suspending the constitution and giving him unchecked power. By the summer all parties, apart from the NSDAP, were dissolved and mass arrests had crushed any opposition. Independent trade unions disappeared, together with all the other democratic institutions of the Weimar Republic. Nazi control was exerted over the whole of the economy and society, including the social welfare and housing institutions (see Neumann, 1942). At first the economic policies, which included an expansion of public works and support and protection for industry, bore a resemblance to similar policies elsewhere. Later, the economy was reoriented towards rearmament, with centralized wage setting and, from 1936, controls on prices (including rents), the diversion of labour from consumption goods production and retailing to armaments industries and a very rapid rise in the number of women workers.

Early Nazi ideology had contained an element of anti-capitalism in its appeal to the 'little man' – peasants, small farmers and *petits bourgeois*. It extolled the virtues of the simple, rural, communal life and was marked by anti-urbanism. As we shall see, all this had some impact on housing policies. However, in practice, the Nazi state developed in a sometimes uneasy coalition with large-scale industry which, for a time at least, benefited from the centralized direction and disciplining of the labour force and from rearmament.

A policy of enforced cartelization, to reduce overproduction and sustain prices, hit smaller businesses but benefited large-scale industry. The Labour Front, which replaced the trade unions and took over their associated organizations, aimed to coopt workers to the regime through holiday and other welfare schemes, including some subsidized housebuilding (Neumann, 1942: 337–74).

Profits and wages were controlled in the drive to increase production and employment, although up to the late 1930s a financially orthodox policy of balanced budgets was pursued. Ultimately, however, all this was subservient to the main objective of maintaining and widening Nazi power, first in Germany and then in the rest of Europe. When ideological preconceptions clashed with the drive for military and political dominance, the latter won out. Thus support for the family and motherhood was contradicted by the drive to push women into the labour force, and anti-urbanism gave way to the dictates of industrial growth and the need for an urbanized workforce. Sadly, the most vicious of these ideological strands, anti-Semitism, was deeply rooted in the German middle class especially and, in combination with nationalism, provided a potent means of sustaining support for the regime.

While the Depression wrought havoc with the German economy and its political system, arguably no more dramatic switch from prosperity to economic ruin occurred than in the USA. Of course, here, democratic institutions survived, but it can be argued that, while most of the other countries under discussion came close to a complete breakdown of the social order in the immediate aftermath of the First World War, America only went through this experience a decade later. As in Europe previously, one can see the social reforms and the extension of workers' rights in the New Deal era as a necessary price that was paid, if grudgingly and on a limited scale, for the avoidance of this breakdown.

Unemployment rose from a little over 1.5 million in 1929 to peak at almost 13 million by 1933, about one in four of the workforce and almost 40 per cent of the non-agricultural workers (Topalov, 1988: 170). According to Sternlieb and Listokin (1987), over one in three of the unemployed were directly or indirectly involved with the building trades (see also Fish, 1979: 177–242). In this same period one in eight farmers lost their properties and the number of banks was almost halved. McCoy (1977: 179) describes how families were broken up under the impact of the Depression and notes that 'one of the common activities of the 1930s was hiding from the landlord because money was unavailable for rent'. He adds, 'the depression was ... the most traumatic experience that the American people had suffered since the Civil War'. In these circumstances, the strong resistance to state intervention weakened, although, as in Europe a decade earlier, most regarded this change as a temporary response to the crisis rather than a permanent alteration of the respective roles of the state and the market. In short, as Piven and Cloward (1971) have argued, the 1930s provided one of those brief periods in American history (the 1960s was another one) when a measure of social and economic reform seemed the only solution to the management of escalating social disorder. As in Europe in the 1920s, when this disorder faded, so did the commitment to reform. However, as in Europe too, there were some enduring social and economic legacies of this period, among them federally subsidized public housing.

Efforts to combat unemployment had already begun in the Hoover presidency. But he resisted more radical plans for major expansion of government spending and stuck to balanced budgets, even after the disastrous army eviction of unemployed and homeless veterans from the Washington 'Hoovervilles' in mid-1932. Hoover did, however, establish the Reconstruction Finance Corporation to support key industries facing collapse and in 1932 the Glass–Steagall Act established the home loan bank system in an effort to prop up the housing finance institutions.

Although Roosevelt had been a reforming governor of New York State, he campaigned in 1932 on a far from radical programme. He promised to reduce government expenditure, balance the budget and protect the currency, while expanding public works, reforming the financial system and controlling agricultural surpluses and prices. Evidently the coherence of his message was less important than the hope which he personally appeared to offer to an electorate desperate for some solutions to the crisis. However, by the time Roosevelt took office in 1933, the social and economic situation had become perilous. The banking collapse has already been described. In addition, large-scale disorders – demonstrations, resistance to foreclosures, riots and more individual acts of violence and theft – now occurred (Sternlieb and Listokin, 1987).

Roosevelt had no coherent programme for dealing with the situation, although many around him had their own conflicting plans. But, as McCoy (1977: 203) describes, he was 'the supreme pragmatist, committed only to personal success and the survival of basic American ideas and ideals'. The subsequent programmes of the first 'hundred days' have already been outlined. Like later measures, including the legislation which established public housing, a great deal of what occurred was shaped by complex negotiations and trade-offs between the different economic and social interests represented in Congress. Much, too, including the public housing programme, was pushing against the boundaries of the constitutional use of federal powers and legal constraints sometimes played a major role in shaping and destroying programmes.

The public works programmes of the first New Deal were massive; for example, the federal Civilian Works Administration supported around 4 million people on 400,000 projects at a total cost of around a billion dollars (McCoy, 1977: 207). The measures to rescue home ownership, which laid the foundations for the phenomenal post-war growth of this tenure, will be described later. The National Industry Recovery Act (later ruled as unconstitutional by the Supreme Court) aimed at a corporatist reorganization and regulation of industry, and also created the Public Works Agency, which played a key role in the emergence of a public housing programme. The administration also pressed ahead with the regulation of agricultural output and prices, especially after violent farm strikes erupted in the autumn of 1933.

By 1934 there was a slight improvement in the unemployment rate and other economic indicators. As this occurred big business's support for the administration began to wane. Conflict between conservative and radical strands in the government and in the country became sharper, with various left- and right-wing populist movements gaining support. There were signs that the AFL might support the formation of a new party and there were advocates of the sort of Red–Green alliance (a Farmer–Labor party) that occurred in Denmark. In 1934 this dissidence pushed Roosevelt towards further reforms, including the creation of the Federal Housing Administration. By now the commitment to a balanced budget had temporarily disappeared.

After the 1934 mid-term elections, a group of Representatives and Senators associated with the Farmer–Labor movement was prepared to press for a radical extension of social policies and economic controls. Many of these demands went well beyond what Roosevelt would agree to, but the reforms that he did adopt aroused further opposition from the right. The situation is illustrated by the landmark 1935 Social Security Act, which established federally funded aid to dependent mothers, the handicapped and the aged, and systems of old age pensions and unemployment insurance (Rimlinger, 1971; Weir, Orloff and Skocpol, 1988). It was attacked by the right as an incursion on their profits and by the left as inadequate.[4] Roosevelt saw these programmes as a means of resolving the social and economic crisis with the minimum necessary levels of federal finance and involvement. Preservation rather than transformation was the objective. An important reform was the 1935 National Labor Relations Act, which recognized the collective bargaining rights of the trade unions and incorporated their interests in the Roosevelt coalition, a significant matter in relation to the subsequent public housing legislation.

In 1936 Roosevelt was re-elected by a huge majority. He made few specific pledges in the election but did promise a return to a balanced budget. Accordingly, there were major cuts in public works and relief expenditure. These contributed to a new recession in 1937, 2 million became unemployed, wages began to be cut again and there was another stock market crisis. The administration was torn between adopting orthodox, deflationary policies or demand stimulation, and at first did very little. By March 1938 unemployment had risen by 4 million in a year and production and the stock market were still falling. Roosevelt again turned to the expansion of relief and public works and, now, public housing construction. However, more radical attempts to restructure and reorganize American industry, for example by enforcing and strengthening anti-trust legislation and by taxation reforms, achieved little. Although some reforms continued, the turbulent social climate of the early and mid-1930s and the wide consensus on the necessity for state intervention had faded away.

In 1938 there were major Republican gains in the elections. This was the climate in which the public housing programme was finally established and began operating. Summarizing the New Deal, McCoy (1977) notes that its objectives were relief, recovery and reform. Of these, least was achieved in relation to recovery. By 1939 aggregate personal income was still below the 1929 level, over 17 per cent were unemployed, only a quarter less than in 1933, one in five were receiving some form of relief, the same proportion as in 1933 and more than in 1936. However, gross national product had risen over the decade, along with labour productivity. The new industries of the so-called Fordist era had further developed, with the use of new technology, mass production techniques and labour deskilling. Overall, though, economic recovery was less advanced in the USA than in the other major industrial societies. McCoy (1977: 308) notes:

> it was plain at the end of the 1930s that the administration was stuck on dead center, neither receding towards classic economic doctrine nor reaching out to implement some new economic theory. The New Deal seemed content to split the difference between Herbert

Hoover and the big-spending ideas of the British economist John Maynard Keynes.

However, '[e]qually significant is that most Americans were also willing to settle for a modicum of recovery'. As in Europe over a decade earlier, if this was not a return to economic normality, at least it marked the point at which the social and political consequences of the economy ceased to pose a threat to the established order. In McCoy's words: 'the New Deal brought neither political nor economic revolution ... It is possible that it staved off violent revolution, however ... [it] provided enough recovery, relief, and reform to regenerate confidence in the nation's political system and revive acceptance of the political system' (McCoy, 1977: 311).

THE ROLE OF HOUSING IN THE ECONOMIC CRISIS AND RECOVERY

In the 1930s the role of housing in the crisis and in governmental responses to housing needs was much more varied than it had been after the First World War. Immediately after 1918, workers' demands did not centre on unemployment but embraced a wider struggle for social, political and industrial rights, including the right to adequate and affordable housing. In the 1930s unemployment was the key issue. Only in the United States, partly as a consequence of its housing market developments in the 1920s, was the collapse of this market a central feature in the broader economic and social crisis. Nevertheless, the development of housing policies and markets in each of our countries was strongly influenced by wider economic and political developments, including the nature of the governmental responses to mass unemployment. In some countries housing became a more or less important element in economic recovery; elsewhere, recovery was obtained entirely by other means, or it hardly occurred at all. When we focus on the history of social housing in the 1930s, the pattern of cross-national variation assumes a further dimension. In the 1930s the possibility of aiding recovery and reducing unemployment by a revivified private market was, in some cases, a more realistic proposition than it had been in the 1920s. In some countries where there were, nevertheless, new programmes of social housing, these no longer substituted for, but complemented, the private market. Particularly in Britain, this recast role involved a clear shift towards the residual conception of social housing.

In France and the Netherlands the stubborn adherence to the gold standard and deflationary policies left no room for the use of social housing construction as an aid to economic recovery. In France, as we have seen, there was no significant programme of subsidized housing until the Loi Loucheur was enacted in 1928. According to Read (1976: 309), the Paris public housing office had, for example, managed to build only 13,000 units up to 1928 and, because of the shortage and high cost of land, these were constructed at high densities on cramped sites. In Sellier's much publicized and praised *cité-jardins*, only 3500 units were completed in this period. More generally, housing construction remained at a low level throughout the 1920s, despite a growing urban population (especially in the Paris region) and extremely high levels of overcrowding and slum housing. Only the construction of *lotissements* boomed: there were estimated to be 180,000 such units around Paris by the late 1920s (International Labour Office, 1930: 202–5, 227).

The Loucheur programme bore the imprint of those concerns which we have already outlined – the encouragement of home ownership, the need to provide some assistance to the middle class and the desire to preserve the largest possible scope for the private sector in housing development. The 1928 law, like its predecessors elsewhere in Europe, did not institute a permanent policy of state-subsidized social housing (for details see Dennery, 1935; Guerrand, 1992: 117–19). Instead, it provided for a five-year programme of 200,000 HBM units and another 60,000 units to be let at 'moderate rents'. The latter units (ILM – Immeubles à Loyer Moyen) had construction costs limits about double the HBM level and rents over three times as high, and were targeted at the middle class. In 1930 a further category was added – HBM améliorée – which, Dennery notes, was intended for the *petite bourgeoisie* (see also Denby, 1938: 217).

The programme was designed to encourage small-scale private owners to construct subsidized housing under state regulation. It provided low-interest state loans (at 2 per cent for the HBM units, compared with market rates of around 8 per cent or more at the time), subsidies to reduce the interest rate to this level on most of the complementary private capital that was required, and up to 15 years' relief from local property taxes. There were also some direct subsidies for large families and the disabled. The support for large families reflected the influence of social Catholicism and the concern about France's low birth-rate.

The subsidy conditions varied, with the greatest support going to the HBM units. There was a mass of detailed allocation regulations.

For example, HBM units were to be let to French nationals with three or more children, while the regulations for the higher rented units were designed to make them accessible to white-collar and other better-off households. The continuing desire to encourage home ownership was indicated by a provision that units could be for sale or rent. However, despite the wish to engage small-scale rentier capital in the programme, the main private participants were Sociétés Anonymes d'HBM, limited-dividend (6 per cent) commercial companies. Some units were also built by various forms of cooperatives. Another type of organization, the Sociétés de Crédit Immobilier, concentrated on supporting individual building for ownership (and some by the other institutions listed above). The emphasis on home ownership is also indicated by the fact that the law intended up to three-fifths of the state credits for the programme to be available for this purpose and it de-emphasized rental construction. However, as Dennery (1935: 32–3) notes, even with state assistance, the high costs of home ownership prevented this goal from being achieved. Even the ILM programme was limited by the lack of effective demand for these higher-rented units. This was the main reason for the introduction of the intermediate level in 1930.

The Loucheur programme provided only a brief interlude in the dismal record of French housing construction in the interwar period, before becoming a victim of the economic crisis. By 1933 about 180,000 HBMs had been constructed, but only around 80,000 of these were built by the Offices Publics, the main providers of the (relatively) lower-rented HBMs. In addition, around 15,000 ILMs and 10,000 HBM améliorée had been constructed (League of Nations, 1939: 85). At the end of this year all state support for new building ceased, and was not resumed on any scale until 1950. Overall, not more than 320,000 HBM units had been constructed, under all the preceding legislation, by 1939 (League of Nations, 1939: 85; see also Denby, 1938: 216–18; Bidemann, 1940).

Surveying the situation at the end of the decade, a League of Nations report (1939) noted that housing output (measured inadequately by the number of construction permits issued) rose sharply as a result of the Loucheur programme during the period 1929–31. Output then fell continuously up to 1938. In Paris, where the largest concentration of poor housing was located, permits for housing construction fell by 90 per cent between 1929 and 1938. The report calculated that, at the end of the 1920s, the rent of a basic newly built unsubsidized apartment in Paris would absorb about one-third of the average annual salary of a worker. In fact, rent controls would have prevented this amount being charged, thus making new private rental housing for the working class an impossibility. In the 1930s this position had worsened for, 'despite the fall in interest rates, the price and wages movements in recent years appear only to have widened the margin between the "economic" rent and the working-class family's capacity to pay' (League of Nations, 1939: 78). This situation created a financial crisis for many HBM institutions, as rent arrears mounted and home owners defaulted on their loan repayments. Local authorities had to guarantee the financial obligations of the institutions; when they became increasingly reluctant to accept this burden, many new construction schemes were abandoned.

In the Netherlands, as we noted in the previous chapter, social housing construction had slowed to a trickle by the late 1920s. The public expenditure cuts after 1931 further reduced subsidized construction, which averaged a little over 1800 units per annum between 1932 and 1937, half the amount built between 1922 and 1930 and less than one-tenth of the numbers built in the peak years of 1920–1 (League of Nations, 1939: 93, 97). As in the later 1920s, these units were mainly built in connection with slum clearance schemes, although the special subsidies to help meet the deficit on slum rehousing schemes were reduced from 1932. In 1934 the linkage of new building to slum clearance was reinforced by a decree which required one slum to be removed for every new unit provided.[5] In addition, some unsubsidized building continued by local authorities and the housing associations, on average 1500 units a year between 1932 and 1937. Falling rents in the private market caused widespread landlord bankruptcies and repossessions. In these circumstances new private construction also declined, especially after 1935, and did not revive during the period of lower interest rates that followed the eventual currency devaluation. In any event, new private housing was beyond the means of working-class households (League of Nations, 1939: 96). As Fisher and Ratcliff (1936: 39) noted, 'the greatest share of governmental assistance has been to housing societies, who have served skilled artisans and white-collar workers' (see also Central Housing Committee, 1935a).

Most of the slum clearance-related housing was built in the three big cities – Amsterdam, Rotterdam and the Hague. Interestingly, as Denby (1938: 109, 117) describes, there were already many signs of the socially problematic nature of this residual social housing. She notes, for example, that there was ill feeling among the residents of areas in which ex-slum dwellers were relocated and the way in which slum clearance resulted in the socio-spatial segregation of the working-class population; thus

[w]ell-to-do families turned out of a district which is being re-
planned, are said to get a suitable dwelling without difficulty in
houses built either by private enterprise or by a public utility society,
while the poorer or less desirable families are housed in dwellings
built for them by the municipality itself.

Here we see again the operation of the system of classification of
the working class and its assignment to different categories of
housing that was a central feature of the housing reformers' pre-
war plans.

The relocation of the poorer and 'less desirable' working class
also involved the imposition of a regime of housing management
and design which sought to reform and regulate behaviour. For
example, the new apartments contained three bedrooms to ensure
the segregation of the parents and their male and female children,
and '[t]he more modern architects are ... engaged in trying to
inveigle families out of the habit of eating and living in their
kitchens, by the subtle tactics of making them too small for anything
but work'. Nevertheless, '[t]his tendency is being stoutly resisted –
the minimum working-kitchen unit" being even more unpopular
among the Dutch working women than it is in the rest of Europe'.
In addition, the most 'undesirable' slum dwellers 'are given the
opportunity of moving temporarily to dwellings on special estates,
built by the municipality and let at particularly low rents'. However,
again there was resistance to this social engineering: '[t]hese estates,
which are meant to be educational, are ... unpopular, as a definite social stigma attaches to those who go there ... in consequence ... they are not full' (Denby, 1938: 113–17).

These 'experimental colonies' were similar in design and operation to those proposed by the early housing reformers for the
lowest stratum of the 'undeserving' working class. Thus Denby
(1938: 115–17) describes an Amsterdam estate of 132 houses, surrounded by a wall, within which the tenants 'are under strict
control'. The housing units were of minimal quality, various activities were organized for the women and children, although 'nothing
[was] done for the men or older boys, who seem to spend their
leisure standing aimlessly at street corners, spitting'.[6] In fact, this
estate was less regimented than one at the Hague, whose inhabitants were locked in at 11 pm. Nevertheless, Denby writes that
the Amsterdam residents 'appear antagonistic to their surroundings
and ... they come into residence with reluctance' (1938: 117).

More generally, in the Netherlands and elsewhere, housing
management was becoming a profession, employing supposedly

'scientific methods' to determine allocations and to regulate tenant behaviour. The principal targets of this management were not the 'respectable' working and middle class but the poor, ex-slum dweller and other low-income households. As van Ellemeet (1935: 270) explained, this management involved supervision of tenants to 'ensure the carrying-through of proper dwelling-customs' and tenant selection based on a detailed examination of applicants' social circumstances, so that the family might 'receive a dwelling best corresponding to its requirements, dwelling customs, buying power etc.' (or rather the requirements defined as necessary by the new professional managers). The reformatory colonies were a first stage in the effort to coerce tenants into socially acceptable forms of behaviour. Once their compliance had been achieved they could be 'promoted' into the normal municipal housing and a slightly less intense and punitive system of control and re-education (The Building Centre Committee, 1936: 280). This was carried out by women housing managers, following Octavia Hill's precepts – a mixture of social work and continual surveillance, through regular inspections, of the housing units and their inhabitants (see also Highton, 1935; van der Kaa, 1935; Central Housing Committee, 1935a; Denby, 1938).

By 1937 there were over 1000, mostly small, housing associations. About 20 per cent were linked to the Catholic social pillar and 10 per cent to the Protestants. No figures are available for the numbers linked to the Social Democrats but these were probably even more numerous (Ministry of Reconstruction and Housing, 1948). Although the associations tended to accommodate the 'respectable' working and middle classes, there were some which performed a more residual role. Thus, a later publication refers to two types of association that were active in the interwar period (Ministry of Reconstruction and Housing, 1950: 11–12). First, the 'workers' associations', housing 'able-bodied' men with reasonable wages – the working-class elite, many of whom were trade unionists. These associations had a considerable degree of tenant self-government. The tenants were good rent payers and there were few social or other problems. By contrast, there were some associations run by 'those who feel inclined to devote themselves to social work' (International Housing and Town Planning Congress, 1937: 171). These accommodated low-income households, including former slum dwellers. Such tenants were 'socially weaker', had more rent arrears and other problems, and required more 'intensive supervision ... to organise the social education of tenants' and a 'vigorous regime' to ensure that the rents got paid.

While the associations remained 'private initiatives', government regulation of their activities increased in the 1930s. In line with its deflationary policies, the government sought to force down the level of rents, as wages and other prices fell. There was, in fact, growing discontent and rent strikes occurred as rents remained high in this situation as a result of high fixed interest rates on housing mortgages. The Social Democrats and the NWR campaigned for the reimposition of rent controls. The government rejected this option but could not force the associations to reduce their rents. The local authorities also objected to the plan, as they would have to meet any shortfall in incomes caused by lowered rents (International Housing and Town Planning Congress, 1937: 161–70). However, many associations were in difficulty because of the unaffordability of their rents, and some were closed down by the government (Hetzel, 1983: 15). By 1934 the government was forced to provide some temporary assistance, reducing the interest rate on state housing loans to 4 per cent. But, in exchange for this assistance, the link of new building to slum clearance was strengthened, as noted above, and the associations were required to repay to the government any surpluses which they might later generate.

These attempts to control and limit the role of the social housing institutions to a residual housing function and to make them instruments of state policy were strongly resisted. The associations saw their role in very different terms – as self-governing alternatives to the private landlord, providing better-quality housing, devoid of any speculative or profit-making element, for the respectable working and middle classes. It was in this context that the left began to develop proposals for a more organized system of mass rather than residual social housing. These were influential after 1945, and involved a major increase in subsidies for housing associations to build 'according to housing need', a planned system of resource allocation for construction, aimed at inducing the local authorities to promote cheap and efficient construction, and limiting building for higher-income groups by a system of licensing. These proposals were incorporated in the 1935 Labour Plan (Abma, 1981). However, the left shared the government's lack of interest in the expansion of social housing as a means of reducing unemployment.

Summarizing this period, Jan van der Schaar (1982) notes that after 1925, social housing was seen as a legitimate alternative to the private market only when it was closely linked to slum clearance and thus to providing a type of housing in which the private market was uninterested. A key assumption was that the private market could and would build housing for the majority of the working class, and that those not benefiting directly would gain access to better housing through the filtering process. However, as almost all contemporary commentaries recognized, this was not the case (see, for example, Denby, 1938: 119–21). The new building that did occur in the 1930s was too expensive for the majority of the working class and filtering up did not occur on any significant scale. Indeed, a 1937 report, referring to the rents charged in the largest Dutch Garden City (outside Rotterdam), noted that these were not only out of the reach of unskilled workers, but also of 'a great many skilled workers in "unprotected" plants, i.e. in businesses which are not protected against foreign competition' (International Housing and Town Planning Congress, 1937: 170). It was this recognition that underlay the left's proposals for a far more ambitious role for social housing as a substitute for the private landlord as houser of the working class and substantial sections of the middle class.

Van der Schaar (1982) notes that there was also some support for a less radical plan. This involved substantial state regulation and planning of social and private market construction, with mass social housing let at cost-covering rents competing with the private sector, thus acting as a price leader throughout the rental market.[7] In their various forms, these wider conceptions of the role of social housing were supported not only by the left-linked housing associations, but also by the Confessional and non-denominational associations. These years mark the emergence of the housing associations and their federations as a distinctive interest group, whose influence on the post-war politics of social housing in the Netherlands has been considerable. However, there remained divisions of interest and approach which have also been of lasting importance. In particular, the Social Democrats located their proposals for an expansion of social housing within their scheme for a state-directed system of economic and social planning. Social housing would become a social service, provided on a universalistic basis, like education or social security. The housing associations would retain their legal status as 'private initiatives' but would, in practice, become the vehicles for a centralized housing policy. These ideas were anathema to the Confessional parties and associations; many of the latter also wished to obtain increased state support, but maintained their opposition to any increase in state control over their activities which might compromise their place in the pillarised structure of Dutch society.

We have already noted that the German social housing organizations were incorporated into the totalitarian organization of the state and society after 1933. This ended not only the legal independence of the workers' housing cooperatives but also their wider role in an autonomous working-class political and social culture. As Feiss (1938: 178) noted, a 'movement intended to reform the physical environment and bring about the social improvement of the lower-income group by democratic means was not compatible with the ideas behind the Nazi movement'. The self-governing structures of the associations were replaced by the hierarchical command and control structures of Nazism and the main associations were reorganized into a large bureaucratized organization called Neue Heimat. This was a key moment in the longer-term evolution of social housing in Germany because, when the trade unions regained control of these organizations after the war, they did not return to the decentralized, self-governing structures of the pre-Nazi period, let alone the wider conception of social housing as a basis for a distinctive working-class social and political culture. Even the name, Neue Heimat, was retained, a 'cooperative' whose demise in the 1980s, described in chapter 5, illustrated the distance travelled by German social housing from its working-class origins and which stood as a potent symbol for its declining reputation and political influence.

Denby's (1938: 122–47) account of German housing describes some of the ideological elements in Nazi housing and other social policies. For example, she refers to the closure of kindergartens and the provision of 'marriage' and 'poverty' loans to encourage women to stay at home with their children. These policies were intended to increase the birth-rate, reduce competition with men in the labour market and stimulate consumer goods production. The loans were available only to those with 'uncompromisingly Nazi views', and the marriage loans, which were tied to the purchase of furniture and other household goods, required the women to withdraw from the labour market. Nazi eugenic policy demanded that successful applicants be free of physical or mental illness.

In line with the anti-urban ideology of the regime, it favoured the development of working-class housing outside the major towns, in small, basic single-family houses in rural colonies that were engaged in subsistence agriculture (Highton, 1935). This was intended to convert the urban working class, or at least the unemployed, into a new 'German peasantry', under the direction of the Ministry of Agriculture (Central Housing Committee, 1935b). In fact, such ideas had a long pedigree in Germany. In 1919 a Federal Settlement Law had been passed to encourage the repopulation of the rural eastern region. In the Depression, before Hitler came to power, they had already gained greater prominence as a way of reducing urban unemployment. Thus, according to Blumenthal (1934: 22), 'since the Reich decree of October 6th 1931, Germany has defined her housing policy as one based entirely on rural homestead settlements'. However, the Nazis also saw this as 'a wise political policy to bind people to the land, since contact between body and earth is less dangerous than intellectual contacts, stimulated by starvation, in the cities'. Therefore, the intention was that all new low-income housing, not just that for the unemployed, should take this form. In these settlements a strong emphasis was put on Nazi indoctrination; as Feiss (1938: 190) noted, '[s]ince all social activities are supervised from the local Nazi headquarters, there is little left for the tenant but to follow Voltaire's advice and cultivate his garden'.

Great emphasis was placed on the construction of single-family houses. The Nazis were hostile towards multi-family housing, seeing it as a breeding ground for socialism, much as the conservative housing reformers had done at the end of the nineteenth century. Thus, according to a contemporary report, the construction of large blocks of flats was stopped in Stuttgart because these 'had promoted subversive politics' (Central Housing Committee, 1935b). Workers were also encouraged to construct their own low-quality housing on suburban plots of land, again with provision for subsistence agriculture. The policy, directed by the Ministry of Labour, also aimed to redistribute employment by reducing full-time workers to part-time status and by creating part-time employment for some of the unemployed.[8] The location of such policies on the wilder shores of Nazi mysticism is illustrated by the words of Professor Doctor Friederich Schmidt, the Director of State Housing Policy: '[t]heir [i.e. the working class] reunion with the soil and their spiritual and bodily restoration is aimed at in the New Germany as an essential measure both as regards state policy, population and political economy' (quoted in Feiss, 1938: 181; see also Highton, 1935).

However, these programmes, which aimed to deproletarianize the working class, were failures, in part because they were met with resistance from their intended victims, and also because private capital was reluctant to become involved with such impractical ideas. The unemployed urban working class had few of the skills necessary to make a success of agricultural production, although the increasingly draconian control and direction of labour power in the Third Reich meant that some received training in 'relief labour camps' (Central Housing Committee, 1935b; International Housing and Town Planning Congress, 1937: 13). By 1935 the regime was already contradicting its own decrees, which stated that the new suburban smallholdings and rural colonies should be built with private capital, by increasing state assistance.

These ideologically driven policies provided no real solution to housing needs when the majority of the employed workforce remained tied to urban industries, and rearmament meant the regime could not ignore the demand for urban housing (Feiss, 1938). Housing output had fallen rapidly in the Depression, from around 315,000 in 1929 to 130,000 in 1932 and 1933, then rising to around 213,000 in 1936 (Fisher and Ratcliff, 1936: 15). As in the Netherlands, and for the same reason, rents had not fallen in line with other prices and wages, thus worsening the low-income housing situation (Schwan, 1935: 132). Such unsubsidized new private building as occurred in the 1930s was too expensive for wage earners. Umrath (1950: 36) refers to 150,000 empty properties in 1932, whose rents were too high for any tenants to afford. Yet he states that, according to census data, the crude housing shortage rose from 600,000 in 1927 to 1.1 million by 1933.

In practice, some resources were still made available for urban housing, with the state providing low-interest (4 per cent) first mortgages of around 25 per cent, guaranteeing second mortgages from the private sector and providing some direct subsidies for the subdivision of buildings (Schwan, 1935: 133). But the loss of the house rent tax revenues from 1931, noted in the last chapter, had been very serious. According to Schwan (1935: 132) this reduced the public support for housing by about 80 per cent between 1930 and 1933. The state loans were provided to the local authorities, who could pass them on to the housing cooperatives or use the social housing organizations which they controlled to do the work. The division between these two sorts of institutions which had emerged before the war, with the former housing skilled workers and the middle class, and the latter concentrating on low-income and slum rehousing, persisted throughout the 1930s. The loans were set at the minimum level needed to produce 'dwellings of the cheapest kind which the necessitous section of the population can afford' (International Housing and Town Planning Congress, 1937: 14). According to figures provided by Feiss (1938: 188–9), around half of all new housing had some government assistance in 1935 and 1936. These data also illustrate the shift which occurred as the impracticability of a purely rural housing policy became evident; thus over half the subsidized units were in subsistence homesteads in 1934, but only around 15 per cent by 1936. No multi-family apartments were subsidized in 1934 and 1935, but by 1936/7 over a quarter of the programme was constituted of such dwellings.

In line with the general system of the totalitarian state, all housing projects were controlled from the centre. Party priorities determined who obtained the new housing; Nazi Party and Labour Front activists were favoured. Some subsidies were also provided for slum clearance and to further the removal of the working class from the cities, because two-thirds of the former inhabitants of cleared areas were required to move to the suburban settlements. Especially in the centrally located renewal areas, the rebuilding had to be in approved neo-medieval styles in order to stimulate 'the value of tourist trade, and ... to return to the "Teutonic tradition and to break away from the Jewish–Bolshevik architecture of the International Style"' (Feiss, 1938: 183). With perhaps unintended black humour, Feiss states that the rumour that pitched roofs were common on new buildings because the Führer had ordered them 'to reduce the velocity of falling bombs' was unlikely to be true, adding that pictures of damage in the Spanish Civil War showed that this form of building offered no protection. Rather, he concluded, it had been primarily determined 'by the romantic tastes of the Führer who is a strong amateur critic of the architectural arts'.

All Nazi housing programmes aimed to reduce the standards and costs of new housing to a minimal level and to increase the proportion of costs met by private capital and by the forced or voluntary labour of the occupants and the unemployed. Although some building by the social housing organizations continued, the intention was to rely mainly on providing some state assistance to the private market. Thus the proportion of housing built by the non-profit associations fell from around 30–40 per cent in the late 1920s and early 1930s to under 20 per cent in the middle of the decade (in addition, housing built by the state and by local authority-owned social housing institutions fluctuated at around 8–10 per cent during this time) (Umrath, 1950: 35).

The aim was to minimize state support for housing but to increase the output of minimal quality housing which would be affordable by a population, vast numbers of whom were in poverty. Blumenthal (1934: 22) notes that the per unit cost limit for the rural settlements was $750, compared with the average cost of publicly aided housing before 1931 of $2500, and that the units normally lacked electricity, flush toilets and other basic facilities. This approach reflects the more Nazi general strategy of raising employment levels while maintaining a low-income workforce. From

1936 the rationale for this policy became closely linked to the wider geo-political aims of the regime, which then implemented a four-year plan whose aim was to put the economy and society on a war footing. All prices, including rents, were frozen at their 1936 levels, thus ending the decontrol of rents on units which had been built since the end of the war (International Housing and Town Planning Congress, 1937: 13).

In Denmark interest rates fell sharply after the devaluation of the krone in 1931 and housing output, which had risen gradually from the mid-1920s, rose sharply up to the mid-1930s. Data (for urban areas only) show that about 11,000 units were completed in 1932, but over 19,000 per annum in 1934 and 1935. Unlike in Britain, where the high level of private housing output achieved by 1934/5 was subsequently sustained, though at a somewhat lower level, by the growth of new consumer-oriented industries, this Danish boom then faltered. Output fell to around 15,000 per annum in 1936 and 1937 (League of Nations, 1939: 51). However, as in Britain, it was the economic policies pursued by government which had the greatest effect on housing in Denmark, by stimulating private building. Housing output in the 1930s was well above its level in the previous decade; indeed, more houses were completed between 1930 and 1935 than between 1919/20 and 1929. Over 80 per cent of the units built between 1930 and 1937 were constructed by private enterprise without subsidies, and a further 10 per cent by this means but with subsidies. Under 3 per cent were built with the aid of subsidies by the housing associations (which also constructed a handful of unsubsidized units) and around 4 per cent by the local authorities. Most of the subsidized construction occurred between 1933 and 1935, amounting in 1934 to almost a quarter of all completions.

The expansion of housebuilding was choked off after 1935 by the increasing balance of payments difficulties that the Danish economy experienced, a feature of this export- and import-dependent economy which continued to have a major influence on housing after 1945. As in Britain, Denmark's so-called 'cheap money policy' after devaluation stimulated housebuilding. But by 1935 the building boom was contributing, through materials imports, to a growing balance of payments deficit and interest rates were increased to stifle demand. The stop–go building cycle entered another phase in 1937 and 1938, after the balance of payments improved, at the cost of higher unemployment. Now the government intervened in the mortgage bond market to increase the supply of funds for housing and boost employment (League of Nations, 1939: 54; Socialt Tidsskrift, 1947).

The limited housing subsidies were tied to the twin (but conflicting) objectives of containing unemployment and managing the balance of payments problem.[9] Thus the rise in subsidized construction around the middle of the decade was achieved by a modest resumption of State Housing Fund loans (some subsidies were also added by the local authorities). These third mortgage loans were available for use by local authorities, social and private landlords and individual home owners. They could cover up to 40 per cent of total costs, except in the case of private landlords, when cover could not exceed 25 per cent, and were at a 4.5 per cent interest rate with 1 per cent annual amortization. The loans were revived in 1938, in the circumstances which have just been described. In addition, from 1933 all new building was exempted from government estate tax. This, plus other tax exemptions, probably reduced building costs by a minimal 3–4 per cent. A more significant long-run feature of new legislation in this period was the power that the government now took to exercise permanent supervision over the activities of the social housing organizations. Any surplus generated by the social housing organizations had to be used for new building and the local authorities had to be represented on their boards of management.

As in the 1920s, the subsidized housing built by the housing associations was beyond the reach of poorer households. Local authority building (mainly in Copenhagen) was the only source of new housing for this group. As in the Netherlands, these units had minimal standards of space and amenities. The sharp contrast between the self-management of the cooperatives, which housed the better-off workers, and the municipal housing estates, has already been noted in the previous chapter. A 1939 report contains some further interesting details (Heiferman, 1939). The tenant contribution on entering cooperative housing was normally the equivalent of a year's rent. Interest was paid on this deposit which was refunded when a tenant left. However, this requirement meant that only the most affluent and securely employed workers could become tenants.

The quality of the cooperative units was still considerably higher than that of units which were built in the 1930s by private enterprise for moderate-income households. Many of the former properties, especially in the suburbs of Copenhagen, which had been extensively developed by the cooperatives since the war, were single-family homes. The limited-dividend housing societies, frequently linked to the trade unions, also provided good quality housing for better-off workers and the middle class. However, at least in Copenhagen where they did most building, these organizations specialized in constructing quite spacious apartments. While the cooperatives were still largely managed by their occupants, tenants appear to have had a waning influence on the management of the housing societies, as the larger and more recently organized ones were centrally directed. By contrast, the municipally owned apartments (largely in Copenhagen) had far fewer rooms and a more basic level of amenities, although these were still far superior to the housing provided in the Nazi programmes or even to the standard HBM units constructed in France. In many cases they had bathrooms, flush toilets, hot water and central heating. Despite the view held by many contemporary housing management experts in other countries that such standards were inappropriate or would not be appreciated by lower-income households, this was not shared by the Danish local authorities or the tenants who inhabited these properties.

When subsidies were again provided in 1938, a more determined attempt was made to target some state support on lower-income housing. The legislation was influenced by concern about declining birth-rates; a government commission that reported in 1935 had stated that family poverty was one cause of this trend (Socialt Tidsskrift, 1947). The new act provided for a six-year programme of third mortgage loans. Around one-third of the units built were to be allocated to larger, poor families. Tenant contributions, set at 5 per cent of building costs, were still required, but the local authorities could now pay these for such households. In addition, the rents of poor families with three or more children could be reduced by 30 to 50 per cent. This subsidy was to be raised from tenants in the rest of the state-subsidized housing built since 1933 by means of a house property tax. As the average interest rate on private third mortgage loans (if these could be obtained at all) was around 10 per cent, the state loans involved a significant subsidy (Graham, 1940: 108). Another important advantage was that they met the wide gap between the proportion of building costs that could be normally covered by private loans (this had fallen to around 50–60 per cent in the economic crisis of the early 1930s) and the full building costs, and that they were repayable over a very long period, i.e. 36 years (Heiferman, 1939). State and municipal guarantees also allowed the proportion of costs covered by private loans to be increased (League of Nations, 1939: 55–7).

To summarize, changes in housing policy played a minor part in the reforms introduced in the 1930s by the Social Democrat/Radical Liberal government. In part, this reflected the moderate brand of reformism adopted by Danish socialists between the wars. The support provided for new social housing was on a limited scale and was closely tied to the use of construction as an economic regulator. For a time the cheap money policy stimulated private sector output. Nevertheless, as the 1938 legislation began to recognize, many poorer working-class households had no access to decent social or private housing and little was done in this period to rehouse slum dwellers (Boldsen, 1935; Socialt Tidsskrift, 1947). As elsewhere, it was wrongly assumed that such households would benefit by filtering up into better-quality housing vacated by those moving to new social and private units.

As we have seen, the economic policies adopted after Britain left the gold standard helped to stimulate a rapid, if geographically uneven, process of growth throughout the 1930s. Housing developments were central to this process which, in certain respects, was similar to that which had occurred in the USA in the 1920s. On the one hand, in the south-east and Midlands of England, the new consumer goods industries, located outside the older town centres, created new jobs, higher incomes and a rising demand for new suburban private housing. On the other hand, in the rest of the country, the older basic industries continued to decline, with persistently high levels of poverty, unemployment and poor housing conditions. Such conditions also persisted in the inner area slums of large cities throughout the country. These urban cores had been little affected by the social housebuilding of the previous decade, for reasons which were noted in the chapter 2. However, by the 1930s, with economic expansion, suburbanization and the rise in road transport, the need to renew and modernize the urban infrastructure, with new roads, retail, commercial and public sector developments, helped to increase the pressure for public action to clear the slums.

The 1930s private building boom was on a remarkable scale and was aided by developments in building society mortgage finance which enabled a high proportion of the cost of housing to be borrowed (Bowley, 1944: 175). Some of this money was used to build rental housing but an increasing amount was provided for individual owner occupiers. With the growth of the new industries and their relatively secure and well-paid jobs, home ownership came within the reach of an increasing proportion of the workforce. [10] Low interest rates (at least in relation to their levels in the 1920s) and the stable real cost of housing throughout most of the boom aided the growth in building, as did a rapid growth in the number of households (Holmans, 1987: 61–5). In the 1920s housing output in England and Wales peaked at nearly 240,000 in 1927/8. The Depression reduced output to around 200,000 in the early 1930s. However, between 1934/5 and 1938/9 annual totals substantially exceeded 300,000, with a peak of 346,000 in 1936/7. By far the largest contribution to this boom was made by private construction, up from 125,000 in 1930/1 to a peak of 286,000 in 1934/5 – a level unsurpassed since (Holmans, 1987: 66).

Nevertheless, after the middle of the decade, private building faltered, so that by 1938/9 private output had fallen to 226,000. The parallel with what occurred in the USA after 1925, with the saturation of effective demand for new private housing, is striking. In both countries the uneven and limited nature of economic growth eventually acted as a constraint on the continued expansion of home ownership. These limits were not overcome until the post-war era. However, a significant difference between the two countries concerned the role of public housing construction in the late 1930s. In this respect British developments had some similarities with those in Denmark and the Netherlands, although the scale of British public housing development was far greater. Between the late 1920s and the mid-1930s local authority output was around 40,000–60,000 units per annum, only rising to 70,000 in 1931/2 as a consequence of the short-lived housing policies of the 1929–31 Labour government, which will be discussed below. However, public housing output rose sharply after 1936, to a peak of over 100,000 in 1938/9, helping to sustain total output when private building was declining (Holmans, 1987: 66–8).

Despite the rising housing standards in the 1930s, as we have already noted, these were confined to certain areas of the country and sections of the population. As Holmans (1987: 72–8) describes, elsewhere poor housing conditions persisted. He estimates that the housing shortage peaked at 1,500,000 in 1925, but was still around half a million by 1939. Overcrowding was an even more persistent and large-scale problem; it had risen between 1911 and 1921 to around 1.4 million and still stood at almost 1.2 million in 1931. Much of the overcrowding was caused by households sharing dwellings, a clear indication of the continuing inadequacy of supply for the lower-income population. Data for the true extent of slum housing are not available for this period, but information collected in 1947 suggests that around half or a little more of the housing stock in the 1930s had no fixed bath or hot water supply to a sink (and only one-third probably had hot water supply to a bath, sink and handbasin). The persisting shortage of lower-rented housing was what led two official committees, in 1931 and 1937, to conclude that the decontrol of the cheapest private rented housing was, as yet, a social and political impossibility.

The formation of the second Labour minority government in 1929 appears to have had rather little effect on the limited policy of continued support for council housing which had been pursued by previous Conservative governments. And yet developments in this period laid the groundwork for a significant policy shift after 1931. On entering office the government cancelled reductions which the previous administration had planned in the 1924 (Wheatley) Housing Act subsidies, but did not stop the already planned termination of the 1923 Act subsidies which, it will be recalled, were designed to help re-establish private building. It therefore continued to provide some support for the type of mass needs building which had occurred in the 1920s and which accommodated the better-off working and lower middle class. However, it also legislated, in the 1930 Housing Act, for a new programme to provide subsidies for housing linked to slum clearance. This was not a part of the government's political programme, but was, as Holmans (1987: 310) explains, 'a departmental measure that had been at an advanced state of preparation ... under the previous government'. Taken in conjunction with the planned reductions in Wheatley subsidies, it looks as if the 'containment' policy (as Malpass, 1986: appendix 1, calls it) of limiting assistance for new public housing to slum clearance purposes, i.e. for the poorest households only, which prevailed in the 1930s, was already emerging in the late 1920s and was delayed only by the 1929–31 Labour government's unwillingness to terminate Wheatley Act building.

Reflecting the high costs of slum clearance and the low incomes of the proposed tenants, the 1930 subsidies were fairly generous and higher than those provided under the Wheatley Act. They took the form, common to all British subsidy programmes after 1919 and up to the 1970s, of fixed annual payments over the period of the building loan (normally 60 years). Nevertheless, there was a marked lack of enthusiasm by local authorities about building housing for the poorest groups of the population. Instead, they preferred to continue using the earlier subsidies to build for the 'respectable' working class (Bowley, 1944: 147–51). However, with the end of the Labour government in 1931, the pressure to redefine the market for local authority housing, shifting it towards a more residual role, intensified (see the detailed account in Malpass, 1986). According to Holmans (1987: 309), there were several stages to this shift of policy direction. In the crisis conditions of autumn 1931, when the Conservative-dominated National government took office and public expenditure cuts continued, the complete cessation of subsidies for new building was considered, but rejected. Instead, the government used administrative means to move local authority building towards a more marginal role and cut expenditure, building cheaper houses for households with children living on low incomes in slum and overcrowded conditions. Permissible space standards were reduced by 20 per cent. As a result of these changes output fell and capital expenditure was reduced by about one-third by 1933.

At this time, as Malpass (1986: appendix 1) documents, there was a shift in official thinking, including among some local authorities, towards a perceived need to target subsidies on poor households excluded from the private market and to removing the competition created by local authority mass needs building. The next stage occurred in 1933 when a more determined move was made to redefine the purposes and nature of local authority building. To prevent further building for the better-off working class, who, the government argued, could now be housed by the private market, the Wheatley subsidies were terminated. However, a new subsidy was provided to support a programme of cheaper, poorer-quality public housing, targeted at those low-income households for whom, it was recognized, private renting was too costly. This was intended to complement the ubiquitous process of filtering which, it was claimed, would also benefit low-income households. Interestingly, Holmans (1987: 311) notes that the rationale which closely linked this policy to a major effort to clear slum housing emerged only during the course of the legislation through Parliament. However, as we have seen, previous developments had begun to make such a link.

A further stage in the policy occurred in 1935, when local authorities, which had already been given the duty to survey slum conditions in their areas and make clearance plans, were given a similar duty to survey and reduce overcrowding. The 1935 Act included a special subsidy to assist the construction of apartments. This occurred because public housebuilding was being reoriented to cater for the lowest-income households. Many such households lived in overcrowded slum housing in city centres, tied to these locations by the need to access low-wage central area employment and an inability to afford the commuting costs from suburban housing. Thus it was necessary to redirect public housing construction from greenfield suburban sites to central redevelopment areas (see the discussion in Ministry of Health, 1938). High land costs and shortages of its supply contributed to the pressure to build multi-storey apartments rather than the terraced or semi-detached 'cottages' that were typical of much earlier British social housing. However, even though the standards in these new units were inferior to the cottage housing, the high costs of construction and the low rent paying capacity of their potential occupants made additional subsidies a necessity. The special subsidy was on a sliding scale, depending on the price paid for the land. In 1938 a common level of subsidy for flats built in connection with slum clearance and the reduction of overcrowding was established.

One further important development occurred in this decade, although its significance became apparent only in the 1950s. Before 1935 local authorities accounted separately for each group of houses that had been subsidized under the various acts. Because of the post-1918 inflation, the houses built in the early 1920s were the most costly to construct and finance. Later houses were cheaper, because building costs and interest rates had declined. Because each account was run on a 'non-profit' basis, the Addison Act houses continued to have high rents while the rents of later, newer units were lower and might even be reduced further as surpluses accrued to the housing account. This problem, a lack of rent 'harmonization', that is, the absence of a rational relationship between relative rents and relative housing quality, later became, as we shall see, a key issue in the other European countries after the Second World War. This was not so in Britain because the 1935 legislation required the local authorities to pool the accounts of all their houses in a single Housing Revenue Account (Jarmain, 1948: ch. 7). In 1935 a key objective was to allow the local authorities to cross-subsidize the rents of older houses by charging higher rents for the newer, cheaper houses. In a later period rent pooling became the major means of cross-subsidizing the rents of newer, more costly housing by charging more for older, cheaper housing. Together with the general power to provide rent rebates for poorer households, which was also now given to local authorities for the first time, and the rejigged subsidies, the 1935 Act signifies an important stage in the reconstitution of council housing as a social service for the poor (rather than a substitute for the private land-lord or home ownership), in which rent levels were related to income rather than to the value of the property (as in the private sector) and with a significant degree of internal cross-subsidy.

However, it must be stressed that there was not time in the short period before the Second World War for the full implications of these changes to become apparent and, as we shall see in the next chapter, the renewed need to build for mass needs after 1945 postponed the return to this conception of public housing by several years. Nevertheless, as Holmans (1987: 311) notes, the withdrawal of Wheatley subsidies in 1933, leaving support only for low-income public housing construction, did induce a somewhat more compliant attitude to the new policies from the local authorities than had occurred in the early 1930s. The institutional interests of the emergent housing professionals may have played a part in this shift. Holmans points out that the local authorities had built up large house-production organizations which would have had to be run down if their efforts had not been diverted into the new programmes. Thus between 1934/5 and 1938/9, 245,000 slums and overcrowded dwellings were demolished and 248,000 units built to replace them. In fact, the rate of slum-linked housing construction almost exactly matched that achieved in the previous years under the 1924 legislation.

Malpass (1986: appendix 1, 51–2) summarizes the developments in the 1930s thus:

> *general needs* housing ... was subject to strong residualizing pressures, initially from the Conservative government in the late 1920s and later from the Conservative dominated National Government from 1931 onwards. These pressures came in various forms which reflected the prevailing economic orthodoxies ... [t]hey also reflected the consistent Conservative Party belief that private housing should not be undermined by municipal competition. Thus council housing was manoeuvred into the position of providing new housing for the poor only ... to be restricted to the bottom end of the market, below the level at which private enterprise could produce decent housing at a profit.

He also notes the role that the driving down of standards and rents played in this process and the new assumption that public housing should not be a lifetime source of accommodation. Instead, tenants should be expected to move out when their children had grown up or when their incomes rose.

Malpass (1986) also highlights another dimension of the marginalization of public housing in this period. This involved restricting the size of the programme, even in relation to its narrowed focus on poor households. Immediately after 1931 the government had aimed to support only a small programme. In 1934, the Labour Party noted that the Minister of Health had told the House of Commons that a programme of 12,000 housing clearances a year would be the maximum necessary. The Party claimed that the government had taken greater action only when it was 'bombarded by protests from all quarters' (The Labour Party, 1934: 16). Even with this increased commitment, Malpass (1986: appendix 1, 59) notes that the total number of slums cleared and rehousing provided in the 1930s scarcely amounted to more than one year's output by the private building market in its peak years. When taken together with the reduced standards of the new housing, he concludes, 'slum clearance meant that a few poorer families obtained access to council housing, but ... what they got was an inferior product'. He also notes that many slum dwellers could have probably paid the higher rents of mass needs housing and that many poor people lived outside the designated clearance and rehousing areas. Slum clearance, Malpass (1986: appendix 1, 60) states, was a policy which dealt with the areas of poorest housing, not necessarily the poorest people:

> [i]t was a policy which arose not as a way of focusing on the poor but in response to the inability of private builders to undertake clearance and rebuilding at a profit ... [it] was about confining council housing to the unprofitable parts of the housing market, and ... about returning to the sanitary role for municipal housing action.

Bowley (1944) also came to this conclusion. It emphasizes the strong continuities in the Conservative conception of social housing from the pre-First World War period.

Therefore, the Conservative rationale for social housing in 'normal times' became clear in the 1930s. It is one which the party pursued throughout the post-war era up to the 1970s. The extent to which the Labour Party adopted a distinctively different approach to the role of public housing is much more difficult to assess, although the common assumption (reinforced by its policies between 1945 and 1951) would be that it maintained a strong and principled commitment to the more or less complete, if gradual, replacement of the private market by public housing. More work probably needs to be done on this question by housing historians, but there does seem, at best, to be a gap between Labour policy statements and its record in practice.

There is some evidence that in the 1930s the party moved towards a more thought-out approach to public housing provision as a substitute for the private market. A mid-decade policy statement contains an enormous amount of detail on the standards required in new working-class housing, showing the impact of the professionalization of housing 'science' in the interwar years. It also contains impassioned references to the need to deal with the slums, strikingly conceived as the 'Cancer of Empire', and sets out policies to provide decent and affordable housing for all, with a strong emphasis on the need for urban and rural planning. A variety of expert evidence is surveyed in arriving at the conclusion that 5–6 million new houses will need to be built over a 20-year period. The failure of private enterprise to build for lower-income groups is condemned, as is the removal of the Wheatley subsidies by the National government. Labour proposes to institute a centrally planned housing drive, in which the local authorities will survey local needs, and devise and execute building programmes. The subsidized programme would amount to 250,000–300,000 houses a year and the implication is that it would largely replace private housebuilding. The government would have powers to control the supply and price of materials and would consult with trade unions to ensure that the public housing could be built.

Many of the proposals in this report were implemented in the immediate post-war period. They imply a far broader and qualitatively different role for public housing than that envisaged by the Conservatives, with the replacement of the private by the public landlord. However, this was to be achieved by state direction of a rationally planned but privately owned construction industry on privately owned land. The main method proposed was the provision of far greater subsidies rather than any more radical socialization of land, construction and finance as well as more state subsidies.[11] The policy document refers to the haphazard and unplanned nature of private development and notes that it cannot build for large sections of the working class. However, the reasons for these defects are not analysed. Although Labour later accepted the need for land nationalization, this reform, and the need for a more adequate system of land use planning, were increasingly seen as necessary by many non-socialists in the 1930s and 1940s. Much of Labour's document reiterates and supports the more general currents in housing and planning reform at this time. In essence, what the party proposed was the reformed and rationalized but still mainly private sector production of housing. Private renting and home ownership would continue, although public housebuilding would provide the main means of meeting new demand.

However, Labour was not in a position to implement such policies, and when it was briefly in office, from 1929 to 1931, it showed little sign of any ambitions to do so. There was, for example, no repetition of Wheatley's attempt to establish the conditions for a major and permanent expansion of mass needs public housing. Indeed, Wheatley was excluded from the 1929–31 government. He had pushed through the 1924 Act in the teeth of opposition from Snowden, the fiscally orthodox Chancellor of the Exchequer at that time and in 1929–31 (Malpass 1986: appendix 1, 54). Wheatley, before his death in 1930, was highly critical of the Labour government for embracing a Conservative-influenced conception of social housing. In particular, he criticized the failure to go beyond cancelling the last proposed Conservative cuts in the 1924 Act subsidies by restoring earlier cuts, thus benefiting the tenants and the local authorities rather than the (richer) section of the population which paid taxes to provide these subsidies. He also criticized the consensus between the government and the opposition over the nature of the 1930 slum clearance subsidy. This was seen by both sides as a limited-duration programme which would remove, once and for all, the slum problem. Wheatley attacked the assumption that 'we ought to approach this problem in a non-party and non-class way', as 'quite nonsensical'. For him, if not for the party leadership, slums were, as Malpass states, 'inherent in the provision of working class housing in capitalist society'.

At the local level, as we have noted, many Labour-controlled (and other) local authorities were reluctant to accept the new, residual role for public housing (see the local studies in Daunton, 1984; see also Bowley, 1944; Jarmain, 1948). Later, they complied with the pressures which the government exerted but in many cases with reluctance. However, a few Labour councils were more enthusiastic about the new policy regime. Thus in 1934 the Labour-controlled London County Council began to press those higher-income tenants who could, it deemed, now afford the private market, to vacate public housing. After the changes in 1935 the Labour-controlled Leeds City Council introduced a highly controversial system of rent rebates. But most local authorities were reluctant to introduce such schemes, partly because of protests from the better-off tenants who had to pay higher rents in order to subsidize poorer tenants (Jarmain, 1948; ch. 10). These were, though, exceptions to the general desire of many local authorities to provide council housing for mass needs. The extent to which this ever amounted to a means of bringing about the more radical replacement of private by socialized housing, which Wheatley would probably have desired, seems highly doubtful. Instead, it was in practice a policy which aimed to meet the needs of the 'core' working class and some white-collar workers who could not afford home ownership or who wished to live in rented housing. In this context, the lack of interest of most authorities in building for lower-income groups alongside the 'Wheatley market' in the early 1930s is illuminating.

As we have seen, the 1930s saw the further development of professionalized housing management. In Britain by the mid-1930s, a little under 20 per cent of all local authorities had appointed formally designated housing managers, many of whom had a background in the property professions or in local authority financial management (Kidd, 1940). The provision of professional training courses, including some university degrees and diplomas, was under way and two professional bodies (the Society of Women Housing Managers, inspired by Octavia Hill, and the Institute of Housing) were developing relevant curricula and professional standards. The first major guidance to the local authorities was provided in an official report entitled *The Management of Municipal Housing Estates* (Ministry of Health, 1938). The report plainly observes that there was no real problem in managing the property built with the aid of the early subsidy programmes. This was too expensive for poor households and was let to the 'better paid artisans and persons of a similar economic status', a 'carefully selected group who, but for the War might have been expected to find their own accommodation' and who were 'an asset and not a liability from the rent-paying standpoint'. Even when some poorer tenants were admitted in the later 1920s, 'the local authority could still pick and choose and selection still went on'. However, the 1930 Housing Act 'introduced an entirely fresh principle in housing administration ... destined in a short time to create great social changes ... the very poorest were to be rehoused'. This required the development of something more than the rather minimal management that had been necessary in the 1920s.

The problem was the adaption of the 'very poorest' to 'the modern houses where they will be given the chance to lead happier and more healthy lives'. Echoing the familiar classification of the working class, the report notes that some households would adapt quickly, some would need 'initial guidance', but 'others without continuous supervision will produce a slum atmosphere' and a very few will be 'beyond reclamation altogether'. The local authority housing manager's role was twofold, to act both as custodian of the public housing resource and, more paternally, as 'counsellor and friend of the increasing number of tenants coming under his charge'. While the former requirement was common to both the private and the public landlord, the interesting development is the enlarged conception of the public sector landlord as a regulator and modifier of tenant behaviour. As we have seen, this conception was also apparent in those other countries where social housing was beginning to be provided for the poorest sections of the working class and, again, it recalls, if in a more muted form, the reformatory impulses of the early housing reformers. Despite the soft language in which much of this report is couched, the inability of many of the new breed of tenants to behave appropriately is clearly stated. Thus, 'unless some steps are taken so to educate the tenants as to secure his cooperation, the landlord, striving to maintain his property, and the tenant destroying it by his neglect, will remain warring parties'.

Although the report rejected the Dutch method of providing isolated reform colonies as a means of disciplining and re-educating 'undesirable' tenants, much emphasis was placed on the need to categorise or 'grade' applicants for council housing. Such grading is still a central feature, in one form or another, of social housing allocation in Britain and elsewhere. The main purpose of this was to ensure that socially deviant slum communities were not transferred *en bloc* into the new public housing estates. Instead, households from these communities should be dispersed among 'families of a good type' and their social networks and former life styles weakened, in order to reduce their resistance to re-education. As a mass of subsequent social studies showed, this engineered breakup of working-class communities was deeply resented by many of those whom it affected, including the 'families of a good type', whose views about being recruited to this project were not regarded as being of relevance. However, in practice, grading has also been used not to impose social mixing but to concentrate less well regarded tenants in poorer-quality social housing. Criteria for selection have included income, life styles, 'race' or ethnicity, and so on.

To summarize, in Britain the economic policies pursued after 1931 helped to stimulate an unprecedented boom in private housing construction. The new consumer-oriented industries, and the employment and incomes which they generated, opened up the possibility of a major transformation in the structures of housing provision, as manifested in the growth of home ownership. This change began to occur only some 30 years later in the other four European countries with which we are concerned. The rapid recovery of parts of the British economy after 1931, and in particular the private housing boom, meant that there was little political requirement for the government to expand social housebuilding as a means of generating employment (despite persistently high unemployment in some areas).

These developments contributed to a major shift in the rationale for council housing provision, making it politically possible to implement the aim, which had been apparent since 1919, of leaving the provision of most working-class housing to the private market and restricting council housing to a residual role, accommodating a limited proportion of the economically, socially and politically marginal urban poor. As we have seen, this conversion was far from complete by 1939 and was frequently resisted by local authorities. After 1945 the renewed need for mass programmes of council housing postponed its resumption for a further decade. Nevertheless, the groundwork for the eventual return to a 'sanitary policy', as Bowley (1944) called it, was laid in the 1930s.

While in Britain private housing boomed in the 1930s, in the United States the collapse of the private housing market and, more generally, the economy, led to the reluctant provision of some federally subsidized public housing. However, a far more significant event was the reconstruction of private housing finance which underpinned the massive post-war expansion of home ownership. The circumstances which led to the collapse of the private housing market and of the banking system have already been outlined. As we have already noted, housing production had peaked in 1925. It then declined to just over 500,000 in 1929. The subsequent collapse was dramatic, down to a little over 93,000 in 1933. Building then began a partial recovery, so that by 1939 it was back near the 1929 level (US Department of Commerce, 1965: table A-1, 18–19). The rate at which many of those who had benefited from the economic growth of the 1920s and from access to home ownership were losing their homes as a result of unemployment and mortgage foreclosure was enormous. In 1933 half of all mortgage debt was in default and foreclosures were running at 1000 a day (Fish, 1979: 186). The need for some form of federal intervention to rescue the situation was evident and it mainly took the form of support for the private housing market.

In contrast to the prolonged controversy which surrounded public housing, there was little opposition to the steps taken by the federal government to reform the banking and mortgage finance system. Detailed accounts of these policies, which began to emerge before the New Deal, have been published elsewhere.[12] Key features of the new system included a reserve bank system for private mortgage finance institutions, federal insurance for savers' deposits, federal mortgage insurance for private loans (through a new Federal Housing Administration, FHA), a federally created secondary mortgage market, and, as a temporary measure, the federal takeover of foreclosed mortgages. These institutions saved the private housing market from virtual extinction and there was a modest recovery in housing production towards the end of the decade. A key development was the 1934 National Housing Act which established the FHA. In 1933 Roosevelt recognized the employment-generating value of a programme to stimulate housebuilding; about one-third of the unemployed were formerly in the building and allied trades and the multiplier effects of new construction were considerable. However, large federal capital expenditures were ruled out and already there was concern over the budgetary costs of the mortgage rescue operation. The idea of trying to use a relatively small amount of public funding to stimulate private housebuilding seemed to satisfy most requirements and appealed to the more conservative and financially orthodox members of the administration.

To a much more limited degree the needs of ex-home owners, the 'submerged middle class' as they have often been called, also contributed to the pressure for federally subsidized public housing, as did the renewed activism of housing reformers. However, the more important origins of public housing lie in the public works programmes which began under Hoover and were enormously expanded under Roosevelt. To a considerable extent the character of public housing was moulded by the opposing interests of the labour unions, whose first concern was employment, and private property interests, whose first concern was to prevent any competition with the private market. Although the 1937 law which established public housing was a victory of sorts for organized labour and the housing reformers, in the longer run the pressures exerted by private property to limit this measure prevented public housing from becoming more than a minor and problematic form of provision.

The detailed history of how public housing emerged in the Roosevelt administrations has been well documented, notably in a blow-by-blow account of the legislative process by McDonnell (1957), from which most of the following details are derived. The first step occurred when the Hoover administration passed an emergency act in 1932 to provide financial support for industry and state and local governments. Some of these funds were available for employment-generating housing schemes, to be carried out by limited-dividend housing corporations. But, in the circumstances of the time, there was little chance that private capital would invest in such corporations and all that resulted was one 1600-unit project in New York City and some rural housing in Kansas (Topalov, 1988: 238).

In 1933 the Roosevelt administration provided far larger-scale funding for state-organized work relief programmes and the Federal Public Works Administration (PWA) was established to finance and administer these programmes directly. The PWA eventually built federally owned public housing in 37 cities, using powers contained in the 1933 National Industrial Recovery Act (NIRA). According to Fish (1979: 211), the inclusion of these housing powers in NIRA was achieved after a leading activist in the reviving housing reform movement persuaded the key Democratic Senator Robert Wagner to insert a clause to this effect. However, this development by no means signified a strong endorsement of public housing by the administration. Indeed, as we have seen, its preference was to revive the private market.

Therefore, the PWA first tried to rely on the privately owned limited-dividend corporations, by providing cheap loans. The programme was an almost complete failure; most proposals which the PWA examined were little more than attempts by private property interests to rid themselves of land which was unsaleable in the Depression. Only seven projects were built, containing just over 3000 apartments, mostly in New York. It was only when this approach failed that the PWA reluctantly turned to the direct financing and development of housing projects and, as its administrator made clear, this was 'in the interest of unemployment relief and recovery' and only where local agencies were unwilling or unable to take the initiative. Eventually the PWA programme resulted in just over 21,000 units of federally built and owned housing in 51 projects. It was bitterly attacked by private property interests (G. Wright, 1981: 226–7). A second element in these early attempts at federally funded public housing arose from programmes to deal with the collapse of the farm economy and employment. These led to the creation of three 'greenbelt towns', new, planned suburban settlements, and some other smaller-scale developments. In these projects 10,900 units were eventually built (Topalov, 1988: 244).

One aspect of the heavy attack which these programmes were subjected to by industrial and property interests involved legal challenges to their constitutionality. In 1935 and 1937 the courts ruled against the federal purchase of land (including by 'eminent domain' – compulsory purchase) for the housing schemes. This contributed to the abandonment of the direct federal construction of public housing and the greenbelt town programme. However, the courts did decide that it was permissible for the federal government to fund slum clearance and low-cost housing, to be provided by local agencies established under state legislation. States could also endow these agencies with the power of eminent domain. These decisions were a major factor in determining the subsequent arrangements for public housing.

As Topalov (1988: 243–66) describes, the early federal housing schemes were also affected by the changing politics of the federal work creation and relief programmes which were responsive both to the changing levels of unemployment and to the balance of political forces acting on the administration. A further factor was the high cost and relatively slow employment-generating capacity of the schemes (Fisher, 1959: 86). After the Democrat success in the 1934 Congressional elections, Roosevelt asked the legislature for new powers to prolong and change the nature of unemployment relief. As McCoy (1977: 229) notes, the new proposals were shaped by Roosevelt's conservative outlook on relief. They involved the establishment of the Works Progress Administration (WPA), to provide public work at subsistence wages for up to 3.5 million workers. Roosevelt wanted to make the maximum impact on unemployment at the minimum cost, and the value of the assistance given to WPA workers was far less than that provided by the PWA.

Meanwhile, the onset of the Depression and the possibilities offered by the federal work programmes for the development of public housing helped revive the housing reform movement which embarked on a long and complex struggle, against the opposition of the private sector, to commit the administration to public housing legislation. McDonnell's (1957) account of this period shows that the public housing reform coalition had three elements. First, local and state government officials who were concerned with the housing situation in their areas; second, the leaders of the building trade unions and lastly, the more progressive wing of the housing reform movement which had led such an attenuated existence in the previous decade (although the conservative older generation, such as Veiller, continued to be extremely hostile to public housing). In 1931 leading housing reformers, based in New York City, began to organize a pressure group for public housing. They drafted a bill and persuaded Senator Wagner, the key legislative figure in many of the major New Deal social reforms, to introduce it into Congress in 1935 (A. Jackson, 1976: 202–24). Building trade unions backed the formation of a second group, which similarly provided Representative Ellenbogen with a draft bill. In 1933 local housing officials had formed their own professional group, which supported public housing in a more discreet fashion. In 1935 the AFL annual convention backed a resolution which called for large-scale, planned, low- and moderate-rent federally subsidized housing. Interestingly, the programme was not to be limited to slum replacement housing but was for mass needs, and workers' housing cooperatives would play a major role in implementing it. The endorsement of subsidized housing by organized labour gave the housing reform coalition the political clout which it had formerly lacked, as it had now engaged a major segment of Roosevelt's political base. However, as Topalov (1988: 271) notes, the eventual outcome was far from that envisaged initially by the AFL.

These first legislative attempts failed in Congress. However, in 1936 Wagner and Ellenbogen collaborated in another bill and in 1937 the final attempt was co-sponsored by Wagner and Steagall, the chairman of the House Committee on Banking and Currency (who was not a supporter of public housing but was a Roosevelt loyalist). The strongest and most vocal opposition came from NAREB (the National Association of Real Estate Boards, which represented local real estate agents) and the National Association of Retail Lumber Dealers. But a more effective strategy was adopted by the US Building and Loan League and the US Chamber of Commerce, which used their influence to limit the legislation, in alliance with a group of Treasury officials and the administrators of the new federal agencies which had been established to support the private housing market. Roosevelt (who would have preferred to extend home ownership to low-income households: see McDonnell, 1957: 128) was at best lukewarm and many key members of Congress remained uncommitted to a permanent programme of public housing in 1935 and 1936. However, after the President's triumphant re-election in 1936, his famous inaugural speech, which referred to 'one-third of a nation ill-housed, ill-clad, ill-nourished', seemed to mark a change of attitude. Even so, Wagner had to take pre-emptive action to introduce his 1937 proposals, after the President had suggested a further round of consultations which would probably have torpedoed any bill. Moreover, at first Roosevelt did not endorse the Wagner proposals, doing so only after strong pressure from the AFL. Later, when the bill was almost lost in the House Committee on Banking and Currency, because Steagall failed to hold hearings (despite being the co-sponsor of the bill), Roosevelt at first failed to ask him to take action. Only strong pressure from Wagner and the AFL, and the President's desire to have some legislative successes in a session where he had been badly defeated on key issues, led him to take this step and ensure that the legislation finally passed through the House.

The public housing programme was shaped by the struggle to obtain administrative and other key support and in the course of its path through Congress. McDonnell plots the complex history of the bill and the interplay of the forces of reform and resistance, as well as of divisions within both these blocs. He makes the

interesting point that the legislative debates were frequently confused and based more on ignorance than any clear appreciation of
Wagner's proposals, among his supporters as well as his opponents!
The outcome was incoherent in many ways, reflecting the differing
interests of the various groups concerned (the first administrator
of the Federal Public Housing Authority applied a phrase first used
by Woodrow Wilson in 1884, calling the act an example of the
'confused and desultory action of the House' (Straus, 1944: 207;
see also Marcuse, 1986b)). As has frequently been noted, this
incoherence is evident in the act's preamble, which defines three
major purposes for the legislation. First, a 'sanitary' conception –
public housing was not oriented to meeting general housing needs
but to enabling the 'elimination of unsafe and insanitary housing
conditions'; second, it would provide some 'decent, safe and sanitary
housing for families of low income'. In these two respects the
programme embodied the conservative conception of social housing
which we have discussed in the European context.

In the third respect it reflected the continuing concern with
employment generation and economic revival, being 'for the reduction of unemployment and the stimulation of business activity'.
In fact, the programme made little contribution to this latter objective in the years up to 1940 and it was the former two objectives
which characterised the post-war development of public housing.
Far from providing a major new source of lower-income housing with a direct federal role in its provision, as, for example,
Ellenbogen had intended in 1935, it amounted to federal support
for localities who were willing to allow a limited programme of
minimal-quality housing to replace slum-cleared units (although not
necessarily to rehouse the low-income households which lived in
such areas), with a low maximum income limit for admission. A
strict link to slum clearance, providing that, for every new unit
built, an old one had to be torn down, the setting of very low
levels of permissible construction costs and of income eligibility
were all inserted in the bill during its passage through Congress
and were accepted as the only means by which the opposition to
the legislation would finally allow its passage. The conception of
public housing as it finally emerged represented a victory for those
forces which had negotiated to limit the programme and to ensure
that it did not compete with the private market. The reliance on
local initiative also provided many opportunities for local property
interests to prevent or inhibit its development. In other words,
the opposition managed to institute the basis for a residual system
of public housing in America from the start.

The act provided for the establishment, subject to state-enabling legislation, of local public housing authorities (PHAs) to build, own and manage housing. There were 60-year government loans, covering up to 90 per cent of the costs of construction; 10 per cent had to be provided by the localities (in fact, PHAs issued tax-exempt bonds to finance their developments, up to 90 per cent of which were bought by the federal government, although it was frequently possible to obtain most of the capital funds required without the government subscribing such a high percentage). The gap between cost-covering rents and the actual rents was met by long-term annual contributions from the federal government and smaller contributions from the local authorities (most partially exempted the housing from local taxes in lieu of this contribution).[13] The bonds were secured against this guaranteed flow of annual contributions and a federal loan guarantee. The act required that tenants should have 'very low incomes', so that they could not 'afford to pay enough to cause private enterprise in their locality ... to build an adequate supply of decent, safe and sanitary dwellings for their use'. The maximum income limits for admission were set at no more than 5 or 6 times the rent plus utilities costs, re-producing the terms of the so-called George–Healey Act of 1936 which had been enacted to cover the PWA schemes.

The early years of the public housing programme continued to be marked by the struggle between reform and reaction. The bill had finally passed Congress at the time when unemployment began to rise in the 1937 recession. One defeat for the reformers con-cerned the low level of resources allocated to public housing by Congress, only $500 million for a three-year programme, half the initial proposal in the bill. But the new recession led, after a strug-gle by the administration, to an expansion of the funding to $800 million in early 1938. By 1940 117,000 units had been constructed in 377 developments, just over 8 per cent of all housing output between 1938 and 1940. However, as Keith (1973: 38–9) notes, the conservative turn in Congress in the late 1930s and antagonism on the part of leading Democrats towards Straus, the federal public housing administrator, led to the defeat of a bill to extend the programme. In 1940 Congress decided that the public housing units still to be completed should be used for housing defence industry workers (later that year the Lanham Act provided for a major programme of war-worker housing). By 1942 the initial programme was all but complete. The public housing stock com-prised around 190,000 units, including about 20,000 PWA units. As 30 per cent of the 1937 Act units were used for housing defence workers, about 120,000 'proper' public housing units had been built. There were also some locally financed units, notably in New York. No new federally subsidized public housing was authorised until 1949 (Housing and Home Finance Agency, 1948: table 22, 26; Keith, 1973: 39).

According to Straus (1944: 10), over 90 per cent of the families housed in public housing fell in the bottom third of the income distribution, a group for which no new private housing was available. The new projects were cheaper than the PWA projects in response to the Congressional requirement for a low-cost, minimum-quality approach, although, as Straus's account shows, his agency tried to resist the pressure from real estate interests (that wished to sell slum property at inflated values to the public authorities) for all the new housing to be located at high densities in the cleared slum areas.[14] Straus provides some interesting details of the economies in design and facilities required to ensure low-cost construction. One by-product of the continuing campaign by real estate interests against new public housing was the suggestion by NAREB – which still regarded public housing as 'undiluted socialism' – that the government finance the purchase and clearance of the slums, making the sites available at a subsidized price for private redevelopment. This was essentially what occurred after public housing was restarted as part of the federal urban renewal programme after the war. As Straus accurately predicted, this policy displaced without rehousing large numbers of low-income households. NAREB also argued that if the federal government was to provide housing subsidies, it should assist poor households to find accommodation on the private market, an idea that was to be taken up from the 1960s onwards, as we shall see.

Unlike European social housing after the First World War, US public housing could not be allocated to better-off sections of the working class; nevertheless, a bias towards the 'respectable' (if poor) working class was evident, although, reflecting the different conception of class in the USA, this group has been labelled the 'submerged middle class' (Friedman, 1980). Silverman (quoted in Fish, 1979: 220) has provided a useful description of this group. He notes:

[i]n the late thirties and early forties, the Local Housing Authorities housed working class families of low income. They were poor, but most of them were employed and accustomed to urban living ... Local Housing Authorities carefully screened out, or imposed quotas on, applicant families receiving relief, those who had unpleasant

social histories or living habits, or those who were not normal families (see also G. Wright, 1981: 230–2).

In effect, public housing provided accommodation for some of the mainly white members of the working class who had fallen on hard times and who had reduced incomes because of the Depression.[15] This (temporarily) submerged 'middle class' included many trade unionists, for whom public housing offered not just accommodation but some increase in construction-related employment. However, after the war, with rising employment and incomes and the benefits of federally assisted access to owner occupation, public housing rapidly lost its rationale as housing for such groups. It then reverted more clearly to the role which seemed inherent in the 1937 legislation and which was reinforced when the programme began again in 1949, providing a limited supply of very low-income housing as an adjunct to urban renewal activities (Fisher, 1959: 171–5). As we shall see, this change profoundly affected the social composition of public housing, its financial situation and, above all, its degree of political acceptability.

To summarize, had it not been for the particular intensity of the Depression in the USA and the pressure that this placed on government for an unprecedented degree of intervention in the economy and society, it is inconceivable that any public housing programme would have been enacted. As in Europe after 1918, the causal connection between crisis and social housing is evident. As in Europe too, the political influence of the small group of pro-public housing reformers, had they stood alone, would have been negligible. McDonnell (1957: 42) quotes one of them saying that a convention of all those working for public housing in 1934 could have been held in a telephone booth. They were able to achieve results only because they took advantage of a favourable conjuncture in the wider, non-housing economic and political context, shaping their specific concern for public housing to the interconnected interests of the President and of organized labour (see Friedman, 1968). Roosevelt had no strong belief in the need for public housing, whatever others in the administration may have advocated. However, it did seem as if public housing construction could make a minor but useful contribution to unemployment relief in the first years of the New Deal. But when these programmes ran into difficulties, there was no immediate desire to provide a more permanent basis for public housing. A grudging commitment came about only at the eleventh hour when the 1937 bill looked like sinking in Congress and the trade unions exerted maximum pressure on Congress and the President. The single most important event was, therefore, the recognition by the AFL, led by the building trade unions, that support for public housing could provide some useful jobs for its members and, perhaps as a secondary benefit, some housing too. As McDonnell (1957: 67–71) notes, the previous craft-based and conservative trade union movement, the base of the AFL, had formerly been opposed to public housing.

However, the public housing legislation was never more than a relatively minor element in the New Deal. Other issues, such as recognition and the provision of social security, were of greater importance to organized labour. Apart from playing a major role in ensuring the passage of the legislation, the unions had little influence on the form of public housing that emerged. This was largely shaped by those who wished for no such programme in the first place, to its lasting disadvantage. The coalition which supported public housing in the 1930s proved to be less enduring than that which ensured its residual character, for, in the era of full employment and rising real incomes after 1945, the white working-class home owner became a far more important base for trade union organization and electoral mobilization than the small minority of increasingly poverty-stricken (and non-white) public housing tenants.

CONCLUSION: THREE MODELS OF SOCIAL HOUSING

By comparison with the 1920s, the 1930s were marked by a more complex and cross-nationally varied pattern of relationships between social housing, structures of accumulation and policy regimes. The need for work, rather than the need for housing, was the dominant concern, and the evolution of housing markets and policies reflected this situation. An additional source of cross-national variation was the state of the private housing market. In some respects, the changes which occurred in this period may be seen as marking a stage in the evolution of a residual role for social housing. However, as we shall see in the next chapter, this outcome was postponed in Europe for many years in the altered circumstances of the post-war world. The collapse in the 1930s of the economic and political assumptions which had accompanied the earlier search for a 'return to normality' gave further impetus to the emergence of a new set of relationships between capital, labour and the state in the 1940s and beyond. In these so-called 'Fordist',

'Keynesian' or 'mixed economy' regimes, the wider conception of social housing which marked its early years after 1918 obtained a new lease of life.

In this context, the most significant factor was the continued transition from economies based on the older, heavy industries, employing a largely male, manual working class with relatively low wages and levels of consumption and/or low-wage agrarian economies, to economies based on new 'light industries' and services, in which there was a rapid growth of white-collar workers and an organized working class with higher wages and levels of consumption and more secure employment. Of course, this transition remained on a very limited and localized scale in the 1930s. And, as we have seen, only in southern England was its impact on housing at all evident. Nevertheless, these changes set the pattern which was to spread after 1945.

The Depression years also saw some important shifts in the political relationships between capital, labour and the state. Again, these were far from universal, but they may be seen as marking an important break with the past. The most obvious change was the abandonment of the belief that the state could stand aside from continual intervention in the functioning of the economy. Of course, the forms that this intervention took were shaped by the particular circumstances of the Depression and of each national situation, as well as by the persistence of elements of economic orthodoxy. In Germany it took a totalitarian form, for example. In most countries, the desire for, if not the possibility of, a return to balanced budgets persisted, the effects of the economic multiplier and of counter-cyclical public expenditure were hardly recognized, and Keynes's finest hour (or epoch) was yet to come. But even in France and the Netherlands, the economic functions of the state grew in significance.

Although the growth of state economic intervention was very largely a reluctant, somewhat haphazard response to the immediate circumstances of the Depression, it was accompanied, also in a patchy and sometimes barely recognized way, by equally important changes, in conception and sometimes in action, in other aspects of the social structures of accumulation. One way of describing these changes is to refer to the growth of corporatism and planning, although this really imposes far too coherent a label on what were, in practice, far more incoherent, fragmented and variable developments. To some extent it may also be argued that these changes were not unique products of the Depression, but rather that they mark a further stage in the development of a new conception of the relationships between capital, labour and the state which had a somewhat premature flowering in the immediate aftermath of the First World War. Certainly, Maier's (1975) study, *Recasting Bourgeois Europe*, which traces the re-establishment of a (fragile) measure of economic and social stability in the 1920s, argues such a case, while concluding that it took the Depression and the Second World War to establish these new relationships firmly. Moreover, Topalov and Magri, in the series of papers referred to earlier, have described how 'advanced' sections of capital and the state, with some participation from reformist social democracy, sought after 1918 to establish a new urban reform project to correspond with their vision of a modernized capitalist economic and social order.

However, the dangers of a Whig interpretation of history are ever present. While the existence of this reformist minority in the early 1920s cannot be doubted, it is clear that the attempt to return to 'normality' in the economic and social order generally, as in matters of housing and urban development, prevailed in the 1920s, and that this general impulse was abandoned, if slowly, reluctantly and in a piecemeal way, only in the 1930s. The new structures and institutions of economic and social regulation emerged in an equally hesitant manner. Nevertheless, we can point, for example, to the growth of the state regulation and reorganization of key branches of the economy such as agriculture in the USA, Denmark, the Netherlands and the UK (and, of course, of almost total regulation, or attempted regulation, of the economy in Nazi Germany). In addition, there were important developments in the political and economic position of organized labour, ranging, for example, from the concessions extracted from capital in the Popular Front agreements in France and the growth of trade union rights promoted by the Roosevelt administration, through the incorporation of social democracy into the system of government in Denmark, to the enforced cooption in the Labour Front in Germany. In each case, although in radically different ways, one can see elements of the incorporation of labour within a changing capitalist economic and social order, in which the state's role in the regulation of capital/labour relations and in the provision of a modicum of social welfare is expanded.

Finally, the 1930s saw a growth in ideas about the role of planning in future economic, social and urban development. Of course, there were only two real examples of such planning in practice. Both involved totalitarian regimes, the Soviet Union and Germany, but both had some influence on thinking in those societies which retained bourgeois democratic institutions. These new ideas, mainly coming from those who were outside government in the 1930s, which were greatly developed during the Second World War, were to prove immensely influential after 1945. In the specific case of housing we have, for example, made reference to the proposals of the Dutch Social Democrats in their 1935 Labour Plan and the British Labour Party's scheme for planned, mass public housing.

However, as we have indicated, the history of the 1930s can also be read in a different way, especially in relation to the eventual destinies of social housing. For, while developments in this decade to some extent prefigured the post-war emergence of the 'Fordist' regime of accumulation and the 'welfare states', in which social housing had a renewed importance in relation to a larger project of societal and economic reconstruction and modernization, we can equally see, with the benefit of historical hindsight, the persistence and development of a more marginal or residual conception of social housing. Certainly, if we focus narrowly on the actual substance of social housing policies and practices in the 1930s, it is the confinement of the tenure to this limited role, rather than a return to the wider conception of its role which existed in the early 1920s, which seems most evident.

To summarize, in so far as new programmes of social housing were initiated in the 1930s, or those established in the previous decade continued, these were no longer targeted at, justified in terms of, or sustained by compelling pressure from broad sections of the working and middle classes. In purely functional terms, social housebuilding was linked, above all, to the contribution which it could make to employment generation (and in Germany also to the economic organization needed to bring about the Nazi's geo-political aims). However, this link was not particularly strong or important in most cases. As we saw in the case of the USA, for example, other forms of public works and assistance to the unemployed were probably cheaper, had a more rapid impact and, for this reason and others, were frequently given a higher political priority.

In some cases, such as Denmark and Britain, the early departure from the gold standard and the adoption of new economic measures in place of deflationary ones allowed a more or less extensive expansion of private housing after the worst years of the Depression. This had as great a positive impact on employment as social housing construction, and was politically far more acceptable to governments which, even in the case of Denmark, still stuck as closely as possible to budgetary orthodoxy. In France and the

Netherlands, where the grim pursuit of economic orthodoxy excluded any real recovery, the possible contribution to employment generation of any expansion of housing output, whether in the social or private sectors, was simply not on the political agenda.

Despite the far more limited role that social housing played in the state management of the Depression, compared with the post-First World War crisis, there are some important features to be noted regarding the way in which this limited role was conceived. Social housing was assimilated into the operations of the state bureaucracy and its management established as one of the emergent urban professions. It was in these years that social housing began to exhibit many of the distinctive institutional structures and social relations which persisted and further developed in the post-war era. At the same time, one can look backwards as well as forwards in time, and see how the legacy of earlier developments helped define these structures and social relations.

The most important point to note is the assignment of a much more limited role to social housing than had been temporarily accepted in the first period when it received major state support after the First World War. The *social* role of social housing, whatever its contribution to employment generation might be, was confined to the housing of a more or less substantial proportion of the urban poor, echoing the residual rationale proposed by the housing reformers before 1914. However, the identification in practice of this population with a limited area, the inner-city slum, indicates, as Malpass suggests, that the real issue was not so much the rehousing in decent accommodation of those in the greatest housing need, not all of whom were concentrated in such areas, but the use of state assistance to achieve the redevelopment and, in many cases, the return to profitable private exploitation of urban areas which could not be cleared at acceptable economic and social costs without this assistance. There is no evidence that the policy which linked small-scale programmes of social housing to slum clearance was mainly driven by the awakened conscience of political or economic elites to the housing needs of the poor. Nor was the satisfaction of such needs at all central to a larger project of sustaining or re-establishing political and social stability, as had been the case in relation to the 'respectable' working class and sections of the middle class in the early 1920s. Instead, in so far as there was any strong impetus behind the 1930s programmes of slum rehousing – and it should be remembered that, even in Britain, these were not on a vast scale compared with the mass of housing poverty and of poor housing which existed – it involved an updated version of a 'sanitary policy' – the removal of 'nuisances', built environment and people, which inhibited both the economic and social 'health' of the city, that is, its efficient functioning as a business and governmental location, as an arena for property investment and as a place of work, leisure and recreation for the better-off urban residents who worked in the public or private sectors, or who benefited from the profits generated by investments in industry, commerce or real estate.

As we have seen, it was widely recognized in the interwar period that the programmes of new social housing which had developed in the early 1920s served only a relatively small proportion of the better-off working class and some sections of the middle class. The more residual programmes of the 1930s, largely linked to slum clearance, were more closely targeted on poorer households, but were even more limited in their coverage. At the same time, as official reports from the ILO and the League of Nations and many national studies made clear, new private sector construction made little or no contribution to reducing the acute shortages of adequate and affordable housing for the households in the bottom half, or perhaps even the lower two-thirds, of the income distribution.

There were two ways in which governments sought to bridge the gap between their claim that mass housing provision could be left to the private market and this reality. The first, which had little or no significance in practice, was the assertion that an enhanced supply of new housing at the upper end of the market would free up cheaper accommodation for lower-income households. In fact, even in those countries where private housing output boomed for a period, such as the USA in the 1920s and Britain in the 1930s, sharply rising rates of household formation largely negated any such filtering effect. The second expedient in some countries was the continued, if reluctant, maintenance or reimposition of some rent controls on lower-cost housing. This obviously made no contribution to increasing the supply of lower-income housing, although its independent influence on reducing the incentives for new construction has frequently been exaggerated. There is little evidence of any great wish of private investors to enter the low-income housing market after the First World War, especially when other more attractive investment media were emerging (see Harloe, 1985). One clear lesson of the 1930s, which helped persuade some governments that major social housebuilding was required after the Second World War in connection with programmes of economic reconstruction and modernization, was that the private housing market would never again perform the role which it had very inadequately discharged, in the first phases of industrialization and urbanization – providing mass housing for the working class.

Along with the retreat from a conception of social housing for mass needs in the social housing programmes of the 1930s went some important shifts in other aspects of the institutions and social relations of provision. Broadly speaking, the management of the social housing built in the 1920s was based on one of two models. The first, which was particularly apparent in Britain, involved the new social landlords behaving like private landlords towards their tenants. The key concern was to select 'respectable' tenants with adequate incomes to afford the rent; the landlord/tenant relationship was limited in its scope, largely commercial in nature and certainly devoid in practice of intensive social control or tutelage, beyond that which might be found in the private sector, despite the wider ambitions of some housing reformers.

The second form of management drew on the workers' co-operative model which had developed around the time of the First World War, notably in Germany, Denmark and the Netherlands. This was characterised, initially at least, by a far greater degree of tenant involvement in management. In some cases the cooperatives were linked to trade union construction enterprises and, as we have noted, they also played a role in the development of a distinctive set of socialist and trade union social, cultural and political institutions. This second model provided a far more radical basis for social housing than the first model, as it might, in time, have led to a wider socialization of housing provision. In recent years, some left-wing critics of bureaucratized social housing have highlighted this lost possibility.[16] However, this form of social housing was also largely the preserve of the 'respectable' working and middle classes, who appear to have been just as selective as the managers of the first model as to which groups were admitted as tenants. Also, by the 1930s, many of the more successful and larger-scale trade union-linked social housing and construction enterprises were moving away from their grassroots origins, becoming more bureaucratized and hiring professional managers. In Germany, all the institutions which were linked to the SPD and the unions were destroyed by the Nazis and were not revived after the war. Only in Denmark has tenant self-management survived into the modern period (or rather, as we shall see, been revived). In this country the strong tradition of producer and consumer cooperatives, originally deriving from the agricultural sector and not the sole preserve of working-class organization, has sustained elements of this distinctive model of social housing management.

The third, residual model of social housing management, which became more evident in the 1930s in countries where programmes of social housing construction became more closely linked to slum clearance and the rehousing of the urban poor, involved not just those elements of property management to be found in the private rental sector, but the additional elements of control, discipline and 're-education' which can be traced back to the proposals of the reforming elites in the period before 1914. A little simplistically, one could argue that if the workers' cooperative model was compatible with a wider project of autonomous working-class cultural, political and economic institutions, whose long-term objective was to contribute to a socialist transformation of society, this third model aimed rather to integrate tenants who were conceived as being on the margins of capitalist society into that society.

Neither the first nor the last of the three models, which might respectively be labelled 'reformist' and 'reformatory', contained within them the transformative potential of the second model. But, with the benefit of historical hindsight, we can see that in most countries the forms of social housing which developed on a far larger scale after 1945 drew very little from this second model. In social housing, as in other aspects of social welfare, the role of self-organized, worker-controlled institutions gradually faded away (for a discussion see de Swaan, 1988: 143–51). Two key influences on this, which became increasingly significant in the 1930s, were the growth of state regulation of social housing institutions and the development of a professional 'science' of housing management, together with the growing influence of these professionals over the evolution of social housing policies. In short, whether targeted at the urban poor or the 'respectable' middle and working classes, social housing became increasingly, like other aspects of welfare provision, an arena for bureaucratically organized and regulated, 'top-down' control, management and policy making. Only in the last 20 or so years have some of the negative consequences of this particular constitution of the structures and social relations of social housing become apparent, providing targets for criticism from both the right and the left.

To conclude, interpreting the significance of the Depression years for the evolution of social housing is not a simple task. Clearly, there was not the same strong link, across most countries, between a growth in social housing provision and the resolution of a societal crisis that there had been in the 1920s. Even in the

USA, where such a connection was the essential basis for the emergence of a programme of federally subsidized public housing, it was more weakly constituted than it had been in most of the other countries after the First World War. However, developments in this decade, some of which were specific to social housing and others of which concerned the broader societal context, had considerable consequences for the development of this form of housing provision over the following half-century. The first legacy from this period was the general growth of the state's role in economic and social management, new patterns of industrial development and changing relationships between capital, labour and the state, all of which prefigured the emergence of the 'Fordist' pattern of full employment, the 'mixed economy' and the 'welfare state' after the war, within which mass programmes of social housing found a new rationale. The second legacy, whose eventual significance became apparent only much later, was the development of, or return to, a much more restrictive conception of social housing as a residual provision for a section of the economically and politically marginal urban poor. The third legacy, relevant throughout the whole of the post-war period to date, was the advancing integration of social housing within the bureaucratized structures of state welfare policy and administration and of professionalized housing management. In future, whether functioning as mass or as residual housing, or as a mixture of the two, the fortunes and constitution of social housing were inseparably linked to such structures. Only in the past 10 or 15 years, in the context of a new phase of major restructuring in the capitalist social and economic order, have these connections become the target for widespread criticism and a conflicting range of proposals for radical change.

NOTES

1   The following account is based on Aldcroft (1978: 1987); Cipolla (1978); Kindelberger (1987); and Mathias and Pollard (1989).
2   The following section draws on Neumann (1942); Cobban (1961); Taylor (1965); Zeldin (1975); McCoy (1977); Kossmann (1978); J. Roberts (1978); Morison, Commager and Leuchtenberg (1980); Berghahn (1982); Blum et al. (1985); Fletcher (1987); and Rying (1988).
3   Although Klein (1975) has argued that public expenditure policy was not as deflationary as is normally suggested.
4   Actually the new schemes were designed to limit the federal role. Insurance benefits were entirely financed by employer and employee contributions and their coverage was inadequate. Due regard was

paid to states' rights, so welfare benefits were based on matching federal–state contributions, thus perpetuating an enormous geographical variation in these payments, which still persists.

5   I am indebted to Jan van der Schaar for providing this and much of the following information on Dutch developments.

6   See also Fisher and Ratcliff (1936: 54), who refer to the targeting of children, 'for more hope is placed in their future than that of their parents'.

7   The idea of planned production was taken up even by those who remained opposed to large-scale subsidies (International Housing and Town Planning Congress, 1937: 171). The use of social housing to act as a price leader in the whole of the rental market became a specific objective of post-war Swedish housing policy.

8   Although later requirements that the new settlers contribute some of their own capital to the housing made the latter objective an impossibility.

9   Interview with Erling Olsen, former Social Democratic Minister of Housing, February 1983.

10   Interestingly, though, Bowley (1944: 86) saw this development as driven by a lack of investment in rental housing, which led many to home ownership 'because it was the only way of satisfying a particular need'.

11   In fact, the issue of finance is ignored completely in the document and it is made clear that the nationalization of any part of the construction industry would be resorted to only if it failed to cooperate with the government.

12   See, for example, Beyer (1963); Keith (1973); Gelfand (1975); US Department of Housing and Urban Development (1976); Fish (1979); G. Wright (1981); J. Mitchell (1985); and Topalov (1988).

13   The act also provided for a second method of federal support – capital grants. For many years the government preferred to make annual contributions. But in the 1980s it switched to providing capital grants for technical reasons concerned with the presentation of the federal budget.

14   But Genevro (1984) has described the successful pressure exerted on the New York Public Housing Authority to do just this. See also Marcuse (1986b).

15   For a detailed local account of the selection processes and racially segregated nature of early public housing in New York City see Marcuse (1986b).

16   Harloe and Martens (1990) contains examples of ideas and projects developed in the 1980s in the USA, the Netherlands and Germany.

4

The Golden Age: Social Housing in an Era of Reconstruction and Growth

The attempt to periodize the changing fortunes of social rented housing is an approximate rather than an exact exercise. Nevertheless, the cessation of the European war in 1945 provides a clear enough starting-point for this chapter. In America and Europe post-war reconstruction involved not just recovery from the ravages of war, but the establishment of a new order within capitalism, a structure of accumulation and policy regime to which the label 'Fordism' has often been affixed.[1] While in 1918 the dominant social forces had favoured a 'return to normality', in 1945 the disastrous political and economic consequences of this choice were widely recognized. The mass unemployment, social unrest and political disintegration of the interwar years had served the interests of neither labour nor capital. So there was little nostalgia for the past. Yet in Europe the devastation of war, added to the destruction of the Depression years, made for a grim situation and a highly uncertain future.

What transpired in the advanced capitalist countries was the longest period of economic growth and rising prosperity since the Industrial Revolution. Unemployment was reduced to minimal levels and economic depressions, involving a reduction in gross national product (GNP), seemed to have been eliminated. Instead, there was only the occasional recessionary interlude in which the rate of economic growth faltered and there was a temporary and

modest rise in unemployment. In retrospect, the fragile foundations
to the 'long boom' are clear. It was built on an impermanent con-
juncture of circumstances, a world economic and political order
and dynamic domestic markets, which was becoming increasingly
problematic by the end of the 1960s. From this point it took around
a decade for the full political and economic consequences of the
ending of the Fordist boom to emerge. So the choice of 1975 as
the end-point for this chapter is a little arbitrary. It corresponds to
the time when the advanced capitalist economies' societies suffered
their first post-war depression, with reductions in GNP, rather than
just a slackening in the growth rate. Unlike previous depressions,
however, the reductions in GNP were accompanied by soaring
rates of inflation – so-called stagflation, to which most governments
had little answer.

In previous chapters we noted the link between economic growth
and rising housing investment in America in the 1920s and in
Britain in the 1930s. After 1945 this pattern became general throughout the advanced capitalist economies. Public and private investment in housing and infrastructure, with its powerful multiplier
effects on consumer and producer industries, generated and fed on
rising levels of employment and real income. In America the role
of private investment in housing was dominant throughout this
period, although its dependence on state support for the financial
and physical infrastructures constituted a new and distinctly different structure of provision. Public housing played no more than a
modest, though controversial and problematic, role in these arrangements. In Europe, the emergence of a radically restructured private
housing market occurred more slowly and less completely. Mass
social housing programmes were adopted by left- and right-wing
governments. However, in contrast to the post-First World War
period, there was now a broader and longer-lasting rationale for
this development, which was linked not merely (or mainly) to a
brief episode of social crisis, but to a longer-term process of economic recovery and modernization.

Nevertheless, while 1945 opened a new era for social housing,
it signified a far less radical break with the past than many then
hoped for. The post-war commitment of most major political and
economic interests to social rented housing was not one of principle but one of expediency. As before, social rented housing was
never intended to supplant the private market, but to meet politically and economically urgent housing needs to the extent and
for the period during which the market was incapacitated. It is
far too crude an analysis to conclude that the growth of post-war

prosperity, and the conditions which enabled dynamic private housing markets to function, automatically resulted in social housing reverting to a more residual role. Nevertheless, by the early 1970s, ironically the peak period for social housing construction in several countries, the economic and social conditions which, since 1945, had provided such a strong rationale for social housing were already in dissolution and its political support was being eroded. Developments in the 1970s intensified the pressure for radical changes in social rented housing and reductions in state support. In several countries the growth of the private market and the end of crude housing shortages seemed to make further large-scale social housing construction redundant. Moreover, it was not just a narrow economic concern to prioritize the private market that made the further growth of social rented housing seem undesirable to many. From this time onwards there was a growing volume of criticism concerning the qualitative aspects of social housing – its location, physical and social environment, structural defects, insensitive management and so on. More generally, this critique, which came from across the political spectrum, reflected rising dissatisfaction with the professionalized and bureaucratized welfare state.

As we shall see in the next chapter, the increasingly powerful promotion of home ownership and limitation of social housing which has occurred over the past two or more decades has some contradictory aspects. Nowhere has the state simply withdrawn all support for social housing, relying on the private market to fill the gap. In this sense there is no correspondence between what has occurred in the last 15 or 20 years and the 1920s. However, both periods were marked by a clear trend towards confining social housing to a residual role. In the United States this has been the role of public housing throughout the post-war period. In Europe the trend developed first and furthest in Britain. Elsewhere, the process has been slower and more inhibited. However, as Murie and Lindberg (1991: 12–13) have concluded,

the post 1945 period saw the heyday of the social rented sector in most of Europe but ... this was over by the mid-1970s. Somewhere between there was a golden age where political support and resources were forthcoming and professionals and organisations in the social rented sector were very influential.

THE AFTERMATH OF WAR

The loss of life in the Second World War was probably three times as high as in the First World War (Milward, 1987: 210–11). However, apart from Germany, which lost around 6 million people, losses in the other five countries ranged from 200,000 in the Netherlands to 500,000–800,000 in France. Economically, these horrific losses were less significant than the destruction of transport and productive capacity by military action and dilapidation. Germany suffered the worst economic devastation, but France and the Netherlands were also severely affected by the conflict and the German occupation. Denmark, although occupied, suffered less economic and physical damage. In Britain the effects of wartime bombing on industry were relatively limited, although the indirect effects of war were considerable. According to Aldcroft (1987: 128–40), the destruction of railways, ports and waterways in Germany, France and the Netherlands, rather than the direct loss of industrial capacity, was a particularly severe problem and resulted, by summer 1945, in production volumes that were a fraction of what they had been in 1939.

At first the prevention of mass starvation in mainland Europe, especially in Germany, took precedence over longer-term reconstruction and recovery. Denmark and Britain had increased agricultural production during the war, elsewhere the situation was grim. Moreover, Europe's devastated economies had no resources with which to pay for the desperately needed food and other imports, most of which had to come from North America. In this period approximately $25 billion of aid, mainly from the USA, was provided to keep European populations alive and to start the revival of economic activity.

As in 1918, only the United States emerged from the conflict with a strengthened economy. On an even larger scale than in the earlier war, the American economy had boomed, as demands for food, shipping and armaments escalated. By the early 1940s war had succeeded, where the New Deal had failed, in bringing about near full employment and rising real incomes. Between 1938 and 1948 the US GNP increased by 65 per cent. In comparison, the French GNP was static, the British had increased by 6 per cent, the Danish by 8 per cent (1940–5), the Dutch by 14 per cent and the German had declined to under half its 1938 level (van der Wee, 1987: 30; Jörberg and Krantz, 1978: 401). While Europe faced the problem of rebuilding shattered economies and societies, the only real problem for the US economy was how this new prosperity might be sustained in the post-war world. The solution adopted, the extension of American economic and military hegemony on a global scale, does not require discussion here. But its practical outcome in Europe, now divided between communism and capitalism, was the institution in 1948 of the Marshall Aid programme and of the North Atlantic Treaty Organization (NATO) in 1949, as well as various economic institutions which followed the 1944 Bretton Woods agreement (Milward, 1987: 362ff.; van der Wee, 1987: 421–49). While in 1918 America had attempted to retreat into economic and political isolation, no such option was possible after 1945. Continued American economic prosperity depended not just on a booming domestic market, but on the ability of US exports to penetrate foreign markets. The protection of Western Europe from communism and the support for economic and political reconstruction, the principal motives behind Marshall Aid, were therefore less purely a 'deeply unselfish act' as one motivated by a strong measure of self-interest. While large-scale American aid helped prevent a potential catastrophe in Europe, America's political and economic hegemony also helped to ensure that radical plans for a new social and economic order which had been widely discussed, for example in wartime resistance movements in occupied Europe and openly in Britain, were stillborn. While the totalitarian imposition of Stalinist regimes in Eastern Europe helped to destroy the credibility of communist parties in the West, even the reformist Social Democratic parties failed, in most cases, to gain the clear access to power which had eluded them in the interwar period. In Britain, where this was not the case, the connections between economic dependency on America and the containment of reform were just as clear.

ECONOMIC RECONSTRUCTION AND MODERNIZATION

By the early 1950s the post-war crisis was over and the European economies entered a longer period of economic transformation. By the late 1960s many Europeans had achieved prosperity comparable to that enjoyed by many, though not all Americans. However, the means by which each country achieved this outcome differed and these differences, together with the political variations discussed in the next section, significantly affected the role and nature of social housing in each nation. But the first and sharpest differences were those which separated America from all five European nations in the early post-war period.

As it had done after 1918, America returned rapidly to a peacetime economy after Japanese surrender in 1946. According to van der Wee (1987: 29–30), this was achieved by good government planning, a major effort to retrain and resettle veterans (the 1944 Servicemen's Readjustment Act, the so-called GI Bill of Rights, provided assistance for employment, education, health and housing), a rapid growth in personal consumption and investment and the government-organized export of American goods and services. By the end of 1946 virtually all wartime economic controls had been lifted, housing rent control being one of the few exceptions. Wartime savings were released for consumption and there was a rapid rate of new household formation. Immediately the war ended this pent-up demand caused rising inflation, falling real wages and a series of major strikes. One consequence was legislation to limit union power (the 1947 Taft–Hartley Act). By the end of the decade inflation was declining and the stage was set for the boom years (Morison, Commager and Leuchtenberg, 1980: 618–26).

Throughout the period under discussion in this chapter, the US economy was sustained by its dominance in international trade and by a rapidly expanding home market. Large-scale immigration resumed, with over 6 million migrants admitted between the end of the war and 1970 (and almost another 4.5 million in the following decade). Overall, the US population grew by about one-third between 1950 and 1970, from just over 150 million to just over 200 million (US Bureau of the Census, 1991: table 1, 7, table 5, 9). A key factor adding to domestic demand, particularly for housing, urban infrastructure and services, automobiles and consumer goods, was the rapid growth of low-density suburban areas. Between 1950 and 1970 the proportion of the American population living in metropolitan areas rose from 56 per cent to 68.6 per cent, while the absolute numbers of the population living outside such areas actually fell. The metropolitan population rose from 84.5 million to 139.4 million. However, the share of this population living in central cities was static at around one-third, while the share living in the suburbs rose from 23 per cent to 37 per cent (Fox, 1985: 51).

Apart from contributing to the boom in domestic demand, this rapidly expanding population provided US industry with a rising supply of labour.[2] This helped keep unit labour costs down and, together with developments in the organization of mass production and technological innovation, resulted in a high level of productivity and competitiveness for many years. America's domination of world trade, resulting in huge balance of payments surpluses, also meant that economic expansion could continue without some of the difficulties that, as we shall see, dogged growing European economies. In fact, the rate of domestic growth in the 1950s could probably have been higher, but the Eisenhower administration rejected Keynesian economics and followed an orthodox policy of balanced budgets. One consequence of these policies was the huge flow of American investment abroad. Another was the maintenance of some unemployment, together with a large, substantially non-white population living below the poverty line, increasingly concentrated in racially segregated inner urban areas.

By the 1960s this pattern of non-inflationary growth was beginning to run into difficulties. Serious balance of payments deficits arose, partly caused by the huge expenditure on maintaining the US military role overseas. This put pressure on the dollar, the key international reserve currency, leading to policies which aimed to maintain its international value, but which restricted growth in the domestic economy. After a recession in the early 1960s, successive Democratic administrations gradually adopted Keynesian policies. This led to the achievement of virtually full employment. Increased public spending and tax cuts in mid-decade avoided a serious recession and the economy started to grow rapidly. However, the effects of large-scale military expenditure on the Vietnam war and the social programmes (including large-scale housing subsidies) of the Johnson presidency, in a situation of full employment, fuelled inflation and led to renewed pressure on the dollar. In the 1950s many economists believed that there was, within limits, an inverse relationship between inflation and unemployment (the Phillips curve). However, by the late 1960s this relationship no longer held in the major industrial nations and prices rose much faster than unemployment fell. In the following decade this combination of high inflation and economic stagnation – stagflation – was a persistent problem.

The rising US deficit mainly benefited the now dynamic economies in Western Europe and Japan, raising their growth rates and providing resources for major developments in public provision as well as increased private expenditure. By the early 1970s the dollar was an increasingly weak currency and, as dollars were sold in favour of the yen, the Deutschmark and other currencies, America's balance of payments problems worsened. The dollar had become overvalued and its fixed parity was abandoned in 1971, when President Nixon suspended dollar convertibility, thus ending the world monetary system established under US tutelage and largely in its economic interests after the Second World War.

From this point the breakup of the relatively settled era of economic growth, full employment and rising prosperity in the leading capitalist economies progressed rapidly. As the weak US dollar continued to affect adversely its balance of payments deficit and increase international liquidity, money supplies and inflation rose sharply in Europe and elsewhere. Raw material and real estate prices rocketed as speculators made enormous profits. Governments struggled to control rising wages and prices, using various policies, including price and wage controls and cuts in public spending. Industry became a battleground, with unions and management seeking to increase wages and dividends respectively. The oil price rise in November 1973 was a part of this struggle, as the oil producers sought to protect their incomes against inflation and the depreciating dollar. In immediate terms it was the combined effect of this price rise in depressing consumer spending and the coincidence of restrictive government policies which led, in 1974/5, to the first post-war depression, with falling GNPs and rising unemployment. As we shall see in the next chapter, the recovery from this depression was shaky, inflation and unemployment fell only to a limited degree and there was a further period of economic crisis as the 1980s began.

The reasons for the ending of the 'long boom' are a matter of intense debate between economists (compare, for example, Aldcroft, 1978; van der Wee, 1987; Lipietz, 1987). However, as in the 1920s, one factor was probably the saturation of effective demand in many of the branches of production which had been at the heart of post-war expansion. In addition, there were declining gains from technological innovation and the new commitments to government expenditure, made in the 1960s and early 1970s, added to budget deficits. The role of military expenditure in the case of the USA has already been noted. However, in the 1970s an increasingly significant factor was the growth of industrial production in the low-wage economies of the Third World. American and other multinational firms relocated production from the high-cost areas of the First World following the exhaustion of the labour reserves which had facilitated high profits and rapid economic growth in several major European economies.

Obviously, economic developments in the European countries with which we are concerned must be viewed against the background of the changing fortunes of the US economy. All five economies shared in the post-war prosperity, although their growth records differed. So, by the early 1970s, a radical transformation had occurred in their relative economic standings. In 1950, despite the long-term decline in its economic fortunes and serious war losses (especially of overseas investments), the British economy was still the strongest in Europe. By 1960, after a decade of rapid growth in Germany, France and the Netherlands, the British lead had been sharply reduced. By 1970 it no longer existed.

Although Britain, alone among the countries with which we are concerned, elected a Labour administration with a massive majority after the war, the 1945–51 Labour government established a pattern of economic policy which, unlike those of countries such as France, Germany and the Netherlands, largely ignored the need for state-led economic modernization and development.[3] Essentially, the Labour government opted, or was forced to opt for, a major expansion of state welfare on the back of an expanding private sector economy. Rather than intervening positively to restructure this economy, the government adopted Keynesian policies of demand management using fiscal and monetary means. At first, however, in order to control the expansion of domestic demand and increase the exports desperately needed to finance the huge foreign deficit, extensive price, import, investment and raw materials controls were retained and in some cases extended. Although there was a wave of nationalization of basic, mainly declining industries, accounting for perhaps 20 per cent of output in the late 1940s, there was no real attempt to use this stake strategically, to steer investment, as, for example, occurred in France. Economic planning, despite some gestures, was never taken seriously by the government, whose room for manoeuvre was severely restricted by the need for major international loans, principally from the USA, and the role of sterling as a reserve currency (see Shonfield, 1974; Hayward and Watson, 1975). From this time forward British economic growth was crippled by the combination of an endemic balance of payments problem and a determination not to devalue the pound. This led to a frequently repeated cycle of rising growth, resulting in rising imports and a balance of payments deficit, being countered by restrictive monetary policies and restricted growth. This stop–go cycle inhibited industrial investment and improvements in productivity.

In the 1950s, under Conservative administrations, the post-war controls were phased out and modest growth, in stop–go cycles, continued. In this period there was a clear trade-off between industrial growth and the maintenance of Britain's international financial standing. The outcome, in favour of the latter set of interests, reflects the frequently noted dominance of financial rather than industrial capital in the British political system. The British economy suffered from poor industrial structure and management, a lack of innovation and apparently no motivation, on the part of labour, capital or the state, to pursue a major process of economic modernization. In certain respects Britain continued to pay a price for its earlier economic development, not only in terms of its ageing capital stock and industries, but also because it was a fully urbanized society, with no great reserves of labour which could be freed from the rural sector to swell the industrial workforce and expand an urban-based domestic market. The population was growing only slowly and the limited immigration of Commonwealth citizens in the 1950s (cut off in the 1960s) had little impact on the size of the labour force. Comparative figures for the five European countries for 1949–59 show that the United Kingdom had the lowest gross investment ratio, growth of GNP and rise in productivity and the second slowest growing labour force during this period (Lieberman, 1977: 91).

By the early 1960s the failure of post-war economic policies was recognized across the political and economic spectrum. In a belated, ill-informed and half-hearted way, successive Conservative and Labour governments tried to combine elements of economic planning with the increasingly difficult maintenance of sterling as a reserve currency and the interests of financial capital. In 1965 a new Labour administration published the first, and so far the only, national economic plan, intending to provide the basis for rapid and sustained growth. Less than a year later it was abandoned, along with many of the government's plans for expanding welfare and other policies, as deflation together with price controls were imposed to stem a balance of payments and currency crisis. Devaluation eventually proved irresistible, occurring at the end of 1967, accompanied by more cuts, controls and tax increases aimed at shifting activity towards exporting. None of these expedients improved the low rate of economic growth. By the early 1970s the British economy, like most others, was experiencing rapidly rising inflation, growth driven by speculation and increasingly desperate governmental attempts to control the situation. The depth of the 1974/5 recession in Britain reflected the long-term weakness of its economy. In these two years gross domestic product (GDP) shrank faster than in any of the other countries under discussion and consumer prices rose faster, by 16 per cent in 1974 and a staggering 24.2 per cent in 1975 (Aldcroft, 1978: 237). Unemployment rose to an unprecedented post-war level, going well over 1 million (5 per cent of the workforce) by the end of 1975 and continuing to rise (Derbyshire and Derbyshire, 1990: 59).

Denmark also had a modest rate of economic growth up to the late 1950s. Like Britain, it had recurrent balance of payments crises, and governmental action to deal with these inhibited growth.[4] In Denmark's case, this was due to its dependence on manufactured imports and agricultural exports. Unlike Britain, Denmark still had a large agricultural sector in 1950. Subsequent Danish growth, as in France, Germany and the Netherlands, partially derived from the shift of activity and population from a rural economy to a modern industrial and service economy. In 1950 the Danish agricultural sector contributed around one-fifth of national output (as it had in 1930) and employed almost a quarter of the workforce. By 1970, after a particularly rapid change in the 1960s, these figures had shrunk to 8 per cent and 11 per cent respectively (Jörberg and Krantz, 1978: 384). Interestingly, though, in Denmark this change occurred without a major increase in urbanization, as it involved the growth of craft and smaller-scale industries, including many closely linked to the agricultural sector.

As we have already noted, Danish economic modernization faced considerable difficulties, given the lack of raw materials and dependence on agricultural exports. According to Jörberg and Krantz (1978: 405), policy makers had two choices when an upturn in growth led to balance of payments difficulties. They could either impose deflationary, growth-inhibiting, stop–go policies, or import foreign capital to meet the deficit, allowing growth to continue. In the 1950s Danish governments stuck to the first, 'British' alternative. This resulted in low growth and a continuing high level of unemployment. In part, the concern to maintain the value of the krone, even at the expense of industrial growth, reflected the strength of the rural exporting interests to which this policy was attuned. Not until the late 1950s, with some loss in the political strength of the rural sector, and with continuing high unemployment and low domestic demand, were the mainly urban industrial interests that supported the alternative policy able to have an impact. From this time the second approach was adopted and the growth rate improved. However, the Danish economy remained subject to balance of payments difficulties through the 1960s. The control of inflation, high interest rates and rising government expenditure became increasingly difficult. Apart from the impact of the latter on the expansion of welfare programmes in the 1960s, deteriorating terms of trade had severely affected farm incomes. Given the continuing political power of Danish agriculture, it is hardly surprising that, as in the 1930s, substantial state aid was provided. By 1968 over one-third of farm income consisted of subsidies.

While Britain failed to restructure its economy after the war, and Denmark did so only after a time and with considerable difficulty, France, the Netherlands and, above all, Germany managed economic modernization with a high degree of success. As we have already noted, of all the countries under consideration in this book, these three were by far the worst affected by the war. In addition, France and the Netherlands had stagnated throughout the interwar years and still retained large agricultural sectors and/ or limited and inefficient manufacturing sectors. Germany was a far more developed industrial economy before the war, but the new state of West Germany suffered from the loss of much of its manufacturing capacity, not just as a result of wartime destruction and plant dismantlement after the war, but also because of the loss of major manufacturing centres, now in communist East Germany. Germany, too, had a large, inefficient agricultural sector. While all three countries experienced remarkable rates of economic growth in the 1950s and 1960s, their economic policies differed considerably. Both France and the Netherlands adopted forms of economic planning, while German policy was strongly influenced by the neoliberal doctrine of the 'social market economy'.

Although French economic planning achieved a worldwide reputation, especially in the 1960s when, ironically, its major contributions to French growth were fading, the Dutch system of economic planning probably involved more extensive state intervention in the private sector.[5] At the end of the war, faced with a ruined economy and high inflation, there was an immediate currency reform and the imposition of price and wage controls. Like Britain and other European countries, the revival of industrial production was inhibited by a lack of foreign currency to pay for imports. Marshall Aid played an important early role in helping to resolve this problem. Meanwhile, a clear decision was taken, recognizing the prospects for long-term decline in agriculture, to complete the development of a modern, industrially based economy. A central planning bureau was established in 1945, the first that used input–output analysis to provide economic forecasts and advice to governmental and other policy makers. More importantly, a wartime legacy of close links between employers and employees was institutionalized in a corporatist system of economic bargaining over wages and prices that involved industry, the unions and the state. The government pursued an active industrial policy, assisting key industrial sectors and regional development. Counter-cyclical fiscal and monetary policies were used to manage demand. The main objective was to expand industry and exports, keeping down inflation and wages to raise international competitiveness. The system of wage and price controls and economic bargaining was remarkably successful in achieving this end. Large-scale industry, such as chemicals, petrochemicals and electronics, developed rapidly, attracting foreign investment. Real wage rises were restrained, despite a high level of employment – the first real wage rise occurred only in 1954. The expansion of the domestic market was aided by rapid population growth, from 9.5 million in 1947 to 13 million by 1970, boosted by a rising birth-rate and the loss of the Dutch colonies. The agricultural sector shrank from about 20 per cent of the economy in 1950 to 7 per cent by 1970. The share of industry increased in the 1960s, then fell back, as the growth dynamic shifted to services (de Vries, 1978: 31–44).

As elsewhere, however, from the 1960s it was increasingly difficult to sustain the 'virtuous circle' of high growth and employment and low inflation (together, by now, with a major expansion of welfare and other state expenditure). Initially, permitted wage increases had been tied to the consumer price index, which is why no rise in real wages occurred at first. But from 1953, increases were linked to productivity rises and, from 1959, after growing pressure from both sides of industry, these were differentiated by industry. With growing prosperity and the increasing integration of the Netherlands within the European Economic Community (EEC), state control over market processes could not be sustained and the consensual mechanisms for wages control faded away, although the Dutch government, like several others, subsequently tried to restrain inflation by unilaterally imposed prices and incomes controls.

While the Dutch managed, for a time at least, to combine high growth and low inflation, the French economy expanded despite high inflation.[6] Again, key factors were the decline of the rural sector, urban population growth and industrial modernization. The population rose from around 40 million in 1947 to 50 million by 1970, the share living in urban communes rose from 59 per cent in 1954 to 70 per cent by 1968, and there was major growth in and around Paris and the larger provincial towns, so that the numbers living in communes with a population of 50,000 or more rose from 9.9 million to 23.7 million. As late as 1954: 28 per cent of the population still worked in agriculture, but by 1970 this figure had been halved (Fohlen, 1978: 77–80, 118).

As in the Netherlands, there had been intensive discussion in the wartime resistance movements concerning post-war reconstruction. Large-scale nationalization and extensive state welfare was envisaged. Communists particularly supported the idea of a planned economy. However, in France, as elsewhere in Western Europe, the experience of the totalitarian Nazi and Stalinist regimes created opposition to command planning. Nevertheless, by 1945 the appalling economic and social conditions, the shortages of raw material and the difficulties of restarting production resulted in at least a partial conversion of key sectors of capital, labour and the state to the need for some form of planning.

As in Britain, the early post-war years saw a series of nationalizations which covered about 20 per cent of the economy. These involved some key economic sectors, including the major banks, and provided the government with a powerful influence over the pattern of new industrial investment. Unlike Britain or the Netherlands, however, price controls were rapidly scrapped, with some exceptions such as rental housing. Immediately after the war, in the conditions of great shortage, there was a high level of inflation, and price and wage inflation continued while the economy grew in the 1950s. In sharp contrast to policies in Denmark and Britain, the French government did little to stop this occurring, using frequent currency devaluations to keep exports competitive and to limit imports.

At first, French economic planning was limited to a few key basic industries (Shonfield, 1974; Hayward and Watson, 1975). The improvement of housing and consumer goods supplies had a low priority. The 'indicative' planning process involved close consultation between government and large-scale industrial producers (with a much more limited role for the unions), the setting of production targets and the use of government grants, loans and its control over the financial system and other parts of the economy to sustain growth in these sectors. The first Monnet Plan led to a rapid rise in employment and labour productivity in the industries with which it was concerned. However, in its early years, this modernization effort involved only a quite limited part of the economy. Moreover, while growth accelerated, wage earners received few benefits, as inflation outstripped pay rises. There was also considerable resistance to modernization by small-scale agricultural and industrial producers.

Only in the last years of the Fourth Republic, and especially after de Gaulle returned to power in 1958, were the political and social barriers to more broadly based modernization overcome.

Now successive four-year plans became more ambitious, setting targets for a wide range of industries, including housing, cars and other consumer durables. The Third Plan, covering 1958–61, set targets not just for basic industries, but also for education, health, housing and urban renewal, all of which needed restructuring, expansion and modernization if economic growth was to be sustained. Subsequent plans attempted to integrate economic and regional planning and to extend further the range of social, cultural and other services which came within its remit.

Despite these escalating planning ambitions, from the early 1960s there was a shift of emphasis away from planning, which had probably achieved its major successes by this point. Nevertheless, government control over the French economy remained extensive up to the early 1990s. Apart from state ownership of the key nationalized industries, it also built up big shareholdings in many private companies and controlled others through setting their investment and pricing policies. In addition, the state controlled the volume of credit in the economy by imposing lending ceilings, operated extensive price controls and established several investment funds to support economic, urban and regional development (V. Wright, 1989: 101–3).

As we have seen, in the 1950s devaluation and import controls were the main means by which governments responded to high inflation while allowing growth to continue. However, with the growth of the Common Market and competition for export trades, the pressure to improve French competitiveness became intense. In the early 1960s, Finance Minister Giscard d'Estaing, an economic liberal, reverted to a more orthodox economic stance, downgrading the role of planning and imposing strict price controls and a wage freeze to stem inflation.

The events of 1968, which led to large-scale wage rises, a political swing to the right, an era of less conflictual relations between industry and labour, and a new investment boom, ensured that the economy continued to grow exceptionally rapidly into the early 1970s. GDP, for example, grew consistently at well over 5 per cent per annum from 1970 to 1973, a better performance over this period than any of the other countries with which we are concerned (Aldcroft, 1978: 234). One measure of the relatively less serious impact of the mid-1970s depression on France was that, alone among our six countries, it did not in technical terms suffer more than a severe recession, as its GDP did not decline in 1974/5, even though industrial production contracted very sharply in 1975 and unemployment rose.

Although France and the Netherlands broke with past economic stagnation to follow a path of growth and economic modernization after the war, the most remarkable achievement was that of West Germany, which combined high growth, full employment, rising prosperity and low inflation for longer than any other nation.[7] German growth started from a very low base, but its phenomenal growth of output in the 1950s, at 7.8 per cent a year second only to Japan, and substantial, if less spectacular, growth in the 1960s, put it in the front rank of the world economies by 1970. In 1950 its per capita GNP was only just over one-third of the US level; by 1970, it was three-quarters of the US level. Productivity rose faster than in most other countries, manufactured exports boomed and inflation was kept way below that existing elsewhere. Between 1950 and 1963 (the year that Adenauer resigned as federal chancellor), unemployment fell from 1.5 million to a little over 100,000 (Lieberman, 1977: 203). In fact, full employment was achieved by the mid-1950s. Germany's rapid growth, low inflation and outstanding export performance led to a strong currency and large balance of payments surpluses, enabling a considerable rise in personal incomes and welfare expenditures to occur by the 1960s.

As elsewhere, growth was fed by a rising population. After the war there were mass inflows of refugees from the East and, until the building of the Berlin Wall in 1961, this influx continued from the German Democratic Republic. Later, around 3.4 million 'guest workers' and dependants flowed in from southern Europe and Turkey to meet the labour demands of Germany's expanding industries. Between 1950 and 1970 the West German population increased from about 50 million to just under 61 million (Flora, Kraus and Pfennig, 1987: 262). While in the immediate post-war period the resettlement of refugees and the reconstruction of ravaged cities and economic infrastructure placed an enormous burden on the economic and political system, there were also some economically beneficial consequences. Apart from the boost that resettlement and reconstruction gave to the economy, the refugees, many of whom had considerable skills and were willing to work hard for low wages just in order to survive, allowed German industry to retain a high proportion of its profits for reinvestment. Industrial growth was also fed by a rapid fall in the agricultural workforce, from 23 per cent of total employment in 1950 to 7.5 per cent in 1970 (Flora, Kraus and Pfennig, 1987: 519, 521). This change, together with the overall population growth, led to a rapid rise in the urban population, adding to the immense demand for new housing which had been created by wartime destruction. In fact, the population living in the larger urban settlements (with populations of 20,000 or more) rose by close to 10 million between 1950 and 1970, almost the same amount as the overall population growth (Flora, Kraus and Pfennig, 1987: 262).

Unlike the more *dirigiste* approach of France and the Netherlands, the German government adopted policies which encouraged and sustained private sector-led growth, while rejecting any overt attempt to intervene more directly to steer its course. The doctrine of the 'social market economy', which was based on neo-liberal economic thinking, was strongly advocated by Ludwig Erhard, the Minister of Economic Affairs throughout the Adenauer governments and the 'father' of the German 'economic miracle' (Lieberman, 1977: 195–201; Leaman, 1988: 48–80). In theory the social market economy involved the creation of a truly competitive market economy, free from government or private monopolies. Government intervention was intended only to curb monopoly power and, perhaps, deal with some of the more negative social consequences of the free competitive market.

Adoption of the social market economy had been only one of several contending views concerning how the German economy might be revived after the war, and was not strongly supported by all the allied occupying powers or by the Christian Democratic Union party which subsequently implemented it. However, in 1948, Erhard, who was then the chief economic policy maker for Bizonia (the US/British-occupied zones of what soon became West Germany), showed what it could achieve. The economy was still in chaos, with high inflation, a rampant black market, a useless currency and no recovery in production. Despite strong opposition, Erhard carried out a radical currency reform and rapidly removed economic controls. Production began to revive immediately, and inflation fell. The adoption of the social market economy by the first federal government was now settled.

Marshall Aid played a crucial role in helping German industry to pay for the imports that it required. But government policies, together with the lack of pressure for rapid wage rises, encouraged new investment. Tax policies allowed industry to retain much of its profits for reinvestment, the independent central bank ran a tight monetary policy, aimed at keeping inflation at an extremely low level, and price and currency stability helped export competitiveness. Especially in the 1950s, private consumption was restricted to allow for the high level of investment.

In fact, although the social market economy was supposed to entail minimal state intervention, this hardly depicts the actual relationship between the state and the private sector in West Germany. The state owned a substantial part of industry, including coal and iron ore mines, electricity and aluminium production and parts of the banking system. However, it mainly left these firms to be run as if they were under private ownership. In order to boost growth and to stabilize the political and social system of the new state, the government channelled substantial funds into industry and social welfare, financing this from the large tax revenues which resulted in budgetary surpluses. According to Lieberman (1977: 53), about 35–40 billion DM was lent, on easy terms, for private sector housebuilding, agriculture, coal mining and shipping between 1949 and 1957. Large tax exemptions were also provided for these and other industries. The expenditure on social welfare, though substantial in relation to national resources, at first provided no more than a basic safety net, although after the mid-1950s the welfare system began to grow more rapidly (Alber, 1986: 13–14).

By the end of the 1950s average earnings had risen by 160 per cent in ten years, the labour force had expanded by 60 per cent, consumption had grown at 6.6 per cent a year, while personal consumption as a proportion of GDP had actually fallen (Lieberman, 1977: 203). However, while the German economy continued to expand far more successfully than many others in the 1960s, it became increasingly difficult to sustain the 'miracle'. By mid-decade, many of the special factors which had resulted in the high growth rate in the 1950s were of declining significance. Also, with full employment, wage costs rose, while productivity gains slowed down. As in the other countries which had grown rapidly in the 1950s, with still relatively low, if growing, levels of social welfare expenditure, the 1960s saw a continuous rise in such spending, which took an ever higher share of GDP (Alber, 1986: 14–16). The independent central bank, still rigorously controlling inflation, managed, by imposing harshly deflationary monetary policies in the mid-1960s, to bring about Germany's first recession in 1966/7.

By 1967 unemployment had risen to just under 700,000 and German economic policy broke away from adherence to the Erhard formulation of the social market economy (Leaman, 1988: 175). The 1967–9 'Grand Coalition' between the CDU and the SPD, followed by the first ever West German federal administration led by the SPD, coincided with, and contributed to, what has been described as an experiment with Keynesian policies, as well as some tentative steps towards a form of economic planning, although these did not survive the mid-1970s recession. In 1967 a new law allowed the government to use Keynesian demand management regulators and, for the first time, counter-cyclical investment programmes were mounted (with substantial funding for new construction, including social housing). The government also tried to establish a form of economic corporatism through so-called 'concerted action', discussions between the state, employers and labour concerning limits for wages, profits and dividends. This was not very successful as the unions felt that they had the worst of the bargaining (as they did in other countries, such as Britain, where this was tried). By the mid-1970s Germany was suffering from stagflation, although less severely than many other countries. Industrial production fell in 1974 and 1975 and GDP in 1975, by which time unemployment was over 1 million, the highest level in 20 years (Aldcroft, 1978: 235; Leaman, 1988: 201).

With the benefit of hindsight one can identify some of the factors which led to the transition from the relatively settled economic world of the 1950s and 1960s to the much more turbulent conditions which have persisted over the past 15 or 20 years. The advantages obtained from labour released by large agricultural sectors, the modernization of underdeveloped industries and rapid population rises, resulted in 'one-off' gains to the economies in which they occurred. The elaborate international economic arrangements which served the US economy so well, and also benefited Western Europe, were destined to break down under the pressure of both changes in the relative economic performance of the advanced capitalist economies and 'external' changes. Market saturation, together with the inflationary consequences of full employment and rising military, welfare and other expenditures, all played their part in the ending of this 'golden age', dominated by 'Fordist' structures of accumulation. Two potent indicators of the declining dynamic of these Western economies are the fall in their growth rates from an average level of around 4.5 per cent per annum in the 1950s and 1960s, a historically unprecedented level, to around 2.8 per cent in the 1970s. By contrast, the average rise in consumer prices in the 1960s was 3.9 per cent, but in the 1970s this had more than doubled to 8.2 per cent, while the average level of unemployment rose from 1.8 per cent to 4.3 per cent.[8]

This era of prosperity involved a distinctive policy regime too, with a far greater degree of state economic intervention and management than hitherto. This was so even in the USA, where the ability of the private sector to expand on a massive scale and dominate world trade after 1945 was sustained by the state's political and military support. Above all, the economic growth of these years was made possible by the expansion of mass consumption in domestic economies and in export markets. The growth of housing investment and consumption, their multiplier effects and the stimulus that they gave to complementary industries were central features of this phenomenon. However, the provision of new housing on a massive scale was not just a response to rising levels of personal incomes and consumption, but was an essential precondition for economic growth, especially in those economies which benefited from population growth and a shift of economic activities from rurally based agriculture to urban-based manufacturing and services employment.

In all six countries under review, state involvement in housing was on an altogether different scale to what it had been before the war. However, the role played by social housing varied considerably. It was shaped not just by the different pathways to economic growth which we have described, but also by political differences which we now consider.

The politics of economic growth

In most of the countries under discussion, the sharp political differences which existed in the interwar years were less evident after 1945. The experiences of war had helped to create closer links between organized labour, capital and the state. In Europe, the immediate post-war crisis helped sustain these links. Subsequently, economic growth, which provided rising profits, incomes and welfare benefits, inhibited the re-emergence of the political conflict and polarization which had occurred in the 1930s, although there were frequent disputes over distributional issues. In this era the ability of the 'mixed economies' of welfare capitalism to function effectively was scarcely questioned, at least by the established political parties and the leaders of industry and labour. The extreme right virtually disappeared from the scene and, while some Western communist parties shared in government in the immediate aftermath of war, the onset of the Cold War ended opportunities to build on this base. The Cold War affected social democracy, which now, if not before, became committed to a moderate reformist path, working within the economic system to change its distributional outcomes through state action. Centre and right-wing parties now accepted that extensive state involvement in the economy and society would continue, in sharp contrast to their views after 1918 or even in the 1930s. In countries which had Christian as well as socialist trade unions, the incorporation of a section of the working class within centre–right Christian Democratic parties helped reinforce this commitment. Not until the economic breakdown of the 1970s did serious cracks begin to appear in these attitudes, with the emergence of a conviction, among some politicians and their advisers, that the boundaries between the state, the market and civil society were in need of radical adjustment.

The existence of some political consensus concerning the broad contours of welfare capitalism did not mean, however, that the nature of this consensus was the same everywhere. Its construction reflected the balance of social forces in each nation, as well as the economic circumstances discussed in the last section. In the United States both these factors, together with the Cold War, meant that the limits to welfare capitalism, or at least to welfare, were more confined than in Europe.[9] As we saw in the last chapter, by the late 1930s the New Deal was in retreat. There had never been a really strong political base for the New Deal reforms. The Democratic Party was an uneasy alliance between a variety of liberal groupings (including rural radicals, organized labour and some black representatives) and political descendants of the white, southern plantocracy which had fought the Civil War. The Republicans were also a somewhat divided party, combining so-called 'Wall Street' Republicans, supportive of a limited federal role in social welfare, and 'Main Street' conservatives, more strongly wedded to a minimal state role in social and economic policies.

The rightward trend in American politics continued in wartime. While in Britain the Labour Party entered the wartime coalition government, played a key role in maintaining trade union collaboration in the war effort and contributed substantially to plans for post-war social reform, in the United States Congress curtailed New Deal social programmes and passed anti-union legislation. Despite this, Roosevelt was re-elected (more narrowly than before) in 1944, promising a post-war bill of economic rights, including federally guaranteed employment, education, medical care, extended social security and 'the right of every family to a decent home'. Truman's intention, on succeeding to the presidency in 1945, was to continue with reform. As we have already noted, the 1944 Servicemen's Readjustment Act, the GI Bill of Rights, offered veterans free education, vocational training, medical care and subsidized housing, and the 1946 Employment Act charged the federal government with the duty of maintaining a high level of economic activity.

However, although there was a relatively smooth economic transition form war to peace, there was a brief period of high inflation, labour militancy and political turmoil over price controls. In the 1946 elections the conservative trend was intensified and the Republicans gained control of both Houses of Congress for the first time since 1928. Major legislation to weaken trade union power ensued. The 1947 Taft–Hartley Act banned the closed shop and imposed a cooling-off period before strike action. Congress also rejected limited-reform Republican proposals for federally aided education and housing. Although Truman campaigned on a reformist programme and won the 1948 election, regaining control of both Houses of Congress, there was no fundamental alteration in the conservative political domination. The modest revival of public housing in 1949, which we shall discuss below, was one of the few elements in Truman's 'Fair Deal' programme to survive the passage through Congress (Jones, 1987: 528).

From the late 1940s reform became not merely unfashionable; for some it became communistic and un-American. Truman himself had responded to the discovery of Soviet spies by instituting a 'loyalty program' in the civil service. An anti-communist witch hunt soon developed, culminating in McCarthyism, which targeted anyone who was suspected of 'fellow travelling', or even espousing social reform. As we shall see later, this campaign, reminiscent of the 'red scare' after the First World War, reinforced opposition to public housing.

After Eisenhower's election in 1952 the limits to the state's role in the economy and society seemed settled. Democratic control of Congress from 1954 onwards made little difference, and the stranglehold of the Southern conservatives on the key Congressional committees persisted until the next decade. On the one hand, Eisenhower (a 'Wall Street' Republican) left in place some of the key New Deal reforms, such as the Social Security Act. On the other hand, there was little desire to extend social policy and a determination to prune expenditure, balance the federal budget and sustain US business interests. This conservative version of welfare capitalism was possible because the dynamism of the economy made greater state involvement in steering its development unnecessary. Also, the rising prosperity of the middle class and large sections of the white working class meant that the 'social wage' was a far less politically potent issue than in Europe. Of course, despite the anti-union legislation, organized labour retained considerable strength and had an influence on the reformist sections of the Democratic Party. However, in practice, the way in which the largely conservative unions managed to extend their members' welfare in the 1950s was by pressing for better wages and fringe benefits.

Much of this new prosperity was used to purchase housing, automobiles and associated consumer durables. About the only major domestic reform that Eisenhower carried through was the 1956 Interstate Highway Act, which provided 90 per cent federal funding for road building (Warner, 1972: 45–52; Hall, 1988: 290–7). This, together with the continuing support for federal mortgage insurance programmes, reinforced the growth of home-owner suburbs on a massive scale. However, these developments contributed to a much more contradictory situation for non-white Americans. On the one hand, the expanding economic opportunities provided new jobs for many black Americans, formerly living in poverty in the South (as well as migrants from the Caribbean and elsewhere). On the other hand, many of the jobs were low-paid and located in declining inner-city areas, where poor housing and urban infrastructure was made worse by the loss of a more affluent population and property tax revenues to the suburbs (Fox, 1985). Federally supported downtown urban renewal worsened this situation. So, modernization of the urban system, occurring as a consequence of economic growth, had highly unequal consequences. The better off increased their share of national income and wealth while, in 1960, around one in four families was still in poverty (Morison, Commager and Leuchtenberg, 1980: 727).

The extent to which John Kennedy's presidency marked a clear break with this conservative version of welfare capitalism is questionable. Kennedy's main concerns were to make the USA more successful in the competition with communism and to speed up economic growth. Moreover, his attempts to extend welfare provision (including the creation of a federal Department of Urban Affairs) were blocked by the powerful combination of Republicans and conservative Southern Democrats (Jones, 1987: 548). In so far as the administration did respond to inner-city poverty and racial discrimination, it has been argued that this was largely a consequence of the growing political significance of minority groups and rising social disorder in segregated urban areas (Piven and Cloward, 1971: 1977). Certainly, the poverty programmes and other reforms did not involve radically redrawing the limits to state intervention in a market-driven system.

In fact, the most significant period of social reform since the New Deal occurred when Johnson succeeded to the presidency. Now more liberal forces began to gain ascendancy in Congress, just as an ex-New Dealer and a highly skilled political operator became President. Amid considerable social and political turmoil, he was able to initiate formerly blocked poverty programmes, civil rights legislation, federal aid to education, the provision of medical care for the poor and the aged, and housing and other urban programmes. He also established the federal Department of Housing and Urban Development. Johnson's 'Great Society' programme briefly shifted the focus of American politics back towards the liberal hopes of an earlier generation of social reformers. However, a new conservative bloc was in formation, based on the Southern and Western states, although its first presidential candidate, Barry Goldwater, was crushed by Johnson in the 1964 election. But the disaster of Vietnam destroyed the Johnson presidency, the civil rights and ghetto revolts which had pressurised the system for social reform were stricken by the assassinations of Malcom X and Martin Luther King, and the liberal cause by the assassination of Robert Kennedy. The climate of disorder and dissent, as well as the accelerating economic problems, provided fertile ground for the emergence of a new, more radical conservatism.

However, the return to a more limited federal role in urban and social policy did not immediately follow the election of Nixon to the presidency in 1968, partly because Congress was still extending programmes and benefits. Nevertheless, two aspects of Nixon's approach to social policy were of lasting importance (Fox, 1985: 206–20). The first was the desire to reduce the role of the federal government, transferring responsibilities to state and local governments and providing block rather than categorical grants. The second was the switch from a 'service' to an 'income' strategy, the substitution of cash grants for specific services, the argument being that this would expand choice and freedom and reduce bureaucracy. Nixon also used the power of impoundment, on a far larger scale than previous Presidents, to prevent money that had been allocated by Congress being expended. As we discuss below, these developments had important consequences for housing policy.

While the United States recovered rapidly from the war and turned its back on any significant extension of New Deal social policies, Britain took almost the reverse course, struggling to come to terms with its weakened economy and, in 1945, electing its first majority Labour government.[10] Labour campaigned on the need for new housing, the reform of social insurance, full employment, economic planning and modernization. In practice, while the government enacted major social reforms, including the first effective town and country planning legislation, controls on industrial location and a mass council housing programme, as we have seen, it lacked the clear commitment to economic planning and modernization which occurred elsewhere in Europe, and was constrained by its economic dependency on the USA and the maintenance of Britain's role as a major military and financial power. According to Morgan (1990: 70), by 1947 '[d]emocratic socialism, Britain's "middle way", assumed a defensive air, its main work already accomplished'.

The Conservative government elected in 1951 recognized the need to accept the broad outlines of the welfare state as established after 1945, together with the commitment to use Keynesian demand management to ensure full employment. As in America, therefore, there emerged a relatively moderate conservatism, vying with an increasingly moderate social democracy. In the 1950s successive Conservative administrations sustained, and modestly extended, many social programmes while avoiding detailed involvement in economic modernization. Apart from the removal of economic controls, which had begun under Labour, the sharpest changes of direction occurred in housing and town planning (Hall, 1980: 99–154). Labour's nationalization of land development values was abandoned and the private housing market was heavily promoted. We discuss these changes below.

Despite recurrent balance of payments crises and the disastrous Suez adventure in 1956, the Conservatives, aided by rising prosperity and full employment, benefited electorally, with easy wins in the 1955 and 1959 elections. By the latter date influential analysts argued that, with rising real incomes and the growth of home ownership, Labour's policies now only appealed to a shrinking section of the traditional working class (Abrams and Rose, 1960). The so-called 'embourgeoisification' of the working class was undermining the electoral base of the party. In fact, as subsequent studies and events showed, this doomsday scenario was false (see, for example, Goldthorpe et al., 1968). However, by the end of the 1950s, much of the Labour Party leadership accepted the need for radical revisions to the party's programme if it was again to appeal to the mass of working-class and a wide section of middle-class voters. What was clear was that Labour needed to move beyond its traditional working-class electorate, like other European Social Democratic parties, if it was to regain power.

The failure of post-war governments to deal with the underlying weaknesses of the British economy, and the sharp contrast between this failure and the success stories in France, West Germany and elsewhere, became increasingly apparent from the early 1960s. This recognition was not, however, matched by an effective political response. One mistake was undoubtedly the earlier decision to remain aloof from the Common Market. When Britain did finally manage to join in 1973, as Larkin (1988: 194) notes, 'its other

industrial members had developed such a head-start that its competition was traumatic rather than a stimulating experience'.

When Labour returned to government in 1964, it campaigned
on a pledge to modernize. In a famous phrase, its leader Harold
Wilson promised that the government would harness the 'white
heat of a second industrial revolution', rejecting past economic and
social conservatism. This message was aimed at the professional
middle class as well as the (relatively) affluent new working class.
Two new ministries were established to spearhead industrial modernization and to produce a national plan. Higher education was
expanded, with seven new universities by 1966. However, as we
have seen, these good intentions faded as domestic expansion was
again sacrificed to maintain sterling's international role. Although
Labour won an increased majority in 1966, its remaining years in
office were marked by the reimposition of orthodox stop–go policies with severe cuts in public expenditure. In addition, there was
now an attempt to control inflation by prices and wages controls.
Political infighting escalated among government ministers and there
was a worsening relationship with the trade unions as Labour
failed in an attempt to legislate for their reform. When devaluation was eventually forced on the government late in 1967, cuts
in public expenditure became even deeper, in an attempt to de-
press domestic demand and expand exports. This finally brought
the balance of payments under control, but did nothing to foster
economic restructuring and growth, nor to advance Labour's social
policy objectives. Labour's brief attempt to remould the British
economy had met with dismal failure.

After a surprise election victory in 1970, the new Conservative
government promised a different route to economic regeneration,
abolishing or curtailing the institutions and policies through which
Labour had attempted to reorganize and modernize industry, cutting
taxes and social expenditure and encouraging competition. At first
this seemed to mark a radical break with the post-war consensus.
However, these policies were rapidly abandoned as the government struggled with the new phenomenon of stagflation. Faced with
powerful union demands for higher wages and rising unemployment,
the government reversed its industry policy, providing major job-
saving subsidies, and tried to establish a form of corporate economic management in consultation with the unions and employers.
Again, wage and price controls were imposed in an attempt to
stem inflation. However, by now, factors beyond the government's
control were rapidly eroding the post-war regime of growth and
full employment, and this foredoomed any attempt to recreate a

consensual approach to economic and social policies. The accession of Britain to the Common Market in 1973 had little immediate impact. By the end of this year the government was in disarray as the inflationary boom ran out of control. As the government sought to resist a miners' strike, a state of emergency was declared and industry was restricted to a three-day week. As a last desperate throw the government called an election on the theme of 'who governs Britain?'. It lost narrowly and Labour returned to power as a minority government.

In Denmark, there was strong resistance to the Nazi occupation and a form of semi-independent government survived until 1943.[11] The pre-war political parties and system were re-established in 1945. In elections in October 1945, the Social Democrats retained their pre-war position as the largest party. Fearing losses to the Communists (who had refused to merge with the Social Democrats), and believing that the war might be followed by a revolutionary period, the party campaigned on a more left-wing programme than in the 1930s, with proposals for a planned economy, nationalization, economic democracy and the expansion of social security. However, as Esping-Andersen (1985: 91) notes, most of the programme concentrated on short-term measures such as rationing, controls and the restoration of economic competitiveness. In the event, the expected political and social crisis did not occur and, while the Conservatives and Radical Liberals lost votes, the Liberals gained ground and formed a minority government with their tacit support. In the 1947 election the Liberals gained more seats, but were replaced by a minority Social Democrat government. Apart from a brief interlude in the early 1950s, the Social Democrats remained in government until the late 1960s, normally in alliance with the Radical Liberals. Regardless of government changes, domestic policies centred on finding solutions to Denmark's economic problems, which have already been outlined. Although, as we shall see, housing policies played a role in this situation, major developments in other social policies occurred only from the late 1950s, when the take-off to sustained growth and full employment began.

For 25 years Danish politics was dominated by the four main 'system parties', the Social Democrats, Radical Liberals, Liberals and Conservatives. No single party obtained a parliamentary majority, so coalition government was essential, with the major left/right divide running between the Social Democrats and Radical Liberals, on the one hand, and the Conservatives and Liberals, on the other. Only after 1957 were the Social Democrats able to form a majority government with the Radical Liberals. This was when the political defences of the farmers were sufficiently weakened for Denmark to embark on a determined policy of economic modernization, social reform and income redistribution.

The lack of a dominant political bloc meant that major policy developments were preceded by negotiations and compromises between the major parties, so much legislation eventually passed through Parliament unopposed. While the Social Democratic Party continued to campaign on its radical post-war programme until the end of the 1950s, its scope for implementing this was highly constrained by the need to sustain coalitions and for political bargaining over policies. Despite their moderation in government, the Social Democrats were unable to regain the peak level of electoral support which they had achieved in 1935. As in the case of the British Labour Party, by the early 1960s the 1945 programme seemed an electoral liability at a time when the party's traditional working-class constituency was being eroded by economic and social developments. So, in 1961, it moved back to a more reformist programme, targeted at the growing mass of white-collar workers. This was unsuccessful, as Elder, Thomas and Arter (1982: 20) note: 'it did little to excite the imagination of a generation that simply assumed the security and prosperity that the Social Democrats had had a large hand in creating'. Instead, the party's base continued to decline as it came under fire from the left for its lack of socialism, and from the right, which began to attract the votes of newly affluent workers, some of whom were becoming home owners.

Housing policy, like other social policies, evolved on the basis of interparty bargaining, although it was a more politically contentious topic than many others (see Esping-Andersen, 1985: 179–86). In 1964, when the Radical Liberals decided to leave the government, the first possibility opened up to form a majority socialist government with the new, left-wing Socialist Peoples party.[12] The Social Democrats decided, however, to remain as a minority government, concluding a new pact on housing policies which, as we discuss later, was a compromise with the right-wing parties. In ensuing elections the Socialist Peoples Party gained considerable support by attacking this 'sell-out' and after the 1966 election the Radical Liberals switched their allegiance to the bourgeois parties. The Social Democrats struggled on until 1968, but were then replaced by a coalition of the Liberals and Conservatives under Radical Liberal leadership. As in Britain, social democracy was increasingly immobile in the face of a worsening economic climate. Now a centre–right government attempted to control inflation and public expenditure. Like the Heath government in Britain, it failed as taxes and spending grew faster than ever and the trade unions refused to cooperate in wage restraint. In 1971 the Social Democrats returned, heading a minority government whose politics were dominated by the fiercely contested entry to the EEC and by a further politically disastrous attempt at housing reform, details of which will be discussed below. The proposed housing legislation led to the formation of a breakaway Centre Democratic Party and new elections in 1973.

This fragmentation of the socialist bloc was one aspect of a wider breakup of the political system, based on the four old parties and grounded in a wide measure of consensus, in practice if not in theory, about social and economic policy. As the economic climate became more turbulent, from the 1960s onwards, political fragmentation and realignment began to occur. As Elder, Thomas and Arter (1982: 98) note, referring to parallel developments in the Scandinavian countries, 'much of the electoral mobility of the 1970s stemmed from a protest against the inability of the established party system to maintain, through a period of declining economic growth, the affluent standards to which the Scandinavians had grown accustomed'. In Denmark the rapidly rising burden of taxation, as welfare programmes expanded while growth faltered, provided the basis for the dramatic emergence of the populist Progress Party, committed to stringent reductions in welfare and other government expenditure. Formed just before the 1973 election, it immediately gained 28 seats in the Folketing, making it the second largest party. This election (dubbed the 'Catastrophe Election') appeared to mark the end of the four-party system. These parties' share of parliamentary seats (already eroded by the growth of the Socialist Peoples Party in the 1960s) fell from 88 per cent to 58 per cent. Although the Social Democrats and Conservatives regained some lost ground later in the decade, both Liberal parties remained severely weakened. In consequence, Danish politics became more polarised and conflictual. Changes in the economy affected these political shifts, weakening the rural and 'old' middle class, the basis for the Liberal parties. The Radical Liberal losses undermined the basis for the former 'Red–Green' coalition. Meanwhile, the growing strength of the new middle class provided support for a variety of centre–right groupings.

While the Danish political system survived the war years, the collapse of the Third Republic in France and the subsequent Vichy regime prevented any such continuity.[13] After the liberation of Paris in 1944, a provisional government was formed, led by de Gaulle and containing Socialist, Communist, Gaullist and other non-socialist Ministers. During the war the Socialists had played the major role in drawing up a programme for post-war social and economic reform, including large-scale nationalization and the extension of social security programmes. In 1945/6 some steps were taken to implement this plan by the provisional government. Some industries were nationalized and social security was reformed. However, wartime demands for economic democracy were watered down. Meanwhile, a unicameral Assembly was elected in October 1945 to prepare a new constitution.

It soon became clear that the system of weak and fragmented government of the Third Republic would be perpetuated in the Fourth Republic. De Gaulle became disenchanted and withdrew to the sidelines, although his political supporters remained active throughout the following years, seeking an opportunity to overturn a political system which, in their view, could only perpetuate a weak executive and a lack of political direction. The left parties and trade unions remained split between the Communists and the Socialists. A new centrist cross-class Christian Democratic party, the MRP, at first attracted many conservative voters who had nowhere else to go following the demise of the discredited traditional conservative parties. Despite the reformist tendencies of the MRP's first leader, it drifted to the right under this influence. Alongside these major groupings, the political scene was completed by the remnants of the pre-war Radical and conservative parties.

It appears paradoxical that, in this system of weak government, any progress could be made with the restructuring of the French economy. Not until the collapse of the Fourth Republic and the return to power of de Gaulle in 1958 was there a government with a clear and central commitment to this goal. In the interim, the long-term economic planning which spearheaded modernization was pushed forward by some politicians and members of the powerful administrative elite which sustained much of the day-to-day development of policies and administration, as it had in the Third Republic.

The political history of the Fourth Republic fell into several phases. The first terminated with the collapse of the Socialist, Communist and MRP coalition which had formed immediately after the war. In May 1947 the Communists were excluded from government, partly under American influence and in exchange for that country's vitally needed financial support. They did not return to government until 1980. The second phase lasted from 1947 to 1951. It was marked by the emergence of the Gaullist RPF, a rightist grouping, paralleling the Communists on the left, excluded from government and inimical to the new constitutional regime. Now the centre of gravity of politics shifted as the Socialists and the MRP became dependent on Radicals and conservatives to form a government. The Socialists were faced with a choice of leaving the governing coalition or remaining increasingly helpless within it, as the Communists continued to attract the votes that it needed to become the dominant governing party. In the third phase, after the 1951 election, there was a further move to the right, as the conservatives, Radicals and MRP formed several governments, excluding the Socialists.

There were several important developments in this period, notably the establishment by Robert Schuman, the long-serving MRP Foreign Minister, of the European Coal and Steel Community, the forerunner of the Common Market. However, the key economic concern was to reduce the high rate of inflation by orthodox means, attempting to cut public and constrain private investment. This hindered economic growth. Throughout the many changes of government, the planning agency (Commissariat Général du Plan) remained largely isolated from these political events. Indeed, the first 'Monnet' Plan (1947–52) and the second 'Hirsch' Plan (1954–7) were never placed before Parliament. The first plan, which set output targets for seven basic industries, achieved most of its targets. The second plan was also restricted to five of the seven basic industries contained in the first plan, and to the two key elements of consumption that were necessary to ensure a basic standard of living for the expanding urban labour force – food (actually meat and wheat) and housing. As we have already noted, later plans, while more wide-ranging and technically sophisticated, were less influential, especially from the 1960s onwards, when the main unions rejected participation in their preparation because of their inability to influence the process and affect distributional outcomes, and because of the hostility of the Ministry of Finance.

By the mid-1950s there was a high level of political fragmentation. The 1956 election was notable for the election of right-wing deputies associated with Pierre Poujade, who led a movement of *petit bourgeois* shopkeepers and small farmers, a formerly powerful socio-political grouping whose fortunes were declining as a result of economic modernization and urbanization. Essentially, there was now a right-wing bloc of conservatives, Gaullists and the MRP and a left-wing bloc of some Radicals and the Socialists, with the Communists and Poujadists outside any alliance. The left remained fundamentally divided, however. So, while the Socialists continued to hold office in a variety of Cabinets until the final collapse of the Fourth Republic, it was unable to press ahead with major social reforms, given its inability to form a left alliance with the Communists, as it had in 1936. There were, however, some improvements in social security benefits and increased support for social rented housing. By now, economic growth was beginning to accelerate, although at the cost of an adverse balance of payments. In this period, too, France signed the Treaty of Rome, becoming a founder member of the Common Market. Less gloriously, it also participated in the Suez adventure and in an increasingly brutal and damaging civil war in Algeria.

In early 1958 the Radical-led government was heavily defeated over its Algerian policy. After several months of political crisis, with rising discontent among the Algerian settlers and the army, some of whom planned a *coup d'état*, de Gaulle returned to head a cross-party coalition (excluding the Communists) with emergency powers and the remit to prepare a new constitution. This received a large majority in a referendum. It provided for a strong presidency and Council of Ministers and a weak legislature, reversing the balance in the Third and Fourth Republics. In the subsequent election the Gaullists won a major victory, with over 42 per cent of the Assembly seats, and various conservative groupings got another 27 per cent. The other Fourth Republic parties were destroyed. De Gaulle was subsequently elected President by an overwhelming majority.

These changes installed a series of strong right-wing governments in France which continued to hold power, in one form or another, for two decades. The major parties in the governing coalition were the Gaullists and a group of conservatives (the Républicains Indépendants) led by the future Prime Minister and President, Giscard d'Estaing. The changes also brought to power the technocratic elite which had been pressing forward with modernization throughout the previous years. Several now gained government office, one of whom, Pompidou, succeeded de Gaulle as President. As V. Wright (1989: 44) comments, Pompidou, who was Prime Minister from 1962 to 1968 and President from 1969 to 1974, while a 'firm political and social conservative' was 'in one important respect ... a radical: he was obsessed by the need economically to transform France, by the need to make his country a great industrial power. And to that end a great deal was sacrificed: the environment and greater social justice were among the victims'. Especially in the early years of the Republic, when Giscard d'Estaing was Minister of Finance, these policies were pursued within a framework of financial orthodoxy, and wages and consumption remained depressed while profits soared.

Workers' dissatisfaction with their limited share in the benefits of economic growth was a key element in the 1968 'events' in France. Although the revolt was started by the students, this was followed by a wave of strikes and plant occupations, riots and other demonstrations. Eventually, the Grenelle agreements between the unions, employers and government brought about a significant rise in wages and some other benefits. However, in the subsequent election, the government increased its domination of the National Assembly, with the Gaullists gaining an absolute majority, the first time any party had done this since 1870. The left and centre parties were reduced to a rump. The new administration responded to some of the grievances which had been expressed through the 'events', with university reform and some extensions of trade union and worker rights. More significantly, de Gaulle finally retired and Pompidou easily won the subsequent presidential election over a deeply divided left and centre. Unlike de Gaulle, who had a limited involvement in the domestic policies of his regime, Pompidou focused on accelerating the modernization of the French economy and society and supported many large-scale building projects, including the poorly planned and serviced suburban housing developments which degraded the environment of major cities and were a source of major social problems in the following decade (see V. Wright, 1989: 63).

After Pompidou's death in 1974, tensions within the governing bloc began to intensify. The Gaullists had their internal tensions and had always been more united on foreign than on domestic affairs. Some favoured a more paternalistic combination of economic and social reform, while others leant towards free market liberalism. However, the major divide was between the Gaullists and Giscard d'Estaing's Independent Republican grouping. In the 1960s the Gaullists were dominant, but Pompidou's death left them in disarray, leading to the election of Giscard to the presidency in 1974. The accession of Jacques Chirac to the leadership of the (frequently renamed) Gaullist party began a period of reorganization, so by the following decade the party was re-established as the leading party of the right. Meanwhile, Giscard moved to consolidate and expand his base, swallowing up the remnants of the Radicals, the political heirs of the long-defunct MRP and other centrist groups to form the Union pour la Démocratie Française (UDF). Throughout the 1970s, the long process of reconstruction of the left was also under way. By the late 1960s the 'old' Socialist Party, the SFIO, virtually ceased to exist. But in the early 1970s a variety of left groupings, including the rump of the SFIO, came

together to form the Parti Socialiste (PS) under the leadership of
François Mitterrand. The PS developed a party programme which
attracted most working-class votes and a considerable proportion
of white-collar voters. By the end of the 1970s the PS had supplanted the Communist Party (PCF) as the dominant party of
the left, reversing the previous situation.

By the mid-1970s the bipartisan character of French politics
was established. It reflected not just the political developments
of the previous decades, but the underlying changes in the economy
and class structure – the decline of the rural and urban *petite
bourgeoisie* and the political parties which represented their interests,
secularization and the spread of education, urbanization and the
growth of a new working class, many of whom now worked in
service industries rather than manufacturing, and a new salariat
of managers and professionals (see V. Wright, 1989: 151–66).

As in France, plans for the post-war modernization of the Dutch
economy and the expansion of welfare were made during the war
years (van Kersbergen and Becker, 1988).[14] There were also wartime moves to reconstruct Dutch politics on a more cooperative
basis (Irwin and van Holsteyn, 1989). However, the pre-war structures reappeared after the war with three Confessional parties,
the two strongest of whom, the KVP and the ARP, continued to
attract a high level of cross-class support from members of their
respective denominations.[15] A key development had occurred in
occupied Holland when, in 1940, the trade union federations and
employers' associations negotiated a secret pact and established
the Foundation of Labour (Wolinetz, 1989). Equally importantly,
the Catholic and Socialist parties agreed to work together in the
post-war government. It had been the refusal of the Catholics to
ally with the Socialists in the interwar period that had excluded
the latter from government until the crisis in 1939 occurred. There
was also agreement across the political spectrum on the need to
abandon the rigid orthodoxies of the pre-war years and to adopt
some of the economic policies prefigured by the 1935 Labour Plan.
A series of corporatist structures, which were particularly strongly
advocated by the KVP, involving capital, labour and the state,
were established to sustain economic modernization. The employers
agreed to recognize the unions and to endorse the full employment
goal. The unions agreed to avoid strikes and not to press their
demands for economic democracy. There were also some welfare
reforms, partly influenced by the Beveridge proposals for the UK,
including a Pensions Act in 1947 and an Unemployment Insurance
Act in 1949.

Van Kersbergen and Becker (1988) suggest several reasons why there was general support for these policy developments, including the impact of the war in radicalizing the more conservative parties, a perceived need for social and economic reform to meet the challenge of communism in the Cold War period, the need for domestic economic modernization to compensate for the loss of colonial revenues from the Dutch East Indies, and the dependence of the Confessional parties, especially the KVP (which espoused the corporatist doctrines of Catholic social policy) on working-class support. Only the Communist Party remained outside this broad consensus, being strongly opposed by all other parties. Partly because of its role in the resistance, the party gained 10 per cent of the vote in the 1946 election, but its support then faded. The Liberal VVD, a true conservative rather than a centrist party, retained its secular, middle-class electorate, based on self-employed traders and shopkeepers, but found it hard to broaden its electoral base (Irwin and van Holsteyn, 1989). It shared in several governments but, after a brief period of cohabitation in government between 1948 and 1952, the PvdA and the VVD refused to participate in the same cabinet, thus both becoming dependent on alliances with the Confessional parties.

These post-war agreements involved several compromises. At first the government was reluctant to accept the Foundation of Labour as significant institution in the system of regulated wages which it established. The PvdA was more strongly in favour of economic planning than the other groups (van Kersbergen and Becker, 1988). In the event, the Socialists had to settle for the establishment in 1950 of a national tripartite Social and Economic Council, to provide advice on economic and industrial policy to the government. Moreover, although a Central Planning Bureau was established, this mainly provided forecasts and did not result in the comprehensive system of democratic economic planning which the PvdA had desired. More generally, the PvdA favoured state intervention in a wide range of economic and social policies, while the other parties continued their pre-war tradition of supporting state aid for 'private initiative'. Eventually, the PvdA moved towards a more moderate reformism, aiming to sustain full employment and growth in a 'mixed' economy by Keynesian means and to expand social welfare (spending on which was also regarded as a useful way of regulating economic demand, at least until the mid-1970s). In these respects there are strong similarities between the Dutch, French, British, German and Danish socialists, all of whom settled for an expanded welfare capitalism in the post-war years.

In the Netherlands, as in Denmark, the Social Democrats were unable to govern, except in a coalition with non-socialist parties. Therefore, the party was forced to accept severe limitations on what it could achieve. The strength of the Confessional parties, especially the KVP, persisted after 1945. In fact, from the onset of universal suffrage in 1917 until 1967, the religious parties together always obtained over 50 per cent of the vote in general elections (Daalder, 1987). After 1945 the Socialists made strenuous efforts to widen the social base of their electorate and to make the transition from a 'workers' party' to a 'people's party' (Wolinetz, 1989). However, surveys in the 1950s showed that the PvdA was unable to attract the support of more than about one-third of working-class voters (Irwin and van Holsteyn, 1989). Like the Danish Socialists, the Dutch party was fated to remain in the minority. In the Netherlands the main reason for this was the cross-cutting influence of religious divisions on the class structure. The dependence of the PvdA on a governing alliance with the KVP led, in time, to a considerable tension within the party, as its left wing had little chance of being included in cabinets or of seeing its policies implemented.

The alliance between the KVP and the PvdA (with varying participation by the other Confessional parties) lasted until 1958. Eventually, however, the PvdA, concerned at electoral losses and the limits imposed by the need for policy compromises, withdrew from government. There followed a series of Confessional–Liberal governments until 1965. After a brief return to a Confessional–PvdA government, another centre–right coalition was formed.

A key feature of these years was the breakup of the system of wage controls. From the mid-1950s the employers and the Socialist and Catholic trade unions had argued for differentiated wage rises, but attempts to include this within the corporate planning and decision-making structures failed (Wolinetz, 1989). In the 1960s, with full employment and rapid economic growth, the pressure for large wage rises proved irresistible. By the end of the decade the unions were strongly in favour of a return to free collective bargaining.

However, despite the growing conflict concerning economic policy, the alternation of centre–left and centre–right governments made relatively little difference as far as welfare policies were concerned, although, as van Kersbergen and Becker (1988) note, the extension of social security occurred 'on Christian Democratic terms' (that is, with a continued emphasis on the importance of 'private initiative'). As Daalder (1989: 15) has noted, the consultations which occurred between the different political representatives of the social 'pillars' that characterised Dutch policy making were sustained by similar links elsewhere. So special interest groups within each pillar formed 'confederal forms of concertation' with their counterparts. These 'special interest groups, cooperating across sub-cultural lines, jointly represented powerful political and social forces. Successive governments found it profitable to share with such interests in the elaboration of new policies, and often to leave them a substantial share of practical execution and daily administration'. Pressure from such groups, together with rising prosperity in the 1960s, led to a considerable expansion in social expenditure, as new programmes were added and benefits increased (including a statutory minimum wage from 1968, to which benefits were index-linked in 1974). Most of these changes were implemented by centre−right governments. One source of pressure for enhanced welfare was the shift to a more radical political and social climate, with the emergence of a more active left, outside and within the PvdA, and growing pressure on the KVP to retain its working-class support by means of social reform (van Kersbergen and Becker, 1988).

By the end of the 1960s cracks were appearing in the hitherto stable system of political parties. The five 'system parties', the PvdA, the VVD and the three Confessional parties (KVP, ARP and CHU) represented the distinctive 'pillars' of the Dutch social structure.[16] But economic changes and secularization began to weaken these structures. As elsewhere, there was also a rapid rise in the number of white-collar workers in the public and other services, to form a new, increasingly secular middle class. One consequence of these changes was a growth in the fluidity of the political system. Another was the merger of the Catholic and Socialist trade union federations, after the former had broken ideologically with the KVP, in 1976 (Wolinetz, 1989). In the mid-1960s one new party had already emerged, the Democrats '66 (D '66), which consisted of dissidents within the PvdA and KVP who were disappointed by the collapse of the centre−left government in that year.

The PvdA leadership came under increasing attack from the left, which pointed to the loss of electoral support suffered by the party and the failure to implement socialist policies owing to the need for compromise with coalition partners. Eventually, the PvdA adopted a more left-wing programme, distanced itself from the Catholics and insisted that it should take the leading role in any new coalition. In the early 1970s it formed an electoral alliance with D '66 and a left-wing faction which had split from the KVP. In 1973 the party was at least able to form a government, which it dominated numerically (the first and only one in Dutch political history so far), with a majority of ministers from the socialist allies and a minority of KVP and ARP members. This lasted until 1977, although it proved incapable of implementing the socialist allies' radical programme, which included measures of industrial democracy, land reform, profit sharing and investment controls. It was still constrained by the need to maintain an alliance with the Confessionals and, like Social Democratic parties elsewhere, lacked a viable programme for dealing with the worsening economic situation. Like other governments, however, it tried using direct wage and price controls, combining these with increased welfare benefits and a rise in the minimum wage.[17] This occurred when growth was fading, inflation rising, the older sections of Dutch industry rapidly declining and when there was increasing confrontation between the two former 'social partners', the unions and the employers. As we have seen, other economies were facing such problems. However, there were some additional features in the Netherlands, where the controlled and rather low-wage system had sustained some labour-intensive older industries, but, in the new era of deregulation and higher wages, a rapid rationalization occurred as employers made labour-saving investments (van Kersbergen and Becker, 1988).

Meanwhile, the KVP had been losing support; its vote shrank from around one-third of the electorate up to 1963 to under 18 per cent by 1972. The CHU vote also fell. This led the Confessionals towards the formation of a single party. By the early 1970s the parties had formed an electoral alliance, and in 1976 they formed a single parliamentary group. A complete merger occurred in 1980 when the Christian Democratic Appeal (CDA) was formed. The new party had a share of the electorate similar to that obtained by the KVP alone in the early 1960s. One consequence of these changes was the marginalization of the 'workerist' elements in the former Catholic and Protestant parties. The new CDA was a considerably more conservative grouping, inclined to seek alliances with the Liberal VVD (whose support had grown as a result of the rise of the secular middle class) rather than with the PvdA, which, in any event, now demanded the leading role in any governing coalition. With these developments it was clear that the basis for the unique combination of pillarised social structures and corporatist and confederal decision making concerning social and economic policy, which had been constructed after 1945, had been further weakened, although as Lijphard (1989) has recently argued, the

Netherlands continued to retain a higher degree of the 'politics of accommodation' than many other democracies.

The post-war reconstruction of the German political system was necessarily a far more radical affair than in any of the other countries with which we are concerned. [18] Not only was a new constitution needed, but, with most Weimar parties thoroughly discredited by their interwar role, a recasting of the non-socialist political groupings as well. The SPD emerged from its years of exile as the main socialist party, rejecting an invitation to unite with the Communists. The latter party survived until it was declared unconstitutional in 1956, although it re-emerged in 1968. However, the division of Germany, which removed its Weimar strongholds in the East, and the Cold War, ensured that it never regained its pre-war significance.

The second major party, which governed Germany for the next 20 years, was the Christian Democratic Union (CDU). This was formed in 1948 by former members of the Catholic Weimar Centre Party and more conservative northern Protestants. Like other Christian Democratic parties it aimed to appeal across the classes and had close links with the Christian trade unions. It was closer to the centrist parties of the Weimar Republic than to the conservative parties which had existed in the 1920s. The latter, like the Communists, had lost some of their former strongholds with the division of the country (Alber, 1986: 96). The connections between the Catholic church and the party were stronger than those with the Protestant churches and the influence of Catholic social doctrines meant that a 'workerist' faction persisted in the party. Indeed, in its first major policy statement, the Ahlen programme, drawn up before the establishment of the new state, the CDU called for large-scale nationalization. As Berghahn (1982) notes, at this time there was strong support for socialism, so non-socialist politicians had to persuade the electorate that capitalism could provide benefits for them, not just for a restricted elite, as had occurred before and during the Weimar period. However, by 1949 the influence of the Catholic labour and socialist elements in the party was weakening. Instead, the party adopted the doctrines of the 'social market economy', under the influence of Ludwig Erhard and Konrad Adenauer, the chairman of the CDU in the British zone and the subsequent party leader and Chancellor. This change came about for several reasons, including the success of the Erhard currency reform, the opposition of the United States to 'socialistic policies', a recognition that the CDU would attract more voters if it appealed to a centre–right constituency rather than attempting to compete with the SPD, and a strong reaction against National Socialism which, as Leaman (1988: 56) notes, 'could be presented as the child of both monopolism and collectivism, thus frightening away all ideas of rational collective solutions which included large scale production and planning'.

The rightward turn of the CDU was evident in the party's 'Düsseldorf principles' of 1949 (see Leaman, 1988: 48–58). These defined the social market economy as one in which the 'endeavours of free and able people are set in an order which yields a maximum of economic advantage and social justice for all', such an order being created by 'genuine competition and independent monopoly control'. As Leaman (1988: 52) notes, '"Social" here does not mean primarily a policy which would involve a wealth-transferring welfare state apparatus, but rather a policy of competition *which indirectly would allow the formation of private social security funds*' (his italics). Among the 16 principles for the 'realisation of the Social Market Economy' were competition guaranteed by controls over monopoly; freely determined prices; freely set but modest wages to allow economic recovery; encouragement for savings-based investment and a simplified tax system to encourage capital formation; and 'private property to be affirmed as the basis for economic independence. The Social Market Economy allows as many able people as possible to own property. Broad property ownership reduces the urgency of nationalisation' (quoted in Leaman, 1988: 53). Explicitly subordinated to these economic principles were some very general 'social political principles' such as the right to work, a six-day week, aid for the integration of refugees and war victims, social insurance as the basis for social security, with public welfare for those in 'proven need', land reform and 'social housing to be developed'. As Leaman notes, there is little in this which went beyond the Weimar constitution, except the commitment to monopoly control and the fostering of competition – a commitment which was never fully implemented (see also Sontheimer, 1972).

Clearly, little remained of the CDU's earlier commitment to social reform and nationalization. Instead, the aim was to establish West Germany as a strong free enterprise economy within the Western alliance, in sharp contrast to the Communist regime in the East. A key objective was to spread property ownership widely among the population, providing a firm material basis for the lasting legitimacy of the new state. As one of the leading neo-liberal economists, Ropke, wrote, these principles aimed at establishing a system 'in favour of the middle classes, in favour of the restoration of property to the widest number of people, in favour of that kind of politics which can be summarised under the headlines of deproletarianisation and decentralisation in the national economy' (quoted in Leaman, 1988: 55).

Although there were several smaller parties in the early years of the new state, they gradually disappeared, mostly by absorption within the CDU. The only significant smaller party which survived and played an influential role in post-war politics (apart from the Bavarian affiliate of the CDU, the Christian Social Union, CSU) was the Liberal Free Democratic Party (FDP). This party, which never obtained more than 13 per cent of the vote but always managed to obtain more than the 5 per cent needed for parliamentary representation, has had deep internal divisions. It is the heir to two liberal traditions: that of the conservative nationalists, who had strong links with large-scale industry, were hostile to the Weimar constitution and many of whom eventually defected to the Nazis; and that of the left Liberals, who were particularly strongly represented before the war in the Hanseatic cities and the south-west. These groups formed the FDP in 1948. Throughout the 1950s, under the domination of the first of these two traditions, the FDP was to the right of the CDU on many issues. Later, the party shifted to the centre–left for a period. Initially, the FDP wanted a centralized state based on liberal economic principles, although it supported social policy as a means of securing social peace. A distinctive characteristic of the FDP has been its rejection, on the one hand, of the collectivism of the SPD and, on the other hand, of the religious affiliations of the CDU. It has drawn its main support, rather like the Liberal VVD in the Netherlands, from the self-employed outside the rural sector and higher-status white-collar employees, including civil servants (Alber, 1986: 97).

At first it seemed likely that the SPD would be the dominant party in the new republic. Like socialist parties elsewhere, the SPD advocated economic planning, nationalization and political neutrality. However, as we have noted, the political climate soon changed, although the SPD only lost the first general election by a small margin. The success of the Erhard currency reform and the scrapping of economic controls, as well as antipathy to state control after the Nazi experience, enabled the CDU, which also wished to integrate Germany in the Western alliance, to gain the electoral advantage. At this stage, neither of the main parties attracted a dominant share of the electorate, but the CDU was just able to form a government with the FDP and the small Deutsche Partei (it had a one-seat majority in the Bundestag). In the 1953 and 1957 elections the SPD programme was even less successful;

its vote remained static, while the CDU/CSU vote increased to just over 50 per cent in the latter year. Like its counterparts elsewhere, the SPD was unable to widen its appeal beyond the traditional working class, or even to attract the Catholic working class. As Conradt (1978: 84) notes, the SPD's historical emphasis on integrating its members through social and cultural organizations had placed it in competition with similar church organizations for the 'hearts and minds' of the population.

In the first federal election about one-fifth of the electorate did not cast a vote. Adenauer was concerned about the lack of attachment to the new democratic and republican order that this seemed to signify, and there was a danger that the anti-democratic forces of the Weimar period would re-emerge. This is why it was important to take active steps to ensure the social and political integration of the new state. Rapid economic growth and rising prosperity were seen as the key means to this end. According to Berghahn (1982), many industrialists remained autocratic and conservative, although pressure from the unions and the reform wing of the CDU led to a limited law on industrial co-determination in 1951. In general, the new political regime was still on shaky foundations in the early 1950s; there were, for example, links between some members of the FDP and remnants of the extreme right.

In the first CDU-led government, the Weimar system of social insurance was restored. Union and SPD plans for a unified national scheme, which would have abolished the distinction between the manual and white-collar workers' schemes, were rejected (for the development of social policies generally, see Alber, 1986). Similarly, the traditional, fragmented health-care system, based on private suppliers, was confirmed. Given the critical state of the economy, the need to resettle 10 million refugees and to get production moving, it is hardly surprising that social welfare benefits at first remained at a low level. The only major initiative in these years, which we discuss later, concerned housing – an area which could not, as yet, be left to the private market and the only industry over which the government was forced to maintain controls.

However, in 1953, Adenauer proposed a fundamental reform of the welfare system. Few of these proposals were implemented because of disagreements between the Social Christian Workers' wing of the CDU and the neo-liberals, who had strong links with the employers. The latter group wanted a highly selective, means-tested policy. But Adenauer sided with the former group for political reasons: to keep the electoral support of pensioners, to blunt opposition to German rearmament from the SPD and the unions with improvements in social policy, and to help sustain the legitimacy of the new state in the face of competition from the alternative social and economic system in the German Democratic Republic (GDR).

Apart from these political reasons for sustaining welfare provision, the revival of the economy, with low wages and non-inflationary monetary policies, was now generating a budget surplus which could be used to finance improvements in benefits. New child allowances were introduced in 1954 and unemployment benefits were improved. Housing subsidies were increased, with more emphasis on the private building of family houses. Above all, there was a major pensions reform in 1957, providing a level of coverage and benefits which most other countries reached only in the 1960s and 1970s. It also helped Adenauer to gain an unprecedented 50 per cent of the vote in the 1957 election, the highest share for any party before or since.

This election helped to precipitate a fundamental reorientation of the SPD. Adenauer had proved adept at labelling the party as a Communist fellow traveller, whose patriotism and adherence to the existing social and economic order was suspect, and its vote had hardly increased at all in the three elections which had been held since the foundation of the state. Now an influential group of state SPD leaders, including Willy Brandt, Helmut Schmidt and Herbert Wehner, argued that the party needed to make radical changes. It must accept the involvement of West Germany in NATO and the Western alliance and, more generally, stress its patriotism. It should drop the Marxist and 'workerist' rhetoric and style which alienated middle-class voters. It had to abandon its commitment to socialist planning and embrace the social market economy. Finally, it needed to turn its back on the attempts to integrate its members not just into a political party, but into a separate culture and way of life in order to woo Catholic voters. At its 1959 Bad Godesberg conference the party made these changes. Like its counterparts elsewhere, the SPD aimed to convert itself from a workers' to a people's party, as the Godesberg programme stated: '[t]he SPD, which was a party of the working class, is now a party of the whole people' (quoted in Grosser, 1974: 235).

Following the adoption of Brandt as its candidate for the chancellorship, the SPD began to make electoral gains. However, its final breakthrough owed much to growing conflict in the CDU after Adenauer's retirement in 1963 and an increasingly difficult economic climate. As we have seen, while the growth rate slowed in the 1960s, full employment brought higher wages and increased welfare spending. The imposition of deflationary monetary policies by the independent central bank led to the first post-war recession in 1966/7. Erhard, who had succeeded Adenauer as Federal Chancellor (to the latter's displeasure), lacked a power base inside the CDU and was discarded as the economic situation worsened and party factions struggled for dominance. Meanwhile, the Free Democrats, who had returned to government in 1961 after a five-year break, began to shift to a centre–left stance as the influence of its conservative faction declined.[19] In 1966 the FDP broke up the government because of differences with the CDU over budgetary policy.

Now, despite internal dissent, the SPD entered into a 'Grand Coalition' with the CDU. The FDP returned to opposition, its leftist wing gained the upper hand and an eventual coalition with the SPD became a possibility. The two major parties entered the alliance for tactical reasons: the SPD wanted to demonstrate its respectability and competence to govern, while the divided and leaderless CDU wanted to retain power. In addition, both parties were concerned with rising popular support for the extreme right-wing National Party of Germany (NPD), which almost entered the Bundestag in 1969, although it then fizzled out, and the growth of the extreme left. The CDU retained the chancellorship, while the SPD held the major portfolios of Economics, Foreign Affairs, Justice and Social Welfare. The new Economics Minister, Karl Schiller, adopted Keynesian policies, restoring economic growth and full employment. Other SPD ministers were equally effective and in the 1969 election the party obtained an increased vote (though still less than the CDU/CSU), enabling it to form a government with the FDP. In the 1972 elections it finally became the largest party and, with the Free Democrats, had a secure parliamentary majority.

The Grand Coalition saw several advances in social policy, such as the expansion of higher education, federal support for health care and improvements in benefits. After 1969, with the resumption of economic growth, there were further reforms and improvements, including changes in housing policy (discussed below). However, many domestic reforms were postponed because of the government's narrow parliamentary majority. The SPD had gained votes because of its increased appeal to middle-class voters and secularization. Also, as Conradt (1978: 119) points out, economic modernization, urbanization and the decline of rural areas, reduced the strongest constituency for the CDU. However, as in the Netherlands, in the

1960s and early 1970s the SPD's left wing became ever more critical of its abandonment of a radical programme.

The increasingly turbulent economic conditions of the late 1960s and early 1970s which have already been described also affected Germany. Renewed growth after 1967 led to a rapid rise in profits and dividends, as the large-scale industrial combines which the CDU had failed to break up seized the advantage. They did so at a point when the trade unions had accepted a policy of wage restraint as part of a corporatist strategy with the employers and the government, in which there was supposed to have been 'concerted action' to restrain profits and wages, accompanied by support for investment and the promise of measures to redistribute benefits to workers and to ensure 'social symmetry' once the crisis was over. As Sontheimer (1972: 51) notes, 'the employers agreed because they benefited from this policy and the unions had to agree in order to ensure full employment'. Wildcat strikes in 1969 signalled the failure of this tripartist approach and undermined Schiller's attempt to manage the economy by Keynesian means. As in the USA, the other latecomer to Keynesian demand management, this approach was adopted just when its ability to control inflation while sustaining growth was declining in every advanced capitalist economy.

From 1969, increased expenditure, especially on education and housing, which had been planned as a counter-cyclical measure, instead acted to overheat the economy. As elsewhere, the inflationary boom of the early 1970s seemed uncontrollable. At the same time the government was under increasing fire from both the left and the right, the latter attacking the social reforms by reviving the anti-socialist rhetoric of the 1950s. In addition, the use of violence by small groups among the extra-parliamentary left contributed to a hostile climate. After the 1972 election the government promised a more active programme of domestic reforms than in its first period, including legislation on co-determination, urban renewal, education and taxation. However, to the dismay of many supporters, relatively little was achieved. Neither Brandt nor the FDP leader and Foreign Minister Scheel were particularly interested in domestic affairs. In addition, there were serious divisions between the governing parties over education, tax reform and co-determination. The FDP was keen to be seen by its middle-class supporters as restraining the excesses of socialism. In 1972 Schiller resigned, after a decision by the government to support policies advocated by the central bank rather than those of its Minister for Economics and Finance. As Leaman (1988: 194) notes, 'his resignation did mark the passing of the co-ordinated techno-cratic attempt to reconcile Germany's monopolised economy with its federal fiscal structure and independent central bank, in order both to manage cyclical and structural problems *and* realise the Social Democrats' ... reform programme'.

Now the government's social policy goals were increasingly sub-servient to the dictates of the central bank, which imposed targets for monetary growth that implied a sharp constraint on rising public expenditure. At this point the world's major economies were plunged into mid-decade recession. In 1974 the more conservative Helmut Schmidt replaced Brandt as the Federal Chancellor. The government now broadly accepted the emergent monetarist orthodoxy concerning economic policy and there was a shift of power from the Social Democrats to the Liberals, as the FDP took over the Economics Ministry and pressed for expenditure cuts. While Social Democrat ministers resisted these demands, as Leaman (1988: 215) notes,

> the junior coalition partner clearly won the ideological battle within the cabinet. The "pragmatism" of the new Chancellor ... forced him to recognise the constraints of coalition government combined with a self-willed central bank and an increasing state debt, and to accept a deflationary approach.

In a conclusion which is not only applicable to Germany but also to the other countries where the Social Democrats were in power in the 1970s, he adds: '[t]he historical dilemma of social democracy in power – caught between its reformist goals and its duty as the fire-brigade of capitalism – expressed itself ... in political paralysis'.

SOCIAL HOUSING IN EUROPE – AN OVERVIEW

After 1945 there was wide political agreement in Europe that some form of mass social housebuilding, on a scale hitherto undreamt of, except, perhaps, by left-wing parties, was a necessity. Only a few largely uninfluential free market diehards disagreed (notably Hayek, 1944; see also D. King, 1987). The first authoritative post-war review of European housing conditions was published by the UN Economic Commission for Europe (ECE) in 1949. This report and its successors provide a useful overview of the evolution of European housing and housing policies and a framework for the subsequent examination of individual countries' experiences (UN Economic Commission for Europe, 1949, 1952, 1954, 1958, 1973, 1976a and b, 1980).

The 1949 report estimated housing needs in 17 European countries. These included all the countries with which we are concerned, except West Germany, which was in the worst situation with only 10 million units in 1950, many of which were little more than temporary shacks or ruins, for 16 million households. The UN report estimated that in its 17 countries the equivalent of six years' housing construction at average pre-war rates had been lost by war damage and destruction. Just to return to the pre-war housing situation would require over 3 million new units. Another 7 million would be required to replace all slum housing and 4 million more to remove chronic overcrowding. This total, over 14 million, represented about one-fifth of the total pre-war 'building wealth' (a standardized measure of the pre-war housing stock). In addition, a further demand for almost 1 million units a year would be generated by the formation of new households and obsolescence (too low an estimate, as it transpired).

On the assumption, which the ECE regarded as unrealistic, that each country could double its pre-war rate of housebuilding immediately, it would take, on average, 22 years to remove the housing backlog. Interestingly, although the projections of demand and supply made by the ECE were incorrect, its suggestion that crude housing shortages would last into the late 1960s or early 1970s proved surprisingly accurate. In 1949, given the European economic circumstances, huge difficulties lay in the path of even the expanded building programme which the ECE saw as the 'probable programme', let alone its more rapid 22-year 'necessary programme'. As the report noted, building on the scale required would involve 'a tremendous effort and something of a revolution in the conception of building' (UN Economic Commission for Europe, 1949: 15). The building industry would need to be modernized and reorganized, the materials industries greatly expanded and there must be new measures for planning and controlling building programmes. There were also more general issues concerning the relationship between housing and general financial and economic policies.

It was self-evident that this extensive agenda required governments to take a lead. The task was beyond the competence or the willingness of private market agencies, even in normal times. In the aftermath of war, with a barely functioning private building industry, virtually no private sector capital or money markets, and rents which, in most cases, remained frozen at pre-war levels, a rapid return to even a partially functioning private housing market and housebuilding industry was inconceivable. Moreover, the desperate need for the European economies to expand industrial production and exports in order to pay war debts and for economic reconstruction and modernization necessitated the maintenance of strict controls over the supply of materials, labour power and money for housing. Production would inevitably be constrained at levels far below the outstanding needs for many years. In this situation, pressure to use the available resources more efficiently was intense, and hence to rationalize design and construction, to gain new economies of scale and to substitute new materials for traditional ones in short supply. All these factors encouraged many governments to place a high priority on social housing construction, using the publicly accountable and controllable agencies which had evolved in the interwar years, building to strictly controlled standards, rather than fragmented, small-scale and less controllable private sector builders and landlords. As Aneurin Bevan, the British Minister responsible for housing in the immediate post-war years, crisply noted: '[i]f we are to plan we have to plan with plannable instruments, and the speculative builder, by his very nature, is not a plannable instrument' (quoted in Merrett, 1979: 239).

The dire economic circumstances severely constrained the first programmes of social housing. However, as we have seen, the initial phase of economic recovery was completed by the early to mid-1950s and there was a transition to the period of steady growth and full employment. Then housing output was expanded and inroads were made in reducing the housing shortage. New social housing construction still played a key role, although the more significant development in the longer run was a reviving private housing market.

At the start of this second period, the ECE again surveyed the European housing situation (UN Economic Commission for Europe, 1952, 1954). The unexpectedly high rate of new household formation had added greatly to the demand for housing. In France, the Netherlands and West Germany, this resulted in a fall in the dwelling per capita ratio compared with 1937 and, using the more important measure of dwellings per household, there had also been a deterioration in Britain. Only the Danish rate of housing construction had just exceeded the rate of new household formation. Moreover, rising employment and real incomes, with relatively low controlled rents, meant that the effective demand for housing was rising even faster than the level of housing needs.

By the early 1950s only very slow progress had been made in raising housing output in Denmark, the Netherlands and Britain, where levels were not much higher than those reached in 1949. In France, as we noted, housing was not included in the Monnet Plan, and output remained at very low levels (even compared with the above three countries). But this was just beginning to change. In Germany, which had the most extreme housing shortage in 1949, rapid steps were, of necessity, taken to expand housing output, which had increased by 250 per cent above its 1949 level by 1953. The 1954 ECE report concluded that, at best, rising housing output was so far resulting, over Europe as a whole, in no more than a cessation in the rising level of unmet needs. One of the main ways in which governments were attempting to cope with this situation was to limit severely the size and amenities of the new housing units. In France and Britain, earlier standards were actually reduced at this time. In the other countries, standards remained at minimal levels.

A few countries, notably Britain, West Germany and, to a lesser degree, the Netherlands, now began to relax investment controls which had inhibited the production of private housing. However, the shortage of private capital still meant that much new investment still came directly or indirectly from the state. Only in West Germany, where, for reasons which we discussed above, there was a strong desire to encourage private housing investment, was there significant use of tax concessions to attract private investment. Almost all new housing received some state support and, as the report noted, 'the difficulty of ensuring that public investment and financial aid is as effective as possible in providing good and cheap dwellings for the occupiers, has contributed to the growth of non-profit-making institutions' (UN Economic Commission for Europe, 1954: 32). It concluded that a further expansion of these enterprises was desirable, 'as an instrument of Government housing policy', because of their competence in housing development and management. Most new private housing consisted of expensive single-family units built for individual owners, outside the major urban areas and centres of rapid population growth. Only in Britain (and, of course, in the USA, which we discuss later) was the phenomenon of suburban home ownership beginning to re-emerge, as controls over private housing production were relaxed and incomes rose.

An important theme that ran through the ECE reports from the early 1950s was the concern among all governments at the increasing long-term burden on public budgets due to the new subsidy commitments. There was also concern about the growing gap between the rents of older housing, many of which had hardly been increased and had fallen in real terms since before the war, and the higher rents of the new housing. Suggestions for rent harmonization were being formulated, that is, relating rents to quality, regardless of age, using surplus income on older units to cross-subsidize newer ones and to compensate private landlords for the losses which they had suffered. Moreover, the later shift away from production to consumption subsidies was clearly foreseen in the 1954 ECE report's reference to the need to 'adopt social measures to enable all categories of the population to pay increased rent' (UN Economic Commission for Europe, 1954: 46). However, the still acute housing shortage made any early abolition of rent controls and subsidies a non-starter, and adjustments in rent policies would be a 'lengthy business'. Nevertheless, the report noted that modest rent increases and/or liberalization of controls were occurring in all five of the European countries with which we are concerned. The report also referred to continuing attempts to reduce the cost of building by improvements in the organization of the building industry, by the use of new materials, prefabrication, modularization and standardization. However, these had not had as dramatic an impact as changes in technology and organization had had on other large-scale industries, so the cost of housing continued to rise faster than the general cost of living.

In the late 1950s, the economic and financial aspects of post-war housing policies were the subject of another major ECE report (UN Economic Commission for Europe, 1958). Any gains from cost reduction had been more than offset by rising standards, sustained by the growth in real incomes now occurring and by the relaxation of earlier restrictions. As the report noted, the sanitary policy which had determined minimally acceptable standards before the war had given way to 'the positive social policy of trying to ensure that all have the opportunity of obtaining a dwelling of high modern standard' (UN Economic Commission for Europe, 1958: 1). In the case of social housing, which still provided a large proportion of most housing, this amounted to a continuing endorsement of a 'mass needs' policy, rather than the residual role which had begun to become more evident in several European countries in the 1930s.

While standards and costs were rising, the report noted that real incomes were growing even faster and full employment had been achieved in most countries, thus improving the ability of many households to afford new housing, although few households could, as yet, afford new privately financed, unsubsidized units. Although an earlier concern that housing investment would compete for resources needed for industry had eased, the report noted that the right balance between investment in housing consumption and 'productive capital investment' elsewhere in the economy remained a problem, as did the general level of domestic investment if inflation was not to rise along with imports, thus affecting the balance of payments and other key economic variables. In an early echo of arguments which were to become much more frequently and forcefully ventilated in some countries after the mid-1970s, the report also pointed to the pressure that subsidies placed on levels of taxation, 'which may in turn affect the supply of ... savings essential to financing productive investment' (UN Economic Commission for Europe, 1958: 9).

All this illustrates that, even though the post-war social housing programmes were on a far larger scale and lasted longer than anything which had occurred in the interwar period, they were still viewed by the experts and officials who contributed to national policy making and to reports such as those issued by the ECE as measures whose longer-term impact on the economy and on government finances was highly questionable. The implicit assumption was still that large-scale social housing programmes were a *temporary* expedient, albeit one that would continue for many years. As a later UN report noted, 'governments hoped they could withdraw once they had built enough replacements for the war years and got the building industry on its feet, and leave housing to the play of the market' (UN Economic Commission for Europe, 1976a: 58). The principal reason for the persistence of this necessity was, of course, the continuing pressure of unmet demand on the part of a wide spectrum of the population, as the interlinked processes of industrial modernization, urbanization, demographic change and rising real incomes fed through into the housing sector. By the late 1950s, the ECE estimated that it would take at least another decade to eliminate the current housing shortage in Europe, not allowing for the increase in household formation occurring from the late 1960s as the post-war baby boom had children. With the benefit of hindsight, it is easy to see that the transition to a Fordist regime of full employment and rising real incomes and consumption had a dramatic and sustained impact on the demand for housing quite unlike anything experienced before (except to a limited degree in the US in the 1920s and parts of Britain in the 1930s), or than was envisaged by most governments and their advisers immediately after the war.

In these circumstances there was still a major need for public investment in housing. Rent controls, even where they were not applied to new building, continued to inhibit the supply of new private capital (Harloe, 1985). In any event, the private sector supply of moderately rented unsubsidized housing was no more attractive a proposition than it had been in the interwar years, especially where it would have to compete with subsidized social housing built to an ever improving level of space and amenity standards. In addition, few European countries besides Britain had financial institutions prepared to lend high proportions of the price of a house over a long term. So, in the second half of the 1950s, between 45 per cent and 65 per cent of all housing investment still came from public funds in four of our five countries, with the Netherlands still the most dependent on the public sector. The only exception was Germany, where public funding amounted to under 30 per cent. Here, policies described below resulted in almost one-third of housing investment coming from personal funds and another 40 per cent from private institutions (UN Economic Commission for Europe, 1958: 39–61).

The continuing dependence of construction on direct subsidies was equally evident. Between 85 and 95 per cent of all new building was aided in 1957 in France, Denmark and the Netherlands. In Britain the proportion had fallen to 58 per cent and in Germany to 52 per cent, owing to the growth of tax-subsidized home ownership in the former case, and tax-subsidized, privately financed rental housing in the latter case. In line with the 'mass needs' philosophy, subsidies were not targeted on the poorest households. In France and Germany the upper limit for admission to social housing was around twice the average income of a skilled worker. In the former country, the ECE noted, over half the new HLM units were allocated to white-collar and other 'higher-income categories'. In Denmark the income limit was set closer to the average earnings of a skilled male worker. In the Netherlands the only restriction, meaningless in practice, was that the new units should be for members of the working class. Even this vague restriction had been removed from the housing subsidy legislation after the war in Britain.

The ECE also reported that productivity rises due to new building techniques were still modest and further improvement in the efficiency of the building industry 'appears to afford wide scope for government policy'. Growing incomes and reviving financial systems were now increasing the possibility for substituting private for public capital. However, the need for subsidies would remain because '[t]he main difficulty ... is that in most countries a dwelling of adequate standard within the means of an average working class income cannot be provided without public financial aid' (UN Economic Commission for Europe, 1958: 73). But there were now pressures, owing to 'the culminative burden of housing subsidies on public budgets', to target future subsidies on those in financial need, rather than to provide more general support. The ECE suggested two means of achieving this, both of which were to find ready acceptance among housing policy makers in the 1960s and 1970s, as the budgetary pressures intensified. First was the provision of individual rent allowances; second was what the Germans called 'degressive' construction subsidies, that is subsidies which reduced over time as, it was hoped, incomes and thus rent-paying capacity improved.

Finally, the predominant issue of the need to cut back on generalized state support for housing gave rise to a new theme in these ECE reports, that is, the suggestion that home ownership should be encouraged as a way of reducing the necessity for the state to supply housing capital. One means to this end would be 'by confining non-profit making rented dwellings to low-income families' (UN Economic Commission for Europe, 1958: 74).

In many ways these reports accurately predicted both the financial difficulties which increasingly affected social housing in the 1960s and early 1970s, and the governmental responses to such pressures. Any suggestion that the transition back to a residual role for social housing began only relatively recently, at least in most European countries, is in danger of overlooking the fact that pressures for such a transition began many years earlier. Among the main reasons why these pressures had limited immediate effect were the political difficulties of abandoning mass social housing while major unmet needs remained; the continuing need for a controlled supply of new housing to meet needs generated by industrialization and urban growth and modernization; and the lack of an adequately functioning mass private housing market and of sufficiently high incomes to support these markets. As these obstacles began to be eroded, the possibilities for change advanced.

By the early 1970s, this situation had been reached, or was beginning to be reached, in all the European countries with which we are concerned. At the same time, the shift from the high growth-low inflation era of the 1950s to stagflation had brought about many of the shifts in housing policy which earlier ECE reports had prophesied. Developments in this latter period were usefully surveyed in a 1980 report (UN Economic Commission for Europe, 1980). This noted that the expansion in Western European housing construction continued in the 1960s and 1970s, aided by rising prosperity, although the trend was broken by the economic crisis of the mid-1970s. Interestingly, there was an identical pattern in the USA. In fact, in five of the six countries with which we are concerned, the peak post-war year for housing output was in the early 1970s, immediately before the crisis. In Britain, the peak occurred a little earlier, in 1968.[20] By now the main period of industrial growth and urbanization was over in the more developed Western societies under discussion in this book. One indicator of this was the rising proportion of building outside urban core areas, as suburbanization took over from primary urbanization (Hall and Hay, 1980). In Denmark, France and the Netherlands the absolute levels of social housing production peaked in the late 1960s or early 1970s. In Britain there was a sharp rise in social output in the late 1960s. The pattern differed only in West Germany, where social home ownership was also important, for reasons to be discussed later.

However, the more important trend concerned the share of social rented housing in all new output. In every country except France, where, as we have seen, housing had only a low priority in the early post-war period, the long-term trend, evident from the early 1950s, was for this share to decline, as the private market recovered and then expanded. In 1950 social housing accounted for over 80 per cent of all new housing in Britain, around 60 per cent in the Netherlands and West Germany and around 50 per cent in Denmark. By the early 1970s, it was around 40 per cent in the Netherlands and Britain, and nearer 20 per cent in Denmark and West Germany. In France the share had peaked at around 30 per cent in the late 1960s and then began to fall away rapidly to under 20 per cent by the middle of the following decade (here, as in Germany, social home ownership accounted for an increasingly large share of social housing output) (see Ball, Harloe and Martens, 1988: 54–5).

While in the 1950s, with limited public and private resources, the main policy objective had been to reduce the crude shortage of housing, building as many units as possible and restricting their quality, size and amenities, in the following period there were significant quality improvements (at least in terms of size and amenities). Between the early 1960s and the mid-1970s in Germany and France the average floor space in new units increased by about 20–30 per cent, when average household sizes were declining. In

Germany and the Netherlands the proportion of new units with central heating rose from between one-fifth and one-third to almost 100 per cent (UN Economic Commission for Europe, 1980: 10–11). In all countries these rising standards were fully reflected in, and frequently led by, changing norms for social housebuilding, adding greatly to its costs. In this respect social housing shared in the more general expansion of welfare benefits which, we have noted, occurred in the 1960s and early 1970s, despite the growing anxiety about the budgetary implications as the economic situation worsened. Unlike earlier or later periods, these years were ones of public and private affluence.

However, while affluence increased the standards of all housing, the forms of construction became increasingly differentiated. An approximate indicator of the growing share of building for home ownership was the rapid rise in the proportion of units built as single- or two-family houses. This rose from around one-third to a half in France between 1960 and the mid-1970s, from near a half to over three-quarters in the Netherlands, and from around 45 per cent in West Germany in 1970 to 70 per cent by 1976/7 (UN Economic Commission for Europe, 1980: 12). In sharp contrast, high-rise building began to account, for the first time, for a substantial proportion of new social housing in the 1960s. Although this trend did not survive long into the next decade, in part because of the rapid appearance of constructional defects and its unpopularity, it has left a baleful legacy. It also contributed a physical dimension to the growth of segregation in housing, between the flat-dwelling social tenant and the single-family house owner (although many other differences of location, income etc. are, of course, important). This separation has been somewhat less obvious where, as in Germany, for example, both the middle-class white-collar and working-class manual workers live in rented apartments, or where, as in Britain, the former live in suburban single-family houses and the latter in suburban detached or semi-detached 'cottage estates'.

The use of high-rise systems building was in part due to the continued drive for higher building productivity, or, at least, for higher output with limited supplies of skilled building labour. However, as Dunleavy (1981) has shown in a study of high-rise in British social housing, it was also the product of powerful lobbying by major construction interests and a consequence of the power that the housing professionals now wielded within the politics of social housing. Social housing, because it was a 'plannable instrument', became the test-bed for most of the innovations in building techniques, new materials and so on which were developed in the post-war years. While there were great advances in the rationalization of private sector building, increased use of machinery and so on, the more advanced (and frequently disastrous) experiments were less feasible in a sector where long production runs were rare and where the builders had to respond to consumers who might go elsewhere, compared with the social housing producers and managers who were often able to dictate what those in housing need should accept.

By the early 1970s, the era of generalized housing shortage appeared to be ending. This suggested to many policy makers that directly subsidized social rented housing was now only needed for 'specific population groups'. The 1980 ECE report lists, as examples, the elderly, isolated households, one-parent families, large families and migrant workers, and those living in pre-1918 housing which required renewal or modernization. Although the existing stock of social housing still accommodated a wide range of low- and middle-income households in most countries, the reorientation of new building away from mass needs towards a more limited role, as housing for the urban poor, is clearly indicated.

However, developments in the 1960s, when the standards and costs of social housing had risen rapidly, created difficulties that continued throughout the next two decades. As the absolute housing shortages faded away and better-off households began to opt for home ownership, the pattern of social housing demand began to change. An increasing proportion of new entrants to the sector came from the low-income groups identified by the ECE report. But these households had a lower rent-paying capacity than the skilled manual and white-collar workers served by social housing in earlier years. So there was a growing gap between affordable and cost rents in the newer social housing. From the early 1970s governments struggled with the consequences of this situation. At the start of the decade, while new building remained at a high level, several countries experienced a novel development, a lack of demand for new social housing, some of which remained empty for long periods, creating financial difficulties for its owners. The report refers specifically to unlet new housing in Denmark, Germany and the Netherlands. The problem was that the new units no longer appealed to better-off households. However, their rents were too costly for the poorer households now trying to enter the sector. Governments had to provide additional subsidies to deal with the situation.

Another aspect of this problem which began to be noticed now, but which became much more significant later, was the disinclination of all but the poorest households, who had little choice in the matter, to accept accommodation on the high-rise, peripheral estates built in the 1960s and early 1970s. In many cases, apart from the frequent lack of communal services and the forbidding design aspects of these estates, they were located far from the inner-city employment markets on which many lower-income households depended and public transport was either missing or expensive.[21] Many of these units, even with additional subsidies, still had high rents, with high utilities costs being a particular problem, especially after the fuel price rises of the mid-decade. The complex and inter-linked social and physical pathology of so-called 'hard-to-let' or 'problem estates' began to develop from this period.

Such problems gave an additional impetus to the efforts, which had begun in the 1960s, to 'harmonize' social housing rents. In most countries, although not in Britain, where, as we have seen, rents were pooled, the rents of individual units reflected the historic costs of their construction. Yet much of the older, cheaper housing was still occupied by the better-off tenants who had gained access to social housing in earlier years. Conversely, the poorer tenants who were increasingly housed in later years faced high rent/income ratios in the expensive, newer housing. The pattern of rents did not reflect the relative quality and locations of the housing stock and there was a regressive distribution of rent burdens. However, as we discuss later, attempts to alter this situation were frequently resisted by social landlords and by older, well-established and better-off tenants.

The rising costs of subsidizing social housing in an inflationary era, accentuated by the declining rent-paying ability of many new entrants into the sector and the 'misallocation' problems just described, led in all countries to the adoption of the solution which had been foreshadowed in the 1958 ECE report – the introduction of rent allowances and the start of a shift from 'indiscriminate' construction subsidies to income-related consumption subsidies. At first allowances were seen as a supplementary measure, alongside construction subsidies, enabling those with especially low incomes, such as the elderly, to afford the rents of new social housing and older units whose rents were being 'harmonized' (i.e. raised). The assumption was that savings would be made on the subsidy bill, as the level and duration of construction subsidies were constrained or reduced, targeting additional assistance, through allowances, on those who were unable to bear the higher rent/income ratios which the new policies were intended to bring about. As we shall see, these policies had mixed effects.

In every country, by the mid-1970s, social housing was beginning to be afflicted by a complex and interlinked series of social and economic difficulties which governments sought, and frequently failed, to remedy. At the same time, while large and politically significant sections of the population continued to live in social housing, and the various social housing agencies and professionals still constituted a powerful lobby, there was a palpable change of emphasis in the politics of housing. Increasingly, governments sought to support home ownership, expanding subsidy programmes in many cases. Diminishing emphasis was placed on social housing construction. As key sections of the electorate, many of whom would previously have entered social housing, began to opt for home ownership (and more affluent social tenants also moved out), the political dividends to be gained from expansive social housing policies waned, while those gained from support for home ownership waxed. The essential context to this shift was, of course, the growth of prosperity and the establishment of the necessary institutional structures, such as dynamic private mortgage markets, for a mass market in home ownership.

The growing prosperity had further significant effects on social housing. In the early post-war years many countries had prioritized industrial investment and housing investment had been tied to the effort to increase the size of the housing stock. By the 1960s, economic growth led to increasing pressure for the modernization of the urban infrastructure, with new roads, offices, retail, leisure and public services resulting in extensive urban renewal and the demolition of slum housing. This removed much of the poor-quality, low-rent housing which had been the main source of accommodation for the urban poor. Urban redevelopment displaced low-income households and it was from this source that many of the new low-income social tenants came, sustaining the social housing construction programmes. Once the worst slum housing was removed, governments switched to supporting the rehabilitation of older but still basically sound housing. There were several reasons for this shift, including the high costs and much criticized social and aesthetic costs of mass clearance and renewal. However, there was also a new source of demand for renovated housing as affluent households entering home ownership preferred central city living in older, more attractive housing rather than suburban locations. The upgrading and 'gentrification' of older housing, frequently aided by subsidies, became a highly profitable activity for private market agencies and for the better-off households that benefited from the large capital gains frequently made from tenure conversion.

Although some efforts were made to prevent the displacement of lower-income tenants from housing renovation operations, the outflow of the urban poor to social housing, frequently to the peripheral estates, continued.

The timing, pace and extent of all the developments which we have been reviewing varied considerably. For example, while all the European countries which we are discussing introduced rent allowances within a few years of each other, the shift towards a more residual social rented sector and the growth of home ownership occurred earlier and more rapidly in Britain than in any of the other four European countries. We now examine some of these national variations.

THE RISE AND FALL OF SOCIAL HOUSING

The most striking differences were between all the European countries, on the one hand, and the United States, on the other. In the USA the growth of home ownership, together with continuing private rental construction, and the restriction of public housing to a residual role, was established by the end of the 1940s. Subsequent developments brought public housing, at least in many big cities, to a point of near-terminal crisis by the mid-1970s (see Struyk, 1980). We have already described the economic and political circumstances which led to the rapid growth of prosperity, the conservative political climate of the late 1940s and 1950s and the opposition to social reform programmes. Between the end of the war and 1949 there was a struggle to pass new legislation to reactivate public housing which was at least as tortuous as that which had occurred in the 1930s. R. Davies (1966) has provided a detailed study of this episode, in which he traces the faltering hopes of the reformers as the economic and political climate changed (see also Friedman, 1968; Keith, 1973; Gelfand, 1975; Fish, 1979).

The opponents of public housing ensured that the 700,000 units of accommodation for war workers that were constructed under the 1940 Lanham Act were sold or demolished after the war. However, the public housing cause gained some fresh support during the conflict. The reformers hoped to break the link between housing and slum clearance that they had been forced to accept in 1937 and legislate for a major programme of new construction, alongside a separate, federally subsidized programme for clearance and renewal. The cleared land would be available for public uses, including housing, or for resale to private developers. However, even the reformers still envisaged public housing as confined to lower-income groups. It would not compete with or replace private housing, but supply decent and affordable accommodation for the unprofitable sector of housing demand. Nevertheless, the opposition to public housing from the real estate and building lobby remained intense. But the New Deal programmes to aid private housing were now acceptable, as one key lobbyist noted: 'we prefer that governmental activity shall take the form of assisting and aiding private business rather than undertaking great public projects'. As R. Davies (1966: 17–18) notes, 'of all the government housing programs, only public housing did not constitute "aid to private enterprise" because it did not encourage Americans to buy their houses'. By the end of the 1940s, in the anti-communist climate which we have described, public housing had even become 'European socialism in its most insidious form' (a phrase that recalls Veiller's rhetoric almost half a century earlier) and 'the cutting edge of the Communist front' (quoted in R. Davies, 1966: 17).

The first important federal policy initiative provided an immediate boost to the private housing industry. The GI Bill of Rights included loan guarantees enabling veterans to buy their own homes. This highly successful programme fuelled the rapid resumption of large-scale suburban construction for home ownership. However, the growing strength of the conservatives in Congress resulted in much more conflict over slum clearance and low-income housing. In 1944 a new Senate subcommittee on housing and urban redevelopment, chaired by the conservative Republican Taft, began to examine the housing question. Reformers and industry representatives had little difficulty in agreeing on the maintenance and extension of federal aid to home ownership, and Taft (who supported public housing, provided it did not compete with the private sector) joined with the tireless Wagner and another Democrat, the southern segregationist Ellender, to present a comprehensive housing bill to the Senate. It contained proposals for a large public housing programme, for a federal commitment to secure decent housing for all, and for subsidized slum clearance and redevelopment.

Truman, a supporter of the 1937 Act, included these commitments in his 1945 Fair Deal programme. Immediately the war ended there was a rapid demobilization and, as veterans returned to urban areas where there were already housing shortages owing to the influx of war workers (few of whom wished to return to the areas from which they had initially migrated), the spectacle of homeless veterans (25,000 in Washington, DC and 100,000 in Chicago, for example) helped fuel the campaign for housing legislation.

However, the anti-public housing lobby launched an intense campaign against the public housing provisions of the Wagner–Ellender–Taft Bill and in 1946 the same opposition managed to cripple a Truman proposal to use the apparatus of wartime controls to build 2.7 million units in a two-year veterans' emergency housing programme. Even though this programme eventually got under way, the fragmented private construction industry could not be organized to deliver the required output and there were problems in obtaining building materials. There was also conflict within the administration, where powerful forces favoured scrapping war controls and a rapid return to an unfettered private economy. The emergency programme lasted only a year before being terminated, along with a construction cost limit on new housing which had been imposed in the immediate aftermath of war, and restrictions on the supply of building materials. Rent controls were eased at the same time. This experience serves to underline Bevan's remark about the unplannable private builder and illustrates the advantages that the European governments had in being able to use existing and politically acceptable social housing agencies, local authorities and non-profit organizations, in the early stages of post-war housing programmes, as well as economic controls. In contrast, in America the same pressures that had resulted in the return to 'business as usual' in housing after the First World War again triumphed.

After a filibuster, the Wagner–Ellender–Taft Bill died in the House of Representatives. Now Truman sought a *rapprochement* with the private housing groups, appointing an emollient administrator, Raymond Foley, to head the federal housing effort. Foley continued to press for a public housing bill, but made it clear that he regarded such housing as a temporary expedient, which could fade away as soon as the private market could build affordable lower-income housing. However, despite continued efforts in 1947–8, Congress would only agree to the establishment of a Federal Housing and Home Finance Agency, the first permanently established national agency with a broadly defined housing policy remit. The Republican-dominated Congress also insisted on a further weakening of rent controls, leading to bitter attacks from Wagner, Truman and others on the failure to respond adequately to the continuing shortage of veterans' housing. In 1947 the public housing issue was seized upon by a new senator, Joseph McCarthy, anxious to gain a national reputation. McCarthy received financial support from William Leavitt, one of the most prominent suburban speculative builders of the post-war period (Parson, n.d.: 12; see also R. Davies, 1966: 68–72). By devious manoeuvres he emerged as the chairman of a Congressional Committee on housing and used this to attack public housing.[22]

In his 1948 election campaign Truman used the Republican opposition to housing legislation and rent controls to good effect, especially after the (renamed) Taft–Ellender–Wagner Bill was again torpedoed in the House of Representatives. In the summer of this year the President summoned Congress to a special session in which he challenged the Republicans to pass the housing bill, a deeply embarrassing manoeuvre for them, as the Republican election platform contained a commitment to just such a bill, despite their record of opposition over the previous years. After Truman's victory, a renewed commitment to housing legislation became a key element in his Fair Deal reform programme. As we saw, the conservative forces in Congress prevented almost all of this programme being implemented. The only major exception was the 1949 Housing Act.

As originally drafted the new bill provided for more than a million units of public housing over seven years, $1 billion in loans and $500 million in capital grants for slum clearance and urban redevelopment and loans for the repair of rural housing. At this time, according to R. Davies (1966: 103), over 2.5 million households still shared accommodation and 5 million lived in slums. At least one-third of urban households had incomes well below the level which made decent private rented housing affordable. What emerged was a six-year, 810,000-unit programme. Interestingly, when opponents of the bill attempted to add a clause forbidding racial discrimination in public housing (which would have resulted in it being opposed by Southern Democrats), liberal supporters voted the clause down, despite their misgivings, in order to save the measure. Despite a frenzied campaign by the real estate lobby, and even a fist fight on the House floor, the bill was eventually passed. The new act also provided federal subsidies for urban renewal with a requirement that provision be made for affordable relocation housing, if renewal involved slum clearance. In the 1950s the already weak provisions of the 1949 Act which linked federal urban renewal subsidies to residential development and/or slum clearance were progressively eroded, and the programme became used as a means of removing socially and racially undesirable groups from downtown areas (leading to the conclusion that 'urban renewal is negro removal') and to underpin prestige projects which benefited real estate and other business interests and their political and official allies (see, for example, Wilson, 1966; Hartman, 1984). As Friedman (1968: 151) notes, the principal focus of the act was not on housing the urban poor, but on physically remaking the cities, in order to provide opportunities for business and real estate, boost the property tax incomes of city governments and satisfy the aspirations of the planning and design professionals. He concludes: 'the act was a planning and businessmens' act, with nods to the housing worriers'. Between 1949 and 1968, 425,000 units of low-rent housing, mainly accommodating minority households, were demolished. In their place only 125,000 new units were built, over half of which were luxury apartments (G. Wright, 1981: 234).

It soon became clear that the 1949 Act was a false dawn for public housing. The high rate of private housing construction (aided by federal insurance) – almost 4.9 million units were built between 1946 and 1950 – reduced the housing shortage for moderate- and middle-income households, thus weakening the social base which had reinforced the housing reform movement in earlier years. As Parson (1984) describes, the trade unions shifted from their pre-war support for public housing towards the suburban home-owner solution for their members and inner-city renewal as a source of jobs. The Korean war and McCarthyism also affected the position of public housing, and the resources available for it. From the start, the public housing legislation was fatally flawed by the compromises which had to be made to the private sector pressures. As before, decisions about whether to authorize public housing agencies were made by each state, and whether to establish such agencies by each locality. This gave the real estate interests many opportunities to frustrate the programme. The most extreme tactics were used to this end. In Los Angeles, for example, leading housing authority officials were accused of communist subversion and dismissed in the early 1950s, crippling the development of public housing in that city (Parson, n.d., 1982, 1983). Many local jurisdictions were forced to hold residents' referenda on individual projects, even after public housing authorities had been established (R. Davies, 1966: 128).

Other aspects of the 1949 Act contributed to the subsequent failures of public housing. Unlike European social housing, it was available only for the very poorest households. In order to prevent any conceivable competition with the private sector, the highest public housing rents could be no greater than 80 per cent of the lowest rents for decent, private rented housing in the locality. Families whose incomes rose above the poverty level were evicted from public housing. Strict cost limits and standards ensured that much public housing was inadequate, poor in both quality and design. The programme was bound down with cumbersome regulations and the federal public housing administration rapidly gained a reputation for inefficiency and incompetence (Fisher, 1959: 148ff.). With few notable exceptions, the programme was also poorly administered locally and housing management remained a very underdeveloped profession, with many smaller housing authorities having no properly trained staff. Even by the 1970s the standards of management were abysmal (Hartman and Carr, 1969; Hartman and Levi, 1973).

Thus the 1949 Housing Act marked more of a retreat for public housing than an advance. Despite its language, the 1937 Housing Act mainly provided accommodation for middle-income and 'respectable' working-class households, many of whom had lost their homes in the Depression. Even though on a very limited scale, this was public housing for mass needs. The 1949 Act redefined the role of public housing as residual housing for the marginal urban poor, especially for some of those (frequently black) who needed to be rehoused from the slums (frequently in racially segregated projects) to facilitate the occurrence of profitable, federally assisted urban renewal (see, for example, Bayor, 1989). As Bratt (1986: 339) has commented, '[o]nce public housing was reactivated, and could no longer claim to be a depression-stimulated support for the temporarily poor, it became clearly defined as permanent housing for people who were more or less separated from society's mainstream'.

In the last years of the Truman presidency attempts to get the public housing programme started on the scale needed for its completion in six years were stymied in Congress. The Eisenhower administration indicated its priorities by staffing the various federal housing agencies with supporters and ex-members of the real estate lobby, and by reducing still further the already modest Truman request to Congress for public housing appropriations (Keith, 1973: 111). In 1952 and 1953 an annual rate of completions of almost 60,000 units was achieved, the product of the Truman effort. Such levels were not reached again until the late 1960s. Annual completions remained in the 10,000–20,000 per annum range through the rest of the 1950s, lower even than the modest requests for new appropriations made by the administration. In the event it took over 20 years, until 1972, to achieve the 'six-year' programme envisaged in the 1949 Act (Bratt, 1986: 338).

In 1953 Eisenhower appointed a committee to review government housing programmes. This advocated a small public housing programme of 35,000 units a year for four years. Even this failed to pass Congress, which authorised a one-year programme of 35,000 units, limited to communities with active slum clearance and urban redevelopment programmes. With this decision the rationale for public housing, as an adjunct and aid to urban renewal, was clearly established. The size of the programme was puny compared to the level of housing needs and has continued to be so. Moreover, administrative action further limited the numbers of units built, for example in 1957 and 1958 to under 30,000, less than half the number for which appropriations were granted.

Eisenhower's so-called 'dynamic conservatism' resulted in a minimal public housing programme throughout the 1950s. At the same time, federal support for urban renewal and the private housing market expanded. As suburban home ownership rose, the residualization of public housing accelerated and the basis for later social and economic problems was firmly established. Reviewing 20 years of public housing, Fisher (1959) noted some of the most ominous trends. In the war years, when the removal of over-income tenants was prohibited, and up to 1948, turnover and vacancies in the public housing stock were very low. Projects still housed a fairly wide range of lower-income households with a reasonable, if limited, rent-paying capacity (tenants had to pay 20 per cent of their income in rent). This meant that the need for federal subsidies was modest, rents covered all operating costs and a high proportion of the debt repayments as well. However, as over-income tenants were forced out in the 1950s, or chose to leave as their incomes rose and private housing became attainable, the concentration of poverty-level households intensified. While in 1950 the federal government had to pay out only 27 per cent of the maximum level of annual subsidies which the legislation provided for, by 1957 this had risen to 78 per cent (Fisher, 1959: 164). While in 1948 25 per cent of public housing tenants had been 'over-income', this had been reduced to 1 per cent by 1957. As Fisher (1959: 165) noted, the clientele for public housing was now restricted to 'among others, families without workers, non-whites, broken families, relief cases and the aged'. Between 1948 and 1957 the proportion of non-white tenants rose from 37 per cent to 48 per cent, many of whom came from urban renewal areas. Between 1952 and 1957 families dependent on welfare benefits rose from 29 per cent to 38 per cent. By the latter date one-third of tenant households had no economically active members and over a quarter were single-parent households. In 1948 the median income of public housing tenants was 44 per cent below that of all urban households, and by 1957 it was 58 per cent below.

So, public housing became identified as housing of last resort for the stigmatized urban poor and, as Fisher (1959: 252) reports, many eligible households in housing need rejected it. At the same time, inadequate public housing management, running poor-quality projects, was unable to deal with the accumulating social and economic problems it faced. These problems were most evident in the big cities, in smaller settlements, notably in the South; small-scale public housing projects presented far fewer difficulties. In every area, bar a few, blacks and whites were mainly housed in segregated projects. As Meyerson and Banfield's (1955) classic study of the politics of public housing location in Chicago showed, public housing helped to reinforce the confinement of black and other minority households within urban ghettoes (see also Bowly, 1978). Not until the civil rights developments of the 1960s was there any real attempt to alter this pattern, but by then the concentration of black households in public housing was so high that desegregation was virtually impossible, even where the will to bring this about existed. [23]

In the last chapter we noted the strong elements of social control incorporated in the management of residualized forms of social housing. While the rhetoric of building communities accompanied early public housing, constructed for the 'submerged middle class', as G. Wright (1981: 234) notes, a sterner tone was struck in the 1950s:

> housing officials still believed that they could reform poor families by situating them in model environments; but the image of that environment, and the tenants' participation in shaping it, changed dramatically. Champions of public housing declared that it would cut mortality rates and stamp out prostitution, reduce crime and eliminate juvenile delinquency – if housing authorities had enough control. There was less rhetoric about building communities and more talk about enforcing order. Housing authorities in cities now preferred massive projects of a unified but distinctive appearance [i.e. distinct from surrounding private housing] to the small projects that blended into the surrounding neighbourhoods. They assumed that a change in scale would help the residents break with their past surroundings and acquaintances.

Instead, these vast and grim projects served further to stigmatize their occupants, as Catherine Bauer (1957) noted sadly, and, like the high-rise projects in Europe, rapidly developed a complex series of interlinked social, economic and physical problems (see, for example, Rainwater's (1970) classic study of the infamous

Pruitt-Igoe project in St Louis). Like their equivalents in Europe, the housing professionals argued that massive high-rise projects provided cheaper housing (for examples of the type of projects that were built, see Bowly, 1978). This was an illusion; even when the units were constructed, the costs of maintaining their deteriorating structures rocketed in the 1960s and 1970s. In these projects tenants were bound round with regulations, according to G. Wright (1981: 237):

> [m]anagement controlled every aspect of the residents' lives – the keeping of pets, the policy about overnight guests, the color of paint on the walls, the schedules for using the washing machines – but it adopted the attitude that spending too much money on safety and maintenance of public facilities was wasteful, since the fundamental problems were too extreme. The tenants recognised the combination of disdain and high-minded belief that public housing could elevate tenants, make them more orderly.

By the early 1960s public housing, despite its continued modest successes, was firmly saddled with a wholly negative public and political image.[24] Although the private sector lobby had been unable to eradicate public housing, it had successfully destroyed its fortunes in the longer run. The new urban programmes of the Democratic administrations of the 1960s, which greatly expanded federally subsidized low- and moderate-income housing construction, shaped these in ways that were acceptable to the building and real estate industries. The federal programmes which provided tax breaks and subsidies for the construction of private rental and home-ownership units resulted in high profits for builders, investors and real estate professionals. They also resulted, from the 1970s onwards, in a major problem of defective units and financially unviable developments, as the federal benefits ran out and project owners defaulted on loan payments (see *Housing Policy Debate*, 1991). The new style federal housing programmes of the 1960s indicated that public housing no longer seemed to be the way forward. Although President Kennedy called for an increased appropriation for public housing, in 1961–3 only 72,000 starts occurred, an average rate less than that in the last year of the Eisenhower presidency (Keith, 1973: 145). One difficulty, as public housing increasingly accommodated non-white tenants, was finding new sites in the teeth of opposition from white residents. Kennedy, as Keith reports, was in any case less concerned with urban affairs than his successor Johnson, who in early 1964 called for a four-year, 200,000-unit public housing programme. He also suggested that public housing authorities should lease 40,000 units of private sector housing. This was the first attempt to remould public housing, to avoid the stigmatizing consequences of project development and to build bridges with the private housing sector. The leased housing scheme had, within a decade, been transformed into the main form of federally subsidized low-rent housing provision, as we shall see. However, in 1964, all the President got was a one-year extension of existing programmes and authorizations for 37,500 additional public housing units. In 1965, after his landslide election victory, the President tried again, this time for a 60,000 per annum, four-year programme and for a rent supplement programme, in which low-income tenants would be subsidized to occupy private sector dwellings. Unsurprisingly, this latter proposal drew support from the private sector interests which had been most opposed to public housing, and was opposed by some public housing authorities and by suburban interests because it did not require local authorization and aroused fears that black households might be relocated to white neighbourhoods. After a struggle, these proposals passed into law as the 1965 Housing Act, although the rent supplement programme was cut in half by Congressional refusal to appropriate funds.

In 1967 the highest number of public housing units in the years since Kennedy had become President was started, although this figure was only 33,400. By now, elderly people were eligible for public housing and the authorities soon discovered that these tenants were far less trouble to manage than poor families (and they were mainly white, whereas the families were mainly non-white). The polarization of public housing, at least in the big cities, with some projects housing white, low-income elderly tenants and other projects, frequently the highest-density and worst-quality inner-city schemes, housing black and other minority households (with high proportions of single-parent households), dates from this period. By the end of 1967 the 1949 Housing Act goal of 810,000 units was still far away; 674,000 units had been completed – and these included units built under the 1930s legislation. Public housing accounted for 1.2 per cent of the national housing stock (Keith, 1973: 184).

In 1968 the administration again tried to increase public housing output, although the schemes for subsidized private rental and home-ownership construction embodied in the 1968 Housing Act took centre stage. In a further attempt to engage the private sector in public housing, and to circumvent the cumbersome bureaucracy of 'conventional' public housing development, Johnson wanted an increased use of 'turnkey' construction, which had begun in 1966.

This involved private developer projects which were sold to the public housing authorities. The 1968 Housing Act, passed by a Congress under pressure from the wave of urban riots following the assassination of Martin Luther King, also set a national housing production goal of 26 million units over the next ten years, 6 million of which were to be for low- and moderate-income households, an annual rate six times the level achieved by all the federal housing programmes for these groups in that year. Throughout the first half of the 1960s, public housing completions remained well below what they had been in the early 1950s, at 25,000–30,000 per annum. Only in the last years of the Johnson presidency was there a significant rise in output, although the main impact of the decisions taken at this time was only reflected in rising output after the Nixon presidency began. Between 1967 and 1971 completions rose from just under 39,000 to an all-time record of over 91,000 (Bratt, 1986: 338). This was still well below the rate envisaged in 1949.

Ironically, therefore, the first Nixon administration coincided with the highest ever levels of public housing output. However, the President was determined to reduce the federal role in housing and urban policy, ending the specific programmes developed under the Democratic administrations and replacing them with a reduced block grant for state and local governments to use according to their own priorities. In general, Nixon's policies reflected his wish to shift federal assistance away from the big city populations, which had not supported him in 1968, to the suburban, white middle class. The administration's deliberate failure to enforce civil rights, housing and education legislation also had this aim in view. Finally, after his landslide victory in the 1972 election, the President took a more radical step, suspending or terminating all federally subsidized housing and urban programmes in January 1973. This led by 1976 to public housing completions falling below 7000, the lowest level since 1950 (when the 1949 programme had just begun).

We shall discuss subsequent events in the next chapter, but increasingly now the plight of the existing public housing stock, rather than the question of new construction, was what occupied the attention of government and Congress (see de Leeuw, 1974; Meehan, 1975; Struyk, 1980). The increasing concentration of poor households in public housing, with high proportions dependent on low welfare benefits, resulted in static rental income. However, as inflation accelerated and as many projects experienced growing dereliction, vandalism, high vacancy rates and so on, the annual federal contributions were no longer sufficient to meet public housing authorities' costs. In this situation there were two, equally damaging, responses. The first was to cut management and maintenance still further to try to reach a balanced budget; this added to the problems listed above. The second was to increase rents to unsustainable levels. That such a financial crisis would eventually occur had been obvious for many years; Fisher's (1959) study, for example, had clearly indicated this (see also Walsh, 1970). The social and political objectives of the public housing legislation, to target this housing at the very poor and avoid all possibility of competition with the private sector, were in contradiction with the economic objective, to limit strictly federal subsidies, according to a formula which took no account of the public housing tenants' ability to pay.

What eventually gave way was the federal commitment to meeting only the costs of debt repayment. In the early 1960s, when public housing first admitted elderly people, the government had provided a fixed rate subsidy of $120 per tenant per annum to assist authorities with their operating costs. This was later extended to handicapped, displaced, large and very low-income families. However, many public housing tenants still faced impossible rent rises and in 1969–71 Senator Edward Brooke succeeded in amending the law to ensure that public housing tenants could not be charged more than 25 per cent of their income in rent and utilities costs. In addition, because this would have resulted in financial disaster for some authorities, the Brooke amendments enabled the federal government to supplement their annual contributions with annual operating subsidies. These rose extremely rapidly, from $12.6 million in 1969 to $102.8 million in 1972, at which point the government sought to devise a funding formula which would, it was hoped, stem this rise by encouraging more effective and efficient public housing management (Bratt, 1986: 339). This Performance Funding System, implemented in 1974, will be discussed in the next chapter. At the same time, the first of a long series of initiatives began which attempted to improve public housing management and deal with the particularly difficult combination of physical, social and economic problems found in some of the worst urban projects. These have been widely criticized for being poorly conceived, sporadically pursued, underfunded and largely ineffective (Kolodny, 1979; Struyk, 1980). The most interesting, if small-scale, development concerned the tenant management of several projects, aided by special federal programmes in most cases (Center for Urban Programs, 1975; Kolodny, 1976; Manpower

Demonstration Research Corporation, 1981). However, these experiments did not lead to a large-scale growth of tenant-managed projects for various reasons (see Harloe and Martens, 1990). [25]

In 1976 a survey of the characteristics of public housing tenants in the large cities, where most of the severest problems were located, was carried out. This showed not just that public housing tenants were very poor but that they were a special group within the poor. According to Struyk (1980: 47), '[t]he archetypical household is black, headed by a female under age 65 living in a household of four people, and has AFDC [Aid for Families with Dependent Children] payments as the primary income source' (i.e. is a single parent dependent on the main form of welfare benefit for such households). Struyk compared the characteristics of public housing tenants and all households whose low incomes made them eligible for federal low-income housing programmes. While 73 per cent of the tenants were black and another 10 per cent of 'Spanish' (i.e. Hispanic) origins, and only 16 per cent were white, over 53 per cent of the eligible were white, 37 per cent black and 8 per cent Hispanic. Half the public housing tenants were female-headed, single-parent families, compared with 32 per cent of the eligible. Some 43 per cent of tenants were dependent on welfare benefits such as AFDC, compared with 16 per cent of the eligible. By contrast, 27 per cent of tenants were dependent on social security benefits (i.e. mainly the elderly), compared with 41 per cent of the eligible.

In effect, public rented housing, at least in major urban areas, had become a form of highly stigmatized ghetto housing for the group within the poverty population which has the lowest incomes of all – black single mothers – and the least chance of finding affordable and habitable private rental housing. By the 1970s US public housing exhibited some of the worst social, physical and economic consequences of a residual social housing system.

Of the European countries with which we are concerned, the furthest progress towards residualization had been made, by the mid-1970s, in Britain. The situation had been very different in 1945, with the first majority Labour government and a massive backlog of housing needs. The residual policy of the 1930s was replaced by a programme of mass (or, as the British government put it, 'general needs') building. Within a few years the government had nationalized development rights and values, instituted a comprehensive system of town and country planning, involving a new towns programme for the relocation of population out of the major cities and controls over the location of new manufacturing industry. All these reforms had in fact been prepared during wartime, by the coalition government (Cullingworth, 1970; Hall, 1980: 99–124). However, there were no links between this physical planning apparatus and economic planning (which, as we have seen, hardly existed anyway). In a country which had already completed the urban-industrial transition, the main concern was to deal with the uneven development that had occurred, steering industry towards the regions where, in the interwar period, there had been high rates of unemployment owing to the decline of heavy industries, dispersing the growth industries which in the 1930s had concentrated in the southern parts of the country.

It was assumed, in Britain as elsewhere, that there would be a low rate of population growth; the enormous boost given to housing demand by the trend to smaller households was not anticipated. Moreover, it was envisaged that most urban development, including housing, would be executed by the public sector. The Labour government restricted private housebuilding and planned for 80 per cent of new housing to be constructed by the local authorities. One indication that social housing would be provided for a broad range of social and economic groups was the removal, in a housing subsidy act passed in 1949, of the reference which had been in all previous housing legislation to council housing as housing for the working classes. Previously, the government had anyway made it clear that 'working classes' referred to 'all sections of the working population' (Marwick, 1970: 355, 359).

According to Holmans (1987: 91–3), the crude housing shortage in England and Wales in 1945 was about 2 million; this was the largest recorded shortage, the figure having peaked in the interwar years at around 1.5 million in the 1920s. Allowing for 'involuntary' sharing households, the 1945 shortage was about 4.35 million, around one-third of all potential households. Wartime destruction accounted for a relatively small proportion of this, about 450,000, although the losses were concentrated in a few major cities. A more important cause was the lack of wartime building and the inherited pre-war shortage. By 1951 there had been very little reduction in the figures. In fact, the crude shortage was not eliminated until the early 1970s and Holmans (1987: 134) comments:

> not until the later 1960s did the balance between dwellings and potential households return to what it had been in 1939. In that sense it took twenty years to make good the effects of the war on English housing, and there is here the reason why shortages affected housing policy so powerfully and for so long.

He adds that even by 1971 there were still concealed households; thus the objective, set out by the Ministry of Reconstruction in 1945, of 'a separate dwelling for every family that wishes to have one' remained unachieved.

The housing shortage was a major political issue in the 1940s and 1950s. In 1945 public opinion polls showed that housing was the single most important issue for the majority of the electorate. Analysis of election manifestos shows that housing was the major social issue highlighted in the Conservative election manifestos in the first four post-war elections (1945, 1950, 1951, 1955) and again in 1970 and the October 1974 election. It figured first in the Labour manifestos of 1945 and 1955 (Perry, 1986: 222). Despite this political pressure, the Labour government set no clear targets for housebuilding; the lack of available building labour, shortages of raw materials and, above all, the economic situation, with the need to channel investment into exports and restrict imports, dominated housing policy (Morgan, 1984: 163–70).

As previously, housing formed a part of the portfolio of the Minister of Health. Not until 1951 was there a separate Ministry, combining housing, local government affairs and planning. The new Minister in 1945, Aneurin Bevan, was mainly concerned with the establishment of the National Health Service, and gave relatively little attention to housing. Bevan did, however, insist that rents were less than those which the Treasury advocated and that the space and other standards of the new houses be raised above the pre-war levels. So the new housing set new standards for rented accommodation and, like the housing built after 1919, but not that built in the 1930s, it consisted mainly of semi-detached (duplex) and terraced (row) properties built at low densities rather than multi-storey, high-density flats. As Morgan (1984: 165) notes, the slow progress of housebuilding soon gave rise to powerful complaints within the government and beyond it. There was a growth of squatting in empty property, including offices in major cities, which the government urged local authorities to take firm action against (Merrett, 1979: 238; Morgan, 1990: 40). In 1946 and 1947, barely 120,000 units of council housing were completed; by 1948 this figure had risen to 190,000. However, the dollar crisis and devaluation of the late 1940s led to a cut-back in housing, so that output fell to an annual rate of around 160,000. It only exceeded the 1948 level in 1953, under the new Conservative government (Merrett, 1979: 320–1).

Despite Bevan's determination to maintain a high-quality house-building programme, with the private sector restricted to no more than 20 per cent of output, pressure to revert to a more limited local authority role and lower standards was already evident in the late 1940s. In part, the reduction of standards, which Bevan eventually conceded, was deemed necessary to maintain output while economizing on finance, labour and materials. Initially, the pressure to diversify the sources of construction was inspired by the slow progress of the local authorities. In the early years of the government, the alternatives of direct government building or building by a National Housing Corporation which would act when the local authorities failed to do so, were canvassed. However, pressure to allow more private building also grew, aided by the fact that the building societies had large sums which could be lent for house purchase. With tight restrictions on the financial aid available for council building and an election in the offing in 1950, Bevan eventually consented to some relaxation of the licensing system for private housing, although private housing completions remained at around 30,000–40,000 per annum throughout the Labour government (Merrett, 1982: 346–7). Almost all of these were for home ownership; significant construction for private rental ceased after the 1930s, even when, in the 1950s, the Conservatives lifted rent controls (Harloe, 1985).

Between 1945 and 1951 Britain came closest to moving from a private to a socialized housing market, at least in relation to new building. Nationalization of development rights and values and control of private construction were the main instruments employed. However, the commitment to socialized housing, and the extent to which it was socialized, were limited. Most of the building industry remained in private hands, although some local authorities carried out 'direct labour' construction. Although most finance for council housing came through the official Public Works Loans Board (PWLB), this in turn borrowed on the private capital markets. Apart from the nationalization of the Bank of England, the major private financial institutions survived and, as we have seen, the Labour government accepted the 'mixed economy' of capitalism and the state's role within it. As Marwick (1982: 184) notes:

> the private sector in key areas of the social services remained vigorous – public schools, private insurance schemes, private medical and specialist services, a capitalist housing market and building industry. These areas were even expanding during the later period of the government ... [when] 'consolidation' led to greater encouragement for private housebuilders.

The apparent failure of the Labour government, with its regime of economic austerity and controls, to provide better living conditions for the population was a potent campaigning issue for the Conservatives in the 1950 and 1951 elections. They promised to lift controls, 'set the people free' and allow the private market to generate prosperity. In relation to housing, this soon led to a policy which promoted home ownership and began to restrict council housing to the more residual role which had been the basis for Conservative policies in the 1930s. However, in the first few years of the Conservative government, there was a sharp rise in council housing completions, which peaked at an all-time high of over 200,000 in 1953 and 1954 before beginning a long decline to 105,000 in 1961 (Merrett, 1979: 320–1).

The reason for the initial boost to council housing, under a government strongly committed to returning housing to the private sector and promoting home ownership, was purely a matter of short-term political expediency and was not, in fact, originally what the party leadership had intended. As we have seen, housing remained a key political issue in the early 1950s and, at the 1950 Conservative Party conference, representatives of the reformist 'One Nation' wing of the party pushed the leadership into an election manifesto pledge that 300,000 houses a year would be built, when, as Morgan (1984: 485) notes, 'the chairman of the conference momentarily lost control'. In the short run, this pledge could be redeemed only by increasing local authority building, which the new Housing Minister, Harold MacMillan, did, cutting space standards to reduce costs (Merrett, 1979: 102).

As we have noted, the government played a passive role in relation to economic development and modernization in the 1950s, content to rely on private sector growth and macro-economic controls. So, the links between housing and economic policies became even more attenuated than in the 1940s. However, economic growth and social change led to a rapid rise in the demand for new housing and in the income available to pay for it. The central objective of Conservative housing and urban policies, in line with their long-held philosophy, was to meet these demands by an expansion of home ownership which was a politically, economically and ideologically preferable form of housing. Now, as between the wars, after the initial crisis caused by the housing shortage was eased, the return to a state-aided private market was desired. Social housing would revert to the residual role which the Conservatives in the 1930s had finally accepted was necessary, as an aid to slum clearance and the largely private redevelopment of urban areas. In this sense, there were obvious parallels with the conception of public housing that had emerged after the war in America.

However, progress towards this goal was not easy in the 1950s and early 1960s, with the continued political salience of housing (Merrett, 1979: 246–54; Holmans, 1987: 91–166; Malpass, 1990: 46–54). For most of the decade, too, the Conservatives held the vain hope that some of the demand for lower-income housing could be diverted to a revived private rental sector. But rent decontrol in 1957 completely failed to stimulate new rental investment; indeed, it accelerated the process of tenure conversion and was a source of political conflict and government unpopularity (Harloe, 1985: 136–7). Not until the 1980s did a more radically right-wing Conservative administration again try to revive private renting as an alternative to council housing.

In 1953 the government had already begun to shift the emphasis away from council housing, announcing that new building for 'general needs' would now be left to the private sector; this would save on subsidies (Merrett, 1979: 248). Furthermore, home ownership was stated to be the form of ownership 'most satisfying to the individual and most beneficial to the nation'. An annual output of about 300,000 was envisaged, and council building would fill the gap between this target and what the private sector built. Local authorities should again concentrate on building units for those displaced by slum clearance. This policy was given teeth in 1956, when subsidies were restricted to slum rehousing and a few other purposes, such as small dwellings for the elderly.

There were several other elements in this reorientation of council housing policy (see Malpass, 1990: 89–94). First, there was pressure to reduce subsidies and target them on the poor. Subsidies were not uprated with inflation, local authorities were no longer required to make contributions to council housing from their general revenues, and rent pooling, available since 1935, was now increasingly used, at government insistence, to cross-subsidize the costs of new units by charging higher rents on older properties. One consequence was that Britain did not face the same necessity for rent 'harmonization' in the inflationary 1960s as did other European countries. Second, after 1955, the state no longer provided loan capital, through the PWLB, for council housing. Instead, it was financed more expensively by direct borrowing on the private money and capital markets. Third, the apparatus of planning and controls which had prioritized council housing and restricted the private market was largely abolished. All building controls were lifted by 1954 and, by the end of the decade, the private land market was fully restored, ensuring that the local authorities paid open market prices.

Finally, with the reversion to a slum clearance role for social housing, there was also a reversion to the higher-density apartment building reminiscent of the 1930s. In the late 1950s, as in the 1930s, the subsidy system was altered to encourage this change. The proportion of houses in local authority dwelling approvals fell from 77 per cent in 1953 to around 50 per cent by the mid-1960s (and was much lower in the big cities, where most of the slum rehousing occurred) (Dunleavy, 1981: table 2.1, 41). Increasingly, these apartments were in high-rise, industrially built blocks. By the mid-1960s, when this building form reached its peak popularity, it accounted for about a quarter of all new units. There were several reasons for this change, including the pressure put on local authorities (sometimes corruptly) by large private sector building firms which had invested in industrialized building; the influence of architectural and planning fashions; the wish to rehouse the slum populations within existing city boundaries (or the reluctance of Conservative rural authorities and suburbs to accept 'overspill' and council housing whose inhabitants might be Labour voters); and the benefits that industrialized techniques seemed to offer to councils that wanted to build more houses but that faced shortages of skilled building labour, much of which was engaged in a private sector construction boom (Young and Kramer, 1978; Dunleavy, 1981). Within a few years much of the high-rise housing was beginning to suffer from the complex of physical and social problems which we have already described. By the 1970s the image of vast, bleak high-rise estates, suffering from physical decay and vandalism, with high levels of social problems, helped to reinforce the generally negative image which council housing had obtained and the stigmatizing effects of residence in some of these areas on their inhabitants (Power, 1987). The fact that the majority of council housing did not suffer from these problems, and that, especially on the many low-rise 'cottage' and other developments which had been built before and after the war, tenants remained satisfied with their housing and living conditions, did not prevent this negative labelling of council housing and tenants, which also reinforced the positive ideology that was attached to home ownership and home owners (see, for example, Saunders, 1990).

This policy shift was accompanied by an increasing polarization in the political debate over housing. While in the 1940s the Conservatives had objected to the stringency of controls on private building, in practice the priority given to council housing was largely accepted. But in the 1950s, when the objective of promoting home ownership and restricting council housing again came to the fore, Ministers encouraged a mythology of the oversubsidized council tenant, implying that anyone who could afford to buy their house should do so (Merrett, 1979: 252). At the same time, Labour became typecast as the party of the council tenant, so that, after it lost the 1959 election, this began to be seen as a particular political liability.[26] In consequence, Labour's attachment to a policy which put council housing first began to wane and its attempts to be seen as a friend of home ownership, alongside the Conservatives, were evident by the early 1960s. By the time Labour returned to government, while the political rhetoric surrounding tenure still divided the parties, the Conservatives had largely seized the initiative, defining council housing as a residual form of provision and home ownership as the 'normal' housing tenure for most households, and Labour had begun to accept this proposition.

The output of private housing rose rapidly in the 1950s, from 22,000 in 1951 to a peak of over 200,000 per annum in the mid-1960s. By 1959 it accounted for more than 50 per cent of output for the first time since the war and by 1961 it was almost up to two-thirds of output (Merrett, 1979: 320–1; 1982: 346–7). However, the Conservatives' policies encountered several difficulties. The housing shortage, as we have seen, remained considerable. Rent decontrol failed to stimulate new private output and led to highly publicized attempts by unscrupulous landlords to remove tenants by force or intimidation in order to relet at higher rents or sell off their properties. In the early 1960s, in response to growing political pressure and public outcry about conditions in London in particular, the government was forced to appoint an influential commission of enquiry (Committee on Housing in Greater London, 1965). Pressure to clear more slums in order to make way for private and civic redevelopment and new roads was growing. Council housing still provided the only source of accommodation for most of those displaced by clearance and the decline in the private rented sector. All this resulted in a limited reversion to subsidies for some 'general needs' housing, although the main objective was that '[a]s real incomes go up, more and more of this need, both for sale and to rent, should be met by private enterprise', with local authorities building 'for the needs which only they can meet' (Merrett, 1979: 253, quoting a 1961 government policy document). The renewed concern with council housebuilding was particularly noticeable in the last years of the Conservative government up to the 1964 election, when the Labour Party campaigned on private rental scandals and the previous decline in council house output.

Labour returned to government in 1964 with a commitment to increasing housing output to 500,000 units a year. Included in this programme was a big rise in council house building, and in 1967 a more generous subsidy system, which protected councils against some of the impact of rising interest rates, was introduced (Holmans, 1987: 336–40). However, by now Labour accepted the Conservative definition of home ownership as the most desirable tenure and sought to ensure that it could no longer be typecast as the party of council tenants and the enemy of the home owner. At a time when increasing proportions of Labour's core electorate, skilled manual workers, were aspiring to, and achieving, home ownership, this made political sense. Like the Conservatives, Labour now saw the council building programme as a temporary expedient, linked to slum clearance and, by implication, as a programme to house those low-income households which could not afford home ownership. In short, the shift to a residualized conception of council housing now stretched across the political spectrum. This was spelt out in the government's 1965 housing policy White Paper, which referred to the need to reduce council building once the slum problem had been overcome. The current expansion of council building was to meet 'exceptional needs' and was a 'short term necessity', but '[t]he expansion of building for owner-occupation ... is normal; it reflects a long-term social advance' (quoted in Merrett, 1979: 255).

The boost in council housing output – completions rose almost 80 per cent between 1961 and 1967 (although in the latter year they remained below the private sector total) – soon fell victim to the economic difficulties which beset the Labour government. Nevertheless, this did enable most of the worst slum housing to be demolished, with many displacees being rehoused in high-rise projects. There was growing criticism of such projects from tenants, housing experts and housing managers, however. The high-rise boom ended in the late 1960s as its social and other costs became apparent. The demise was accelerated after the collapse of a high-rise block in the East End of London in 1968 led to the disclosure of the scandalously low standards of construction which had often been incorporated in these schemes.

By the end of the decade, there was a widespread consensus among housing agencies and experts and across the political spectrum that the emphasis should shift away from clearance and council rehousing towards the rehabilitation of the existing older housing stock. This was a reaction to the criticism of the physical and social effects of mass clearance and high-rise, high-density renewal. It was reinforced by the pressure on public expenditure and a belief that rehabilitation would be cheaper than redevelopment (A. D. Thomas, 1986: 64–70). In addition, with the conversion of an increasing proportion of private rental housing to home ownership, there was a political dividend to be gained from subsidizing these new owners to modernize and improve their accommodation. There was also rising political and community-based conflict when local authorities tried to enforce their clearance (J. G. Davies, 1972; Dennis, 1972).

Although governments had attempted since the mid-1950s to redefine council housing as a residual sector, their ability to ensure that this occurred was still limited. In particular, there were limits on the ability to enforce the targeting of subsidies on low-income households within the council sector. Historically, rent policy had been a matter for the local authorities alone, subject only to a general provision that rents should be set at 'reasonable' levels (Malpass, 1990: 57–113). Although subsidy levels were at times cut back to try to narrow the range of households for whom the local authorities built and to raise the share of income coming from rents, councils were partially able to circumvent this by making contributions from their general revenues to council housing. Rent pooling also helped those councils which had a large stock of older housing to maintain their building programmes. Moreover, while the Labour Party nationally was now committed in the longer run to a limited scale of new building, many Labour-controlled local authorities still had a strong ideological commitment to public housing, and also saw at first hand the continuing needs in their areas.

By the time that the Conservatives returned to power in 1970, the absolute shortage of housing was no longer evident, so political pressure for a mass council building programme had faded. Now it was commonly held that the main requirement was for a limited programme of council housing for 'special needs', that is, for distinctive groups of poor people in limited areas of the country, mainly the inner areas of the big cities. In addition, the two decades of promotion of home ownership as the most socially desirable tenure, the labelling of council housing as second-class accommodation for the poor and the unpopular slum clearance programmes, aided by the high-rise disasters, meant that the agenda of housing politics firmly centred on owner occupation, with each party vying to prove that it would do most for home owners.

In these circumstances, the new government initiated a more determined effort to confine council housing to a residual role, although it did so in a politically inept manner which created a short-lived but intense bout of political conflict and resistance from councils and their tenants. In the 1972 Housing Finance Act it removed the power of local authorities to set rent levels (Malpass, 1990: 114–25). These would now be determined by the same means that had existed since 1965 for rent setting in the private sector. The intention was to increase council rents sharply to quasi-market levels. All previous subsidy regimes, which were still applied to those units that had been built during the time when they were operative, were phased out and a new and more limited subsidy provided, which was intended to allow new building only where this remained absolutely necessary, such as in the major cities. The new regime of higher rents and lower subsidies was accompanied by a national rent rebate scheme, whose costs were split between central and local government, to target additional means-tested assistance on poorer households that could not afford the new rent levels. More generally, the intention was to increase pressure on better-off tenants to move out and become home owners. It was the prospect of higher rents which led to an intense campaign by tenants and many Labour local authorities against the new act (Sklair, 1975).[27] The national leadership of the Labour Party was careful not to endorse the more radical protests, but it did pledge to return the rent-setting power to local authorities and to revise the subsidy arrangements when it returned to government. We consider these changes in the next chapter.

A more minor theme, which later became significant, was an attempt to find an alternative to the private landlord, which the Conservatives now seemed to accept could not be revived, as a provider of lower-income rented housing. Given the ideological distaste for any further extension of council housing, especially when provided by Labour councils, and concern about rigid and bureaucratic local authority housing management, interest began to be shown in reviving the housing associations, which had languished as almost a forgotten corner of the housing system since the First World War (Malpass and Murie, 1987: 154–61). In the early 1960s the Conservative government legislated to increase their activities. The associations were also promoted by some influential housing activists who had links with leading associations and who recognized that they were more palatable to the government as a source of new rented housing than private landlords or local authorities. However, it was not until attention turned to large-scale housing rehabilitation that the associations were seen as one of the main vehicles for bringing about this programme, especially in the inner cities. Generous subsidies were made available in the 1974 Housing Act, prepared under the Conservative government but passed, with slight amendments, when Labour returned to power. These changes appeared to provide support for independent, non-profit bodies, like those in Denmark, the Netherlands and Germany, and to reduce the degree of political control over social housing. In fact, they increased government control. Associations in receipt of the new subsidies were supervized by the Housing Corporation, a nominally independent body, but one over which the Ministry exerted greater control than the locally elected councils.

Local authority output, which had begun to decline after Labour's public expenditure cuts in the late 1960s, fell further, to 88,000 in 1973, the lowest level since 1946. At the same time, the economic boom of the early 1970s, with high inflation, rising incomes, easy credit and low real mortgage interest rates, stimulated a speculative private housing boom. In 1972, 228,000 private units were started, the third highest level since the late 1930s and one not exceeded since (Merrett, 1982: 346). House prices increased at an unprecedented rate, doubling in the three years from 1970 (Merrett, 1982: 298). Eventually, the boom collapsed and by 1974 private sector starts were at their lowest level since the early 1950s.

Despite the various setbacks and delays suffered by the strategy of restricting the role of social housing over the years, and the surface rhetoric of party political differences, the persistent tendency towards residualization is evident. Even in the late 1940s, the Labour Party had a limited conception of socialized housing, essentially embracing only the ownership and distribution of the housing stock rather than its production and financing, and leaving space for the private housing market to begin its dynamic post-war expansion. Meanwhile, the Conservatives always regarded mass council housing as a short-term expedient, pending the recovery of the private market. Sharp political differences persisted over the detailed treatment of council housing, although not over the increasingly large tax subsidies for home ownership. By the 1970s, political support for council housing was waning. This was re-inforced, and in turn helped to reinforce, a decline in public support for social housing. While in earlier years opinion polls had shown strong support for increased council building, this now became, along with expenditure on welfare benefits for the poor, a less popular preference than, for example, more spending on health and education. In the minds of much of the population, council housing became associated with the well-publicized problems of high-rise 'sink' estates, despite the fact that these only accounted for a tiny proportion of the actual stock (Power, 1987). Home ownership became strongly associated with values such as 'choice', 'freedom' and 'self-reliance'. In inflationary times the economic motive for investment in housing became important. In the 1960s and 1970s public opinion surveys showed a steady rise in the proportion of households aspiring to home ownership (Holmans, 1987: 198–201).

Along with the emergence in political and popular discourse of a sharp differentiation between home ownership and council housing, there were important changes in the composition of council house tenants, as this sector became increasingly redefined as housing for the poor. Holmans (1987: 167–204) provides some interesting data on this transition. In the early 1950s council tenants tended to be drawn from the better-paid manual occupations, with low proportions of retired people and others not in employment. Comparisons of income by tenure for 1953/4 and 1963 show that the proportion of council tenants in the lowest-income brackets rose considerably over this period for two reasons: the start of major council building for elderly people and the role that slum clearance played in transferring poor households from private rental housing to the council sector. In the 1960s and 1970s, as Holmans (1987: 189) notes, 'with more and more of the households with sizeable and stable earnings becoming owner-occupiers, those households that were tenants were increasingly only those with only low earnings, or no earnings at all'. By the mid-1970s, the concentration in the council sector of households with high levels of ill health, unemployment and other problems was apparent.[28] A potent indicator of the growing gap between council tenants and home owners, apart from the widening income differential as the aggregate of council tenants got poorer, was the relative change in levels of those who were outside the labour market and dependent on state benefits. In 1962 17 per cent of home owners were economically inactive, but only 11 per cent of council tenants. This reflected the number of retired home owners and the extent to which council housing was still allocated, above all, to what might be described as the core working class, employed family heads. By 1978 the proportion of the economically inactive in owner occupation had risen only to 19 per cent, while that in the council sector had virtually tripled to 30 per cent, as it became increasingly inhabited by those on the economic margins. In 1954 21.5 per cent of all recipients of the main form of welfare payments for low-income households (supplementary benefits, as they were later called) were in council housing, 10.7 per cent in owner occupation and the remaining 67.8 per cent in private renting. As the private rented sector declined, diverting low-income tenants into council housing, and as better-off council tenants (and the better-off groups who would formerly have become tenants) opted for home ownership, these proportions shifted. By 1960 one-third of all recipients of supplementary benefits were in council housing, 51.7 per cent were in private renting and 12.5 per cent in home ownership. In the 1960s and 1970s, as we have seen, the pace of residualization quickened; by 1976 58.9 per cent of all supplementary benefit recipients were in council housing, 23.7 per cent in private rentals and 17.4 per cent in home ownership (see also Murie, 1983). The outcome of 25 years of policy evolution could not be more graphically illustrated than by these figures.

In Denmark, as we have seen, some steps were taken just before the war to tie social housing subsidies to the accommodation of lower-income households.[29] This policy continued in the early war years; in 1941 a provisional act provided aid for private building in slum clearance areas (Department B, 1971). However, as in Britain, the post-war shortages caused a reversion to a larger-scale policy of building for a broader range of incomes. Preparations for this had been made during the war. In 1940 the government established a Housebuilding Committee whose report was published in 1945. It advocated an expansion of social building on several practical grounds. First, it could supply lower-income groups with a better standard of affordable housing than other agencies; second, a high output of affordable social housing could affect rent levels throughout the market; third, social agencies were better able to undertake large-scale, planned developments which would include adequate community facilities; finally, these agencies would plough back surpluses into further housing construction – to a degree, they could be self-financing (Greve, 1971).

Another important development occurred in 1941 when the unions, with government backing, formed an organization to promote housing associations which later also provided them with management and technical services. The development of cooperatively organized housing services, which had occurred in the inter-war years, was extended through this and other organizations after the war. A further important influence on later policy was a report entitled 'The Housing Movement of the Future', issued by the Federation of Housing Associations (closely linked to the Social

Democrats). This adopted a broader perspective than the government's report, linking the need for an increased supply of lower-income housing to economic development, arguing for a rise in real wages in order to increase housing consumption and reduce inequalities. It also supported state-controlled allocation and rents and the appropriation of rising property values through taxation. In the conditions of post-war shortage, controlled allocation was adopted, only being completely eliminated in the 1970s, and rent controls, which had been reintroduced in 1939, also persisted in changing forms (Harloe, 1985: 130–5). However, the more radical proposals, which sought a major extension of the socialization of housing, were not adopted (Greve, 1971: 27–47).

The post-war history of Danish social housing was moulded by the key economic and political factors which we have already discussed, notably the constraints imposed by the political system on social democracy, with the need to assemble multi-party agreements for new policy developments, and the recurrent balance of payments crises and high levels of inflation and interest rates. In addition, owner-occupied housing formed an important sector in the Danish housing system at an early stage. This derived from the nature of the rural economy and society, with many small independent producers. After 1945, home ownership continued to expand, although, as Vestergaard (1982) has explained, in the early decades this was less because ownership was in itself invested with the positive associations that we have described in the British case, and more because a key issue in the politics of housing and in public pressure for increased housing output was the desire to occupy a single-family house with a garden. Indeed, this was a more important issue after 1945 than the growth of social or private housing *per se*. However, from the 1960s onwards, the distinctions between social rented housing and home ownership which we discussed in relation to Britain did have growing salience in Denmark.

Although there was a pressing need to build in 1945, existing housing standards were probably higher and the shortage was less extreme than in the other countries under review in this book. Denmark suffered relatively little war damage, and did not have the massive problems of demobilization and refugee resettlement that other countries faced. Some building, mainly of social housing, had continued in wartime, at an annual rate of about 10,000 units a year in total (Vestergaard, 1982). Nevertheless, by 1945 there was a considerable housing shortage, and a rapid reversion to the private market was no more feasible than elsewhere. The shortages of building resources and the difficult economic situation dictated much the same mixture of financial and physical controls over housing production, standards, allocation and pricing as elsewhere in Europe. In 1946 the Liberal minority government passed a Housing Act which provided long-term, low-interest state loans for social and private rented housing. However, there was cross-party agreement that state support for private landlords was purely temporary, necessary in the immediate situation, but eventually to be phased out.[30] There was a general concern that such aid would only inflate prices, rents and profits, if these were not controlled. In fact, the loan conditions for private rental building were less favourable than those for social housing and such construction ceased to be subsidized in 1958 (Harloe, 1985: 183). The act also set higher standards for subsidized housing. According to Vestergaard (1982), the average size of social units in the 1930s was 50–60 square metres, rising to 73 square metres in the period 1946–56 and reaching 99 square metres by 1970. As we have noted before, such increases, together with other quality improvements, substantially contributed to the rising cost of social housing in the post-war period. The act also continued a limited scheme of rent subsidies for large families in social housing (Ministry of Housing, 1968: 33).

Attitudes towards the longer-term role of social housing were more divided. On the one hand, the Social Democrats, with their links to the unions, the social housing federation and the other constituent elements in the social housing movement which we have described, supported the priority given to social housing. However, as we have seen, their ability to pursue reformist policies was continually restrained by the necessity for political compromise. On the other hand, the Liberals and Conservatives largely shared the desire of their right-wing counterparts elsewhere in Europe for a return to the private market in housing, as soon as this was feasible, and for a social sector restricted to housing the urban poor.[31]

Throughout the late 1940s and most of the 1950s, the resources for housebuilding were severely restrained by low growth, persistent unemployment and balance of payments difficulties. However, as elsewhere, economic and demographic developments added to housing demand, so even in the 1960s it was estimated that there was a shortage of between 100,000 and 200,000 units. Only after the shift of economic policy in the late 1950s, with accelerating growth and full employment, were these constraints eased. However, balance of payments difficulties still affected the level of housing output. Total production remained within the range of around

20,000–25,000 units per annum until 1958, then rose to an annual total of 40,000 in 1965, around 50,000 by the end of the decade and a post-war peak of over 55,000 in 1973, just before the mid-decade economic crisis, after which levels fell back to those of the early 1960s (Danmarks Statistik, various years).

In the years following the 1946 Housing Act, before the private capital market was re-established, around 90 per cent of housing output was aided by state loans. Most social rented housing was built by the housing associations, although in the first few years some local authorities also built a significant number (mainly in Copenhagen). Between 1949 and 1958 the associations constructed just over 100,000 units, around 46 per cent of all new housing (Danmarks Statistik, various years). There was no clear secular trend. Instead, the figures show the impact of recurrent balance of payments crises and deflationary cuts in public expenditure, as output fluctuated across successive cycles. In the early 1960s social housing output fell back from the levels which it had reached in the late 1950s and its share of all output fell even faster as private building increased. But for about a decade from the mid-1960s the absolute level of social housing construction rose to its highest post-war levels, at around 10,000–14,000 units per annum. However, its share of all output remained lower than it had been in the 1940s and 1950s. Between 1960 and 1974 about 160,000 units of social housing were built, but this now amounted to only a quarter of all output (Danmarks Statistik, various years).

These figures show that, as in Britain, the dominance of social housing faded as economic growth and prosperity reinforced the political and economic forces leading to the re-establishment of the private housing market. And, as in Britain too, this mainly took the form of home ownership. Like the British Labour Party, the Danish Social Democrats eventually came to terms with the situation and followed housing policies which, while retaining social housing assistance, endorsed the trend towards home ownership. In fact, conflict over housing policy was at the centre of the wider political struggle on several occasions and, Esping-Andersen (1985) has argued, the compromises which were forced on the Social Democrats contributed to their fading political fortunes in the 1960s and 1970s.

From 1953, as we have seen, the Social Democrats returned to power, where they remained, frequently in alliance with the Radical Liberals until the late 1960s. After the immediate post-war period, conflict over housing policy grew. As Esping-Andersen (1985: 183–4) writes, '[t]he bourgeois parties, backed by powerful interest organisations, held that controls were no longer needed now that the shortage problem had been eased. The free market, they argued, should be permitted to regulate prices and credit for new building'. They also argued that the free market would be better than the social sector in providing the variety of choice required by the population. Here the salience of the demand for single-family houses and gardens, rather than the apartments mainly constructed by the housing associations, becomes evident.

As elsewhere, the rising budgetary costs of housing assistance led to insistent pressure, from the early 1950s, for its reduction. The need to cut subsidies and scrap rent and building controls, the policy adopted in the 1950s by the British Conservatives, was strongly advocated by Liberals and Conservatives. The difficult economic circumstances of the country also put direct pressure on the Social Democrat-led governments, who were unable to pass any major housing legislation without the opposition parties' agreement. In 1954 the interest rates on state loans were raised to market levels and annual subsidies were provided, calculated according to the floor area of the units (Ministry of Housing, 1968, 1974). In 1955 a start was made on lifting rent controls and reducing the system of compulsory housing allocation. This led in 1958 to a multi-party housing pact, in which the return to a private market-led housing system was clearly indicated. As in Britain in 1956, state housing loans were abolished. Most capital for social housing was now borrowed from the reviving private bond market via the peculiar Danish system of mortgage credit institutions. As a minor gesture towards an equitable approach, the taxable values of owner-occupied houses were increased. More significantly, the proportion of a house purchase loan that could be borrowed on the private bond market was increased from around 30–40 per cent to 75 per cent (this involved first and second mortgages). In addition, third mortgages were made available through a special fund, operated mainly by the banks under government supervision. Housing associations could obtain up to 94 per cent of the building costs in mortgage loans, compared with 85–90 per cent for private building. Interest rates rose to the market level of around 5–6 per cent, compared with the previous rate of 2–2.5 per cent on government loans (Greve, 1971: 46).

After 1958, with the opening up of the private mortgage market and the relaxation of controls, plus increased economic growth and rising incomes, the private construction of single-family houses for owner occupation rose rapidly. Owing to its balance of payments situation, interest rates also rose sharply, especially in the inflationary 1960s and early 1970s. Fuelled by rising welfare expenditure and the costs of servicing the National Debt, the marginal rate of tax also grew steadily to around 55–60 per cent by the early 1970s (Vestergaard, 1982). As mortgage tax relief was available at the marginal rate, the drive towards home ownership, which itself contributed to rising house prices, was strongly facilitated. Land speculation was widespread, the price of building plots, which had doubled in the 1950s, rose almost fivefold in the 1960s and similarly in the 1970s. The price of one-family houses rose by about 65 per cent in the first decade, 200 per cent in the second and only slightly less fast in the third (Vestergaard, 1982). Attempts by the Social Democrats to control these processes were thwarted. In 1960 licensing was introduced for all housing construction in the main urban areas, as part of a more general set of building controls. These were phased out by 1966. Annual quotas for social housing were introduced in 1961 (Vestergaard, 1992: 41). In the aftermath of the 1958 changes, the Social Democrats had planned to restrict speculation in land and housing. But in 1963 their legislation to control land and house prices was defeated in a referendum, after a concerted campaign by the farmers, landowners, builders and financial interests, backed by all the non-socialist parties. Attempts were also made to impose (generous) limits on the maximum size of new units and on the construction costs of smaller units. However, under pressure from the right, from property interests and the growing body of home owners, taxes on capital gains due to rising land prices were abolished in 1964/5. One politically contentious consequence of the speculative boom in housing and land, which the Social Democrats sought to control, was the 'freehold conversion' of private rented flats, involving their sale for home ownership and the collection of large profits by the agents who arranged such 'breakups' (Harloe, 1985: 302–3).

After the defeat of the land control bill in 1963, the Radical Liberals left the governing coalition. From 1964 the Social Democrats governed alone, having rejected the possibility of a left alliance, as we earlier described. By now the party was under attack from both the left and the right. Its housing policies were a central theme in these attacks. The new left Socialist Peoples Party (SF) made electoral gains and strongly attacked the 'anti-social' 1958 housing reforms. At the same time, the Social Democrats required support from other parties to develop new policies. As Esping-Andersen (1985: 185) notes:

[i]n contrast to what happened in 1958, the social democrats were now caught in the dilemma of having to choose between a new housing compromise with the left or, as previously, with the right. They opted for the latter, a decision that probably more than any other helped to bring about their electoral demise.

There ensued a new housing pact in 1966. By now the rising costs and rents of new housing were giving rise to a distorted pattern of rents and to pressure to 'harmonize', thus economizing on subsidies. At the same time, inflation made it increasingly difficult to sustain new social housing construction, and the phenomenon of vacant new social units which could not be let because of their high rents began to occur (Ministry of Housing, 1968). According to a 1968 report, by the early 1960s the limited regime of rent allowances for large families and the subsidies for new construction reduced the rent of a new social unit for a low-income, two-child family only by an inadequate 20 per cent. The 1966 pact addressed these issues. It introduced a degressive system of social construction subsidies for a construction quota set at 13,000 units per annum, well above the then current levels of social output. The subsidy or 'interest guarantee' met the gap between the market rates paid on loans and 6.5 per cent; after six years, the full subsidy was scaled down over the following three years and ended completely after nine years.

This system set initial rents below what they had been before 1966. In 1974 it was calculated that rents were reduced to 60 per cent of full cost levels for the first six years (Ministry of Housing, 1974). However, eventually the full cost of construction would be reflected in the rent and ultimately rents would be set at market levels. At the same time the rents of older social and private rented housing were to be 'harmonized', that is, progressively raised to market levels, and the proceeds, in the case of social housing, used to help finance new building. The average planned increase was about 20 per cent in social housing, although it was far higher in Copenhagen. The average rise planned for private rental housing was around 40 per cent (Ministry of Housing, 1974; Harloe, 1985: 134–5). The intention was to focus new social housing construction more narrowly and move away from a mass needs policy. Thus the social housing fund was to provide loans for, among other purposes, slum clearance and urban renewal. The new system provided for 97 per cent of the cost of new social housing to be met by loans (94 per cent from the private market, 3 per cent from the new social housing fund), which was subject to the interest guarantee. This left 3 per cent to be found from the tenants' deposit which had continued after the war. In addition, a system of 'graded rents' (housing allowances) was introduced to cushion the impact of higher rents on low-income households in social and private rented accommodation.

To summarize, the new policy attempted to increase in social housing construction while economizing on subsidies, targeting assistance on low-income households and cross-subsidizing new housing by higher rents on older units. The rent rises were to be phased in over an eight-year period, ending in 1974. The assumption was that the inflation of the mid-1960s would be temporary, that the rate of price rises and the level of interest rates would decline, while incomes continued to rise. The increased rate of construction would also result in a 'housing reserve' which would moderate price rises. The belief was that the rental market could finally be deregulated in 1974 and a cost rent regime in social housing, and market rents in private housing, be established.

This did not occur. Inflation and interest rates increased, so the gap between the rents of older and new housing widened. The high cost of social rented housing owing to inflation and rising standards meant that, even with a rapidly accelerating subsidy burden, the rents of new units became too expensive for many lower-income households. By the early 1970s about 15 per cent of new social flats were standing empty, associations were suffering serious financial problems and the level of building began to fall. The degressive subsidy system placed additional pressure on lower-income households, as their rents increased and the system of graded rents was not adjusted fast enough to compensate. In fact, by the late 1960s, it was already evident that the 1966 pact was a failure and additional measures had to be taken to limit the impact of rising rents in the newer housing. In addition, political resistance managed to prevent a corresponding increase in rental values which had been planned for existing home owners; eventually this was only imposed on new housing built after 1969.

The pact was a disaster for the Social Democrats. The housing associations and tenants objected to the abandonment of historic cost rents and the cross-subsidy to new building. Clearly, this was not in the interests of the majority of tenants, many of whom benefited from low rents in relation to their rising incomes (Greve, 1971: 36–7). The tenants argued that proceeds from higher rents should be used to improve their housing. There was strong opposition to the pact from the labour movement, led by the left-wing SF. Despite the optimism of the Social Democratic Housing Minister, who stated 'we have eliminated one of the largest and most complicated political conflicts' (quoted in Esping-Andersen, 1985: 185), this was not so. In local government elections the Social Democrats incurred heavy losses while the SF gained. Looking back on the episode in 1976, Esping-Andersen (1985: 188) reports that the Social Democratic Finance Minister in the 1966 government stated:

> the agreement on housing was one of the party's major tactical and political blunders. Krag [the Prime Minister] refused to seek support from the SF, and this forced us to settle for legislation which was less beneficial to the working class, which overwhelmingly benefited homeowners, which did not do much to better the conditions of renters, and which did not result in the establishment of a public housing fund.

In the early 1970s, when the Social Democrats had returned to office, they came under constant pressure from the unions and the SF to remove the home-owner tax privileges and increase governmental control over housing finance. However, attempted reform bills were defeated and by now the party, like the British Labour Party, had to face up to the consequences of the spread of home ownership among key sections of its own electorate. One result of this period was the right-wing split from the Social Democrats in 1973, with the formation of the pro-home owner Centre Democratic Party which opposed a government bill to reduce the home-owner deductions gradually. This led directly to the fall of the government and to the 'Catastrophe Election' whose outcome we have already described. Following the formation of another minority government, negotiations commenced for a new housing pact which was announced in 1974. This will be discussed in the next chapter.

By this point, inflation was at an unprecedented level. In 1973 and 1974 building costs rose by around 40 per cent and the interest rate rose from 12 per cent in early 1973 to 17.5 per cent in mid-1974 (Ministry of Housing, 1975). The problem of the high rents and high public expenditure costs of the newest social rented housing (subsidies under the 1966 scheme rose more than tenfold between 1967/8 and 1974/5), which was now proving difficult to let, especially when it was in high-rise blocks, had already resulted in 1972 in a sharp reduction of space standards; the maximum area of an average unit was cut from 100 square metres to 85 square metres and the annual building quota for subsidized production was cut by about half (Rasmussen, 1981). Building activity began to collapse from the boom levels which it had reached in the early part of the decade. Social housing completions fell by 38 per cent from the peak post-war year of 1971 to 1975. The private boom was sustained a little longer, peaking in 1973, but then falling by the same percentage in just two years (Danmarks Statistik, various years).

In his major study of Scandinavian social democracy, Esping-Andersen (1985) argues that the compromises that the Danish Social Democrats made with the non-socialist parties, which fostered the private housing market in the 1960s and 1970s, contributed to the fading support for the party. He suggests that 'Danish housing policy has stimulated divisions between renters and homeowners, and it is likely that this helped produce social democratic decomposition' (Esping-Andersen, 1985: 247). Interestingly, the electoral data which he presents shows how the disadvantages that these policies brought to the party changed as the trend towards home ownership progressed. Thus the 1966 reforms helped to push tenants towards the Socialist Peoples Party. However, in the mid-1970s, the attempt to reduce home-owner tax breaks alienated working-class Social Democratic voters who had now become home owners, and they moved towards the right. As Esping-Andersen notes, the Social Democrats eventually created a clientele wedded to tax-privileged home ownership. At the start of the 1970s a majority of public opinion was in favour of abolishing the home-owner tax subsidies. By the end of the decade there was massive opposition. In an even more dramatic measure of the impact of these housing policies, Esping-Andersen shows, by a regression analysis, that, while social class had a powerful relationship with voting choice in 1960 and housing status (i.e. tenure) had hardly any significance, these relativities began to change slowly in the 1960s and very rapidly in the 1970s, so that by 1975 housing status appeared to be marginally more important than social class. Housing policies helped to polarise and split the Social Democrats' electoral base, pushing those who remained tenants to the left and first-generation working-class home owners to the right. Data for 1960, 1970 and 1977 show this shift in the housing circumstances of the working class. In the 1960s the home-ownership share among skilled manual workers rose from 30 per cent to 41 per cent, and by 1977 by another 9 per cent to 50 per cent (Danmarks Statistik and The Institute for Social Research, 1979: 245).[32]

These policies began to bring about change in the social and economic composition of the social rented sector, with consequences that became more apparent later. However, much of the post-war social housing continued to be allocated to relatively better-off groups of the economically active population with families, such as the skilled manual working class and moderate-income white-collar workers. Especially before the introduction of the graded-rent scheme in 1966, the rising rent levels and the high standards of the new housing acted to restrict access to lower-income groups. The systems of tenant deposits also acted as a filter, although some loans, with easy repayment terms, to meet these deposits were available for very low-income households (Ministry of Housing, 1974). Data for 1970 on the composition of the private rented and social sectors reflect this situation. Around 60 per cent of households in social housing consisted of married couples with one or both partners economically active, compared with only just over 40 per cent in private renting. Almost half the social tenants were white-collar and skilled manual workers, compared with just over one-third of private renters. Conversely, households with no children, many of them elderly, were concentrated in private renting (Harloe, 1985: 94–9). Throughout most of the period which we are reviewing, private renting continued to be the main form of housing for many of the poorest households. Only as this sector declined and as the better-off manual and white-collar workers moved into owner occupation did the socio-economic composition of the social rented sector begin to change. In this respect Danish developments paralleled those in Britain, although the change was slower and began to occur later.

As we noted in relation to the interwar period, there was a division between the cooperative housing associations whose management, at least at the local level where allocation was largely determined, was strongly influenced by tenants and the so-called self-governing associations, which had strong links with the local authorities. In the early post-war years there was a rapid rise in the number of associations. Many of the new associations were in this second category; they built for mass needs and had less close links with the unions and the Social Democrats than the older associations. These associations were mainly responsible for the larger estates of social housing built with industrialized methods. In so far as lower-income households filtered into social housing, they were mainly housed by these associations. However, the post-war housing policy regime did require all social landlords to accept some lower-income households, including those displaced by slum clearance schemes.[33] But such tenants tended to be concentrated in the older, less desirable but cheaper stock, and later in the expensive but unpopular high-rise projects.

Unlike much of the social housing which was built in France, Britain and especially the USA, the planning and design of Danish social housing and the provision of communal and other facilities was generally of a high standard (Skriver, 1981; Lundgaard, 1981). In the 1950s and 1960s, for the reasons which we discussed in the case of Britain, the government encouraged the development of non-traditional and industrialized construction methods by offering extra subsidies (Jantzen and Kaaris, 1984). The social housing sector provided the main opportunity to develop such methods. In the early 1970s the government established five-year programmes of industrialized social housing construction to encourage the use of these methods and to provide a stable market for the firms operating in this field, who also exported their systems, thus helping solve the balance of payments problem (Ministry of Housing, 1974). As elsewhere, it was hoped that the adoption of industrialized building would lower costs, but this did not occur. In the 1970s, as in Britain, low-rise but high-density industrialized developments were increasingly preferred (Rasmussen, 1981). However, the high-rise, peripheral developments of the 1960s, built to generous space and other standards with high rents, became difficult to tenant in the early 1970s. Later, some developed a complex series of physical and social problems, like their counterparts elsewhere.

In the Netherlands the shortage of housing in 1945 was far more severe than in Denmark, because of damage and loss of output during the war, and because of the pre-war situation. The 1947 census put the housing shortage at 300,000 units (van Weesep, 1981). However, it was the economic situation, as already described, which determined the housing policies that were adopted. As in Britain and Denmark, housing output had to take second place to investment in new production for export. In addition, rent controls formed an important element in the low-wage policy. Government control of the housing market was virtually total, with controlled investment, rents and housing allocation. This system set aside the provisions of the 1901 Housing Act and was based on three laws passed to deal with the post-war emergency, concerned with reconstruction, rents and housing allocation. They reversed the pre-war policy of minimal state involvement in housing but in several respects took up ideas, such as planned house production, that had been discussed and argued for by the unions and the Social Democrats in the 1930s, and were included in the 1935 Labour Plan. Annual production targets were set by the central government and allocated regionally according to the shortage in each area (van der Schaar, 1982).

This was not, despite the presence of the PvdA in government, seen as the basis for a long-term socialization of housing. As we have already noted, the party's wish for a major shift away from a private economy was thwarted after the war. However, according to van der Schaar, the Social Democrats did not show that much interest in developing distinctively socialist housing policies and for many years after the war the Housing Minister came from the KVP.[34] As Priemus (1981: 300) writes in relation to the post-war controls:

> [t]he general feeling ... was that this drastic approach to the problem was to be only temporary. As soon as the shortage had been alleviated, it was expected that the situation would be 'normalized', and policies could be liberalized. The post-1918 experience with housing development was still fairly fresh in the public mind; then the shortage had been made up quickly, and was followed quite unexpectedly by overproduction in the 1930s. This sobering experience produced apprehension about stepping up building capacity too much.

In fact, as we have seen, there were major differences regarding the development of the Dutch economy after the First and the Second World Wars. After 1945 urbanization and industrialization, the influx of population from the colonies and the rapid rate of new household formation perpetuated the housing shortage, and the pressure for a major government role in housing, for many years. The post-war history of Dutch housing is repeatedly punctuated by over-optimistic statements from politicians that the housing shortage would soon be over.

Official data on the housing shortage showed it falling from 318,000 in 1947, to 252,000 in 1956: 221,000 in 1960: 185,000 in 1964: 91,000 in 1967 and 49,000 in 1970 (Priemus, 1981: 302). Up to the late 1950s, housing production was severely limited by the economic situation; annual output was negligible before 1948, then fluctuated between 55,000 and 68,000 per annum between 1951 and 1956, rising briefly to almost 90,000 per annum in 1957/8, before falling back for the next five years. But there was then a rapid increase to around 120,000 per annum in the second half of the 1960s and a further sharp increase in the early 1970s to a post-war peak of 146,000 in 1974, after which production collapsed sharply as the economic crisis took effect (Priemus, 1981: 302, 344). Within these secular changes, there were shorter-term fluctuations in housing output, as the government used social housing as a counter-cyclical economic regulator.

In the 1950s all housing was built with the aid of direct government subsidies, a situation which changed after 1960. Between 1961 and 1967 one-quarter to one-third of output came from the private sector, without direct subsidies. However, the level of private building then fell away as output rose, to around 15–20 per cent of total production. Throughout the whole period social rented housing provided the largest proportion of output, accounting for around 50 per cent in the 1950s. Its share then fell as private unsubsidized construction was stepped up in the early 1960s, but it rose later in the decade as this building fell away. The third major form of construction was directly subsidized 'premium' housing for private rental and sale. In the late 1940s and early 1950s this had a much smaller share of building than social rented housing, but from mid-decade it accounted for about 45 per cent of output, falling away to around a quarter in the mid-1960s as unsubsidized private building expanded. However, as the economic conditions worsened in the late 1960s and 'pure' private building declined, the private housing drive was sustained by a sharply increased level of premium housing. In the first half of the 1970s this became, for the first time, the largest source of new housing. By this point the majority of these premium units were for home ownership rather than private rental (van Weesep, 1982).

Social housebuilding, and, more generally, directly subsidized production, played a larger and more sustained role in the Netherlands than in any of the other five countries. At no time did 'purely' private housing (which did, however, receive indirect tax subsidies) account for more than 35 per cent of output (in 1963). Social rented housing was particularly important in the 1950s and in enabling the level of housebuilding to rise sharply in the mid-1960s. Subsidized private housing was turned to when pure private output was negligible, in the 1950s, or flagging, from the late 1960s (Priemus, 1981; van Weesep, 1982).

These changes took place within a system in which the government set annual targets for housing output, taking account of the state of the economy and the regional distribution of housing needs, manipulating the social housing quotas and the premiums and quotas for subsidized private housing, and operating a system of construction permits. A further dimension to this control was provided by the large-scale municipal ownership of land. Most local authorities bought up land ahead of housing needs, prepared it for development and controlled its disposal to the various forms of developer. This, together with their planning powers, gave the local authorities a major influence on the pattern of housing development.

Municipal land ownership was a long-established tradition, going back well before the Second World War, and was not a politically divisive issue or particularly associated with a specifically Social Democratic approach to housing and urban development, although there were divisions over the price paid for expropriated development land. The Socialists pressed for compensation at current use value (the 1977 government fell apart over this issue). Municipal land ownership also enabled the authorities to cross-subsidize land for social housing and other purposes from the proceeds of sales or leasing to private builders. However, as unsubsidized private housebuilding expanded and builders were able to choose where they located new projects, these negative controls became rather less effective (van der Schaar, 1982).

Nevertheless, the Dutch housing market remained, throughout the post-war period, under a greater degree of public control than any other with which we are concerned. These controls not only affected housing production, but also, through the systems of rent control and housing allocation, the pricing and use of large parts of the existing stock (Harloe, 1985: 121–5). As elsewhere, government also played a big role in setting new housing standards and promoting non-traditional forms of building. In the 1940s and 1950s these were mainly used to save on skilled labour and to use alternative materials; they only became associated with high-rise construction and with the erroneous belief that these methods might save money in the 1960s. The high-rise boom was ended by the Confessional–Liberal government in 1967 as a result of the unpopularity of the large, industrially built high-rise estates. In the 1970s the new methods continued to be used in low-rise housing. In every period the social rented housing sector acted as a pioneer for new developments in building technology, design, materials and organization (van der Schaar, 1982).

In the late 1940s the government estimated future housing needs, taking into account projected population changes and the need for replacement units. Plans had to be scaled down because of the economic situation and an annual production rate of around 65,000 per annum to 1970 was set (Ministry of Reconstruction and Housing, 1948). This rate was achieved by the early 1950s but, as the housing shortage persisted, it was soon recognized as insufficient.[35] The new subsidy system for social rented housing, introduced in 1947, provided annual payments to meet the gap between controlled rents (set at the level which they would have been in 1940) and costs. At first, competing demands on state finances resulted in the capital required coming from the private market, although through the agency of the local authorities, who bore the risks incurred and by this means had a powerful control over the associations' building plans. The 1947 legislation also provided for premium subsidies for private rental developers which were to last for ten years, after which it was believed rising rents would cover the revenue gap. In a first attempt to stimulate home ownership, premiums for this purpose were made available in 1953, but rising interest rates and a financial crisis in 1958 stifled the initiative. In time, various changes were made in the rental premiums; thus, in 1955, lower premiums were introduced to stimulate the production of housing that could be let at freely set rents and in 1960 the system was altered to provide a small lump sum payment plus degressive annual payments. From 1961 housing associations were allowed to build premium rented housing. Owners were also helped by a system of municipal mortgage guarantees.

At first, as after the First World War, the local authorities carried out a considerable proportion of building themselves. They accounted for the largest share of social rented output up to the early 1950s, but from the early 1960s the housing associations became, by a narrow margin, the major social housebuilders. The associations always pressed for a return to 'private initiative' in social housing and for a loosening of local authority controls. From the mid-1960s, after measures were taken to prioritize association building and eliminate local authority activity, this dominance increased, so that by the early 1970s the associations were responsible for about 85 per cent of output. Local authority building was sustained the longest in the big cities of the Randstad, where the housing shortage remained most acute and where major slum clearance later occurred.

The rent freeze was first broken in 1951, and in subsequent years further relatively small rent rises were allowed. However, the low-wage policy continued to limit rent levels. By the early 1960s the rent increases had resulted in rather more than a doubling of the level of controlled rents in 1951. But, as these were at 1940 levels, the depth of the social housing subsidies remained substantial. There seems to have been a broad consensus over the housing policy that had been established in the late 1940s during the long period of Confessional/PvdA government which lasted until the late 1950s. Interestingly, as we noted above, the Housing Ministers of this period came from the KVP, not the PvdA. In fact, the KVP controlled the Ministry, in successive centre–left and centre–right governments, from 1951 to 1974.

All parties, except the Liberals, who had little influence in this period, supported social rented housing. As we have seen, the pillarized structures of Dutch society resulted in housing associations and federations linked to the Social Democrats and to the religious parties, especially the KVP. So support from social housing was strongly entrenched across most of the political spectrum. However, there were some differences. The Confessionals, led by the KVP, which played the most influential role, wanted to encourage private housing, alongside a housing association sector based on the 'private initiative'. They sought to raise rents and promote home ownership. The first attempt at this latter policy, with the aid of premium subsidies, came to an early end in 1958 owing to a financial crisis. The PvdA had a less influential role in housing policy but it was more reluctant to raise rents and return to the private market and supported the continuation of local authority building, much of which was done in the larger cities which it tended to control, notably in Rotterdam and Amsterdam.

Despite these differences in principle, in the 1950s the overriding priority of establishing economic growth and full employment required continuing large-scale government support for housing and, despite the wish of the non-socialist political forces for a reversion to the private market, this had to be postponed. The housing shortage, and public pressure for increased building, was probably the main social policy issue. There was, however, political conflict over rent policy (leading, for example, to the collapse of a government in 1955), as rent rises failed to compensate for rising costs, the economics of private landlordism suffered and new investment in this sector remained very low. The premium system was an attempt to encourage such investment.

After the Socialists left government in 1958, under pressure because of the compromises which they had been forced to accept while in office, the subsequent centre–right governments, encouraged by the growth in incomes following the gradual breakdown in the system of wage control, opened a new phase in housing policy with the aim of returning to the free market in housing. However, progress was highly constrained by the continuing housing shortage and the requirements of economic policy. A further important goal was to return the responsibility for the provision of social rented housing firmly into the hands of the 'private initiative' housing associations, going back to the framework set out in the 1901 Act. This, too, was not easy to achieve.

A first attempt was made by Van Aartsen, who was Housing Minister from 1959 to 1963.[36] He wanted additional rent increases to enable subsidies to be cut, but was defeated by strong opposition inside and outside Parliament. The next Minister, Bogaers (1963–6) accepted that, before the free market could be re-established and rent controls ended, a major increase in output to eliminate the shortage would be required. Given the disincentives to increased private rented investment that rent control still posed, and shortages of private capital plus high interest rates which made even premium subsidized housing hard to expand, the main means of achieving this end was, ironically, to increase the annual quota of social housing. Under Bogaers (whom Priemus has called 'a real build-ing minister'), this task was energetically pursued. Interestingly, Bogaers came from the labour wing of the KVP, and one reason for the expansion of housing expenditure at this time (and of social expenditure under a Minister with a similar background) was to paper over the cracks that were beginning to appear in the KVP and attempt to retain the allegiance of its labour wing. The aim was to achieve the required housing stock by 1970, after which the free market could be restored. An element in the Bogaers pro-gramme, as elsewhere at this time, was the use of industrialized building. Extra subsidies were granted to builders willing to use these methods and extra quotas to municipalities which were willing to have them build in their areas. This was another reason for expanding social housing: it was a more 'plannable instrument' for the promotion of industrialized building than the private developers (Harloe and Martens, 1985).

The effort seemed to pay off. From 1964 official estimates of the shortage began to decline more quickly than in the previous decade. At the same time, rising building and land costs, together with the rising standards of the new social housing units, resulted in a rapid increase in housing subsidies. This led the government to begin an effort to loosen and lift rent controls in the private and the social sectors and to economize on subsidies. In 1965 a scheme of degressive annual subsidies was introduced, the aim being that full cost rents would be charged after ten years (Lundqvist, 1992: 42). Priemus (1981) notes that the government recognized that this would make new units very costly and prevent lower-income households gaining access to them. However, in principle at least, it believed that filtering could be relied on to provide accommodation for such groups as the market expanded.

Already from 1964 more frequent rent rises had occurred. However, rents still lagged behind income growth in this boom decade. In 1967 a start was made on the complete decontrol of private sector rents and of housing allocation (which covered much of the home ownership sector as well) on an area-by-area basis. But all social housing rents remained under control, as did private rented housing in the area of highest shortage, the Randstad. These changes contributed to the sharp rise in private housebuilding in the 1960s, although in the latter part of the decade when the economic situation began to become less favourable, the government was forced to increase the premium subsidies to sustain overall housing output. As van Weesep (1982) points out, never before had a government supported so much subsidized housing output as in the late 1960s. It is interesting to note that this occurred during a period of virtually unbroken centre–right government.

The policy of returning the responsibility for social housing to the associations and eliminating local authority building took some time to achieve. After the war, with the system of planned housing production and the local authority controls over dwelling allocation, land availability, the approval of state loans to associations and so on, the associations' status as 'private initiatives' was much weakened. In 1958 the government had appointed an expert committee to examine the role of the associations. The aim was to restore their private character, as a part of the overall plan to revert to a private housing system and reduce state involvement. The committee's report was completed in 1962, but various factors, including the resistance of the local authorities, held up its publication until 1964 (Hetzel, 1983). Its main recommendations, along with a new system of land use planning, were incorporated in legislation in 1965. This reaffirmed the principle enshrined in the 1901 Housing Act, that the associations were 'private initiatives', not simply tools of government housing policy. The report looked forward to the time when the associations could build without the aid of subsidies, using surpluses from their existing housing. However, this would only be possible after rent controls ended. It also recommended that the associations again become the main social housebuilders; local authorities should build when and where the associations were unable to do so. This priority rule was incorporated in legislation in 1965, but it took until 1969 to implement. Since then, much of the local authority stock has been transferred to associations. As we shall see in the next chapter, changes being implemented in the 1990s may complete the transition, or reversion, recommended in the 1964 report.

These changes strengthened the position of the associations and their two federations. In order to broaden the financial base of the associations, the committee recommended that they be allowed to build premium subsidized housing for sale and rent (acting, in effect, as private landlords in this respect). This was permitted from 1968, and from 1975 they were allowed to build in the unsubsidized sector as well. According to van der Schaar (1982), this change involved a broadening in the base of the associations' activities, as they began to house some better-off, middle-income and professional households which had previously been accommodated in the higher-quality subsectors of the private rental sector (now in decline). Two further provisions were also intended to increase the freedom of action of the associations. The first reversed the policy, in force since 1934, that required surpluses to be repaid to the government. This change allowed reserves for new investment to be accumulated. Also the power of local authorities to control the associations' activities was weakened when the government set nationally uniform rules for loan conditions and municipal control. However, the degree of control over the associations' activities, given that they were still dependent on subsidies, remained high in relation to many financial matters, such as the levels of approved costs for management and maintenance, accounting and administrative arrangements, the purchase and sale of real estate, rent setting, tenant security and so on. Nevertheless, these changes reinforced the ability of the associations to resist attempts, for example, to impose rent pooling or to target their social rented accommodation solely on lower-income groups.

By 1967, with the return of a new centre–right government after a brief centre–left interlude, the new administration, convinced that the earlier policies were at last ending the shortage, began to move more rapidly towards the decontrol of the housing market. Private housebuilding expanded, aided, as we have noted, by subsidies, and the social construction quota was cut back. In Britain and Denmark, the first steps to reduce government support for social housing were taken in the 1950s, when the interest rates on state loans were raised to market levels, soon to be followed by the requirement that this capital be obtained on the private market. In the Netherlands, the first of these steps occurred only in 1968, when market rates became payable, thus equalizing the treatment of new private and social rented housing which also had the same scheme of degressive subsidies. However, the regime of state loans for social housing (which had been reintroduced in 1958, when others were already abandoning this policy) lasted until the 1980s. The degressive subsidies did nothing to reduce the increasing problem of disparities between the rents of older and new housing. Moreover, as inflation accelerated in the late 1960s and housing costs rose, the scheme exacerbated the growing problem of the affordability of the newer housing. Like Denmark, the Netherlands had no system of rent pooling. Interestingly, the

Social Democrats proposed such a system after the war, but the 'private initiative' housing associations resisted this, fearing the loss of their better-off tenants.[37] Despite these changes aimed at economizing on subsidies, the shift to market interest rates and the sharply rising cost of new social housing, the effect of quality improvements and inflation, resulted in a rapid rise in the subsidy bill.[38] Overall, the cost of new social housing rose by just under 70 per cent in the 1950s, more than doubled in the 1960s and nearly tripled in the 1970s (van der Schaar, 1982).

In 1971, with a continuing boom in the private sector, the government moved a stage further in its strategy by adopting a similar policy of rent harmonization to that which had occurred in Denmark earlier. Here, too, the policy was intended to eliminate the 'misallocation' of subsidies, and reduce them, by raising the rents of older housing. A points index, based on the standards and rents of social housing built in the last five years in the region concerned, was developed. Initial rents in the social sector were based on this index. Annual rent increases in both rental sectors were decided by the government and linked to cost increases in the social sector. Rents of existing housing which were below the 'correct' level, as determined by the points index, could be raised to the 'harmonized' level, after which the annual trend rate would apply. The system was compulsorily applied in social rented housing and could optionally be used by private landlords (Priemus, 1981).

The harmonization policy aimed to raise rents overall, not just to relate them more closely to quality. This was seen not only as a way of reducing subsidies but also of making the filtering system work properly, encouraging better-off households in the older units that had benefited from low rents to move out into higher-priced and newer housing, including home ownership. As elsewhere, the new policy was coupled with the introduction of housing allowances for low-income households. As in other countries, too, when they began in 1970, allowances were seen as a supplement to the building subsidies, aiding the minority of really poor households, although their significance expanded later (Priemus, 1981).

At the same time, a search for a means of stemming the escalation of construction subsidies began. The solution, eventually enacted in 1975, was to introduce a complex scheme of degressive subsidies, known as the dynamic cost rent system. This scheme was first proposed by housing experts, including the civil servant who headed the Ministry of Housing, at the beginning of the decade. Dynamic cost pricing reduced the 'front loading' of interest

payments, that is, it altered the pattern of housing loan repayments, so these rose over time as, it was assumed, incomes and
therefore rent-paying capacity would also rise (Floor, 1972; Priemus,
1981). By these means, the rents of new units could be set at
below what they would have been with the traditional annuity
repayment system. When a centre–right government was formed
in 1971, the new Housing Minister took up these ideas, setting
out his proposals in an official memorandum in 1972. They caused
widespread protests. The dynamic cost system, which was also
intended to apply to new private rental housing, was regarded as
unworkable by the main institutional investors in this market, as
it was based on calculation of long-term movements in costs and
income which were bound to be inaccurate and which, if wrong,
might seriously affect the profitability of their investment. The
left parties and the housing associations were opposed because
the rent rises inherent in the new system of dynamic cost subsidies
and harmonization for the existing stock contained no guarantee
that private landlords would not simply raise their profits, rather
than reinvesting in the improvement of their housing; because no
changes were proposed in the heavy direct and indirect subsidies
for home ownership; because of the rigidly built-in future rent
rises; and because under the proposed regime new units would
still be unaffordable to those on lower incomes.

Opposition to harmonization and the new subsidy proposal were
among the reasons why the succession of Confessional–Liberal
governments ended in 1973 and the PvdA, which had campaigned
as a party opposed to the return to the private market, took power,
although, as we noted before, this government operated in highly
constrained circumstances. In 1974 the new administration modified the new rent and subsidy proposals without abandoning them
(Priemus, 1981; Harloe and Martens, 1985). The objective of
withdrawing the state from the housing market was rejected and
rent liberalization stopped. The dynamic cost system was modified
by the addition of a system of building subsidies to lower initial
rents. Rent increases would no longer be linked only to rising
building costs and new rents would be set at a level thought
to be affordable, 8 per cent of costs in the first instance. Subsequent increases would be related to changes in building costs
and incomes, but the government set no clear formula as it wished
to bear in mind macro-economic considerations (van der Schaar,
1982). Location subsidies were introduced to cut the cost of land
and thus the initial costs in high-cost areas; this especially aided
urban renewal in central city areas (seen as a way of improving

the housing situation of low-income groups). Housing allowances, which had been available only for limited categories of accommodation and had been seen as a temporary means of helping tenants adjust to higher rents, were made available for all low-income tenants. There was also a proposal for a 'filtering levy', a tax on tenants with low rent/income ratios, but this was rejected in Parliament.

The unpopular system of rent harmonization was revised. Now there was to be a uniform scheme covering all rented housing, ending the distinctions between areas where rents had been liberalized and where they were still controlled, and between social rented and private rented housing. It consisted of two elements. First, all rents would be set by the points system, with phased increases over several years to take rents to the 'harmonized' level. Second, the government would set an annual trend rent increase, established now in the light of cost increases and other considerations. Private landlords could simply accept the trend rent increase, or they could seek further increases by the points system. Housing association rents were to be raised to the appropriate level and then be subject to trend rate increases, however. These policies were implemented in 1975. Although the revised dynamic cost subsidy system was applicable to private rented as well as social rented building, in practice private investors shied away from it and all but ceased to build.

Despite these changes, the shift of emphasis away from a dominant role for directly subsidized housing, with social housing as the key sector, towards home ownership and market-oriented rents, was not in its essentials changed after the PvdA returned to power, although in its public statements the government rejected the previous strategy of a long-term return to the private market in housing and a withdrawal of the state, arguing that public intervention was necessary as a matter of principle, to attain a just distribution of housing standards and costs (van Weesep, 1982: 31). However, by now, as elsewhere, the Social Democrats also supported the expansion of home ownership, for similar reasons to those which we have described in relation to other countries (Harloe and Martens, 1985). It provided a new form of premium, targeted at lower-income purchase of housing constructed by the associations for sale.

This government also presided over a speculative boom in private housebuilding, a neat contrast with the boom in social housing output which had occurred under centre–right governments in the 1960s! It also acted in other ways to promote home ownership.

For example, it ensured that most housing for home ownership remained outside the housing allocation system in the areas where that still existed; it kept permissible land costs for social housing low, thus encouraging the local authorities to sell more land for home ownership, in order to cross-subsidize new social rented housing; and it also pressed local authorities to zone more land for home ownership in their land use plans. At the same time, sales of formerly private rented housing for home ownership were running at a high level and new social housebuilding declined. In short, the reorientation of housing production away from social housing towards the private market, mainly in the form of home ownership, continued much as before, despite the proclaimed commitment to social housing and the state regulation of the market contained in the 1974 policy statement.

Nevertheless, the transition towards a private market in housing and moves to harmonize rents, reduce subsidies for construction and target them on low-income households, began later and occurred more slowly in the Netherlands than elsewhere. Many controls continued to be used; for example, in 1974, when the housing shortage again increased in certain stress areas, a modified form of allocation control was reintroduced (van Weesep, 1982). There are various interrelated reasons for this continuing high level of state involvement (Harloe and Martens, 1985). First, the persisting political importance of the housing shortage, driven by demographic and economic change, which made rent controls and subsidies an imperative. These may be seen as one aspect of the wider role which planning and government controls played in post-war Dutch developments, as explained earlier. Second, the pivotal role of the KVP in housing policy and more generally with respect to social policies. Third, the political strength of the social rented housing sector itself, with two influential federations, linked to the PvdA and the Confessional parties respectively, who played a major role in the housing policy advisory committees – bodies which reflected the Dutch system of pillarized democracy more generally. The social rented sector also had political clout just by virtue of its size; it was the largest housing sector by the mid-1970s. So the tenants of social housing formed a large and important part of the electorate, and still included many of the better-paid manual and white-collar employees who, in Britain for example, were increasingly home owners. The ability of social tenants to influence housing policy by, for instance, resisting rent harmonization can be understood in the light of this situation.

As a result of these circumstances, although the drive towards home ownership was evident from the 1960s, there was much less evidence by the mid-1970s of residualization in social rented housing in the Netherlands than in Britain, for example. According to van der Schaar, for most of the post-war years Dutch policy involved building relatively high-quality and high-cost accommodation, including in the social rented sector, for middle-income households – groups that are economically and politically important. Filtering would solve the problem of lower-income demand, provided that housing output was at a sufficiently high level.[39] There were, however, indications of a gradual shift in the early 1970s, when home ownership was expanding rapidly and the general housing shortage seemed to have ended. Suggestions were then made that social housing construction should mainly be for low-income, 'special needs' groups. The 1974 reforms were influenced by this special needs objective. The argument was that social justice required that poorer households receive a greater share of housing subsidies (van Weesep, 1982; Priemus, 1987a). In any event, the decline of private renting and slum clearance did result in an increased flow of lower-income households into social housing. Many of these households were relocated on the less popular but expensive high-rise peripheral estates, as elsewhere (de Jonge, 1985). But, while the private rented sector's share of the housing stock declined steadily over the post-war period, from around 60 per cent in 1947 to 20 per cent by 1975, home ownership grew rather slowly, from 28 per cent to 39 per cent, and social rented housing rose from 12 per cent to 41 per cent (Lundqvist, 1992: 50). So, although the private rented sector declined sharply as a source of housing for a wide range of income groups, the extent to which the higher-income demand was met by home ownership was far less in the Netherlands than in Britain or even Denmark. Instead, social housing expanded not just to house a high proportion of lower-income groups, but many better-off households as well.

Nevertheless, there was stratification within the social rented stock. Many associations, especially those not so closely tied to the big local authorities, tried to minimize the extent to which they rehoused 'problem' or low-income tenants, including those from the ethnic minorities (such as the Surinamese who immigrated in the 1960s and 1970s), guest workers from Southern Europe and North Africa, and those from urban renewal areas or with medical problems (van der Schaar, 1982). There were conflicts between the local authorities and the associations over who should control allocation, with a wide variety of agreements being more or less willingly entered into. Many associations wished to offer vacancies in better-quality and more popular housing to existing tenants and less desirable property to local authority nominees, from the waiting lists of those in urgent need. Many of the latter ended up in the local authority-owned part of the social housing stock, which by the 1970s, given the restrictions on local authority building, tended to contain a high proportion of older, poor-quality and cheaper, smaller housing. In addition, as we have noted, after the introduction of housing allowances some of these households were also accommodated in less popular high-rise, peripheral estates. The legal requirements which governed associations' allocation policies were fairly vaguely drafted, referring only to the need to let properties to those who had difficulties in finding accommodation, with some priority for low-rent units to be let to lower-income households. This rule was successfully obstructed by some of the associations. Anyway, its observance was made less imperative for a time by the improved access to more expensive housing opened up by the provision of housing allowances, although the resistance of many associations to housing ethnic minorities and the growing costs of allowances later resulted in a renewed governmental concern to enforce these provisions.

Data on social housing tenants from 1967 to 1975 show that there was a concentration of households in the child-rearing years, although increasing numbers of the elderly and young households began to appear in the 1970s. Income data from 1964 to 1975 show the effects of rising home ownership among the better-off households and the growing income gap between social tenants and home owners.[40] In 1964 the median incomes of owners and social tenants were both between 7500 and 9000 guilders per annum, while in 1975 the tenant median was between 21,000 and 24,000 guilders per annum and that of owners was between 24,000 and 27,000 guilders per annum. Data from 1956 to 1975 show that in 1956, only businessmen and the 'free professionals' had a home ownership rate of (just) over 50 per cent, rising to 70 per cent by 1975. The rise among white-collar employees was spectacular, from only 15 per cent in 1956 to 45 per cent by 1975, and among manual workers from 17 per cent to 32 per cent. The growing divide in access to ownership between white-collar workers and manual workers is evident.

Thus, even though the social sector retained a relatively wide range of social, occupational and income groups, the trend towards a polarization between home ownership and social housing is clear.

The former sector changed from one which accommodated only the higher-earning and status businessmen and professionals to one dominated by white-collar workers, while the social rented sector moved from accommodating white-collar and manual workers to one which increasingly accommodated manual workers and the economically inactive. The share of white-collar workers in social rented housing fell from 31 per cent to 25 per cent between 1967 and 1975 (earlier data for this sector are not available), that of manual workers fell only a little, from 42 per cent to 39 per cent, while the share of the economically inactive rose from 23 per cent to 34 per cent. These figures show that, while the marginalization of the social rented population, with the narrowing of its income and class composition, was much less evident and developed more slowly in the Netherlands than in Britain, similar tendencies were evident in the 1960s and 1970s.

After the Liberation in 1944, housing conditions in France were worse than in any other of the countries with which we are concerned, except Germany. According to Butler and Noisette (1983: 38), there was a shortfall of about 1.15 million dwellings in 1945 (including 452,000 destroyed by war) and another 1.436 million were damaged by the war. The initial policy response was similar to that which occurred after 1918, an extensive programme of reconstruction of lost and damaged property. There was very little other new building. Reconstruction simply reproduced housing of the type and in the locations in which it had existed before the war (Duclaud-Williams, 1978: 127). In view of subsequent economic developments and the growth of urbanization, the policy was highly questionable. Almost 400,000 units were constructed under this programme, which continued into the 1960s although at an insignificant level after the late 1950s (Duclaud-Williams, 1978: 148–9).

In general, as we have noted, housing had low priority in the immediate post-war years, although the backlog and the new demands generated by demographic and economic change were enormous. In nine years, from the Liberation to the end of 1953, annual housing output averaged 54,000 units; just over 5000 per annum were HLM rental units and another 2300 were HLM units for home ownership. In 1954 only 160,000 units were completed, production then rose to around 300,000 per annum from 1958 to 1962, there followed a further rapid rise to around 400,000 by the mid-1960s, then another sharp increase to around 500,000 per annum in the first half of the 1970s. From the late 1950s, when a determined effort to increase housing production began, the output of HLM rental units played a major role, accounting for around a quarter of annual output up to the mid-1970s. The highest absolute levels of completions occurred earlier in this decade, then more emphasis began to be placed on HLM building for home ownership (Duclaud-Williams, 1978: 148–9).

Like the Dutch government, the French government provided direct subsidies for a high proportion of all post-war housebuilding. It also retained a high degree of control over the supply of credit to the housing market. There were several reasons for this. First, the long history of rent controls in the private sector, which continued after the Second World War, limited the willingness of private capital to invest in housing (Harloe, 1985: 131–4). However, the retention of low rent/income ratios helped to blunt some of the pressure for higher wages and so contributed to economic growth. A second, related point is that, as salaries and wages remained low in the 1950s and early 1960s, extensive subsidies were required to make new housing affordable for large sections of the population. At the same time, governments realized, after the early post-war years, that an improved housing supply was an essential condition for economic growth and urbanization. As we saw, the second national plan recognized this fact. Finally, even when incomes began to rise in the 1960s, there were several obstacles to a freely functioning private housing market, for example, the lack of long-term private mortgages and a mass housebuilding industry. So state involvement in, and promotion of, private housing through credit supply, subsidies and other means remained extensive.

All this is reflected in the share of housing output (including HLM) which received direct subsidies. Up to the mid-1960s it amounted to around 90 per cent. Then there was a notable growth of unsubsidized private building; even so, by the mid-1970s, it only amounted to about a quarter of all new building. At this time around a half to two-thirds of new housing consisted of directly subsidized private rental and owner-occupied housing, outside the HLM sector.

There were three major pieces of legislation in the immediate post-war years.[41] In 1948 a rent control law provided for a staged series of rent increases in existing private rental units (and a similar system was extended to the 320,000 or so HBM units built before 1939) (Magri, 1977: 18). New units, including social housing, were not affected by this law, which intended to link rents to incomes rather than costs. The rents remained low in relation to incomes, but governments found it politically difficult to move to full decontrol in the 1950s. However, area decontrol began in

1959 and proceeded slowly into the 1970s. The second major measure, enacted in 1950, established the directly subsidized 'intermediate' sector, which, as we have noted, played a major role in post-war housing production (Harloe, 1985: 176–82). It provided annual subsidies for 20 years and loans from the Crédit Foncier, a juridically private but state-controlled bank, established in the nineteenth century and reformed after the war to finance this private sector housing (and through which the Ministry of Finance could control the volume of credit going into a large part of the private housing market, in line with its broader macro-economic and investment priorities). The loan and subsidy arrangements for this sector were subsequently changed on many occasions but, from the start, the main aim was to encourage home ownership, although the loans and subsidies were also used for rental housing. This emphasis on home ownership was, of course, most strongly endorsed by the parties of the centre and the right but, according to Duclaud-Williams (1978: 216), the Socialists did not oppose the growth of the subsidized private sector, seeing any form of provision as better than none in the circumstances.

The third new law, enacted in 1947, simply re-established the pre-war HBM system (renamed HLM – Habitations à Loyers Modérés in 1950). However, as we have noted, this resulted in very little building over the next few years. These three measures were enacted during the period of 'Third Force' governments from 1947 to 1951, during which the Socialists increasingly found themselves prisoners of a centre–right majority, following the breakup of the Socialist/Communist/MRP alliance. The rent law and the re-enactment of the HBM regime, both of which aimed to ensure low-rent working-class housing, were passed while the left was still relatively strong (Magri, 1977: 27). However, little more in the way of a positive attempt to raise housing production was considered and, according to Duclaud-Williams (1978: 124–7), there was not much political discussion of the housing situation or pressure for change in the late 1940s. As Butler and Noisette (1983: 38) note, economic reconstruction and constitutional issues dominated early post-war political debates. But the housing situation was very bad; later, the 1954 census found 22 per cent of the population living in acutely overcrowded conditions and 42 per cent of all dwellings without an internal supply of running water (over twice the British level in 1951). A 1953 survey showed that one-third of the population was dissatisfied with its housing conditions. Yet housing did not figure prominently in any of the immediate post-war elections, an interesting contrast with the situation in the other European countries under discussion. But this does seem in line with the curiously high degree of passivity regarding housing in the interwar years, even by the left. Much more political heat surrounded the housing reconstruction programme, whose defects have already been noted (Duclaud-Williams, 1978: 127).

By the early 1950s there were signs that political pressure was beginning to mount for an increase in housing production, and there was growing popular discontent of the shortages. So, despite the shift to right-wing governments after 1952, this discontent and an increasing recognition of the links between housing supply and economic growth, led to some action. An important obstacle to greater output was the continued dominance of small-scale property capital and land ownership in France; this industry was like most others in this respect (Topalov, 1987). There were difficulties in respect to land acquisition and, as economic growth took off, rapidly rising land prices. Eventually, as we shall see, the modernizing regime of the Fifth Republic took action to resolve these problems.

In 1953 Pierre Courant, whom Duclaud-Williams regards as the most able Housing Minister of the Fourth Republic, proposed a package of reforms, the so-called Plan Courant. This stressed the need to expand housing for owner occupation, to industrialize and standardize building, to improve the power to expropriate housing land, to raise the rent levels and to establish a 1 per cent *patronal*, a payroll tax on all employers with more than ten employees to provide funds for workers' housing.[42] While some aspects of the Plan were watered down by the legislature, these were important reforms. In addition, there were also changes in the system of loans and subsidies established in 1950, which had not been sufficiently generous to make it a success (Harloe, 1985: 179).

A further important development was the higher priority which housing received when it was included in the 'Hirsch' Plan, for reasons that have already been explained. This plan aimed to raise housing output from the 1952 level of just under 75,000 units to an annual rate of 240,000 by 1957. In the event the plan was overfulfilled, with an annual rate of 270,000 by 1957. This was still far below the necessary level to deal with the mass of overcrowded and poor housing and meet the rising demand occurring as a result of urbanization and demographic change. The Third Plan, which ran from 1958 to 1961, raised the target for the latter year to 300,000 units – 316,000 were actually completed. The Fourth Plan set a 1965 target of 400,000 and, again, this was exceeded (Lieberman, 1977: 16–18).

Although a good deal of this new housing was built by the HLM organizations, there was considerable conflict between the main providers of HLM rented housing, the Offices Publics (especially where these were in left-dominated areas), and central government over the extent to which their new production was targeted on providing for the expanding industrial sectors rather than more general needs. Attempts to enforce targeting were fiercely opposed by the national HLM federation, which had close links with the left, and the government struggled to bring the social landlords under a stronger form of control. One of the main motives for the development of the 'intermediate' sector was to provide a more directable instrument for the satisfaction of industrial needs. A variety of organizations were active in this sector. These included the privately based HLM societies (which concentrated on home ownership and higher-rented housing) and a range of parastatal organizations, legally private and independent bodies but, in fact, directed by a combination of the state and major financial interests (for a detailed description see Harloe, 1985: 105–7). Many of these organizations (and some Offices Publics) used the 1 per cent *patronal* to help finance their projects. They were particularly active in building schemes for the employees of the expanding industries. The employers, in exchange for their contributions, were able to nominate employees to a proportion of the new units. These organizations' role was especially important in the Paris region: between 1954 and 1958 most new rental housing in this area was produced by them. They built projects for, among others, the Simca, Renault and Peugeot workforces. In the 1950s most of these units were rented; later, more were for home ownership.

Further changes in housing policy occurred during the Mendès-France government in 1954–5. Mendès, who was a committed economic modernizer and who, in some respects, foreshadowed the strong executive style of the Fifth Republic, took power at a time of political crisis with an unusually strong mandate and special powers to rule by decree (Larkin, 1988: 238).[43] He brought in new arrangements to regulate urban development and expand the parastatal developers' activities. There was a big increase in the loans allocated by the Ministry of Finance for new housing (Larkin, 1988: 245). The policy of expanding housing output, now with rather more emphasis on HLMs, continued during the Socialist-Radical cabinet, under the Socialist leader Mollet, which was formed after the 1956 general election, and during the subsequent short-lived governments in the last years of the Fourth Republic (Larkin, 1988: 254ff.). Thus, in 1957, a law was passed to increase the housing programme, as indicated in the national plan, with a five-year programme for the HLM sector, and the provision of 'collective equipment' (i.e. urban infrastructure), including new powers to facilitate the expropriation of land. Finally, in 1958, another law established priority zones for urban development (ZUPs), which will be discussed below (Butler and Noisette, 1983).

Throughout this period the basic principles of the HLM subsidy system remained similar to those which had evolved before the war and had been re-enacted in 1947. This housing received low-interest, very long-term state loans. However, there were important changes in the details of this scheme and in other matters, notably rent setting. The 1947 law had modified the pre-war provisions of the Loucheur Act, providing 2 per cent loans for 60 years covering 90 per cent of building costs. This regime applied only to the small number of HLM units completed up to 1953. As Magri (1977: 209) notes, this and schemes which followed from 1953 involved a policy of low-cost housing provision, linked closely to the varying needs of industry. The state supplied the capital for this housing for many years, out of the Treasury budget. Up to 1963 the terms of these loans were very generous; thus, between 1953 and 1960, they covered 85 per cent of the costs at an interest rate of little over 1 per cent (plus 2 per cent per year amortization) with a term of 45 years. Supplementary finance came from the 1 per cent payroll tax, the Crédit Foncier, the state savings banks or the state itself. However, the high rate of inflation did create some financing problems as the main loan was calculated on the basis of fixed price levels which were not raised as fast as inflation. This and other factors meant that the state loan covered only 75 per cent of costs by 1963 and increased the recourse to more expansive forms of supplementary finance.

In the 1950s, a range of HLM units, with varying standards of equipment, was built (see Magri, 1977: 197–213). The 1947 Act set space standards at well above the pre-war levels. However, by 1953 these had been much reduced and only regained the lost ground by the early 1960s. With the exception of the mandatory provision of a bathroom, the first post-war standards for equipment did not make much advance on those set before the war. But in 1961, a new higher-rented category, ILN (Immeuble à Loyer Normal), was added, which was more spacious and better equipped. As we shall note later, HLM units tended to be let to better-off manual and white-collar rather than low-income households. However, apart from the concentrations of poorer households which still lived in inner-city slums, in the 1950s many also inhabited

the *bidonvilles*, the successors to the pre-war *lotissements*, on the out-
skirts of major cities. In this decade the number of poor and
extremely badly housed households was augmented, as rural migrants moved to the expanding city industries and away from the
declining agricultural sector. The HLM programme was expanded
to take some account of these low-income needs. In 1951 a 'reduced
standard' category of building was authorised for households from
slum clearance areas and those 'not used to ordinary living'; these
were very small and lacked amenities, and not many were actually
built. After various further changes in the 1950s, two new categories were created in the 1960s to cater for such households: in
1961, PSR (Programme Social de Relogement) and in 1968, PLR
(Programme à Loyer Réduit) The financial terms for the various
types of HLM housing were differentiated, with PSR being funded
by interest-free, 53-year loans in order to keep rents down.

As we have noted, the 1947 Act had set rents in the existing
HBM stock by a system similar to that applied to the pre-1948
private rental sector. But these rents, based on the surface area
and amenities of each unit, took no account of the costs of provision. While, in the private rented sector, the landlord was left
to cope with these problems, if HLM landlords ran deficits the
state would ultimately have had to bail them out. In 1953, in the
period of Conservative government after the collapse of the Third
Force, the Laniel government, which had been granted special
powers and had taken a hard line to quell a strike over public
sector economies, attempted to set cost rents (i.e. rents which met
the gap, after subsidies were deducted from costs) on a building-
by-building basis (Larkin, 1988: 174). There was strong opposition
from the HLM movement and the government backed down. In
1955 a new law, which was opposed only by the Communists,
established that rents would be set by the individual HLM landlords within maximum and minimum levels decreed by the state
(Duclaud-Williams, 1978: 129). However, the overall requirement
was that each landlord had to balance its annual budget. As the
government raised these levels and as the costs of new building
increased rapidly owing to the high level of inflation, the cross-
subsidy of new units by older ones became obligatory; in other
words, a form of rent pooling developed. Nevertheless, rents remained rather low and well below the government maxima in the
1950s.

The main objectives of policy in the 1950s were clear: to expand
the supply of relatively cheap housing in order to meet the needs
of an expanding economy. Standards were kept low in order to

maximize the use of available resources but in conditions of great
housing shortage, there were plenty of applicants for the new housing. State guidelines regarding eligibility were not very restrictive.
Up to 1954 there was a general rule that applicants should be
'less fortunate people and especially workers primarily dependent
on wages' (quoted in Duclaud-Williams, 1978: 131). Throughout
the 1950s and beyond there was a constant struggle between the
HLMs and the state over the control of allocations. The state
argued that HLM units (principally the 'ordinary' rented units)
were being allocated to many households that did not really need
them and that lower-income households and other categories (such
as key workers) were excluded. The HLMs argued that the financial conditions set by the state did not allow such groups to be
housed. To some extent this contest was really about the general
issue of control and the government's desire for key workers to
be housed, because neither most HLMs nor the state were, in
practice, all that concerned about housing the poor. Nevertheless,
the matter became controversial in 1953 when a priest, Abbé
Pierre, shot to fame as the leader of a campaign to force some
action to be taken on behalf of the homeless. The Abbé attacked
the HLMs for their exclusivity and in 1954 the government tried
to impose a points system for allocation. Like the Laniel administration's rent proposals, it involved a considerable reduction in the
autonomy of the social landlords who strongly opposed it. The
scheme had to be withdrawn, and its adoption was made discretionary in 1955, which meant that it was never used (Duclaud-
Williams, 1978: 133). In theory, the situation changed with the
advent of the Fifth Republic. In 1958 maximum income limits were
set, leaving the HLM organizations free to set lower-income minima
for admission. In practice, it was these minima which were more
important, as the organizations needed to cover their costs. So
many poorer households were excluded. The maximum limits were
very high; work done for the Sixth Plan (1971–5) suggested that
70–80 per cent of the population came within the limits then
applicable (Duclaud-Williams, 1978: 135).

The setting of maximum income limits in 1958 was accompanied
by a measure that was intended to encourage 'over-income' tenants
to move into the private sector: a rent surcharge known as the
sur-loyer. Predictably, the HLM organizations opposed this change
and, as they were not forced to adopt it, did not do so for many
years. An attempt by the activist Housing Minister Albin Chalandon
to enforce the *sur-loyer* in the late 1960s led to widespread objections, including some from Gaullist deputies, and was promptly

dropped (Duclaud-Williams, 1978: 139). From 1947 to 1961 about half the HLM housing was allocated to manual workers, especially those in the more skilled and better-paid categories. The other half went to white-collar workers, including a considerable proportion of the higher-status and better-paid employees in this sector. This concentration on middle-income demand did not change in the following period up to 1968. In fact, the proportion of less-skilled manual workers fell and that of middle-income white-collar workers rose as the rents were increased in this decade. However, there was a slight decline in the proportion of the higher-paid groups as opportunities in the private housing market began to open up.[44]

As we have noted, after the return of de Gaulle and the formation of the Fifth Republic, the drive for economic modernization accelerated, especially after Pompidou became Prime Minister in 1962. Social policy became closely linked to this objective. At the same time, especially with Giscard d'Estaing at the Ministry of Finance (from 1962 to 1966 and 1969 to 1974), the government's economic and expenditure policies were characterised by a more orthodox adherence to liberal doctrines. What resulted in the case of social housing was a further drive to raise output, but to tie this more closely to the government's overall objectives and to use state aid in a more targeted manner.

The housing shortage remained severe in the early years of the new Republic, worse, in fact, than in any of the other countries with which we are concerned. In 1958 the estimated shortage was 4 million units, not allowing for slums and overcrowding. Around 25 per cent of manual and agricultural workers were overcrowded and 13 per cent of middle-income white-collar workers, compared with 4–8 per cent of the various upper-income groups (Butler and Noisette, 1983: 41). In these circumstances it is not surprising that HLM housing provided a major source of accommodation for middle-income and even upper-income white-collar, professional and managerial workers.

The advent of the Fifth Republic, and the influential role that the technocratic elites played in its policies, led to major reforms in land use policies from the late 1950s and the adoption of suitably technocratic solutions to the production of mass social housing (Butler and Noisette, 1983: 70–107; Power, 1993: 44–51). We have already referred to the obstacle to large scale urban development projects caused by fragmented land ownership and weak expropriation powers. In 1958 a new law established Zones d'Urbanisation Prioritaire (ZUP).[45] Once a ZUP was declared, land prices were frozen and the land was purchased, either by the state or by the local authorities, operating through a variety of the legally private but publicly controlled parastatal bodies. The land was then serviced and sold to chosen developers, many of whom built social housing. Especially in the Paris region, these new areas fitted into a wider plan whose aims were to reorganize the use of land for housing and industry in order to accommodate and facilitate economic growth and change (Hall, 1984: 68–85).

These arrangements were changed as the ZUPs were found to have several drawbacks. Apart from growing concerns by the late 1960s at the poor quality of many of the developments, especially high-rise, industrially built housing projects, the administrative procedures to establish a ZUP were slow and cumbersome and there were many opportunities for what Butler and Noisette (1983: 88) call 'guerrilla wars' between the agencies involved. In the late 1960s Minister Chalandon launched a new attack on local property interests, which continued to obstruct many developments, through the establishment of ZACs (Zones d'Aménagement Concerté), which reduced the ability of local interests to intervene in development and increased the directive role of the developers. (He also tried, unsuccessfully, to tax away some of the profits being made by private interests on the rising value of development land.) After Giscard became President there was an even clearer desire on the part of the administration to sustain the interests of large-scale industry, finance and property development. However, by now, the conflict between the Gaullists and the Giscardian liberals was increasingly evident, and Giscard was, of course, dependent on both these groups. The Gaullists were largely dependent on the votes of just those groups of the population, such as the small-scale property owners, which the 'modernizing' property and development policies most threatened. So, in the mid-1970s, there was something of a return to the previous situation, at least in relation to the balance of power between local political and landed interests, on the one hand, and the state and development capital, on the other, with the institution of ZIFs (Zones d'Intervention Foncière), which provided for the local authority pre-emption of land in development areas, but at market prices (not very effective as few communes had the legal, political or financial means to establish a coherent development strategy) (Butler and Noisette, 1983: 97–103).

For reasons of speed and to reduce costs, there was more concentration on the use of industrial building techniques for the mass production of social housing in France than in any of the other countries with which we are concerned. The use of off-site production techniques, cranes travelling along railway lines from block to block and other heavy construction machinery, seems only to have been rivalled by Eastern Europe and the Soviet Union. In order to provide the scale of programme which the private construction firms using these techniques required for profitability, large sites were necessary. Given the price of land, these were inevitably located at the urban periphery in ZUP and their successors. From the late 1950s most HLM units, especially those in the lower- and middle-rented categories, were built in large projects (the *grands ensembles*), on such sites. The average ZUP housing development contained over 5000 units and around 750,000 units were built in 140 of these developments (Power, 1993: 52). They were frequently poorly planned, monotonous in appearance, with block after block of high-rise, reinforced concrete apartments, lacking good transport, shopping and other social and commercial facilities. In all, between 1960 and 1980 HLMs completed around 2.5 million units, mostly by industrialized building techniques. Some 75 per cent of all HLM projects had 800 dwellings or more and the peripheral ZUP-type *grands ensembles* ranged from 2000 to 10,000 dwellings per project, mostly apartments, although in the 1970s there was a gradual reversion to more low-rise housing (Emms, 1990: 86–90).

All these changes involved attempts to 'rationalize' and coordinate the arrangements for large-scale housing and other developments. As Butler and Noisette (1983) show, the changes in policy which led from ZUPs in the late 1950s to ZIFs by the mid-1970s and to large-scale industrialized building were influenced by the conflict between various sections of capital. The state faced various pressures: the desire to modernize the economy and to meet the needs of industrial capital; the need to maintain the political support of small property owners who were strongly entrenched in many local authorities; the need to obtain investments by large-scale building, development and financial capital; and, finally, the need to make some response to popular pressures in relation to the inadequate supply of housing and, later, to the poor environment and quality of much that was built in the development zones. Broadly speaking, the reformers of the Fifth Republic aimed to break with the small-scale structures of land ownership and building production which were a constraint on the expansion of housing output and the renewal of the built environment. In short, the aim was to modernize the production of the built environment by working with leading sectors of large-scale financial and industrial capital, as occurred throughout the rest of the economy. In housing, the aim was to establish a large-scale modern private market system, centred increasingly, from the late 1960s, on an expansion of home ownership. Substantial effort was also put into reforming the structure and functioning of the financial institutions concerned with housing construction and purchase.

As Topalov (1987: 234–304) has shown, the public and parastatal housing developers, together with the system of direct subsidies for private housing, were used as important agents in achieving these objectives, helping, for example, to sustain the drive towards the private market at times when economic and other conditions retarded purely private sector building (as occurred between 1965 and 1968, for example). Interestingly, the Socialists proposed little in the way of an alternative strategy. While, in 1963, the leading Socialist politician Gaston Deferre (who later stood unsuccessfully for the presidency) put forward a proposal for municipal land ownership with compensation at existing use value, and the new Parti Socialiste proposed a land tax and municipal land disposals on 99-year leases in the 1970s, as Butler and Noisette (1983: 103–6) note, no attention was paid to changing the capitalist organization of building production. Only the Communists developed policies for reorganizing the basis for the production of housing and the building industry generally. However, as Duclaud-Williams (1978: 36) writes, '[a]t no time in the postwar period has the French Communist Party advocated the nationalisation of private residential property ... the party has always envisaged ... the continuation of the system of landlord and tenant and that of owner-occupation'. We shall discuss the policies adopted by the PS, when it eventually gained power in the 1980s, in the next chapter.

The modernization of housing, planning and development was accompanied by new subsidy and financing policies which were very similar to those adopted elsewhere at this time. These aimed to reduce the dependence of social housing on state-provided capital; raise rents in order to economize on subsidies and encourage better-off households to move into the private housing market; and target social housing assistance on a more limited range of households. However, given the housing shortage, which persisted into the 1970s, and the resistance of the HLM movement to many of these changes, it took until the late 1970s to achieve them all.

As elsewhere, the space and internal standards of social housing were improved in the 1960s and 1970s, as incomes rose. This added considerably to the costs of new construction. At the same time, rising prosperity began to make it possible for the government to reinforce efforts to restrict the social rented sector to lower-income households, diverting the middle-income demand into the intermediate subsidized and unsubsidized private sectors. Up to 1963, there was a single maximum income limit for admission to all HLM housing, except the ILN units (which had a higher limit). But then a lower maximum income limit was set for the admission of single-earner households to HLM housing and in 1968 it was proposed to lower the maxima for all entrants into ordinary HLM housing and set an even lower limit for PSR housing. The officially stated objective was to limit access to only the less-favoured population groups. But Butler and Noisette (1983) contend that, in reality, it was an attempt to penalize workers who had just received large wage rises as a result of the Grenelle agreements. If the new limits came in, many middle-income manual and white-collar workers would either have to leave HLM housing for more expensive units in the 'intermediate' sector, or pay the *sur-loyer*. Opposition from the HLM movement stopped this change occurring. However, from 1969, the income limits were indexed to construction costs and also diversified, being 10 per cent higher in the Paris region, set at 25 per cent below the ordinary HLM limits for the lower-quality, low-income units and 50 per cent above for some higher-quality and higher-rented units, with no limits for those of the highest quality of all. The intention was to reduce access to standard HLM housing by better-off workers who were to be accommodated in the less-subsidized, higher-rented types. In fact, the rising costs of construction and the rising rents of new units resulted in a reduction of access by lower-income groups to the standard units. Instead, they were concentrated in the older, poorer-quality and cheaper stock. However, they still tended to pay a higher proportion of their incomes in rent than the better-off households in the higher-quality and newer housing (Magri, 1977: 149–57; Barou, 1992: 44–57). Overall, the proportion of white-collar workers in the HLM sector increased and the proportion of unskilled and semi-skilled manual workers fell. So government policy produced a contradictory outcome: the role of HLM housing in catering for middle-income demand was consolidated rather than reduced. At the same time, there was a growth of segregation – by income, socio-economic position and housing type/location and quality – within the sector.

The financing and subsidization of HLM housing changed in the 1960s in line with the new objectives of government policy. These changes formed part of a wider process in which the heavy reliance of the housing sector on state finance was converted, by the end of the 1960s, into a system of housing finance dominated by the private sector banks and other financial institutions, but with continuing state support. These institutions became central to the operations of housing finance – collecting savings, distributing loans and realizing profits, as Topalov (1987: 331–50) succinctly concludes. In 1966 the regime of cheap Treasury loans for HLMs was ended (partly to cut the budget deficit). Instead, the finance now came through a new body, the Caisse aux Prêts HLM (CPHLM), a subsidiary of the Caisse des Dépôts et Consignations (CDC), the state bank used for financing local government and other public bodies, which collected funds from the state savings banks. Deposits in these banks were made mainly by small savers on modest incomes. They received a low interest rate which in the inflationary 1960s and 1970s was often negative in real terms. Therefore, the relatively cheap finance allocated to the HLMs was, in effect, subsidized by many of the types of household who lived in this sector (Topalov, 1987: 335–6). The CDC and the CPHLM became the main providers of a mixed system of finance to HLMs. Loans covered 50 per cent of the approved costs of PSR units, 60 per cent of 'ordinary' HLM units and 100 per cent of ILM and HLM ownership units. Capital grants provided the rest of the finance for the first two types of housing, up to 95 per cent of approved costs. Interest subsidies were provided to reduce the costs of the loans for the higher-rented categories. The cost of this finance was increased in comparison with what it had been before 1966 and the repayment periods reduced. A total of 5 per cent of the costs had to come from the HLM landlord's own resources or from the previous sources of supplementary finance (Pearsall, 1984: 27). Moreover, the CDC/CPHLM finance was calculated on the basis of construction cost limits set by government. These were not raised in line with inflation, so increasing recourse had to be made to more expensive supplementary finance. There were also cost-saving reductions in the quality of construction. Further changes were made in the late 1960s and early 1970s which increased the cost of HLM finance still further. The result was that rents rose sharply while new building fell away.

The policy of reducing direct subsidies for social housing, targeting those which remained on lower-income households and encouraging the growth of the private housing market, gave rise to a significant increase in the production of HLM housing for ownership, much of it built by the organizations which were also active in the intermediate sector. This sector, rather than HLM rented production, became a clear government priority after 1969. Along with this shift went a much sharper differentiation in the financing terms of the HLM housing types and a growth in their number. While in 1961 there had been three types of HLM housing, by 1970, there were seven. In 1972 there was a new development, which paralleled changes occurring in other countries, when the interest subsidies payable on higher-quality, higher-rented ILM units became degressive (Magri, 1977: 210–13).

The 1960s and 1970s also saw efforts, as elsewhere, to raise rents and reduce the gap between the rents of older and newer property (Magri, 1977: 129–43). Between 1963 and 1972 the rents of the oldest HBM units rose faster than those of the units which had been built in the 1950s. At the same time the higher level of building-cost inflation also led to very rapid rises in the rents of new HLM housing. Given the income growth which was occurring, these changes had a fluctuating effect on rent/income ratios. In the early 1960s these tended to fall, then they rose sharply from 1964 to 1968 as the new financial arrangements took effect, finally dropping a little and eventually levelling out by the early 1970s (following the wage rises after the 1968 'events'). However, the rent/income ratios in the new units continued to be high and rising.

By this point, the government's rent and subsidy policies had resulted, as elsewhere, in new units standing vacant because their rents were too costly. From 1974 rent arrears and tenant protests over high rents multiplied (Topalov, 1987: 245). Increasingly, those higher-income households which had previously lived in HLM housing, including the higher-rented types, found it advantageous to move into the home-ownership market, with or without the benefit of the direct subsidies which the government supplied to this sector (or if this was beyond their reach, into the HLM ownership sector) (Topalov, 1987: 351–81).

In 1963 the government had sought to reform the legal and institutional structures which governed HLM housing, in order to ensure that it complied with the role which the state defined for it, as the supplier of housing tied to the needs of the expanding economy. The representation of local councils on the boards of directors of HLMs was weakened and the control of the state strengthened, at least in theory. Departmental Prefects were given some say in lettings policies and were able to nominate to HLM vacancies. However, the HLM movement vociferously opposed these changes, and Pearsall (1984: 16) remarks that, in practice, many of these enhanced controls could still be evaded.

Summarizing the changes which occurred between the 1950s, on the one hand, and the 1960s and early 1970s, on the other, Magri (1977) suggests that, in the 1950s, state policy was driven by the need to provide a sufficient output of minimal-standard housing in order to allow the process of economic reconstruction to go ahead and contain public discontent about housing conditions. The high level of housing production was achieved by keeping standards, and hence costs, relatively low. This housing was available in a fairly undifferentiated way to a wide range of income and social groups, who paid low proportions of their incomes in rent. From the 1960s policy changed, with a wide diversification of housing types and financing schemes and a big rise in non-HLM production. The overall objective was to encourage the growth of the private housing market and to aid this by a more clearly differentiated structure and range of types of housing with differing quality levels and degrees of state support. One objective was to raise rent/income ratios in the HLM sector to encourage outward mobility by the better off, although this was frustrated by the relatively slow development of private housing production during the 1960s owing to the impact of accelerating inflation on building costs and house prices. This new pattern also matched changes in the labour force, with the growth of white-collar and service workers and sections of the better-off skilled working class. The new structure of housing production, with the increasingly differentiated locations for the different types of housing, reinforced and reflected the increasing diversification of the labour force. Magri suggests that, in this respect, housing policies even contributed to class fragmentation and the effective exercise of social control in this period, although whether this was a deliberate aim seems less clear.

These and other changes resulted, in the 1960s and early 1970s, in an increasing polarization in the housing situation of the French population (Barou, 1992). Low-income households became concentrated in the pre-1948 private rental stock and in the lower-cost, poorer-quality older HBM and HLM units. At the other extreme, higher-income households moved into the expanding home ownership sectors, the unsubsidized sector and that part of the 'intermediate sector' which provided houses for sale subsidized with Crédit Foncier loans and premiums. Meanwhile, the middle-income groups moved into the newer and higher-rented HLM subsector, the HLM ownership sector and the 'intermediate' rental sector, which was also aided with Crédit Foncier loans and premiums. The poor were increasingly segregated spatially into centrally located areas of decaying and old private rented housing and into the poorer-quality HLM units, now including some of the more problematic *grands ensembles*. As the French economy had expanded, it had drawn in an increasing number of guest workers from Southern

Europe and North Africa, who were paid low wages for mainly unskilled jobs and who formed a large sector of those remaining in poverty in the 1970s. Such households also began to find their way into the peripheral low-quality HLM estates during this period (Emms, 1990; Power, 1993).

Therefore, while much of the HLM sector continued to house a range of middle-income households (indeed, for the reasons mentioned, much of the better HLM stock became even more exclusively the preserve of such households), other parts began to be converted to a form of residual housing for economically, socially and politically marginal sections of the population. Concern about the deteriorating *grands ensembles* had begun to be expressed from the late 1960s. There was mounting criticism of the gigantic urban development and renewal projects which were a hallmark of the Pompidou presidency and the product of his drive to modernize the urban system, along with the rest of the economy. Increased emphasis began to be placed on the need to improve the quality of urban life (*cadre de vie*), shifting from quantitative to qualitative policy objectives. In part, this was a reaction to the political radicalism which had been exhibited by some of those who lived in the *grands ensembles* in 1968. It became an important theme in the campaign which Giscard d'Estaing waged for the presidency in the early 1970s. By the time he came to power, as in other countries, the policy of industrialized high-rise building had been abandoned and the first proposals were emerging for new policies to deal with the social and physical problems that had begun to develop in these projects. We shall return to this topic in the next chapter.

Giscard, as a technocrat and an economic liberal, was hostile to the high degree of state intervention in the economy which had marked the Gaullist years. As Derbyshire (1990b: 40) remarks, he sought to combine technocratic, long-term strategic planning with a competitive, deregulatory, freer-market approach at the micro level and sought generally to instil greater market and price consciousness into the French system. At the same time, he had a commitment to a welfare safety net for the poor similar to that advocated by the more paternalist conservatives in other countries.

Up to this point, despite the changes which we have described, the fundamental basis for the financing and subsidizing of social housing had evolved along lines set in the early post-war period, when the main objective had been to increase new construction as rapidly as possible for mass needs. Despite the growing pressures placed on better-off households to move out of social housing into the private sector, there had been no radical reform aimed at reorienting the sector to perform a more limited role housing low-income groups. This now changed. In 1975, two reports were prepared, one by Simon Nora, a senior Inspecteur des Finances, which recommended new policies for housing rehabilitation, targeting public assistance on those who were least well off, and calling for a more general reform of housing policy along these lines. The second, prepared by Raymond Barre, a neo-liberal, monetarist economist (who then became the Finance Minister and, from 1978, Prime Minister), provided a plan for this reform. This aimed, in a far more systematic way than hitherto, to follow the path which we have seen occurring elsewhere, targeting subsidies, through a system of housing allowances, on low-income households, raising rents and cutting back on state assistance (Pearsall, 1984: 38–40). We shall discuss these changes, which were enacted in 1977, in the next chapter.

While the priority given to industrial investment in France immediately after the war delayed the expansion of housing production, this was not possible in West Germany. The wartime destruction and damage suffered by urban housing, infrastructure and communications, the influx of refugees and, above all, perhaps, the shaky political and social foundations of the new state, necessitated a major effort to increase housing output from the first years of the federal republic. Moreover, with mass poverty and low wages and a severe lack of private capital, there was a universal acceptance of the need for the state to take the leading role in the housing sector. We noted earlier that housing was the major social policy area in which the government was actively involved in the early post-war years, and the only sector of the economy in which it was forced to maintain controls. As Wollmann (1986: 138) notes, even Erhard was prepared to except housing and real estate from the free market and put them under a form of 'emergency rule'. He adds:

> so housing control, a rent freeze, tenure security on existing rental housing and a price freeze on real estate ... were carried on way into the fifties, expressing the political decision of the ruling Christian Democrats that the interests of landlords and owners of real estate had, at least temporarily, to step aside, as long as this was deemed necessary in order to provide low-rent shelter ... and to contribute, through low real estate prices and low rents, to keeping the wage level and, thus, the industrial production cost level down which, in turn, was regarded to be an indispensable precondition for the economic recovery of post-war Germany.

However, as we have seen, the doctrines of the social market economy involved a rejection of collectivism and laid great emphasis on the encouragement of private investment and property ownership. These were seen as the keys to the establishment of a vigorous and rapidly growing capitalist economy, the basis for the legitimacy of the new state. In its Düsseldorf principles the CDU committed itself to the development of social housing, but the manner in which this occurred was strongly influenced by these broader economic and political considerations. The overall objective was embodied in the first statement by the new federal government in September 1949, in which housing was a major topic. Adenauer said:

> [t]he situation on the housing market that prevents the social and ethical recovery of the German people ... will be tackled by us with all out energy. We are ready to support housing construction ... by providing public subsidies ... By cautiously modifying and lifting the administrative control over the existing housing stock and the measures of rent control we shall proceed to reactivate private capital for housing investment. If we do not succeed in engaging private capital again in housing construction, a solution of the housing problem will not be possible (quoted in Wollmann, 1986: 138–9).

Thus the long-term intentions were clear from the start: to return housing as soon as practicable to the private market and to encourage the spread of small-scale property ownership by private landlords and for home ownership. Housing subsidies were needed to stimulate the major construction programme that was urgently required but, as far as possible, this programme should be financed by private savings and investment and the housing owned and operated by private individuals and companies. Wherever this was not possible, the government looked to a revival of the non-profit housing institutions, legally private entities, to provide social housing, not the public authorities (actually the term 'non-profit', though frequently used, was a misnomer – see below). Given these objectives, direct social housing subsidies were made available to any institution or individual that accepted government rules regarding standards, costs and other matters. Moreover, the subsidies could be used for rental housing or for home ownership (Marcuse, 1982: 92–4; Jaedicke and Wollmann, 1990; Boelhouwer and van den Heijden, 1992: 120–1). Crucially, in the light of later history, the status of these units as social housing would last only for a limited period, while the subsidized loans were repaid and for some time after that. Eventually, the properties would revert to the 'free' private sector, or, if they were owned by the non-profits, would then only be subject to the legal provisions regarding non-profit housing (these had been enacted by the Nazis in 1940, and the law continued to operate after the war).

Apart from the social subsidies, the government used techniques to stimulate private sector housing similar to those which it employed elsewhere in the economy, providing substantial tax breaks and other inducements for savings and investment.[46] From 1952 these included premiums for households who invested their savings in Bausparkassen, institutions that also provided such households with housing loans; depreciation allowances for investors in new housing; property and sales tax breaks; and deductibility for tax purposes of private loans for financing housing. Alongside the social rented sector there was also a tax-subsidized 'intermediate' private rented sector which, in addition to benefiting from depreciation allowances along with all new private rental units, received property and land acquisition tax reliefs (Harloe, 1985: 183–5).

Therefore, housing policy was oriented towards maximizing the flow of private investment into housing and to reducing the role of direct state support at the earliest possible opportunity. This is why, unlike a country such as France, where public expenditure on social housing grew over time, the share and significance of social housing expenditure in Germany was highest in the early years of the republic and then declined more or less continuously. In 1950 public sources contributed 44 per cent of the total cost of housebuilding, but by 1975 only 7.5 per cent. By contrast, the share financed by the capital market rose from 42 per cent to 77 per cent. Interestingly, at both dates around 15 per cent came from other sources, mainly from households' own resources.[47] So most home owners have had to contribute a higher proportion of their own resources to buy than in countries such as the USA or Britain, which have had more developed systems of institutional housing finance than Germany. This requirement, together with the high quality, highly regulated standards and fragmented organization of the building industry, and hence high costs of German housing construction, has been an obstacle to the spread of home ownership, even in the prosperous years from the early 1960s onwards (Ball, Harloe and Martens, 1988: 87–129; Boelhouwer and van der Heijden, 1992: 130). One consequence has been to sustain the demand for better-quality social and private rented housing.

While Germany had perhaps an even greater need than the other European countries which we have already discussed for a massive increase in new industrial investment after the war, unlike these countries this did not rule out an equally rapid increase of investment in new housing production. To understand why this was possible we have to recall the more general economic situation in the 1950s. First, there was the deliberate policy of keeping wages and consumption low and diverting much of the benefits of economic growth into investment, with a fiscal regime that encouraged the reinvestment of profits. Second, there were highly conservative, neo-liberal fiscal, monetary and expenditure policies, which resulted in low inflation and a high budgetary surplus that could be used to assist housing. Finally, Germany had the significant advantage, unlike, for example, France or Britain, of having no costly colonial and military commitments to divert resources from the expansion of the domestic economy.

In addition to these general considerations, there were some housing-specific factors which help to explain how the output of new units could be expanded so rapidly. First, policy was driven by quantitative rather than qualitative goals: the pressing need was to maximize the number of units produced. Unlike countries such as Britain or Denmark (but not France), where the aim was to raise the output and the quality of new housing, in Germany the 1950s saw a lot of fairly poor quality and cheaply constructed new housing. Only when the available resources and incomes rose in the 1960s was there a rapid transition to much higher standards. Second, the very fact that most areas of social policy were a low priority for increased public expenditure in the early post-war years meant that the one which was not, housing, could receive substantial government support out of the budgetary surpluses. Finally, housing construction was in itself, of course, a major sector of the industrial economy which the government sought to foster. It contributed greatly to the growth of a wide range of basic and consumer industries and provided much manual employment for the mass of refugees which had flooded into the country after the war; by 1958, over 2 million were employed in the construction industry (Leaman, 1988: 113). And, as in France and the Netherlands, a low-rent housing policy was seen as a vital adjunct to keeping production costs down and aiding economic development (Marcuse, 1982: 94). So, to a greater extent than would have been the case with many other forms of social provision, raising housing output contributed significantly to the overall goal of sustained and rapid economic growth.

About 2.5 million dwellings had been destroyed in the war in the area of the new republic and many were seriously damaged (Emms, 1990: 115). In addition, there had, of course, been a pre-war shortage of urban housing which had been exacerbated to by the lack of building in the war years. But the shortages were made far worse by the population influx and by later demographic and migratory developments which have already been described. In 1950 the country had an unparalleled shortage of housing, with some 16.65 million households occupying just over 10 million units (Emms, 1990: 114). Many of these units were badly damaged. The rapid growth of housing output was remarkable, outstripping all of the other European countries with which we are concerned. Housing production was already over 200,000 in 1949, the first year of the new state. By 1953 it was over 500,000 and by 1956 it reached 591,000. Output then fluctuated until a new peak of 623,000 in 1964. During these years the economy went through three four- to five-year business cycles and, allowing for lags in housing completions, the variations in output fit this pattern. However, as we have seen, in the mid-1960s the economy suffered its major interruption in the record of continued growth. Housing output then fell sharply, from 605,000 in 1966 to 478,000 in 1970. The early 1970s saw, as we noted, another economic boom, this time fuelled by speculation and signifying a grossly overheated economy. Housing output soared to the remarkable total of 714,000 in 1973 before collapsing to under 400,000 by 1976 and staying below this level for the rest of the decade (von Einem, 1981: 10). Despite this outstanding record of new construction, the acute shortage which existed after the war, together with the population developments in the 1950s and 1960s, to which we have already referred, meant that there was still a crude housing shortage of almost 3.4 million dwellings in 1961 and of just over 1 million in 1970. Not until the second half of the 1970s was the number of households in excess of the number of dwellings, by around 600,000 in 1980 (Emms, 1990: 114).

Some idea of the extent of this building programme can be gained from comparing Germany and France – the latter being the closest to Germany in terms of population and post-war housing shortages. Between 1950 and 1959 almost 5.2 million dwellings were constructed in West Germany, compared with only just under 2 million in France (including all units built since the Liberation) (von Einem, 1981: 10; Duclaud-Williams, 1978: 148–9). French post-war output did not exceed 5.2 million until 1968. However, unlike France, where, as we have seen, social housing accounted for around a quarter of all output throughout much of the 1950s and 1960s, the high level of German building and the successful use of tax incentives for private housing investment allowed the government to begin reducing the share of social housing in new building from an early stage. The output of new social housing, including for home ownership, reached a peak level of just over 317,000 in 1952 and then fell more or less continuously to 137,000 in 1970. Output then rose a little in the early years of the Brandt government, up to around 170,000 by 1973 before continuing its decline. Its share of total output fell continuously from an even earlier point. Between 1949 (the first year for which figures are available) and 1952 its share was just under 70 per cent. Then, as the new provisions for stimulating private investment took effect and housing output rose, the share of social housing declined rapidly. By 1955 it was around 50 per cent. In the 1960s, when Germans were able to benefit from economic growth, with rising wages and enhanced consumption, including housing, social housing output contracted as private building grew (aided by rent decontrol from 1960). In 1960 social housing still accounted for about 45 per cent of output, but by 1970 it accounted for only 28 per cent (von Einem, 1981: 10).

Two further aspects of these statistics are important. First, the split between social housing for rent and for ownership and, second, the division between non-profit social housing and that built by commercial agencies and individuals. Unlike France, where the share of social housing for home ownership remained low in the 1950s and expanded more slowly and later than the share of social rented housing, social home ownership in Germany always accounted for a significant proportion of all new social housing. Moreover, while the absolute levels of production of social ownership units declined from around 60,000 per annum between the mid-1950s and the mid-1960s, the output of social rented housing fell more rapidly, so the relative importance of social home ownership increased. Thus, in 1950, it accounted for around 17 per cent of all new social housing; by 1960 the share was 24 per cent, by 1970 33 per cent and by 1975 it was 43 per cent (von Einem, 1981: 10).[48]

The share of the non-profit associations in housing output, not surprisingly, was highest in the 1950s, accounting for between 35 per cent and 47 per cent of all completions output in 1950–4. From 1955 to the late 1960s it accounted for around 25–30 per cent of output, before declining more sharply in the early 1970s to around 15 per cent by mid-decade.[49] However, the non-profits were not confined to just constructing their own social rented housing. They also built 'own account' rental housing outside the subsidy system and a considerable proportion of the social housing which was purchased by individual home owners. Under the law which governed their non-profit status they were required to continue building housing, but this did not have to be subsidized social housing and, in fact, some associations never used the social subsidy systems.[50] Whether they built social housing or not, they were still exempted from income and corporation tax on their revenues (up to the late 1980s, when a radical change occurred; see the next chapter). Some of the larger associations became major builders of housing (and urban infrastructure) for other agencies as well. About 15 per cent of non-profit building between 1955 and 1974 was not on 'own account'.[51] In the 1970s they also became involved in running urban renewal projects. In addition, they managed rental housing which was owned by others and projects occupied by home owners; in 1985, about 425,000 dwellings were so managed (Emms, 1990: 128). By the mid-1980s, the non-profits owned about 9 per cent of all private rented housing in West Germany and 60 per cent of all social rented housing. In total they owned 13 per cent of the housing stock, 9 per cent consisting of social rented housing and 4 per cent consisting of rented housing built without the social subsidies (Emms, 1990: 20). Within the total holdings of the non-profit sector, rather less than one-third was owned by cooperatives and over two-thirds by limited liability companies (we shall discuss the significance of this division later and in the next chapter). Local authorities were also able to use social subsidies, but they rarely did so directly, usually operating through non-profit, limited-liability companies which they controlled.

At the end of the war the occupying powers took emergency measures in response to the housing crisis, imposing rent controls and compulsory dwelling allocation. Then the new Land governments and the local authorities began the repair and reconstruction of damaged buildings. The social housing subsidy system was one of the first pieces of legislation of the new republic, drafted and passed in a few months at the end of 1949 and beginning of 1950. It was the first time that Germany had had a national law providing for publicly subsidized housing (Wollmann, 1986: 139). Despite the Länder's wish to retain the primary responsibility for housing, the acute nature of the housing shortage led most political parties to agree on the necessity for a strong federal role, especially in relation to finance (the private capital market was virtually non-existent) and subsidies. The SPD supported the legislation; as

Wollmann (1986: 139) notes, it even accepted the provision that private investors could receive social subsidies, although this departed from the interwar practice, when only limited-dividend corporations and cooperatives had received such assistance. Only a few state-level Social Democratic politicians were critical, seeing this as a step towards the privatization of social rented housing and a threat to the non-profits. The act referred to the urgent task of the federal and Land governments, cities and towns to support new housing construction which would be appropriate for 'wide sectors of the population' (Wollmann, 1986: 139). It established the distinctions between social, tax-subsidized and 'free financed' housing which have already been mentioned. For social housing it provided low-interest loans and subsidies for builders who were prepared to accept a limited return on their equity, to let the properties to households which met the income criteria for eligibility, to charge the controlled rents applicable and to build to set space standards (not too generous at first). In addition, this housing received similar tax subsidies to those of the purely tax-subsidized sector (and non-profits received further tax reliefs by virtue of their status). Given the situation, it is hardly surprising that, as elsewhere at this time, the income limit for access to social housing meant that about 60 per cent of the population was eligible for this 'first subsidy system'. The income qualification only applied on entry, and no account was taken of subsequent increases in tenant incomes.

Under the new constitution housing continued to be a joint area of competence for the federal and Land governments and, with the exception of the later national housing allowance scheme, federal law lays down the broad guidelines for the operation of subsidy systems, leaving the Länder to determine the details of how these are applied. The Land governments also provide a substantial proportion of the actual resources; by the 1970s this amounted on average to about one-third of the subsidy bill, although some contributed a good deal more.

Under the first subsidy system construction was financed by a combination of first mortgages obtained from non-state sources, state loans and grants and the owners' own resources. In the early years, before a fully functioning capital market had been re-established, the first mortgage might cover 25–30 per cent of costs, the state loan 45–50 per cent and the owners would invest the balance (a minimum own investment of 15 per cent was required). The profit on this equity was limited to 4 per cent on the minimum 15 per cent and 6.5 per cent on sums above this while the units remained as social housing, although non-profits, by virtue of the general legislation which established their status, were permanently bound to distribute no more than a 4 per cent return to their shareholders, reinvesting any extra surplus in housing (or, as many critics later alleged, frequently paying inflated salaries and 'perks' to their staff) (von Einem, 1981). Maximum rent levels were set by the legislation, and individual Länder then established the actual rents charged, taking account of local circumstances and the extent to which the Länder and municipalities also provided loans and subsidies. Cost rents were calculated, with allowances for depreciation, management, maintenance, interest payments and other expenses plus the owners' return. Subsidies met the gap between cost rents and controlled rents. The cost rent regime applied to each unit; rent pooling was not permissible.

In 1953 the first amendments were made to the legislation.[52] These clearly indicated the longer-term aim of a reversion to the private market, allowing the early repayment of the state loans by private builders of social housing. After a transitional period such units would then become part of the free market housing sector (without early repayment the period during which the units would be subject to 'socially binding' rules regarding tenant eligibility and rents was about 50 years). The act also removed rent controls on tax-assisted housing and included a clause giving priority to subsidies for home ownership.

In 1956 a second major housing act marked another move towards the private housing market by seeking to reduce the dependence on state-provided capital (paralleling the similar development in Britain at this point). The act envisaged an annually declining contribution from federal funds for housing. Now subsidies were made available to reduce the interest payments on private sector loans (and public guarantees of repayment were provided). Initial rents were no longer to be determined by statute but by a calculation of the full costs of provision minus initial subsidies. Subsequent increases in costs were to be met by raising rents; before it had been up to the Länder to provide additional subsidies to meet rising costs. This cost rent system built into German social housing the same problem that occurred elsewhere: the wide variations in the rents of comparable units which had been constructed at different times. The rent gap between units built immediately after 1950, which had very low rents, and those constructed after 1956 soon became apparent.

The system of cost rents and guarantees made investment in social rented housing an almost risk-free proposition. Moreover, profits were not in reality limited to 4 per cent, because the arrangements for the calculation of other costs, such as management services provided by the landlords, also allowed a margin of profit. There was, in addition, the long-term prospect of reversion to the free housing sector and capital gains (see G. Winter, 1979, and Krätke, 1989, for analyses of the many ways in which private investors, managers and financiers involved in non-profit housing have been able to make substantial profits). Non-profits have also benefited from the rising market values of the housing and land that they own and have been free to set up for-profit subsidiaries. The dramatic collapse of the largest non-profit, Neue Heimat, in the 1980s, which we shall discuss in the next chapter, showed just how these opportunities for profitable activity could be exploited by a corrupt management.

The 1956 Act increased the proportion of social housing financed by the private sector, although state capital was still required. More generally, the act was designed to stimulate home ownership. Its formal title, the Housing Construction and Family Home Act, indicates this intention. Higher subsidies were provided to encourage the production of new units for home ownership, although these were to be used in conjunction with private capital formation, that is, with owners' own savings and commercial loans, not state loans, unlike social rented housing. The act referred in a very direct way to subsidized housing construction not just as a way of meeting housing needs but of sustaining family life and creating a stake in the system through property ownership by 'connect[ing] the broad masses ... to the land and soil through the promotion of owner-occupation, particularly in the form of family homes' (quoted in Wollmann, 1986: 139; see also Jaedicke and Wollmann, 1990: 148). Moreover, the influence of Catholic social doctrines was particularly evident in the reference to support for housing which would foster 'a healthy family life, particularly for families with many children'. As Wollmann (1986: 140) notes, an aim of the legislation was 'that "healthy families" should live on a landed property of their own and should [remember the Cold War situation of the 1950s] have a "stake in the [Western] system"'. He adds that a second aim was to get potential home owners to mobilize their savings and self-help potential, enabling the state to reduce its financial commitments to housing and opening up new opportunities for private banks and the building industry. This approach was part of a wider CDU policy of privatization, exemplified by the later selling-off of state enterprises such as Volkswagen, with the aim of stimulating share ownership by individual households, especially those on modest incomes, who received a special discount. In a statement in 1961 Adenauer directly linked property ownership and social stability, saying that '[t]he wide distribution of private property is one of the preconditions for the stability of our free economic and social system' (quoted in Wollmann, 1986: 140). There was little political controversy over the increasing emphasis on home ownership. The SPD gave a higher priority to social housing and to the social organizations than the CDU, but Wollmann suggests it was already being influenced by the evident political popularity of the government's moves to expand home ownership. This probably contributed (along with the new pensions legislation) to Adenauer's landslide victory in the 1957 elections. He also notes that at the local level housing policies seemed to be shaped more by variations in socio-economic and housing circumstances than by a strong ideological commitment to one form of housing provision or another.

By the early 1960s the government concluded that the post-war housing emergency was ending, despite evidence that there was still a major housing shortage. Despite considerable opposition, including from the labour wing of the CDU, in 1960 it legislated for the so-called Lücke Plan (the federal Minister of Reconstruction at the time) to begin removing rent and security controls on housing built before 1948 (the measure was called the Act for the Dismantling of the Housing Emergency System) (Wollmann, 1986: 141; Leutner and Jensen, 1988: 151–2). The intention was to allow vacancy decontrol as the crude housing deficit in localities fell below 3 per cent, in other words, while there was still a considerable housing shortage in these areas (Harloe, 1985: 136). No provision was made to protect tenants from eviction and many private landlords issued notices to quit, in order to relet at higher rents or force tenants to pay more. The legislation was strongly opposed by the SPD and tenant organizations. One consequence of decontrol was that speculative capital flooded into the housing market and there was a very rapid inflation in housing prices and rents. While the prices of rents, clothing and food more or less rose at the same rate in the 1950s, from 1960, while clothing and food prices continued to inflate at similar rates, rents rose much faster. By 1970 rents had risen by 250 per cent compared with 1950, while clothing and food prices had increased by well under 150 per cent. By 1980 the differential was even greater, with a 400 per cent rise in rents compared with a 200 per cent rise in the other two indicators. Sharp increases in rent/income ratios were experienced in these latter decades (Marcuse, 1982: 97).

The changes made in 1960 also involved a weakening of the system of dwelling allocation in which local authorities determined the order of priority for housing and allocated to vacant units in the private and social sectors. Now landlords were given a greater freedom to select tenants, provided that they came within the income limits for eligibility, although local authorities could still nominate tenants to a proportion of the vacant units which they had helped to subsidize. Also in 1960 the Federal Construction Act terminated the price freeze on real estate which had been implemented in the post-war emergency and ended the strong powers of expropriation and land use planning which had also been a part of the emergency system of public controls over urban development. Now the free land market was restored, even where compulsory public acquisition was concerned, and local authorities' planning powers were severely restricted. These changes added to the rapid inflation in land and property prices.

The neo-liberal faction in the CDU, led by Ludwig Erhard, intended to go further with these policies by privatizing that part of the social rental stock which was owned by the limited-liability companies controlled by city governments. A plan for this was announced by Erhard's government in 1963. However, there was strong opposition from within the CDU, led by the party's 'social committees', which represented its Catholic labour wing. What ensued was the reverse of what Erhard had intended – legislation which entrenched the cost rent and eligibility conditions for social housing, prolonging its status as a 'special rental market' apart from the 'normal market' (Wollmann, 1986: 141–2).

In 1967 two important changes were introduced by the Grand Coalition government. First, for similar reasons to those we have discussed in relation to other countries, the government activated powers, contained in the 1956 Housing Act, to implement a degressive subsidy system. Subsidies were to last for 12 years, being reduced by 25 per cent every three years. As elsewhere, it was believed that future trends in inflation and incomes would ensure that the subsequent rent rises were affordable for most households, a new rent allowance system (see below) aiding the very poorest (Marcuse, 1982: 95–8; Emms, 1990: 135). The second major change in 1967 was the introduction of a 'second subsidy' system. The intention was to stimulate further the development of home ownership by opening up subsidies to higher-income groups. The scheme used the mechanism of interest-subsidized private sector loans introduced in 1956. The second subsidy scheme supplemented rather than replaced the first scheme and the income limits for eligibility were raised by 40 per cent above those applicable for the first scheme, covering around three-quarters of the population. The aim was to provide a shallower subsidy, targeted at middle- rather than low-income households (Marcuse, 1982: 95; Papa, 1992: 53–8). One objective was to encourage better-off households in the more highly subsidized social rented sector to move into home ownership. Such households were not subject to the income limits for access to the second scheme. In this respect the policy was very similar to that of the French government at this time. This was also seen as a way of tackling the problem of the 'misallocation' of subsidies which rent harmonization was intended to solve elsewhere. In Germany, as we have noted, the cost rent system did not allow the use of rent pooling or harmonization.[53] In any event, the structure of ownership of social rented housing, with many small, private landlords, was hardly suited to approaches which worked best when applied to relatively large holdings of social housing, built over many years. And, as we have seen in the Netherlands and Denmark, long-established, relatively prosperous social tenants were reluctant to cross-subsidize new housing by paying increased rents. Instead, increasing recourse was made to assisting new lower-income entrants to the social sector to occupy expensive new housing with the aid of housing allowances. In Germany a similar resistance to paying higher housing costs was experienced and the growing problem of the lack of affordability of the degressively subsidized new housing units was resolved, not by inducing better-off tenants to move into them, but by increased use of housing allowances and supplementary subsidies for lower-income households.

Over time, the share of social housing output which received the more generous support available under the first subsidy system was reduced, so that, by the mid-1970s, about half the (by then) much reduced social housing output was produced under the second scheme (Marcuse, 1982: 93). Like its counterparts elsewhere, the degressive subsidy was based on an over-optimistic projection of inflation and tenant incomes. The high and rapidly rising rents of costly social housing built in the 1960s and their unaffordability, without substantial expenditure on housing allowances and/or supplementary subsidies from the Länder and local authorities, became a considerable problem in the next decade. One consequence of the combination of degressive subsidies and the cost rent regime in social housing was that its rents tended to rise faster than those of private rented housing. There was growing discontent from tenants over this situation.

A restricted provision for housing allowances had first been made in 1960. Their availability was extended in 1965, in the context of the withdrawal of rent controls from the private rented sector, although they soon became an important means of making the newer social rented housing affordable for lower-income households, as in other countries (Harloe, 1985: 204). At first, as elsewhere, allowances were seen as a supplementary measure which would only be necessary for the poorest households. The costs were shared between the federal and Land governments on a fixed basis, unlike the building subsidy schemes, and there were no locally determined variations in the scheme.[54] Expenditure on housing allowances and the number of recipients mushroomed in the 1970s (Papa, 1992: 70-1).

On finally coming to power at the head of a government in 1969, with an ambitious programme of social reforms, the Social Democrats enacted a new form of rent regulation in the private sector and a new tenant protection law. They also increased the subsidies for the housing allowance scheme and, rather like the British Labour Party a few years earlier, announced an expanded housing programme which included social housing construction in regions where the housing shortage still persisted. However, while social housing played a part in this expanded building, by now the Social Democrats envisaged a major growth in private housing output for rental and ownership. As we noted above, in the over-heated boom years of the early 1970s output did expand to a remarkable 714,000 in 1973, although the expansion of social housing completions was much less dramatic, up from a low point of 137,000 in 1970 to 169,000 in this peak year (Marcuse, 1982: 93). One consequence of this boom period was that guest workers flooded into Germany's inner cities. By 1973 there were 2.5 million in the country (van der Wee, 1987: 162). This intensified housing shortages and provided a new source of demand for low-income rented housing (von Einem, 1981: 14).[55] When the economic boom collapsed about half a million new units remained unsold and many builders and investors who had speculated on a continuing rise in house prices were bankrupted. At the same time, as we noted earlier, the Social Democrats were forced to abandon many of their reform plans, including the expansion of social housing. Nevertheless, the trend towards social home ownership continued so that, while in the 1950s and 1960s (under CDU-led governments) around three-quarters of new social housing was for rental, in the 1970s, under SPD-led governments, the share fell from 57.5 per cent at the start of the decade to 28.6 per cent at the end (Wollmann,

1986: 142), as support was switched from the first to the second subsidy system. In the course of this change the regional social rented housing programme announced in 1971 was transmuted into a programme to boost social home ownership. The increasing concentration on subsidizing home ownership in the 1970s mainly benefited better-off households and led to an increasing degree of polarization. Thus the rate of home ownership among the lowest two deciles in the household income distribution fell from 29.3 per cent in 1965 to 25.7 per cent in 1978, while that of the highest 20 per cent rose from 45.1 per cent to 54.1 per cent (Wollmann, 1986: 142).

So the government augmented a system of state assistance which was designed to promote home ownership and to shift subsidies from social rented construction to individual housing allowances, in other words, to target assistance. Thus it improved the housing allowance system, but in 1972 ended the provision of state loans for social housing construction. Now all new finance came from the private sector, and the state only provided degressive subsidies to reduce its costs (Leutner and Jensen, 1988). This added to the rapid rate of increase of rents in the newer social housing and to the pressure on Land and local governments to provide additional capital resources. There are close parallels between the evolution of the SPD's approach to housing in the 1960s and 1970s and those of other social democratic parties, notably the British Labour Party, which had opposed private rental decontrol in 1957 and, on returning to office in the mid-1960s, had enacted new tenant security and rent regulation laws, but continued to sustain the shift in housing policy away from social renting to home ownership.

The Social Democrats did, however, introduce new federally funded urban renewal and regional development programmes (Kennedy, 1984: 59), which involved a far greater federal intervention in these matters than hitherto. From the mid-1970s subsidies were also provided for housing modernization. These changes were a part of the wider concern of the government to move away from the limited state role envisaged under the doctrines of the social market economy towards a greater involvement in planning social and economic change (von Einem, 1981: 4). As Konukiewitz and Wollmann (1983: 4) explain, the new policies were inspired by the growth of concern about the limitations that an outmoded urban infrastructure was beginning to put on the continuation of economic growth. New roads, hospitals, parking and educational facilities all received major federal funding as a part of this effort at modernization. These changes, besides feeding the real estate boom to which we have already referred, facilitated large-scale, disruptive urban renewal, like that which had occurred in America in previous decades, followed later in the decade by gentrification. They also provided an opportunity for some of the larger non-profit organizations to enter a new field of activity, as the building of social housing on peripheral sites tailed off in the 1970s.

The 1960s saw, as elsewhere, considerable recourse to high-rise, industrialized construction, especially by the larger housing associations in satellite cities settlements which were developed around the major cities (Kennedy, 1984: 61–4; Emms, 1990: 134–6; Power, 1993: 127–31). Non-profit housing organizations, many of whom had close links with Social Democrat city governments, played a major role in these developments, not just by building housing, but by providing other facilities and infrastructure, organizing the planning and development process and so on. About half of all the social rented stock built between 1965 and 1975 is on such estates (Emms, 1990: 144). By the early 1970s, as the housing shortage eased, some of the new and costly dwellings in these unpopular peripheral estates became very hard to let, like their counterparts in France, Denmark and the Netherlands. As in these countries, rent allowances provided an apparent solution to the problem. Subsequently, many low-income households, including guest workers, were rehoused in areas, some of which suffered the same complex of social and physical problems which occurred elsewhere.

The policy of promoting home ownership, and rising incomes, resulted in a sharp rise in home ownership from the late 1960s. The share of home ownership among white-collar and manual workers rose from around 25 per cent in the mid-1960s to over 40 per cent by 1978 (Kennedy, 1984: 65). However, this meant that the majority of such households still lived in rental housing, much of it in the social sector. As we have already noted, the main constraints on a more rapid expansion of home ownership were the relatively high costs of housing in relation to wage levels (the average house price is around eight or nine times average net income, compared with a ratio of three to four in France and Britain, for example (von Einem, 1981: 19)), and the lack of a housing finance system which could provide loans covering a high proportion of house prices. It still remained necessary for households to find a considerable proportion of the cost of house purchase out of their own savings. Moreover, until the Social Democrats changed the system in 1977, the main tax reliefs were linked to new construction, reflecting their original purpose in the conditions of immense post-war housing shortage. So the average age at which

Germans purchased their first house remained high; in 1979 40 per cent were between 40 and 60 years old, 40 per cent were between 30 and 40 years old and only 12 per cent were under 30 years old (Kennedy, 1984: 65). This meant that most households, whatever their economic status and incomes, spent a considerable time in rented housing. So both the social and the private rented sectors retained significant proportions of better-off households and neither developed on a large scale the social, economic or political features which are the characteristics of residualized housing elsewhere. However, as in the Netherlands, France and Denmark, by the mid-1970s there were signs of a residualization of sections of the social housing stock, notably in some of the high-rise peripheral projects which have already been discussed.

Better-off social tenants have tended to concentrate in the accommodation owned by private investors and the housing cooperatives. The latter are normally based in a single locality, have relatively few dwellings, and are highly selective in their allocations policies, letting only to their members. Most members have to pay a fairly high, though refundable, charge of up to 5 per cent of the dwelling cost on entry. All these factors result in the exclusion of most lower-income and/or 'problem' households. The main source of housing for such households has therefore been the larger-scale limited-liability companies, sponsored by employers, unions, churches and especially the local authorities which controlled about one-third of the stock in this sector and had nomination rights to these dwellings (Krätke, 1989: 286–7). However, even in the case of the latter, it was frequently alleged that the local authorities had limited power to enforce their allocation priorities on the professional managers that run 'its' housing association.[56] According to Emms (1990: 130), the limited-liability and joint-stock companies had an average dwelling stock of around 4000 units, and many are much bigger (compared with an average of around 850 dwellings for the cooperatives). It is this group of social landlords which was responsible for most of the peripheral high-rise construction in the 1960s and early 1970s and thus owns the bulk of the residualizing portion of the social rented housing sector.

THE RISE AND FALL OF SOCIAL HOUSING

After the Second World War the need for a return to mass programmes of social housing construction, on a scale far beyond that of the interwar years, was accepted by governments of all political complexions in Europe. Moreover, unlike the period after the First World War, this response was not just a temporary reaction to a period of acute social unrest, a brief interlude before the return to business as usual in housing, as in the economy generally. Of course, the war added to the acute shortages of low-income housing which had existed in the 1930s, and these shortages were a major social and political issue which required state intervention, at least until a functioning private housing market re-emerged. However, now a new and powerful reason existed, alongside the political salience of the housing shortage, for many governments to sustain social housing construction – its contribution to economic modernization and urbanization. In addition, social housing investment became one of the tools of economic management, being frequently used to help maintain the new commitment to full employment.

In most countries this combination of factors helped to sustain programmes of social housing construction into the 1960s. Economic modernization and growth, together with demographic changes, including the trend to smaller households, maintained the shortage of housing to the end of the 1960s. In several countries public and private housing investment remained restricted, because of the pressure on state budgets for investment in industry, infrastructure and other welfare programmes and because of the relatively low levels of disposable households available for spending on housing. However, the picture began to alter as the effects of economic modernization and rapid growth resulted in rising private and public sector resources. On the one hand, this resulted in sharply rising expenditure on social programmes and, in several cases, social housing output expanded, as governments promised finally to eliminate housing shortages. On the other hand, the preconditions for a major upsurge in private housing output began to be established. Two further factors which influenced the changing commitment of governments to social housing, and the form which this took, were the increasing economic difficulties which we discussed earlier in this chapter, and the shift, as crude housing shortages were eliminated and the urban-industrial transition more or less completed, towards social housing construction linked to the modernization of the urban system and thus to slum clearance.

As we have seen, the significance of each of these general factors affecting social housing programmes and the exact timing of their effects varied considerably. Moreover, neither the political nor the economic imperatives which sustained mass social housing in Europe were operative in the United States. Here, social housing rapidly became confined to a residual form of provision for particular sections of the urban poor. Its overall significance, even as housing for the poor, remained marginal.

By the mid-1970s, the conditions which had underpinned the post-war expansion of social housing were rapidly being eroded. The impact of economic modernization and urbanization in increasing the demand for rental housing had declined. At the same time, home ownership was expanding rapidly, promoted and aided by governments of all political complexions. While larger-scale urban renewal continued, increasing emphasis began to be placed on the rehabilitation of private housing (and some older social housing) rather than clearance and replacement. Moreover, the onset of stagflation and the increasing resort to austerity policies, involving deep cuts in public expenditure, reduced the public resources available for social housing. In addition, the continuing budgetary costs of the expensive and, as it became all too apparent, problem-ridden social housing constructed in earlier years resulted in a shift in government support from the production to the consumption of such housing.

Also, the politics of housing was undergoing a transformation. With home ownership increasingly within the reach of large sections of the population, conservative and centrist parties, which had always maintained a long-term preference for this form of provision, began to move away from the support for mass social housing. Social democratic parties failed to bring about the transition from a private to a socialized housing system. In fact, this had rarely been a serious objective when they served in government. Economic growth and industrial restructuring led to important changes in the class structure and eroded the traditional social base on which these parties had depended. As the radicalism of the immediate post-war period gave way to an era of full employment and rising prosperity, the electoral prospects of most social democratic parties seemed to dim. In almost every case they responded by seeking to broaden their appeal, moving from being workers' to 'people's' parties, and accepting the main principles of the mixed economy of welfare capitalism. They abandoned whatever pretensions they had once had to large-scale socialization of the economy and state planning, confining their argument with the right to distributional issues – the extent to which the state should modify the distributive outcomes of the private market. Now, as they sought to attract middle-class white-collar voters, and as many among their traditional working-class constituency became home owners, these parties embraced the conservative preference for home ownership. Whatever ideas that they might have had, in the immediate post-war era, for replacing the private market in housing and land by a semi-socialized system, these now gave way to a conception of social housing which, in practice, was scarcely different in any fundamental respect from that held by non-socialist, centre and right-wing parties. The politics of social housing became confined to arguments between left and right over matters such as the size of the construction programme and the level of subsidies and rents, over the relative generosity of state assistance, rather than over more fundamental issues regarding the revival and growing dominance of the private market.

In these respects the politics of housing reflected the broader acceptance by social democracy of the boundaries between the state and the market (and the acceptable relations between the two) in the system of welfare capitalism which was established after 1945. Even within the social housing sector, these limits were clearly evident, as the degree of socialization of housing production remained severely restricted and even declined over time owing to, for example, the removal of land price controls, the use of private finance and of private construction firms. In some cases, notably Germany and France, much of this housing was also in private, capitalist ownership as well. Mass social housing benefited the private sector in other ways, too. It provided a useful, controllable instrument for the state-inspired drive to modernize housing production, which favoured large-scale construction firms. Developments such as high-rise industrialized building would not have occurred in a housing market where consumers had some degree of choice, but, for many years at least, social housing consumers had to accept whatever the producers, architects and planners, housing managers and politicians, gave them. Although the high-rise 'revolution' was a dreadful failure, many of the technical and organizational developments, together with the productivity gains through the use of standardization, prefabrication and the substitution of unskilled for skilled labour, which it incorporated were transferred to low-rise construction in the private sector. In addition, social housing construction provided an important basis for the revival of the construction industry after the war and, at times when private orders declined, a means of sustaining activity and profit levels.

Another feature of post-war social housing, accepted by social democrats, as by non-socialists, was the further growth of large-scale, professionalized and bureaucratic housing management. Little survived of that part of the early social housing reform movement which had been based on workers' self-organization and management and on making a contribution to wider processes of political mobilization and acculturation. Indeed, in Germany, where such initiatives had been most evident in the first decades of the century, the SPD and the trade unions consciously turned their backs on any wider societal role for social housing as they sought, like others elsewhere, to broaden their appeal and to incorporate new sections of the labour force and the electorate. Only in Denmark, and to some extent in Germany, was the tradition of small-scale, locally based cooperative housing retained, in which tenant democracy, in theory at least, persisted. However, by the 1970s, few of these projects retained any of the broader social objectives of earlier workers' housing initiatives; many became professionally managed with tenants having little influence over their affairs. Frequently, their main concern was to preserve and defend the benefits which such housing provided for their existing tenants (by, for example, the control of allocations to exclude 'unacceptable' lower-income and other households and by resisting rent harmonization), rather than to pioneer and represent a radical alternative to the mass-produced, large-scale, bureaucratically and professionally managed products of welfare capitalism.

Of course, the extent to which the increasing political support for mass home ownership translated into a rapid growth in the proportion of the housing stock in this sector varied considerably. Economic and political circumstances combined to produce different outcomes, as illustrated by the contrasting examples of Britain and Germany, two countries which were governed for long periods by parties strongly committed to home ownership. In addition, some countries, such as Germany, France and the Netherlands, provided assistance to sustain private rental housing, although this did not stem the long-term decline of this sector which accelerated as, first, the support for social housing and, later, for home ownership, left it competing on increasingly unequal terms (Harloe, 1985).

A further important variable in the fortunes of social rented housing was the degree to which it had a broad base of political support. This, in turn, partially depended on who lived in such housing. In the mainland European countries social housing organizations exerted a considerable influence on most political parties for many years, operating through their federal bodies, because they provided a major source of accommodation for many white-collar and skilled manual workers and because of the inclusion of some sections of organized labour within parties such as the Dutch and German Christian Democrats, although, in the longer run, the

Catholic social doctrines which had the greatest influence within these Christian workers' sections, with their emphasis on sustaining family life, also tended to provide ideological support for home ownership rather than social rented housing.

However, despite these national differences across Europe in the political, economic and institutional context to social rented housing, it is the broad similarities of circumstances and the many parallel developments which seem most striking. These findings are thrown into sharp relief by the very different post-war history of US public housing. In the United States, as in Europe, economic growth, full employment, rapid urbanization and major demographic changes created a high and sustained demand for new housing. However, the political and economic conditions which allowed a rapid growth of home ownership occurred here a generation before they appeared in most European countries. So, from the start, the possibility of a mass programme of social housing for general needs was inconceivable. Instead, public housing rapidly became defined as a residual form of provision, very largely being used (in the big cities at least) as an adjunct to private sector, state-assisted urban renewal operations, rehousing the most stigmatized sections of the urban poor. Moreover, the generalized political hostility to public housing, whipped up by the real estate industries, ensured that the accommodation that was provided came in a form and with a financial structure that was almost pre-programmed to fail and to amplify the stigmatization of its tenants. The crisis which public housing faced from the late 1960s onwards was an all too predictable outcome of the way in which it had been re-established in 1949.

Ironically, just when the crisis in US public housing was becoming apparent, European social housing seemed to be flourishing. In several countries the 1960s saw an increase in the output of social housing and, in every case, by a considerable improvement in the space and other standards of what was built. These changes were made possible by the increased revenues which governments had available for social expenditure and by the rising incomes of those sections of the population which, it was assumed, would inhabit the new social housing. However, these developments occurred just at the point when the complex combination of circumstances that had underpinned the post-war expansion of social housing was beginning to unravel. First, the mass housing programmes of previous years, together with the virtual completion of the rapid transition to modern, urban-industrial economies, were at last reducing the major shortages of housing that had affected broad sectors of the population. Moreover, the rising real incomes of these groups and the revival of a dynamic private housing market, heavily aided and promoted by all governments, opened up home ownership to groups that had formerly been dependent on rented housing. The advancing breakup of the post-war economic order also had important consequences for social housing. High inflation provided an additional inducement for those households that could afford home ownership to buy rather than rent. These pressures peaked in the brief but hectic boom years of the early 1970s when the speculative real estate market was at its height. At the same time, the decline in growth rates, evident from the 1960s onwards, together with the high cost of the extension of social welfare provision which had occurred in this decade, put increasing pressure on governments to make those changes in the financing of social housing which had already been discussed in the previous decade in reports by the ECE and others – raising rents and reducing subsidies, and targeting assistance, through housing allowances, on lower-income households. The higher rents contributed to the other factors, already noted, which encouraged middle-income households to opt for home ownership rather than social rented housing. One paradoxical consequence was that some of the new and costly social rented housing which had been con- structed in the 1960s and 1970s began to be occupied by low income households, rather than the better-off tenants whom it had been envisaged as serving.

A consequence of these changes was that, while in many cases the existing stock of social rented housing continued to accom- modate a fairly wide range of income and social groups, the nature of the new demand for social rented housing began to shift, away from the better-off manual and white-collar employees towards lower-income households, including those who were outside the labour market altogether. This change was by no means as rapid in some countries as in others. Nor was it welcomed by the social landlords and their existing tenants, who frequently resisted a redefinition of the role of social housing. These trends and the conflicts which surrounded them became even more apparent after the mid-1970s, as we shall see in the next chapter.

A further factor which contributed to the declining role of social housing in relation to the housing of better-off sections of the popu- lation was the changing perception, by some housing consumers, of the relative attractiveness of social housing and home owner- ship. Of course, the rhetoric which surrounded the promotion of home ownership as a form of housing which offered choice and independence was overblown. However, the fact remains that much of the expensive social housing built in the 1960s, while it achieved high standards of space and internal amenities, was in high-density developments (frequently high-rise and peripherally located as well) which were rejected by households who now had the incomes to afford the single-family housing provided by the private sector. For many households the choice between paying high rents and rapidly rising heating and other costs for such housing, or buying a preferred form of housing which was also (apparently) an ever appreciating capital asset, was not a difficult one – they opted in increasing numbers for the latter. Moreover, while such households were prepared in the early post-war years of housing shortage to accept the bureaucratic and insensitive management regimes which tended to accompany the growth of large-scale social housing organizations, such methods were increasingly unattractive for households which now had the opportunity to escape to what was frequently perceived as the realm of freedom and self-determination in the private sector. The contrast between the two sectors was undoubtedly exaggerated by those political and economic interests which had most to gain from the growth of home ownership, but that there was some material basis for this contrast cannot be denied.

To summarize, there was a shift from a situation, after 1945, when a conjunction of factors supported and, for many years, sustained the expansion of social housing for mass needs to one where this combination began to break down. With the breakdown there was also the beginning of a redefinition of the role of social housing, back to the more limited conception as a source of housing for economically marginal groups excluded from access to the private market, which was a persistent theme in conservative visions of housing reform from before the First World War. What reinforced this transition was not just the changing material conditions and the political shifts which made home ownership increasingly accessible to many middle-income households, nor the ideological discourses which supported this development. In addition, by the 1960s, economic modernization and developments in the politics and economics of housing itself were creating a growing replacement low-income demand for social housing. One consequence of economic modernization and growth was the pressure that resulted for urban modernization and growth and therefore for large-scale urban renewal (and later, in the case of housing, for the upgrading of older housing with the replacement of low-income tenants by higher-income owners or tenants). Urban renewal reduced the stock of low-income private rental housing, which had been the major source of accommodation, rather than social housing, for many poor households. More generally, the decline of private rental housing added to the demand for social housing. In addition, there were various other demographic and social changes, such as the growth of the aged population and of single-parent households which added to low-income housing demand. As we shall note in the next chapter, the ending of full employment and the development of polarised labour markets in the late 1970s and 1980s also added to this low-income demand. A further factor was the influx of low-income ethnic minority households and guest workers, encouraged by governments in the 1960s as their growing economies demanded a fresh supply of labour, but who remained locked into low-income jobs, many of which proved insecure after the mid-1970s, when unemployment began to climb.

So, from a situation where social housing accommodated a wide range of middle-income households, it began to provide the main source of housing for an increasing proportion of low-income households, while those who might have occupied such housing in a previous era became home owners. It is important to emphasize yet again that this transition has been, and continues to be, a gradual process. In none of the European countries with which we are concerned has social housing become purely the preserve of very low income households as in the USA. Nowhere, either, does social housing as a whole have the same degree of financial and social problems that US public housing exhibited by the early 1970s. And it retains a wider and more substantial basis of political support in Europe, too.

The changes which we have been describing were most evident in the changing pattern of demand from those seeking access to social housing. Existing social housing tenants were still drawn from a much wider range of incomes and occupational backgrounds, many of whom benefited from relatively low, historic cost-related rents. In fact, the changes in the nature of the population becoming social housing tenants led to an increasing segmentation of the sector. Low-income households first concentrated in that part of the older social rented stock which was poor quality and therefore relatively affordable by them (as we have already noted, better-off established tenants were often reluctant to move out of cheaper, better-quality older housing). In many cases, it was envisaged that the costly and supposedly higher-quality units built in the 1960s would enable internal filtering to occur, freeing up older and cheaper units for less well off households, but this did not occur.

Instead, with the aid of housing allowances, such units were increasingly allocated to poorer tenants, who had no alternative but to accept them. The result was concentrations of multiply disadvantaged households – ethnic minorities, single parents, the unemployed and so on – on these estates. In later years, as we shall show in the next chapter, the problems of such residualized segments of the social housing stock bore similarities with those which typified much of the big city public housing sector in the USA.

These developments were limited before the mid-1970s, even though many of the changes which were recasting the role of social housing were in train. Later developments, such as the emergence of New Right economic and political doctrines, the decline of manufacturing industry and the growth of a 'post-Fordist', service-based economy, with an increasingly polarised labour market, accelerated the transformation of social housing. Nevertheless, by the mid-1970s, with the breakdown of the structure of accumulation and the growth of unresolvable tensions in the compact between labour, capital and the state which had underpinned the 'long boom' and the policy regime of welfare capitalism, the golden age of social housing was over.

NOTES

1 Although, as we have seen, the foundations for the new system were being laid in the interwar years.
2 The following account is based on Aldcroft (1978); Cipolla (1978); and van der Wee (1987).
3 The following discussion draws on Shonfield (1974); Lieberman (1977); Aldcroft (1978); van der Wee (1987); and Morgan (1990).
4 The following discussion draws on Aldcroft (1978); Jörberg and Krantz (1978); Esping-Andersen (1985); and van der Wee (1987).
5 The following discussion draws on Shonfield (1974); Aldcroft (1978); de Vries (1978); and van der Wee (1987).
6 The following discussion draws on Shonfield (1974); Lieberman (1977); Aldcroft (1978); Fohlen (1978); van der Wee (1987); and Larkin (1988).
7 The following discussion draws on Shonfield (1974); Lieberman (1977); Aldcroft (1978); van der Wee (1987); and Leaman (1988).
8 Figures calculated from Aldcroft (1978: 234, 237); and van der Wee (1987: 77).
9 The following discussion draws on Morison, Commager and Leuchtenberg (1980); Blum et al. (1985); Jones (1987); and Derbyshire (1990a).
10 The following discussion draws on Marwick (1970, 1982); Morgan (1984, 1990); and Derbyshire and Derbyshire (1990).

11   The following discussion draws on Miller (1968); Fitzmaurice (1981); Logue (1982); Elder, Thomas and Arter (1982); Esping-Andersen (1985); Rying (1988); and Einhorn and Logue (1989).

12   This party was formed in 1960 by former Communists and dissenting Social Democrats.

13   The following discussion draws on Ardagh (1977); Larkin (1988); V. Wright (1989); and Derbyshire (1990b).

14   The following discussion draws on Lijphard (1975); Daalder (1987); Gladdish (1991); and Andeweg and Irwin (1993).

15   The third party, the Christian Historical Union, based on the Dutch Reformed Church, was less successful, many of this church's adherents voting for the PvdA and some for the ARP and the Liberal VVD (Irwin and van Holsteyn (1989)).

16   Lijphard's (1975) characterization of the Netherlands as a 'pillarized' society and arguments concerning the degree of 'depillarization' in recent decades have generated an extensive critical literature. See Daalder (1987, 1989); Lijphard (1989); Middendorp (1991); and Andeweg and Irwin (1993).

17   Interestingly, the Minister for Social Affairs in the government was from the ARP and was an ex-member of the Christian trade union movement.

18   The following discussion draws on Grosser (1974); Conradt (1978); Berghahn (1982); Fletcher (1987); Ardagh (1991); and Derbyshire (1991).

19   It was also concerned about losing its separate identity if it only continued to ally with the CDU, and had formed several governing alliances with the SPD at state level in the previous decade.

20   See Ball, Harloe and Martens (1988: 54–5) for comparative trends in the six countries.

21   See Power (1993) for a detailed study of these problems in Denmark, the UK, France and Germany; see also Emms (1990), who also covers the Netherlands, and Prak and Priemus (1985), who include the USA.

22   Interestingly, he favoured a policy adopted by the Nixon administration 25 years later, i.e. cash subsidies to lower-income households for private rental accommodation.

23   The lengthy Gautreaux law suit, fought in order to force public housing desegregation in Chicago, had only limited success, although the children of families that were relocated as a result to suburban housing did benefit. See Bowly (1978); Polikoff (1978); Lazin (1979–80); and Rosenbaum (1991).

24   Although many smaller public housing authorities, and some big city ones, were generally regarded as well run. See Struyk (1980).

25   Most of the projects had to struggle with a framework of national and local policies and regulations that were less than helpful, as well as difficulties which arose from the nature of the projects and their low-income populations (interviews with tenants and managers of

the St Louis Housing Authority and Jersey City Housing Authority, National Tenant Management Demonstration Program, and Robert Kolodny, June 1976; William Law (Jersey City Housing Authority), June 1983).

26 As Abrams and Rose (1960: 44) noted, commenting on a survey of voters, '[o]f all working-class Labour supporters nearly half (46 per cent) live in council dwellings; among other members of the working class the ratio ... is much less – 26 per cent ... municipal tenants strongly identify themselves with the party which ... has come to be regarded as a supporter of subsidised housing'.

27 The government eventually enforced the act, in a few cases suspending local authorities' housing powers and operating through special commissioners which it appointed.

28 Indeed, there appeared to be an association between living in council housing and higher levels of mortality and unemployment that was independent of social class, as later research discovered. See Murphy and Sullivan (1986).

29 This section draws on interviews with Bent Fjord (Ministry of Housing), Hans Skifter Andersen (Danish Building Research Institute) and Erling Olsen (Social Democrat MP and former Minister of Housing), February 1983.

30 Interview with Lars Østergaard (Ministry of Housing), 1978.

31 See note 30.

32 Interestingly, the figures for home ownership among unskilled workers over these years were very similar.

33 The Minister could require that 20 per cent of social housing vacancies be made available for slum rehousing. By the 1970s such households could also receive additional subsidies to meet the new higher rents in social housing (Ministry of Housing, 1974).

34 Interview with Jan van der Schaar (University of Delft), April 1983.

35 The following details are drawn from Priemus (1981); van Weesep (1982); and van der Schaar (1982).

36 See note 34.

37 See note 34.

38 The average floor space of Housing Act dwellings hardly rose between 1948 and 1952; indeed, it declined for a year or two, then rose by over 20 per cent to peak in the early 1970s, after which it fell back a little (van der Schaar, 1982).

39 See note 34.

40 The following figures derive from van der Schaar (1982 and are based on official housing censuses and housing demand surveys.

41 A detailed account of post-war policies up to 1972 is contained in Magri (1977), from whom many of the following details are taken.

42 By the 1970s the sum collected in this way was very large; in 1975, it exceeded the state's budgetary allocation for housing (Pearsall, 1984: 18).

43   Giscard d'Estaing was a member of Mendès-France's economic think-tank.

44   For a detailed analysis of the changing socio-economic composition of HLM tenants see Barou (1992).

45   The following details draw on an interview with Joseph Comby and Vincent Renaud (Ministère de l'Urbanisme et du Logement), June 1983.

46   Leaman (1988: 118) shows how income tax was cut back sharply in the 1950s, especially on higher incomes, as part of the policy of reducing the tax burden in favour of capital accumulation.

47   Information supplied by Eberhard Mühlich (Institut Wohnen und Umwelt, Darmstadt).

48   Additional data supplied by Eberhard Mühlich (Institut Wohnen und Umwelt, Darmstadt).

49   See note 48.

50   Interview with Dr Hannig (Gesamtverband Gemeinutziger Wohnungsunternehmen), January 1984.

51   Based on official data, I am indebted to Peter Marcuse (Columbia University) for this information.

52   I am indebted to Peter Marcuse (Columbia University) for supplying these and subsequent details of the early post-war housing legislation.

53   Although from 1968 some increases in the cost rents of older units occurred owing to increases in the interest rates payable on their debt, and from 1974 rent pooling could occur on a project-by-project basis, but this hardly enabled any significant cross-subsidy to occur (interview with Neue Heimat, Dortmund, January 1977).

54   The various problems – of coverage, eligibility and take-up rates which accompany means-tested benefits such as housing allowances are well known and apply to all the schemes introduced in the countries with which we are concerned. In addition, allowances have proved an inadequate substitute for production subsidies when there is a need to stimulate new investment in housing. In the German case an additional problem has been the imposition of maximum limits for the subsidizable rents. The actual rents paid by low-income households have frequently exceeded these maxima, leaving tenants to meet the 'top slice' of the rent themselves. See the discussion of these issues in Ball, Harloe and Martens (1988: 70–2).

55   Although a ban on primary immigration was imposed when the boom collapsed in 1973.

56   Interview with Neue Heimat, Dortmund, May 1977.

5

Residualism Revived: Social Housing in the Contemporary Era

The ultimate significance of the most recent period in the history of social rented housing cannot yet be fully evaluated. In some ways it is tempting to see the years since 1975 as a rerun of the reversion to the more limited, residual model of social housing that occurred after the mid-1920s. However, in the five European countries under review in this book, social rented housing accounted for a far larger proportion of the housing stock by the mid-1970s than 50 years earlier. It accommodated a far larger number of households and a wide range of social and income groups. Large-scale, well-established social housing organizations had a significant influence on the politics of housing, and most political parties and governments, whether of the left, centre or right, now accepted some level of social housing as a permanent component of national systems of housing provision.

In the 1920s and 1930s, when the size and significance of the social housing sector was still extremely limited, the retreat of the state from its early post-war programmes of mass social housing was a relatively simple action, signalling the return to a private housing market. In the 1970s, while the desire of governments to rely on the private market (now with extensive state support) for most housing provision became increasingly clear, disengagement from major commitments to social housing could not be so easily achieved. Even if it had wanted to, no government could abandon its large-scale subsidy commitments, let alone matters such as rent regulation, the provision of demand subsidies, the financial and administrative supervision of social rented landlords, a concern for the physical and social conditions in the existing stock and so on. In short, the extent of state involvement in social rented housing was on a wholly different scale from that which existed in the 1920s and any reorientation of the sector was bound to be a protracted and complicated affair. In any event, the institutionalization of social housing interests within national politics and state bureaucracies meant that there was likely to be significant resistance to state disengagement.

The outcome of these contending forces, those making for a restructuring of social housing into a residual form of provision, and those resisting this tendency, has taken varied forms in each of the countries with which we are concerned. The most dramatic developments within the European nations have occurred in Britain and Germany, although by the early 1990s, the residualization of social rented housing was also well established in France. In Denmark and the Netherlands a shorter distance had been travelled along this road. In the USA successive administrations tried to go further and dissolve the public housing sector, although it managed to survive.

In the previous chapter we described the gradual erosion of the social structures of accumulation and the policy regime which was the basis for the golden age of mass social rented housing. From the mid-1970s the pace of change quickened as the economic and political context within which social rented housing policies were determined was transformed. The dynamic economic growth of the previous decades gave way to a far more turbulent situation. Full employment gave way to persistent structural unemployment, which never reverted to the low levels of the previous era, even when the economies recovered from recession. Faltering growth, high unemployment, ageing populations and other factors placed new demands on state welfare expenditures, while the scope for financing these expenditures was curtailed. Underlying many of these changes were some profound alterations in capitalist economies and the world economic system – deindustrialization and the rise of high technology and service industries, with a more polarised distribution of occupations and incomes, in the older advanced economies, together with the rise of the newly industrializing economies and a new international division of labour and economic power.

As the problems caused by these changes became more intractable, the political regime which accompanied the post-war expansion of welfare collapsed. As Gourevitch (1986: 29–32) puts it, the historic compromise between labour and capital (and agriculture) which involved policies of demand management, welfare and stabilization started to fall apart. While social democratic parties governed alone or in coalition from time to time, right-wing political forces were in the ascendant. Moreover, the revival of free market, liberal economic and political ideologies not only transformed many right-wing parties from within, but also influenced the nature of social and economic policies more generally. Old arguments which condemned state intervention as inefficient, ineffective and undemocratic were revived and taken seriously again. Privatization, decentralization and state disengagement now appeared on the political agenda, although these policy labels frequently concealed a trend towards stronger central control over certain aspects of welfare provision (D. King, 1987).

These changes had wide-ranging consequences for social rented housing. These will be discussed in detail later, but several features stand out. First, there was an ever increasing concentration of low-income households in social rented housing and, within this broad grouping, there was a growth of certain of the poorest and most vulnerable categories, such as ethnic minorities, the elderly and handicapped, single-parent households and so on. The share of tenants who were largely or wholly dependent on welfare and other state income transfers grew. Second, the pressures on somewhat better-off households to leave the sector increased as supply subsidies diminished, rents rose and state support was targeted on the poorest households through housing allowances. Third, the problems of an ageing and, in many cases, poorly designed, planned or constructed social rented housing stock combined with the growing social and economic difficulties of some of its tenants to result in the increasingly frequent emergence of 'troubled', 'problem' or 'hard-to-let' social housing projects. This was merely the most dramatic indication of a wider process of internal differentiation within social rented housing, between the older established, more socially and economically (but not ethnically) mixed tenants who had moved into the sector in the previous era, and the poorer, disadvantaged groups who increasingly looked to social housing as their principal form of accommodation. As we shall see, economic and administrative processes tended to ensure that many of the latter group were concentrated in sections of the social housing stock which were more or less segregated from those occupied by the former group. Fourth, this internal differentiation has, in some cases, been accentuated by a more radical separation, as privatization transfers parts of the social stock out of the sector altogether. However, as yet, privatization has proved a step too far for some of the countries with which we are concerned. Finally, a more widespread development has been the decline in the supply of new social rented housing, although several governments have temporarily reverted to larger programmes of new investment, not primarily in response to the considerable growth of unmet low-income housing needs, but for macro-economic reasons, including support to the housing industry at times when the private market has collapsed, for employment generation and to meet various other exigencies. But these temporary reversals have not marked any fundamental change in direction.

Restructuring has many complicated, contradictory and prob-lematic consequences for social housing organizations, tenants and governments. For example, there is a contradiction between policies which, on the one hand, encourage higher-income households to leave social rented housing, with the aim of targeting assistance on the neediest groups and limiting 'indiscriminate' state aid, and, on the other hand, the growth of severe deprivation and physical deterioration in parts of the stock, which gives rise to new and costly special purpose programmes. Moreover, the rapidly acce-lerating expenditure on housing allowances, owing to rising rents and the growth in poverty, has largely negated the impact of reductions in supply subsidies on levels of public expenditure. Many social housing organizations have been caught in a related trap. On the one hand, they are being forced by policy and housing market developments to accommodate increasing numbers of lower-income households; on the other hand, this presents them with increasingly difficult financial and management problems, such as escalating rent arrears, the need for new expenditures on community programmes, social work, security provision and rehabilitation. The expensive building and design mistakes of the 1960s and early 1970s and the more normal deterioration of the older stock have added to their financial difficulties.

Finally, the influence of social housing organizations and tenants on the politics of housing has been waning. Housing has slipped down the political agenda in most countries. In part this results from the elimination of acute housing shortages. But it also re-flects the far greater importance now placed on policies relating to economic growth, unemployment and inflation. In addition, in most countries, the problems of maintaining adequate state-funded education, health care, pensions and other income transfers affect larger and more politically significant sectors of the population than the problems of social rented housing. The post-war welfare states were largely a response to the needs and the political weight of the better-off working and middle classes, not the poor. So it is hardly surprising that, as social rented housing becomes a far less relevant form of provision for the former group, its political fortunes should fade. In some cases the loss of influence has been quite dramatic, in other cases less so. And in some cases social housing organizations are actively seeking to counter this loss, by, for example, transforming themselves into private sector landlords or by diversifying their activities while retaining some commitment to social provision. In other cases, organizations are trying to come to terms with being the functional equivalent of the bottom end of the private rented sector in an earlier period – landlords of last resort.

ECONOMIC RECESSION AND RESTRUCTURING

The turbulent economic conditions which the six economies have experienced since the mid-1970s provide the first and most basic key to understanding the changes in social rented housing which we have just outlined.

Despite the depth of the recession in 1974/5, there was a relatively rapid recovery of the major world economies – led by the USA, Japan and West Germany, which had emerged with low inflation and strong balance of payments surpluses.[1] However, this upturn did not signal a return to long-term economic expansion. Growth rates remained below former levels and the long-term decline in European rates, closer to those experienced by the USA, continued (see also Aldcroft, 1978: 234). While there were various immediate factors which helped to limit recovery, such as rising energy costs, the basic post-war structural transformation of the European economies was over, or rather, a new phase was beginning. Opportunities for rapid increases in productivity and growth by the modernization of manufacturing industry, the incorporation of agricultural labour forces into industry and so on had vanished. Instead, the older manufacturing economies, with outdated plant and methods and with relatively high levels of wages, came under increasing competition from the new economic superpower, Japan, and the newly industrializing countries (NICs). In Europe, only Germany maintained its manufacturing base more successfully, although even here there was a sharp decline in its rates of return. The sheer size of the US economy meant that it

continued to be a major economic power, even as its older manufacturing base began to collapse. Deindustrialization caused by
the decline of manufacturing added to persistent unemployment
in the countries with which we are concerned.

A new pattern emerged – flagging long-term growth rates, weak
recoveries from repeated recessions, levels of unemployment far
higher than in previous decades, even at the height of the recoveries, and the persistent presence of inflation. In the late 1970s
the average unemployment level in the OECD (Organization for
Economic Cooperation and Development) countries was double
that of the period 1962–73, current output was running at 5–15
per cent below full capacity and export growth and productivity
were declining. Yet inflation rates in the 1970s were more than
double the level of the 1960s (and in Britain more than three times
as high). Moreover, even the relatively weak recovery after the
mid-1970s, in conditions of high unemployment and low capacity
utilization, could not be sustained without a rapid return to the
high inflation rates of the early 1970s (Aldcroft, 1978: 237).

It was the structural changes already discussed, rather than the
exigencies of the moment, which presented governments with new
and far more intractable problems of economic management than
hitherto. As Aldcroft (1978: 251–2) writes:

> [t]hey were faced with a whole host of problems, many of them
> occurring simultaneously, namely inflation, rising unemployment,
> stagnating output, balance of payments difficulties, rising public
> sector deficits, currency disorders ... not since the interwar period,
> and even then prices and unemployment had not risen together,
> had there been a period in peacetime when so many adverse influ-
> ences converged.

In these circumstances Keynesian demand management policies,
which had worked reasonably well when there was an underlying
strong growth dynamic, seemed to provide no solution. Indeed,
attempts to stimulate economic recovery by expansionary fiscal
and monetary policies only set off renewed inflation and balance
of payments difficulties.

From the mid-1970s governments moved towards a new economic
orthodoxy – monetarism. They were searching for a way back to
non-inflationary growth. Earlier in the decade many governments
had tried to employ incomes policies and price controls within
a Keynesian framework. However, the manifest failure of these
attempts led, from the late 1970s, to the adoption (in various forms)

of policies which owed their intellectual lineage to Hayek and Friedman rather than Keynes (Lipietz, 1987: 133–64). These placed the control of inflation and the restoration of the external balance above full employment and growth and operated through control of the money supply, radical reductions in public expenditure growth rates and public sector deficits, and, more broadly, action to reduce the role of the state in the economy and widen the scope for the private market. Although these policies became identified with the rise of so-called New Right policies and administrations, they had frequently begun to be adopted by centrist and social democratic governments beforehand.

The costs of these policies, in terms of high unemployment and reductions in state welfare, were considerable. In many cases governments found the full rigours of the monetarist remedy politically unacceptable. In addition, the technical problems which arose in exercising monetary control were considerable. Falling incomes and profits resulted in lower tax revenues and rising welfare costs, so the struggle to restrain government deficits intensified. Inflation was only squeezed out of the economies with great difficulty and at a high cost in terms of lost growth, incomes and employment. High interest rates boosted inflation and restricted new investment and recovery. Moreover, inflation returned when governments tried to stimulate a recovery. In fact, some governments adopted purely defensive policies, aimed at keeping inflation in check, not just as their main priority, but almost their sole one.

Throughout the 1980s and beyond governments struggled and failed to find a way back to sustained growth and low unemployment. By 1980 a new recession was in full swing, with declines in GDP in Denmark, Britain and the USA and sharp falls in growth in the other three countries. Unemployment began to rise rapidly while money (but in many cases not real) wages also accelerated. Governments intensified efforts to restrain inflation, adding to the depth of the recession. By now financing the welfare state in an era of low and uncertain growth was widely seen as an almost intractable problem, thus reinforcing growing acceptance of neo-conservative prescriptions for a radical restructuring and reduction of state provision (OECD, 1981). It was in this period, too, that some of the labour market consequences of manufacturing decline and the rise of increasingly services-based economies began to become apparent. On the one hand, relatively well-paid, skilled male manual and associated white-collar jobs were disappearing as a result of manufacturing decline. On the other hand, the expansion of services employment, especially in sectors such as banking and finance and, in the 1970s at least, in the public sector, failed to replace this 'missing middle'. The new services employed a minority of highly educated and paid professional and technical workers and a far larger number of low-paid, low-skilled workers, many of them women and ethnic minorities. Frequently, these jobs were part-time and poorly paid, insufficient to provide a family wage. In the 1980s, during the period of economic recovery, further service jobs were created, especially in consumer services, which expanded owing to the purchasing power of the new service class (or 'yuppies' as they came to be called). This increasingly polarised employment structure, whose lower tier of poorly paid and highly exploited workers was augmented by the persistently high level of unemployment and by the growth of low-income pensioners, had major consequences for urban and welfare policies and expenditure, including social rented housing (Fainstein, Gordon and Harloe, 1992). One obvious example was the upward pressure that the rising demand for income-related welfare benefits placed on public expenditure.

In early 1983 the UN Economic Commission for Europe (1983: 1) noted that the recession of the previous two to three years had been the longest and deepest for 50 years. While recovery was now expected, it was obstructed by a new factor, which became a recurrent difficulty, that is the reluctance of consumers to switch from saving to spending in an era of economic insecurity. Moreover, the continued desire to restrain public expenditure meant that governments had abandoned a major mechanism for stimulating recovery. More generally, the impact of monetarist policies during the early 1980s was procyclical, deepening the recession. The growth of international debt problems and falling commodity prices cut Third World imports, adding to the worldwide recession. The resultant fragility in the international banking system, with widespread losses and bad debt provisions, intensified the problems as well. Increasingly, unemployment began to affect geographical regions and groups of workers which had, in former times, been protected from the worst effects of economic downturn.

Faced with this situation, faith in the monetarist experiment became increasingly strained (Lipietz, 1987: 165–74). Several governments, such as those in the UK, Germany and the USA, began to relax the rigour of monetary controls, largely perhaps because of the political costs of rising unemployment. Nevertheless, this was a relatively limited change because of the fear of renewed inflation, which had eventually abated in the early 1980s. In most cases (though not the USA), the use of fiscal policies to aid growth was abjured and the efforts to restrain public expenditure continued with, for example, the suspension of wage indexation in France and Denmark and low limits for public sector pay in Denmark, West Germany, the Netherlands, Britain (and the USA).

High interest rates, coupled with falling inflation, meant that the real cost of borrowing remained at very high levels, something of particular concern for housing markets. In the early 1980s real rates ranged from over 9 per cent in Denmark to 3.5 per cent in the Netherlands, compared with rates of under 1 per cent to under 3 per cent throughout most of the 1960s and early 1970s, the period of rapidly rising housing output which we analysed in the previous chapter (UN Economic Commission for Europe, 1983: table 1.2.9, 22). This increased the real cost of housing and other finance has persisted into the 1990s as lenders are no longer prepared, in the new and uncertain economic era, to accept the poor returns that they formerly obtained. The deregulation of financial markets in the 1980s also removed legislative barriers that had helped sustain cheap housing capital (Ball, 1990).

Much of the new investment that did occur was linked less to an expansion of output than to a need to rationalize production and shed labour in order to respond to the increasing competition from Japan and the newly industrializing low-wage economies. By 1982 unemployment rates in the six countries ranged from 6.8 per cent in West Germany to 11.2 per cent in Britain (UN Economic Commission for Europe, 1983: table 1.3.1, 25). Productivity was far below pre-1974 levels and many economists began to suggest that the advanced industrial economies had undergone a 'system shift' to higher levels of unemployment and lower productivity.

Developments in Japan and the USA underpinned the economic recovery of the mid-1980s. The growth of Japanese production and investment at home and overseas reflected the real strengths of this economy. The US expansion was built on the shakier foundations of Reaganomics. This involved continued attempts to cut social programmes, a massive expansion of defence expenditure and radical tax cuts for companies and the better off to stimulate private sector growth. What resulted was a major growth of activity and new jobs (though most were low-paid and part-time), but also a rapid rise in the budget and balance of payments deficits. These problems have continued to dog American economic policy into the 1990s. However, American and Japanese expansion helped to stimulate the world economy. But recovery was far weaker in Europe, which lacked Japan's high-performing economy or America's fiscal regime. A factor which added to European difficulties was the high US interest rates, necessary to fund the deficit, and an overvalued dollar which reduced the competitiveness of European exports and increased imports from the USA. Increasingly, there was also concern to avoid domestic policy changes which would result in adverse exchange rate adjustments between European trading partners, the problem which the European Monetary System (EMS) tried and failed to solve.

By the middle of the decade inflation rates were falling back to levels closer to those of the late 1960s and early 1970s. Productivity was rising, though mainly as a result of labour shedding and the loss of uncompetitive enterprises. So the renewed growth was not based on major new investment and output, which alone could have reduced the high levels of unemployment closer to pre-1975 levels. In the second half of the decade recovery continued, peaking earliest in Britain, where GDP rose by 4.8 per cent in 1987, and in 1988 or 1989 elsewhere (although Denmark, which grew rapidly in the middle of the decade, then entered a prolonged period of economic crisis with falls in GDP in 1988/9) (UN Economic Commission for Europe, 1990: table 2.2.1, 35).

By the late 1980s several years of growth had resulted in high levels of capacity utilization and, at last, unemployment began to fall. At the same time, inflation rates rose and governments resorted to raising interest rates and further public expenditure restrictions. In fact, the growth of public consumption expenditure remained at low levels, even when growth and rising private consumption expenditure resumed in the latter part of the decade. In Germany the collapse of the socialist states to the East at the end of the 1980s led to a massive inflow of immigrants, around 720,000 in 1989 alone, and a big boost to private consumption and inflationary pressures. The subsequent political unification of the two Germanies and the consequences of economic unification added to these pressures.

In fact, the economic growth of the later 1980s was built on shaky foundations. We have already referred to the way in which US growth was based on massive borrowing abroad. But elsewhere, too, the boom was frequently based on heavy and costly borrowing. Financial deregulation had resulted in far easier access to credit for households and the corporate sector. These were the years of the junk bond and the leveraged buy-out. In the real economy, as we have noted, most of the new jobs were in low-paid service occupations, a high proportion of which involved part-time female labour. Meanwhile, high unemployment persisted among groups affected by the continuing 'rationalization' of manufacturing industry.

Long-term and youth unemployment remained especially high. According to the ECE report for 1989/90, 75 per cent of the new jobs created in Western Europe and North America in the 1980s upturn were female and almost two-thirds of all the new jobs for women were part-time. Fully 75 per cent of all the new jobs were part-time, in fact (UN Economic Commission for Europe, 1990: 63–4). The prosperity which some experienced in this period was one in which much of the population did not share. Instead, they were trapped in long-term unemployment, in low-paid, part-time jobs, or were outside the labour market, dependent on welfare payments and public services which had been the target of repeated reductions and restrictions and, in some cases, more radical attack through privatization and other means.

In 1989 business confidence and activity began to contract across Europe and in the USA. Activity had been in steep decline in Britain since 1988 and even in Germany, which had the strongest economy in Europe, economic growth began to decline. Now the precarious nature of the debt-financed expansion became evident, with accelerating company failures and banking losses. In many cases, too, notably with respect to housing, households had financed rising consumption by borrowing. As unemployment and economic insecurity increased, households cut back on consumption to pay off debts, thus deepening the recession. Rising interest rates created problems for debt-encumbered businesses and households, providing a further twist to the situation. One feature of this debt deflation was a loss of asset values, as the inflated prices paid in the boom years collapsed. This had particular relevance in the British and American housing markets, and in some Nordic countries, with the appearance of widespread 'negative equity', as owners found that the value of properties fell below the purchase price and frequently below the value of the outstanding mortgage. In Britain the ratio of household debt to GDP rose more sharply than anywhere else, from 40 per cent in 1980 to 80 per cent by 1990, by which time there was a rapidly rising level of mortgage default and repossessions. In the USA (as well as in Sweden, Norway and Finland) the reckless lending policies of the 1980s, encouraged by financial deregulation, led to the collapse of financial institutions and threats to national banking systems which required costly state intervention. The hugely expensive rescue of the US Savings and Loans institutions from the late 1980s was the most publicized of these events, and was a substantial contributor to the large budget deficit (OECD, 1992: 41–9).

By late 1992 the *OECD Economic Outlook* (1992) described a gloomy situation and predicted that any recovery over the next few years would only be very weak. Unemployment in the OECD countries would continue to rise, with a growing proportion of long-term unemployment (which had fallen in the late 1980s). Disinflation would continue, except in Germany, where the effects of reunification were still feeding through into price rises. Many commentators suggested that this problem had been accentuated by the failure of the Christian Democrat/Free Democrat government to take action at the time of reunification. Instead, the politically independent Bundesbank kept German interest rates high in order to restrain inflation. From 1991 there was a sharp disjunction between the German situation and that in other weaker European economies, which needed lower interest rates to aid recovery. The consequence, between 1991 and 1993, was growing turmoil in European currency markets and the breakdown of the European Monetary System, initiated when Britain and Italy left the system in the autumn of 1991, devalued their currencies and began to lower interest rates. Finland and Sweden also allowed their currencies to devalue after losing battles with currency speculators. Countries which remained, for the time being at least, inside the Exchange Rate Mechanism (ERM), such as France and Denmark, were caught in a trap. With falling inflation and the need for a stimulus for their domestic economies, they were nevertheless unable to reduce interest rates because of the impact that this would have on currency values, tied to that of the Deutschmark through the ERM. In Europe generally, recovery was crucially dependent on developments in the German economy and in its economic policies, and by 1993 the German recession was still deepening.

High interest rates, depressed production, high unemployment and falling tax revenues all added to governmental borrowing and indebtedness in Britain, Denmark, France, Germany and the USA. In the Netherlands there was some reduction since the late 1980s, but from a very high level. In fact, the rise in governments' indebtedness began in 1974 and continued through the following years. Only in Britain was there a fall in net debt in the 1980s, as the Thatcher governments restricted public spending and repaid debt, but by the early 1990s Britain again had a rapidly accelerating debt. As the OECD (1992) noted, these deficits were structural rather than purely cyclical. In response, most governments seemed likely to impose a new round of public expenditure cuts and, in some cases, tax rises, in the mid-1990s.

Moreover, the Maastricht Treaty, concluded at the end of 1991, which marked a further stage in European integration, committed the European Union (EU) nations to reduce their public sector borrowing requirements (PSBRs) to 3 per cent of GDP by 1994, adding further urgency to the need for public expenditure cuts. The OECD (1992) also noted the pressure that the needs of ageing populations were putting on public expenditure and that this was stimulating a search for new, supposedly more cost-effective ways of providing public services, for example by bringing about more competition and increasing managerial autonomy. An important contributor to rising welfare expenditure was the pension reforms of the era of the 1960s and early 1970s, the full costs of which, given their 'pay as you go' financing, were only incurred many years later. Another problem was the rising cost of health care, a major topic, for example, in the Bush–Clinton presidential contest in late 1991.

The long period of economic instability since the mid-1970s had resulted in a much slower growth in real wages, so by the early 1990s labour's average share of national income in the OECD countries was back to the levels of the late 1960s. However, despite rising profits and rates of return, many companies were reluctant to invest, especially to hire labour, because of the uncertain economic future.

While describing these general developments, we have already referred to some more specific national patterns. In fact, the average annual GDP growth rates of the six economies with which we are concerned, between 1976 and 1990, all fell in the range of 2–3 per cent per annum, a clear indication of the long-term decline in their growth rates (UN Economic Commission for Europe, 1990: table A1, 374). In a reversal of the previous rank order, the USA was at the top of this growth league, with an annual rate of just under 3 per cent, owing to faster rates of growth than in the European countries in the late 1970s and during the deficit and debt-financed boom of the mid-1980s. Within Europe there was a division between France and Germany, the two strongest economies, with growth rates averaging around 2.5 per cent, and the other three nations. Neither France nor Germany suffered as deep a recession in the early 1980s as Britain. Nor did their growth decline as precipitately towards the end of the decade. Britain, Denmark and the Netherlands had average growth rates of between 2.1 per cent and 2.25 per cent. In Britain's case, a weak recovery from the 1970s recession had been compounded by an even deeper recession in the early 1980s, enhanced by the Thatcher government's monetarist policies. This was followed by a faster revival than most other Western economies in the middle of the decade, and then a faster return to recession. Danish economic performance had been even more problematic as the country struggled with recurrent inflation and balance of payments difficulties. Growth rates were low in the late 1970s and, while the country recovered faster than almost any other from the recession in 1980/1, this upturn collapsed in 1986 and the economy stagnated for the rest of the decade. The Dutch economy grew slowly throughout the whole period (apart from the recession years of 1981/2) with annual rises in GDP only exceeding 3 per cent in 1984 and 1989/90.

Over this period there were far higher unemployment rates than hitherto. In the early 1970s they had ranged between 1 and 3 per cent in the five Western European countries and around 5 per cent in the USA (which historically had had higher rates) (UN Economic Commission for Europe, 1990: table A12, 385). In all six countries there was a strong upward trend from the mid-1970s to the mid-1980s, from around 3 per cent on average in the European countries to three times this level a decade later, and from around 5.5 per cent to 9.5 per cent (in this case by 1983) in the USA. Only in the USA was there much reduction in this level during the economic upturn of the middle and later 1980s. In Europe the long-term structural nature of unemployment was revealed as economies which had resumed growth maintained high levels of joblessness. Only at the very end of the decade was there a marked downturn in unemployment, but, as we noted above, this was not sustained into the 1990s.

One of the most dramatic changes to occur in the six economies concerned the relationship between wage and price inflation. In the early 1970s, before the full force of the inflationary surge was felt, wages were rising far faster than prices. The subsequent events, with high unemployment, declining trade union power and the imposition of monetarist policies, transformed the situation. By the 1990s consumer prices were rising far slower than they had since, in most cases, the early to mid-1960s, as were wages. The effects of this change on real wages varied: data for hourly earnings in manufacturing industry and consumer prices suggest that they continued to rise in the five European countries, but fell in the USA. However, even where they grew, the rate of growth was far lower than in the earlier period and more uncertain. In fact, the most rapid increases in real income occurred among the higher-paid service workers, not those in the contracting manufacturing industries. Moreover, the widespread cuts in income maintenance and other benefits (by, for example, breaking indexation to wage rises and by various restrictions in payments and eligibility) meant that the poorest in these societies fared worst. Clearly, the temporary economic revival of the 1980s, based on an increasingly polarised labour market and a persistent high level of unemployment, had similarly polarizing effects on the distribution of incomes. However, there was little indication that social and economic policies in the 1990s would find an adequate response to what was variously labelled the 'underclass', the 'two-thirds society', 'social exclusion' or the 'new urban poverty'.

THE POLITICS OF ECONOMIC INSECURITY

In the interwar years economic insecurity had a polarizing effect on many national political systems. There was a growth of the extreme right and the extreme left, vying for the support of those classes, notably the working class and the *petite bourgeoisie*, who suffered the poverty and unemployment that the post-war welfare states largely succeeded in eliminating. History did not repeat itself in the 1980s. On the one hand, the growth of the non-social democratic left, which had occurred in the 1960s and early 1970s, was decisively reversed. On the other hand, while in some countries the growth of extreme right-wing movements (campaigning on racist anti-immigrant or anti-guest worker platforms) was significant, nowhere had they achieved the successes of their forerunners.

Nevertheless, as we have already noted, there was a clear break with the orthodox politics which had been established after 1945, in which most centre, right and social democratic political parties shared many common assumptions about the appropriate relations between the state and the market and the necessity for the mixed economy of welfare capitalism. In contrast, after the mid-1970s, the ground began to shift as governments tried and failed to sustain the trinity of rising incomes, low unemployment and expanding welfare provision. The major challenge to the established politics of the welfare states came from a revival of liberal economic and political theories by those who were identified as the New Right by many commentators (Mishra, 1984: 26–64; Levitas, 1986; D. King, 1987). In fact, the New Right took rather different forms in the two countries, Britain and the USA, in which many of its leading mentors and adherents were located. Moreover, the strongly ideological politics of Reagan, in the USA, and Thatcher, in Britain, were more weakly mirrored elsewhere. Indeed, in France, the main adherents of New Right policies were out of government from the early 1980s (except for 1986–8).

Nevertheless, from the late 1970s New Right ideas had a pervasive influence well beyond their homelands. One reason for this was the ideological vacuum which opened up after the failures of governments of the moderate left and centre–right to solve the conundrum of rising welfare costs and falling public and private resources, in a situation of growing economic turmoil after the early 1970s. Lipietz (1987: 133–45) has referred to this as the period of social democratic crisis management, noting that such governments were in power in Britain and West Germany (as they also were in the Netherlands and Denmark), that there was a Democratic President in the USA and that the centre–right French government followed similar policies. However, as we have seen, social democratic parties had abandoned any more radical, socialist ideas by this time and were left intellectually bereft by the new economic circumstances, being subsequently unable to mount a convincing challenge to New Right ideas. At the same time, many centrist and moderate right parties moved away from the old political compact with the social democrats, although few went so far or so fast as the British Conservatives or the Reagan Republicans.

The eclipse of social democracy during the 1980s, with one apparent exception, is quite striking. In Britain, after a Labour government had held on, eventually as a minority government, until voted out of office in 1979, the Conservatives won four general elections in a row. In Germany the SPD-led government struggled on until 1982 and then collapsed owing to the withdrawal of support from the FDP, which had moved towards the right in the late 1970s and who now joined a CDU-led government which continued into the 1990s. In the Netherlands there was a PvdA-led coalition government from 1973, but with a majority of non-socialist ministers in the cabinet. This collapsed in 1977 and, in a historic shift from its traditional alliance with the PvdA, the Confessional CDA allied with the right-wing VVD. CDA-led centre–right administrations continued until 1989 when the PvdA re-entered government as the junior partner. In Denmark the long period of almost uninterrupted participation of the Social Democrats in government was ended in 1982, to be replaced by a coalition based on the (relatively moderate) KF and the more radical right Venstre. The only apparent exception to this general political sea change occurred in France, where the uneasy coalition between the Gaullists and the Giscardiens ended with the victory of the PS in the 1981 presidential and legislative elections. With the exception of the period of *cohabitation* in 1986–8, when a Socialist President and a Gaullist Prime Minister shared power, the PS continued in government until 1993, when it was routed in Assembly elections and seemed close to breakup. However, as we shall see, the attempt to implement a distinctive social democratic solution to French economic and social problems did not survive beyond the early 1980s.

Within all these right-wing governments ideas and policy options which, whether recognized by their advocates or not, owed a distinct debt to the influence of New Right thinking, had far more significance than hitherto. As D. King (1987: 9) notes:

> [t]he core of New Right liberal political and economic tenets is the superiority of market mechanisms as a promoter both of economic prosperity (because of the supposed greater efficiency of the market in the allocation and use of scarce resources); and of the maximisation of individual freedom through the limiting of state intervention: freedom must be market-based freedom rather than state-imposed.

Monetarism became associated with such views because of the limited role which it assigned to state control of market forces. A belief that state-provided welfare had failed and had had undesirable consequences, for example failing to target benefits on those who most needed them and restricting individual freedom, was also asserted. Among the more cerebral strands in New Right thinking were public choice theories, developed in the main by American political theorists, which assumed that the growth of the welfare state was mainly at the instigation and for the benefit of politicians, who used it to buy votes, and bureaucrats, who used it to improve their budgets, prestige and incomes. And theories of 'political overload' suggested that the burden of welfare and other state expenditure had now outstripped the capacity of slowly growing economies to finance them, targeting the role of special interest groups such as the trade unions and state bureaucracies in this situation (A. King, 1975; Offe, 1984).

At a time when restraining the expansion of public expenditure and controlling inflation preoccupied all governments, any doctrine which suggested that the control of inflation through the money supply was the golden key to eventual economic success and that the growth of state expenditure was positively harmful was bound to have an impact, however variously it was filtered through distinctive national political traditions and ideologies. In fact, only in Britain, under Margaret Thatcher, was there a fairly coherent and wide-ranging implementation of New Right economic and welfare policies. In the USA, as we have already seen, the economic policies followed by President Reagan were hardly the pure milk of monetarism and Democratic control in Congress blunted some of the more radical proposals for federal withdrawal from welfare provision.

Nevertheless, whether from ideological conviction or as a more pragmatic response to circumstances, many of the principal features of the New Right programme for diminishing the role of the state in the economy and in welfare provision were evident in all of the countries with which we are concerned. Apart from persistent attempts to cut back welfare expenditure, action to target benefits on the poorest in society and remove them from the rather better-off sections of the working class were common (although less attention was paid to targeting services and benefits, such as housing tax reliefs, which disproportionately aided the middle class) (Marklund, 1988: 44–51). Privatization of state-owned assets was also much discussed and implemented in some cases. In addition, there was a tendency for national governments to withdraw from or limit their role in service provision, devolving responsibility to subnational governments, arguing that decentralization was a way of ensuring that provision would be more sensitive to locally varying needs. However, decentralization was frequently accompanied by severe restrictions on the resources which local government had available to sustain the services. Finally, there were attempts to introduce market 'disciplines' into welfare provision, for example by allowing private sector organizations to compete for the supply of services and by encouraging or requiring existing providers to adopt quasi-market processes. As we shall see, privatization, decentralization and the marketization of provision had a considerable impact on social rented housing. However, the detailed political circumstances in which the new lines between the state, the market and social housing provision were drawn varied considerably.

Even in Britain, where the election of Margaret Thatcher in 1979 marked a decisive political turning-point, there had already been, as we have seen, a decisive shift in economic policies towards monetarism, under the 1974–9 Labour government.[2] This government, when first elected in 1974, had the largest number of seats in Parliament, but was unable to form a majority government. Later that year it obtained a tiny overall majority after a second election. In the early 1970s the left wing within the Labour Party had grown in strength. Its ideas inspired the party's 1974 election manifesto, which called for increased public ownership in industry, price controls and an agreement with the trade unions which exchanged voluntary wages restraint for improved welfare expenditure and a national minimum 'social wage'. Despite its narrow majority, the government began to implement this programme, ending the miners' strike which had destroyed the previous Conservative government, imposing price controls, promising a major increase in pensions and implementing a previously agreed 'social contract' with the unions. By 1975, however, under the impact of the worsening economic situation, this programme, which entailed large increases in public expenditure, began to unravel. Rapidly rising inflation and balance of payments deficits marked the onset of the mid-decade recession. Unemployment began to rise and production fell. At first the government opted for a Keynesian solution, trying to support sagging demand. This involved large-scale international borrowing to fund the deficit, support for export industries and the social contract. Much of the increased welfare and industrial expenditure was to be met by raising income taxes on high earners.

It was when these economic policies failed that the first signs of an emergent monetarist economic orthodoxy began to appear. This probably originated in the Treasury civil service, which had been pressing for deflationary policies and cuts in public expenditure. Widespread tax rises and public expenditure cuts occurred in 1975 and commitments to new public ownership initiatives and to state–industry planning agreements faded away. The balance of power in the government shifted decisively away from the left. In 1976, Harold Wilson, the long-serving Labour leader and Prime Minister, resigned to be replaced by the right-of-centre James Callaghan. More significantly, in early 1975, after a bitter battle, the Conservative leader Edward Heath, blamed by many for his U-turn away from radical to more consensual policies, was ousted by the candidate of the increasingly influential right wing of the party, Margaret Thatcher. Within six months of his election as leader, Callaghan's government faced its decisive crisis. This was set off by the plummeting value of the pound on the foreign exchanges and by the rapid exhaustion of national currency reserves, expended in a vain attempt to stem the decline. As in 1931 and 1966/7, a Labour government faced a stark choice: to devalue the currency or to obtain new international credits in exchange for drastic cuts in public expenditure. As before, after considerable internal conflict, it chose the latter course, being forced into a two rounds of deep expenditure cuts in one year as a condition for International Monetary Fund (IMF) and other loans. This reversal of previous economic policies marked the abandonment of Keynesian demand management and the commitment to full employment. Apart from the cuts in public expenditure, welfare and other programmes were now 'cash limited', that is, provided with no adjustment for unforeseen inflation. In many cases, cash limits resulted in real cuts in expenditure.

By 1977, following by-election losses, the government was again in a minority in the House of Commons. Now it only stayed in office on the basis of an informal pact with the small centrist Liberal Party. The radical programme on which Labour had been elected was completely abandoned as the government struggled to control the economic situation and hang on to power. Economically, it benefited from the recovery in the late 1970s, with falling inflation and unemployment, a positive balance of payments and rising production. But the early success which the government had in maintaining its corporatist social contract (despite the expenditure cuts), which restrained wage rises, could not be sustained. Meanwhile, at grassroots level, the party was coming increasingly under the influence of its growing left wing, which gained control of many Labour-run big city councils. At the same time, the Conservatives, under their new leader, were adopting a New Right programme, much of it developed by influential political think-tanks and pressure groups. The new programme involved the rejection of Keynesian demand management and much of the previously accepted framework of the welfare state, in favour of monetarism, privatization of state assets, and a breakup of the corporatist relations which had existed between trade unions, the government and industry.

Despite the recovery from recession, the social security costs of unemployment and of programmes to stem job losses meant that, even with the stringent public expenditure cuts after 1975, public spending continued to rise. But as economic conditions eased, strains arose in the agreement with the unions over wage restraint. In winter 1979 (which went down in British political mythology as the 'winter of discontent'), there were widespread public and private sector strikes. The government was already in a precarious state as a result of the ending of the 'Lib-Lab' pact in late 1978, and when the wave of strikes led to major pay rises, the Conservative leader was able to exploit the claim that Labour was a prisoner of the trade unions, whose power was destroying the economy. In March 1979 the government lost a parliamentary vote of confidence (the only such defeat since the first Labour government fell in 1924), and resigned. The Conservatives returned to power after the subsequent general election with a respectable majority.

The Conservative election programme reflected the sharp turn towards New Right policies under Margaret Thatcher. It promised to redraw the boundaries between the state and the citizen, cutting public expenditure and income taxes, curbing trade union power and supporting a return to 'traditional' moral values with increased expenditure on law and order. Reducing inflation by controlling the money supply and expenditure cuts was the predominant economic priority; high unemployment was a necessary, if temporary, price that had to be paid for long-term prosperity. Large-scale privatization of state-owned assets and deregulation would see an 'enterprise culture' set free and reduce the dead hand of the state over the market (Young, 1986).

While not without internal conflicts, the Conservative governments of the 1980s and early 1990s pressed ahead and implemented much of this programme. The least successful element was monetarism, which was slowly abandoned, although the commitment to restraining inflation and cutting public expenditure remained. But a long list of state assets was privatized and the sale of council houses proved electorally popular, eventually becoming accepted, therefore, across the political spectrum. Meanwhile, the Labour Party tried to come to terms with the new political age. A significant right-wing faction split away in 1981 to form a short-lived Social Democratic Party, which allied itself, uneasily, with the Liberals (Drucker, 1986). After long internal battles the centre-right control of the Labour Party was gradually reasserted. However, in successive general elections in 1983, 1987 and 1992, the Conservatives, aided on some occasions by political fortune (notably the so-called 'Falklands war' in 1982), managed to defeat ever more moderate Labour proposals for expansionary economic policies and additional welfare benefits.

We discuss the Conservatives' housing policies later, although the government's imposition of ever tighter controls on local government spending and taxation was of particular relevance to the prospects for social housing. This campaign, particularly directed at so-called 'loony left' councils in the early part of the decade, went beyond mere expenditure control as the big city metropolitan authorities, which were Labour strongholds, were abolished and council activities and assets were curtailed (Lansley, Goss and Wolmar, 1989). Increasing stress was placed on the need for councils to obtain 'value for money' in service provision by introducing market competition for the supply of services which frequently pitted the councils' own workforces against private contractors. In many cases service provision became 'contracted out' to private suppliers. In addition, as the proportion of central contributions to local expenditure fell and rigid controls were exercised over local taxation, user charges for many local government services were introduced for the first time and/or increased, in some cases to market levels. High levels of unemployment and an ageing population placed new demands on the public and social services, and increasing difficulties were experienced in maintaining them as resources were reduced or, at best, increased more slowly than demand. The government also restricted local authority powers in urban policy and land use planning. Instead, it looked to the private sector to take the lead, in deprived inner-city areas, by establishing Enterprise Zones, with tax breaks and other inducements for industrial and real estate investment, and several Urban Development Corporations, which assembled land for private development and assumed the planning powers formerly vested in the local authorities (Stewart and Stoker, 1989).

In the middle of the decade the government benefited from the economic recovery, although, as we have noted, the benefits of this recovery were unequally distributed. The contrast between the affluent South and the depressed older industrial regions of the North, Scotland and Wales was increasingly apparent (Smith, 1989). On the one hand, these were the years of high incomes and rapid wealth accumulation for a minority of those working in the dynamic financial and professional services, real estate and consumer services sectors, and improvements in incomes and standards of living for a larger section of the white-collar workforce in growth industries and regions. On the other hand, there was a rising mass of low-income earners in these growth industries and in the declining manufacturing sector as well as the unemployed and others dependent on barely adequate state benefits (Cooke, 1989; Fainstein, Gordon and Harloe, 1992). However, there was relatively little protest about this increasing social and economic polarization, although from the early 1980s there were outbreaks of urban riots and other large-scale disorders. More organized protest had little effect, especially after the defeat of a year-long miners' strike in 1984–5. With increasingly restrictive controls on trade unions, the power of organized labour to influence government policies was virtually eliminated. In 1979 the Conservatives had managed to capture the votes of the 'middle mass' of the electorate with their promise of an end to the political and economic chaos of the previous decade. The party subsequently managed to hang on to much of this vote, even in the 1992 general election when a new recession had bitten deep into the employment and well-being of this group, so that a Labour victory was, at last, confidently predicted by almost all politicians and political analysts.

By the 1987 election Margaret Thatcher dominated her government and party, all real opposition having long since been crushed. Her wish to bring about a permanent shift in economic and social life, away from collectivism towards market-based individualism, was quite explicit. Now the Conservatives' election manifesto promised to push the reduction of the powers of local authorities and the application of New Right policies to public services a stage further with new arrangements (subsequently enacted) allowing state schools to break away from council control and become self-governing entities, as well as more radical proposals, which we shall discuss later, to reduce and eventually eliminate local authority housing ownership and to remove most regulation from the private rented sector. By the early 1990s the basic public utilities – water, gas and electricity – were all privatized, and the railways and the coal industry were following this course. Changes in the National Health Service (NHS) stopped short of privatization, which would have alienated most middle-class voters. However, 'market disciplines' were introduced into the running of the service, with the creation of an 'internal market' that divided health-care organizations into 'purchasers' and 'providers' (also introduced into local authority-run social work services) and enabled hospitals to become 'self-governing trusts' (N. Johnson, 1990).

Despite all this, by the early 1990s Thatcher's grip on her party and the country was failing. Much unpopularity was generated by an unworkable reform of local government taxation, the community charge, or 'poll tax', which alienated many middle-class Conservative voters. There was increasing conflict between the Prime Minister and her associates, who were hostile to further European integration, and other senior ministers. Moreover, as the recession which began in 1988 rapidly deepened, the administration's economic management was questioned as a government-stimulated consumer boom went out of control, inflation rose and the balance of payments went into deficit. The main response was to raise interest rates sharply, which helped bring about a collapse in the housing market and more unemployment as investment dried up. From late 1988 the Labour Party moved ahead of the government in public opinion polls and the personal popularity ratings of the Prime Minister also began to collapse.

In 1989 an obscure backbench Member of Parliament challenged Thatcher in the annual elections for the party leadership (normally just a formality). This was the prelude to a far more serious challenge the following year and the replacement of Thatcher by John Major, a protégé of the former Prime Minister although less identified with her right-wing conservatism. Nevertheless, there was little change in the direction of the government's policies in matters such as health, education, housing and law and order. The control of inflation remained central to economic policies, although there was growing criticism of the lack of response to rising unemployment. Entry into the European Monetary System, which Thatcher had been forced to concede, only increased the government's economic difficulties as it had to maintain high interest rates to keep within the system. Meanwhile, public expenditure rose under the impact of the recession and the public sector deficit rocketed, while further austerity policies were postponed long enough to win the 1992 election.

This surprise victory resulted in the new government having a far smaller majority than its predecessor, and in a governing party deeply split between a Thatcherite, anti-European minority and a pro-European majority which supported the new Prime Minister. As already described, in late 1992 the government was forced to concede a devaluation of the pound, leaving the European Monetary System. Interest rates were rapidly reduced to stimulate the economy, but in 1993 stringent public expenditure cuts and increased taxation were imposed in order to reduce the budget deficit. This, and the running battle within the government's ranks over European integration, threatened to end the long period of Conservative political hegemony.

While a right-wing administration survived, albeit in weakened form, in Britain in the early 1990s, the 1992 American presidential election, which saw the defeat of George Bush by the Democrat Bill Clinton, marked the end of twelve years of Republican administration. Whether this also marked the start of a longer break in the succession of Republican Presidents which had begun in 1968, and which had only been interrupted between 1976 and 1980, remained to be seen. Moreover, Clinton did not make many promises to expand the welfare programmes which had, since Roosevelt, been espoused by the Democrats. Instead, the reduction of the huge budget deficit and the revival of the American economy were the main bases for the Democratic election programme. The principal target for reform in the field of social policy was the costly and inefficient American health-care system, strongly protected by those vested professional and business interests which profited from it.

In 1976 there had been a similar presidential victory for a Democratic candidate, Jimmy Carter, who, like Clinton, had also started as an outsider in the pre-election battle for the Democratic candidature.[3] Like Clinton, too, Carter came from the South, a region which, together with the West, had benefited from the shift away from older industries to the new 'Sunbelt' combination of services and technologically advanced manufacturing (Perry and Watkins, 1977). By the 1970s the shifts of population which had occurred as a result of this economic restructuring meant that the Sunbelt states held the key to success in presidential elections.

Carter's close election victory over the Republican incumbent Gerald Ford owed a great deal to the consequences of the enforced resignation of President Nixon in 1974 after the Watergate affair. Ford found himself opposed at every turn by a Democratic-controlled Congress, and the election came before the full effects of the economic recovery from the 1974/5 recession were felt. Ford was also under pressure from the emergent leader of the New Right within his party, Ronald Reagan.

Carter, a former governor of Georgia, was an outsider in Democratic party politics. He promised to make government more accountable to the people and stressed the need for a new morality in the administration. He promised a national health-care system and other social welfare measures, as well as action to reduce unemployment. However, Carter's economic objective, to reduce the federal budget deficit, meant that large-scale new spending was ruled out. Instead, he wished to make changes in taxes and social welfare to target resources on the poor. He failed to gain sufficient support in Congress for this approach and his reform programmes were blocked, notably a wide-ranging attempt to legislate for energy conservation which offended many vested interests. His popularity began to slump and never recovered.

By 1978–9, following the rapid recovery of the US economy, inflation began to rise again, exacerbated by the new oil price rise, and industrial production was falling. The result was cuts in health and public works expenditures and calls for wage restraint. But these policies accentuated the economic downturn and increased criticism of the administration, which was dealt a final blow by the taking of American hostages in Iran and an ill-fated attempt to rescue them. The virtual abandonment of welfare and urban reforms as the fight against inflation became the main priority of the administration after 1978 also resulted in growing opposition to the renomination of Carter in 1980 from the liberal wing of the Democratic party, led by Edward Kennedy.

During the Carter years Ronald Reagan had consolidated his position as the Republican candidate for the presidency. More generally, New Right ideas and advocates had gained ground among elite and popular opinion. The increasing political significance of the Sunbelt states has already been noted. It was in these areas, particularly in the affluent suburbs, that the new ideology took root. A key event was 'Proposition 13', passed in a California state referendum in 1978, which placed a cap on state expenditure and required cuts in state taxes and expenditure. This tax- and expenditure-cutting movement spread rapidly to other parts of the country. In the USA, unlike Britain, the economic aspects of New Right thinking (based, in this case, on supply-side theories) were reinforced by a moral element, born-again fundamentalist Christianity, propagated by media evangelists leading movements such as the Moral Majority. These movements provided a potent basis for Reagan's presidential campaign which he skilfully exploited, also drawing on a more traditional source of right-wing rhetoric, anti-communism.

Reagan's election programme was similar to that which had seen Thatcher victorious in 1979 – cuts in direct taxes and welfare expenditure, the withdrawal of federal government from many programmes, deregulation and an increase in defence spending to counter the communist threat. Like Thatcher, too, he attracted working-class votes away from the opposition party. He won the election by a landslide and the Republicans gained control of the Senate for the first time in many years. As in Britain, this election marked a decisive shift away from the politics and economics of the previous era. However, as in Britain too, the ground for this shift was prepared during the previous period of Democratic rule.

Unlike Thatcher, however, Reagan had to work with a House of Representatives controlled by the Democrats. It was therefore not possible to push ahead with his programme as rapidly and radically as did his British counterpart. He promised to cut taxes, reduce non-defence spending and balance the budget – an inconsistent mixture, as it later transpired. However, in 1981, he succeeded in getting Congress to approve major budget cuts, focusing on programmes which mainly served the poor rather than those which benefited sections of his core electorate, and supply-side tax cuts. Further expenditure cuts followed, while the economy continued to decline and the budget deficit rose as a result of reduced tax revenues and increased defence spending. Federal regulation of key industries, such as energy and transport, were loosened and an attempt was made to decentralize many federally run welfare programmes to state and local governments, reducing the proportion of expenditure on them met by the federal government. The administration also tried to obstruct moves to expand 'affirmative action' over civil rights and failed to activate the powers that it already had to pursue such rights.

Mid-term elections in 1982 reduced the ability of the President to control Congress. From this time proposals to make further deep cuts in welfare expenditure were strongly resisted. But from 1983 the economy revived and unemployment began a fall that lasted for the rest of the decade. This growth was aided by the tax cuts and by the abandonment, in 1982, of the central tenet of monetarist economics: tight control of the money supply. Reagan also failed to reduce the budget deficit. Indeed, it began to grow rapidly, as did the current account deficit, which had been eliminated by Carter's restrictive economic policies. Now the growth of the deficit was spectacular, from a positive balance of $6 billion in 1981 to a deficit of over $100 billion by 1984, rising to over $140 billion in 1987. It was accompanied by a rising budget deficit which reached $185 billion by 1984 (UN Economic Commission for Europe, 1990: table A7).

The divisions within the Democratic Party that had opened up in the Carter years continued during Reagan's first term and during the process of choosing a challenger to the President in the 1984 election. The eventual candidate, Walter Mondale, was unable to attract back the voters which had left the Democrats in 1980 and the President was re-elected by the biggest margin on record, 49 states to one. However, although the Republicans won some more seats in the House of Representatives, they did not gain control. Their majority in the Senate was lost in the mid-term elections in 1986.

Following the 1984 election, the administration proposed dealing with the budget deficit by further large-scale cuts in welfare spending, targeted on the poor, as well as a reduction in higher income tax rates. Congress rejected the plan and opted for fewer welfare cuts and a reduction in defence spending, together with a measure that would enforce further budget cuts in subsequent years and which aimed to eliminate the deficit by the early 1990s. If operated, this would inevitably lead to further reductions in welfare and defence spending. In subsequent years the struggle between the President, who wished to sustain defence, cut social spending and privatize federal assets, and Congress, which wanted to protect the social programmes from further erosion, continued, with the latter being more successful than the former. Nevertheless, there was little support in Congress for more than this holding action and for the restoration of programmes and expenditure that had been eliminated in the first Reagan term.

The last years of the Reagan presidency were overshadowed by the 'Irangate' scandal, the illicit sale of arms to Iran by federal agents. By now the administration's push to impose the New Right agenda was over and Congress initiated modest reforms in matters such as welfare and health-care arrangements, although the looming federal budget deficit reinforced fiscal conservatism. As in Britain, the gap between rich and poor widened in the 1980s, as the real incomes of the better off had risen sharply while those of the poor had declined. A wide range of federal welfare programmes had been drastically cut. As we discuss later, support for low-income housing fell by 70 per cent, one of the largest cuts of all. Conditions in America's inner cities became ever more desperate, with rapidly rising rates of poverty, drug addiction, ill health and crime among, in particular, the black and Hispanic populations – the so-called urban underclass (Jencks and Peterson, 1991).

The development of the Democratic Party in the 1980s mirrored that of the Labour Party in Britain, a period of internal division giving way, under the pressure of the successful right-wing politics of its opponent, to a reassertion of centre–right control over organization and policies by the end of the decade. However, this realignment did not enable the Democrats to attract back a sufficiently large number of the 'Reagan Democrats', those voters who had defected to Reagan, in the 1988 presidential election. Despite the fact that the Republican candidate George Bush had neither the appeal nor the New Right credentials of Reagan, he was pitted against a candidate, Michael Dukakis, whose programme was also distinctly conservative. However, it was represented by clever Republican campaigning as being far more radical. Bush won the election, although by a smaller margin than had Reagan in 1980 and 1984, and he failed to regain Republican control of the legislature.

The new President's cabinet contained relatively few representatives of the New Right; among them, however, was the Secretary of the Department of Housing and Urban Development, Jack Kemp, a leading politician with presidential ambitions. We shall discuss the impact that this had on federal housing policies later, but Kemp's appointment ensured that a more activist approach would be substituted for the stagnation (and, it was now revealed, corruption) in federal urban policy making and administration which had occurred under Reagan. More generally, though, Bush, unlike Reagan, had no distinctive domestic policy agenda. His main concern was with the rapidly unfolding events that surrounded the collapse of the socialist bloc as well as the conflicts in the Middle East. Meanwhile, the domestic policy agenda was increasingly focused on the budget deficit and, from 1989, the onset of a new recession.

In France, the growth of New Right conservatism focused on one of the two parties forming the nucleus of the centre–right bloc that sustained Giscard d'Estaing when he was elected to the presidency in 1974.[4] This was the Gaullist party, led by Giscard's first Prime Minister, Jacques Chirac, which adopted yet another new name in 1976 when it became the RPR (Rassemblement pour la République). The RPR had more seats in the National Assembly than the President's Independent Republican Party. In fact, Giscard had only become President because of divisions within the Gaullists following the death of President Pompidou. These centred on conflict between the traditional wing of the party, which combined nationalism and state intervention in economic and social policies, and Chirac's neo-liberal wing, which espoused the New Right economic agenda. On the left, François Mitterrand, who had almost beaten Giscard in 1974, continued to rebuild the PS around a left social democratic political platform, although his alliance with the Communists broke down for a period after 1977.

Giscard was a member of France's elite administrative cadre which has had such wide-ranging influence on policy making under all post-war governments. He was an economic liberal, but also had a social programme which aimed to improve conditions for the very poor, for women and for other disadvantaged groups. He also favoured a reduction in some of the many state controls over civil society. He combined a continuing commitment to the state's role in modernizing the French economy with a less regulative approach to individual enterprises.

A rapid start was made on this programme after 1974, with changes in laws governing abortion, the voting age and other civil rights, and improvements in welfare benefits and the statutory minimum wage. But many of these programmes were opposed by the right wing of the governing bloc and were only carried through the National Assembly with support from the opposition. Moreover, Giscard was soon engulfed by the consequences of the 1974/5

recession, first deflating in order to curb inflation, and then re-
flating to combat rapidly rising unemployment. In 1976 the conflict with Chirac, who opposed social reform and wanted more a
nationalistic foreign policy, came to a head and the Prime Minister
resigned. Outside government Chirac and his party worked even
more assiduously to frustrate Giscard's policies, and the President
tried, in turn, to marginalize the Gaullists within his government
(Machin and Wright, 1982). The new Prime Minister, Raymond
Barre, a monetarist economist (whose influence on housing policies
will be discussed below), was unpopular with the electorate and
regarded as high-handed and arrogant. Barre began to introduce
monetarist policies, before this occurred in Britain and the USA.
He deflated, with a combination of price freezes, tax rises and
high interest rates to control the money supply, accepting that
this would cause a sharp rise in unemployment. Barre also aimed
to reduce drastically, though not abandon, state intervention in
the private economy, to allow older industries either to die or be
'rationalized', and to privatize some state assets.

Despite the gains made by Giscard's party (or rather, his centrist
coalition, which campaigned as the Union pour la Démocratie
Française, UDF) in National Assembly elections in 1978 (which
also saw the Socialist Party outpoll the Communists for the first
time in over 40 years), Chirac's support was still needed to pass
legislation. By now all the early social and civil rights reformism
had evaporated, with successive rounds of expenditure cuts and
the first attempts to implement deregulation and privatization. As
the recession of the early 1980s took hold, French policy followed
a course very similar to that being pursued in Britain, with more
expenditure cuts and the prioritization of inflation control at the
cost of more unemployment. Unlike Thatcher, however, Giscard
had to face re-election in 1981.

Despite internal conflicts within both the main political blocs,
the presidential contest was a rerun of the 1974 election. This time,
however, Mitterrand won and in subsequent National Assembly
elections the Socialists and Communists gained a large majority.
However, the Communist Party (PCF) was eclipsed by the PS in
both elections and its influence on the new administration (in which
it held some Ministries) was marginal. The Communists' inclusion
did, however, protect the government from a source of possible
opposition. Data on voters' opinions showed that there was considerable antagonism towards Giscard's abandonment of reform
and the Socialists' promises of further social and economic reform
had considerable appeal, not just to those of the left, but to centre

and even some right-wing voters (Machin and Wright, 1982). In short, Mitterrand captured the support of some sections of the population, such as the new middle class, who were, in other countries which had had socialist governments in the later 1970s, now moving towards right-wing parties (Schmidt, 1990).

The new government aimed to make major changes in the French economy and society. These included substantial income redistribution and the expansion of welfare provision for the less well off, state control of major industries, their modernization and the expansion of workers' rights. Decentralization was also a major objective. In a first burst of reform taxes on the rich were increased, along with welfare benefits and the minimum wage, restrictions on civil rights were removed and retirement and holiday provisions improved. But the first major reform was the 'Deferre Law', passed in 1982, which established directly elected regional councils, reduced the power of the Prefect and gave regional and departmental councils new powers to develop and finance their own policies (Ashford, 1990: 46–65). However, state control of locally provided services remained considerable and housing was not one of the devolved responsibilities. The most radical policy was the nationalization, in 1982, of key industrial and financial sectors. This was intended to ensure not only that they were modernized and became internationally competitive, but that, unlike multinationals, the employment and profits that they generated would remain in France.

Alongside these basic changes the government implemented a short-term economic recovery programme which was radically at variance with developments elsewhere in the early 1980s. Apart from the stimulus to income and consumption which has already been mentioned, monetarist controls were abandoned, there was a new housebuilding programme and an expansion of public employment and industrial development. In part this was to be paid for by increasing consumer and high-income taxation, in part the government allowed the public sector deficit to rise in a counter-cyclical manner. However, the programme was fiercely resisted by industry and the banking sector. It resulted in plummeting share values, a falling currency and the drying up of industrial investment.

As the other leading nations pursued restrictive monetarist policies, the expected rise in French exports failed to materialize. Instead, unemployment continued to rise, accompanied by double-digit inflation, high interest rates (to protect the currency) and growing balance of payments and budget deficits. By mid-1982 the bold attempt to break out of recession was abandoned, with cuts in welfare and other expenditure, currency devaluations and price and wage freezes. Within the government there was a shift of power away from the left and in 1984 Prime Minister Mauroy, who was on this wing and had been a close associate of Mitterrand for many years, was replaced by a young technocrat from the social democratic faction, Laurent Fabius. At the same time the PCF withdrew from the government. A more important political development was that rising unemployment led to a revival of anti-immigrant politics, spearheaded by the National Front, led by Jean-Marie Le Pen, which made spectacular gains in the 1984 European election and in other contests.

In several respects the new government's policies bore a re-markable similarity to those being adopted in Britain and the USA. Reducing inflation was the first priority and more public expenditure cuts ensued. Income and company taxes were reduced and the managers of state industries were given more autonomy, price deregulation continued and exchange controls were eased. Finally, there was a small-scale programme of privatization of state-owned companies. As in Britain, these policies had some of the desired effects, reducing inflation, the budget and trade deficits and stabilizing the currency. However, as in Britain too, unemploy-ment continued to rise and there was particular concern at the levels of youth and long-term unemployed, some of whom were homeless.

By 1986, when a new National Assembly was elected, the Socialist Party's popularity had plummeted and it had incurred heavy local election losses. Chirac had finally emerged as a major figure on the right and had added to his reputation by being an activist Mayor of Paris. By now the RPR had adopted most of the main elements of the New Right programme, although, while this attracted support from the far right, it also alienated many nearer the political centre. The UDF had always had a strong neo-liberal wing, rather like the German FDP, although, like the latter party, it took a more 'liberal' line over issues of individual social and civil rights than its conservative partners (Schmidt, 1990). Mean-while, the PCF continued to disintegrate, riven by internal splits and losing support to the PS and, in some cases, now to the ex-treme right. The PS was also divided between those who wanted a new alliance on the left and those who wanted to realign the party decisively around a moderate social democratic programme and an alliance with centrist political groupings. In the event, the main proponent of the latter approach, Michel Rocard, was defeated at the 1985 party congress. However, with Mitterrand's support, the party did realign itself around a moderate social democratic programme.

The election resulted in a narrow victory for the RPR/UDF, but the PS retained its position as the largest single party (Cole, 1986). The PCF had its worst result since the 1930s and ended up with 35 seats, the same as the National Front, which gained seats for the first time. The Front attracted votes from those sections of the population – workers, *petits bourgeois* and farmers – who had lost out economically (Schmidt, 1990). During the election the right had campaigned on the familiar New Right package, income and wealth tax cuts, denationalization, deregulation, reductions in public expenditure and law and order. The Socialists defended their policies, claiming that the right-wing programme would lead to social disorder, citing the recent riots in British cities as a warning. Despite these differences, Mitterrand declined to resign after the election, leading to an uneasy period of *cohabitation* between the new Prime Minister Chirac and the President. The key posts in Chirac's Cabinet were filled by his own party and the UDF was confined mainly to less important portfolios, although the major Ministry of Equipment, Housing and Transport went to this party.

Chirac took immediate steps to implement his programme, reducing exchange and price controls, abolishing rent controls and the wealth tax and making it easier for firms to sack their workers. The government also began a large-scale programme of the privatization of state-owned industries, including those banks which had been taken over in the first post-war government led by de Gaulle. A tough law and order policy reduced civil rights and was particularly directed against illegal (and many legal) immigrants. However, while the Prime Minister managed to push these changes through the National Assembly, the President made clear his disapproval of many aspects of policy, and projected himself as a figure above politics and as guardian of the national interest. Soon his popularity began to rise and that of the Prime Minister, who also had a far from united coalition with the UDF, declined.

In the winter of 1986–7 the government faced increasing difficulties over a controversial plan to restrict university entry and over public sector wage restraints, and there were large-scale strikes and mass demonstrations. While some modest social reforms were introduced, the focus on privatization and strong law and order policies remained. Chirac's position continued to weaken, mainly as a consequence of the economic situation. By now unemployment was rising, and there was a growing trade deficit and little growth in the economy. Pessimism about the future of the economy was widespread. Moreover, the privatization policy became derailed following the collapse of the major stock markets in the autumn of 1987 (initiated by the 30 per cent fall on Wall Street on 'Black Monday', 19 October).

By early 1988, however, there were the first signs of economic recovery. As elsewhere, this was aided by deregulation of the financial system, and, as the stock market revived, a new wave of privatization of state industries occurred. As in Britain, these asset sales helped to sustain public expenditure while reducing the public sector borrowing requirement and allowing taxes to be cut. It was thus possible to keep inflation down while economic growth accelerated. The political standing of the government therefore began to revive, but the President had now managed to establish himself as a statesmanlike figure, above party politics, appealing to a wide section of the electorate. There was little opposition within the Socialist Party to inhibit Mitterrand's campaign for re-election to the presidency in 1988. In contrast, the right-wing bloc was split, and a growing number of right-wing votes were being commanded by the National Front.

Eventually, there were three candidates from the right. Chirac, Barre and Le Pen. Chirac, who emerged as the main challenger, campaigned on a New Right platform, while Mitterrand adopted a far more centrist approach than in 1981, promising to try and form a centre–left government if re-elected. Now there were no radical proposals, only a vague appeal to social justice and some limited social reforms. The President's campaign centred on his personality rather than on the policies of his party. This tactic paid off. In the first round of voting the right-wing vote split, while Mitterrand was well out ahead. The National Front vote increased sharply to just under 15 per cent. In the second round, while Chirac obtained the grudging support of the rest of the 'conventional right', he also needed to attract National Front voters. His attempts to do this, for example by showing sympathy to the racism of some voters and taking a hard line on immigration and law and order, alienated many other potential supporters. In the event, Mitterrand was re-elected by a substantial margin.

However, this victory did not signify a return of the electorate to social democratic policies. Indeed, many now questioned whether the election results of the early 1980s were more than a short-term response to the poor record of the previous government. As elsewhere, economic changes were undermining the traditional working-class base of support for the left, with sharp falls in manufacturing employment and the rise of new growth industries and regions specializing in high-technology manufacturing and advanced services. After the election, Mitterrand pursued his strategy of trying to form a centre–left government, splitting away centrist support from the right-wing bloc. However, his new Prime Minister, Michel Rocard, was unable at first to bring more than a handful of centrist politicians into the government, which remained dominated by Socialists who had served in the 1981–6 administrations (but he did bring in a substantial number of non-party Ministers).

In the subsequent National Assembly elections the PS campaigned on a moderate programme which included a new minimum wage financed by a wealth tax, and improvements in education, housing, research and development, and employment programmes. In contrast, the divisions on the right persisted. The elections resulted in the PS having the largest share of seats, but just short of an overall majority. This result was seen as being advantageous to the President's strategy of constructing a government which would have to seek support from the moderate wing of the UDF, and the non-PS component in the Cabinet was increased. The right was almost equally split between the RPR and the UDF. The PCF declined still further and the National Front vote fell sharply, with the result that it had only one deputy elected.

While Rocard headed a minority administration, it could govern with support from the Communists and some elements of the centre–right. It put forward a very limited programme of social reforms and called a halt to some of the more ideological elements of Chirac's policies, notably privatization. However, there was no radical shift in policy stance, unlike that which had occurred in 1981. Policies such as financial deregulation and the easing of political controls over state industries continued. In addition, there were tax cuts to encourage industrial investment and a continued reliance on tight control over public spending and the money supply, policies which won the approval of business and the financial sector. By now the PS had finally committed itself to a market-led economy and began to consider a coalition with the centre or even parts of the right (Schmidt, 1990).

However, the following years saw a gradual disintegration in the government's position. A striking development, first evident in local and European elections, was the rise of support for France's two green parties, together with renewed support for the anti-immigrant policies of the National Front. In 1991, in an attempt to revive the government's flagging fortunes, Rocard was replaced by Edith Cresson, France's first woman Prime Minister. At the same time, divisions began to open up within the PS over policy matters and the endorsement by the government of a 'social market economy', barely distinguishable in many respects from the policy stance of the moderate right, and between rival contenders for the left nomination for the presidency in 1995 (or when Mitterrand retired, which many now thought should be before this date). By spring 1992 the attempt to rekindle support by the appointment of Edith Cresson had badly misfired and she was replaced by the experienced former Minister of Finance Pierre Bérégovoy. However, the government had lost the support of the new middle class and many workers as well and the PS was soundly defeated in elections for the National Assembly in 1993. After this Chirac's nominee, Balladur, formed a new right-wing government. Mitterrand remained in office, while the remnants of the PS plunged into open warfare as Rocard sought to form a new centre–left grouping.

By the mid-1970s the German Social Democrats, in alliance with the FDP, were firmly established in office.[5] However, although the subsequent recession affected Germany less than many of the other countries with which we are concerned, by the time of the 1976 Bundestag election, the SPD polled its lowest total of votes for over 20 years and the coalition's majority fell to ten seats. But internal divisions between the CDU and the CSU weakened their political impact over the following four years while the standing of the government, especially of the Chancellor, Helmut Schmidt, rose.

By now, as elsewhere, the public sector deficit and the tax burden on households were rising rapidly (Alber, 1986: 36). Much of this was caused by the increasing costs of social insurance and other welfare programmes in an era of slower growth and rising unemployment. The government now switched from expansionary welfare policies to austerity. By the early 1980s these measures had actually begun to reduce the level of social expenditure, absolutely and as a proportion of GDP. The government had four aims: to cut public debt, to shift public expenditure from consumption to investment, to reduce taxes and stimulate the private market, and to curb inflation (Alber, 1986: 114). There were wide-ranging reductions in the coverage and level of welfare benefits. According to Alber (1986: 116), over 80 per cent of all post-war curtailments in the welfare state up to 1982 occurred in the period from the mid-1970s. As elsewhere, this change of direction in social policies pre-dated the advent of right-wing administrations in the 1980s. Schmidt, unlike Brandt, came from the right wing of the SPD and had a reputation as an effective government manager. Under his leadership the Keynesian experiments of the first period of Social Democratic rule were abandoned in favour of tight fiscal and monetary policies (Paterson, 1981).[6] Schmidt worked closely with successive FDP Economics Ministers, despite the alienation that this caused among some Cabinet colleagues and party members (Dyson, 1981; Padgett, 1987).

The divisions on the right resulted in the nomination of Franz-Josef Strauss, the leader of the Bavarian CSU, as candidate for the chancellorship in 1980, a man widely regarded as a dangerous and extreme right winger. In the 1980 election, the government regained a similar majority to that which it had had before the 1976 election. However, the balance of forces within the coalition altered as the SPD vote remained static while the FDP vote increased sharply (one reason being its growing attraction for the 'new middle class' (Pridham, 1981)). In addition, there was a new political force, the Green Party, which was formed in 1980. This drew on a rising tide of concern and grassroots organizing (*Burgerinitiativen*) around local environmental and other issues during the 1970s. The growing impact of the Greens had adversely affected the SPD vote, especially among the younger age groups. More generally, the growth of the Greens was an aspect of what Padgett (1987) calls the erosion of the 'social democratic paradigm', owing to the collapse of the economic foundations which underpinned it. This was accompanied by an increasing attack on the paradigm by both the right and the left, in Germany as elsewhere. However, the critique had a varied impact, adding to the popularity of the Greens but also encouraging the increasingly neo-liberal stance of the FDP. One common element in left and right critique was the assertion that government had been captured by powerful, well-organized interests, including bureaucratic state agencies (Kitschelt, 1991). However, the identities of the oppressors and the oppressed varied with the political ideology of the critic.

Within a short time the government was beginning to fragment. On the one hand, there was increasing disaffection with the Chancellor's policies from the SPD's left wing, especially its youth movement, and clear identities of interest between the Greens and this section of the party. In addition, the SPD's relationship with the trade unions was at a low ebb, with growing opposition to the coalition's economic policies (Padgett, 1987). On the other hand, the FDP was pressing for a further shift towards deflationary monetarist policies (Dyson, 1981). The recession of the early 1980s widened these divisions and destroyed the government.

In many ways the governmental response to the new recession was similar to that adopted by the right-wing governments in Britain and the USA. Domestic public expenditure was cut back sharply while defence spending continued to increase. The government looked to the private rather than the public sector to spearhead recovery, so it reduced taxes on the private sector. There was concern about the falling competitiveness of the German economy compared with Japan and the newly industrializing countries, together with a belief that the growth of welfare and other public expenditure had 'crowded out' private investment and raised company taxation and production costs, and that powerful interests – the trade unions, the bureaucracy and so on – needed to have their power curtailed. State support should be targeted on new, dynamic sectors of production or on modernizing older industry. The welfare state needed restructuring, reducing the power of special interest groups, decentralizing responsibilities to subnational governments, to private agencies or to self-help organizations. However, unlike the British and American governments, the German government sought to work with 'responsible' unions that accepted the need for change, for greater flexibility in working practices and for the introduction of new technology (Esser, 1986).

As the recession deepened and the popularity of the SPD continued to fall (it lost control of West Berlin in 1981, one of its electoral heartlands), intra-party dissent grew, while the FDP Ministers argued for still tighter economic policies. From 1981 the FDP, whose political stock was also falling, prepared to abandon the SPD and form a new alliance with the CDU. In autumn 1982 the conflict came to a head when the FDP Economics Minister proposed further deep cuts in welfare expenditure which were unacceptable to the SPD. The FDP left the government. It soon lost a vote of confidence in the Bundestag and resigned. The CDU leader, Helmut Kohl (who had a Catholic labour background), then assumed the chancellorship at the head of a CDU/CSU/FDP government. The new government began a programme of further welfare cuts while preparing for an election in the spring of 1983. This was one of the most divisive campaigns in the history of the state. There was a major conflict over defence and the stationing of new missiles in West Germany. But Kohl also proposed a radical change of direction (*Wende*) in social and economic policies, with the familiar New Right package of cuts in social expenditure, support for industry with tax cuts and a reduction of the role of the state in society. In contrast, the SPD, which had a new leader, wanted to raise taxes on high earners to pay for job creation and other programmes, having moved away somewhat from its former monetarism in response to conflict within its ranks, and the growing problems of the declining industrial cities and regions which were its electoral heartlands (Paterson, 1981, 1986). The SPD remained just the largest party in the Bundestag, but with an even lower vote than in 1976. The most notable change was the success of the Green Party, which entered the Bundestag for the first time, polling almost as many votes as the FDP (which had been discredited by its abandonment of the SPD) and drawing support from former SPD and young voters (Pappi, 1984). However, the overall result was a triumph for the new coalition which had a large majority over the combined forces of the SPD and the Greens.

At first the new government was a rather shaky construction, with major divisions between and within its constituent elements. It was soon enmeshed in several scandals, including the discovery of illegal contributions to party funds by industrial interests, which forced the resignation of leading figures in the CDU and the FDP. At the same time the CDU's traditional brand of centre–right, Christian Democratic politics came under increasing pressure from the two other parties in the government, the FDP and the CSU. These were the main standard bearers for New Right policies, wishing to press ahead with privatization, deregulation (including changes in labour law) and further cuts in domestic expenditure. However, they differed over foreign policy and law and order, with the FDP maintaining its traditional, more (socially) liberal approach. At first, the main aspects of the government's programme to be implemented were cuts in welfare expenditure and limited deregulation, such as the reduction of rent controls. But from 1986 larger-scale privatization and financial deregulation were instigated. By this stage Kohl was becoming more cautious about welfare cuts as state election results had shown that they were unpopular (Conradt, 1993).

The main opposition forces, the SPD and the Greens, were internally divided, in part over the issue of 'Red–Green' coalitions, the first of which occurred in the state of Hesse in 1985. The SPD was also split over environmental and defence issues and over economic policy, with some still supporting Keynesian demand management and the goal of full employment and the restoration of welfare cuts, and others who broadly accepted government policies in this area (Padgett, 1987).

As the economy recovered in the mid-1980s, the government regained popularity. By 1986 inflation had almost been eliminated, production was rising and unemployment falling, although, as elsewhere, there was persistent long-term unemployment and the benefits of growth were unequally distributed. In particular, there was a growing disparity between the areas of high unemployment and declining heavy industry in the North and the areas of new science-based and high-technology industry in the South. In the inner areas of the larger industrial cities, some with high concentrations of foreign workers, there was serious economic and social deprivation, the product of an increasingly polarized economy and society.

In late 1986 the revival in the government's fortunes was aided by a further scandal when the largest social housing organization, Neue Heimat, owned by the trade union federation and with close links to the SPD, collapsed as a result of speculation and corruption among its top management. As we shall see later, this had major consequences for social housing. However, its immediate impact was to alienate many of the SPD's traditional supporters, leading to a serious collapse of its vote in Land elections. It also turned the party's links with the unions from an asset to a liability (Padgett, 1987).

The rightward drift in the coalition's policies was reflected in its programme for the 1987 Bundestag elections which stressed the need for further privatization, tax cuts and stronger law and order policies. The main beneficiaries from the election were the FDP and the Green Party, which increased their representation in the Bundestag. The Greens again attracted many former SPD and new voters (G. Roberts, 1987). Under the increased influence of the FDP, the new government introduced major changes in taxation, cutting income and company taxes. Despite its election victory the CDU's poll standings again began to decline, owing mainly to divisions within the government over its response to the new disarmament initiatives by the Soviet Union, now led by Mikhail Gorbachev. The SPD and the FDP welcomed this change, while the CSU opposed it and the CDU temporized. The former two parties benefited electorally from their stance. A notable development was the revival of several far right political parties which gained votes from the unemployed and other groups, such as farmers, who had not benefited from the economic revival of the mid-decade. In European elections in 1989 the leading extreme right-wing party, the Republicans, polled almost as well as the Greens and won six seats in the European Parliament. One factor which strengthened support for the extreme right was the flow of ethnic German refugees and asylum seekers from Eastern Europe that began in mid-decade and reached around 850,000 in 1989 alone. The extreme right played on feelings of resentment among sections of the population who believed that the newcomers were competing for jobs and housing. Like the French National Front, the extreme right began to attract votes away from both the conventional right-wing parties and the SPD (Minkenberg, 1992; Westle and Niedermayer, 1992). It also provoked increasingly frequent clashes with left-wing groupings and there was a growth of racially motivated violence.

From this point onwards the political consequences of the collapse of the Communist government in East Germany dominated the political agenda. In mid-1989 there was a rapid growth of mass demonstrations in favour of democratization in the GDR. Following a visit by Gorbachev in October the East German leader Erich Honeker was forced to resign. For a brief period the reformist wing of the Communist Party assumed power, legalizing independent parties, removing restrictions on travel to West Germany and allowing the Berlin Wall to be torn down. However, by December the party was forced to relinquish power, leaving government to be carried on by an interim administration, led by the liberal, reform Communist Hans Modrow. At the same time, in both Germanies, pressure for a rapid movement towards reunification gathered momentum. In November Chancellor Kohl, drawing on this popular upsurge, proposed a plan for confederation, leading eventually to unification. By early 1990 the interim East German government accepted the goal of reunification.

During the subsequent few months, while negotiations continued between the two Germanies and with the Soviet Union, the USA and the other Western allies, the accelerating economic disintegration and political turmoil in East Germany, accompanied by continuing mass migration to the West, led to a headlong rush to reunification, without any interim stage. This accelerated after the first (and last) free election in East Germany held in March 1990, which was a triumph for the 'Alliance for Germany', in effect the East German CDU. The new government, which included Social Democrats and Liberals, had one task: to bring the negotiations for reunification to a speedy conclusion. In July, despite strong opposition from the Bundesbank to the terms, economic and monetary unification took place, with East German wages, pensions and small savings converting at 1:1 and other savings, debts and liabilities at 2:1. This had two effects: given the comparative strengths of the two economies, it added greatly to inflationary pressures in the West and ensured that East German industries, with their low productivity but with wages moving closer to West German levels, were completely uncompetitive, leading to their rapid collapse. By the end of 1991 the Eastern workforce had declined by 25 per cent, there were a million unemployed, another million in subsidized jobs and 500,000 had migrated to the West (Conradt, 1993).

Following the conclusion of negotiations with the Soviet Union and the Western allies in September, and with the pressure of accelerating economic collapse, the two Germanies were finally reunited on 3 October. This involved the takeover of East by West Germany. The first elections for the unified state were held in December. By now the CDU's declining fortunes had undergone a remarkable revival, as Kohl's drive for reunification had won him mass support. In contrast, the SPD's fortunes had waned as it tried to argue that a slower progress to reunification would be preferable (Kitschelt, 1991). In fact, the rapid disintegration of East Germany probably made this impossible.

In a campaign notable for the success with which the CDU managed to convince voters that the rapid modernization and privatization of East German industries would pay for the costs of reunification without federal tax increases, the SPD's protests that this was fraudulent fell on deaf ears. The governing coalition won around 55 per cent of the vote and had a three-figure overall majority in the enlarged Bundestag. However, this large majority was mainly the result of the heavy vote for the CDU in the East, the SPD actually getting more votes than its rival in the West. But it still had its worst result here since 1957 (Kitschelt, 1991). A worrying feature of the election was the continuing support for the Republican Party, although it failed to gain enough votes to win a seat in the Bundestag. For the Greens, which decided not to ally with the East German Greens until after the election and which also opposed rapid unification, the contest was a disaster. It was eliminated from the Bundestag, although its Eastern allies gained some representation.

The mood of post-unification euphoria soon dissipated, however, as problems, many of which the SPD had foreseen, mounted in 1991 and 1992. The run-down state of the physical and industrial infrastructure of the new Eastern Länder, and the agreement to raise wages and benefits to Western levels, imposed a huge financial burden on the Western economy. In the short term the costs of unification were met by special subsidies from the federal government (raiding, among other sources, state pension funds, and borrowing, thus increasing the budget deficit). However, the longer-run plan was for these costs to be met through the established system which redistributed funds from the richer to the poorer Länder.

The consequence was that all the Western Länder would become net contributors to the scheme, entailing a severe financial squeeze on their own expenditure. Moreover, the confident claim by the government that reunification would be financed from the proceeds of privatization and the modernization of industry in the East soon proved to be a chimera. By 1991 it was clear that little East German industry would survive and that mass unemployment would accelerate and persist. Few investors wished to open new plants in the East and the government offered only limited inducements to encourage them to do so. Instead, West German industry boomed, selling its products to eager new consumers in the East. This flood of purchasing power, created by the terms of economic unification, together with the rising budget deficit, stimulated inflation, as the Bundesbank had feared it would. One consequence of the imposition of high interest rates by the bank, in an attempt to control these pressures, was the disintegration of the European Monetary System in 1992/3. Meanwhile, Germany's public debt reached $1000 billion by 1992, the highest ever level, and the economy plunged into recession.

Rising unemployment and growing resentment concerning the takeover by the West led to a rapid fall in the popularity of the government in the East and mass demonstrations in 1991. There was a further growth of far right violence (including racially motivated murders) against foreigners who became scapegoats for an increasingly embittered population. The government also became ever more unpopular in the West as the real costs of reunification were realized. Despite the immediate stimulus which reunification had given to the Western economy, rising inflation and high interest rates, together with a growing competition for housing and jobs, now had their effect. In addition, the government reneged on its election promise not to raise taxes, imposing new consumer, income and business taxes in 1991. Its falling popularity meant that by 1991 it had lost outright control of all but one of the 16 Land governments and the SPD controlled the upper house of Parliament, the Bundesrat. Once again, an SPD/FDP alliance seemed a possibility.

As we described in the last chapter, the 1973 Dutch election led to the formation of a government headed by the PvdA and its left-wing allies, but which also contained Ministers from the KVP and the ARP.[7] The mid-decade recession left a legacy of higher levels of unemployment, despite increased government support for industry. These subsidies, plus the rise in welfare benefits which occurred because of the recession and following the expansion of such programmes in the 1960s and early 1970s, increased the budget deficit. But the economic problems were assumed to be 'conjunctural', so it was anticipated that the deficit would only be a temporary phenomenon. However, while in 1973 there had been a budget surplus, by 1979 the deficit amounted to 13 per cent of the budget and showed no sign of falling.

On entering office the government had taken over a package of measures from the preceding administration which aimed to cut the deficit and bring inflation under control. It included wage and price controls, a profits freeze and measures to reduce unemployment. The resort to direct control over wages and prices followed the final collapse of the corporatist system of wage setting (Wolinetz, 1989; Padgett and Paterson, 1991: 200). The government's programme contained measures to reduce social and economic inequality and increase democracy. It aimed to increase public control of finance and investment, and enhance worker participation in industry. It also improved social benefits by indexing them to average rather than minimum wages and adding further supplementary benefits.

However, like its counterparts elsewhere, the Dutch government soon began to move towards the new, post-Keynesian economic orthodoxies. After 1975 it adopted a policy of 'selective growth' which involved action to improve profits, freeze wages, stimulate private investment and tightly restrict the growth of public expenditure. As Gladdish (1991: 152) comments, '[t]he year 1976 might be regarded as a watershed in post-war economic policy. From then on governments would be committed to restricting public sector growth in favour of private sector expansion'. However, despite this change, the government remained resistant to breaking the indexation of social benefits to wage rises.

The government almost ran its full term, but in early 1977 the Confessional Ministers resigned in opposition to a land expropriation bill. In the subsequent election, the PvdA received over one-third of all votes, its best ever result. However, it was excluded from the new government because the VVD had also polled well, and so the CDA was therefore able to form a centre–right, Christian Democrat/Liberal government under its leader, van Agt. One reason why the Confessional–Socialist government did not continue was the pressure which was exerted on the leadership by the left wing of the PvdA, which opposed the policy U-turns of previous years, not to compromise during the negotiations to form a new administration following the election (van Mierlo, 1986). In addition, the merger of the Confessional parties diluted the influence of the labour wing of the former Catholic Party, and hence the predisposition to ally with the PvdA, and strengthened the inclination for an alliance with the VVD (Wolinetz, 1989). This was a political turning-point as it set a pattern that was to persist until the late 1980s (with a brief interlude in 1981/2). So the PvdA 'breakthrough' of the 1970s, rather than marking a new pattern in Dutch politics, was merely a pause in the party's long exclusion from government which began in the late 1950s. By contrast, a firm basis was now established for a centre–right governing bloc which transcended the decreasingly significant divide between religion and secularism in Dutch society.

The new government, like its predecessor, was committed to reduce unemployment and inflation and to contain public expenditure and the budget deficit. Unemployment had been around 6 per cent in the second half of the 1970s, rising sharply to 15 per cent by 1983. By 1981, despite the attempts, from 1975, to cut back public expenditure, its share of GDP had risen from 45 per cent at the start of the 1970s to 61.5 per cent. The new government's policy, which placed deficit reduction and expenditure cuts to the fore, regardless of the consequences for employment, was strongly influenced by claims that the rising size and costs of the public sector were squeezing out private investment, reducing profitability and competitiveness. In addition, academic studies had shown that Dutch industry was overreliant on declining manufacturing industries, which were losing out in the face of low-cost competition from newly industrializing nations. In consequence, it was argued, state support should be shifted away from these sectors (where it often served to sustain employment rather than improve competitiveness) to technologically advanced industries. It was also suggested that the link between private and public sector wages should be severed and that social welfare benefits should be recast in order to provide greater discipline and a greater incentive to work (Wolinetz, 1989). However, the government retained some commitment to trying to protect the purchasing power of those on the lowest incomes. Nevertheless, it made deep cuts in public sector wages and social security costs.

By 1981 the country was entering its worst post-war recession; GDP fell by 1.4 per cent in 1981 and unemployment again climbed. At this point the government's term ran out. Domestic policies played a relatively small role in the subsequent election. But the PvdA was now widely seen as an extremist party by an electorate that was moving rightwards, and its vote fell. However, the governing parties lost just enough seats to prevent them from forming a new administration, so a shaky coalition ensued, including the PvdA but excluding the Liberals, with whom it had always refused to cooperate. As before, the CDA leader, van Agt, was Prime Minister. This administration lasted only a few months, however, collapsing over the opposition of PvdA ministers to public expenditure cuts. There followed an even shorter interlude with the two remaining government parties in coalition (CDA and D '66) before Parliament was dissolved and an election was called for the autumn of 1982.

This resulted in a change in the strengths of the two right-wing parties, with the VVD increasing its share of the vote while the CDA vote fell even further. The PvdA made small gains but the overall result meant that the CDA–VVD government could be re-established, under the leadership of the new CDA leader Lubbers, but with an increased number of VVD Ministers in the Cabinet. The government's dominant priority was to reduce the budget deficit and free up the private sector. It now took more drastic action to achieve this end. The indexation of welfare benefits and public sector wages to average wages was suspended. There were also across-the-board cuts in public sector wages and benefits and more general reforms in the social welfare system to reduce expenditure on health, education and other services. Corporate taxes were reduced. According to Wolinetz (1989), trade union resistance to these changes was weakened by rising unemployment. He comments that these policies finally severed the post-war consensus between government, the unions and the employers, in which the government provided generous social benefits and public sector wages linked to the private sector. Now the unions were left to do as well as they could in negotiations with individual employers. By 1986 the deficit had been reduced to 8 per cent, inflation was almost eliminated but unemployment had scarcely fallen at all.

In the 1986 election, despite unemployment of around 12 per cent, the differences between the governing parties and the PvdA over economic policy were limited, although the latter did favour some expansion of spending to reduce unemployment and the introduction of a shorter working week (Gladdish, 1987). The CDA and the PvdA gained seats, at the expense of smaller parties and the VVD, many of the latter's voters now switching to the CDA. This result allowed Lubbers to form a new administration, but the Liberals had a marginally reduced share of Cabinet seats. However, this continuity of government masked a more important sea change in the nature of centre–right politics in the Netherlands. The formation of the CDA had loosened the former KVP's close links with the Catholic 'pillar' and by the 1980s the party was moving away from the commitment to a considerable degree of collectivism, towards a more conventional conservative political philosophy (van Kersbergen and Becker, 1988). The coalition with the VVD, a party of free marketeers opposed to more than minimal state intervention (but, like the German FDP, with a more 'progressive' attitude to matters of individual freedom), accelerated the CDA's rightward shift. Undoubtedly, this shift also reflected the more general waning of support for the politics of the postwar welfare states and for collectivism.[8] This helps explain, for example, the emphasis that the Lubbers governments placed on decentralization, deregulation and the privatization of state assets after 1982, all these being seen as a means of reducing governmental 'overload', and the influence that special interests had had over economic and social policy (Daalder, 1989).[9] However, few of these policies were pursued as rapidly and radically as elsewhere. This meant that the CDA was still able to form coalitions with the PvdA or the VVD, as the electoral situation demanded.

The second Lubbers government planned to reduce the budget deficit further, ending industrial subsidies, freezing public sector pay and increases in wages, and cutting health-care costs. It promised not to increase taxes or social security contributions, while reducing unemployment and eliminating inflation. In 1987 a reformed social security system came into being, with lower and shorter-duration unemployment benefit and other cost-cutting changes (van Kersbergen and Becker, 1988). Like the other Western economies, the Dutch economy revived in the late 1980s, with very low inflation and a falling deficit. However, high unemployment persisted. Social security expenditure was considerably reduced but, as high levels of dependency persisted, savings occurred by allowing average benefits levels to fall.

By its last year in office the government's sustained movement towards the neo-liberal stance advocated by the VVD was evident. The 1989 budget, while it stressed the need to combat unemployment, also promised income tax cuts, a reform of health care, the introduction of market forces into the sector, and cuts in assistance for students and the young, single unemployed. However, there were some strains between the CDA and the VVD. As the economy revived in the late 1980s the strong commitment to austerity policies, which had bound both parties together since 1982, seemed less necessary to the Confessionals than to the Liberals. In fact, though, the government finally broke up in 1989 over a relatively minor disagreement relating to environmental policies (Wolinetz,

1990). The PvdA, which, like the British Labour Party, had suffered from its left-wing reputation and which had opposed public expenditure cuts in the 1980s, was anxious to re-enter government and thus to project an image of fiscal responsibility. Under a new leader, Wim Kok, it now stressed the need to support the private market and to restrain the size of the public sector, while doing more for the poor and improving health, education and the environment. It wanted to fund these by cancelling tax cuts and cutting defence expenditure, and announced its readiness to enter a government with the CDA. The election resulted in no change in the number of CDA seats in Parliament, and a small fall in the PvdA representation as a result of its failure to attract new young voters, unlike the CDA, which now also had many non-religious supporters. In contrast, the Liberals lost heavily. After the usual negotiations, the third Lubbers government was formed, excluding the VVD but including the PvdA. Wim Kok became Minister of Finance in a government still committed to much the same approach to social and economic policies as that adopted by the centre–right administrations of the 1980s.

In Denmark, as we noted in the last chapter, the 'Catastrophe Election' in 1973 resulted in a sharp decline in support for the four old 'system' parties and a rise in support for smaller parties and the new party of the taxpayers' revolt, the Progress Party.[10] From 1973 to 1982 there were four minority governments, none of which lasted their full term. The first, from 1973 to 1975, was a Liberal administration, while the other three were Social Democratic (including an unprecedented coalition with Venstre in 1978/9). During these years the pre-1973 pattern was, to some extent, re-established. But the Progress Party remained a significant presence in the Folketing. However, there were significant changes within the left and the centre–right groupings. The Venstre vote declined to about half its 1960s level (except in the 1975 election), and the Radical Liberals, who had done well in the early 1970s, reverted to the lower level of the previous decade. In contrast, the Conservative Party made a major comeback from its losses, with almost as many voters as the Liberal parties by the early 1980s. On the left, the Social Democrats recovered strongly, and by the end of the 1970s they were approaching the 40 per cent share of the vote around which their support had hovered for most of the previous 50 years.

The 1981 election marked the start of a new collapse in this vote. Not only were the Social Democrats, like their sister parties in Britain, Germany and the Netherlands, faced with the difficulty of managing an increasingly turbulent economy; they also had an ageing membership and no longer appealed to many young voters. Many of these voters were, however, still on the left, and the main beneficiary was the somewhat more leftist Socialist People's Party. After 1981 the rise of the Conservative Party accelerated, and in 1984 it polled almost 25 per cent of all votes, its best ever result, leaving it far ahead of the combined votes for the Liberal parties. The main result of these changes was that, as elsewhere, the 1980s became a decade of right-wing government, although all were minority administrations. In 1982 Poul Schluter became the first ever Conservative Prime Minister, forming a minority government with Venstre and two smaller centre parties. This coalition survived further elections in 1984 and 1987. However, after another election in 1988, called after a defeat on defence policy, Schluter's new government consisted of a coalition of three of the four old 'system' parties, KF, Venstre and RV. In 1990 there was yet another election. The Prime Minister hoped, by this means, to gain additional bargaining power over the Social Democrats with respect to economic policies. This was a failure as the Social Democrats gained seats and KF fell back. Schluter now formed a minority coalition which excluded RV and which was in an even weaker position than its predecessor.

In fact, by 1990, there had been a considerable shift in the balance of power between the two main right-wing parties. In the 1984 election KF reached its post-war high point with 42 seats in the Folketing, about double the number held by Venstre. In each subsequent election KF lost seats, down to 30 after the 1990 election. Meanwhile, the Venstre vote remained solid and in 1990 it obtained 29 seats. However, RV lost out heavily, down to a post-war low of seven seats by 1990, and the Social Democrats eventually managed to regain much of the support which they had previously lost. By 1990 they held 69 seats, their best position since 1971, though still rather less than they normally obtained in the 1950s. Many of their gains were at the expense of SF, although this party remained the fourth largest in Parliament. So the right-wing government now faced a left-wing bloc that was now only a few seats short of an overall majority. [11]

The backdrop to these political changes was, of course, the persisting economic difficulties which Denmark experienced during and after the mid-1970s recession, to which succeeding governments responded much as elsewhere. In Denmark's case, however, the reliance of minority governments on gaining extra support in Parliament to pass legislation added to the difficulties. By 1974, with accelerating unemployment, high inflation and an increasing balance of payments deficit, the minority Liberal government failed to gain acceptance of a package of drastic public expenditure cuts and a wage freeze. The succeeding minority Social Democrat government adopted policies similar to those being tried by the British Labour government – an incomes policy agreed with the unions, some measures to sustain jobs, expenditure cuts and a tight monetary policy, with limits for the growth of the money supply. [12]

Successive minority Social Democrat governments were under pressure from two sides. First, from the unions, which objected to the incomes policy and the limited nature of attempts to sustain employment (and whose pressure eventually forced the Social Democrats into opposition in 1982). Second, from the Liberals, Conservatives and other bourgeois parties, which pressed for deeper expenditure cuts, reductions in taxation and a tight restraint on wages. In 1975 the government had concluded a pact with other parties on economic policies which was based on over-optimistic predictions of an economic recovery. A new pact, to impose a stricter wage norm and more expenditure cuts, only scraped through the Folketing in 1976 and led to an outbreak of unofficial strikes. A price and wage freeze was then imposed until 1977 and unofficial strike leaders were prosecuted. Early in 1978 the government proposed a new package of housing, defence and economic policies which failed to get through Parliament, leading to the 1978 election. It was in this election that the Social Democrats regained most of the votes lost in 1973 and were thus able to assemble a majority in the Folketing for their policies, at first in a remarkable coalition with Venstre.

These deflationary economic policies led to a decline in inflation, but high wage rises continued, accompanied by high unemployment. Moreover, the balance of payments deficit was reduced only modestly and temporarily. So similar economic policies were again embraced. At the same time the main centre–right parties came together to form the coalition which took power in 1982 (in fact, the unprecedented formation of a Social Democrat–Liberal government in 1978–9 was an attempt by the Socialists to detach one of the partners in this coalition). These political developments were accompanied by increased questioning of the combination of economic growth and welfare state expansion which had been the aim of most political parties before the mid-1970s. By the end of the decade, apart from the populist, right-wing, anti-welfare state impact of the Progress Party, there was also criticism from the left and the centre in Danish politics and calls for decentralization, de-bureaucratization, small-scale production, a greater concern for the environment, and so on. Many of these themes had first emerged during the campaign against Denmark's membership of the Common Market in the early 1970s. The growth of support for smaller, newer parties of the left and the right partially reflected these changes in social and political thinking.

Despite the cuts in public expenditure under the Social Democratic governments, social expenditure continued to rise (Johansen, 1986: 361; see also Marklund, 1988). The public sector deficit increased very rapidly in the early 1980s; debt service rose from 7.6 per cent of total public expenditure in 1980 to 12.8 per cent in 1983. The first Schluter administration had, on the one hand, to woo the populist, anti-welfare state Progress Party, yet, on the other hand, it also needed RV votes. This party supported some expenditure cuts, but also wanted to preserve the core of the welfare state. In fact, the lack of stable government majorities in the 1980s gave rise to a growing trend for administrations to stay in office, even if defeated in Parliament. This meant that in some areas policy was effectively controlled by the opposition rather than the government (Bille, 1989).

Nevertheless, in the teeth of opposition from the unions and the Social Democrats, the Schluter governments, like their Dutch counterparts, suspended wage indexation, and hence the indexation of welfare benefits (except pensions) (A. Thomas, 1986). This had a considerable impact on reducing expenditure and the standard of living of beneficiaries, the real value of unemployment benefits, for example, falling by 15 per cent in two years. By 1985 most social security benefits (except pensions) had lost 20 per cent or more of their real value in the five years since 1980.[13] In addition, there were reductions in the coverage and level of income support programmes and increased social insurance and other charges. An increasing tendency to target benefits on low-income households was also evident. Reviewing Danish developments in the first half of the 1980s, Marklund (1988: 35) concluded: 'Denmark has gone through a rather dramatic reduction in its welfare costs. It has also moved away from its traditionally universal, high coverage and generous welfare benefits towards a much more selective, restrictive and residual social policy'. As elsewhere, the strongest campaigners for a radical restructuring and reduction in the scope of the welfare state came from the neo-liberal Venstre rather than the more moderate KF. It is notable, for example, that the Conservative Prime Minister in the 1980s, Poul Schluter, took care to distance his politics from those of Thatcher or Reagan, denying any intention of radically restructuring and reducing the welfare state.[14]

SOCIAL HOUSING IN DECLINE

In the last chapter we described the principal factors which caused the erosion of governmental commitments to mass social housing programmes, some of which pre-dated the economic restructuring and the breakdown in the political compact over the mixed economy of welfare which has occurred since the mid-1970s. The failure to contain inflation and public expenditure while maintaining a commitment to expansionary welfare programmes paved the way for a politics of welfare which sought to redraw the boundaries between the role of the state, on the one hand, and the market and the individual, on the other. At the same time, economic restructuring created increasingly polarized societies, with a rising mass of low-income households excluded from paid employment or engaged in insecure and poorly paid work. Moreover, the polarizing effects of economic change have been augmented by the consequences of economic and political upheavals. In America, there has been a rising migrant flow from Central and South America (including the Caribbean) and East Asia.[15] Some of these migrants rapidly established themselves in America's open economy. Many more were trapped in inner-city ghettoes, in low-paid jobs in the formal or informal (including criminal) economies, or dependent on eroding welfare benefits. In Europe, from the mid-1980s onwards, there was a new source of mass immigration consequent on the breakup of the socialist states, with a rising tide of asylum seekers and economic migrants. At the same time, many who had earlier been sucked into Western Europe's expanding economies from Southern Europe and the Third World were expelled from employment, or even more firmly trapped at the bottom of a polarized labour market.

This growing mass of low-income households has been augmented by demographic and social changes. In most countries there has been a rising proportion of the elderly and, as a result of modern medicine and improved standards of life, of the very elderly. Between 1970 and 1990, the share of the population over the age of 65 grew by between 20 per cent and 30 per cent in almost all of the countries discussed in this book, and only in France was there more stability (US Bureau of the Census, 1991:

table 22, 18; Boelhouwer and van den Heijden, 1992: table 2.4, 28). There has been a decline in the proportion of 'conventional' family households and a rising share of single-parent and other single households, many of whom have low incomes. The share of single-person households in the six countries rose from around 17–25 per cent in the late 1960s and early 1970s to between 24 per cent and 33 per cent by the mid-1980s, a remarkably rapid change. These and other demographic and social changes (such as those concerning fertility rates) resulted in a major increase in the number of households, and hence the demand for accommodation. Between 1970 and 1987 the number of separate households grew by almost 50 per cent in the Netherlands and the USA (1970–90), 30 per cent in France and around 22 per cent in West Germany, the United Kingdom and Denmark (US Bureau of the Census, 1991: table 56, 45; Boelhouwer and van den Heijden, 1992: tables 2.1 and 2.3, 24–5).

Of course, not all these additional households had low incomes. There was, for example, a notable growth of small, dual-earner households, with both partners working in those sectors of the economy, mainly in services, where there were expanding opportunities for well-paid, white-collar employment. Many such couples chose to limit the size of their families, delay having children, or remain childless. Rising incomes and the reduction or elimination of child-rearing expenses meant that these households had extra resources to invest in consumption, including housing. In tight urban housing markets, this 'yuppy' generation had an important impact, outcompeting less well-off households for a limited housing supply, inflating prices and giving rise to tenure transfers and gentrification (Harloe, 1992; Harloe, Marcuse and Smith, 1992).

However, at the other end of the spectrum, many gains of the era of full employment and welfare state expansion were reversed, with an inexorable growth in the number of households in poverty. The measurement of poverty is a notoriously controversial and difficult issue, involving not just factual matters but also questions of definition and values. However, the European Community (EC) estimated that the number of poor in the EC rose from 38 million in 1975 to 50 million a decade later. These figures are affected by shorter- as well as longer-term economic changes and by nationally varying social welfare policies. Thus between 1980 and 1985 the proportion of those in poverty in West Germany fell a little, as its economy recovered and there were rather less welfare cutbacks than elsewhere; in France economic recovery and the improvements in welfare programmes in the early period of the Socialist government led to a significant fall in the very high levels of poverty which existed in 1980 (but, at 15.7 per cent in 1985, still far above the German level of just under 10 per cent). In contrast, the persistence of high unemployment, slow growth and the effects of welfare reductions in the Netherlands led to a small rise in the proportion in poverty (and a larger numerical rise, given population growth). In the United Kingdom New Right economic and social policies made a larger impact, with a rise in the poverty population from 14.6 per cent in 1980 to 18.2 per cent in 1985 (Atkinson et al., 1993: table 1, 3). In the USA, similar factors resulted in the share of population below 125 per cent of the federally determined poverty level rising from around 16 per cent in the late 1970s to over 20 per cent by 1983, before falling back as the economy recovered (US Bureau of the Census, 1991: table 745, 462). Interestingly, while poverty rates for non-white minorities remained far higher than for whites, the percentage rise in the rate among the white population was greater than that of the minorities, possibly reflecting the fact that economic restructuring destroyed many blue-collar manufacturing jobs in the 'rustbelt' cities. By contrast, most of the new jobs created in the USA and elsewhere in the 1980s were, as we have seen, part-time and/or poorly paid. The onset of a new recession in the late 1980s has certainly added to poverty in all six countries.

Despite the considerable demand for housing generated by these changes, housing investment's share of GDP stagnated or declined after the middle of the 1970s in all the European countries, although it fluctuated more widely in the USA (US Bureau of the Census, 1991: table 700, 433; Boelhouwer and van den Heijden, 1992: table 2.10, 30). At the same time, the cost of housing increased as a proportion of household budgets. In Europe the sharpest rise occurred in the Netherlands, where housing costs as a percentage of total household expenditure rose by 30 per cent between 1975 and 1987. In France, West Germany and Denmark the rise was around 17–20 per cent and in the UK 11 per cent. By the late 1980s housing costs accounted for around 18–20 per cent of total household expenditure in most of the European countries, but was considerably higher, around 26 per cent, in Denmark (due largely to the very high interest rates in this country) (Boelhouwer and van den Heijden, 1992: table 2.11, 31). Traditionally, American households have paid larger shares of their income and expenditure for housing but in the 1980s the collapse of regulated mortgage markets and house-price inflation, at a time when real incomes were contracting, led to a dramatic rise in home-owner costs and a continuing rise in the already very high level of renter costs. Thus the average cost of home ownership for first-time buyers, as a percentage of their incomes, rose from around 10 per cent in the mid-1970s to a staggering 35 per cent by the mid-1980s before falling back somewhat. Meanwhile, the proportion of income spent on rent by all tenants grew from under 25 per cent to around 30 per cent (Joint Center for Housing Studies, 1991).

Housing production fell from the high levels which it had reached in the late 1960s and early 1970s. In the European countries only the Netherlands, which, it will be recalled, had a very rapid growth of households, sustained levels of housing production in the 1980s that were fairly close to the levels of the early 1970s (though still below them). Elsewhere, the decline in output was greater. In 1989 West German output was 45 per cent below the 1975 level; in France the fall was 37 per cent, in Denmark 34 per cent and in the UK 27 per cent. US housing output, being almost totally dependent on the private market, followed the cyclical development of the economy, recovering in the late 1970s to the levels of the early 1970s (around 2 million per annum). The recession of the early 1980s caused an even sharper collapse, with a weak recovery in mid-decade followed by another decline as the recession of the early 1990s set in (US Bureau of the Census, 1991: table 1369, 720; Ministry of Housing, Physical Planning and the Environment, 1991: 41; Boelhouwer and van den Heijden, 1992: table 2.17, 35).

The level of social housing completions varied considerably. In some countries, there was a decline across the whole period. In others, for reasons we shall describe, governments continued from time to time to increase levels of output for macro-economic reasons, principally to alleviate unemployment, especially when the private housing market was in recession. Nevertheless, these revivals were a temporary phenomenon, not the sign of a reversion to large-scale social housing programmes in response to rising lower-income demand. In Denmark the annual quota for non-profit housing fell from around 13,000 in the early 1970s to 7000 by 1980; it then rose to 12,000 in 1982 as the government sought to counter a collapse in private building and rising unemployment, before falling back to the 1980 level by the end of the decade (Ministry of Housing and Building, 1990; Ghékiere, 1991: 89). In Germany the long-term decline in social rented construction accelerated, with a major fall in output from around 81,000 in 1975 to about 14,000 in 1988. This decline was only reversed, temporarily, in the early 1990s, for reasons which we shall discuss below. In Germany, too, a rising share of *all* social housing constructed was for owner occupation. In the 1960s and early 1970s seven out of ten new social units were for rental and three were for home ownership. By the later 1980s these shares were reversed, and the total annual output of social housing had shrunk by 75 per cent since 1970 (Jaedicke and Wollmann, 1990: table 3.4, 134). In France social rented housing output fell from around 110,000 in the middle of the 1970s to around 50,000–60,000 by the time the Socialists came to power. The new government's commitment to social housing did not, however, result in any significant rise in this level of output over the following decade. Instead, production slowly declined as austerity policies were adopted, while major cuts occurred in the social ownership sector. This form of social housing had been prioritized by the centre–right governments of the 1970s as a part of their drive to expand home ownership, so that by 1980 two out of every three new social units were in this subsector. By 1989 there were slightly fewer units built for ownership than for rental, by which time the total social programme amounted to just under 100,000 units, a fall of about two-thirds since the mid-1970s (Duclaud-Williams, 1978: 148–9; Ghékiere, 1991: 130).

The remarkably high growth in the number of households in the Netherlands meant that pressure to sustain new construction remained greater than in other countries. In the 1970s, when home ownership expanded rapidly, social rented housing completions fell from a peak of over 60,000 per annum just before the mid-decade recession to about 23,000 by 1979. However, in the early 1980s, the collapse of private housing output and rising unemployment led the centre–right government to permit a temporary rise in social rented construction, to over 60,000 units in 1982. It also expanded subsidized private sector housing. Later in the 1980s, as private unsubsidized building slowly recovered, the subsidized forms of production were cut back. By 1989 social rented production was moving back to the 1979 level (Harloe and Martens, 1985; Ministerie van Volkshuisverting en Ruimteligke Ordening en Milienbeheer (MVROM), 1991: 58; Lundqvist, 1992: 54–5).

No such fluctuations accompanied the precipitate decline in British social housing production. In its first years in office the 1974–9 Labour government expanded output, and completions rose up to a peak of 170,000 in 1977. Thereafter the decline was rapid, down to around 110,000 by 1979, then falling continuously to around 30,000 by the late 1980s, at which point most new building was carried out by housing associations rather than local authorities. Over the period from 1975 the share of social housing in total output had fallen from around 45 per cent to under 15 per cent (Emms, 1990: table 1.4, 19; Harloe, 1990: figure 2.1, 98; Ministry of Housing, Physical Planning and the Environment, 1991: 53).

The share of public and other directly subsidized low-income housing in American housing output has, of course, always been far lower than in the European countries. In the 1980s public housing completions were reduced to a minuscule level. Public housing construction had expanded modestly under the Carter administration, and there were around 46,000 starts in 1981, a fourfold increase over the 1978 level. However, by 1987, starts had fallen to under 6000, the lowest level (bar one year in the 1950s) since public housing was re-enacted in 1949. The total number of additional low-income housing units, under all urban and rural federal subsidy programmes, for which Congress had made financial provision fell from around 500,000 in 1977 to around a quarter of this level throughout the 1980s. An increasing proportion of these commitments consisted of housing vouchers and other forms of subsidy which reduced the rents of existing privately owned units rather than supporting new construction (Lazere et al., 1991). Overall, federally subsidized new (public and private) housing construction fell from a peak of 237,000 (14.6 per cent of all construction) in 1979 to 40,000 (0.6 per cent of all construction) in 1988. Excluding rural housing programmes, the fall was even more dramatic, from 153,000 in 1979 to a mere 9000 by 1988 (Marcuse, 1990: 353; Lazere et al., 1991: 32–3; Karn and Wolman, 1992: 86).

As we have noted, housing-cost burdens increased after the mid-1970s owing to a variety of factors. On the one hand, large sections of the population had incomes which were declining in real terms, or increasing far slower than in the previous period. On the other hand, a declining supply of new housing and a shift, especially after mortgage market deregulation in the 1980s, to much higher real rates of interest, and periods of high house-price inflation, raised housing costs. In addition, many poorer households were affected by reductions in housing subsidies. The pattern of housing subsidies shifted, as governments switched from support for new investment to consumption subsidies. As we have noted, many governments embarked on this change in the belief that it would reduce their overall financial commitment to housing. However, the economic and housing market conditions of the past two decades, which have resulted in a growing problem of housing affordability for many low-income households (including many new entrants to the housing market, not all of whom will remain low-income households in the longer run), have made it difficult to achieve this objective. Instead, governments have been locked in to subsidizing existing housing consumers, and existing housing consumption, at the expense of new investment and new entrants to the housing market. A rising proportion of direct housing subsidies has taken the form of means-tested rent or housing allowances. While these allowances have to a growing extent been narrowly targeted on low-income households, with cut-backs in eligibility and the depth of the subsidy, this has not prevented a rapid rise in the total amount of expenditure devoted to them, as more and more households become eligible because of the growth of poverty and rising housing costs. Meanwhile, regressive indirect tax subsidies have continued to grow over the long term, although changes in interest rates and house prices have, of course, caused shorter-term fluctuations. Frequently, the tax subsidies have been insufficient to enable moderate-income households and new entrants to the housing market to become home owners, while providing excessive support for the better off and those already established in the sector. By the early 1990s, in some countries, there were moves to cut back these indirect subsidies, but without any redistribution of assistance to less well-off or would-be home owners.

While comparable data on governmental housing expenditures are hard to assemble, Papa (1992) has recently attempted this task for the major Western European nations (these figures are for current expenditure, with no adjustment for inflation). In Denmark, between 1980 and 1990, expenditure on property subsidies doubled, while that on housing allowances increased almost fourfold. At the start of this period about 45 per cent of direct subsidies went on housing allowances; by 1990 this had risen to over 60 per cent and direct subsidies rose from 2.5 per cent to 3.7 per cent of total government expenditure (unfortunately, Papa does not have figures for indirect subsidies). West German data are especially deficient, but between 1982 and 1988 the levels of assistance (subsidies and loans) for new investment in social housing from federal and Land governments fell by 60 per cent, while housing allowance costs rose by 40 per cent. In 1982 over 75 per cent of total direct social housing subsidies were for investment; by 1988 this share had fallen to around 50 per cent. In France there was a similar development; property subsidies increased by 120 per cent between 1978 and 1988, while housing allowances grew by a remarkable 800 per cent following a major reform in the late 1970s. In 1978 property subsidies amounted to 85 per cent of total direct subsidy expenditure; by 1988 this share had fallen to under 60 per cent. Meanwhile, housing expenditure took an ever rising share of total government expenditure, up from 3.77 per cent in 1978 to 4.85 per cent a decade later. In fact, indirect subsidies grew more slowly than direct subsidies, so that their share of total assistance declined from about 50 per cent in 1978 to 30 per cent in 1988 (still, they more than doubled in this period).

In the Netherlands the high level of state support for subsidized social and private construction meant that there was a very rapid growth of property subsidies, up by 400 per cent between 1975 and 1990. However, housing allowance expenditure grew even faster, by 660 per cent. But it still accounted for only 17 per cent of all direct subsidies at this latter date. Indirect subsidies increased over fourfold during this period, mainly in the second half of the 1970s when the home-ownership market was booming. As in France, but to an even greater degree, direct housing subsidies took an increasing share of total government expenditure, up from 3.3 per cent in 1975 to 7.8 per cent in 1989.

In Britain central and local government property subsidies for council housing fell by over 50 per cent between 1980/1 and 1988/9, although this was partially offset by a rise in assistance for new investment by housing associations (three-quarters of total support went to the former sector in 1980/1, but only 38 per cent by 1988/9). By this latter stage most council housing subsidies were used to rehabilitate the existing stock. Over the same period tax reliefs for home ownership rose from a level that was roughly equal to local and central council housing subsidies to over five times this level and three times the level of council and housing association subsidies (Lundqvist, 1992: 33). However, housing allowance payments almost tripled between 1980/1 and 1986/7 (Leather and Murie, 1986: 29). Their share of direct housing subsidies rose from around 27 per cent to around 60 per cent. Despite deep cuts in production subsidies for social housing, the rising bill for housing allowances resulted in the share of direct subsidies in total government expenditure remaining close to 6 per cent for much of the decade.

In the USA the balance between support through the tax system for private housing (mainly home ownership) and direct subsidies for low-income rental housing remained massively in favour of the former sector. Between 1976 and 1992 federal spending on low-income housing rose from about $7.2 billion to $19.5 billion, while tax subsidies rose from $25.2 billion to $75.9 billion (at 1992 constant dollars). However, this rise in federal outlays on low-income housing largely reflected increased expenditure as units for which funds were appropriated some years previously had to be refinanced. New commitments can be measured by budget authorizations. These fell sharply in the 1980s, from over $60 billion in 1977/8 to around $11 billion in 1990 (Dolebeare, 1992: graph 1). [16] Outlays on low-income housing as a proportion of the total federal budget remained at less than 1.5 per cent throughout these years. The influence of Congress in sustaining even this level of low-income housing assistance is indicated by the fact that the government requested less than Congress appropriated in every year from 1983 to 1990 (Dolebeare, 1992: graph 10). Overall, the outstanding budget authority for low-income housing dropped from $49.7 billion in 1980 to $20.2 billion in 1991 (in constant dollars). Of this amount, a small and declining share was available for new public housing, $7.45 billion in 1980, $1.3 billion in 1991. From 1987 onwards there was also a small programme to provide emergency aid for America's growing numbers of homeless persons. Apart from this, the only programmes that were sustained during the 1980s were funding for public housing operating subsidies (which could not be abandoned without bankrupting the public housing authorities) and assistance for the massive task of repairing and modernizing the existing public housing stock. Each of these received an average annual budget allocation of $1.75–$2 billion during the 1980s and early 1990s (Dolebeare, 1992: table 2).

The overall effects of problems of housing affordability, and the end of an era when there were the conditions for a rapid expansion of home ownership, are indicated by changes in the tenure distribution between 1970 and 1990. In the 1970s home ownership's share of the total housing stock grew in all five European countries, by 7 per cent in the Netherlands, 6 per cent in the UK, 5 per cent in Denmark and by 2 per cent in France and Germany. In the 1980s the picture was much more mixed, the share declining by 1 per cent in Denmark, staying static in Germany and growing far more slowly, by 3 per cent, in the Netherlands. However, France made up for its earlier slow growth with a rise of 7 per cent and in Britain there was a remarkable growth of 10 per cent, so that by 1990 the home-owner share, at 65 per cent, was above the then current American level. A good deal of this growth was a direct consequence of social rented housing policies which we shall discuss below (Ministry of Housing, Physical Planning and the Environment, 1991: 45–7; Boelhouwer and van den Heijden, 1992: table 2.20). This contrasting pattern was also evident in the USA, where the home-ownership rate increased from 62.9 per cent in 1971 to 65.6 per cent in 1980, but then fell back to 64.1 per cent in 1990 (Joint Center for Housing Studies, 1991; Karn and Wolman, 1992: 43).

There were equally significant contrasts between the 1970s and 1980s in relation to social rented housing. In the 1970s the proportion of the stock accounted for by social housing increased by 2 per cent in Britain, 3 per cent in Denmark, 4 per cent in France and by almost 8 per cent in the Netherlands. Only in West Germany was there no growth. Note, though, that in most cases home ownership expanded its share of the housing stock more rapidly. In the 1980s, the sharp reduction in new social rented construction, coupled with privatization, actually reduced the share of social housing in Britain and West Germany, by around 4 per cent and 5 per cent respectively. In the other three countries its growth rate was much reduced, to 1 per cent in Denmark, 2 per cent in France and 4 per cent in the Netherlands (Kroes, Ymkers and Mulder, 1988; Ghékiere, 1991; Ministry of Housing, Physical Planning and the Environment, 1991: 47). In the USA the reduction in the supply of new public housing to a trickle diminished its minimal share of the total housing stock. In 1989 there were about 1.36 million units of public housing, 1.45 per cent of the overall stock and 4 per cent of all rental housing. The net increase in public housing between 1970 and this date had only been about 172,000 units (Struyk, 1980: 5; US Department of Housing and Urban Development, 1992b: figure 1).

These figures illustrate the decline in the fortunes of social rented housing. As described in the last chapter, the foundations for this decline were laid in the 1970s. However, the full consequences of change only became evident in the 1980s and early 1990s. To examine these developments in greater detail we now consider each country in turn.

Before it regained power in 1974 the British Labour Party had promised to repeal the previous Conservative government's 1972 Housing Finance Act, but had no clear idea of what to put in its place.[17] The government's first concern was to redeem its pledge to repeal those parts of the 1972 Act which linked council rents to those in the private sector and removed local authorities' rent-setting autonomy. It also wanted to increase the level of council house building. These objectives were achieved by new but temporary subsidy legislation, passed in 1975.

Potentially, the most significant development was the establishment of a fundamental review of housing finance and subsidies, covering all the main tenures (Harloe, 1978). The initial expectation was that this review, carried out by civil servants but with expert outside advisers, would result in a radical reform of housing subsidies, including the tax subsidies for home ownership. Work done for the review showed just how regressive the home-owner subsidies were and also indicated that the distribution of subsidies for council housing construction were not well directed at the areas of greatest need. A particular concern was to find resources to support the rising investment in housing which the government had promised. The inflation of the late 1960s and early 1970s, with rising house prices and interest rates, had resulted in a rapid increase in direct and indirect subsidies, but an increasing proportion of this expenditure was supporting housing consumption rather than investment. This trend seemed likely to accelerate without major reforms.

However, the review was strongly influenced by the rapid deterioration in the government's economic and political circumstances. By 1976, as we have seen, the government had abandoned its reformist programme and its main energies were devoted to maintaining a shaky grip on power and coping with the economic crisis. The brief period when radical housing reforms might have been possible had passed and there was strong opposition within the Cabinet to any reform of home-owner subsidies, especially after a formerly safe Labour seat was lost in a by-election, allegedly because of fears about such reform.

By the time the review reported, in 1977, the social rented housing programme had become a victim of successive rounds of public expenditure cuts. Up to 1974/5 there were no major controls on local authority housing expenditure. Now controls were imposed. In this respect, as in others, the Labour government laid the foundations for a more radical attack on the local authority housing role after 1979. The review abandoned any attempt to institute major changes in housing finance (Department of the Environment, 1977). *Any* reform of home-owner subsidies was emphatically rejected as no more than 'theoretical or academic dogma' – a stance that found the full approval of the Conservative opposition in Parliament. Moreover, Labour's abandonment of mass social housing policies, already evident in the 1960s, was more clearly articulated than ever. Making much of the elimination of crude housing shortages and the growth of home ownership, social rented housing was envisaged as a supplementary form of provision, targeted at limited areas where lower-income housing shortages remained and at deprived groups. The main thrust of government policy should be to expand home ownership, as this was the tenure which most households preferred.

The principal reforms which the review advocated concerned social rented housing. A minor element was the proposal for a Tenants' Charter to modestly enhance the rights of council house tenants and to improve local authority housing management, which was increasingly regarded as inflexible, bureaucratic, inefficient and paternalistic. There was also a concern to renovate and improve existing low-income housing and target aid on those who remained in poor conditions. This was to be achieved by a system of local authority housing investment planning, four-year rolling plans incorporating local authority bids for central government subsidies and permissions to invest. Much was made of the new freedoms that the local authorities would have under this system, which replaced a mass of detailed controls over individual programmes with a block grant. Now, it was claimed, local authorities could decide what housing was best suited to the particular needs of their areas. Detailed decision making would be decentralized to the localities.

In fact, the new system institutionalized the stronger central control over local authority housing expenditure that had already developed. Between 1974/5 and 1978/9 housing public expenditure fell by 20 per cent, faster than all other major areas of public expenditure. Spending on capital investment fell even faster, by 35 per cent (Lansley, 1979: table 4.6, 124–5). Increasingly, expenditure was used to keep local authority rents down. In part, this reflected the government's commitment to the social contract with the trade unions, as well as the perceived need, at a time of high unemployment and the accelerating concentration of low-income tenants in social housing, to protect these households against rapidly rising housing costs.

A deficit subsidy for council housing was introduced, which involved further incursions by central government into local authority housing finance. Each year the government determined how much of the growth in local authority expenditure on housebuilding, management and maintenance would be met by subsidies and how much would be met by a 'local contribution', that is, from rents and local taxation. This was a clever way of controlling central expenditure while avoiding the principle to which Labour had objected in the 1972 Housing Finance Act, the loss of local authority control over rent levels. However, it put in place new mechanisms for controlling local authority housing activities which were to be fully exploited by the successor Conservative governments.

Indeed, the changes which resulted from the policy review were broadly welcomed by the Conservative opposition when the government brought forward its legislation in the dying months of its term in office. They were very close to proposals made in a Conservative policy paper in 1977 (Harloe, 1978: 13). As one of the expert advisers to the review commented, in a critique of its proposals:

> [a] key aspect of the new system of HIPS [Housing Investment Plans] ... is that central government will now have a much better means of monitoring local policies and exercising strategic control over levels of expenditure. It is evident that the Treasury saw much of merit in the ... proposals for this reason. Local authorities may well reflect on what a two-edged weapon their new 'freedom' might become. A government which chose radically to reduce public housing expenditure will now find it easier to do so (Harloe, 1978: 12).

More generally, it was suggested:

> [v]ery little of the Labour Party's traditional enthusiasm for public housing is now reflected in the present government's ... proposals ... Public housing is implicitly seen as an ambulance service, concentrating its efforts on the remaining areas of housing stress and dealing with a variety of 'special needs' ... This defensiveness about public housing, which ... seems to be based on an underlying conviction that there *is* something rather undesirable about it, may now leave the way clear for its gradual eclipse (ibid.).

As Malpass (1990: 134) concludes:

> [b]y their failure to come to terms with what had been happening in housing finance, the Labour governments of 1974–9 left the way clear for a radical reforming government of the Right. They almost succeeded in taking the politics out of housing. But, more than that, they actually set up the network of controls on capital spending, and the outlines of a public sector subsidy system which provided the Thatcher governments with the tools they needed for their version of the reform of housing finance.

In the years that followed these reforms soon went beyond housing finance. The objective was to end the local authority role as the major provider of social rented housing, by preventing new council housing construction and by privatizing the existing council housing stock through sales to individual tenants or to private landlords and by transfers to housing associations. In future, in so far as new rental housing was required, it would be provided by the associations and by private landlords (in practice, mainly the former). Eventually, the local authorities would be reduced to an 'enabling' role, supporting private sector and association provision. By the early 1990s this radical transition had been substantially accomplished. However, the housing policies of the successive Conservative governments evolved through several stages.

The issue which received most attention during the first Thatcher government, up to 1983, concerned the Conservatives' major housing proposal in the 1979 election, the 'right to buy'. This measure, enacted in 1980, allowed all local authority tenants of more than two years' standing to buy their housing on easy terms. The purchase price was based on assessed market values discounted according to the number of years that a tenant had occupied council housing, up to a maximum of 50 per cent (later increased). The policy, opposed fiercely by some Labour local authorities and more weakly by the national party, was popular and helped to ensure the re-election of the government in 1983, after which the Labour Party abandoned its outright opposition. By 1990 almost 1.2 million council houses had been sold, accounting for one-third of the growth of home ownership since 1980 and this year (Audit Commission, 1992: 5). Sales, which amounted to about one-fifth of the stock that had existed in 1980, plus the drastic reductions in new social rented building in the 1980s, resulted in the sharp fall in social housing's share of the total stock noted earlier. Moreover, as various studies showed, sales were selective, disproportionately involving the better portions of the stock and the better-off tenants, for example those in full-time employment in the more prosperous parts of the country, occupying single-family houses, rather than the unemployed and others on very low incomes living in inner cities or other declining areas, in high-rise flats with defects and a poor environment. In short, the sales policy contributed to the concentration of poorer households in social rented housing, living in poorer-quality housing projects (Malpass and Murie, 1987: 277–86; Forrest and Murie, 1988).

The extension of home ownership, which the right-to-buy policy involved, was the central objective of the Conservatives' housing policies in their first term. Policy towards the remaining council housing was mainly determined by the government's monetarist stance, with severe reductions in public expenditure. The government took up the mechanisms which the previous Labour government had fashioned, using them to exert even stronger controls to enforce reductions in investment and subsidies than Labour had intended. Using Labour's deficit subsidy system, but abandoning the requirement that local authority housing accounts should be non-profit making along with Labour's relatively low rents, the government rapidly increased the share of the deficit that had to be met locally, cutting the central government contribution. In the government's first term council house rents rose on average by 119 per cent, while retail prices rose by only 55 per cent (Malpass, 1990: 140). At the same time, central government subsidies fell by 84 per cent in real terms and by the end of the period most local housing authorities received no central subsidy for council housing. In principle, this rising requirement for a local contribution to support social housing could have been met from raising rents or from raising local taxation. However, the government also introduced the first of an increasingly stringent set of controls over local authority expenditure and taxation, ending local councils' freedom to set their own levels of local property tax and determine their own spending plans. The interaction between the new controls over local taxes and expenditure and housing subsidies was very complex, but it resulted in most of the costs of reduced subsidies being borne by tenants through rising rents. In addition, some councils began to make surpluses on their housing accounts which they could transfer to their general revenues. So council tenants subsidized local expenditure and other local tax payers.

However, this high-rent policy, together with the growing mass of low-income tenants in social housing, led to a major rise in the number of tenants dependent on means-tested housing allowances and in the cost of this provision. In 1976 less than 50 per cent of council tenants were dependent on allowances; this proportion had risen to two-thirds by 1985 (Malpass, 1990: 145). In short, there was a radical switch from all but the most limited subsidies for new investment in social housing to consumption subsidies. Interestingly, the latter were now regarded as a form of income support and were the responsibility of the Ministry of Social Security, not the Housing Ministry. This change symbolizes the transition from a mass needs social housing policy to a form of residual welfare provision for the economically marginal population.

While these changes occurred in subsidies for council housing, cuts were also made in the borrowing for capital investment permitted to the local authorities. A 30 per cent cut in 1980/1 was followed by another 15 per cent in the following year (Forrest and Murie, 1985: 103). By the middle of the decade capital spending was under half the level it had reached in the peak years of the

Labour government. Now over three-quarters of this expenditure was for improvements to the existing local authority stock and grant-aided improvements to the private stock, compared with only 20 per cent in the mid-1970s (Emms, 1990: table 1.9, 33). Increasingly, capital spending was financed from the receipts for council housing sales (at a rate also controlled by the government).

The government succeeded, therefore, in reducing council building to a trickle. Any new low-rent housing was to be provided by a small programme of building by non-profit housing associations. These were aided by capital grants which reduced the cost rents in new building to affordable levels and by some operating subsidies. The capital programme for the associations was increased in the first year of the Conservative government to a level which supported the construction of around 10,000–15,000 new houses per year, far less than the number lost by the reductions in local authority housing capital expenditure (Boelhouwer and van den Heijden, 1992: 180–1). However, this modest programme of housing association building became an increasingly important source of what new social housing there was. Association building accounted for about 10 per cent of all new social rented housing in 1975, but by 1990 it accounted for two-thirds. Meanwhile, the total social rented building programme had shrunk by 75 per cent (London Research Centre, 1991: 5; Boelhouwer and van den Heijden, 1992: 181).

By the middle of the decade these policies were beginning to run out of steam. The limits set by household incomes to the attempt to privatize council housing by individual sales were being reached. Moreover, as fewer and fewer local authorities received housing subsidies, the ability of the government to enforce higher rents was weakened, so rent increases tailed off. More generally, there was a recognition, first expressed by the some of the influential right-wing think-tanks that contributed to Conservative policy formation, that new means were needed to reduce the local authority housing role further. There was also a realization that there would be a continuing need for some form of rental housing for those who could not afford home ownership (Harloe, 1987: 199–202).

Therefore, the second stage of Conservative housing policies aimed to recreate a viable private rented sector, which would include non-profit housing associations and 'responsible' private landlords. Substantial changes were made in policies towards private rented housing, including the removal of virtually all effective controls over rents and security, and some assistance for new building through tax subsidies. However, the government was unwilling to provide the major subsidies for new investment by profit-making private landlords which would be required to achieve the revival of the sector. Moreover, few major private investors wanted to become involved in a difficult business which they did not understand. So, from the late 1980s, the main reliance for new social housing was placed on the housing associations, with efforts, which we shall describe below, to reduce the proportion of public investment and attract some of the private investors that had earlier refused to cooperate.

However, the most striking addition to housing policies, which began in earnest in mid-decade, was a concerted effort to transfer control of the remaining council housing stock to non-local authority landlords, such as tenant cooperatives, housing associations and the private sector (Harloe, 1990: 117–19). New legislation in 1986 began this process, although there was considerable resistance, for example, to proposals to transfer run-down estates to independent housing management trusts and little wish by tenants to exercise new rights to 'opt out' of local authority control. But further legislation occurred in a third stage of housing policy evolution after the 1987 election. These policies were part of a general assault on the remaining bastions of socialism, the Labour local authorities. More generally, they formed part of the policy of privatizing local authority and other welfare state services and the introduction of market mechanisms into those which remained, a radical alteration of the boundaries between the state and the market which affected almost every aspect of social provision.

The government paper which introduced the 1988 Housing Act spelt out the new role of the local authorities as 'enablers' rather than providers of social rented housing thus:

> the future role of the local authorities will essentially be a strategic one, identifying housing needs and demands, encouraging innovative methods of provision by other bodies to meet such needs, maximising the use of private finance, and encouraging new interest in the revival of the private rented sector (Secretaries of State for the Environment and Wales, 1987: 14).

A key element in achieving this objective, further limiting the scope for local authority housing activity and ensuring that the costs of social housing provision were met out of rents, not central or local subsidies, was the 'ring fencing' of local authority housing accounts, which was enacted in 1989. This prevented housing account surpluses from being used to reduce other local government expenditures or taxes. Instead, they were to be used to reduce central government expenditure on housing allowances. So, somewhat better-off tenants now subsidized income support for the less well off. As these subsidies were now chargeable against the local housing account, most accounts were again in deficit, as they had been in the early years of the government. The government was therefore again able to use its determination of the proportion of the deficit to be met locally, i.e. out of rents, to bring about a further rapid rise in rents and reductions in central subsidies.

At the same time, as already noted, changes were made in the subsidy scheme for the housing associations (Karn and Wolman, 1992: 173–4). These required the associations to find a proportion of the capital for new investment from private sector lenders at commercial interest rates. The aim was to 'stretch' a relatively small amount of government subsidy as far as possible. But the subsidy was much shallower than before, so rents had to rise. Changes were made in housing association rent setting to allow higher rents to be charged, and tenant security was reduced to the same limited level which applied to the private rented sector. These changes provoked a widening split within the national federation of housing associations between those who eagerly accepted the invitation from the government to become large, quasi-commercial providers of rented housing at higher rents, serving a mixture of low- and middle-income households, and those who retained a strong commitment to the provision of good housing at affordable rents for those in the greatest housing need.

Within this general picture of declining support for social rented housing and, more generally, low-income housing provision, there were only two areas where the Conservative governments of the 1980s developed new programmes. The first consisted of, on the one hand, a series of fragmented responses to the rising tide of homelessness, the product of the growth of poverty, and, on the other hand, reductions in the supply of low-rent housing. These policies included well-publicized initiatives to reduce the number of homeless people living and sleeping on the streets of the major cities, especially in London, which was the most visible consequence of the housing and economic policies which have been described in this chapter.

The second consisted of programmes to improve the physical and social conditions on the most deprived council housing estates (Emms, 1990: 50–9; Power, 1993: 224–8). These estates varied in their nature and location. Many were high-rise peripheral or inner-city, industrially built blocks dating from the 1960s and early 1970s; others were low-rise housing built at other times in these or other locations. A combination of bad design and location, a lack of maintenance and inadequate management plus the increasing concentration of low-income tenants in these projects resulted in a complex mixture of social, economic and physical difficulties. Problems such as crime, vandalism and the breakdown of the more settled social networks and structures which had existed on most social housing estates in earlier years added to the complex pathology of these areas.

The government funded a series of programmes which aimed to improve the management and physical conditions of the estates, many of which had high levels of empty, unlettable properties and rent arrears. It was in these areas, above all, that the effects of the reduction of social rented housing to a residual provision for the economically marginal were experienced in a concentrated form. In the 1980s the difficulties that the local authorities had in managing such areas, and their stocks more generally, were worsened by the lack of sufficient government funding for adequate management and maintenance. This was not offset by the relatively small amounts of special funding made available for the worst-off projects, so there was a steadily growing backlog of repairs and maintenance, exacerbated by the discovery of expensive defects in some of the industrialized schemes built in previous decades (Cantle, 1986; A. D. Thomas, 1986).

Work to identify the extent and nature of these areas, euphemistically called 'difficult-to-let' estates, had begun in the mid-1970s. In 1979 a pilot scheme, the Priority Estates Project, was started on three estates. By 1987/8 about 250 schemes were in progress or had been completed and a special unit within the Ministry, called Estate Action, was established to run them (Department of the Environment, 1984: 1987). The cost of the programme had risen from £50 million in its first year to around £190 million in 1989/90. However, this should be compared with an overall backlog of repairs and maintenance which ran into billions and which was increasing, according to an official source, at about £900 million per annum in mid-decade (Cantle, 1986: 80).[18] A key element in these remedial programmes was the decentralization of housing management to the estate level. Physical upgrading, remodelling of projects, environmental improvements and measures to improve security were all employed in flexible combinations adapted to local circumstances. In some cases an attempt was made to create jobs for local residents. However, the main objectives were

narrowly targeted on improvements in physical and social conditions and in management, not on linking these to local economic
development. Some Estate Action projects did result in major improvements in physical and social conditions and in management,
while others were less successful.

Some Estate Action projects involved the establishment of tenant
management cooperatives and the complete transfer of management
responsibility from the local authority. More generally, as we have
noted, encouragement for such transfers fitted in with the government's wish to run down the local authority housing management role. By the end of the decade there were about 120 tenant
management cooperatives (Emms, 1990: 58). Some had received
a great deal of publicity, especially those in Glasgow and Liverpool.
However, only a relatively few tenants appeared willing and had
the time and other resources to take control of their own housing,
so this remained a numerically insignificant development.

Following the fourth Conservative election victory in 1992, the
growing pressure on the local authorities to divest themselves of
their remaining stocks of social rented housing, and on the housing
associations to take over the major role as providers of a limited
supply of new social housing and as managers of much of the
former local authority stock, reached the point where many authorities began to accept the end of their role as social housing landlords and the confinement to a limited 'enabling' function. Now
some authorities began to set up housing associations to take over
their stock. For many this was seen as the only way to escape increasingly restrictive government controls on local authorities and
ensure that this source of social rented housing survived (Kleinman,
1993). In some respects British social housing had turned full circle,
back to the situation in late Victorian and Edwardian England
where the legitimacy of direct local authority housing provision
was not accepted and reliance was placed on a limited programme
of provision by non- or limited-profit organizations. What differed
a century later was, of course, the provision of some state support
for such organizations and substantial expenditure on means-tested
housing allowances.

While many of the changes which had occurred in the 1980s,
at least after the first impact of the right-to-buy legislation, had
met with little effective opposition from the other major political
parties, there were continuing attempts by pressure groups, by
expert commissions and others to argue for a change in direction,
involving reforms of housing subsidies (especially the regressive
home-owner subsidies) and more support for new investment in

social housing (Harloe, 1987: 1990). As the lack of affordable accommodation became more evident, especially after the widespread mortgage defaults and repossessions which accompanied the recession of the late 1980s and early 1990s, housing again became a somewhat more important issue, with increased media coverage, for example. However, no very coherent alternative to the government policies came from the two main opposition parties, Labour and the Liberal Democrats. In the 1983 general election Labour's opposition to council house sales had added to its unpopularity. In the mid-1980s the party drew up a new housing policy document which promised increased investment but was vague about the reform of subsidies and how the increased expenditure would be funded. Much emphasis was placed on the less costly extension of tenants' rights. Opposition to the right to buy was dropped, although Labour promised to replace housing lost from the social sector by this means.

Between the 1987 and 1992 elections both the Liberal Democrats and Labour continued to criticize the lack of new social housing and promised to increase investment, mainly by enabling the accumulated capital receipts from council house sales to be used for this purpose. The Liberal Democrats also campaigned for a radical reform of housing subsidies, ending mortgage tax relief for new house purchase and replacing it by a means-tested housing allowance for tenants and home owners. Labour also made much of the need to reform housing subsidies, in effect conceding the mistake which the party had made 15 years earlier. However, Labour was still vague about how it would change the system. Moreover, sensitive to the oft-repeated claim by the Conservatives that Labour was a party of high taxation, which helped them to win three elections (and in 1992 an unexpected fourth victory), a far more restrictive view was taken of the possibility that there could be a major expansion of social rented investment should the party regain office. Ironically, both before and after the 1992 election, it was successive Conservative administrations which began the long-delayed process of trimming away the tax subsidies for home ownership, helping to deepen the worst recession in the home-owner market that had ever been experienced in Britain. These changes did not result in resources being diverted into new housing investment or more adequate forms of support for low- and moderate-income housing consumers as, for example, the Liberal Democrats proposed. Rather, they were the outcome of a long campaign by Treasury officials, economic commentators and others who had regarded the growth of home-owner tax subsidies with disfavour, combined with the growing difficulties that public sector finances experienced as the recession took hold and there was a reversion to deep expenditure cuts and a deflationary macro-economic policy.

In the early 1990s the Audit Commission (1992), an official body established in the 1980s to oversee local authority expenditure and to make recommendations on how to achieve better 'value for money' in service provision, produced the latest of a series of reports on local authority housing services. Earlier reports had dealt with housing management, maintenance and policies towards accommodating the homeless. They were highly critical of deficiencies in all these areas. Now the Commission tackled the broader issue of how the local authorities could reshape their role and become 'enablers' rather than providers of social housing. Apart from its detailed findings and suggestions, the Commission's report estimated future housing needs and the likely supply, given current policies. It concluded that about 60,000–90,000 new units of social or other rented housing would be needed annually over the following decade, but that only 50,000–60,000 would be forthcoming, mainly from the housing associations. Moreover, the current and likely future level of capital expenditure by the local authorities on maintaining the 4 million or so homes that they still owned was inadequate.

The Commission examined various ways in which the authorities might stretch the meagre resources that they were likely to have available to meet rising needs for lower-income housing. Among the strategies suggested for raising more resources were increases in local authority rents (although, as the Commission noted, the net revenue gain, discounting the increased means-tested benefits that this would entail, would only be about 30 per cent of the gross increase), the use of capital receipts, and successful bids for special programme funding such as that allocated for Estate Action projects (although the Commission noted that bidding was expensive and time consuming, with no guarantee of success). The report also suggested that the authorities had to become experts in manoeuvring among a plethora of mainly small-scale and fragmented possibilities for obtaining modest additions to the supply of rental housing. First, there could be further gains in the efficiency of local authority housing management, ensuring that vacated properties were relet promptly and unauthorised tenants removed, for example (on some inner-city estates with high levels of unemployment, the illegal occupation of council housing had become a useful source of accommodation for those unable to gain access by conventional methods and a source of income for tenant 'landlords').

Second, the authorities could use the resources that they did have to support more housing association building, in exchange for an increase in nomination rights. They could also encourage lower-cost home ownership. Finally, there might be advantages in handing over the entire local authority housing stock to housing associations. The Commission reported that up to 130 local authorities were considering this option.

Despite these and other small-scale possibilities for the expansion of rented housing and for the repair and improvement of the existing stock, many would be extremely costly to pursue and administer. The bleak conclusion could not be avoided, as the Audit Commission (1992: 92) wrote:

> [a]ll of these steps would ease the difficulty that local authorities
> face in preparing and implementing their local strategies. But they
> would not change this report's central message, which is that current
> investment and the pursuit of best practice by the local authorities
> will reduce but not eliminate the shortfalls either in the provision
> of social housing, or in the maintenance of council housing and in
> the repair of private housing.

As we have noted, there was only a small growth in the American public housing stock after the mid-1970s.[19] Most additional directly subsidized low-income housing involved federally subsidized privately owned housing. By 1989 there were about 2.7 million such units, compared with 1.36 million units of public housing (US Department of Housing and Urban Development, 1992a: 3). The switch in emphasis away from public to subsidized private housing, as we have seen, began in the 1960s but the real turning-point occurred after the Nixon housing moratorium in 1973 and the establishment of the Section 8 programme in the 1974 Act. As Marcuse (1990: 353) comments, '[t]he 1974 act placed the private sector formally on the throne, even if it was not until the Reagan administration that it received its full purple robes, crown, and scepter'.

The Section 8 programme was designed as a step towards the Nixon administration's goal of abandoning construction subsidies for social rented housing and limiting assistance to income-related subsidies which would enable low-income households to rent privately. An elaborate housing allowance experiment was devised to test the validity of this approach. It generated a great deal of information and controversy, but appeared to show that supply-side subsidies were still essential because of the lack of adequately located, decent and affordable private housing, the unwillingness or inability of private landlords to upgrade their stock to minimally acceptable levels, and the pervasive effects of racial discrimination in housing markets (Struyk and Bendick, 1981).

Section 8 was a hybrid, containing elements of supply- and demand-side subsidies. Like housing allowances, it provided subsidies to meet the gap between the required rent (federally determined 'fair market rents' were used) and the proportion of tenants' income which, it was assumed, could be afforded for housing (set as 25 per cent of 'adjusted' income, later 30 per cent). However, like supply-side subsidies, the payments were made under long-term contracts to the landlords, not the tenants. Landlords were free to select tenants who met the income criteria for eligibility. The programme was supervized by local public housing authorities and only they could evict tenants. Some 30 per cent of tenants had to have incomes below 50 per cent of the area median, the rest could have incomes up to 80 per cent of this level (Fox, 1985: 214–15; Harloe, 1985: 194–5). Section 8 took two forms. First, the 'existing' programme involved already built units, thus coming closest to a pure housing allowance. Second, Section 8 payments could be used for new or substantially rehabilitated units, therefore coming closer to a housing supply subsidy. This second scheme resulted from Congressional concern that the supply of low-income housing was inadequate.

By the mid-1970s there were, therefore, three main low-income subsidized programmes: public housing, Section 8 new and Section 8 existing housing. The administration wished to terminate all new public housing construction (although Congress prevented this), subsidize as few new Section 8 units as possible and limit subsidies for Section 8 existing housing, until a pure housing allowance programme could be devised. As we shall see, there was considerable continuity between this policy and that later pursued by the Reagan and Bush administrations. However, while the Carter administration made no significant changes in the Section 8 legislation, it operated the programme in a rather different manner, expanding new production.

The Section 8 programme fitted into the more general framework for federal urban policies enacted in 1974. This swept away many categorical programmes, notably the urban renewal programme, and replaced them with a block grant to the localities for community development. This 'new federalism', echoing later developments in other countries, was promoted as a means of decentralizing decision-making power from the federal government to the

localities, enabling them to devise housing and other urban programmes best suited to local needs. In practice it was an attempt
to reverse the expanding federal involvement in urban policies.
A key aspect of this new policy, seen in the Section 8 scheme,
was to use limited amounts of public money to attract private
investment in the inner cities through public/private partnerships
(Fox, 1985: 210–20, 243–9).

This new emphasis was shared by the Carter administration
which added a further programme – Urban Development Action
Grants – to encourage the use of block-grant funding in public/
private partnerships. In sharp contrast to the Democratic administrations of the 1960s, the fiscally conservative Carter administration
sought to restrict federal urban expenditure, and rely on less costly
inducements to the private sector to underpin its urban policies.
Nevertheless, within narrow limits, there was an expansion of
federally subsidized housing provision, including some public housing and more extensive use of Section 8 new build/substantial rehabilitation subsidies. Public housing starts rose from a low point
of about 11,000 in 1978 to over 40,000 per annum in 1980 and
1981 (Marcuse, 1990: 353). Section 8 subsidies were provided for
around 225–250,000 new or rehabilitated units per annum between
1976 and 1980, while allocations for Section 8 existing housing
fell from around 200,000 to 90,000 (Dolebeare, 1992: graph 2).[20]
The use of Section 8 in this way was less a major policy decision
than a product of the influence of those in Congress, the Department of Housing and Urban Development (HUD) and elsewhere
who believed that there was a pressing need to increase the supply of low-income housing. Unlike public housing, new Section 8
units tended to house only those sections of the poor, such as the
elderly and, more generally, white households, that were seen as
less problematic to manage than, for example, minority families.[21]

However, the succeeding Reagan and Bush administrations returned to an even more radical implementation of the original
intentions of the 1974 Housing and Community Development Act
(Struyk, Mayer and Tuccillo, 1983). We have already noted the
cut-backs in federal expenditure and public housing output in the
1980s. The stated intention, only obstructed by Congress, was to
eliminate support for new supply and restrict assistance to a lower
level of support for existing housing than had occurred even in
the late 1970s. The administration fought a long Congressional
battle to change this form of support from Section 8 existing subsidies to housing vouchers, which provided less adequate support
with shorter-term contracts (five years rather than 15). Accordingly,

the allocation for Section 8 existing/vouchers fell from 90,000 in 1979 to 23,000 in 1982, it then fluctuated at levels of around 40–80,000 per annum into the early 1990s (Dolebeare, 1992: graph 12).

From the start of the Reagan administration there was a familiar scenario in Washington, in which the administration proposed the virtual elimination of almost all low-income housing programmes, except those necessary for the maintenance of the existing federally supported stock (see below), and low-income housing pressure groups and their supporters in Congress fought to preserve some low-income housing subsidies. These defensive struggles meant that there was no major new low-income housing legislation until 1990. Low-income housing policy was an obvious target for the Reagan administration. It established a commission of (friendly) experts to examine the low-income housing situation and make recommendations (The President's Commission on Housing, 1982). Its agenda was to recast federal housing policies in a New Right mould, with strong emphasis on deregulation and private market solutions, thus to 'create a housing sector that functions ... with minimal government participation' and to ensure that 'the genius of the market economy, freed of the distortions forced by government policies and housing regulations ... can provide for housing far better than Federal programs' (The President's Commission on Housing, 1982: xvi–xvii). The report asserted that federal low-income housing programmes had focused on housing production and were costly and inefficient. The problem was not inadequate supply but affordability. Hence, 'housing aid to the disadvantaged ought to take the form of a consumer-oriented housing payments programme to provide to the household the wherewithal to make its own housing decisions' (The President's Commission on Housing, 1982: xvi). This took the form of a small-scale programme of vouchers, but there was a grudging recognition that, in hard-pressed housing markets, localities might also need to support some new construction (Karn and Wolman, 1992: 227).

The Commission concluded that the federal government should withdraw from its involvement in public housing, transferring full responsibility to the localities and allowing them to decide what to do with the projects. The report highlighted the growing financial dependency of public housing on operating subsidies; thus operating costs had increased by around 220 per cent between 1969 and 1980. At the same time, the average incomes of public housing tenants had continued to fall, down from over 60 per cent of national median family income in 1950 to around one-third in 1969 and to 28 per cent by 1980 (The President's Commission on Housing, 1982: 33). A key problem was the substantial number of 'troubled' projects, especially among the large, older family projects.

The Commission outlined five options for dealing with the public housing stock: first, to retain the projects as public housing but with strictly limited operating subsidies; second, to sell the projects to private owners, including tenants, the proceeds from these sales to be reused for low-income housing assistance; third, to 'deprogram' projects that were unviable, selling them off with or without demolishing the units and providing the tenants with relocation assistance and income-related subsidies; fourth, to raise rents and eliminate the operating cost subsidy, restoring the position to that which had existed before 1969 – tenants would receive income-related subsidies, enabling them to remain in the units or find private housing; and fifth, to develop specially tailored solutions suitable to local circumstances.

In practice, the Reagan and Bush administrations were not able to make much headway with a radical reduction of the public housing sector and of federal involvement. Therefore, apart from the regular struggle to prevent the elimination of new construction subsidies, the main focus for the politics of public housing in the 1980s and early 1990s concerned the level of federal subsidies for operating costs and modernization. By the early 1980s there was considerable dissatisfaction with the Performance Funding System (PFS), which set operating subsidies, and the modernization programme (Struyk, 1980). According to a Congressional Budget Office report (1983: xiii), PFS probably underestimated some of the legitimate operating costs of the larger urban public housing authorities (thus compounding problems of undermaintenance and deteriorating finances). Moreover, the separation of modernization and operating subsidies encouraged public housing authorities to cut back on routine maintenance, thus solving short-run budgetary problems, in the belief that when projects had deteriorated sufficiently conditions could be made good through modernization funding. The large public housing authorities, in particular, argued that the modernization programme was insufficient. Furthermore, being discretionary, receipt of funding depended on the decisions of HUD bureaucrats and there was no attempt to develop a comprehensive approach.

The administration's answer to these problems was to replace the discretionary modernization funds by a formula funded approach, eliminating the worst 100,000 units and providing reduced support for the rest. This would be a part of a single federal sub-sidy, covering operating and modernization costs, whose level would be the same as that provided through the voucher system for private tenants. As the Congressional Budget Office (1983: 37, 55) pointed out, this took no account of the possibility that the costs of operating public housing, owing to the nature of its tenants and the services provided, might be higher. If implemented these proposals would have bankrupted many public housing authorities.

Essentially, the Reagan administration's approach to public housing was similar to that of the Thatcher governments. However, it had to accept the fact that wholesale privatization of the exist-ing stock was impractical, given the inability of most tenants to afford the purchase of their units and the unattractiveness of most projects to the private investor. In any event, a majority in Con-gress continued to regard the preservation of the existing stock of public housing, if not its expansion, as important, rejecting the administration's view that the supply of low-income private rental housing was adequate and that the only problem was affordability (Silver, McDonald and Ortiz, 1985; Karn and Wolman, 1992: 228).

In 1983 the administration tried and failed to implement its proposals for the recasting of public housing subsidies. Congress permitted only incremental modifications in the PFS.[22] At the same time it strengthened constraints over the sale or demolition of units. Subsequently, the administration accepted the reality of Congressional opposition to its more radical plans and settled for persistent attempts to chip away at PFS subsidies and eliminate all new construction. For example, in 1986 it tried (but failed) to freeze existing levels of federal assistance to low-income housing, cutting PFS by a sixth and stopping virtually all modernization. While Congress never accepted such draconian reductions, the financial fortunes of public housing depended on the outcome of an annual round of legislative lobbying by low-income and public housing pressure groups.

During the Reagan years the federal Department of Housing and Urban Development was a governmental backwater, having little political visibility or importance. Moreover, for most of the 1980s, housing was also low priority for the legislature. However, in later years this began to change, especially as a result of the rising numbers of homeless people on city streets and the growing visibility of campaigns on their behalf. These led to various forms of federal assistance. However, these programmes did not aim to expand the supply of affordable permanent housing; instead, for example, they financed temporary shelter provision.

The second important change occurred with the arrival of the Bush administration in 1989.[23] HUD was now headed by a politically ambitious former Congressman, Jack Kemp, who had a strong commitment to applying New Right politics to the resolution of inner-city problems. HUD adopted a far more active stance than it had under Reagan. Kemp's main objective, close to that adopted by the Thatcher government, was to expand low-income home ownership. The wider social and economic purposes behind this policy were expressed by him in 1989: '[h]ome-ownership is essential to the American dream, and by giving people an equity stake in their neighborhoods, we will introduce economic incentives and improve behaviour' (quoted in Karn and Wolman, 1992: 232). Previous federal programmes were seen as fostering dependency, but federal support for low-income ownership would spread the socially beneficial virtues of 'family self-sufficiency' (Stegman, 1990; US Department of Housing and Urban Development, 1992b).

Accordingly, the Bush administration's housing agenda combined that of the Reagan administration (restraining federal assistance and increasing deregulation), with an expansion of low-income home ownership, increased though inadequate support for homeless programmes, and more attention to the preservation of existing low-income housing, with a particular focus on improving conditions in the most 'troubled' public housing projects. The centrepiece of the Kemp plan was a programme packaged as 'Home-ownership and Opportunity for People Everywhere' (HOPE). This was to provide grants for low-income purchasers with a particular focus on sales of public housing and other vacant and foreclosed federally assisted properties.

At the same time, the swell of support within Congress for a new low-income programme led to a proposal to provide federal funding to states and municipalities for the production of new low-income housing (the HOME programme). After the usual lobbying, dealing between the administration and Congress and committee hearings, there emerged the first major housing legislation for many years, the 1990 Cranston–Gonzalez National Affordable Housing Act, which contained the, by now much amended, HOPE and HOME programmes (Housing and Development Reporter, 1990). The act provided $1 billion in 1991 and just over $2 billion in 1992 for local schemes to increase low-income housing supply, principally rental units. The HOPE provisions allowed more limited support for public housing home-ownership programmes of $68 million in 1991 and $380 million in 1992 (expanding small-scale experiments initiated in 1985 which had revealed many problems, including the lack of affordability of home ownership for most tenants (Rohe and Stegman, 1990)).[24] There were provisions to prevent involuntary displacement of tenants and to ensure that sales proceeds were reused for low-income housing purposes. Two smaller-scale programmes provided for sale of other federally owned stock to its tenants.

The administration placed a renewed emphasis on encouraging tenant management of public housing projects. As we noted, a few of these projects developed, with federal assistance, in the 1970s, but the number had not increased significantly in the following years. Most objective evaluations of tenant management highlighted the many difficulties that such projects faced and the limited resources and willingness of tenants to become involved in them (Manpower Demonstration Research Corporation, 1981; Peterman, 1989; Monti, 1989; Harloe and Martens, 1990; M. Chandler, 1991). However, the expansion of tenant management had obvious attractions to an administration bent on increasing 'family self-sufficiency'. In 1992 this led Kemp to put forward a programme entitled 'Perestroika for Troubled Public Housing' (US Department of Housing and Urban Development, 1992c). This measure, which failed in Congress before the administration left office, proposed a 'radical restructuring' of public housing, strongly reminiscent of some of the changes that the British Conservatives had made in council housing legislation in the later 1980s. Its target was the relatively few but large-scale public housing authorities that were in severe difficulties owing to the state of their stock and their finances. Modernization funds would be top-sliced to provide the programme funding. Tenants could opt out of public housing authority management in favour of non-profit or private landlords or establish tenant management corporations, with some funding for rehabilitation and redevelopment. Just management or management and ownership could be transferred. Meanwhile, several of the largest public housing authorities remained in a precarious state and the lack of adequate operating and modernization subsidies meant that a significant number of units remained vacant, unfit for habitation. Increasing concentrations of mentally ill people were located in some projects, following deinstitutionalization. Public housing was also used to accommodate homeless families. These changes added to the difficulties of public housing management (which remained generally poor) and of its tenants.

Taken together, the housing initiatives of the Bush administration amounted to a more determined effort than those of the Reagan administration to privatize public housing. In the last years of the Bush presidency there was a continual struggle between the administration, which wished to expand the HOPE programme and restrict the HOME programme, and the housing lobby, which wanted to achieve the opposite goal. There were, for example, challenges to the legality of HUD interference in properties which were owned by the public housing authorities and about the basis of compensation for lost units. More generally, it was argued that public housing home ownership would require massive federal subsidies. These would better be used to expand the number of assisted rental units.

American public housing remained what it had been for many years, a fully residualized sector. In the 1980s and 1990s rising low-income housing needs meant that the demand for public housing, especially for the better projects, remained high. Its tenants remained among the poorest in the nation. In 1992 HUD published an illuminating collection of statistics which compared the characteristics of tenants and units in the various federally subsidized low-income housing programmes (US Department of Housing and Urban Development, 1992a). This showed that public housing accommodated more black and Hispanic households than the programmes which subsidized private rental housing. Public housing tenants also had less formal education (over half did not finish high school) and three-quarters of all households were female headed. Public housing tenants had lower median incomes ($6571) than tenants in the two private sector programmes, vouchers and Section 8 ($7060 and $8074 respectively). Only one-third of public housing tenants gained their main income from employment, and most also received other assistance such as Food Stamps. About one-third of public housing tenants lived in large apartment blocks and public housing was concentrated (70 per cent) in central cities. Resistance to locating public housing in the suburbs had been intense, but was rather less in the case of Section 8 projects. There was a strong racial dimension to this resistance (Wacquant, 1992). About a half of all public housing tenants complained of poor neighbourhood conditions (mainly crime and litter/housing deterioration). The level of complaints was somewhat less among the other tenants; significantly, they were mainly concerned about noise and traffic.

Nevertheless, for many tenants public housing still offered better-quality, more secure and affordable housing than they could have obtained in the private sector (Bratt, 1985; Stegman, 1988). By the early 1990s there were about 1 million applicants on the waiting lists. But conditions in some of the larger projects were grim and worsened in the 1980s as poverty, crime, drug addiction and trafficking increased. In an article published in 1989, strikingly entitled 'Hell in a very tall place', an *Atlantic Monthly* reporter described conditions in some of the worst high-density, high-rise projects run by the New York City Housing Authority – generally regarded as one of the most effective and well run of the large public housing authorities (Vergara, 1989). The reporter visited 60 projects and 140 separate buildings. He notes that some projects were too dangerous for him to walk through, because of the location of 'crack supermarkets' in them. Tenants struggled to organize resistance to this development, but the most stable and active residents tended to move out eventually. Old people were particularly vulnerable, waiting for people whom they trusted to ride with them in the elevators, where much mugging occurred. In some cases any removable fixtures and fittings, including doors, were removed and sold to support drug habits. All the housing authority employees that the reporter spoke to believed that crime in the projects was getting worse and their task was becoming more difficult. Much of the change was attributed to the collapse of local industries and unemployment. Overall, the housing crisis had resulted in around 33,000 families sharing apartments without authorization and many more sleeping in roofs, stairways, basements and elevators. There were 180,000 on the waiting list (for a stock of 178,000 units, 94,000 of which were located in the poorest, most crime-ridden and physically devastated areas of the city). Federal cuts in housing and other welfare benefits, which had increasingly resulted in only the very poorest being aided, had accelerated the change from a mixed-income, mostly working population to dependent, female-headed households as working families, which now received no assistance and paid 'market-rate' rents, moved to private housing in better neighbourhoods.

The 1970s marked a turning-point in the fortunes of social rented housing in France.[25] As Barou (1992: 58) notes, the decade began with feverish levels of new construction, aided by large-scale subsidies, and ended in an atmosphere of doubt and questioning, with falling levels of construction and growing concern about conditions in the *grands ensembles*. The high building rates of previous years, plus declining birth-rates and slowing immigration, meant that, by the early 1970s, the crude housing shortage had been eliminated and a large part of the population was well housed – major achievements, given the state of French housing 20 years earlier. By 1978 there were almost 2.4 million rented HLM units, a 60 per cent rise since 1970, increasing the share of social rented housing in the stock by 40 per cent, to 13.3 per cent.

However, these aggregate statistics concealed a less optimistic picture, as the Nora report, which we mentioned in the last chapter, disclosed. As Barou (1992) demonstrates, in the 1950s and 1960s a disproportionate share of the new social rented units had not gone to 'families of modest resources' (as the legislation put it), but to better-off white-collar workers, whose numbers grew as the French economy modernized. As we have noted, HLM landlords ignored maximum income limits for admission and substituted minimum levels which excluded many poorer households. The requirement for balanced budgets and the lack of any general income-related housing subsidy encouraged this situation.

By the 1970s there were growing complaints that HLM housing had lost its social role (although this ignored what that role had always in practice been). In addition, there was disquiet about the huge blocks of high-rise, industrially built flats located on inadequately serviced peripheral sites – the *grands ensembles* or '*brontosaures*', as Barou calls them. Over the next two decades the social composition of HLM tenants changed radically. At first the new housing was occupied by newly formed households, with a high proportion of young white-collar and many skilled manual workers. But, as these households grew older and their incomes rose, they tended to move away from the increasingly unpopular *grands ensembles*, to be replaced by those population groups that had been excluded. As Blanc (1993) notes, this process was selective, affecting the least desirable estates most severely and creating vacant units which became a serious drain on HLM finances. HLM landlords were caught in a dilemma, fearing the management and financial difficulties that would be caused by a growing concentration of low-income tenants, yet finding that such tenants, with the aid of housing allowances, especially after 1977, were the only section of the population that still wanted to occupy their vacant stock. So they were increasingly forced to move in the direction that the government desired, changing from mainstream providers of housing to landlords of last resort for the urban poor (see Power, 1993 for a discussion of the management problems).

However, this transition was not evident to the many critics of the sector in the 1970s when the Nora report, published in 1975, and concerned with the problem of rehabilitation, established the basis for a radical reform of the housing policies which had led to the biased socio-economic composition of HLM housing (Nora and Eveno, 1975). Nora reported that, despite the elimination of the crude housing shortage, there were still 16 million poorly housed people in France, including a high concentration of the elderly and less-skilled workers. Although most of these households were in private housing, there was also a growing number in deteriorating units in *grands ensembles*. In 1973 an interministerial group had been established to examine this problem, leading to developments which we discuss below.

The Nora report reflected the shift in emphasis which occurred on the election of Giscard to the presidency in 1974, away from Pompidou's drive to modernize the French economy and society by means of large-scale initiatives towards a mixture of neo-liberal economics and a concern for the environment, preservation and human-scale development (which led to the cessation of huge social housing projects). There was a restricted concept of the state's role in welfare provision, targeting benefits on the poor. Accordingly, Nora concluded that housing subsidies were being misallocated, for new building rather than for rehabilitation, and for assistance of the better off rather than the poor. Nora claimed that the market could provide housing for most of the population. So state assistance should be restricted, targeted on the poor and on the rehabilitation of poor-quality housing.

This meant that a radical revision of housing finance and subsidies was required. The task was entrusted to the monetarist economist Raymond Barre, soon to become Giscard's Prime Minister, who reported in 1977 (*Revue de l'Habitat Sociale*, 1978; Boelhouwer and van den Heijden, 1992: 217–19). Many aspects of the Barre analysis echoed those made in the 1970s and 1980s in the other countries with which we are concerned: housing programmes were too complex, bureaucratic, rigid and centralized. Subsidies were poorly targeted and housing public expenditure had an inflationary effect. It would be more efficient to leave housing provision, in the main, to market forces. In the longer term all existing subsidies, including those obtained through the tax system, should be replaced by income-related allowances. These proposals were strongly opposed by the HLM federation, whose own report argued for an expansion of social housing construction to encompass a wide variety of household types and forms of tenure, and more state assistance for building and for housing consumers (Galarza, n.d.).

However, such criticisms had little effect. In 1977 the government initiated a new system of housing subsidies which subsequent Socialist and right-wing administrations maintained. The key principle was that housing provision should be largely a matter for the market, not the state. Consumer payments should more closely reflect the real price of provision, therefore rents and mortgage interest rates should be increased. Public expenditure should be reduced and redirected to those in the greatest need, by means-tested allowances, and to improving the stock. Home ownership should be promoted, especially among moderate-income groups, thus increasing choice, and the system of housing finance and administration simplified. As Galarza (n.d.) comments, the policy was predicated on a liberalization of rents. This was seen as the *sine qua non* for the efficient operation of the market. The new subsidies for rehabilitating older rental housing were short-term measures that would lubricate the transition of older inner-city areas from low- to high-rent neighbourhoods, with a corresponding change in their population. The administrative measures which aimed to decentralize decision making to the local level, accompanied by at least a rhetorical commitment to increasing public participation (a hallmark of Giscardian urban policies), could be viewed more cynically as an attempt to increase levels of social control and place greater responsibilities and burdens on the localities. However, in practice, the decentralization of housing policies in France was rather limited as, mainly for macro-economic reasons, housing finance and subsidies remained centrally controlled and allocated.

Various new loans were made available, tailored to these purposes (Papa, 1992: 119–35). Low-income non-profit construction, by HLMs or other organizations, was eligible for subsidized Prêts Locatifs Aidés, and grants were provided to meet around 20 per cent of the costs of renovating social housing (within a cost limit). Contracts were agreed between the state and the owners, setting out the terms under which this assistance would be available, including matters such as rent levels and allocation. Departmental Prefects were given wide-ranging powers to set the contract terms and to intervene if they were not adhered to (although, following pressure from the HLM movement, President Mitterrand later reduced this discretionary power). A key aspect of the new regime was that the construction subsidies incorporated in the new loans were much lower than in previous schemes, so rents were closer to market levels. However, the new units were targeted on poorer households. Thus a new system of more generous housing allowances, Aide Personnalisée au Logement (APL), was provided. At first APL was available only for new or rehabilitated housing subject to the new contracts. But it would gradually become universally available, replacing the more limited housing allowances that already helped some low-income households in the rest of the housing stock.[26] In some ways APL was like the US Section 8 subsidy, being paid directly to the landlord, not to the tenant. APL was also available for less well-off home owners who were in receipt of new types of subsidized loans aimed at increasing moderate-income owner occupation.

Over the following years eligibility for APL was extended and the costs of the subsidy rose rapidly. These costs were inflated by the growth in the stock eligible for subsidies (about half the units built after 1977), the policy of raising housing costs ever closer to market levels and the growing poverty of social housing tenants, hence their need for deeper subsidies.[27] Between 1980 and 1987 the number of recipients of rental APL rose from 47,000 to 861,000 (and home owners from 208,000 to 940,000) and the cost from around 1.2 billion francs to 19.7 billion francs. By 1986 about a half of all HLM tenants received one of the two main housing allowances (APL and ALF, Allocation Logement Familiale) and about 40 per cent of all rent payments were met by these subsidies (for comparison, about two-thirds of English council housing tenants got housing allowances, accounting for 50 per cent of the rent roll (Emms, 1990: 86)). The rising costs of APL, the costs of subsidizing renovation and the subsidized loans for lower-income home owners (which added considerably to the share of home ownership in the stock) resulted in a rapidly rising level of housing expenditure.

Undoubtedly, this unexpected outcome was affected by the break with the conditions of full employment and rapidly rising real incomes for most of the population which had existed in the 1960s and early 1970s. The assumption that such conditions would continue had provided the starting-point for Barre's assessment of what was needed to replace the state by the market in housing provision (Ghékiere, 1991: 147). As it turned out, the intention of the 1977 legislation, to reduce housing subsidies, clearly failed and their rising level became an ever more problematic issue for the government.

A further important change brought about by the Barre report was the gradual withdrawal of the state from the provision of housing loans and the increasing importance of private sector housing credit. In addition, the growth of an international and increasingly deregulated financial system, together with the ability of individual savers to shop around for the best rate of return, made maintenance of the traditional state-dominated system of housing finance, based on low-interest individual savings accounts, increasingly untenable (Ghékiere, 1991: 144–5). This was very important for the HLM organizations which relied heavily on cheap credit to build at affordable rents. The problem intensified after further deregulation was introduced in 1985.

The Socialists were elected in 1981 with a programme which promised to make housing a priority, to improve living conditions and boost employment.[28] They proposed a new land tax and, alongside the continuance of APL, new subsidies for construction and a reform of the indirect tax subsidies. They also proposed to reform landlord/tenant legislation. The government envisaged a rapidly rising level of new and rehabilitated HLM units. In fact, after 1982, housing expenditure became a principal target for austerity policies. Moreover, the plans to reform housing subsidies and taxation encountered opposition from inside and outside the government and were abandoned (Galarza, n.d.). In the early 1980s, however, the administration improved the level of housing allowances, along with other social benefits, and expanded efforts to deal with the problematic estates. But the only radical change concerned the private rented sector. New protection for tenants was introduced in 1982, amid strong opposition from the right and from landlords.

The brief period of right-wing government from 1986 to 1988 made few changes, apart from the suspension of the 1982 legislation on private rents and security, further deregulation of private housing finance and a weak attempt to raise the level of sales of social rented housing (which had long been possible but which was, in practice, insignificant). Clearly, housing was not a priority issue for government in the 1980s and, after its initial opposition to the Barre reforms, the formerly powerful HLM federation largely accepted them (Boelhouwer and van den Heijden 1992: 219).[29] In fact, as we shall see below, the most important developments now concerned conditions in the existing stock, not new construction.

Housebuilding was one of the hardest-hit victims of the economic recession of the early 1980s. Loans for new HLM building became a target for successive public expenditure cut-backs. Between the early and the late 1980s housing completions declined from just under 400,000 per annum to around 250,000–290,000, and new authorizations for HLM rented units fell to well below the levels that existed when the Socialists first took office, from around 60,000 to 37,000 in 1989 (HLM building for ownership fell even more, from 115,000 to 46,000). The overall share of housing starts directly subsidized by the state fell from 45 per cent in 1980 to 29 per cent in 1989 (Ghékiere, 1991: 130). Governments also struggled to trim the escalating bill for APL. Following an expert report in 1987, the level of APL for new entrants to the stock was cut while being maintained for existing tenants. The less generous ALF scale of assistance was also substituted for the more generous APL scale in the case of new units from 1988. However, this provision was also extended to all social rented tenants.

The post-1977 system of social housing finance and subsidies accentuated the difficulties that many social landlords had in balancing their budgets. The rapidly rising rents faced by HLM tenants who were not eligible for income-related assistance provided a strong incentive for them to move out, to buy their own units or to rent in the private sector, especially when they were located on the deteriorating, unpopular *grands ensembles*. Because of the poor conditions on some projects and because high rent levels reduced demand in some cases, the number of vacant units began to rise. There were also growing problems of rent arrears caused by rising rents and an increasingly low-income population. By the mid-1980s it was estimated that 35–40 per cent of HLM institutions were in financial difficulties (Boelhouwer and van den Heijden, 1992: 224). One response was to cut costs by reducing management and maintenance, thus aggravating the difficulties in the longer run. Another way of improving HLM organization finances was to impose a *sur-loyer* on higher-income households. In the 1980s an increasing number of HLM organizations did this, but it added to the pressures on better-off tenants to quit the sector.

The changes in the socio-economic composition of HLM tenants from the 1970s onwards are striking. As Barou (1992) shows, the proportion of families with children declined and the share of single persons and one-parent households rose significantly between 1978 and 1984. At the same time, most of the new movers into social housing came from less-qualified and younger sections of the population. One source of this demand was the rapid rate at which private rented housing was being converted to home ownership, with the aid of the new system of housing loans (Ghékiere, 1991: 131). Most of the outmigration from HLM projects was of better-off, middle-aged households, leaving an ageing lower-income population of long-term residents behind. The declining income and rent-paying capacity of HLM tenants is indicated by the fact that, in 1984, 59 per cent of them had incomes that were below the national median, compared with 48 per cent in 1978 (Emms, 1990: 95). By 1988 the concentration of an economically marginal population in social rented housing was even more clear cut. Thus the sector's share of all households in the bottom three income deciles had doubled between 1978 and 1988, from 9.9 per cent to

18.6 per cent (in 1978 low-income households were underrepresented in the sector, compared to their representation in the entire stock. By 1988 the position was reversed). However, data for 1984 to 1988 concerning the socio-economic composition of HLM tenants suggest that in this period of economic turbulence, high levels of unemployment and economic insecurity, the declining incomes of social housing tenants were now due less to differential migration than to a deterioration in the economic circumstances of those who had stayed in the sector.[30] Within the HLM sector, conditions varied a good deal, as Barou's (1992) more detailed analyses show. There was a contrast between newer APL-aided projects, where many of the poorest lived, and older projects, which retained a considerable proportion of longer-term residents paying rents which, though rising, were still relatively modest. In addition, although almost 95 per cent of the units were apartments, many older projects consisted of small blocks with fewer problems of environment or construction than the larger projects of the 1960s and early 1970s. About 25 per cent of all HLM units were located in the peripheral priority planning zones (Emms, 1990: 88). It was in these areas that most of the troubled projects were located.

A further important element in the changing circumstances of HLM housing was the growth of ethnic minority occupation (Blanc, 1992: 1993). Economic recession and high unemployment helped to ensure that many of the non-white migrants that had been sucked into the expanding French economy in previous decades remained trapped in low-wage employment or were unemployed. These groups became increasingly dependent on HLM, especially units whose rents were reduced with the aid of APL. By the 1980s many of these non-white occupants were not immigrants but had been born in France. However, official statistics only enable us to identify the proportion of foreign-born among the tenant population. These show that almost a half of all households whose head was born outside France or another EC country lived in social rented housing by 1989 (or 33 per cent of all non-French-born heads, up from 25 per cent in 1979) (Barou, 1992: 116–19). As Barou points out, the declining attractiveness of HLM housing for French-born households, who had enough income to choose another housing solution, plus the effects of high rents and APL, accelerated the outmigration of traditional residents and the inmigration of ethnic minorities and other low-income households. As he notes, this change vastly improved the housing situation of many ethnic minority households who had previously been dependent on the worst of the private rented sector. However, the combination of high rents and APL on post-1977 projects (including the modernized stock) meant that these became the estates on which the sharpest ethnic concentration occurred.

This change added to the financial and social problems of the HLM stock. The increasing ethnic mix led, on a significant number of well-publicized projects, to racial tensions and violence between white and non-white populations (Blanc, 1992: 1993). This situation was exploited by far right politicians, notably the National Front (which called in the 1988 presidential election for HLM housing to be reserved for French nationals). It also encouraged racially discriminatory allocation practices by landlords, concentrating non-white tenants in 'ghetto' areas, away from white tenants, or trying to avoid accepting them altogether. A further problem was the large size of many of these non-white households, leading to high child densities on projects and high levels of overcrowding in units which had been designed for smaller French-born families (Emms, 1990: 90–3). Only a minority of social rented housing consisted of such 'troubled' projects.[31] But the increasing frequency of out-breaks of disorder and violence in such areas, together with their growing social, economic and physical problems, came to dominate political and public attention. This served to accelerate the declining status and reputation of the sector as a whole and the re-shaping of large parts (though not all) of it as a residual tenure for the economically marginal population (see Blanc, 1993: 212, on the emergent 'two-tier HLM system').

As elsewhere, governments struggled to devise special programmes to alleviate conditions on the worst estates (Power, 1993: 79, provides a useful chronology). The first initiative, following the interministerial review noted earlier, occurred in 1976. This Habitat et Vie Sociale (HVS) project aimed to build partnerships between the various local and central bodies responsible for social housing projects and the services that they required, using exist-ing funding to improve conditions in about 80 of the worst-affected projects. The emphasis was almost entirely on physical improve-ments and little headway was made with resolving the underly-ing economic and social problems (Galarza, n.d.; Emms, 1990: 98–110; Power, 1993: 71–87).

According to Emms (1990), subsequent policy initiatives were largely driven by the politics of the situation, responding to media coverage and public and political criticisms which arose following outbreaks of disorder and violence. Thus in 1981 there was a wave of violence on several large estates. The government commissioned three expert reports, on youth, security and problem neighbour-hoods (Dubedout, 1983). The latter resulted in the transforma-tion of HVS into a larger programme under the Commission Nationale pour le Développement Social des Quartiers, led by its author, the Socialist mayor of Grenoble who had been involved in various local initiatives (in 1988 the Commission was renamed the Délégation Interministerielle à la Ville). Emms (1990: 98) describes this Commission as 'a political initiative to deal with an evident and serious problem, but one on which there was very limited quantified information about the nature and seriousness of the management problems which the HLM organisations were facing'. Although stress was placed on involving local residents in these initiatives, and some schemes did do so, more generally as Blanc (1993: 211–12) notes, HLM management remained paternalistic and authoritarian with little real tenant participation (inclusion of tenants on HLM boards, following legislation in 1982, made little impact on this situation).

The Commission aimed at a broad-ranging strategy of inter-vention to improve the social, economic and physical conditions and the management of projects. Its method was to coordinate action by the long list of Ministries (11 in all) that had some stake in service provision in these areas, together with the local authorities and the HLM landlords. Much emphasis was placed on decentralized decision making and there was a strong representa-tion of local politicians on the Commission. But project funding was drawn from the existing budgets of the Ministries, with the lion's share being housing subsidies for the improvement of the dwellings. In many cases the hoped-for coordinated approach did not emerge and sectional interests prevailed. In any event, co-ordinating the programmes and priorities of so many agencies proved an almost impossible task, and the attempt to turn round projects, whose main difficulties were caused by more fundamental social and economic changes, through small-scale targeted pro-grammes proved inadequate in most cases (for an exception see Stébé, 1993). By the early 1990s the programme was generally acknowledged to be a failure, at least with respect to its wider social and economic objectives.

By the end of the 1980s it was recognized that, owing to the economic changes, there was an increasingly polarized social struc-ture in France. While most people remained in employment and some continued to enjoy rising standards of living, a growing mass were trapped in poverty, living in poor housing or being homeless. In addition, by now, many moderate-income households had increasing problems of housing affordability. Decontrol of private rents by the 1986–8 government had added to the long-term trend of rising housing costs and housing cost/income ratios.[32] At the same time, new units were standing empty because they were unaffordable by those in the greatest housing need. Generally, there was a rapid increase in the number of homeless households, estimated at 20,000–25,000 in Paris alone by the early 1990s (Boelhouwer and van den Heijden, 1992: 227).

In 1989 an official report noted the impact of the economic changes in reducing housing access for low-income groups, who were becoming economically and socially marginalized, including many who were now in difficulties with the mortgages that they had taken out on new HLM ownership units. The report stressed the need to expand the housing programme to around 300,000 units per year and to target the type of housing constructed and its cost levels at less well-off households (output had become increasingly targeted at the better off in the previous decade). It also stressed the need for more social rented housing, to develop a coherent system of local housing planning and to counter social, financial and ethnic segregation (Boelhouwer and van den Heijden, 1992: 226–7). However, despite various promises concerning new funds for housing provision in the late 1980s and early 1990s, these had to be contained within the overall austerity policies of the government. So, in practice, they amounted to little and the main focus of housing policy became an enhanced attempt to target expenditure at the least well off. In 1990 funding was made available for a small-scale programme that enabled HLM organizations to purchase older, cheaper (and poorer-quality) private rented housing and let the units, unimproved, at modest rents. HLMs were also empowered to take over the long-term management of private rented units.

In the last crisis-racked years of the Socialist government, before its stunning defeat in 1993, there was a plan to expand the housing programme and raise the share of social rented housing. Although in 1990 the government did announce an increase in the housing budget, this was later cut back. More attention was paid to other elements in the 1989 report's recommendations. Thus, while the decentralization initiative of the early 1980s had not encompassed housing finance and subsidies, there was a subsequent growth of forms of local housing planning. This was given further impetus by urban disturbances in suburban Lyons and Paris in winter 1990 involving young ethnic minority and white residents on some of the most disadvantaged *grands ensembles*. These events inspired the 1991 Loi d'Orientation pour la Ville which formalized local housing planning requirements and made them obligatory for large urban areas and certain other high-growth localities. It also extended the programme of special treatment for social housing estates and appointed a new Minister for Cities (without a Ministry) to coordinate the drive against social 'exclusion'. Extending the notion of contracts introduced in 1977, local housing plans were to contain an agreement between local and central government, based on the assessment of local needs and programmes which targeted public resources on those in the greatest need. However, early evaluations of these plans suggested that they had not so far had much impact on government funding allocations and so were not taken very seriously by most local politicians. Moreover, there was little opportunity for public involvement in the planning process and few localities had either the staff or the skills to prepare plans. Whether the 1991 law would eventually improve the situation remained doubtful (Laboratoire du Logement, 1991; Goodchild, Gerrichon and Bertrand, 1992).

Alongside these developments, several other limited changes were introduced in the late 1980s and early 1990s in response to the low-income housing crisis and the increasing financial difficulties of HLM organizations. Low-income tenants and those in receipt of social security benefits received new housing allowances which enabled them to pay their rents, and HLM organizations were able to write off accumulated rent arrears. Some extra assistance was also provided for basic improvements in low-rent housing, with low-income occupancy conditions attached (Boelhouwer and van den Heijden, 1992: 228–9). In addition, the 1990 Loi Besson required *départements* to draw up plans (Plans d'Occupation du Patrimoine Social) for housing low-income households and established a 'Housing Solidarity Fund' to be used in conjunction with the plans, extending and giving a legal status to earlier existing funds which assisted in the payment of rent arrears and provided rent guarantees for poor tenants of social and private rented housing. The Fund could intervene in various ways: not only could it prevent some of the worst-off households from becoming or remaining homeless, but it could also shore up the finances of low-income landlords that were suffering from rising rent arrears. There were no general rules for eligibility; cases were reviewed by a committee of officials which had discretion in whether or not to provide help (OPAC des Vosges, 1992). The perception that there was a growing section of the population which was being marginalized or excluded from mainstream society by contemporary economic developments, heightened by concern about the continuing outbreaks of disorder and the rise of the National Front, and the need to reintegrate such groups within mainstream society, provided much of the impetus behind these policies. However, they were accompanied by a continuation of the fiscal austerity which had characterised the Socialist governments since 1982. Moreover, as Ghékiere (1991: 148) points out, such measures to refocus resources on low-income households raised questions about how the housing needs of middle-income groups, which had also suffered in the previous decade, would be met.

As we saw in the last chapter, the basic framework within which West German housing policies had evolved was settled in the immediate post-war years.[33] Direct state intervention in the market, through subsidies for social construction and rent and security controls, was regarded as a temporary response to the post-war emergency. Even the federal housing ministry was regarded as a temporary agency (and plans to abolish it were almost implemented in the early 1960s, when the housing emergency was officially declared at an end). So the decline in social rented housing output was built into policy from the outset (Novy, 1991). Moreover, much of this housing was built by private investors and would leave the sector when the 'socially binding' conditions that were attached to the receipt of subsidies expired. However, the majority of the social rented stock was owned by the non-profit housing landlords, whose tax-exempt status provided a second and apparently permanent form of assurance that their stock would remain in the social rented sector. The non-profits had a significant influence on housing policy, with links to the trade unions (notably through the biggest non-profit, the trade union Neue Heimat) and the SPD, but also to the Christian Democrat bloc.

As we shall see, this system was broken up in the 1980s and further affected by the dramatic events accompanying German reunification. However, as we noted in the last chapter, in the early 1970s housing and urban policy had been a high priority for the Brandt government. The aim was to expand production, including social housing, but with an increasing emphasis on social owner occupation. But, following the transition in the German economy and economic and social policies after the mid-decade recession, output declined more or less continuously. By the early 1980s it had fallen to about half the 1973 peak of over 700,000, rising to about 400,000 in 1984 and then collapsing to a little over 200,000 by 1988. Finally, under the impact of new measures to alleviate housing shortages, it rose to 315,000 by 1991.[34]

Recession and the austerity policies adopted by the Schmidt government between 1976 and 1982 accelerated the long-term shift away from large-scale direct state intervention to expand the supply of housing for the mass of the population, towards a more limited policy, supplementing market provision and targeted on low-income groups. This shift was reinforced by earlier high levels of building and the high costs of construction and finance. By mid-decade, rising costs resulted in a rapidly accelerating public expenditure bill and rising numbers of vacant, high-cost, new rented and owner-occupied properties. The official conclusion that the crude housing shortage ended in 1976 provided an additional rationale for cutting social housing completions by a third between 1975 and 1982, to just below 100,000 (Papa, 1992: 60).

Like other governments, the Schmidt administration adopted two main methods of refocusing its housing policy. First, it placed increased emphasis on means-tested housing allowances as a way of targeting assistance on the poor.[35] Second, it switched from subsidizing new building to tax-subsidizing housing improvements in the older stock, where many of the poorer households lived. However, as elsewhere, the wave of housing improvement which then occurred frequently involved gentrification and the displacement of existing low-income tenants by better-off tenants or owners. This became a potent source of community-based activism in many German cities in the ensuing years (see, for example, Katz and Mayer, 1985). These changes were broadly in line with the policies advocated by the opposition CDU/CSU, although they would have gone further than the government in cutting back demand subsidies, prioritizing home ownership and relying on housing allowances for aiding the poor. From 1980, when the FDP had an increased influence within the administration and the new recession led to further pressure on public expenditure, the movement towards a market-led housing policy accelerated under the aegis of the FDP Minister for Economic Affairs, Lambsdorff (whose own, more radical, proposals for the reorientation of housing policy were later implemented).

The switch from a mass to a targeted federal housing policy was accompanied by an increasing concern about the 'misallocation' of social rented housing, that is, the extent to which housing was unavailable for poor households due to its continued occupancy by better-off tenants (Ulbrich and Wullkopf, n.d.). Of course, as in France, this was no accidental outcome of social housing policies which had been targeted on the 'middle mass' of the population and had fostered the development of social housing organizations which, with some exceptions (notably those controlled by city governments), did not see the provision of housing for the poor as their principal role. But proper regard for this history did not prevent the growth of criticism about the non-profit sector's lack of a truly social role during the 1980s. In 1982 the Schmidt government introduced legislation which enabled Land governments to impose an additional rent on 'over-income' social housing tenants. The proceeds were to be used for additional social housing construction. This provision was gradually adopted by most Länder during the following decade, partly because it provided some badly needed finance for social housing. A further criticism of social rented housing was the lack of rent harmonization. The strict policy of 'cost' rents meant that better-off tenants in older social housing, with rents which reflected historic costs, benefited, while new units with high cost rents were unaffordable by low-income households. As Ulbrich and Wullkopf (n.d.: 4) explain, the problem could have been resolved by rent pooling. This had been advocated from the 1960s onwards, but the influence of longer-established tenants on social housing management and on the politics of social housing prevented the change from occurring.

More significant changes, which worked in the opposite direction, were also introduced by the government in 1980 and 1982. These enabled social landlords to accelerate the repayment of their subsidized loans (which originally had a 60-year term). According to Ulbrich and Wullkopf (n.d.: 6), '[t]his legislative change was more concerned with short-term finance rather than high principle'. It reduced the average outstanding repayment period from 30 years to 15 years, thus bringing forward the time when there would be a rapid privatization of social housing. Between 1981 and 1986 about 760,000 units left the social rented stock for this reason (Häussermann, 1991: 11).

Summarizing the shift in policy in the 1970s, Boelhouwer and van den Heijden (1992: 126) conclude that, compared with the beginning of the decade, by 1980 'housing was obviously on the political defensive'. They cite several reasons for this: the growth of a market-oriented culture within government, especially as a result of the FDP's influence, and the impact of the oil crises of 1973 and 1978 on economic policy and the purchasing power of households. They note: 'at the beginning of the 1960s there were seemingly hardly any financial limits to policies of reform, whereas at the end of the 1970s the reduction of the national debt was the paramount political issue'.

The centre–right coalition government which came to power in 1982 soon announced a further reduction in the federal housing role. It stated that, with the end of the crude housing shortage and rising incomes, most people would now be served best by the private market (aided by enhanced tax subsidies). Moreover, as elsewhere, this policy of central government disengagement was accompanied by the wish to decentralize (or rather, devolve) residual responsibilities for lower-income housing provision to state and local governments. Again, the possibility of abolishing the federal housing ministry was considered, although it survived (Novy, 1991; Heinz, 1991). The centrepiece of government policy was the promotion of home ownership and private sector building for ownership and rental (Boelhouwer and van den Heijden, 1992: 127–30). Private sector rent controls were eased. This had the effect of increasing rents at a faster rate than inflation, in the hope of stimulating private building. Despite relatively favourable economic conditions in the second half of the 1980s, this did not happen, however, mainly because investors had been caught after the 1970s boom with large stocks of unsold housing and they were extremely cautious about the future level of demand for new housing, given projections of a falling national population over the next decades. Nor was the policy of expanding home ownership to a 50 per cent share of the housing market successful. In the 1980s it was simply too costly for many households. Instead, they competed for the limited supply of affordable rented housing.[36]

In contrast to its intended expansion of aid to the private market, the government cut back further on subsidies for new social housing and increased the share of these units that were for home ownership. By 1988 production was down to about 41,000 units, a quarter of the 1970 level, and under half the level which had been constructed in 1980. Many state governments, including those run by the SPD, followed this pattern. In 1988 federal subsidies for new social rented construction were abolished. In future the federal government would only support new social construction for home ownership (and at a steeply declining level); any new social rented housing would have to be subsidized by the states and localities. It was argued that as there was no longer an overall dwelling shortage and as incomes were rising, public assistance could be concentrated on low-income home ownership (always the CDU preference, as we have seen), leaving the less well off to be more selectively and effectively supported by housing allowances (Häussermann, 1991). However, very few households claimed these allowances: a Düsseldorf study showed that over 80 per cent of eligible households failed to claim (Häussermann, 1991: 13). Moreover, the allowances mainly benefited the elderly, being, in effect, a form of supplementary pension, and not the growing mass of younger low-income households (although the latter's share grew in the 1980s, with rising poverty among those still in employment and long-term unemployment). Finally, the assistance was insufficient, excluding heating and other service costs and still leaving recipients paying a higher share of their incomes for housing than other households. In the 1980s, as many household incomes stagnated or grew far more slowly than hitherto, and as rents, especially in the degressively subsidized stock, increased faster than the growth in incomes, the deficiencies of the federal housing allowance led to the development of supplemental rent allowance schemes, financed by state and local governments.

Behind these policy changes there was, as Jaedicke and Wollmann (1990) reveal, a more radical debate within the coalition government about the future of social rented housing and the non-profit sector (Ulbrich and Wullkopf, n.d.; Krätke, 1989). One important factor was the increasing influence of neo-liberal economic ideologies and the New Right, with the emphasis on the political and economic benefits to be gained from the free market and the inefficiency, restrictiveness and bureaucracy of welfare state institutions. The social housing landlords were an obvious target for such a critique. We have already referred to the growing concern about the 'misallocation' of social housing but, as elsewhere, there was also widespread criticism, across the political spectrum, of other aspects of the social housing system. One of these concerned the rules for determining 'cost' rents which in fact enabled the social landlords to accumulate large surpluses. While the non-profits could not distribute these as dividends (beyond the modest level of 4 per cent on shareholders' own capital), they could be used for empire building, and to pay high salaries and fringe benefits. Several of the non-profits, but especially the largest, Neue Heimat, diversified into a range of building, planning and other urban development activities, in Germany and elsewhere, that enhanced the status and salaries of their executives but were far removed from the original purposes of the non-profit housing organizations.

Of course, the associations and their well-financed federation rejected such criticism. However, once the post-war housing crisis had ended and it seemed likely that the housing needs of the majority of the population could be met by the private market, the powerful political position of the non-profits began to weaken. On the one hand, some critics could no longer see any rationale for social housing organizations with a special mission, enshrined in legislation, which provided them with certain privileges in relation to private landlords, notably exemption from taxation. On the other hand, there was criticism from a younger generation on the left, many of whom were involved in the community-based movements in German cities in the 1970s and 1980s, that the non-profits were organizations that served their managers and the professions rather than those in housing need, and that they were quasi-capitalist rather than decommodified housing providers (G. Winter, 1979; Krätke, 1989). Moreover, over time, the initial restrictions on the size of social rented units and the other uses to which surpluses could be put were eroded. Profits could be reinvested, for example, in housing for sale and commercial building, or invested in stocks and shares. Many of these developments had occurred with the sanction of SPD governments.

There was also concern about the lack of tenant involvement in management and that most new social housing had become far too expensive for those in the greatest housing need. In fact, much of the non-profit housing stock was in competition with the private sector for the middle-income households that many of its managers preferred to house, if only because they could meet the high rent levels. Local authorities were largely powerless to intervene in allocation procedures. Though they had nomination rights to some non-profits, most of the households in the greatest housing need, for which the authorities had to find accommodation, were rehoused in the authority-controlled communal associations. Even when the authorities did have nomination rights to other than their own non-profits, they had to nominate three tenants for each vacancy, from which the landlord selected one. According to Häussermann (1991: 8), in 1989 the local authorities had nomination rights for 1.6 million social rented units. The landlord chose the tenants for the other 3 million units, paying close attention to rent-paying capacity, the absence of social or personal problems and the ethnic origins of applicants (Kreibitch, 1986).

The gradual disintegration of support for the non-profits was brought to a head by the collapse of Neue Heimat, as a result of corruption and mismanagement in the 1970s and early 1980s, when its top managers embarked on increasingly risky for-profit developments (which were legal, provided that the profits were not distributed) and also embezzled large sums for their personal benefit: as Ulbrich and Wullkopf (n.d.: 7) put it, 'losing touch with commercial reality and succumbing to megalomania' (see also Power, 1993: 132–42). When it collapsed Neue Heimat had debts of 17 billion DM (*Financial Times*, 11 August 1986). The collapse caused enormous embarrassment to the trade unions and the SPD. The unions had to sell their bank and insurance company in order to meet the losses incurred. Further odium was heaped on the unions after a bizarre attempt in 1986 to sell Neue Heimat to a Berlin bakery owner for 1 DM. Eventually the stock of about 300,000 units was disposed of in a piecemeal fashion to other non-profits and state governments.

Meanwhile, the government was split between those such as representatives of the labour wing of the CDU and the Housing Ministry who wanted to retain non-profit organizations but strengthen their commitment to the social housing role, and the neo-liberals who argued that these organizations' privileged tax status provided an unfair advantage which ought to be ended. Their aim was a free market in housing, with no subsidies or rent controls. The contention was that any increase in rents which this produced would lead to an enhanced supply of housing, making the rise only temporary. Moreover, greater economic efficiency and intensified competition would be to the eventual benefit of tenants (Krätke, 1989; Novy, 1991). The first group proposed that the non-profits be required to contract with the local authorities to house people on the local waiting lists. In exchange for accepting this social role, the tax benefits would be retained. When proposed by a government commission and the Länder in 1984 this proposal was strongly opposed by the non-profits, who had no wish to be shifted from their traditional role as housers of middle-income households with only a limited commitment to housing those on the lowest incomes and in the greatest housing need. Instead, the associations argued for the maintenance of their tax-free status but a greater degree of freedom to charge higher rents in the older properties in order to cross-subsidize new units. However, they also wanted to retain rules for determining 'cost' rents which would still allow substantial surpluses to be generated.

Eventually, the debate was resolved along neo-liberal lines. Apparently the decision, in 1988, to abolish the tax-privileged status of the non-profits (except for cooperatives) was something of a coup by the neo-liberals. The federal Housing Minister was not involved in the decision, which was taken as part of a wider-ranging reform that aimed to reduce tax subsidies across the board. The immediate circumstances of the decision are explained by Ulbrich and Wullkopf (n.d.: 7) thus:

the Finance Minister, Stoltenberg, committed himself to cutting the subsidy bill ... he tried to cut the subsidies for shipbuilding, but failed: his own constituency relied heavily on shipbuilding! He then turned to the not-for-profit housing movement, drawing attention to the tax concessions that it received – even though they were trifling compared with other tax concessions. The Government and the Christian Democratic Party were far from united on the issue, but the combination of the Neue Heimat 'scandal' and a widespread belief that there was no longer any housing shortage tipped the balance.

Perhaps unsurprisingly, given the negative image of the non-profits, there was little opposition to the virtual abolition of the sector. And the non-profits were divided: many welcomed the changes because they were no longer tied to the 'socially binding' non-profit rules. They were now free, as private sector organizations, to make profits and to compete with the private market for the more solvent demand. The only remaining restrictions were the temporary obligations, now rapidly running out, imposed through the subsidy system. One consequence of the abolition of non-profit status was the creation of a new set of private landlords with large assets that had been built with the aid of subsidies. Some shareholders, who had had no right to this capital or to more than a very restricted share in the non-profit income, received large windfall benefits. There was a growth in speculative trading in shares of the former non-profits (Novy, 1991).

Therefore, by the late 1980s the social housing sector was in dissolution. Essentially, there were now three separate groupings. First, there were the social rented dwellings which were owned by 'traditional' private landlords. These were rapidly falling out of the sector, as the socially binding conditions expired, becoming a part of the private rented sector with market-level rents. Second, there was that part of the non-profit sector which had retained this status, the cooperatives. Most cooperatives were small scale and highly selective in their dwelling allocation, excluding low-income applicants in favour of more 'respectable' and solvent sections of the population. As Häussermann (1991: 12) comments:

[t]hose who are members of cooperatives have a permanent right to occupancy and can even bequeath it to others. The cooperative may not make a profit, the members take part in management. Because of their internal structure, however, cooperatives are socially very selective and require a commitment of personal capital and social competence which the weakest groups on the housing market usually do not possess.

Finally, there were the newly privatized former non-profits. As we have noted, many of these were now certain to follow the path of the first group, shedding their social role and becoming normal commercial landlords. However, within this group there was a wide range of ownership, including the local authorities and socially oriented organizations such as the churches that retained a commitment to housing those in the greatest need.

The radical steps taken in the 1980s to reduce the scale of the social rented housing sector resulted in a more rapid and extensive privatization than that achieved by the other main proponent of this approach, the British Conservative governments. Thus, of the stock of around 4 million social rented dwellings existing in 1984: 1.5 million were owned by private landlords and so would join the private market, at an accelerated rate after the changes which occurred in 1980/2. Cooperatives accounted for about 30 per cent of the 2.5 million units owned by non-profits, so about 800,000 units retained non-profit status after the changes in 1988, but, as we have noted, without any commitment to serving those in the greatest housing needs (or even to serving a mixture of middle- and lower-income households). This left about 1.7 million units owned by the former non-profits, many of which also seemed destined in the 1990s to rejoin the private market. According to Krätke (1989: 286), on the basis of data from 1983/4, about 700,000 of these units were owned and managed by the local authority-owned social housing companies (although they also managed many units which they did not own). These would remain as social housing. The outcome of changes within this last sector are hard to predict but it was expected that by the mid-1990s the social rented sector would be half the size that it had been a decade earlier, and still declining. According to one estimate, by the year 2000 there would be, in all, about 1 million social rented units (Häussermann, 1991: 12).

One consequence of this sharp reduction in the sector was likely to be a growth of social segregation in German cities. Unlike some of the other countries with which we are concerned, prior to this period there had been relatively few areas of concentrated low-income settlement in social rented housing. This was a positive consequence of the allocation policies which we have described. In fact, the largest low-income concentrations occurred not in social housing but in areas of older inner-city accommodation, which had, for example, housed many of the migrant workers that had come to Germany in the 1960s and 1970s. One consequence of the switch from new housing to subsidies for renovation that occurred from the mid-1970s was the gentrification of some of these areas, and a growth in the low-income demand for social housing by those who were displaced. Increasingly, such households concentrated in those newer, peripheral social rented estates which were costly and unpopular, with the loss of better-off households who could move elsewhere (and who were not eligible for rent allowances to reduce the high rents) (Emms, 1990: 153–83; Power, 1993: 127–31). The loss of much of the social rented stock following privatization seemed likely to accentuate this development. Moreover, conflicts between ethnic minority residents and white households similar to those that occurred in France were also happening in Germany in the late 1980s and early 1990s. Much of the support for the ultra-right Republican party came from such areas (Häussermann, 1991: 17).

In a detailed study of the effects that these changes were having on the low-income housing market in Hanover, Kreibitch (1986) concluded that by the early 1990s the local authority would only have about half the social rented stock that it had had in 1977 available for allocation to those in the greatest housing need. Much of this housing, mostly owned by the local authority's own housing association, would be on unpopular peripheral estates. According to Kreibitch this 'assignment' housing would 'serve the same problematic purpose as council housing in Great Britain', as 'a second-class service which caters for the less skilled and unemployed', a residualized form of provision (see also Kreibitch, 1991, on Cologne). The problems of these areas were first recognized towards the end of the 1970s when the German Association of Cities coined the term 'estate in crisis' to describe them (Schuler-Wallner and Wullkopf, 1991). In 1985 there was an investigation into the large, high-rise, high-density, peripheral social housing estates which had been built in the 1960s and 1970s. A total of 233 such estates (having 500 or more units per estate) were identified, covering 500,000–600,000 units; about 450,000 of these were social rental units, 10 per cent of the total social rented stock, but half of all such housing built between the mid-1960s and the mid-1970s. Local authorities had nomination rights to about 60 per cent of these units (Emms, 1990: 153–84; Grieff and Ulbrich, 1991). The estates were not popular places to live, and were especially disliked by families with small children.

By the 1980s there was increasing evidence of structural defects and of the concentration of 'problem' families in such areas. These families were frequently in severe and urgent housing need, so the local authorities tended to relocate them in the least popular social housing where vacancies most frequently occurred. However, unlike France or Britain, for example, there was no significantly funded national programme to deal with the problems of these areas, only scattered experiments and local initiatives. Most social housing management remained resistant to developing new, less bureaucratic and more participative structures. To some extent the concern about these estates, particularly on the part of their non-profit landlords, was linked less to the underlying social and economic problems of their inhabitants than to the appearance of vacant units in the first half of the 1980s, when the housing market was roughly in balance, as those tenants that could move out did so and others declined to move in. This created a financial problem for the landlords, hence their wish to make some improvements. When the housing market again became tight in the late 1980s the concern to improve conditions tended to fade as the vacant units filled up.

Just at the point when the federal government stopped assisting new social rented housing construction in 1988, evidence emerged of a new housing shortage, especially in the bigger cities (Ulbrich and Wullkopf, n.d.; Schuler-Wallner and Wullkopf, 1991).[37] Soon public and media attention began to put pressure on the federal government for some response (Catterall, 1990). According to Häussermann (1991: 9–11), there were several causes of the 'new housing need'. First, the existing supply of dwellings was less than the estimate accepted by the federal government when it decided to stop assistance, as a 1987 housing survey subsequently revealed. Second, the demand projections were also wrong. These assumed a slowly declining population, whereas the flood of immigrants from Eastern Europe and the GDR, plus the rising headship rates of the West German population, more than compensated for any decline. Much of this new demand was for low-income housing. Third, the falling rate of private and subsidized construction contributed to the lack of supply. Moreover, while low-income demand grew especially rapidly, an increasing share of new production was for higher-income households. Häussermann estimated that in 1990 the supply of low-income social housing was about half what was needed, if the latter figure was based on income eligibility criteria (and this did not take account of 'over-income' tenants in the existing social stock).

The growing housing shortage and high rents affected not just the very poor, but also many younger households with moderate incomes entering the housing market for the first time, especially in the bigger cities and the more prosperous regions. By the end of the 1980s it was estimated that about 800,000 households in West Germany were homeless, or living in bed-and-breakfast or other temporary accommodation. Moreover, about 800,000 had rents which took 40 per cent or more of their incomes (after taking account of housing allowances). There were also another 200,000 households at imminent risk of becoming homeless in the former GDR. In addition, about 1.1 million households in the whole of Germany still lived in unsatisfactory housing (lacking bath/WC and/or overcrowded). Many of those in the worst situation were migrants from the East, refugees and former guest workers (data from Schuler-Wallner and Wullkopf, 1991: 14–15). There was a huge rise in the numbers in urgent housing need after 1989, with the breakup of the GDR and the other socialist countries. This situation was one aspect of the development of what the Germans called the 'two-thirds' society. On the one hand, a majority continued to benefit from rising incomes and improving living conditions. On the other hand, there were the 'new poor' – the unemployed (swelled by rapidly rising numbers in the Eastern Länder as their economy collapsed), single-parent households, low-income young workers and large families (Kirchner and Sautter, 1990).

The situation intensified the pressure on the government, from a variety of charitable and other groups, for measures to improve the supply of housing for 'socially disadvantaged and disintegrated groups'. However, as Schuler-Wallner and Wullkopf (1991: 2) pointed out: '[a]lthough housing supply for lower income groups has become an increasing problem, the propensity to take measures in favour of social groups who possess hardly any lobby has decreased'. Instead, the government responded to the shortage of housing and the growing political pressure for action with measures that were mainly directed to sections of the population in housing need which had a strong political voice – such as younger, middle-income white-collar and skilled manual employees who were being priced out of the housing markets of the bigger cities. This was the group which had traditionally benefited most from the post-war social housing programmes. In autumn 1989 the government announced a change in its policies (Boelhouwer and van den Heijden, 1992: 130–8; Papa, 1992: 57–60). Its main aim was to increase the housing supply by encouraging more private building and investment through improved tax deductions for new rental units and for the conversion and subdivision of buildings. Very little of this new housing would be affordable by lower-income households. In addition, some federal subsidies were again provided for social rented housing construction. However, the new 'third' or 'inter-changeable' subsidy system which was adopted involved more limited assistance than the first or second subsidy schemes. The new subsidy had flexible rules which allowed the Länder to provide a variable level of assistance to social housing investors and to stretch the amount available (half came from the federal government and half from the states and localities) as thinly as possible in order to meet the government target of 500,000 new social rented units by the mid-1990s. The duration and size of the subsidy (usually no more than about ten years), rent levels and other conditions were negotiated between the authorities and the investors. In some cases the income limits for social housing eligibility could be set aside. So it was clear that this programme was targeted at the more politically important middle-income demand rather than the poorest households. Also, it soon became clear that the private sector was unlikely to increase production to the levels which the governments had predicted when the new policies were announced in 1989/90.

In fact, the policy relied, for the alleviation of the low-income housing problem, on stimulating the supply of middle-income housing, in the belief that some of the units vacated by those occupying the new units would filter down to the poor, especially when it created vacant units in the existing social rented stock. But there was no reversal of the policies which were leading to the rapid privatization of large sections of the social rented stock. This meant that the modest increase in new social rented supply was outweighed by the contraction in the pre-1990 stock. Moreover, privatization, higher rents and the loss of social restrictions on letting not only reduced opportunities for low-income households to enter the sector; they also increased insecurity for many existing tenants in the newly privatized units. These tenants had only limited security of tenure and many were under pressure from speculators who had bought up former social rented housing blocks for resale or renting. The ability of the new landlords to charge market-level rents also acted as an increasingly important cause of displacement from these properties (Boelhouwer and van den Heijden, 1992: 137).

There were tensions within the governing coalition over housing policy, with some wishing for a more radical reversion to the market and others resisting this. The SPD largely accepted the general direction followed by government policies, however. Meanwhile, privatization and the earlier withdrawal of the federal government from support for social rented housing had left the states and local authorities with increasing responsibility for trying to meet the growing mass of housing needs, but with declining resources. As Heinz (1991: 102–3) notes, the limited and fragmented local initiatives were a far cry from the mass housing policies of the past; instead, '[l]ocal low income housing policies ... rely, to a growing extent, on a series of instruments, limited in time and practicality, with an emergency function'. A more major concern for mainstream local politics was infrastructural, environmental and cultural improvements, aimed at bettering the localities' ability to compete with other areas for employment and economic activity. Both nationally and locally, the limited responses to the new housing crisis of the late 1980s and early 1990s were seen as purely temporary, emergency measures which should not interrupt the long-term goal of post-war German housing policy, namely, a return to the free market in housing. However, this 'free market' was, as many German housing market analysts have shown, in reality sustained by an increasing volume of housing subsidies targeted on upper- and middle-income home ownership, mainly through the tax system (Häussermann and Siebel, 1991).

An important factor, apart from the continued ideological adherence to private market solutions, which severely limited the scale of the response to the new housing shortage, was the growing burden placed on public expenditure by reunification, which we discussed earlier. One aspect of this burden was the vast cost of modernizing the crumbling former state housing estates in the East. Over half the former GDR stock pre-dated the Second World War and it had been allowed to deteriorate as the regime concentrated on new building. Unfortunately, much of this new building consisted of industrialized blocks which were also in a very poor state. Some 25 per cent of the East German stock lacked an inside WC, compared with only 2 per cent in the West, and there were many other deficiencies (Grieff and Ulbrich, 1991: 5). Although the policy was to raise rents considerably, thus providing some resources for modernization, this would also add to the public expenditure bill for housing allowances.

As we saw in the last chapter, the PvdA-led government which came to power in the Netherlands in 1973 set out its new housing policies in 1974.[38] These provided the basis for Dutch housing policies until the late 1980s (Priemus, 1987a; Boelhouwer and van den Heijden, 1992: 60–5). The policy was formulated by centrist and socialist Ministers and, according to Boelhouwer and van den Heijden (1992: 62), 'reflected their view of the capacity of the government to better society, and, reflecting too the spirit of the 1970s, it envisaged increasing involvement by the government in

many aspects of social and economic life'. So it rejected the previous centre–right policies which envisaged only a temporary expansion of state-subsidized new construction. Instead they asserted
a permanent role for government, to ensure a just distribution of
accommodation. This entailed production and consumption subsidies
and increased allocation controls. The aim was not just to ensure
that new social housing remained affordable for those on average
incomes, but also to improve quality and choice for all households.
In order to achieve this, housing allowances were extended to cover
all but the most expensive rented housing. In addition, the right
to apply for separate accommodation through the allocation system
was opened up to young, single people. This added considerably
to demand in the following years (Priemus, 1981: 342–3).

As we described in the last chapter, a system of dynamic cost
price subsidies was introduced in 1975. This system entailed long-
term forecasts of movements in prices and wages when estimating
the future cost for the government budget of the units subsidized
in this way. It was soon clear that these estimates had been too
optimistic, as the Dutch economy entered the troubled economic
conditions which have persisted since the mid-1970s. Moreover, private investors withdrew from rental housing construction. Instead,
they lent funds to help finance the expansion in home ownership
that occurred after 1975. This took the share of home ownership
from 35 per cent in 1971 to 42 per cent in 1981 (after which, as
we have seen, it stagnated). One reason for this growth was the
entry of the post-war baby-boom generation to the housing market,
during a period when real incomes were still rising and were expected to continue doing so, when high inflation rapidly eroded
the real value of mortgage debts, and when, with rising house
prices, housing investment became a very attractive method of
saving (Priemus, 1987a: tables 1 and 2, 18–19). The easing of
credit control in the early 1970s enabled banks and other institutions to vie with each other to lend on easy terms. The boom in
home ownership soon became driven by speculation, as consumers
and investors anticipated ever rising prices, fuelled by financial
institutions' provision of credit (Harloe and Martens, 1985). As we
noted, this market collapsed abruptly, as the Dutch economy nose-
dived in the late 1970s, shortly after the government lost power
in 1977.

As the initial forecasts on which the dynamic cost system had
been based were far too optimistic, the government was forced to
introduce ad hoc additional subsidies to keep the cost of new social
rented housing at affordable levels and sustain production. In the

later 1970s rents rose more slowly than building costs, leaving a growing gap to be met by subsidies. Thus central government supply and demand subsidies for all forms of rental housing (but mainly social housing) rose remarkably, from around 325 million guilders in 1970 to well over 3 billion guilders by the end of the decade (Boelhouwer and van den Heijden, 1992: table 3.12, 72). This escalation limited the funding available for new construction during a period when, as we have seen, the government was forced to follow increasingly austere economic policies, so contributing to the reversal of its initial intention to expand social housing output. By 1979 the output of social rented housing had fallen to around 23,500 units a year, compared with almost 56,000 when the government had taken office. The collapse in private rented housing output, following the withdrawal of private investment, was even more severe, down from around 40,000 to a mere 8000 units (Priemus, 1981: table 14, 344). In the social rented sector the rents of new accommodation were set at between 10 and 17 per cent of tenants' incomes and there was increasing recourse to consumption subsidies; the number of households receiving rent allowances rose by 30 per cent between mid-decade and 1980/1 and government expenditure on this scheme by 85 per cent (Papa, 1992: table 3.1, 15). The escalating burden of subsidies caused by the dynamic cost system continued to create difficulties for the right-wing governments in the 1980s, at a time when the principal economic policy objective was to reduce the government deficit.

Even though its long-term housing policy objectives differed from those of the preceding centre–right governments, in practice the 1973–7 government also placed much emphasis on expanding home ownership, especially among moderate- and lower-income households, by means of a new subsidy scheme which encouraged housing associations and other non-profit developers to build for sale to such households. Summarising this period, Lundqvist (1992: 45) writes:

> [t]he Left–Center coalition of 1973–77 intervened to increase hous-
> ing availability and affordability, only to leave the subsidized rental
> construction crumbling and the private – and increasingly expensive
> home ownership market thriving.

The centre–right government which came to power in 1977 wished to pursue again the objective of returning responsibility for most new housing provision to the private market, by promoting home ownership and by selling social rented housing (although the new Minister, Brokx, soon dropped the latter policy, partly because of the strong opposition that it raised) (Lundqvist, 1992: 53-9; Boelhouwer and van den Heijden, 1992: 65-70). However, the new government was faced with the worst recession that the Netherlands had experienced in the post-war era, with rising unemployment, high interest rates, falling real incomes and a collapse in the private housing market (average house prices fell by 30 per cent between 1978 and 1982), together with the rapidly escalating budgetary costs of the subsidy system which had to be propped up with a complex series of ad hoc subsidies (notably those which supported urban renewal housing targeted at low-income groups in the major cities).

The effect of this situation was to delay the desired policy shift for much of the subsequent decade. Instead, like the centre-right governments in the 1960s, the administration was forced, particularly by pressure from Parliament, to increase assistance for new production, raising social housing output to compensate for the virtual disappearance of private building (Harloe and Martens, 1985). By 1982 the output of social rented dwellings accounted for 53 per cent of all completions and between 1981 and 1984 85-90 per cent of all new housing output was directly subsidized. Even in 1987, with a slowly recovering private unsubsidized sector, two-thirds of output was still directly subsidized (about half in the private and half in the social sector) (Lundqvist, 1992: table 3.5, 54). In part, this policy reversal was dictated by the politically determined need to counter rising unemployment through what was in effect a public works programme. But it was also a response to the re-emergence of a housing shortage in the late 1970s, caused by demographic changes, including the growth of small households, enhanced demand from younger age groups, a widespread unwillingness to enter owner occupation because of its financial risks, and the increasing unaffordability of new private construction for low-income households, on the one hand, and the declining levels of private housing output, on the other (Priemus, 1981: 342-3).

This policy reversal cut across government plans for across-the-board reductions in public expenditure, announced in 1981, which entailed higher rents, increased rent harmonization and cuts in housing allowances, as well as reductions in funding for new social rented and subsidized home ownership units. A subsequent attempt to cut the social rented programme by 2500 units was rejected by Parliament, which demanded an increase of 3000 units. This was forced through the Cabinet by the housing Ministers, who threatened to resign if the increase was not accepted (Boelhouwer and van den Heijden, 1992: 67). Nevertheless, as Lundqvist (1992: 54) points out, some aspects of the 'forced' interventionism of this government did reflect its longer-term priorities. For example, in 1979 it increased the direct premium subsidies for new private housing production.

After the interim government led by van Agt, Lubbers became Prime Minister, with Brokx returning as Housing Minister. In 1983 the government began again on the path which its predecessor had initially intended. There was a cut in the housebuilding pro-gramme, mainly affecting the social rented sector. It reduced the ceilings for housing allowance eligibility and made other cost-cutting changes. But, despite these changes, housing expenditure continued to increase its share of public spending. The number of housing allowance recipients continued to climb, up to 900,000 by 1987, from 14 per cent of tenants in 1980 to 30 per cent in 1987 – the product of rising rents, on the one hand, and high un-employment and the growth of poverty, on the other. Direct hous-ing subsidies doubled between 1980 and 1985 and reached 9.3 billion guilders by 1987, while tax subsidies for home ownership rose rather less rapidly owing to the slow recovery of demand and house prices (Papa, 1992: 14–16, table 3.6, 28). However, annual social housing quotas were reduced over the rest of the decade, although not those for subsidized home ownership. But there was now less emphasis on encouraging lower-income households to buy, given the financial risks in the changed circumstances of the 1980s. A more radical attempt to cut the burgeoning levels of housing public expenditure was contained in a 1985 policy document which examined how to cut expenditure by 20 per cent or more in the forthcoming years (Boelhouwer and van den Heijden, 1992: 56). A start was made in 1986 with the ending of state loans for social housing construction and more reductions in the annual quota for new production, aimed at saving 1.5 billion guilders by 1990. In addition, further reductions were made in the eligibility for, and levels of, assistance provided by the housing allowance, targeting this ever more narrowly on the poorest households. The earlier policy of limiting post-allowance rents to 10–17 per cent of tenant incomes was abandoned during the 1980s as too costly (Priemus, 1990b).

In fact, even while housing expenditure was rising, some steps were taken, from the early 1980s onwards, towards reducing the role of the central government in housing provision. Moves began to decentralize responsibilities from the centre to the local author-ities, which entailed the introduction of a system of standard costs in 1986. Also, the financial risks of developing social housing began to be shifted from the government to the localities and to tenants, through the debudgetization of housing loans noted above, and in other ways which will be discussed below (Fleurke and de Vries, 1990; Lundqvist, 1992: 55–8). In the late 1980s, with the recovery of some private unsubsidized output and the increasing influence of neo-liberal economic and social policies within the government, more radical plans were announced for the disengagement of the state from housing provision in the 1990s. The decentralization of responsibilities for housing planning and the distribution of subsidies to which we have just referred had begun following government proposals in the early 1980s for the widespread decentralization of many government programmes and for privatization and deregulation, in the belief that this would reduce government overload and increase efficiency. But many of the initial proposals for radical decentralization had been watered down to ensure a continuing level of substantial central involvement and control.

The decisive shift in housing policy occurred only when the long-serving Housing Minister Brokx (from the Catholic wing of the CDA) was replaced by a new, ex-ARP politician, Heerma, following allegations of fraud over construction grants.[39] The parliamentary commission which investigated this situation added pressure to the impetus for change by suggesting that the government could no longer effectively control the mass of specific housing programmes that were under its direct supervision (Priemus, 1987b, 1990a). Heerma, an able and energetic politician, was strongly committed to reshaping housing policies and shifting the boundaries between the public and the private sectors in favour of the latter. In 1988 he published his proposals in a consultative memorandum (for details see Priemus, 1990a; Boelhouwer and Priemus, 1990). This was followed by definitive policies being presented to Parliament in 1989. At this point the government coalition collapsed, to be replaced by a centre–left administration as the PvdA returned to government. Heerma retained his position as Housing Minister, together with the policies which he had developed in the previous administration. These were only slightly modified as a result of the re-entry to government of the Social Democrats, for example by a small increase in the social rented housing quota (although this was again cut as austerity policies were tightened early in 1990) (Priemus, 1990a).

Apart from the long-pursued wish to redraw the boundaries between the state and the market in Dutch housing provision, as

Priemus (1990a) notes, the policy proposals were driven, on the one hand, by the desire to reduce public expenditure and especially the ever rising levels of housing public expenditure, and, on the other hand, by the belief that the large-scale housing shortage of the early part of the decade had now eased, so that a reduction in governmental support for housing was politically viable again. In fact, Heerma envisaged a further fall in housing output, from an average of around 110,000 in the 1980s to 80,000 per annum in the second half of the 1990s. The policy memorandum painted a rosy picture of the prospects for the Dutch housing market in the 1990s, with only a slow growth in demand due to demographic factors, low interest rates and a reasonable level of economic growth. It predicted a steady rise in real incomes, shared by those in employment and the welfare-dependent.

It was against this background that the government believed that there could be a fairly unproblematic expansion of the private housing market, and a reduction in the state's role to one which sought to help the private housing market work more effectively. Responsibility for securing adequate housing was, in the first instance, to be the duty of the market institutions and individual consumers. As Boelhouwer and Priemus (1990: 107) note, the key concepts were deregulation, decentralization and self-reliance. Direct government assistance should be confined to households with below-average incomes through a limited programme of subsidized housing and rent allowances (although the levels of benefit were frozen in 1991 in a further round of budget cuts). Much of the expansion in private output would be in home ownership. Rising incomes would mean that rents could rise more rapidly than hitherto, thus reducing levels of subsidy. However, as Priemus (1990a) noted, as the recession of the early 1990s was gathering momentum in the Netherlands, an alternative economic scenario might be one of stagnant or even declining incomes, rising interest rates and a new slump in private building, reducing the affordability of home ownership, especially for those on moderate incomes, and leading to sharply rising rent/income ratios in the social rented sector. Moreover, if income growth was not as predicted by Heerma, the rising rents would increase the housing allowance burden. Already in 1990 there were about 950,000 claimants, one in four of all tenants, although changes in the scheme had pegged back the rate of increase in its costs (Priemus, 1990b: 170). One group which had lost out as a result of these cuts (and also reductions in minimum wage laws) was young single adults, whose entitlement to housing, which, as we noted, was greatly improved in the mid-1970s, was now virtually abolished.

The new policies, adopted in the early 1990s, involved the following changes. First, a sharp cut-back in the level of new social rented housing production, with increasing reliance on the free sector, mainly in the form of home ownership. Second, reductions in the budget of the Housing Ministry, mainly spent on rented housing, of 2.5 billion guilders a year up to the year 2000, compared with a rising total of indirect subsidies for home ownership over the same period. Third, a policy of raising rents faster than the rise in operating costs, to reduce the subsidies paid for existing housing, probably leading to sharply rising rent/income ratios for many households. Some attempt at even-handedness was made by modest increases in taxes on home ownership. Fourth, a target of 55 per cent home ownership by the year 2000, which Heerma initially proposed would be contributed to by sales of 10,000 units of social rented housing per annum, aided by a write-off of a part of the rising debt that dynamic cost-financed units incurred in the first decades of their operation.

Another major feature of the new policies was the changed treatment of the housing associations. First, there was the declining level of subsidies for new building. This also involved the replacement of the expensive dynamic cost system, which entailed long-term annual subsidy contributions by government, taking up 60 per cent of the housing budget by 1988, by a cheaper system of fixed annual payments for a limited period, whose duration would be linked to the level of interest rates. Second, there were some incentives to encourage, though not require, sales to sitting tenants. Third, there were changes in the nature and role of the sector which, in some respects, are reminiscent of the original conception of social rented housing in the 1901 Housing Act, and echo those proposed in the early 1960s, as discussed in the last chapter. Thus it was assumed that the financial reserves of the associations, aided by rising rent revenues, would grow substantially in the 1990s, enabling the financially weaker associations to be aided by contributions, through a new housing solidarity fund, from the stronger associations. In addition, the withdrawal of state loans in 1988 had already been accompanied by the expansion of a guarantee fund to encourage the private sector to supply loans. This had been set up in 1984, when government loans for housing improvement were abolished, with a government contribution to the initial capital. But from 1988 the fund was wholly reliant on contributions from the associations. The overall objective was to increase the degree of financial self-reliance, with a reducing governmental contribution. The associations were also to be given more autonomy in other respects; for example, they no longer needed to get local authority approval for sales. But this autonomy did not include the ability to evade a new requirement to target their activities on lower-income households. However, as Boelhouwer and Priemus (1990: 118) note, given the large proportion of the Dutch housing stock in the social sector and the lack of any policy of forced privatization, even these new policies were hardly likely to bring about the rapid reduction of social renting to a residual form of provision, serving only the poor. Nevertheless, the policy of targeting was to be reinforced by putting pressure on above-average income tenants to move out of social housing and into the private sector. In part this would be achieved by the new rent regime. But Heerma had wanted to go further, suggesting that tenancies might in future be granted on a time-limited basis and could be revoked as incomes rose. This coercive policy was eventually dropped as it aroused strong opposition.

The same mixture of decentralization and deregulation, together with the maintenance of strategic controls by central government, also characterized new policies affecting the local authority housing role. Thus the government scrapped its detailed project-by-project scrutiny of housing programmes, replacing this by annual block grants whose distribution to different types of housing project was determined locally, in the light of local assessments of need. Local authorities were to act, like their British counterparts, more as 'enabling' bodies and become less involved in controlling or directly providing housing. New measures were taken to divest the big cities of their remaining social housing stocks: these were to be transferred to new or existing housing associations. Localities had stronger powers to determine the rules of the allocation system, however. But these new local powers (or rather, greater responsibilities but declining central government resources) were accompanied by the retention or strengthening of central strategic controls. These included tighter controls on cost limits for new subsidized housing, the new regime of higher rents which the local authorities were to police, the attempts to restrict allocations to lower-income groups, and the possibility of legislation which would limit local authorities' power to control the nature of local housing developments.

These policies combined a decline in central government support for social housing with greater reliance on the private (indirectly subsidized) market and on consumption subsidies. They embodied an apparent commitment to decentralization and deregulation but, in reality, the maintenance of strong central controls helped ensure this 'liberation' (Lundqvist, 1992: 53–63). As van Weesep and van Kempen (1992) have suggested, from the mid-1980s there was a shift towards reliance on filtering to provide much of the future supply of low-income housing. Lundqvist (1992: 61) notes that these changes reflect the political shifts which occurred in the 1980s – the realignment of the CDA towards the right, the influence of neo-liberal ideas about the relationship between the market and the state, and the determined attempt to reduce public expenditure and debt. However, the institutional strength of the housing associations, based on their legally independent status as 'private initiatives', the considerable support that they continued to obtain from the Social Democrats and the Confessional bloc, and the fact that they still housed many in the 'middle mass' of the population, not just the poor and politically weak, made it politically infeasible to run down the sector by, for example, forced privatization. Thus, despite the fact that the VVD, in power with the CDA from the late 1970s to the late 1980s, had long pressed for this policy, it was unable to succeed. All that had been achieved by the early 1990s were some very tentative attempts to encourage social rented housing sales (Boelhouwer and van Weesep, 1988).

Opinions varied about just how radical a change these new policies would bring about, especially as the initial economic forecasts soon proved ill founded in the new recession. However, there was remarkably little opposition to them from the political parties, housing agencies, interest groups or consumers. In part this was due to the skill with which Heerma drew up and promoted his new policies. In addition, housing now had a lower political and public priority. As Boelhouwer and van den Heijden (1992: 77) conclude: '[h]ousing now has to compete more fiercely with other issues facing the government, the environment and transport for instance, which clearly have greater political priority'. One indicator of this shift was a parliamentary resolution passed in 1987 which asked the government to investigate the feasibility of large-scale social housing sales to finance environmental and infrastructural improvements (Priemus, 1991: 4).

By 1990 the persistent attempts to reduce the size of the state's financial commitments to housing finally began to be realized, with a decrease in housing expenditure in real terms and as a percentage of all public expenditure (van Weesep and van Kempen, 1992). In the following years considerable progress was made in implementing the Heerma reforms. We have aleady referred to the general lack of strong opposition, but the main social housing federation, the NWR, generally accepted the Heerma proposals as well, attracted by the increased independence, especially from local government, that they entailed and the opportunities to operate in a more entrepreneurial manner. The new subsidy system, which began in 1990, shifted any costs due to later changes in interest rates from the central government to the local authorities, and ultimately to the associations and their tenants. One consequence was likely to be a change in the culture and management of the housing associations, with a decline in the importance of the building and construction professionals who had a project-linked philosophy, and greater emphasis on quasi-commercial and financial skills and management. According to an NWR official, decisions about whether and what to build would be increasingly influenced by market-derived criteria similar to those which concern private housing developers (van Harten, 1991). This seemed likely to lead to a growth in the size of associations and a reduction in their number, as the smaller and weaker ones were taken over by the stronger ones. In many ways these developments parallel those affecting the housing associations in Britain, described earlier in this chapter.

The system of local authority block grants began in 1992. At first it consisted of four budgets, for social rented or subsidized owner occupation and gut rehabilitation (the largest budget); for other renovations, handicapped and student accommodation; to reduce rents in existing dwellings; and to reduce costs in certain high-cost localities. The government abandoned any attempt to set precise targets for housing output, leaving these to be determined by local decisions about how to deploy the budgets. Many local authorities welcomed the greater freedom that these changes brought about, although they were also accompanied by a devolution of financial risks. As Priemus (1991: 8) has pointed out, this will mean that the associations will no longer be willing to sustain or increase output when high interest rates choke off private building, for they will face similar risks to those of private investors. Also, the freedom of the local authorities might still be constrained in one key respect – the choice between financing new social rented or directly subsidized home-ownership units. Minister Heerma made it clear that sanctions might be imposed if the local authorities financed 'too few' of the latter units.

Commentators have suggested that these new policies, in conjunction with the growth, as elsewhere, of a polarised economy, in which the better off continue to benefit from rising real incomes while poorer groups lose out, may increase social and spatial segregation in Dutch cities (van Weesep and van Kempen, 1992).

However, despite the clear intention of the government to change the role of social housing, this large-scale sector still showed far fewer signs of residualization by the early 1990s than that of most other countries.[40] The political and legal context to Dutch social rented housing prevented any centrally determined mass privatization of this stock, as has occurred in Germany and Britain. Instead, Heerma's strategy involved an attempt to return to the concept of a self-sufficient social rented housing sector, with minimal state subsidies (apart from housing allowances). This may be seen as an alternative method of achieving the objective of state withdrawal to that of large-scale privatization by tenant sales and/or by converting social landlords into normal commercial operators. This approach, which echoes the original conception of the associations as 'private initiatives', is a more feasible form of (re)privatization, given the Dutch conditions. In addition, while social rented housing continues to accommodate significant sections of the middle-income population and most associations are asset rich, have strong balance sheets and a high proportion of good-quality stock, a policy of increased self-sufficiency is financially more viable than in a system where social housing has already been reduced to a residual role, serving only low-income housing consumers, with a deteriorating stock of less desirable accommodation (in 1985, for example, the associations had financial reserves of 7.6 billion guilders, equivalent to 82 per cent of their annual rent roll and an operating profit of 0.8 billion guilders (van Weesep and van Kempen, 1992: table 8, 15)).

However, within the social rented sector, especially but not only in areas of unpopular high-rise development in the major urban areas, a residualized subsector did emerge from the 1970s onwards, housing an increasing concentration of low-income population, including many ethnic minorities. Yet, despite the intense publicity given to dramatic examples of high-rise 'problem' estates, notably the Bjilmermeer in suburban Amsterdam, the scale of the problem was quite minor.[41] High rents, poor housing quality and poor locations were some of the factors contributing to the declining middle-income demand for these properties and their use as housing of last resort for low-income groups.[42] Various remedial programmes were instituted to deal with these problems, including major renovations, rent reductions and programmes to reduce heating costs. In addition, from the mid-1980s more attention was paid to innovative management strategies, involving the familiar mix of enhanced coordination between the various agencies involved in managing problem estates and their residents. Although not all of these initiatives were successful, by the early 1990s the problem seemed to have been contained, in part because of the cessation of the rapid movement of many better-off tenants into home owner-ship, which had occurred in the 1970s, in the uncertain economic and housing market conditions of the 1980s and early 1990s.

More generally, however, changes in the 1980s and 1990s in the housing allowance and local housing allocation systems, aimed at targeting assistance on the poor and ensuring that low-income households do not occupy higher-rented housing (thus requiring larger rent subsidies), have increased tendencies towards segrega-tion in Dutch housing (van Weesep and van Kempen, 1992). The Heerma policies, if they succeed in refocusing the role of social housing, will accentuate this development. Nevertheless, the poli-cies may be thwarted by a failure to realize the ambitious plans for the expansion of home ownership and the wish to make the associations more self-sufficient, which will most readily be achieved if they continue to house an economically mixed population. Cer-tainly, the NWR has argued that this must be sustained (Nationale Woningraad, 1990). One factor which will aid associations' reten-tion of such households is the relatively high esteem in which social housing and social housing landlords (most of which still operate on a relatively small scale and in a single locality) are still held. This means that social housing is still seen as a desirable form of accom-modation by many households who do have some choice in the housing market. In turn, this helps to sustain the entrenched in-fluence that the social rented federations still have on government policies and their ability to resist changes which would damage their position.

As we described earlier, the latter half of the 1970s saw a suc-cession of weak, minority governments in Denmark, mainly led by the Social Democrats, struggling to come to terms with unem-ployment, inflation and balance of payments deficits.[43] The mixture of policies and pressures was much the same as elsewhere. Changes in housing policy, like much else, remained dependent on negotia-tion between the leading parties, inside and outside the government, in order to assemble the necessary parliamentary majorities.

In the last chapter we examined the reasons why the 1966 hous-ing pact failed and how the mounting pressure to reduce public expenditure led to deep cuts in social rented housing output from 1972. High inflation and interest rates greatly increased the cost of new housing and the subsidy commitment. Between 1970 and 1974 the mortgage interest rate was never below around 11 per cent, rising by 1974 to almost 16 per cent, and to 21 per cent by

1982. Housebuilding costs rose by over 60 per cent between 1971 and 1975 (and in the succeeding five years by over 70 per cent) (Vestergaard, 1982). The initial cost rents of social units, which were mainly financed (95 per cent) through borrowing on the bond market, became increasingly unaffordable. This, plus the rapid increase in housing supply in the early 1970s, led to new social rented units staying vacant.[44] In 1974, following a 12-month freeze on public building, the annual social housing quota for the next five years was fixed at 8000 units under a new housing pact, intended to last until 1979 (Ministry of Housing, 1974: 23–5). This pact envisaged a falling demand for new housing, due to the economic conditions and a reduction in population growth, to about 40,000 new units per annum. In 1973, the peak year for post-war housing production when almost 56,000 units were built, around 13,000 units of social rented housing were completed. By 1979 there had been a sharp contraction in total housing production, down to around 31,000 completions, with under 5000 new social rented units (Boelhouwer and van den Heijden, 1992: table 6.3, 154). So even the more modest programme which had been planned fell victim to austerity policies and to contracting private investment.

The new housing pact accelerated the removal of rent and allocation controls in the private sector and reformed rent determination in areas where controls continued, setting rents which covered all outgoings plus a 7 per cent yield on the assessed value of the property. These rents were considerably higher than had been charged hitherto. In addition, restrictions on the conversion of private rented units to condominiums were largely removed (some were reimposed later, following speculative activity and poor-quality modernization. In 1979 further conversions were prohibited). The need to provide deeper subsidies for the social rented sector to ensure affordability was accepted. A new system was based on what were, in effect, capital grants covering 23 per cent of total costs. A 3 per cent contribution from tenants was continued, the remaining 74 per cent to be met by commercial borrowing from the mortgage credit institutions. The government limited its increased subsidy bill by cutting the annual quota and by requiring part of the grant to be provided by the local authorities and by a national fund which received part of the rent increases occurring in pre-1963 social housing; together these amounted to 13 per cent of the total costs (in the early 1980s the fund's contribution was replaced by more government assistance so that the fund could invest in improving the older rental stock). The government also continued the interest guarantee scheme adopted in 1966, meeting the difference between 6 per cent and the interest rates charged by the mortgage credit institutes. However, this annual subsidy was now withdrawn at a faster rate than hitherto, with a full guarantee of the difference for only the first four years, compared with six years previously (Ministry of Housing, 1983).

The new pact, like its predecessor, embodied a compromise between the wish of the non-socialist parties to free up the private market and the left's wish to sustain some level of new social housing output. The latter wanted to balance the rent increases by reductions in the indirect tax subsidies for home ownership, but no definite proposals were included in the pact beyond the establishment of a review of the tax rules and a plan to raise the officially determined rental value (on which owners paid a mainly very small imputed income tax). A subsequent attempt by the government to legislate for the gradual removal of home-owner tax subsidies could not gain majority support in Parliament, so home ownership continued to benefit from rapidly rising levels of indirect subsidy. Given the very high marginal income tax and interest rates, the stimulus to housing consumption, speculation and high house-price inflation from this system was substantial, as was the impact on government finances and general interest rates in the bond market, the main source of financing for the government debt. There was increasing concern about the volume of funds flowing into housing and the shortage of affordable credit for industrial investment which could help Denmark reduce its balance of payments deficit and unemployment (Ministry of Housing, 1984: 39–40). However, political resistance to radical reforms remained intense.

The changes in rents and subsidies as a result of the 1974 pact still left the government with a rising bill for housing and facing persistent pressure to reduce new social rented housing output, as indeed occurred. Expenditure on the graded-rent (housing allowance) scheme was increased as its coverage was extended following the new political agreement. In part this was a response to the increasing divergence between the assistance given to home owners and to tenants. It was more feasible to restrict the divergence by increasing the latter, rather than reducing the former (Boelhouwer and van den Heijden, 1992: 156–7). By 1980 about a quarter of all tenants benefited from graded rents, and there was an especially generous scheme for the elderly. Another source of the growth in expenditure was the modification in the arrangements for the withdrawal of interest-rate subsidies for social rental housing, noted earlier. In the late 1970s, as part of a more general prices and incomes policy, the timescale for withdrawal was linked to movements in prices and wages. This extended the phase-out period from the originally intended eight years to about 17 years (Ministry of Housing and Ministry of the Environment, 1979: 11). Even so, the housing finance system remained heavily biased in favour of home ownership. In 1979 the government calculated that the average cost of occupying an owner-occupied unit over 30 years was substantially below the rent that would be paid by a tenant in a similar unit (Ministry of Housing and Ministry of the Environment, 1979: 9). This bias helps to explain the rising share of home ownership which occurred in Denmark in the 1970s. But the growth in home ownership and, more generally, rising housing standards were not only costly in terms of government expenditure; the average housing cost/income ratio rose sharply from 14 per cent in 1970 to 19 per cent by 1980 (Ministry of Housing and Ministry of the Environment, 1982: 46).

In the early 1980s, the last period before the advent of the centre–right governments of that decade, housing developments were dominated by the collapse of the overheated private housing market as the new recession took hold. Unemployment in the building industries and bankruptcies soared. By 1982 inflation was 10 per cent and mortgage interest rates around 20 per cent, at a time when real incomes were falling for many home owners. The fall in housing output between 1978 and 1982 was the sharpest of any Western European country at this time (Ministry of Housing, 1984: table 3, 86). In this situation the government responded, essentially for macro-economic reasons, in a similar manner to its counterpart in the Netherlands. New funds were provided for urban renewal and energy conservation, and the social rented housing quota was rapidly increased from 7000 units in 1980 to 12,000 by 1982. In addition, direct subsidies were provided for a further 6500 units for young people and the elderly (the latter were developed by the local authorities, although they often used the non-profit organizations as their agents) and for owner cooperatives (Ministry of Housing and Building, 1988: 78–80; Boelhouwer and van den Heijden, 1992: table 6.1, 149). The cooperative programme developed out of the political conflicts in the previous decade over the selling-off of privately rented blocks by their landlords and was strongly advocated by Venstre (Vestergaard, 1982). From 1980 landlords who wished to sell were required to offer their tenants the right to purchase the property and establish an owner cooperative before selling to others. In addition, subsidies were now provided to enable newly built owner cooperatives, essentially a form of collective home ownership, to be established (the subsidies compensated for the fact that cooperative owners were not eligible for home-owner tax subsidies). Support through the social subsidy system for a form of home ownership was a new departure in Danish housing policy. Despite their social subsidies, the new co-operatives accommodated middle-income households, squeezed out of home ownership, rather than low-income households, and were not subject to local authority supervision or to any obligation to house less-advantaged households, unlike the housing associations (Ministry of Housing, 1988; Power, 1993: 286–8).

These policy shifts meant that, while in 1978 the social sector's share of output had reached its lowest level since 1950 at just over 16 per cent, four years later it accounted for the highest share since that year, at just under 49 per cent (Boelhouwer and van den Heijden, 1992: table 6.3, 154). Apart from the macro-economic reasons for this change, the collapse of the home-ownership market caused a large fall in house prices and a rising tide of repossessions. This shifted demand back to the rental sectors, with long waiting lists for admission to social housing.

As in the Netherlands, this boost to social rented housing occurred under a centre–right government and was a temporary expedient, only postponing the longer-term aim of reducing the state's involvement and increasing reliance on the private market. As the home-ownership market began a modest recovery from 1983 onwards and building industry unemployment fell, the social rented housing quota was gradually reduced, back to around 9–10,000 between 1983 and 1988, and 7000 in 1990 (Boelhouwer and van den Heijden, 1992: table 6.1, 149). Throughout the 1980s, as Boelhouwer and van den Heijden (1992: 168–9) note, housing policy was driven by the central priority for the government, that of reducing inflation and the balance of payments deficit (which rose from an already massive 12 billion Danish krone (DKR) a year in the late 1970s to 20 billion DKR, or \$2.1 billion by 1982: 4 per cent of GNP (Ministry of Housing, 1984: 12)), reducing public expenditure on housing and other welfare programmes, and facilitating private sector growth. Within this context, the Housing Ministry had relatively little influence, although in the early 1980s, when the Minister was a member of the Centre Party, as we have seen, social housing production expanded. It will be recalled that, at this time, the government was dependent on the support of the Radical Liberals, who would agree only to limited public expenditure reductions and wanted to preserve the core of welfare state

services. Despite this, some deep cuts were made in welfare benefits, and within the government the Venstre Ministers pressed for
neo-liberal restructuring and reductions in the state's role.

In 1986 a Liberal whose aim was to implement these policies
was appointed as Minister of Housing (Boelhouwer and van den
Heijden, 1992: 158). In particular, he wished to institute a major
programme of privatization of social rented housing through a
similar policy to that adopted in Britain. It was not, however,
possible to gain the necessary support for this proposal, although
the government did establish a commission to investigate the feasibility of social housing sales (Boelhouwer and van den Heijden,
1992: 158). In the event, this Minister's tenure of office was brief.
Between 1987 and 1990 three further politicians held the post,
partly as a result of the rapidly changing governments during
this period and partly because of the low political status that now
attached to the post.

During these years there were two major changes in housing
finance, both driven by Denmark's economic crisis. In 1982 the
system of social housing subsidies was reformed (Ministry of Housing, 1984; Papa, 1992: 78–84). The extremely high interest rates
in the late 1970s and early 1980s, together with rapidly inflating
building costs and increased social housebuilding, meant that the
Danish government, like that of the Netherlands, faced a rapidly
escalating subsidy bill over many years. Expenditure on the interest
guarantee scheme rose by almost 75 per cent to nearly 2 billion
DKR between 1978 and 1982. Discussion of index loans had begun
in the 1950s. In the 1970s there had been attempts to institute
these in order to reduce the 'front-end' loading of interest payments
under a normal annuity scheme, and hence cut the budgetary
costs of the interest guarantee scheme. However, the bond market
resisted this innovation. But in 1982, after considerable political
debate, indexed loans were made compulsory for all directly subsidized new housing and the interest guarantee scheme was abolished. Market resistance was overcome by offering tax concessions
to the mortgage credit institutions on the index loans for subsidized
housing. However, a parallel scheme to provide index loans for
home ownership was unsuccessful, owing, in part, to consumer
resistance. At first the capital grant was maintained at 23 per cent.
This was reduced in 1984 by cutting the government contribution,
so that now the grant covered 18 per cent of costs, two-thirds
paid by central and one-third by local government. Some 2 per
cent of funding still came from tenants' deposits, leaving 80 per
cent to be financed on the bond market (later the government

ended its contribution and the system consisted of 94 per cent index-linked loans, 4 per cent local authority capital and 2 per cent tenant deposits).

Like the Dutch dynamic cost price system (and similar schemes elsewhere adopted during these years), the new system altered the conventional pattern of repayments which, assuming future growth in incomes and prices, stays nominally fixed but falls in real terms over time, to one in which the nominal interest payments rose but stayed level in real terms. The index loans carried a low nominal rate of interest, still paid by the government, leaving rents to repay the capital. In the early years of the debt repayment the 'excess' interest due (i.e. the gap between the nominal and the market rates) was capitalized. One purpose of the scheme was to reduce the immediate impact of housing subsidies on the government budget, thus allowing the enhanced rate of social housing output to be sustained. In addition, the scheme entailed an indexation of tenants' repayments of capital, on a similar basis to that which operated under the interest guarantee scheme. This enabled the initial rents of new units to be lowered as well (the basis for this calculation was not altered when the index loans were increased to 94 per cent). However, as with all such schemes, the eventual outcome depended on future and unpredictable movements in wages and prices. The 1982 reforms left the system of graded rents in place, although the costs of this also escalated rapidly, by 65 per cent between 1980 and 1983, up to 2.3 billion DKR, and it continued to rise to about 5 billion DKR by 1989 (Ministry of Housing 1983; Papa, 1992: table 6.2, 76–8).

Meanwhile, despite their increasing cost and regressive nature, the home-owner tax subsidies remained in place. This was only one aspect of a system which allowed deductions of interest on all loan repayments. By the early 1980s, the top tax rate, which had risen considerably in the 1970s, as the problems of funding public expenditure worsened, stood at 70 per cent. The tax losses were enormous and, as events in the 1970s had demonstrated, the system encouraged massive speculation and over-investment in housing, especially at the top end of the market by higher-income house-holds, while those on more modest incomes benefited far less and in many cases struggled to maintain high housing repayments (Ministry of Housing, 1984: 33; Einhorn and Logue, 1989: 222). Much of the subsidy served only to raise house-price inflation, benefiting the providers and financiers of housing, not consumers. Moreover, the system contributed to intense competition for capital and the maintenance of Denmark's extremely high interest rates.

By the middle of the 1980s there was agreement among the major political parties that a reform of the tax system could no longer be avoided. By now the country had the highest per capita national debt in Europe (Boelhouwer and van den Heijden, 1992: 160–1, 166–7). In 1986 the government, supported by the Social Democratic opposition, instituted a rigorous austerity policy which included: a plan to limit income growth to levels below those of other industrial countries, with the aim of improving the competitiveness of the economy; restricting the size of the public sector by privatization and improving its efficiency; reductions in income taxes and in government expenditure to pay for this loss of revenue, reducing direct and indirect subsidies especially to sectors of the economy, such as construction, which did not contribute to exports; and reducing the trade deficit, changing taxation by a new charge on consumer-oriented loans, to encourage a switch from consumption to investment.

These reforms radically increased the cost of home ownership, with changes in the financing system that raised initial repayments and a reduction to 50 per cent in the marginal rate applicable to home-loan interest deductions. The nature of the changes meant that first-time buyers and recent purchasers were particularly hard hit. Although the tax changes included a reduction in rates of income taxation, rising local authority taxation virtually wiped out the gains, and house sales, which had risen very sharply in anticipation of the changes, fell to even lower levels than in the early 1980s. At the same time repossessions rose to an even higher number than before. As in Britain, many home buyers were unable to move, locked into housing which had lost value and for which there were no buyers. A further blow to the sector occurred in 1990 when various mortgage frauds came to light. As elsewhere, sharp practices had been facilitated by the intense competition for borrowers which had developed in the 1980s, leading to a lack of proper scrutiny of loan applications and inflation in loan costs. New legislation reduced competition after the scandals were exposed. Overall, the prospects for a rapid recovery in the home-owner market, after the crises of the previous 15 years, seemed slight (Boelhouwer and van den Heijden, 1992: 161–5).

By 1990 there was a wide measure of political agreement on the need for a further stage in the development of the economic policies followed in the late 1980s, with more reductions in the higher rates of income tax.[45] However, there was no agreement on whether this should be financed by further cuts in welfare expenditure, already severely reduced after a decade of austerity policies, or by increases in wealth and company taxation. The Ministries of Housing and Finance advocated the former solution, arguing that there was no longer any need to support the expansion of housing supply and that subsidies for new construction of social rented and cooperative housing should be abolished. In addition, the large-scale sale of social rented housing was again proposed. However, as we discuss below, the ownership of this housing by legally independent housing associations, as in the Netherlands, made such a policy difficult to implement. In addition, reductions in the existing housing subsidy bill and in housing allowances were also proposed (Boelhouwer and van den Heijden, 1992: 166–9).

Following the next election, these plans began to be implemented, though less drastically than had been originally proposed. The annual social rented housing quota was reduced from 7000 in 1990 to 4000 by 1992 and smaller cuts were made in other subsidized programmes.[46] This resulted in a shift of emphasis within the reduced programme: for the first time social rented housing accounted for only a minor share of the subsidized output. In effect, this was a form of privatization of new socially subsidized production, as around one-third would now be in the ownership cooperative sector (cooperative owners paid a 20 per cent deposit and the remaining 80 per cent was in the form of the subsidized index loan). The government also lengthened the repayment period for social rented housing loans, while keeping rents at the levels previously charged, thus reducing its annual budgetary commitments (Papa, 1992: 81). Drastic reductions in housing allowances proved politically impossible to implement, so the government settled for a salami-like strategy, beginning to remove additional payments, beyond the basic rent, from the housing costs admissible for subsidy (Boelhouwer and van den Heijden, 1992: 169). Only a programme for subsidizing urban renewal and improvement, which had been expanded in the 1980s partly for employment reasons, remained intact.

As in the Netherlands, despite the country's economic situation and the domination by the right in the 1980s, with the development of neo-liberal policies for welfare state restructuring, social rented housing did not suffer the same degree of privatization and residualization as elsewhere. Attempts to privatize the stock by mass sales made little headway and for much of the 1980s a government which, in principle, wished drastically to reduce new social rented housing construction and subsidies could not do so. However, as in the Netherlands also, cut-backs were only postponed, as the reductions in the social housing quota in the early 1990s illustrate.

And, in fact, projections of future demand towards the end of the century suggested that the switch from new building to renewal and rehabilitation, which the government also aimed to achieve, had a good deal of validity.

There are other parallels with the Netherlands. First, the crises in the home-ownership market made many housing consumers wary of house purchase and sustained demand for good-quality rented housing, much of which was in the social sector. The unpopular, industrially built portion of the stock was relatively limited and all such construction ceased after the mid-1970s, when there was a return to smaller-scale, low-rise projects with a strong emphasis on good planning and environment (O. Svensson, 1988). These units were smaller than many built in the previous period, with a greater concern to ensure that they were affordable by the type of tenants likely to occupy them (Kristensen, 1985; Andersen, 1992). Unlike their counterparts elsewhere, Danish housing associations have sustained a position (which they intend to maintain) as competitors with the private sector for the provision of middle-income accommodation, alongside their role in relation to less-advantaged households. Associations have been conscious of the need to maintain this competitive position by, for example, instituting high levels of environmental and building improvement through the 1980s and 1990s, so that they can still attract sections of the population which could pay for private market housing but which choose, instead, to occupy social housing.

Second, from the late 1980s government moved towards an alternative to mass privatization as a means of bringing about state disengagement from the social rented sector. As in the Netherlands, this involved the establishment of a more financially self-sufficient sector, in which the considerable assets represented by the accumulated stock and the annual surpluses generated by rent income are applied to the rehabilitation of the older stock and the support of such new construction as may be necessary (Vestergaard, 1992; Boelhouwer and van den Heijden, 1992: 168–9). We have already noted that from 1982 surplus rent income, accumulated in the National Building Fund, was used to aid rehabilitation and the Fund subsequently took over support for this activity completely, as the government phased out the subsidies. By the early 1990s it was anticipated that government subsidies for new construction might also be phased out, to be replaced by assistance from the Fund. Also, as in the Netherlands, central government sought to decentralize its financial, planning and regulatory responsibilities to the local authorities. We have also noted the reduction and then cessation of government contributions to the capital subsidy for social rented housing, leaving only a local authority contribution. In addition, when, in the 1980s, the new programme of assisted housing for the elderly was developed, the government placed the prime responsibility on the local authorities for deciding how much should be constructed, limiting the number of units that it was prepared to support, leaving the localities to assist any additional units (Ministry of Housing and Building, 1988). Finally, in the early 1990s, much of the detailed supervisory responsibility for the non-profit housing associations was devolved from the government to the local authorities and further decentralization was being discussed.

Various factors have contributed to the maintenance of Danish social rented housing as a mass rather than a residual form of provision. Some have already been mentioned: the high quality of much of the sector, the continuing demand for rental housing from a wide range of income groups, and the fact that it is owned by independent organizations and is thus private property which cannot be compulsorily sold off as a result of legislation. However, two further important factors are the decentralized institutional structures of Danish social housing and the high degree of tenant involvement in its management, increased by legislation in the mid-1970s and mid-1980s (Cronberg, 1986; Salicath, 1987; Power, 1993: 274–84). Interestingly, up to the 1970s the associations had been marked by erosion of earlier cooperative structures, the growth of management bureaucracy and a lack of effective tenant involvement that also marked, for example, developments in Germany, as well as the post-war growth of welfare state institutions more generally.[47] The subsequent reforms were not so much the product of factors specific to Danish housing as an outcome of the more general critique of the overcentralized and powerful welfare state bureaucracies which fed variously into New Right, Green and some socialist agendas (Einhorn and Logue, 1989: 276–8). In Denmark it was a Social Democrat-led government that began the break with this system, not by privatization but by an attempt to increase democratic control while sustaining a social housing sector.

Each non-profit association operates in a single locality (Salicath, 1987; Ministry of Housing and Building, 1990; Andersen, 1992). Their average holdings are only around 1100 dwellings. While the associations are supervized by the local authorities, each individual estate forms a financially separate and largely self-sufficient section within the association, with a high degree of tenant participation in decision making over matters such as the annual budget, levels of rehabilitation, and management and maintenance. By the early 1990s elected tenants also formed the majority on the central boards of directors of the associations (in some cases alongside local authority nominees) and there had been a reduction in the degree of autonomy of most of the professional managers, compared with the situation before the reforms began. Clearly this form of tenants' democracy, which has grown considerably as a result of the legislative reforms, provides a powerful counter to the growth of centralized and overbureaucratic administration and hence to one of the most frequent claims of right-wing critics, that, in comparison with the private sector, social rented housing limits the autonomy and freedom of choice of tenants. The tenants' involvement in Danish social housing, plus its generally high quality and ability to retain a social and economically mixed occupancy, has made it much more difficult for the sector as a whole to be stigmatized and politically marginalized. In addition, the rule which states that each section must be financially self-sufficient, in the sense that rent income must balance outgoings, net of subsidies, and that associations must be strictly non-profit, so there is no opportunity to generate surpluses that can be diverted elsewhere (as in Germany), also protects the sector from the political attack and economic expropriation that have occurred elsewhere. Any remaining surplus, after sections have put by the sums needed for longer-term repairs and modernization, is transferred to the overall organization but can only be used for other social housing purposes. As Andersen (1992) has noted, this situation also encourages a relatively high level of tenant participation in the management of the sections, not for ideological but for material reasons.

Nevertheless, within this system, various pressures were evident from the 1970s onwards. There was an evident tension between the role of the associations in accommodating low-income households in housing need, which the government envisaged for them and about which local government was also concerned, given its responsibility to find accommodation for such households, and the wish of tenants and the housing managers to retain a social mix and the considerable degree of economic self-sufficiency which this provides (Vestergaard, 1992: 40–1). Local authorities could and did nominate tenants to one-third of the vacancies in the social stock. However, individual sections were often resistant to what they saw as the possibility of overconcentrations of low-income households in their projects and, in particular, to the housing of 'problem' families. Apart from social and racial prejudice, there was an obvious economic dimension to this resistance as, for example, households which incurred high rent arrears adversely affected the budgets of individual projects and the rents charged.

More generally, as Andersen (1992: 15) notes, in this structure 'there is a greater risk that managers and other employees – and in part the (tenant) volunteers – want to follow their own objectives instead of the ideological (ie socially oriented) objectives that founded the organisation'. In so far as the dominant control within housing associations is vested in professional managers and the normally more articulate, better-off sections of the tenant population, the claims of the less well-off tenants and lower-income, poorly housed potential tenants may be disregarded.

Another possibility might be a growth in segregation within the social rented sector, with the emergence of some 'sink' estates, housing concentrations of low-income and problem households, while other sections provide better-quality housing at relatively low rents for more solvent and 'respectable' households. But one factor which limited this possibility was the rule that required each sector to balance its budgets. This would inhibit any such segregative process and encourage a policy of social and economic mixing within each estate. In addition, there was a framework of rules which inhibited discriminatory tenant- or management-driven allocation policies.

Despite these strengths, the growth of home ownership led to a narrowing of the income mix of tenants in social rented housing, with a growing concentration of low-income tenants and fewer better-off ones over the period 1970–85, according to the results of an official report published in 1987 (Boligministeriet, 1987; Boelhouwer and van den Heijden, 1992: 165–6; Power, 1993: 294–5). This showed a growth in the underrepresentation of self-employed and professional workers over the period and a switch from over- to underrepresentation of higher-qualified white-collar workers. Less well-qualified white-collar workers remained overrepresented in 1985, but less so than in 1970, while skilled manual workers (who probably had higher wages) moved from being over- to underrepresented. The representation of the unemployed moved in the reverse direction. Finally, there was a growth in the overrepresentation of unskilled workers. So, more as a consequence of wider changes in housing provision than as a result of central government-enforced restructuring of social housing, a growing tension between social housing as mass housing and the alternative, more limited low-income role, was emergent.

As elsewhere, the growth of socially and economically disadvantaged households from the mid-1970s, in combination with the existence of some large, high-rise, high-density, industrially built estates which proved unpopular with most tenants, did result in social housing having a number of what the Danes referred to as 'socially depressed' estates (Kristensen, 1985; Vestergaard, 1990). These combined a defective environment and buildings with high vacancy and mobility rates and high concentrations of low-income and socially disadvantaged tenants, who filtered into these units because they were where most of the vacancies available to the social services departments of local authorities occurred. Associations often cooperated in this process, because at least it resulted in vacant units being occupied, and hence the losses to the associations being reduced. The situation led to conflicts between local authorities, especially in the Copenhagen region, where areas with high levels of social rented housing (mainly under the long-term control of Social Democratic administrations) faced an increasing inflow of lower-income households from adjoining areas with low levels of social housing (normally under right-wing control). To inhibit this process some of the former municipalities attempted to enforce minimum income requirements on incoming households applying for social housing in their area (Vestergaard, 1992: 40). Frequently, however, the associations with the greatest problems were opposed to such rules because of their need to fill unpopular vacant units.

These problems caused considerable financial difficulties for some associations and led to extensive government-sponsored research into their problems and new policies in the 1980s (Kristensen, 1985; Vestergaard, 1990, 1991, 1992; Power, 1993: 293–301). As Vestergaard (1991: 3) notes, the scale of the problem was far smaller than in many of the other countries discussed in this book, amounting to 25,000 units on some 80 estates built in the heyday of industrialized construction, i.e. 1965–75. The government responded with individually tailored packages to rehabilitate and improve the estates, and to rearrange their loans on more advantageous terms which financed the physical improvements and reduced rent levels, which, as elsewhere, were particularly high on these projects, built to high internal standards of space and amenity during a time of high inflation, on the assumption that they would accommodate relatively well-off tenants rather than the low-income households that filtered into them as those who had more choice went elsewhere. These remedial schemes were designed, planned and carried out with a high degree of tenant participation through the section-level organizations. There were also various initiatives to provide more social services and better management support to such estates. In the early 1990s a large-scale evaluation project was under way to judge whether the schemes had succeeded, and whether, if successful, they had merely diverted problems to other parts of the social rented stock.

CONCLUSION: RESIDUALIZATION OR REFORMATION?

Since the mid-1970s the shift back towards a contemporary version of the restricted, residual model of social housing provision, targeted on the poor, has become evident in all the countries with which we are concerned. Of course, this was no new development in America, and in Europe the transition was far swifter and more far reaching in some countries than others. We shall return to these variations below. However, in country after country, the period was marked by a common pattern – deep cuts in new investment; moves, on the one hand, to privatize sections of the stock and, on the other hand, to narrow the socio-economic profile of those whom the sector accommodated; policies of decentralization and attempts by government to reduce its political and financial responsibility for the sector.

In this chapter we have described and analysed the social, economic and political context within which this transition occurred. The history of these years, with successive recessions, high levels of unemployment, the growth of economically and socially polarised societies, the rise of racial and other forms of social conflict, and rising levels of poverty, contrast oddly, at first sight, with a situation in which national housing systems became increasingly centred on home ownership, a form of provision whose growth is heavily dependent on just those economic conditions – full employment, rising real incomes and property values – which became increasingly difficult to sustain after 1975. However, while the material preconditions for mass home ownership worsened, the drive towards this form of provision, and away from mass social rented housing, intensified.

Therefore, this latest period yet again demonstrates that the relationship between social housing policies and housing needs is, at best, very indirect. From the First World War onwards, mass programmes of social housing have been strongly linked to wider developments in society and in the economy and to the existence of particular forms of housing need whose satisfaction has strategic significance within this broader context. In the period since 1975, in most countries and at most times, there has been no such con-juncture. In most cases the steady growth of what has been var-iously labelled 'the new urban poor', the 'underclass', the 'two-thirds' society and so on, has posed few real problems for economic systems which, in many sectors, have been expelling rather than attracting labour and in which the new industries have little or no need for many of the skilled manual and middle-income occupations which, as we have seen, provided much of the demand for mass social housing between 1945 and the 1970s.

Politically, the new poor have also posed few lasting problems. In country after country, social democratic governments struggled and failed to sustain their vision of economic growth, full employ-ment and the welfare state, giving way to an era of right-wing political dominance, marked to a greater or lesser degree by the adoption of a neo-liberal politics which had had no place in main-stream political life since before the Second World War (or earlier). Now social democracy became pushed to the margins, its political base slipping as the traditional working class was restructured out of existence and sections of the middle class, which it had begun to attract in the affluent 1960s, turned to parties of the right which seemed to offer solutions to the problems of high inflation, sagging economic growth, state bureaucracy, trade union power and so on.

Social democratic parties struggled but failed to come to terms with the politics and economics of the era, being unable to forge a new social base among the disadvantaged, increasingly fragmented by gender, racial and ethnic distinctions and demography. At the same time, they failed to move from an increasingly ineffective defence of the economic and social framework of the post-war welfare states to a new set of principles and ideas that might have challenged the ideological dominance of the New Right, and pro-vided a basis for reclaiming the political allegiance of the 'middle mass' of the electorate. The emergence of social democratic parties as parties of government after 1945, together with the growth of the welfare state (under governments of all political shades) had been intimately linked to the political allegiance and the social needs of this middle mass, not those of the poorest in society (although the latter had surely benefited as well). Now these links were disintegrating, although, as the onset of a new recession in the late 1980s indicated, with ever deeper reductions in public ex-penditure and social welfare cutting into the social wage of middle-income groups, the ability of the New Right politics and economics to consolidate its position and to consign social democracy to oblivion, or at least to being little more than a less radical adherent to the same ideology, seemed problematic.

In the late 1920s, as the first era of mass social housing ended, in a world where the state was far less deeply involved in housing or other forms of social provision, where large-scale private renting still existed and where social rented housing accounted for no more than a small proportion of working-class accommodation, state disengagement from this form of provision was relatively unproblematic. Some 60 years later, although the policy objective was not very different, the process was far more complicated and difficult. In the European countries social housing now accounted for a major share of low- and moderate-income housing provision, and hence for a major and continuing governmental commitment in financial and political terms. While new entrants to social housing increasingly consisted of low-income sections of the population with relatively little economic or political power, the concerns and the political weight of longer-term tenants continued to be of considerable importance in many countries, as did those of the social housing professionals, federations and other linked interest groups. Even in America, where the political clout of public housing tenants was minuscule, the public housing professionals and lobby groups managed to mobilize enough political support in the legislature to thwart administration plans for the abolition of the federal role in low-income housing provision.

Apart from these political factors, governments were, of course, locked into long-lasting financial commitments to social rented housing. Fewer of these commitments were, however, linked to the expansion of the sector. Instead, they were concerned with sustaining affordable rents for an increasingly impoverished social housing population, and providing some level of investment to counter stock deterioration. These growing commitments highlighted the principal contradiction at the heart of many governments' policies towards social rented housing during this period. Ideologically and financially driven policies led them to adopt various means of targeting social rented housing more narrowly, so that it served the poor rather than those on middle incomes (who, it was believed, could afford to buy or rent privately). This would encourage self-sufficiency and save on public expenditure. Moving rents closer to free market levels, or at least to levels which reflected the costs of provision, would encourage the better-off tenants to move out into the private market (thus increasing levels of indirect subsidies, a consequence largely ignored in this scenario). Major savings on 'indiscriminate', 'bricks and mortar' subsidies would accrue, although some additional expenditure would be necessary for income-related housing allowances to lower rents to affordable levels for a reasonably small number of the least well-off tenants.

Such policies began to emerge in the first part of the 1970s. They *might* have worked in the 1980s and 1990s if the economic conditions of this earlier period had persisted, if poverty, low wages and unemployment had remained relatively small-scale phenomena and the purchasing power of even the less well-off social rented tenants had kept up with escalating housing costs and rents. However, as we have seen, this did not happen. Instead, social housing accommodated growing concentrations of low-income households, increasingly dependent on means-tested housing allowances. These social consequences of policies which restructured social rented housing as a residualizing form of provision for the poor involved the state in new financial commitments which it found hard to evade. In some respects, therefore, social rented housing became more rather than less state-dependent. Apart from the escalating level of consumption subsidies, the combination of low-income occupancy, economic and social deprivation with, in many cases (notably on the problem estates), a deteriorating housing stock and a lack of internally generated resources for its improvement (i.e. from rents), led to new and pressing demands for state subsidies. In purely economic terms the rationale for reducing social rented housing to a residual form of provision for the poor was far from evident, especially as it involved an expansion in direct and indirect state assistance for home ownership. Moreover, as we have suggested in this chapter, some of the social costs of this transition, at least in those countries where it has gone furthest, have been considerable.

Alongside policies which aimed to narrow the section of housing needs accommodated by social rented housing, there were also policies of privatization, which aimed to reduce the sector by transferring its ownership and moving it from the non-market to the market sectors, either home ownership or private renting. The extent to which privatization formed a major element in the housing policies of right-wing governments during this period, and the extent to which they were able to implement these policies, varied significantly. Moreover, where privatization did occur, it took various forms. These differing outcomes were determined by a complex interaction between diverse social, economic, political and institutional factors, within the social rented sector, in the rest of the housing market and beyond the housing system altogether. In certain important respects the legal and institutional structures of social rented housing, which emerged in the first decades of the century, and which we discussed in the early pages of this book, had a material impact on the differing prospects for privatization.

The detailed discussion of national circumstances in the previous sections of this chapter have referred to many of these variations. It remains to draw out and highlight some of the major contrasts here. In America, the Reagan administration might not initially have thought that resistance to its privatization plans would have been too difficult to overcome. However, it was thwarted by the continuing ability of the expert low-income housing lobby, which included public housing professionals, to mobilize Congressional resistance. Also, the Reagan and Bush administrations were faced with the ultimate contradiction. In order to privatize in any way that would have been socially and politically feasible, more rather than less federal spending would have been necessary in order to subsidize the very low income tenant populations' purchase of its accommodation or purchase by private market agencies. Here the complete residualization of public housing by the later 1950s closed off a privatization strategy which was adopted 30 years later. In addition, the federal government faced considerable legal obstacles to any centrally imposed privatization of public housing, even if it had been willing to provide the heavy subsidies required, owing to the fact that this housing belonged to legally independent public housing agencies, subject to state, not federal, laws. While the support for public housing at state and local levels had, in most cases, never been strong (and in many jurisdictions there had been great hostility), the rising tide of poverty and deprivation in the 1980s, especially in the larger cities which had significant public housing stocks, meant that many local politicians wished to preserve all forms of lower-income housing provision against erosion, including public housing. This resulted in little enthusiasm for the federal governments' attempts to privatize during this period.

In Europe, as we have seen, the largest-scale privatizations occurred in Britain and the former West Germany, although they took very different forms in the two countries. In Germany a significant proportion of the social housing stock had been destined from its inception eventually to become privatized, and policy changes in the 1980s only speeded up this process. However, the more radical change was the removal of the 'socially binding' obligations and tax privileges from the 'non-profit' sector (except cooperatives). A crucial factor was the political vulnerability of the subsector, especially after the Neue Heimat scandal, and more generally a growing belief that it had lost its earlier social mission, a view shared by many across the political spectrum. The desire of many social housing managers to have restrictions lifted so that they could pursue more entrepreneurial activities, moving closer to operating as commercial landlords, is evidence that this was, indeed, the case. The changes in the 1980s resulted in the reduction of social rented housing to two distinct forms of provision: cooperative housing, serving sections of the better-off working and lower middle class, and a relatively small, residual stock under the control of the local authorities which continued to house a high proportion of low-income groups.

As we have seen, the reversal of policy direction from the late 1980s onwards, with the restitution of a federal–state programme of shallow subsidies for new social rented construction, was more apparent than real, as the major process of privatization of the existing stock continued unabated. Moreover, the nature of this programme illustrates, yet again, the close relationship between social housing development and the housing needs of middle-income, politically significant groups of the population rather than those of the politically marginal poor. While the new 'third subsidy' system has frequently been seen as a response to rising low-income housing needs and to the flow of immigrants from the East into West German cities, in reality it was a response to a growing shortage of affordable housing for middle-income groups in these cities and was designed to produce units with rent levels appropriate to this group. Moreover, as most forecasts of housing market supply and demand predicted that the inability of the private market to cater for these groups would not persist beyond the mid-1990s, the programme was explicitly intended to be no more than a temporary expedient to deal with the political and social consequences of a short-term crisis.

In Britain, the form of privatization was conditioned by the legal and constitutional circumstances of council housing, owned by public rather than private sector landlords who were constitutionally subordinate to central government. This meant that many of the obstacles to a government determined to privatize the sector which were present in other countries, even as we have seen in the USA, were absent. However, two other factors were also significant. First, the growth in previous decades of mass home ownership, which provided a viable and increasingly popular housing solution for many middle-income households, more of whom elsewhere remained in social rented housing. Second, the political weakness of council housing, which had been accentuated by loss of better-off tenants and its increasingly low-income, residual character, which had always been seen by the Conservatives as an inferior form of provision to that of home ownership, and which, from the late 1960s onwards, was increasingly so viewed by the Labour Party (especially at the national rather than the local level).

For differing reasons, privatization strategies were far less advanced in France, the Netherlands and Denmark, although in every case the wish of central governments to withdraw from their previous extensive involvement in social rented housing was evident. A common characteristic of the three countries was the greater degree to which social rented housing had gained and retained support across the political spectrum, and the relatively limited influence on government policies exerted by those parties which did adopt a more radical New Right approach to housing policy. In each case too, the position of social rented housing was sustained, to some degree at least, by developments elsewhere in the economy and the housing market – the recourse to new programmes of social housing investment for macro-economic reasons during the recession of the early 1980s and the crises in the home-ownership market which slowed down the further expansion of this tenure in the 1980s and early 1990s, inhibiting the outflow of better-off households from the rental tenures.

In each of these three countries, there were more nationally specific features affecting the prospects for privatization as well. In France, apart from the exceptional circumstance of a Socialist government throughout much of the 1980s, the shift to the private market in housing provision occurred in part within the social sector, with increased emphasis in the early part of the period on social home ownership (plus a generous system of direct and indirect state support for private market home ownership), although this could not be sustained as economic conditions worsened and even heavily subsidized home ownership was increasingly unaffordable by the groups at which it was targeted. Significantly, however, even the Socialist government failed to carry through its initial plans to expand social rented construction. Instead, it maintained in all essentials the housing policy framework, strongly influenced by neo-liberal economics, which had been established under the Giscard presidency. In any event, from the 1970s onwards there was a rapid transition in the nature of French social rented housing, towards a residual sector, housing low-income tenants for whom home ownership, even with the aid of heavy subsidies, was unachievable. However, the crushing victory of the right-wing parties in the 1992 National Assembly elections may result in some form of privatization of even this stock being attempted.

In the Netherlands, despite the ideologically driven desire to privatize of one of the major partners in government during much of the period, there were many obstacles to its proposals to sell off social rented housing. First, social rented housing had maintained a considerable degree of cross-party support, especially in the pivotal Christian Democratic party. The large proportion of the housing market accounted for by the social rented sector, which meant that it accommodated sections of the electorate from which this and other centre and centre–right parties drew support, provided a continuing basis for the political muscle exerted by the social housing federations and other interest groups. Second, developments in the home-ownership market after the end of the 1970s inhibited the outflow of these better-off households from the sector, helping to sustain its socio-political base. Finally, the legal and constitutional status of the housing associations, as 'private initiatives', provided a substantial obstacle to any forced privatization, even if the government had been willing to attempt such a course of action. However, despite these obstacles, by the end of the 1980s the Dutch government was moving towards disengagement from support for social rented housing. But this took a particular form, not the wholesale transfer of social housing to the market sector, but, rather, an attempt to revive something of the original conception of Dutch social rented housing as a 'private initiative', largely self-sufficient, with a limited financial involvement by the state, although it would continue to play a greater regulative role. This rather sophisticated approach to state disengagement was developed by a highly effective Housing Minister with great political skill and sensitivity to the particular socio-economic, political, legal and historical context to Dutch social rented housing. By the early 1990s the likely success of this strategy was still unclear. Much probably depended on whether the Minister's predictions for a recovery in the economy and the private housing market in the rest of the decade proved accurate, or whether the maintenance of a mass social rented housing sector with a substantial level of state support continued to be a politically unavoidable necessity.

In many ways the most interesting example of those countries where privatization made least headway in the 1980s and early 1990s was Denmark, which did have a government committed to increasingly radical cuts in welfare state provision, and even in tax subsidies for home ownership, but where new social housing construction continued at a significant level and the desire of one of the governing parties, the Liberals, to implement mass social housing sales had no chance of succeeding. As we have seen, the sustained governmental support for new social housing construction in the early and mid-1980s was driven by macro-economic considerations and was a purely temporary expedient which ended as the economy recovered from recession. However, in the long run, the more significant obstacle to privatization was provided by the particular nature of Danish social rented housing. As in the Netherlands, it had managed to retain a considerable section of moderate- rather than just low-income tenants which, in itself, meant that the political influence exerted by the sector was maintained more successfully than in countries where this was not the case. Also, as elsewhere, successive crises in the home-owner market helped sustain this position. However, an additional important strength of Danish social housing was provided by its localized and decentralized institutional and management structures, which had been reinforced by the implementation of 'tenant democracy'. This, together with a high degree of financial self-sufficiency, which had allowed there to be considerable investment in improving and upgrading the stock, and a reputation for providing (in most cases) high-quality accommodation, which competed with what the private market could offer, meant that Danish social rented housing was far less vulnerable to the sort of criticism that social rented housing was prone to elsewhere – that it was poor-quality housing, bureaucratically and insensitively managed, which offered housing consumers little choice.

All this meant that in Denmark, even more clearly than in the Netherlands, overt privatization was not a viable strategy for a government which, by the later 1980s, like its counterparts elsewhere, was also looking to reduce its involvement in social rented housing. Instead, as in the Netherlands, the emphasis was on a reorientation of the social sector rather than its transfer to the private market. One aspect of this change was the development of a socially subsidized owner cooperative sector, a bridge between social renting and full home ownership, which accounted for an increasing proportion of new social housing quotas over the period. Another feature, which, as we have seen, occurred in all the other countries with which we are concerned, was the decentralization of many of the detailed responsibilities for regulating and supporting lower-income rented housing from the central government to the local authorities. Finally, as in the Netherlands, there were policy changes which shifted social housing organizations away from continued dependence on state support towards a greater degree of financial self-sufficiency, using internally generated resources to fund an increasing share of new investment in the sector.

Despite these important national variations, it is evident that in every country the most recent history of social rented housing has been marked by a movement away from the mass model of provision towards the more limited, residual model which, as we have argued throughout this book, is more likely to prevail in advanced capitalist societies with dominant private housing markets in periods when there is no compelling political or economic reason for more wide-ranging collectivist or semi-socialized state intervention in housing supply (rather than support for market forms of provision). However, while broadly similar macro-economic, social and political features of the advanced capitalist countries over the past 20 or so years can be pinpointed as the ultimate cause of these common features of development in national systems of social rented housing, cross-national variations in the nature and extent of state disengagement and of the reversion to the more restricted model of social rented housing provision have been crucially affected by distinctive, nationally specific structures of provision and developments within them, as well as by nationally specific political, economic and social structures. These include the historically inherited legal status and institutional format of social housing, the political, social and ideological status of the sector, developments in the private housing market, features of wider constitutional, governmental and political systems, the use of social rented housing investment as a part of macro-economic policies, and so on.

However, by the 1990s, while the trend towards the residualization of social rented housing was far more advanced, and even complete in one case, in four countries – the USA, Britain, France and the former West Germany – than in the Netherlands and Denmark, it was apparent everywhere. As we have seen, even in Denmark and the Netherlands there was an increasing concentration of lower-income households in the sector and the loss of middle-income tenants or sources of new demand. In every case, too, this result had been brought about largely as a result of deliberate state action which had aimed to channel housing demand away from the social sector towards the private market. We have traced many of the adverse, even contradictory, social, economic and budgetary consequences of these policies for the social housing landlords and governments. These were intensified by concurrent changes in national economic circumstances, the growth of increasingly polarised economic systems with levels of unemployment, poverty and housing need not seen in the previous decades of the post-war welfare states and private housing markets whose ability to extend their activities to progressively lower levels of the income distribution, as had occurred in the 1960s and 1970s, and even earlier in Britain and America, was severely inhibited after the late 1970s.

The logic of the argument which this book has sought to sustain regarding the socio-economic and political circumstances in which mass rather than residual social housing has been developed suggests that any major reversal of these trends must be dependent on a renewal of a political and/or economic imperative requiring such provision, and that this will be linked to the satisfaction of the housing needs of at least a section of that majority of the 'two-thirds' societies of contemporary advanced capitalist nations which earlier provided the social and political basis for mass programmes of social rented housing. As we noted above, the recent restitution of federal subsidies for social rented housing in Germany is a potent indicator of this relationship, although only a temporary reassertion of it.

A more likely scenario is continued movement towards the residual model of provision with, ironically, continuing high levels of dependency on state support for income-related subsidies, for programmes to resolve or at least contain some of the more unacceptable and disruptive consequences of the residual role and so on. Even in Denmark and the Netherlands, where governments seek to withdraw state support and revive something of the initial design for a self-sufficient social housing sector, a major withdrawal from income-related and other forms of support is likely to be an impossibility. Moreover, the extent to which state disengagement will be possible will relate to the degree to which the financial self-sufficiency of the social housing organizations can be sustained and developed. And this in turn will depend on the ability which these landlords have to continue housing sections of the middle-income population. Government policy poses an evident contradiction here, on the one hand desiring to reduce state support and foster self-sufficiency, and, on the other hand, wishing to target social housing provision on the poor and those in the greatest housing need. In these countries social housing managers face an evident dilemma: whether to give way to pressures for a more socially targeted role, leaving middle-income demand to go elsewhere, or to retain a more socially and economically mixed tenant population. As we have seen, the social housing organizations in both countries wish to resist the imposition of a purely residual role by government and they have some capacity to do so, even though they are under increasing pressure.

In fact, while these organizations were able more or less successfully to carry out a broadly defined social role, housing not just some of the poor but many middle-income households as well, up to the current period, their circumstances have now altered. On the one hand, there has been the unremitting growth of low-income demand, resulting not only from economic and demographic changes, but also from the continuing decline in low-income private rental housing. On the other hand, there is no longer continued large-scale state support for new social rented housing construction which might have enabled some of this burgeoning demand to be accommodated alongside the maintenance of provision for better-off households. Instead, governments are looking for a switch of priorities within an existing or, at best, slowly growing stock of social rented housing. One consequence of this situation has been a growth of segregation within social rented housing stocks, via allocation processes which concentrate low-income groups in less desirable, poorer-quality estates. Alongside segregation there is also evidence of the growth of formal or informal processes which have the aim of limiting the incursion of low-income households into certain parts of the social rented stock occupied by better-off or longer-established tenants. In many cases these also involve direct or indirect racial discrimination or other forms of discrimination against socially stigmatized sections of the low-income population.

In these countries the eventual outcome may well be a separation between a residualized subsector within social rented housing and a relatively small-scale sector which retains a wider socio-economic base. In such circumstances one could speculate about the possibility of a 'German solution' being adopted, with the complete splitting-off of the latter subsector, either in a form of co-operative, tenant-controlled housing, catering for middle-income groups with little or no commitment to housing the poor, and/or in a fully commercialized form. Meanwhile, a relatively small-scale residualized sector would remain, heavily dependent on state support within a policy framework which ensured that it concentrated on accommodating economically, socially and politically marginal sections of the population. However, a very important factor that is likely to inhibit any such development is the high degree of commitment which most social housing organizations and their representative bodies still have to maintaining a broadly based social role, housing a range of low- to moderate-income groups, not just the better off, and their continuing ability to mobilize external support for this view. In contrast, many German social landlords and managers welcomed the moves to end their social obligations and thus their enhanced ability to concentrate on accommodating more solvent sections of the population, together with the opportunities for personal and corporate gain that this offered. The only significant exceptions were the local authority-owned organizations, whose mission was largely determined by the legal responsibilities of local government regarding low-income housing needs and who were under increasing pressure as a result of the privatization of much of the rest of the social housing stock.

If the future course of development of the former mass social housing sectors in these countries is, as suggested here, one of increasing residualization, a lack of new additions to the stock and, in some cases, a continuation of their current decline, absolutely and as a proportion of the entire housing stock, the growth of low-income housing needs, so evident in the 1980s and early 1990s, is likely to be sustained for the rest of the century and beyond. However, unlike previous periods when social housing output was severely restricted and when mainstream private market provision was out of reach of large sections of the population, the changes which have occurred in post-war housing markets have eroded the traditional source of low-income accommodation in capitalist societies, the private rented sector. The next few years may well see the growth of newly constituted or revived forms of low-quality low-income private housing provision, alongside limited residualized social sectors. The current recourse in many countries to the use of redundant non-residential accommodation, welfare 'hotels', night shelters and so on as 'solutions' (or means of warehousing) homeless individuals and families is reminiscent of solutions which have been adopted by the state from time to time ever since the nineteenth century to manage socially and politically unacceptable manifestations of housing and social deprivation. In addition, in the USA and Britain especially, poor-quality home ownership now accommodates certain sections of the low-income population. Finally, in some areas, notably the larger cities, there is likely to be a growth of exploitative, poor-quality but affordable private rental housing. Slums and overcrowding were the main consequences and ways of responding to the nineteenth-century housing crisis; a century later, they may again begin to play this role.

More promisingly, there might be another parallel between the early years of social housing and the conditions in which it emerged, and the contemporary situation. As we saw earlier in the book, there were two distinctive, although interconnected, strands to early social housing reform movements. First, the approach adopted by the reformist elites, many of whose conceptions were later absorbed into state-subsidized systems of social rented housing, whether this took the form of mass or residual provision. Second, the alternative 'workers' cooperative' model, based on self-organization, control and management by the tenants themselves. As we have described, with the partial but important exception of Denmark, this second model scarcely survived in the era of the mass welfare state after 1945. However, in the 1980s and 1990s, in countries such as Britain, West Germany, the USA and the Netherlands, new, localized and mainly small-scale forms of social housing began to emerge which, in terms of their social base, orientation and forms of organization and self-management, had some affinities with the workers' cooperative model (Harloe and Martens, 1990; Novy, 1991: 31–5). In some cases new, tenant-managed and controlled forms of social housing arose outside the existing social sector altogether, as groups of housing consumers who were excluded from social housing, and/or who found the bureaucratic style of its management unacceptable, collectively sought alternative solutions. Among these groups there were some who wished to live in ways that conflicted with the regulative and financial structures which surrounded conventional social rented housing, for example sharing facilities rather than occupying wholly private, family-based spaces, combining work with residence and so on. In other cases forms of tenant-owned and/or managed housing arose among groups of low-income households who had no alternative, if they were not to lose their accommodation, but to take it over (such situations occurred, for example, in a few public housing projects and in landlord-abandoned private rented blocks in the USA). In the European countries such developments were mainly associated with state-supported initiatives targeted on 'problem estates'.

A notable feature of many of these developments, especially those which have been initiated by groups of younger, more highly educated activists, is that, with few exceptions, they have taken place outside the framework of social democratic politics. If anything, their roots lie in the politics of the new social movements, linked, for example, to environmental or civil rights issues or inner-city struggles against urban renewal, which have developed from the 1960s onwards and which have often been as opposed to social democratic policies and governing regimes as to right-wing ones. Again, with few and localized exceptions, mainstream social democratic housing politics and policy formation have remained locked into a now largely bankrupt, increasingly feeble defence of bureaucratized forms of welfare state-directed social housing provision and acceptance of dominant conservative ideologies which, as we have seen, have never sanctioned any permanent incursion of social rented housing into serving those groups of the population which can be housed by the private market at tolerably acceptable costs and standards. Any possible basis for a radical, social democratic alternative to this dominant ideology and conception of the role of social rented housing, based on bottom-up rather than top-down structures of ownership, control and management, and building on the rash of innovative projects which have emerged over the past 15 or so years, has been rejected, or simply overlooked. Indeed, in some cases, the apparent congruence between the emphasis on self-reliance and autonomy inherent in such projects and the conservative emphasis on similar virtues has led to some support for their development from right-wing governments and hostility, or at least deep suspicion, from social democratic parties. In fact, many of these projects combine elements and principles of organization, ownership and control which cut across the conventional ideological spectrum, combining a degree of collectivism which is wholly alien to conservative political thought with a degree of self-reliance and autonomy which social democracy lost sight of in its transition from the political organization of the oppressed, excluded from the governing system, to a place within that system as a collaborator in the development of the welfare state and of bureaucratized welfare state housing, and, more recently, in the radical alteration and partial dismantlement of these structures.

It is not yet possible to draw any major conclusions about the scope and significance of these new forms of social housing provision, or their prospects for growing to become a major alternative to mainstream forms of state-subsidized and regulated social rented housing. A more detailed review and analysis of innovative social housing projects, their problems and limitations and their prospects for survival and growth, has been published elsewhere (Harloe and Martens, 1990). However, an acquaintance with the history and eventual demise of the early workers' self-help housing projects, as well as with some of the conflicts and difficulties that these contemporary projects already face, poses a series of doubts and questions concerning their future evolution. First, it seems unlikely that these small-scale experiments, many of which are already dependent on obtaining state support in order to exist at all, can expand to become a major new source of lower-income housing without vastly increased state subsidies. In the era of welfare state expansion, increased state support was accompanied by increasing state regulation and direction, and by increasingly professionalized and bureaucratized forms of management with declining tenant independence and control.

Second, as we have seen, the early workers' cooperatives were located within the wider social, cultural and political structures of the organized working class, the core of which was constituted by skilled manual workers and the lower middle class in the expanding white-collar sectors of employment. So these self-organized forms of social housing provision were, to a greater or lesser degree, socially selective. In other words, they did not aim to house the very poor; these groups remained in slum housing owned by private landlords, at least until more residual forms of social rented housing began to be developed, with state subsidies, in conjunction with slum clearance. To some extent, of course, this selectivity was less apparent, at least to many contemporary commentators, at a time when the mass of the working class, including organized, skilled workers, were scarcely much better off than the urban poor. Today, as we have seen, rather similar patterns of social selectivity operate in those parts of the 'conventional' social rented housing stock which are most successfully resisting the residualizing trend. Close examination of many examples of the new, innovative forms of social housing provision in the contemporary era suggests that a precondition for their survival and stability may well be careful tenant selection. There may be several bases for this selectivity, for example the possession of a certain level of stable income and assets to meet quite high rent levels and other payments required on entry; the possession of personal and educational resources which enable tenants to participate in the active management and development of the projects; or the lack of certain social and financial characteristics which are felt to threaten the viability of the project in question, such as low and unstable incomes, a history of rent arrears, criminal or other behaviour which is deemed anti-social, or even racial or other ascribed characteristics which are regarded as unacceptable by existing tenants.

Finally, questions may be asked about whether those projects, which mainly involve very low income households and which come about less from any initial desire to develop autonomous forms of tenant-controlled housing than from necessity and from their exclusion from mainstream forms of state-subsidized housing, are much more than devices by which the poor can be induced to manage one aspect of their own poverty, reducing pressure on the political system to respond in more adequate ways. One indicator of whether such projects manage to transcend their essentially defensive origins is the degree to which they result in an empowerment of those involved; whether, for example, they have spin-off effects, providing tenants with new skills and confidence that enable them to improve their personal social and economic situations, or providing the collectivity with additional political clout and a basis for levering additional resources from local and central governments to repair and modernize their housing, improve its social and physical environment, develop recreational, educational and other facilities, or attract associated economic development and employment. By making such gains, several of these projects have demonstrated their potentiality to be more than just devices for getting the poor to manage their own poverty.

However, while it is not difficult to point to many of the possible limitations on these new forms of social housing provision – their small scale and often fragile constitution, their tendency to practise forms of selection and discrimination which bar access to many of those in the greatest housing need – such criticism is, to a considerable degree, misdirected given the situation they face. In an era when the economic and political structures and assumptions which underpinned the post-war expansion of the welfare states, and the post-war growth of mass social rented housing, have been swept away, and when the dominant parties across much of the political spectrum have abandoned or greatly weakened their commitments to social justice and greater equality in housing provision, as in other areas of social need, accepting the emergence of 'two-thirds' societies and tolerating the growth of poverty, homelessness and unmet low-income housing needs, the context within which these attempts to chart a new path for social rented housing are struggling to survive is nearly as unpromising as that faced by their predecessors at the turn of the twentieth century.

NOTES

1　This section draws on the annual Economic Survey of Europe (UN Economic Commission for Europe, 1976a and b, 1981, 1985, 1990) and OECD (1992).

2　The following section draws on Byrd (1986); Morgan (1990); Derbyshire and Derbyshire (1990); and Peters (1993).

3　The following section draws on Blum et al. (1985); Jones (1987); King (1987: 136–63); and Derbyshire (1990a).

4 The following section draws on Larkin (1988); V. Wright (1989); Derbyshire (1990b); and Safran (1993).

5 The following section draws on Derbyshire (1991); Ardagh (1991); and Conradt (1993).

6 But large tax cuts were used to revive the economy in 1978.

7 The following section draws on Daalder (1987); Middendorp (1991); Gladdish (1991); and Andeweg and Irwin (1993).

8 It is notable, for example, that while most voters in elections of the 1960s and 1970s favoured the formation of centre-left coalitions, in 1982 far more favoured a centre–right coalition (van Mierlo, 1986).

9 See Tommel (1992) on the decentralization of regional policy, and the shift from state-led to market-led approaches.

10 For a discussion of factors causing the rise of this party see Einhorn and Logue (1989: 19–21). The following section draws on this work and on Elder, Thomas and Arter (1982); Daalder (1987); and Damgard (1992).

11 After the 1990 election the KF and Venstre held 59 seats while the Social Democrats and SF held 84 seats. The Social Democrats alone could now outvote the government, which could assemble a majority that could beat the left bloc only with all the (three) small centre parties and the Progress Party (whose vote in the 1980s and early 1990s remained far below its 1970s levels).

12 When agreement proved impossible wage settlements were imposed in 1975, 1977 and 1979 by the Social Democrats. Einhorn and Logue (1989: 246–7) point out that when Schluter's bourgeois government did the same in 1985, there was a general strike.

13 Real wages also fell in these years, but more slowly.

14 Interestingly, a voters' survey in 1984 showed that only 10 per cent more KF voters felt that cuts in social programmes had not gone far enough, compared with the proportion that felt they had gone far enough. In contrast, the balance of opinion in favour of more cuts among Venstre voters was 8 per cent (Johansen, 1986: 370).

15 Asian immigration to the USA almost quadrupled between the 1960s and the 1970s, and then grew by about another 50 per cent in the 1980s (US Bureau of the Census, 1991: table 5, 9).

16 They then rose somewhat owing to renewals of earlier commitments to federally subsidized private rented units.

17 The following section draws on Merrett (1979); Malpass (1986, 1990); and Holmans (1987).

18 Although until new controls were imposed at the end of the decade there was a period of rising expenditure and a reduction of the backlog, using receipts from council house sales (Audit Commission, 1992: 14).

19 The following section draws on interviews with Joe Feagin (University of Texas), Rick Goldstein and Susan Judd (US Department of

Housing and Urban Development), Robert Kolodny and Peter Marcuse (Columbia University), Cushing Dolebeare (Low Income Housing Coalition), Mary Nenno (National Association of Housing and Rehabilitation Officials), Ray Struyk and Jack Goodman (Urban Institute), Wayne Sherwood and Elizabeth March (Council of Large Public Housing Authorities) and Florence Roisman (Attorney, Washington, DC), July and October 1983.

20   These data include a very small number of public housing units.

21   According to The President's Commission on Housing (1982: 13), 77 per cent of all new Section 8 units built in 1979 were one bedroom or 'efficiency' units.

22   Details of the annual struggles between Congress and the administration are usefully documented in Low Income Housing Information Service (various dates).

23   The following section draws on interviews with Chester Hartman (Poverty and Race Research Action Council), Peter Marcuse (Columbia University), Mary Ann Russ (Council of Large Public Housing Authorities), Marjorie Turner (Urban Institute) and Jill Khadduri (US Department of Housing and Urban Development), May 1992.

24   The first year allocation was later increased to $161 million.

25   This section draws on interviews with Pierre Strobel and Françoise Taieb (Ministère d'Urbanisme et du Logement), Christian Topalov (Centre de Sociologie Urbaine) and Michel Lachambre (Union Nationale des Fédérations d'Organismes d'HLM), June 1983.

26   Allocation Logement Familiale, originally introduced in 1948, and Allocation Logement Sociale, dating from 1971.

27   By 1984 average HLM rents in the post-1977 stock were about 87 per cent of private rent levels, compared with about 65 per cent in the pre-1977 units, although no allowance is made here for quality variations (Emms, 1990: table 2.7, 85).

28   The following section draws on interviews with T. Lacroix (Institut National de la Statistique et des Etudes Economiques), Michel Conan (Centre Scientifique et Technique du Bâtiment), Christian Topalov (Centre de Sociologie Urbaine), Maurice Blanc (Centre Universitaire de Cooperation Economique et Sociale), Laurent Bertrand (Laboratoire du Logement), J.-F. Marchal (Office Public d'Aménagement et de Construction des Vosges) and Nancy Bouché (Ministère de l'Equipment et Logement), September 1992.

29   Boelhouwer and van den Heijden suggest that this changed at the end of the 1980s; it did not, however.

30   I am grateful to T. Lacroix (Institute National de la Statistique et des Etudes Economiques) for supplying these unpublished data derived from the 1978: 1984 and 1988 Enquêtes-logements.

31   Although it was quite a large minority, consisting of at least 400 projects by the early 1990s (Power, 1993: 79).

32 Although the private rent increases were moderated by further legislation in 1989, subletting at higher rents was common in hard-pressed urban housing markets.

33 This section draws on interviews with Dr Uli Pfeiffer, Mrs Hofflich-Heberlein, Eugen Dick (Federal Ministry of Housing and Building), Dirk Schubert and Hans Harms (University of Hamburg-Harburg), Drs Hachmann, Hannig, Schindele and Heinen (Gesamtverband Gemeinnütziger Wohnungsunternehmen), Dr Menrath and Mr N. Burkhard (Deutscher Verband für Wohnungswesen), Uwe Wullkopf and Eberhard Mühlich (Institut Wohnen und Umwelt), January and May 1977, January 1984.

34 I am grateful to Dr Rudi Ulbrich (Institut Wohnen und Umwelt) for these data.

35 The scheme was updated to allow for rising rents and incomes in 1978 and 1981, although it remained relatively small scale, being received by around 6–7 per cent of all households, 10 per cent of which were home owners. It was increasingly inadequate in the 1980s, as we note later (Papa, 1992: 53–6).

36 The 1987 census showed only a slight rise to 42 per cent. Interestingly, in 1987 the government reformed owner-occupier subsidies in a way which reasserted the CDU's long-term ideological concerns with sustaining the family and private property ownership. Home ownership was no longer regarded as an investment but as a consumption good. Tax relief on mortgage interest and an imputed income tax were abolished and replaced by a tax allowance for home owners with children. However, the existing indirect subsidy which was obtained by setting a depreciation allowance against income tax was retained in a revised form. This increased the depreciable sum and allowed for an accelerated rate of depreciation (Papa, 1992: 64–7).

37 The following section draws on interviews with Hartmut Häussermann (University of Bremen), Uwe Wullkopf, Rudi Ulbrich, Joachim Kirchner, Eberhard Mühlich (Institut Wohnen und Umwelt), and Stefan Krätke, August, September and October 1992.

38 This section draws on interviews with Jan Conijn (Institute for Building Economics), Jan van der Schaar, Hugo Priemus and C. Adriaansens (University of Delft), N. van de Berg and J. van der Moer (Nationale Woningraad), Mr van Rijn and Mr Fornier (Ministry of Housing), and Bert de Graaf (Gemeente Rotterdam), April 1983.

39 The following section draws on interviews with Jan van der Schaar (University of Amsterdam), Hugo Priemus (Research Institute for Public Sciences and Technology, Delft), Frank Bonfrere (Amsterdam Housing Department), Jan van Weesep and Frans Dieleman (University of Utrecht), Edo Arnoldussen (Platform Gemeentelijke Woningbedrijven), Mr de Kam and Mr Harten (Nationale Woningraad) and Gerard Andriesen, June–July 1992.

40 Although housing analysts who were interviewed in 1992 pointed to

several indirect indicators of such a shift and, in particular, growing segregation within the social rented stock.

41   See Prak and Priemus (1985); van Kempen (1986); Heeger (1987); Priemus (1988, 1989); Elsinga and Wassenberg (1991); and Adrianow (1992).

42   However, the exact combination of factors which brought about this result varied from estate to estate; for example, the older lower-rise estates often had low rents but suffered from increasing dilapidation, while many newer estates provided high-quality accommodation but at high rents and in unpopular locations and environments (the Bjilmermeer was one example of such an estate) (Priemus, 1988).

43   This section draws on interviews with Erling Olsen (former Social Democrat Housing Minister), Kurt Jeppersen (Union of Tenants in Denmark), Hans Skifter Andersen (Danish Building Research Institute) and Jens Lunde (Ministry of Housing), February 1983.

44   Another factor which contributed to their unpopularity was that many of them were in high-density, industrially built projects.

45   The following section draws on interviews with Hedvig Vestergaard, Hans Skifter Andersen, Ivor Ambrose and Ole Kirkegaard (Danish Building Research Institute), Asger Munk (Ministry of Housing), Inger Bonnesen (National House Building Agency), Keld Adsbol (Social Housing Federation), Finn Barnow (Royal Danish School of Architecture), Niels Peter Thomsen (Dansk almennyttig Boligselskab) and Kim Harboe, August 1992.

46   Data supplied by the Ministry of Housing.

47   Interview with Bent Fjord, Ministry of Housing, February 1983.

6
Social Housing and Theories of Social Policy

This last chapter returns to some of the issues outlined in the Introduction. It moves beyond the detailed consideration of social rented housing to discuss the implications of our findings for theories of capitalist welfare state development. It concludes that such theories should pay more attention to the specific characteristics of individual areas of social provision for human needs, such as housing.

THEORIES OF SOCIAL POLICY

Theories of social policy development in the advanced capitalist societies fall into two broad categories: first, those which concentrate on cross-national similarities; second, those which focus on cross-national differences.[1]

The first group includes theories which link welfare state development to economic growth, industrialization, the spread of democracy or citizenship rights, modernization and so on.[2] Functionalist theories are also frequently classified within this first group. There are Marxist and non-Marxist variants. The Marxist versions stress the functionality of social policy for the maintenance of the capitalist regime, through its impact on accumulation processes and on maintaining legitimacy. Non-Marxist versions stress the role of social policy with respect to social and system integration.[3]

These approaches are frequently criticized for their inability to account for national differences in welfare state development. In fact, this may not be an inherent weakness, at least with respect to the functionalist approaches.[4] But there have been few attempts to test such theories empirically and historically across a range of comparable countries. As Skocpol and Amenta (1986: 135) note, with respect to one variant: 'neo-Marxist grand theorists have largely rested content with abstract conceptual elaborations tied to illustrative case materials for one nation at a time'.

In recent years this criticism has led to new approaches which do focus on such differences. These take various forms. One of the earliest and most influential was the 'power resources' or 'labourist' theory, developed by Korpi (1980: 1983), Esping-Andersen and Korpi (1984) and others, which sought to explain welfare state development in terms of the presence or absence (and the degree of success) of a wider social democratic project to transform the social order through, in part, the provision of solidaristic, universal benefits to wide sectors of the population, not just the working class. This form of class analysis has been criticized, for example by Baldwin (1990), for being merely a special case, mainly applicable in practice to Sweden, of a more general approach which links welfare state development to changing class relations.

Most recently, Baldwin (1990) has stressed the key role played by sections of the middle class in the development of universalist, solidaristic social policies ('institutional' welfare states) and in transcending a more residual conception of the welfare state. The latter form of welfare provision, he argues, exists in most advanced countries to satisfy the functional prerequisites for the continuation of the capitalist system. What determines the detailed nature of this residual system is not of concern to Baldwin. His main interest, like that of Korpi, is to explore the determinants of the institutionalized welfare state. And yet, as he notes, '[n]ot all, in fact very little, social policy has been solidaristic' (Baldwin, 1990: 21). He also comments, in passing, that various social policies mainly benefit the middle class, not the poor, for example many aspects of family policy.

An examination of variations in social policy in terms of whether national systems amount to residual or institutionalized types of 'welfare capitalist regime' also lies at the heart of Esping-Andersen's recent studies, first of variants within the institutional Scandinavian welfare states (1985), and then with respect to a wider and more diverse selection of nations (1990).[5] Esping-Andersen identifies three 'worlds of welfare capitalism' – the socialist, the

conservative-corporatist and the liberal. Denmark and the Netherlands are included in the socialist cluster, France and Germany
in the conservative-corporate one, and the USA in the liberal
grouping. Britain is less easy to allocate, displaying some characteristics of the liberal and the socialist regimes. The nature of
social welfare provision varies across the three regimes. As already
indicated, in the ideal-typical socialist welfare state there will be
a high degree of decommodification, with universalistic social
benefits available to all or most citizens as of right. The liberal
welfare state will be marked by a preponderance of means-tested
benefits, which are barely adequate to maintain individuals above
the poverty level and which are stigmatizing. The main concerns
shaping welfare provision in the conservative-corporatist regime
will be the preservation of existing status and economic distinctions, engendering loyalty to the state and the nation and support
for traditional social structures, notably the family. In practice, of
course, actual national systems will only approximate to these ideal
types.

Esping-Andersen's work combines quantitative and qualitative
historical studies, but he develops two statistical indices which, he
claims, confirm the reality of this tripartite division. The first is
a measure of decommodification, the extent to which welfare has
been disconnected from market provision, and hence from levels of
individual purchasing power and the distribution of incomes (a
trend most developed in the socialist cluster and least in the liberal).
The second is a measure of the extent to which the welfare state,
by redistribution, has countered inequality and social stratification
arising from the labour market position of individuals.

While Esping-Andersen's analysis is elegant, it is not always very
convincing. For example, his 'decommodification score' ranges 18
advanced capitalist countries along a continuum, with Australia and
the United States being least decommodified and (unsurprisingly)
Sweden being most decommodified. There are no clear breaks in
the series, hence little justification for the tripartite division that
Esping-Andersen imposes on it (his index of stratification is rather
more convincing in this respect). He also has to do occasional violence to history, for example the large-scale growth of decommodification and equalizing tendencies in the Netherlands since 1950
is attributed to the strength of that country's Social Democratic
party – hence its allocation to the socialist cluster (Esping-Andersen,
1990: 53). This explanation downplays the important role played by
the Confessionals, especially the Catholics (as Castles and Mitchell,
1991: 23, n.1, note).[6] More generally, Castles and Mitchell (1991)

have critically reviewed some aspects of the empirical basis for Esping-Andersen's classification in the course of arguing for a fourth world of welfare capitalism, while accepting the general thrust of his approach.

A different perspective is advocated by Skocpol (Evans, Rueschemeyer and Skocpol, 1985), who emphasizes the need to take account of the state itself as an actor when examining the cross-national variation in social policies.[7] Skocpol and Amenta (1986) have highlighted two broad areas for investigation. First, the autonomous impact on social policy of the organizational structures and capacities of states. Second, the political effects of previously enacted policies. However, this second consideration is hardly a distinguishing characteristic of a 'state-centred' approach. The 'feedback' effects of earlier social policies and institution building on later developments is evidently an important consideration for a wide variety of analytical approaches which are not 'state centred' (see, for example, the works of Esping-Andersen and Baldwin). The question of whether autonomous or semi-autonomous state action has a major impact on forms of welfare provision can only be answered empirically. Skocpol has tried to do this, especially when explaining the evolution of American social policy (Weir, Orloff and Skocpol, 1988; see also Hage, Hanneman and Gergan 1989). However, this account grounds state formation and its subsequent impacts on social policy in the context of wider socio-economic and political changes. So the state-centred approach seems to promise rather more than, in practice, it delivers. In fact, as Gourevitch (1986: 62) observes, 'the impact of state structure, however great, cannot be shown independent of some understanding of the society it is meant to affect'.

HOUSING AS SOCIAL POLICY

A detailed comparison and critique of these theoretical approaches to social policy development and cross-national variance is beyond the scope or requirements of this study. Instead, the aim is to consider whether any of the theories provides an adequate basis for understanding the development of housing policies and provision, especially social housing, and, conversely, to consider some of the implications of the housing case for such theories.

The first step is to summarise the main findings of this study. These are:

1   Social housing has nowhere accounted for more than a minor share of all housing provision. Quantitatively, it has been most important in the Netherlands and in Britain and least important in the United States. France, Germany and Denmark fall between these two extremes.

2   Two models of provision have been identified – the 'residual' and the 'mass' models. A third variant, the 'workers' cooperative' model, faded away in the second half of the century. This latter model was largely the product of what Esping-Andersen (1987a: 81–3) has termed the ghetto model of organized working-class social, economic and political development, abandoned in favour of reformist, coalition-building conventional politics as its limitations became obvious.

3   The residual model of social housing provision involves small-scale building programmes, targeted on the poor. Historically, they were closely linked to slum clearance. More recently they have served the 'new urban poor', many of whom are outside the labour market and excluded from private market provision. Residual social housing tends to be a more or less stigmatized form of provision which accommodates politically, socially and economically marginalized groups. It therefore shares many of the characteristics which analysts have more generally attributed to the residual welfare states.

4   The case for state action to provide or support the provision of re-sidualized forms of social rented housing was increasingly heard in the years before the First World War in Europe (though it was strongly opposed in the USA). However, developments during and after this war led to a different form of provision (see below). But, as the ability of the private rented sector to supply sufficient cheap and poor-quality accommodation for the urban poor declined, what seems (so far) to be a permanent state commitment to some level of residual social housing provision became institutionalized. Thus, in a sense, this form of provision may be seen as 'normal' in many advanced capitalist countries.

5   The 'abnormal' form of provision has been mass social rented housing. Typically, this has involved large-scale programmes of social rented housing, much less closely targeted on the poor. Such housing has frequently been managed in a rather less controlling or paternalistic way. Little or no stigma has been attached to its occupancy. Histor-ically, means-tested subsidies have played a small part in such pro-grammes. Instead, they have been assisted with 'indiscriminate' bricks and mortar subventions.

6   At any particular point in time, most social housing systems consist of a combination of mass and residualized forms of provision. Only the American system has, for most of its history beyond the first few years, been unequivocally residual. However, the major growth of mass provision has only occurred under historically specific circum-stances which involved periods of generalized societal crisis and/or restructuring for capitalist regimes. The first and shortest period oc-curred in the crisis years immediately after the First World War.

Then the main function of mass social rented housing was to aid the restoration of the status quo. In the United States, where the post-war crisis was less severe and was dealt with by other means, mass social rented housing did not emerge. Instead, a rather similar, if weaker, development occurred in the 1930s, under the crisis conditions created by the Depression.

7   The second, far longer period during which the mass social housing model was dominant stretched from the end of the Second World War to the mid-1970s. Again, the connections between housing provision and wider issues was evident. Now, however, mass social housing was not linked to an attempt to revert to the *status quo ante*, but to the reconstruction and restructuring of the capitalist economy and, in some cases, to completing the transition from rural-agricultural-based to urban-industrial societies. More generally, mass social housing was an element in the wider expansion of the welfare state and a part of the post-war settlement between labour and capital.

8   These connections between periods of mass social housing development and capitalism's 'requirements' should not, however, be understood in a crudely functional manner. That is, developments in social housing cannot be 'read off' as an inevitable consequence of such requirements. There is no necessary connection between crisis and restructuring, on the one hand, and mass provision, on the other. For example, the Depression did not lead to a renewal of large-scale mass provision in most countries, nor has the turbulent period since the mid-1970s. In each country, there were specific historical circumstances which resulted in mass social housing programmes being implemented. But two general conditions were of central importance. First, a situation in which the private housing market was unable, for various reasons, to provide adequate housing solutions for sections of the population. Second, when unmet housing needs among these sections of the population had a wider significance for the societies and economies in which they existed, whether in terms of heightening social tension and crisis (after the First World War and in the USA in the 1930s), or in terms of economic modernization (after 1945).

9   The poor were not a strategically significant group in relation to mass social housing. Rather, the main groups targeted by such housing were the organized or 'respectable' working class and sections of the middle class. This was the grouping (or cross-class alliance perhaps) that, as has been demonstrated, underpinned other aspects of the welfare state where there was a movement from residual to more universalistic, institutionalized forms of provision. However, mass social rented housing was at best a very flawed form of universalistic provision, since it tended, by one means or another, to exclude many of those who were poorest and in the greatest housing need. One way of viewing the difference between universalistic income transfer programmes, for example, and mass social housing, is to recognize that the former

extended welfare benefits beyond the poor, to the middle strata. The right to welfare thus granted encompassed both groupings. In contrast, mass social housing provided a benefit for the (lower) middle strata but severely restricted access by the poor.[8] Instead, as the century progressed, some of the poor were accommodated in the forms of residual social housing which we have described, and, in the most recent period, in degraded stock which was originally built as mass social housing for better-off groups. In many countries, for example the Netherlands, there was an explicit recognition that mass social housing was not mainly for the poor. They would have to rely on private market filtering to improve their housing situation, as better-off tenants moved into the social sector.

Therefore, there are some broadly similar reasons why there have been parallel developments in the national histories of social rented housing. Of course, there have also been many national differences, and any satisfactory analysis of social rented housing has to take account of both similarities and differences. Among the important differences are:

1   The extent to which mass social housing provision was perceived by the dominant political and economic groupings, and hence by the state, as an important element in the resolution of crisis or the implementation of restructuring. The most obvious contrast here is between the American and the European situations after both world wars. But there are also many more fine-grained variations, for example the immediate recognition of the need for social housing in the Netherlands and Germany after 1945, compared with its delayed recognition in France (and also the delay in the latter country in the 1920s).

2   The state of the private housing market and its ability, with or without state support, to provide accommodation for key sections of the population. Linked to this has been the ability of larger or smaller sections of the population, in specific periods of housing policy development, to afford private rather than social housing. These matters involve many separate considerations, for example developments within the building industry (and, more generally, the arrangements for private housing production) and within financial institutions which tend to extend or to restrict access to market provision. They also involve more general features of national economies which affect prices, incomes and employment. Again, compare the difference between America and the European countries after both world wars, or the difference between Britain and the other European countries in the 1950s and 1960s.

3   The strength of political support for social rented housing. This tends to be weak when such provision is purely residual. Mass social rented housing has prospered when it is supported by the organized working class and sections of the middle class. But the extent and durability of this coalition of interests has varied cross-nationally. It existed only

fleetingly in the USA. It soon proved fragile in Britain, where council housing and its tenants were seen as the preserve of the Labour Party, and this party was more likely to be in opposition than in government. It has been more durable in countries such as the Netherlands and Germany where the existence of Christian Democratic parties, with a cross-class appeal and with long periods in government, has resulted in broadly based support for social rented housing (although there has been an erosion in recent years).

4　Institutional and legal variations affecting the forms of social rented housing provision (including, but not only, the nature and capacities of the state). There are many instances of the significance of such variations. For example, they have affected the extent to which national policies could be implemented in the face of resistance from social housing providers. They have affected the extent to which social housing organizations have been able to accommodate certain sections of the population and exclude others. In the most recent period, as we have seen, they have either facilitated or impeded efforts to privatize social rented housing. Many of these institutional and legal parameters were established in the early years of social rented housing, before or soon after the First World War. This historical legacy has constrained subsequent developments, helping to establish the range of feasible policy options for governments and political parties. However, such factors are more accurately seen as constraining rather than decisive forces when we view the development of social rented housing in broad cross-national terms, in relation to the two dominant models of provision and the reasons for their changing significance in different historical periods.

5　Finally, there are the effects of ideological differences. Such differences are embedded in the political, institutional and legal aspects of social rented housing. Ideology has helped to shape the way in which policy choices, institutional structures and rules are formed. Again, these ideological differences are long standing and persistent. They derive from conceptions of the relationship between the individual/family, the state and the market, many of which pre-date the advent of social rented housing. Virtually none are 'housing specific' (except, perhaps, those which relate to aspects of housing planning and design, and even these frequently reflected wider ideological developments, as do ideological preferences for home ownership). Examples include the impact of liberal notions of the roles of the state, the market and the individual on American policy; the rather different impact of Catholic family-centred doctrine on French and German social housing policy; and of cross-ideological corporatism on Dutch policies. However, one of the most striking features of the politics of social housing has been the weak impact of distinctively social democratic ideologies. As we have noted on many occasions, social democracy failed to develop, let alone to implement when in power, a radically decommodified model of social rented housing provision which, to use Esping-Andersen's terminology, would break the connection between market position and housing circumstances for the great majority of the population, providing housing as a right of social citizenship for all. The reasons for the lack of a social democratic conception of social housing to go alongside its espousal of decommodified, universalistic and solidaristic systems in other parts of the welfare state are discussed below.

Before considering general theories of welfare state development in the light of these findings, it is important to outline some general characteristics of the relationship between the state and the rest of the housing market. The first point to note is that this relationship has more or less continuously expanded since the First World War, so that in recent decades most housing policy has not been concerned with social but with market forms of provision. Increasingly, too, state housing expenditure has been for the support of private market production and consumption. A further cross-nationally similar characteristic is that much of this financial support has taken the form of tax (indirect) subsidies for consumers and, in some countries, for the producers and providers of private market housing. As many economists have pointed out, such subsidies have two main beneficiaries. In so far as they effectively lower the price of housing for consumers, they do so in a manner which is regressive with respect to income. In short, they provide most for the better off and least for the poor. However, in free markets with constrained supply, much of the subsidy is capitalized into the housing price, hence it benefits landowners, builders, financial institutions and other producer interests.

When viewed as a whole, therefore, the most striking characteristic of housing policy, especially in comparison with income maintenance policies (the study of which frequently provides the basis for general theories of welfare state development), is that it tends to sustain rather than weaken the link between individual/family housing welfare and labour market position, and thus between market-determined patterns of social stratification and inequality. Even the mass social housing programmes were limited in this respect. And residual social housing policies are relatively easily accommodated within policy regimes whose main thrust is to underpin market provision. Moreover, it is worth noting that almost all social housing – whether of the residual or the mass type – has provided major profits for the private owners of land and financial and building capital. Indeed, from time to time, some of these interests have been supporters of expanded social housing provision, when alternative private market opportunities have been lacking.

HOUSING AND THEORIES OF SOCIAL POLICY

Are any of the recent theories of social policy development compatible with these findings? And do the findings highlight any weaknesses or omissions in the theories? Again, it is only possible to discuss a few key issues in this chapter.

The first point concerns the value of theories which aim to explain cross-national similarities and those which focus on differences. The social housing example indicates that this is an unhelpful division, or at least that any comparatively based theory that aspires to explain the overall development of a field of social policy, not just selected aspects, has to account adequately for similarities and differences. There is a danger that some recent contributions which have marginalized the analysis of cross-national similarities may simply not 'see the wood for the trees'. Of course, whether the similarities *are* less significant than the differences is an empirical question. It may be possible, for example, to speak of the three (or more) worlds of welfare capitalism with respect to other areas of social policy than housing (and to other areas than income maintenance programmes). But this has to be demonstrated. At the very least this comparative study of housing policy should serve to make one cautious about accepting purportedly general theories of welfare state development which mainly derive from a consideration of what determines cross-national differences in selected areas of social policy.

One of the best recent comparative studies of state policies which has been acutely aware of the need to focus on similarities and differences is Gourevitch's (1986) analysis of economic policies during periods of crisis – *Politics in Hard Times*. His general conclusion is echoed by this study of housing policies: '[e]ach country is affected by these twin factors: the force of epochs, which cuts across the particularities of circumstance, and the force of national trajectories, which expresses the features specific to each nation's history' (Gourevitch, 1986: 217). To understand the development of social housing in the six countries with which we have been concerned, it was as important to identify and trace the significance of some general political and economic changes in all advanced capitalist societies as it was to grasp the nationally specific circumstances in which these changes were experienced and which shaped the responses to them.

One consequence of this is that the earlier theories of social policy development, which focused on similarities and underplayed differences, should not be discarded as necessarily of little explanatory value. Baldwin (1990: 37) makes a rather similar point when he refers to the fact that different theories are concerned with different levels of explanation. However, his main concern, to examine why solidaristic income maintenance policies developed in some countries at some times, subsequently leads him to focus on the explanation of differences rather than similarities.

The findings of this study suggest that the Marxist theories which, in varying shapes and forms, link capitalist social policy development to the functional imperatives of accumulation and legitimation, do have some relevance to the understanding of cross-national similarities. Certainly, we have shown that there were links between accumulation/legitimation, on the one hand, and the nature of social housing policies, on the other (connections which much neo-Marxist theory has assumed *must* exist, but has rarely bothered to demonstrate empirically and historically, at least in a systematic manner). But it is equally clear that the conception of the class basis for social policy which many of these accounts embodied (basically a struggle between the working class and the monopoly capitalist class) was impossibly simplistic. No study which attempted to understand the nature and development of social housing policies as just a product of the strategies and power resources of these two classes would be able to make much headway when confronted with the reality of what was provided, in which form, when and to whom.

A further limitation of these Marxist theories, highlighted by Skocpol and Amenta (1986; see also Esping-Andersen, 1990: 14), is an uncertainty about the link which they make between social policy development and *capitalist* societies, rather than advanced industrial societies more generally (and the former state socialist countries in particular). In what sense, if any, are the accumulation/legitimation determinants of social policy specific to capitalist rather than all advanced industrial regimes? As this study only concerns capitalist societies, the question is difficult to answer in a fully convincing way. However, the 'force of epochs' which impacted on social rented housing as well as other aspects of social policy were certainly events within the history of the development of capitalism. The state socialist regimes had their own course of development which also resulted in a need for social (or rather, state) housing, driven by their own economic, political and ideological causes. Just because there were links between state socialist housing development and demands linked to accumulation and legitimation, one cannot assume that the analysis of state socialist and capitalist housing policies should be subsumed within some more general order theory of social policy development linked to industrialization and its imperatives, abstracted from specific features of the two systems. Instead, it is useful to note that the model of economic development adopted by most state socialist regimes mirrored that adopted by many capitalist regimes in some important respects, notably the focus on spatially concentrated industrial development, the formation of an industrial working class and the consequential need to provide for rapidly growing urban populations. Given these parallel developments, the existence of some congruities between some forms of capitalist and state socialist housing provision is not surprising. However, there were also many salient differences, for example regarding the degree of socialization of housing production, the rules which governed its allocation and the sharply differential treatment of private housing in the state socialist and the capitalist countries respectively (see, for example, Szelenyi, 1983; Andrusz, 1984; and Marcuse, 1991: 103–16). The more general point is that the relationship between the state, the market and the individual was differently constructed under state socialism and this profoundly affected the nature of social provision, including housing.[9]

We have already expressed doubts about whether the strong version of Skocpol's state-centred approach has much to offer when we seek to explain macro-level changes in social policy. Certainly, the forms adopted by social rented housing in, for example, the United States, on the one hand, and Britain, on the other hand, have been influenced by the differential capacities and constitutional position of their respective central states. More generally, we can point to the significance of cross-national differences in the constitution and powers of all the agencies which are involved in the structures of social housing provision. Consider, for example, the relative autonomy of German, Dutch or Danish housing associations compared with the subordination of British local authorities to the central state. But such differences are merely one set of factors which may or may not be of significance when comparing national structures of provision. There is no case for elevating them to a privileged theoretical status, as Skocpol appears to advocate. As Baldwin (1990: 47) notes, 'crucial decisions of welfare policy may have been taken by administrators ... different state structures may encourage or impede solutions, but ... in the final analysis, larger social forces have nonetheless significantly determined the nature of the legislation adopted'.

A similar conclusion must apply to theories which seek to privilege social democracy (or any other class-based political grouping) as the driving force behind extensions of social housing policy beyond a minimal, residual level. In fact, the more interesting historical finding is that the impact of social democratic parties on housing politics and policies has been severely restricted. In this respect, the history of social housing policy bears out Baldwin's (1990: 8–9) contention that

> such an account formulated in terms of the working class's strength and organisation is but one instance of a broader logic of social interest behind the welfare state and its development. Workers were often that group most concerned with social policy, but they have not been the only one. Nor, in a broader comparative analysis, have their interests been more than a single factor, amongst many competing ones.

Baldwin adds: 'to the extent to which social policy has ever gone beyond economically and politically functional minima, it is hard to deny the role played by the middle classes'. As we have seen, the existence of strategically significant working- *and* middle-class housing needs has been an important factor during periods when large-scale programmes of social rented housing developed. The presence (or absence) of sections of the middle class with a stake in social rented housing provision has helped to sustain support for this form of provision by bourgeois political parties. Of course, analysts such as Korpi and Esping-Andersen have recognized the significance of cross-class coalitions in the development of forms of the welfare state which go beyond the merely residual, but the implicit or explicit assumption has tended to be that the left and the right have adopted cross-nationally similar and fixed strategies. Thus Esping-Andersen and Korpi (1984: 181, 185) write:

> the opposed strategies of the Right and the Left concerning the institutional development of social policy can be expected to be broadly similar across nations. Labour movements have tended to strive for institutional structures which unify as large sectors of the population as possible into the same institutional contexts, and the Right has favoured attempts to divide the population through the creation of separate programmes and institutions for different sectors and groups ... socialist labour movements attempt to create 'institutional' welfare states ... Bourgeois forces, in contrast, strive for "marginal" types of social policies.[10]

But this is an historically and nationally (and perhaps programmatically) contingent argument. In relation to mass social housing it certainly fits the period of major expansion in Britain after the Second World War, for example. But it hardly fits the Dutch, French or German experiences during this period.

One further aspect of this quotation needs to be challenged. This is the assumption that social democracy, on behalf of its supporters, has an inherent interest in solidaristic social reforms. Korpi, Esping-Andersen and others have been strongly influenced in arguing this case by the particular circumstances and strategy adopted by Swedish social democracy, by the 'People's Home' ideology. As we noted in the Introduction, in this country the development of solidaristic social policies was central to a sophisticated strategy for mobilizing support for social democracy as, it was hoped, the prelude to a socialist transformation of society. However, such a strategy has been more clearly articulated and more consistently pursued (aided by long periods in government) by the Swedish Social Democratic Party than by any other such party elsewhere. As Esping-Andersen and Korpi (1984: 181) recognize, the circumstances facing social democratic parties in other countries have not provided them with this possibility to anywhere near the same extent.

But more importantly, the assumption that the organized working class and its political representatives *necessarily* have an interest in pursuing solidaristic social policies needs to be questioned. In fact, as Esping-Andersen (1987: 81–3) himself has pointed out, the early 'ghetto strategy' adopted by many social democratic parties was exclusionary. It sought to include neither the unorganized poor within its orbit, nor sections of the bourgeoisie. The failure of this strategy certainly caused a change of direction in social democracy, with a greater general concern for universalistic and solidaristic social policies.[11] However, it is important to specify, in each case, the scope and limits of this concern. In this context there may be a significant difference between the nature of social insurance programmes and, for example, social housing. We return to the topic later, but this difference occurs because insurance programmes involve the pooling of risks and contributions, so there is frequently an evident benefit to be gained by an insecure working class in promoting solidaristic social insurance policies which will pool their contributions and risks with those of the middle class (as Baldwin's (1990) study shows). But the applicability of this argument is much less immediately obvious in the case of social housing, although it is true that social housing sectors that have managed to retain middle- as well as working-class households, and maintain support from bourgeois as well as social democratic parties, have been more resilient. But few would claim that this was consciously part of a solidaristic strategy adopted by social democratic parties, at least in the six countries discussed here.[12]

An equally significant point is that the social democratic espousal of mass social housing policies has not necessarily implied any particularly strong commitment to housing sections of the population with the lowest incomes and in the greatest housing need. Indeed, there has frequently been resistance by tenants, social landlords and the organizations which represent them (many having close links with trade unions and social democratic parties) to extending solidarity *down* the social structure. This suggests that more attention needs to be paid to patterns of social closure when examining social democratic (not just right-wing) class-based strategies for social policy development. In this context, Parkin's (1979) reference to strategies of exclusion, by which collectivities with privileged access to rewards try to exclude those who do not qualify for membership of the collectivity, is of obvious relevance. One also needs to pay attention not just to the official policies and ideologies of social democratic parties, but to how their working-class electorate actually behaves and the impact that this has on policy formation. Finally, there is another conceivable basis for social democratic strategy which is to foster individual upward mobility within a still-stratified system. In practice, as Parkin notes (1975: 121–8), most social democratic parties have substituted this 'equality of opportunity' for more radical visions of equality in relation to key aspects of their social and economic programmes.

In fact, it is hard to see much evidence in the history of social housing policy for the impact of solidaristic objectives, whether espoused by social democracy or any other politico-social grouping. There is even less evidence that the better-off working and middle classes supported solidarism and universality of provision. Instead, as already indicated, the politics and administration of mass social housing provision were frequently exclusionary and tenants supported this. Also, in more recent times, social rented housing has been profoundly affected by the spread of 'equality of opportunity' in the rest of the housing market, promoted by social democratic as well as bourgeois parties. The growth of state support and encouragement for home ownership, extending access to the lower middle and working classes, largely on the basis of regressive tax subsidies, is a strategy which facilitates individual mobility 'up' the housing system, not equality across the system. This is not to claim that the initial adoption of such a strategy was a conscious or a whole-hearted decision by social democratic parties. Rather, such parties responded to pressure from below, warming to home ownership as some of their core electorate shifted into this sector. In short, as the stake which their supporters had in the provision of mass social housing declined, social democratic housing policies shifted accordingly. The consequences have been spelt out in the later chapters of this study.

This picture, of housing policy underpinned by shifting rather than by more fixed class alliances and needs, is, in many essentials, close to that adopted by Baldwin (1990: 10), who notes: '[t]o speak of the welfare state's social basis is therefore misleading except within narrowly circumscribed temporal and geographical limits. In broader comparative basis, the welfare state has been founded on differing combinations of social bases'. This suggests that Esping-Andersen's attempt to delineate three regimes of welfare capitalism 'with different logics and developmental trajectories' imposes too rigid and invariant a categorization. Certainly, it is hard to fit the housing policies adopted by the six countries which we have studied in this book into this tripartite division. Granted that the US case can be assigned to the liberal pigeon-hole, and that one can, for example, see elements of the conservative/corporatist approach in French and German social housing policies. But some aspects of this approach are at least as evident in Dutch housing policies, which Esping-Andersen mistakenly typifies as a socialist regime. As we have already noted, there is not much evidence that any of the social rented housing systems that we have examined – even that of Denmark – came close to fitting into Esping-Andersen's socialist category. In fact, rather than trying permanently to assign systems of social housing provision to a fixed ideal typology, it is more important to note that the six housing systems are all developing (or fully exhibit) characteristics associated with the residual, 'liberal' model. Of course, the speed and manner in which this is occurring varies considerably. But this is due to nationally specific combinations of political, economic and institutional factors and historic legacies: in short, to distinctively constructed structures of housing provision. And the analysis of the dynamics of structures of housing provision is not helped by any fixed categorization of regime types, especially as these have not been constructed with empirical reference to the history of housing markets and policies. Instead, we have found it more useful to construct three broadly drawn ideal typical modes or models of social housing provision (mass, residual and workers' cooperative) and explore the manner in which they occur in differing national combinations at differing times.

THE SPECIFICITY OF HOUSING IN THE WELFARE STATE

As we have suggested, some recent welfare state theories seek to privilege certain causal factors above others. The state-centred approach of Skocpol and the labourist approach evolved by Korpi and subsequently built upon by Esping-Andersen all make such choices. In addition, many studies, including that by Baldwin, have a particular concern with examining the reasons for solidaristic, universalistic social policies. Because Sweden has been held to be the model of such a welfare state, and because, implicitly or explicitly, many social policy analysts wish to go beyond analysis, endorsing this model as an ideal against which other welfare states should be evaluated, there is a sense in which the analysis of welfare state development has been 'Swedocentric' (as Esping-Andersen, 1990: 17, admits), that is, captured by a particular case and a particular set of questions.[13] Also, partly because of practical problems (data and other information availability – see, for example, Wilensky, 1975: 7–9), and partly for these theoretical reasons, most of the more ambitious cross-national studies of welfare state development have concentrated on income maintenance policies (although Esping-Andersen, 1990, also examines labour market and employment policies).[14] As we have already suggested, social insurance programmes, by the very nature of the insurance principle, are most likely to be a fruitful area for examining the spread of universalistic and solidaristic policies. In addition, as they were historically the mainsprings of early welfare state development and continue to be at the centre of welfare policies and spending, the attention which has been paid to them is understandable.

However, there is no reason to believe, in the absence of contrary evidence, that theories which have been developed to account for cross-national variations in one, albeit major, aspect of the welfare state will be equally applicable to other sectors, let alone to the overall 'regime' (if such a holistic conception is thought to be empirically identifiable and/or of analytical utility). Nor is it evident that research which focuses on exploring the reasons for solidaristic welfare provision will necessarily be asking all the right questions and seeking all the required answers to a different issue, whether this be the more holistic theme of the general nature of national welfare systems or more specific themes concerning aspects of welfare provision where these questions of solidarism and universality are of less relevance.

This suggests that, as Hage, Hanneman and Gergan (1989) have indicated and as we noted in the Introduction, there is a need to pay greater attention to the differing characteristics and dynamics of the individual parts of the welfare state (see the useful discussion in Heidenheimer, Heclo and Adams, 1990: 349–54). One starting-point, in the case of housing, is to reflect on some of the reasons why the barriers to the socialization of housing provision, and hence to greater degrees of decommodification and reductions in inequality, appear to have been so high, in comparison (at least in many countries) to the socialization of some income-related programmes, health provision, education and so on. To provide a compelling set of answers to this question would require detailed comparative studies of each of these areas of the welfare state, not just a long book on social housing policy. But one can at least provide some pointers.

First, there is the obvious but important fact that housing is property and in capitalist societies the defence of all forms of private property rights is deeply entrenched. It is a reasonable prediction, therefore, that housing policy proposals which threaten to abolish or seriously abrogate such rights are likely to face fiercer opposition than proposals to socialize and/or decommodify forms of education, health care or pensions.[15] Of course, this is not to say that in certain countries at certain times major private market suppliers of education, health care and pensions have not opposed the extension of state provision (the case of health care in the USA is notorious). However, it can hardly be denied that the private ownership of land and property lies at the heart of the capitalist system, alongside industrial and financial capital which also have an abiding interest in the maintenance of private housing production and markets. In this respect, there might be similarities between the obstacles to housing socialization and, for example, those facing plans to socialize the ownership of industry or agriculture. It is no coincidence that in all these areas the main impact of state policies has been to regulate and assist rather than to supplant private ownership.[16]

A second characteristic of housing is that there always has been some form of private market provision available, however low its standards, for the vast majority of the population. Historically, this was not the case for services such as health care, education, pensions and other social insurance benefits. In these areas state provision developed, more or less adequately, to meet demands for which, at the time, the private market was unwilling or unable to cater. From the start, therefore, the growth of social rented housing was seen as a direct and dangerous competitor with, in particular, the private landlord. We have seen how this helped to ensure that social rented programmes were constrained (most notably of all, of course, in the USA).

A further consideration relates to another aspect of the fact that housing is a form of real property. It is an asset against which money can be borrowed. This means that the capital cost of housing can be met by a continuing stream of far smaller payments. In this way, either indirectly through rental or directly through mortgage payments, private market provision can be brought within the means of the majority of the population (frequently aided by state subsidies). So some form of private market solution is financially feasible for the mass of the population, at least in 'normal' times. Of course, it has been precisely in 'abnormal' times that recourse to mass social housing has been most likely. By contrast, the consumption of health care, education or income maintenance provision does not also entail the simultaneous possession by individual households of a real property asset which can stand as security for a loan. Of course, there are ways of financing the provision of such services through the private market, for example by long-term contributions to individual pension funds (which may or may not involve some pooling of risks).[17] And the growth of private pension funds in recent years, as the mass of the population benefited from full employment and rising real incomes, has been notable. So the viability of forms of private welfare provision is not fixed for all time. However, it is less easy to see an immediate opportunity for profitable private sector provision of education, unemployment and disability benefits for the broad mass of the population. It is because retirement is a predictable event and it occurs towards the end of life, when most private pension beneficiaries have been contributing to their pension fund for many years, that the growth of such funds has been possible. But education comes before adult life in the labour market and disability and unemployment may strike at any time. The timing and extent of ill health is also unpredictable at the individual level and, as those who are dependent on private health insurance schemes discover, their coverage is frequently inadequate. Of course, these distinctions between housing and other forms of social provision are somewhat crudely and incompletely drawn. Nevertheless, they suggest that there are differently constituted risk and cost factors associated with different forms of social provision.

There are two conclusions that can be drawn from these considerations. The first reinforces the view that social policy theorists need to pay far more attention to the specific nature of individual types of social provision. Among the questions that need to be asked are to what extent will those major programmes that seek to socialize and decommodify provision conflict with core capitalist interests; are there means of making the cost of some form of private market provision affordable by most households or only a relatively few; and are considerations of cost and risk likely to make state provision more or less imperative?

Thus it is essential to recognize that some part of the variance in the relations between the state, the market and the individual in welfare provision may derive from the specific nature of the service concerned. Indeed, the outer boundaries to state involvement in some aspects of welfare provision in advanced capitalist countries may be rather less determined by cross-nationally variant factors of class relations, politics and institutions than by cross-nationally similar factors, such as those discussed above. So the construction of theories of the welfare state in advanced capitalist countries needs to be built on empirical and historical work which does not assume that a limited range of social programmes is an unproblematic 'indicator' or 'bearer' of more generalisable features of welfare state constitution and development. This implies that more theorised cross-national studies are needed of a wider range of forms of welfare provision. But it also implies a need for more comparative studies of individual programmes which explore the programmatic variance in the actual and likely potential outer boundaries to state intervention and their implications for policy development. Of course, if questions concerning whether there are significant 'intrinsic' (or at least deeply entrenched) differences in the nature of different forms of social provision in capitalist societies are to be satisfactorily explored, such studies also need to be cross-national. Comparisons between forms of provision in a single country may confuse nationally specific and 'intrinsic' factors. However, as Heidenheimer, Heclo and Adams (1990: 353) conclude, '[u]p to now there have been very few systematic attempts to compare functionally different policy areas cross-nationally'.

The second conclusion is that the extremely constrained role that has been played by (semi-) socialized housing in our six advanced capitalist countries (and it is even more constrained in many other such countries) is hardly surprising. Briefly and crudely put, a major expansion of such provision on a permanent basis would provide a radical challenge to core capitalist interests. Moreover, means, however inadequate, have evolved (with state support) for providing some private market accommodation for the majority of households in most countries at most times. In short, pressure for a universalistic, decommodified housing system has never been overwhelming, given the availability of private market alternatives. And powerful forces at the centre of the capitalist economic and political order would line up to oppose any such possibility.

THE SWEDISH CASE – BUILDING THE 'PEOPLE'S HOME'

In this respect the fate of social democratic housing policy in Sweden provides a useful test case. As Esping-Andersen (and others) have argued, this country provides us with the most developed example of a decommodified, solidaristic, socialist world of welfare capitalism. And some analysts of Swedish housing policy have also pointed to the system created by the Social Democrats in the post-war years as a model of reformist socialist housing policies (in fact, the only one), which has radically reduced the power of private capital in housing and greatly weakened the unequal distribution of housing services and costs which results from the unequal distribution of incomes (see, for example, Headey, 1978, or the more sophisticated analyses of Dickens et al., 1985, and Heclo and Madsen, 1987). However, more recent developments in Swedish housing policies and the growth of more critical evaluations of aspects of that country's welfare state, including housing, indicate that, despite the many achievements of Swedish housing policy, its decommodifying and redistributive achievements have been distinctly limited.

One of the most interesting studies in this respect is contained in Esping-Andersen's (1985) comparative examination of three Nordic welfare states – Sweden, Denmark and Norway. Much of the book is concerned with exploring why social democracy took root more successfully in Sweden than, in particular, Denmark, and why social democratic welfare and other reforms went further in the former than in the latter country. Esping-Andersen concludes that Swedish social democratic housing policy was more successful than the policies advocated and implemented by their Danish counterparts.[18] However, for our purposes, the interesting conclusion is that even the Swedish housing policies proved to be severely limited. Indeed, the main section of the book where he discusses these policies is entitled 'Sweden: from socialised housing to reprivatisation'. And he states that social democracy has had 'an inability to manufacture a solidaristic housing policy'. Despite housing being a highly politicized issue after the war and the fact that it is a central component in determining people's living standards, the post-war reforms 'did not appear to be a dramatic political rupture' (Esping-Andersen, 1985: 246, 182). But Esping-Andersen does not reflect on what might lie behind this interesting finding, merely referring to the difficulty of designing such a policy. However, it is probably this lack of achievement of a solidaristic housing policy, even in the model Swedish social democratic welfare state, that partially accounts for the omission of any consideration of housing policies and expenditure from his later work on the three regimes of welfare capitalism.

Other more specialized works provide greater detail on some of the ways in which Swedish social democratic housing policies have been constrained. For example, Elander and Strömberg (1992) have examined the implications for housing and land policies of the fact that the boundaries of Swedish social democracy 'have always been defined within the borders of a capitalist economic basis'. One consequence was the lack of any attempt to socialize the ownership of land. Instead, reliance was placed on weaker and not particularly 'socialist' controls over its use. Meanwhile, '[o]nly by way of exception has the landowners' security of tenure been quashed – the formal ownership of land has virtually always been "hard currency" in decisions on housing development' (Elander and Strömberg, 1992: 113).

By contrast, Elander and Strömberg note that post-war social housing provision did represent a more radical break with capitalism with respect to the distribution if not the production of accommodation. They highlight several ways in which social democratic governments subsequently prevented privatization and maintained social housing as a universalistic form of provision, not a residual form targeted on the poor. However, by 1980, the social housing sector 'proper' (the stock owned by municipal housing companies) amounted to only about 20 per cent of all Swedish housing (Lundqvist, 1992: table 5.3, 98). About another 15 per cent was owned by cooperatives, most of which have also been regarded as a part of the social housing sector and whose federative organizations are part of the wider social democratic bloc – the 'Popular Movements Coalition' (Bengtsson, 1992: 93). So, after over three decades of social democratic housing policies, about 60 per cent of the Swedish housing stock still remained in the private sector, two-thirds of it in home ownership, a pattern which is similar to that of the Netherlands, for example. Moreover, as elsewhere, post-war production shows a familiar pattern, with a large share and large-scale production of social (municipal and co-operative) housing up to the mid-1970s, followed by a rapid decline in total production, with a sharp rise in the share of construction for home ownership, in the rest of this decade (Lundqvist, 1992: table 5.2, 96). In the 1980s municipal building stabilized at around a quarter of all new output, while there was a resurgence of private rented construction, some growth in the share of co-operative building and a fall-back in building for home ownership (Lundqvist, 1992: table 5.5, 104). By 1989 about three-quarters of new building was for private renting, home ownership and the cooperatives.

By the 1980s cooperative housing had obtained many of the attributes of private sector housing. As Bengtsson (1992) has described, the dominant form of such housing in Sweden is the 'tenant-owner' cooperative. New building by rental cooperatives was prohibited in 1930. Originally, the two main cooperative federations enforced rules which prevented members making capital gains from the sale of their units. However, under pressure from their members, restrictions on resale prices were abandoned by the late 1960s. By the 1980s Lundqvist, Elander and Danermark (1990: 456–7) found that

> the cooperative sector has undergone several changes – never codi-fied in the Cooperative Housing Act – which have given it a much more speculative character ... as prices have continued to soar in the 1980s ... cooperative tenant-owners benefited ... Of utmost importance here is the changing attitude towards cooperative flats by banks and other money-lending institutions. Nowadays they look at membership certificates in co-operative societies ... in exactly the same way as a deed for real estate, thus accepting it as collateral for long-term loans to finance the purchase of a cooperative flat. The development of further 'commodification' – or 'privatisation from within' – of a housing sector which has traditionally been considered 'social' ... means that not just the 44% of owner-occupied housing, but also the 16% of cooperatives are now providing their inhabitants with the possibility of a favourable economic outcome from housing.

So the post-war policies left the private market in place, together with private land ownership and housing production. The main strategy was to use the provision of state housing loans (with conditions attached) and a system of municipal housing planning and building controls, in conjunction with a large-scale programme of social housing construction by municipal housing companies and cooperatives, as a means of providing affordable housing for all sections of the population. Private building received less preferential treatment.[19] Clearly, the broader objectives of solidaristic and universalistic provision helped to shape housing, as they shaped other areas of social provision. The plan was to eliminate all housing shortages within 15 years. However, Lundqvist (1992: 90) notes that this 'grandiose social engineering plan' soon 'collided with harsh economic realities'. The escalating costs of the subsidized state loan scheme placed increasing pressure on the state budget. Raising the costs of these loans would help solve the fiscal problem, but at the cost of a weakening of the redistributive goals of the policy. As Lundqvist comments:

> [i]t is interesting to find that the Social Democrats wavered between radical, across-the-board privatisation alternatives and painstakingly detailed measures which rendered the public–private mix a patchwork. Despite the social rhetoric of the 1946–47 program, there was no adherence in principle to *general* production subsidies.

In fact, as early as 1956, the report of an official commission recommended a shift from general subsidies to selective and supplementary housing allowances targeted on those in 'real need'. In short, Swedish housing policies faced similar pressures and considered adopting similar solutions to these problems as were discussed elsewhere.

In practice the move to selectivity occurred only slowly. Lundqvist (1992: 91–2) refers to

> a process of successive financial and regulatory changes to patch up the public–private balance of Swedish housing, covering but not really solving the fundamental cracks at the base caused by the inflationary tendencies not really acknowledged as a problem by the Social Democrats ... this took three main forms; (a) successive reductions in general production subsidies; (b) gradual increases in selective subsidies to needy households, and (c) some steps towards rent deregulation. Furthermore, taxation of home ownership began to develop into a general subsidy to housing consumption in the owner-occupied sector.

Interestingly, although the tax subsidies for home ownership were in some sense an inadvertent product of the general nature of the tax system, Lundqvist notes that over time the government acted to increase their generosity.

The rapid restructuring and growth of the Swedish economy and the accompanying large-scale rural to urban migration led, as in other countries, to the need for a large-scale housing programme in which social rented production played a key role. In Sweden this resulted in a plan to build a million homes over ten years (the 'Million Programme') which ran from 1965 to 1974. As elsewhere, too, the budgetary costs of this programme, accentuated by rising inflation and interest rates, caused a further shift from general to selective subsidies (and to the introduction of 'parity loans' in 1968, similar in principle to the Dutch dynamic cost system). Also, rent regulation was replaced by a corporative system of rent setting through negotiations between landlord organizations and the state.

In many ways, therefore, the course of housing policy in postwar Sweden was not so dissimilar to that which occurred in other European countries. The public/private mix was not radically different and the dilemmas faced by governments, and their response to them, were also similar. The close link between economic modernization and social rented housing was also evident. The level of control over, and government intervention in, the whole of the housing market was greater than in many other countries, but not noticeably more so than in the Netherlands, where housing policy was strongly influenced by the non-socialist Confessional parties, especially the Catholics.

In the case of Denmark and the Netherlands the 1960s and 1970s saw largely unsuccessful attempts by social democratic parties to sustain redistributive housing policies which upheld the goal of providing access to affordable and decent housing for all. In both countries these parties were in a weaker political position than that of the Swedish Social Democrats, being either excluded from government or forced to share power with bourgeois parties. In addition, they came under increasing pressure from sections of their own electorate to sustain or even increase assistance for home ownership as voters increasingly opted for private housing. By contrast, in 1975 the Swedish Social Democrats were able to implement an attempt to return to the original objectives of post-war housing policy through a new system of housing finance. This provided interest-subsidized loans for all forms of production, but the subsidies were varied according to the requirements of a 'solidaristic rent' objective. That is, equal rents were to be set for units of equal use value, regardless of the historic costs of their production. In addition, the system aimed at 'tenure neutrality' with regard to housing costs, with lower support for home ownership through the loan scheme to compensate for the continuing tax subsidies. The public regulation of housing production was also strengthened. However, as Lundqvist (1992: 94) explains, the loan system, which provided some subsidies for all forms of new housing, was enormously expensive in an era of high inflation and interest rates. Moreover, as Lundqvist, Elander and Danermark (1990) show in detail, 'tenure divisions in terms of housing outcomes' became more pronounced. There was also growing socio-economic segregation as white-collar workers concentrated in home ownership and blue-collar workers in rental housing.

By 1982, when the Social Democrats returned to power after a period of government by the bourgeois parties (who left the subsidy system in place), the escalating housing subsidies had become a serious problem. There had, under Social Democrat pressure, been the first limitation of home-owner tax subsidies in 1981 (the marginal rate for deductions was limited to 50 per cent). However, more radical reductions in support for home ownership were difficult because, as Lundqvist (1992: 102) notes, by now, as elsewhere, the party could not afford to ignore the growing political strength of the home-owner lobby which opposed further subsidy cuts. The Social Democrats were dependent on attracting some home-owner votes to win elections and they, along with the other parties, 'found it necessary to issue "letters of privilege" to the homeowners, reassuring them of their status'. But cutting the subsidies for social housing would be opposed by the Popular Movements Coalition, jeopardizing the party's power base. So, instead of radical changes, the government levied a tax on all the existing stock in order to redistribute resources to new production and sustain (or rather, re-establish) its affordability for broad sections of the population. In fact, this tax increased the costs of housing for most households.

However, as in France, the economic and fiscal conditions of the 1980s subsequently forced the Social Democrats into radical policy changes. In housing the new policies were similar in many respects to those adopted by the centre–right governments in Denmark (with social democratic support) and in the Netherlands. Thus, the loans on older social housing units were made degressive; state loans were debudgetized and a new institution established to obtain housing credit on the open market; reforms were implemented to cut the top marginal rate of tax and, to compensate for the loss of revenue, there were deep cuts in production subsidies for rental and cooperative housing; housing allowances were increased to protect those on the lowest income from rising rents; finally, home-owner tax subsidies were again reduced.

All this amounted to an attempt to reduce the level of the state's financial support for the whole of the housing market and to rely increasingly on individual households to meet their own housing costs. As Lundqvist (1992: 107) notes, the argument had shifted from redistribution and 'tenure neutrality' to the view that all housing subsidies had become an unsustainable burden on the economy and the public finances. The public role shifted from giving general subsidies to all housing to providing selective and supplementary subsidies for 'market-weak' households. So, the redistributive and solidaristic objectives of Swedish housing policy have given way to a mix of policies which are very similar to those adopted elsewhere. Interestingly, as Lundqvist explains, this shift has occurred despite opposition from the formerly powerful set of social housing organizations, historically closely linked to the Social Democratic Party. As he comments:

[t]o paraphrase Orwell; the affiliates of the 'Popular Movements Coalition', once politically treated as 'more equal than others', go from room to room, but no longer can they tell whether they really are in the 'Peoples' Home' they and the Social Democrats once set out to build (Lundqvist, 1992: 111).

CONCLUSION: SOCIAL HOUSING AND SOCIAL JUSTICE

The fact that the People's Home has proved incapable of construction even in Sweden, the epitome of the solidaristic welfare capitalist regime, lends weight to the conclusion that, in capitalist societies, there are likely to be severe barriers to the incorporation of housing within solidaristic, universalistic systems of welfare provision. As has frequently been noted, social democracy has been accommodated within capitalist societies, but under certain conditions. Thus Giddens (1978: 286) comments: the boundaries of state intervention are set within limits which do not 'transgress the essential character of the organisation of economic activity'.

In housing, as we have argued, this rules out a radical decommodification of provision which would entail the socialization of private property and capital. Swedish social democracy went further and had more opportunities than other social democratic parties to implement its vision of a solidaristic housing policy. However, this largely involved state regulation and subsidization of a 'mixed economy of housing', in which private capital retained a key role.[20]

And in the long run even this system broke down under the overriding effects of the 'force of epochs'.

More generally, the history of 'actually existing' social democracy suggests not only that any project radically to decommodify housing would be incompatible with the terms on which reformist socialism has been incorporated within the capitalist order, but that the absence of social democratic visions of such policies itself reflects the entrenched power of the private market. In this respect the construction of housing policy agendas in capitalist societies is surely a prime example of the exercise of power through the 'mobilization of bias' and even through Lukes's (1979) 'third dimension' of power which involves not just the suppression or deflection of radical demands but a system which moulds the very nature of the demands themselves. [21]

Therefore, general and deeply entrenched features of the capitalist societies provide the key to understanding why only a residual conception of social housing provision has been institutionalized in these societies and why such housing has been provided on a larger scale for wider sections of the population only under specific and temporally limited historical conditions. Of course, these links between capitalist development and social housing provision are constructed in complex and cross-nationally varying ways. There has been no automatically operative or simply constructed causal chain linking capitalism and social housing. Nationally varying economic, political and housing market developments, patterns of urbanization, ideological factors, institutional arrangements and historical legacies have all been significant. The structures of social rented housing provision are nationally and temporally specific, even though the outer boundaries to their development are more uniformly set, with only occasional opportunities for their temporary and limited alteration.

In the present era, while all the systems of social housing which we have reviewed in this book seem to be converging on a residualist model, these nationally specific differences continue to affect the pace and the nature of residualization. To state that a process of convergence is occurring does not imply that social housing everywhere will be reduced to a uniformly and comprehensively residualized form of provision. The establishment of structures of social housing provision created institutions and interests which will continue to have their own nationally varied consequences for the fortunes of the sector. However, any radical reversal of the residualizing trend is only likely to occur if the emergent phase of capitalist development gives rise to a new rationale for social rented housing production targeted on sectors of the population who are in the economic and political mainstream rather than at the margins. Such a development would, on the evidence of past history, probably be no more than a temporary phenomenon, leaving the dominant means of provision of housing in capitalist societies – the private market – in place and available to resume its role as the mainstream housing provider in due course. For social housing to develop beyond this level of significance, to supplant the private market permanently, would require a historically unprecedented and radical shift in the boundaries between the state, the market and the individual. In an era when these boundaries have been shifting in an entirely different direction, it would be Utopian to suggest that this could occur. Indeed, the only sensible prediction must be that the 'People's Home' will remain a distant dream.

NOTES

1 Skocpol and Amenta (1986) provide a concise and critical review of the various approaches.
2 For example, see Flora and Alber (1981) (modernization and democratization); T. Marshall (1963) (citizenship); O'Connor (1973) and Gough (1979) (neo-Marxism); Wilensky and Lebeaux (1958) and Wilensky (1975) (functionalist/level of economic development).
3 The similarities between both approaches with respect to this distinction are obvious, although the basis for its construction is radically different (see Lockwood, 1976). For a comparison of Marxist and functionalist theories of welfare (including the version associated with 'convergence theory'), see Mishra (1977).
4 See, for example, Wilensky (1975). Whether one finds Wilensky's explanation of the reasons for the cross-national differences convincing is, of course, another matter. More generally, an emphasis on the functionality of social policy need not imply that these functional 'needs' are satisfied in a cross-nationally uniform manner. Nor does Marxist functionalism imply any such uniformity. The problem, rather, is the tendency to adopt teleological explanations which derive causes from consequences, which are uninterested in how (and to what extent) social policies come to serve functional ends, and so ignore the sources and nature or cross-national variations.
5 This latter work involves a more developed version of Korpi's class-based analysis, which Esping-Andersen (1990: 16–18) criticizes on several grounds, notably its failure to take account of the significance of differing cross-class coalitions for social policy formation. Nevertheless, the close links between the development of social democracy and the growth of the institutionalized welfare state remain in this work.

6 Wilensky (1981) has examined the impact of leftism, Catholicism and corporatism in welfare state development in a number of countries, concluding that Catholicism has shaped welfare state developments (i.e. led to their growth) far more than left power. Both have fostered corporatism.

7 One of the most ambitious attempts in this vein – to develop cross-national explanations of variations in a range of social policies based on the 'thesis of the active state' – is provided by Hage, Hanneman and Gergan (1989).

8 Of course, many of the 'respectable' working-class tenants of social rented housing subsequently *became* poor, as ill-health, unemployment or retirement caught up with them. But many experienced upward economic mobility as well. However, the significant point being made here is that their status and income at the point of entry determined whether they entered social housing at all.

9 The effects of the state and the market on housing under state socialism (in Hungary) are illuminatingly debated by Szelenyi (1983, 1987), on the one hand, and Hegedus and Tosics (1983), Hegedus (1987, 1988) and Tosics (1987, 1988), on the other hand. For general discussions of the specificity of state socialist welfare see Ferge (1979) and Szelenyi and Manchin (1987).

10 There is an evident elision here between the liberal, marginalist strategy and the 'conservative-corporatist' one, which involves divisive social policies. This reflects two distinctive ideological legacies in right-wing politics. In later work, Esping-Andersen (1990) is far clearer on this issue.

11 As Esping-Andersen (1987a: 83) explains, this shift essentially arose out of a calculation by social democratic leaders 'that the goal of absolute political majorities would probably never be reached unless they were willing to forge alliances with alien social classes'. Certainly, this explanation helps us to understand, for example, the 'Red–Green' coalitions in the 1930s in Denmark and Sweden. However, other social democratic parties followed other strategies. For example, in Britain's 'first past the post' electoral system there was every reason for the Labour Party to believe that it could form a majority government without such a coalition and the SPD and the PvdA long held such aspirations in Germany and the Netherlands, respectively. More generally, as Przeworski (1985) has argued, the policy compromises which class coalitions impose on social democracy may or may not make the strategy electorally beneficial. As he shows, historically the Swedish Social Democrats benefited from a coalitional strategy while the German SPD did better without such alliances (the existence of the Communist Party, to which disaffected working-class voters could migrate, being a crucial consideration). Of course, in the years after 1945, all social democratic parties aimed to incorporate sections of the expanding white-collar salariat into their electoral base – hence

the movement towards redefinition as 'people's parties'. But this was not a matter of 'forging alliances with alien social classes'.

12 Although some social housing institutions, especially in more recent times, show some signs of a recognition that their continuing ability to house sections of the middle class and their political fortunes are linked.

13 Whether this conception of the decommodified, solidaristic Scandinavian welfare state is accurate is another question. Baldwin (1990: 60) suggests that the truth is more complex.

14 Of course there is a growing volume of cross-national studies of specific fields of social policy (there are many references to these in Heidenheimer, Heclo and Adams, 1990, for example). But they mostly consist of fairly undertheorised programme descriptions and histories or, if they are more ambitious, focus on 'middle-range' theorization which attempts to provide narrowly based explanations of cross-national variations, only weakly related to more general considerations of welfare state and societal development.

15 Interestingly, in the twentieth century the private housing sector which has been most deeply 'attacked' by state action has been the private rented sector, especially at its bottom end. By and large, this part of the stock is owned by small-scale, petty bourgeois landlords, a class whose economic and political power has been in decline more generally. See Harloe (1985) for a full analysis of this point.

16 There have, of course, been some attempts to socialize parts of these sectors, most of which have been defeated in the long or short run. In this context, it is interesting to trace the fate of the Swedish Social Democrats' proposals for the gradual socialization of Swedish industry through the Meidner plan for wage-earner funds (see Tilton, 1990: 228–35).

17 But only states were able to contemplate the establishment of 'pay-as-you-go' income maintenance benefits, the means by which welfare provision could be rapidly expanded after the war without postponing the receipt of benefits for a generation.

18 Esping-Andersen evaluates social democratic policies in Norway as the most solidaristic and egalitarian. Exceptionally, these involved measures to extend home ownership to the mass of the population, not social rented housing. The reasons relate to specific ideological features of Norwegian society and attitudes to all forms of rental provision. However, as various other analysts have described, the redistributive objectives of Norwegian housing policy have become increasingly compromised with, in the 1980s, the deregulation of cooperative housing, a sharp reduction in the proportion of new production financed by state loans, a shift from general to selective subsidies and so on. As we shall see, there are some close similarities between Norwegian and Swedish developments in this period (Torgerson, 1987: 123–4; Nagel, 1992: 83; Lundqvist, 1992: 65–88).

19　As indicated already, political support for these policies was underpinned by the housing wing of the Popular Movements Coalition – the interlinked structure of party, union and consumer interests which was a central characteristic of Swedish social democracy. In the case of housing this included the building unions, the housing cooperatives, the tenants' association and the larger urban local housing authorities, all of whom benefited from the policies which they supported. More generally, housing policies evolved through a corporatist system of bargaining between the government (and the housing wing of the Popular Movements Coalition) and a bourgeois coalition of producers, private landlords and home owners (Dickens et al., 1985: 49; Lundqvist, Elander and Danermark, 1990: 451–2).

20　Dickens et al. (1985) provide an interesting analysis of the 'groundrules' for the establishment of the 'corporatist reality of social democratic capitalism' in Sweden. In the case of housing labour benefited from reduced costs, higher quality and access while big building firms and materials suppliers were the main capitalist beneficiaries. They claim that, by contrast, landowners and landlords were 'frozen out'. But developments in Swedish housing policy make this assertion questionable, at least for the more recent period. And the system of housing finance involved state subsidies for private sector loans (the state loan covered only the lesser part of the cost of new housing). So, while Swedish housing policy regulated and placed some limits on profitable housing activity, it also benefited specific producer interests by providing a high and reasonably stable level of subsidized demand.

21　The prime example is the process by which, in some countries, home ownership has come to be seen as the *naturally* preferred form of housing, rather than one which, for historically contingent reasons, happens to be preferable. Private market housing interests have contributed to the establishment of this belief. So, too, have some sociologists; see, for example, a recent attempt to ground the preference in considerations of the universal human need for 'ontological security' (Saunders, 1990).

Bibliography

Abma, R., 1981, 'The Labour Plan and the Social Democratic Workers Party', *The Low Countries Historical Yearbook XIV*, The Hague, Martinus Nijhoff.

Abrams, M. and Rose, R., 1960, *Must Labour Lose?*, Harmondsworth, Penguin Books.

Adrianow, S., 1992, 'Social management in Great Britain, France and the Netherlands', Delft, OTB Research Institute (mimeo).

Alber, J., 1986, 'Germany', in P. Flora (ed.), *The Western European Welfare States since World War II*, Volume 2, Berlin and New York, de Gruyter, 1–154.

Aldcroft, D., 1978, *The European Economy 1914–1980*, London, Croom Helm.

—— 1987, *From Versailles to Wall Street 1919–29*, Harmondsworth, Penguin Books.

Andersen, H., 1980, 'Organisations, classes and the growth of state intervention in Denmark', *Acta Sociologica*, 23(2–3), 113–31.

—— 1992, 'The role of non-profit housing opportunities in European housing policy and their political and historical background – the case of Denmark', lecture given at Temple University, 9 July, mimeo.

Andeweg, R. and Irwin, G., 1993, *Dutch Government and Politics*, Basingstoke, Macmillan.

Andracheck, S., 1979, 'Housing in the United States: 1890–1929', in G. Fish (ed.), *The Story of Housing*, New York, Macmillan, 123–76.

Andrusz, G., 1984, *Housing and Urban Development in the USSR*, London, Macmillan.

Ardagh, J., 1977, *The New France. A society in transition*, Harmondsworth, Penguin Books.

—— 1991, *Germany and the Germans*, Harmondsworth, Penguin Books.

Aronovici, C., 1914, 'Housing and the housing problem', in C. Aronovici (ed.), *Housing and Planning*, Philadelphia, American Academy of Political and Social Science, 1–7.

Ashford, D., 1986, *The Emergence of the Welfare States*, Oxford, Basil Blackwell.

—— 1990, 'Decentralising France: how the Socialists discovered pluralism', *West European Politics*, 13(4), 46–65.

Ashworth, W., 1954, *The Genesis of Modern British Town Planning*, London, Routledge and Kegan Paul.

Atkinson, A., Gardiner, K., Lechene, V. and Sutherland, H., 1993, *Combating Poverty in France and the United Kingdom*, London, Suntory-Toyota International Centre for Economics and Related Disciplines.

Audit Commission, 1992, *Developing Local Authority Housing Strategies*, London, HMSO.

Baldwin, P. 1990, *The Politics of Social Solidarity*, Cambridge, Cambridge University Press.

Ball, M. 1986, 'Housing analysis: time for a theoretical refocus?', *Housing Studies*, 1(3), 147–65.

—— 1990, *Under One Roof. Retail banking and the international mortgage finance revolution*, Hemel Hempstead, Harvester Wheatsheaf.

Ball, M. and Harloe, M. 1992, 'Rhetorical barriers to understanding housing provision: what the "Provision Thesis" is and is not', *Housing Studies*, 7(1), 3–15.

Ball, M., Harloe, M., and Martens, M., 1988, *Housing and Social Change in Europe and the USA*, London and New York, Routledge.

Barou, J., 1992, *La place du pauvre. Histoire et géographie sociale de l'habitat HLM*, Paris, L'Harmattan.

Bauer, C., 1934, *Modern Housing*, Boston and New York, Houghton Mifflin.

—— 1957, 'The dreary deadlock of public housing', *Architectural Forum*, May, 140.

Bayor, R., 1989, 'Urban renewal, public housing and the racial shaping of Atlanta', *Journal of Policy History*, 1(4), 419–39.

Bell, D., 1973, *The Coming of Post-industrial Society*, London, Heinemann.

Benevolo, L., 1971, *History of Modern Architecture. Volume 2. The Modern Movement*, London, Routledge and Kegan Paul.

Bengtsson, B., 1992, 'Not the middle way but both ways – cooperative housing in Sweden', in L. Lundqvist (ed.), *Policy, Organization, Tenure. A comparative history of housing in the small welfare states*, Oslo, Scandinavian University Press, 87–104.

Berghahn, V., 1982, *Modern Germany: society, economy, politics in the twentieth century*, Cambridge, Cambridge University Press.

Beyer, G., 1963, *Housing and Society*, New York, Macmillan.

Bidemann, J., 1940, *Housing Agencies in France. Functions and organisation*, New York, New York City Housing Authority (mimeo).

Bille, L., 1989, 'Denmark: the oscillating party system', *West European Politics*, 12(4), 42–58.

Blanc, M., 1992, 'From substandard housing to devalorised social housing: ethnic minorities in France, Germany and the UK', *European Journal of Intercultural Studies*, 2(3).

—— 1993, 'Housing segregation and the poor: new trends in French social housing', *Housing Studies*, 8(3), 207–14.

Block, F., 1987, 'Social policy and accumulation: a critique of the new consensus', in M. Rein, G. Esping-Andersen and L. Rainwater (eds), *Stagnation and Renewal in Social Policy*, Armonk and London, M. E. Sharpe, 13–31.

Blum, J., McFeely, W., Morgan, E., Schlesinger Jr, A., Stamp, K. and Woodward, C., 1985, *The National Experience: a history of the United States*, 6th edition, San Diego, Harcourt Brace Jovanovich.

Blumenthal, Y., 1934, *Germany: economic aspects of low cost housing*, New York, Housing Study Guild (mimeo).

Board of Trade, 1908, *Cost of Living in German Towns*, London, HMSO.

—— 1909, *Cost of Living in French Towns*, London, HMSO.

—— 1911, *Cost of Living in American Towns*, London, HMSO.

Boelhouwer, P. and Priemus, H., 1990, 'Dutch housing policy realigned', *Netherlands Journal of Housing and Environmental Research*, 5(1), 105–19.

Boelhouwer, P. and van den Heijden, H., 1992, *Housing Systems in Europe. Part 1. A comparative study of housing policy*, Delft, Delft University Press.

Boelhouwer, P. and van Weesep, J., 1988, 'On shaky grounds: the case for the privatisation of the public housing sector in the Netherlands', *Netherlands Journal of Housing and Environmental Research*, 3(4), 319–33.

Boldsen, M., 1931, 'Development of housing in Denmark', in *The Social Importance of Housing Now and in the Future*, Stuttgart, Verlag Julius Hoffmann, 100–04.

—— 1935, 'Housing in Denmark', *Danish Foreign Office Journal*, 176 (September), 121–26.

Boligministeriet, 1987, *Den almennytigge boligsektors rolle paa boligmarkedet*, Copenhagen, Boligministeriet.

Boligselskabernes Landsforening, 1973, *Non-profit Housing in Denmark*, Copenhagen, Federation of Non-profit Housing (mimeo).

Bommer, J., 1931, 'Holland. Building by public utility housing associations', in *The Social Importance of Housing Now and in the Future*, Stuttgart, Verlag Julius Hoffmann, 335–6.

Bowley, M., 1944, *Housing and the State 1919–44*, London, George Allen and Unwin.

Bowly, D., 1978, *The Poorhouse. Substandard housing in Chicago 1895–1976*, Carbondale and Edwardsville, Southern Illinois University Press.

Boyer, M., 1983, *Dreaming the Rational City*, Cambridge, Mass. and London, MIT Press.

Brahl, O., 1931, 'Municipal building enterprises. Germany', in *The Social Importance of Housing Now and in the Future*, Stuttgart, Verlag Julius Hoffmann, 191–7.

Bratt, R., 1985, 'Controversy and contribution: a public housing critique', *Journal of Housing*, September/October, 165–73.

—— 1986, 'Public housing: the controversy and the contribution', in R. Bratt, C. Hartman and A. Meyerson (eds), *Critical Perspectives on Housing*, Philadelphia, Temple University Press.

Bullock, N. and Read, J., 1985, *The Movement for Housing Reform in Germany and France 1840–1914*, Cambridge, Cambridge University Press.

Burnett, J., 1978, *A Social History of Housing 1815–1970*, Newton Abbott, David and Charles.

Butler, R. and Noisette, P., 1983, *Le logement sociale en France 1915–1981*, Paris, La Découverte/Maspero.

Byrd, P., 1986, 'The Labour Party in Britain' in N. Paterson and A. Thomas (eds), *The Future of Social Democracy*, Oxford, Clarendon Press, 59–107.

Cantle, T., 1986, 'The deterioration of public sector housing', in P. Malpass (ed.), *The Housing Crisis*, Beckenham, Croom Helm, 57–85.

Castells, M., 1978, *City, Class and Power*, London and Basingstoke, Macmillan.

—— 1989, *The Informational City*, Oxford and Cambridge, Mass., Basil Blackwell.

Castles, F. and Mitchell, D., 1991, *Three Worlds of Welfare Capitalism or Four?*, Canberra, Australian National University.

Catterall, T., 1990, 'Housing has its borders', *Roof*, 15(1), January–February, 24–6.

Center for Urban Programs, 1975, *Tenant Management Corporations in St Louis Public Housing: the situation after two years*, St Louis, Center for Urban Programs.

Central Housing Committee, 1935a, *Summary of Consular Reports on Housing Problems in the Netherlands*, Washington DC, CHC (mimeo).

—— 1935b, *Summary of Consular Reports on Housing Problems in Germany*, Washington DC, CHC (mimeo).

Chandler, A., 1978, 'The United States: evolution of enterprise', in P. Mathias and M. Postan (eds), *The Cambridge Economic History of Europe Volume VIII, Part 2*, Cambridge, Cambridge University Press, 70–133.

Chandler, M., 1991, 'What have we learned from public housing resident management?', *Journal of Planning Literature*, 6(2), 136–43.

Cipolla, C. (ed.), 1978, *The Fontana Economic History of Europe. Contemporary economies. Volumes 1 and 2*, Glasgow, Collins/Fontana Books.

Clark, J., 1931, *The Cost of the World War to the American People*, New Haven, Yale University Press.

Cobban, A., 1961, *A History of Modern France. Volume 2: 1799–1945*, Harmondsworth, Penguin Books.

Cole, A., 1986, 'The return of the right: the French election of March 1986', *West European Politics*, 9(4), 225–32.

Committee on Housing in Greater London, 1965, *Report*, London, HMSO.

Community Development Project (CDP), 1976, *Whatever Happened to Council Housing?*, London, CDP Information and Intelligence Unit.

Congressional Budget Office, 1983, *Federal Subsidies for Public Housing: issues and options*, Washington, DC, US Government Printing Office.

Conradt, D., 1978, *The German Polity*, New York and London, Longman.

—— 1993, 'Germany', in M. Hancock, D. Conradt, B. Peters, W. Safran and R. Zariski, *Politics in Western Europe*, Basingstoke, Macmillan, 183–288.

Cooke, P. (ed.), 1989, *Localities. The changing face of urban Britain*, London, Unwin Hyman.

Cronberg, T., 1986, 'Tenants' involvement in the management of social housing in the Nordic countries', *Scandinavian Housing and Planning Research*, 3(2), 65–87.

Cullingworth, B., 1970, *Town and Country Planning in England and Wales*, 3rd edition, London, Allen and Unwin.

Daalder, H. (ed.), 1987, *Party Systems in Denmark, Austria, Switzerland, the Netherlands and Belgium*, London, Francis Pinter.

—— 1989, 'The mould of Dutch politics: themes for a comparative enquiry', *West European Politics*, 12(1), 1–20.

Damgard, E., 1992, 'Denmark: experiment in parliamentary government', in E. Damgard (ed.), *Parliamentary Change in the Nordic Countries*, Oslo, Scandinavian University Press, 18–49.

Danmarks Statistik, various years, *Statististike Efterretninger*, Copenhagen, Danmarks Statistik.

Danmarks Statistik and The Institute for Social Research, 1979, *Living Conditions in Denmark. A compendium of statistics*, Copenhagen, Danmarks Statistik and The Institute for Social Research.

Daunton, M., 1983, *House and Home in the Victorian City*, London, Edward Arnold.

—— (ed.), 1984, *Councillors and Tenants: local authority housing in English cities 1919–1939*, Leicester, Leicester University Press.

Davies, J. G., 1972, *The Evangelistic Bureaucrat*, London, Tavistock.

Davies, R., 1966, *Housing Reform during the Truman Administration*, Columbia, University of Missouri Press.

Dawson, W., 1914, *Municipal Life and Government in Germany*, London, Longman, Green and Co.

de Jonge, D. 1985, 'Problems of post-war flats in the Netherlands', in N. Prak and H. Priemus (eds), *Post-war Public Housing in Trouble*, Delft, Delft University Press, 133–45.

de Leeuw, F., 1974, *Operating Costs in Public Housing. A financial crisis*, Washington, DC, Urban Institute.

De Swaan, A., 1988, *In Case of the State*, Cambridge, Polity Press.

de Vries, J., 1978, 'Benelux 1920–1970', in C. Cipolla (ed.), *The Fontana Economic History of Europe. Contemporary economies – 1*, Glasgow, Collins/Fontana Books, 1–71.

Denby, E., 1938, *Europe Re-housed*, London, George Allen and Unwin.

Dennery, E., 1935, *La question de l'habitation urbaine en France*, Geneva, Société des Nations.

Dennis, N., 1972, *Public Participation and Planners' Blight*, London, Faber and Faber.

Department B, School of Architecture, 1971, *The Housing Problem in Denmark*, Copenhagen, School of Architecture.

Department of the Environment, 1977, *Housing Policy: a consultative document*, London, HMSO.

—— 1984, *Local Housing Management. A Priority Estates Project survey*, London, HMSO.

—— 1987, *The PEP Guide to Local Housing Management*, 3 volumes, London, Department of the Environment.

Derbyshire, I., 1990a, *Politics in the United States. From Carter to Bush*, Edinburgh, Chambers.

—— 1990b, *Politics in France. From Giscard to Mitterrand*, Edinburgh, Chambers.

—— 1991, *Politics in Germany. From division to unification*, Edinburgh, Chambers.

Derbyshire, J. and Derbyshire, I., 1990, *Politics in Britain. From Callaghan to Thatcher*, Edinburgh, Chambers.

Devine, J., 1992, *The Causes of the Great Collapse of 1929–33: an interpretative essay*, Los Angeles, Loyola Marymount University (mimeo).

Dickens, P., Duncan, S., Goodwin, M. and Gray, F., 1985, *Housing, States and Localities*, London and New York, Methuen.

Dolebeare, C., 1992, *At a Snail's Pace. FY 1993*, Washington, DC, Low Income Housing Information Service.

Drucker, H., 1986, ' "All the king's horses and all the king's men." The Social Democratic Party in Britain', in W. Paterson and A. Thomas (eds), *The Future of Social Democracy*, Oxford, Clarendon Press, 108–26.

Dubedout, H., 1983, *Ensemble refaire la ville*, Paris, La Documentation Française.

Duclaud-Williams, R., 1978, *The Politics of Housing in Britain and France*, London, Heinemann.

Dunleavy, P., 1981, *The Politics of Mass Housing in Britain 1945–1975*, Oxford, Clarendon Press.

Dyson, K., 1981, 'The politics of economic management in West Germany', *West European Politics*, 4(2), 35–55.

Earl of Shaftesbury, 1883, 'The mischief of state aid', *Nineteenth Century*, XIV, 934–5.

Einhorn, E. and Logue, J., 1989, *Modern Welfare States. Politics and policies in social democratic Scandinavia*, New York, Praeger.

Elander, I. and Strömberg, T., 1992, 'Whatever happened to Social Democracy and planning? The case of local land and housing policy in Sweden', in L. Lundqvist (ed.), *Policy, Organisation, Tenure. A comparative history of housing in small welfare states*, Stockholm, Scandinavian University Press, 105–20.

Elder, N., Thomas, A. and Arter, D., 1982, *The Consensual Democracies? The government and politics of the Scandinavian states*, Oxford, Martin Robertson.

Elsinga, M. and Wassenberg, F., 1991, 'Tackling crime and vandalism on post-war housing estates: the Dutch approach', *Netherlands Journal of Housing and the Built Environment*, 6(2), 159–75.

Emms, P., 1990, *Social Housing. A European dilemma?*, Bristol, School for Advanced Urban Studies.

Engels, F., 1973, 'The housing question', in K. Marx and F. Engels, *Selected Works. Volume 2*, Moscow, Progress Publishers, 295–375.

Englander, D., 1983, *Landlord and Tenant in Urban Britain 1838–1918*, Oxford, Clarendon Press.

English, J. and Norman, P., 1974, *One Hundred Years of Slum Clearance in England and Wales – policies and programmes 1868–1970*, Glasgow, University of Glasgow.

Esping-Andersen, G., 1985, *Politics against Markets*, Princeton, Princeton University Press.

—— 1987a, 'Citizenship and socialism: decommodification and solidarity in the welfare state', in M. Rein, G. Esping-Andersen and L. Rainwater (eds), *Stagnation and Renewal in Social Policy*, Armonk and London, M. E. Sharpe, 78–101.

—— 1987b, 'The comparison of policy regimes: an introduction', in M. Rein, G. Esping-Andersen and L. Rainwater (eds), *Stagnation and Renewal in Social Policy*, Armonk and London, M. E. Sharpe, 3–12.

—— 1990, *The Three Worlds of Welfare Capitalism*, Cambridge, Polity Press.

Esping-Andersen, G. and Korpi, W., 1984, 'Social policy as class politics in post-war capitalism: Scandinavia, Austria and Germany', in J. Goldthorpe (ed.), *Order and Conflict in Contemporary Capitalism*, Oxford, Clarendon Press, 179–208.

Esser, J., 1986, 'State, business and trade unions in West Germany after the "Political Wende"', *West European Politics*, 9(2), 198–214.

Evans, P., 1976, 'Raymond Unwin and the municipalisation of the Garden City', *Transactions of the Martin Centre for Architectural and Urban Studies*, University of Cambridge, Volume 1, 251–74.

Evans, P., Rueschemeyer, D. and Skocpol, T. (eds), 1985, *Bringing the State Back In*, New York, Cambridge University Press.

Fainstein, S., Gordon, I. and Harloe, M., 1992, *Divided Cities: New York and London in the contemporary world*, Oxford and Cambridge, Mass., Basil Blackwell.

Feiss, C., 1938, 'What of housing in the Third Reich 1936–7?', in

C. Woodbury (ed.), *Housing Yearbook 1938*, Chicago, National Association of Housing Officials, 178–92.

Ferge, Z., 1979, *A Society in the Making*, Harmondsworth, Penguin Books.

Fish, G. (ed.), 1979, *The Story of Housing*, New York, Macmillan.

Fisher, E. and Ratcliff, R., 1936, *European Housing Policy and Practice*, Washington, DC, US Government Printing Office.

Fisher, R., 1959, *Twenty Years of Public Housing*, New York, Harper and Row.

Fishman, R., 1977, *Urban Utopias in the Twentieth Century*, New York, Basic Books.

Fitzmaurice, J., 1981, *Politics in Denmark*, London, Hurst.

Fletcher, R. (ed.), 1987, *Bernstein to Brandt*, London, Edward Arnold.

Fleurke, F. and de Vries, P., 1990, 'Decentralizing public housing in the Netherlands', *Netherlands Journal of Housing and Environmental Research*, 5(1), 29–48.

Floor, J., 1972, *Rents, Subsidies and Dynamic Cost*, The Hague, Ministry of Housing and Physical Planning.

Flora, P. and Alber, J., 1981, 'Modernization, democratization and the development of the welfare states in Western Europe', in P. Flora and A. Heidenheimer (eds), *The Development of the Welfare States in Europe and America*, New Brunswick and London, Transaction Books, 37–80.

Flora, P. and Heidenheimer, A. (eds), 1981, *The Development of the Welfare States in Europe and America*, New Brunswick and London, Transaction Books.

Flora, P., Kraus, F. and Pfennig, W., 1987, *State, Economy and Society in Western Europe 1815–1975. Volume II. The growth of industrial societies and capitalist economies*, London, Macmillan Press.

Fohlen, C., 1978, 'France 1920–1970', in C. Cipolla (ed.), *The Fontana Economic History of Europe. Contemporary economies – 1*, Glasgow, Collins/Fontana Books, 72–127.

Forrest, R. and Murie, A., 1985, 'Restructuring the welfare state: privatization of public housing in Britain', in W. van Vliet, E. Huttmann, and S. Fava (eds), *Housing Needs and Policy Approaches. Trends in thirteen countries*, Durham, Duke University Press, 97–109.

—— 1988, *Selling the Welfare State*, London, Routledge.

Foster, J., 1979, 'How imperial London preserved its slums', *International Journal of Urban and Regional Research*, 3(1), 93–114.

Fox, K., 1985, *Metropolitan America: urban life and urban policy in the United States 1940–1980*, Basingstoke, Macmillan.

Friedman, L., 1968, *Government and Slum Housing*, Chicago, Rand McNally.

—— 1980, 'Public housing and the poor' in J. Pynoos, R. Schafer and C. Hartman (eds), *Housing Urban America*, 2nd edition, New York, Aldine Publishing Company, 473–84.

Galarza, M., n.d., *Housing and the Crisis: rehabilitation policies in France*, London, London School of Economics (mimeo).

Gauldie, E., 1974, *Cruel Habitations*, London, Allen and Unwin.

Gelfand, M., 1975, *A Nation of Cities. The federal government and urban America, 1933–1965*, New York, Oxford University Press.

Genevro, R., 1984, 'Site selection and the New York City Housing Authority, 1934–1939', *Journal of Urban History*, 12(4), 334–52.

Gershuny, J. and Miles, I., 1983, *The New Service Economy*, London, Francis Pinter.

Ghékiere, L., 1991, *Marchés et politiques du logement dans la CEE*, La Documentation Française.

Giddens, A., 1978, *The Class Structure of the Advanced Societies*, London, Heinemann.

Gilbert, B., 1970, *British Social Policy 1914–1939*, London, Batsford.

Ginsburg, N., 1979, *Class, Capital and Social Policy*, London and Basingstoke, Macmillan.

Gladdish, K., 1987, 'The centre holds: the 1986 Netherlands election', *West European Politics*, 10(1), 115–19.

—— 1991, *Governing from the Centre. Politics and policy-making in the Netherlands*, London, Hurst and Company.

Glyn Jones, W., 1986, *Denmark: a modern history*, Beckenham, Croom Helm.

Goldthorpe, J., Lockwood, D., Bechofer, F. and Platt, J., 1968, *The Affluent Worker: political attitudes and behaviour*, London, Cambridge University Press.

Goodchild, B., Gerrichon, Y. and Bertrand, L., 1992, *Local Housing Strategies in France*, Nancy, Laboratoire logement (mimeo).

Gough, I., 1979, *The Political Economy of the Welfare State*, London and Basingstoke, Macmillan.

Gourevitch, P., 1986, *Politics in Hard Times: corporative responses to international economic crisis*, Ithaca and London, Cornell University Press.

Graham, J., 1940, *Housing in Scandinavia. Urban and rural*, Chapel Hill, University of North Carolina Press.

Greater London Council, 1980, *A Revolution in London Housing*, London, Greater London Council.

Grebler, L. and Winckler, W., 1940, *The Cost of the Great War to Germany and Austria-Hungary*, New Haven, Yale University Press.

Greve, J., 1971, *Voluntary Housing in Scandinavia*, Birmingham, Centre for Urban and Regional Studies.

Grieff, R. and Ulbrich, R., 1991, *Housing Supply and Housing Policy in the Federal Republic of Germany and the Future of Large Housing Estates in the East and West German Laender*, Darmstadt, Institut Wohnen und Umwelt (mimeo).

Grinberg, D., 1982, *Housing in the Netherlands: 1900–40*, Delft, Delft University Press.

Grosser, A., 1974, *Germany in Our Time*, Harmondsworth, Penguin Books.

Guerrand, R.-H., 1967, *Les origines du logement sociale en France*, Paris, Editions Ouvrières.

—— 1992, *Une Europe en construction. Deux siècles d'habitat sociale en Europe*, Paris, La Découverte.

Hage, J., Hanneman, R. and Gergan, E., 1989, *State Responsiveness and State Activism*, London, Unwin Hyman.

Halévy, E., 1961, *Imperialism and the Rise of Labour*, London, Ernest Benn.

Hall, P., 1980, *Urban and Regional Planning*, Harmondsworth, Penguin Books.

—— 1984, *The World Cities*, 3rd edition, London, Weidenfeld and Nicolson.

—— 1988, *Cities of Tomorrow*, Oxford, Basil Blackwell.

Hall, P. and Hay, D., 1980, *Growth Centres in the European Urban System*, London, Heinemann.

Hancock, M., 1993, 'Sweden', in M. Hancock, D. Conradt, B. Peters, W. Safran and R. Zariski, *Politics in Western Europe*, Basingstoke, Macmillan, 289–456.

Hardach, G., 1987, *The First World War 1914–1918*, Harmondsworth, Penguin Books.

Harloe, M., 1978, 'The Green Paper on housing policy', in M. Brown and S. Baldwin (eds), *The Year Book of Social Policy in Britain 1977*, London, Routledge and Kegan Paul.

—— 1979, 'Marxism, the state and the urban question: critical notes on two recent French theories', in C. Crouch (ed.), *State and Economy in Contemporary Capitalism*, London, Croom Helm, 122–56.

—— 1981, 'The recommodification of housing', in M. Harloe and E. Lebas (eds), *City, Class and Capital*, London, Edward Arnold, 17–50.

—— 1985, *Private Rented Housing in the United States and Europe*, London and Sydney, Croom Helm.

—— 1987, 'Manifestoes for change? A critique of recent proposals for housing reform', in M. Brenton and C. Ungerson (eds), *Year Book of Social Policy 1986–7*, Harlow, Longman, 196–214.

—— 1990, 'Great Britain', in W. van Vliet (ed.), *International Handbook of Housing Policies and Practices*, New York, Greenwood Press, 85–126.

—— 1992, 'Housing inequality and social structure in London', *Housing Studies*, 7(3), 189–204.

Harloe, M. and Martens, M., 1984, 'Comparative housing research', *Journal of Social Policy*, 13(2), 255–77.

—— 1985, 'The restructuring of housing provision in Britain and the Netherlands', *Environment and Planning A*, 17, 1063–87.

—— 1990, *New Ideas for Housing. The experience of three countries*, London, Shelter Books.

Harloe, M., Issacharoff, R. and Minns, R., 1974, *The Organisation of Housing. Public and private enterprise in London*, London, Heinemann.

Harloe, M., Marcuse, P. and Smith, N., 1992, 'Housing for people, housing for profits', in S. Fainstein, I. Gordon and M. Harloe (eds), *Divided Cities: New York and London in the contemporary world*, Oxford and Cambridge, Mass., Basil Blackwell, 175–202.

Hartman, C., 1984, *The Transformation of San Francisco*, Totowa, NJ, Rowman and Allanheld.

Hartman, C. and Carr, G., 1969, 'Housing authorities reconsidered', *Journal of the American Institute of Planners*, 35 (January), 10–21.

Hartman, C. and Levi, M., 1973, 'Public housing managers: an appraisal', *Journal of the American Institute of Planners*, 39 (March), 125–37.

Harvey, D., 1989, *The Condition of Postmodernity*, Oxford and Cambridge, Mass., Basil Blackwell.

Häussermann, H., 1991, *Housing and Social Policy in Germany*, Bremen, Bremen University (mimeo).

Häussermann, H. and Siebel, W., 1991, 'Housing and social welfare policy', in A. Norton and K. Novy (eds), *Low Income Housing in Britain and Germany*, London, Anglo-German Foundation, 127–42.

Hawkes, D., 1976, 'Garden cities and new methods of construction', *Transactions of the Martin Centre for Architectural and Urban Studies, University of Cambridge*, Volume 1, 275–96.

Hayek, F., 1944, *The Road to Serfdom*, London, Routledge and Kegan Paul.

Hayward, J. and Watson, M. (eds), 1975, *Planning, Politics and Public Policy*, Cambridge, Cambridge University Press.

Headey, B., 1978, *Housing Policy in the Developed Economy*, London, Croom Helm.

Heclo, H. and Madsen, H., 1987, *Policy and Politics in Sweden. Principled pragmatism*, Philadelphia, Temple University Press.

Heeger, H., 1987, 'Post-war high rise: difficult to operate', *Netherlands Journal of Housing and Environmental Research*, 2(3), 263–80.

Hegedus, J., 1987, 'Reconsidering the roles of the state and the market in socialist housing systems', *International Journal of Urban and Regional Research*, 11(1), 79–97.

—— 1988, 'Inequalities in east European cities: a reply to Ivan Szelenyi', *International Journal of Urban and Regional Research*, 12(1), 129–32.

Hegedus, J. and Tosics, I., 1983, 'Housing classes and housing policy: some changes in the Budapest housing market', *International Journal of Urban and Regional Research*, 7(3), 467–94.

Heidenheimer, A., Heclo, H. and Adams, C., 1990, *Comparative Public Policy*, 3rd edition, New York, St Martin's Press.

Heiferman, R., 1939, *Housing Agencies in Denmark. Functions and organisation*, New York, New York City Housing Authority.

Heinz, W., 1991, 'The role of local authorities in meeting housing need', in A. Norton and K. Novy (eds), *Low Income Housing Policies in Britain and Germany*, London, Anglo-German Foundation, 83–108.

Hentschel, V., 1989, 'German social and economic policy, 1815–1939', in P. Mathias and S. Pollard (eds), *The Cambridge Economic History of Europe. Volume VIII*, Cambridge, Cambridge University Press, 752–813.

Hetzel, O., 1983, *A Perspective on Governmental Housing Policies in the Netherlands*, The Hague, Ministry of Housing.

Highton, J., 1935, *Working Class Housing on the Continent*, London, HMSO.

Hildebrand, K., 1978, 'Labour and capital in the Scandinavian countries in the nineteenth and twentieth centuries', in P. Mathias and M. Postan (eds), *The Cambridge Economic History of Europe. Volume VII, Part 1*, Cambridge, Cambridge University Press, 590–628.

Hill, O., 1871, 'Blank Court or landlords and tenants', *Macmillan's Magazine*, XXIV, 456–9.

Hirst, F., 1934, *The Consequences of the War to Great Britain*, Oxford, Oxford University Press.

History of the Ministry of Munitions, 1976, *Volume 5, Part V. Provision for the Housing of Munitions Workers*, Brighton, Harvester Press (microfiche).

Holmans, A., 1987, *Housing Policy in Britain: a history*, Beckenham, Croom Helm.

Housing and Development Reporter, 1990, *Summary of Cranston–Gonzalez National Affordable Housing Act*, Washington, DC, Warren, Gorham and Lamont.

Housing and Home Finance Agency and Office of Housing Economies, 1948, *Housing Statistics Handbook*, Washington, DC, US Government Printing Office.

Housing Policy Debate, 1991, volume 2, issue 2, special issue on preserving low-income housing opportunities.

Hyldtoft, O., 1992, 'Denmark', in C. Pooley (ed.), *Housing Strategies in Europe 1880–1930*, Leicester, Leicester University Press, 40–72.

International Housing and Town Planning Congress, 1937, *Rents for the Working Classes*, Frankfurt, International Housing Association.

International Labour Office, 1924, *European Housing Problems since the War 1914–23*, Geneva, ILO.

—— 1925, *The Housing Situation in the United States*, Geneva, ILO.

—— 1930, *Housing Policy in Europe. Cheap home building*, Geneva, ILO.

Irwin, G. and van Holsteyn, J., 1989, 'Decline of the structured model of electoral competition', *West European Politics*, 12(1), 21–41.

Jackson, A., 1976, *A Place Called Home*, Cambridge, Mass. and London, MIT Press.

Jackson, K., 1981, 'The spatial dimension of social control. Race, ethnicity and government housing policy in the United States, 1918–68', in B. Struve (ed.), *Modern Industrial Societies. History, policy and survival*, Beverly Hills and London, Sage Publications, 79–127.

Jacobs, M., 1976, 'The political economy of public housing', MA thesis, New York, Columbia University.

Jaedicke, W. and Wollmann, H., 1990, 'Federal Republic of Germany', in W. van Vliet (ed.), *International Handbook of Housing Policies and Practices*, Westport, Conn., Greenwood Press, 127–54.

Jantzen, E. and Kaaris, H., 1984, 'Danish low-rise housing', *Scandinavian Housing and Planning Research*, 1(1), 27–42.

Jarmain, J., 1948, *Housing Subsidies and Rents*, London, Stevens and Sons.

Jencks, C. and Peterson, P. (eds), (1991), *The Urban Underclass*, Washington, DC, Brookings Institute.

Johansen, L., 1986, 'Denmark', in P. Flora (ed.), *Growth to Limits. The Western European welfare states since world war II*, Volume 1, Berlin and New York, de Gruyter, 293–381.

Johnson, N., 1990, *Reconstructing the Welfare State*, London, Harvester Wheatsheaf.

Johnson, P., 1968, *Land Fit for Heroes. The planning of British reconstruction 1916-1918*, Chicago, University of Chicago Press.

Joint Center for Housing Studies, 1991, *The State of the Nation's Housing 1991*, Cambridge, Mass., Joint Center.

Jones, M., 1987, *The Limits of Liberty*, New York, Oxford University Press.

Jörberg, L. and Krantz, O., 1978, 'Scandinavia 1914-1970', in C. Cipolla (ed.), *The Fontana Economic History of Europe. Contemporary economies – 2*, Glasgow, Collins/Fontana Books, 377-459.

Jurriens, R., 1981, 'The miners' strike in the Dutch province of Limburg (21 June-2 July 1917)', *The Low Countries History Yearbook XIV*, The Hague, Martinus Nijhoff, 124-53.

Karn, V. and Wolman, H., 1992, *Comparing Housing Systems*, Oxford, Clarendon Press.

Katz, S. and Mayer, M., 1985, 'Gimme shelter: self-help struggles within and against the state in New York City and West Berlin', *International Journal of Urban and Regional Research*, 9(1), 15-46.

Keith, N., 1973, *Politics and the Housing Crisis since 1930*, New York, Universe Books.

Kemp, T., 1972, *The French Economy 1913-39*, London, Longman.

—— 1989, 'Economic and social policy in France', in P. Mathias and S. Pollard (eds), *The Cambridge Economic History of Europe, Volume VIII*, Cambridge, Cambridge University Press, 691-751.

Kennedy, D., 1984, 'West Germany', in M. Wynn (ed.), *Housing in Europe*, Beckenham, Croom Helm, 55-74.

Keynes, J., 1919, *The Economic Consequences of the Peace*, London, Macmillan.

Kidd, K., 1940, *Four Million Tenants. A study of English public housing management*, Chicago, National Association of Housing Officials.

Kindelberger, C., 1987, *The World in Depression 1929-1939*, Harmondsworth, Penguin Books.

King, A., 1975, 'Overload: problems of governing in the 1970s', *Political Studies*, 23(2), 284-96.

King, D., 1987, *The New Right. Politics, markets and citizenship*, Basingstoke, Macmillan.

Kirchner, J. and Sautter, H., 1990, *The Integration of Ethnic German Migrants from the GDR in the Labour and Housing Markets in the Old Federal Republic of Germany*, Darmstadt, Institut Wohnen und Umwelt (mimeo).

Kitschelt, H., 1991, 'The 1990 German federal election and national unification', *West European Politics*, 14(4), 121-48.

Klein, P., 1975, 'Depression and policy in the thirties', *Acta Historiae Neerlandicae VII*, The Hague, Martinus Nijhoff, 123-56.

Kleinman, M., 1993, 'Large scale transfers of council housing to new landlords: is British social housing becoming more "European"?', *Housing Studies*, 8(3), 163-78.

564   Bibliography

Köhler, P. and Zacher, H. (eds), 1982, *The Evolution of Social Insurance 1881–1981*, London, Francis Pinter.

Kolodny, R,, 1976, *Searching for New Answers in Housing Management*, Trenton, State of New Jersey.

—— 1979, *Exploring New Strategies for Improving Public Housing Management*, Washington, DC, US Government Printing Office.

Konukiewitz, M. and Wollmann, H., 1983, 'Urban innovation – a daughter of crisis? From infrastructural to social needs. The West German case', Berlin, Free University (mimeo).

Korpi, W., 1980, 'Social policy and distributional conflict in the capitalist democracies: a preliminary comparative framework', *West European Politics*, 3(4), 296–316.

—— 1983, *The Democratic Class Struggle*, London, Routledge and Kegan Paul.

Kossmann, E., 1978, *The Low Countries 1780–1940*, Oxford, Oxford University Press.

Krätke, S., 1989, 'The future of social housing – problems and prospects of "social ownership"', *International Journal of Urban and Regional Research*, 13(2), 282–303.

Kreibitch, V., 1986, 'The end of social housing in the Federal Republic of Germany? The case of Hanover', *Espaces, Populations, Sociétés*, 2(1), 85–97.

—— 1991, 'Housing needs now and in the 1990s', in A. Norton and K. Novy (eds), *Low Income Housing in Britain and Germany*, London, Anglo-German Foundation, 63–82.

Kristensen, H., 1985, 'Danish post-war public housing in trouble: trends and strategies', in N. Prak and H. Priemus (eds), *Post-war Public Housing in Trouble*, Delft, Delft University Press, 147–52.

Kroes, H., Ymkers, F. and Mulder, A., 1988, *Between Owner-Occupation and Rented Sector. Housing in ten European countries*, De Bilt, NCIV.

Kuisel, R., 1981, *Capitalism and the State in Modern France*, Cambridge, Cambridge University Press.

Laboratoire du logement, 1991, *Evaluation et valorisation des programmes locaux de l'habitat*, Nancy, Laboratoire du logement.

Landes, D., 1969, *The Unbound Prometheus*, Cambridge, Cambridge University Press.

Lansley, S., 1979, *Housing and Public Policy*, Beckenham, Croom Helm.

Lansley, S., Goss, S. and Wolmar, C., 1989, *Councils in Conflict. The rise and fall of the municipal left*, Basingstoke, Macmillan.

Larkin, M., 1988, *France since the Popular Front: government and people, 1936–1986*, Oxford, Oxford University Press.

Lash, S. and Urry, J., 1987, *The End of Organised Capitalism*, Cambridge, Polity Press.

Lazere, E., Leonard, P., Dolebeare, C. and Zigas, B., 1991, *A Place to Call Home*, Washington, DC, CBPP/LIHS.

Lazin, F., 1979–80, 'Policy, perceptions, and program failure: the politics of public housing in Chicago and New York City', *Urbanism Past and Present*, 9 (Winter), 1–12.

League of Nations, Economic Intelligence Service, 1939, *Urban and Rural Housing*, Geneva, League of Nations.

Leaman, J., 1988, *The Political Economy of West Germany, 1945–1985*, Basingstoke, Macmillan.

Leather, P. and Murie, A., 1986, 'The decline in public expenditure', in P. Malpass (ed.), *The Housing Crisis*, Beckenham, Croom Helm, 24–56.

Lee, J., 1978, 'Labour in German industrialization', in P. Mathias and M. Postan (eds), *The Cambridge Economic History of Europe. Volume VII, Part I*, Cambridge, Cambridge University Press, 442–91.

Lescure, M., 1992, 'France', in C. Pooley (ed.), *Housing Strategies in Europe, 1880–1930*, Leicester, Leicester University Press, 221–39.

Letwin, W., 1989, 'American economic policy, 1865–1939', in P. Mathias and S. Pollard (eds), *The Cambridge Economic History of Europe, Volume VIII*, Cambridge, Cambridge University Press, 641–90.

Leutner, B. and Jensen, D., 1988, 'German Federal Republic', in H. Kroes, F. Ymkers and A. Mulder (eds), *Between Owner-Occupation and Rented Sector. Housing in ten European countries*, De Bilt, NCIV, 145–82.

Levitas, R., 1986, *The Ideology of the New Right*, Cambridge, Polity Press.

Lieberman, S., 1977, *The Growth of European Mixed Economies 1945–1970*, New York, Wiley.

Lijphard, A., 1975, *The Politics of Accommodation*, 2nd edition, Berkeley and London, University of California Press.

—— 1989, 'From the politics of accommodation to adversarial politics in the Netherlands: a reassessment', *West European Politics*, 12(1), 139–53.

Lipietz, A., 1987, *Mirages or Miracles. The crises of global fordism*, London, Verso.

Local Government Board, 1919, *The Housing Problem in Germany*, London, HMSO.

Lockwood, D., 1976, 'Social integration and system integration', in G. Zollschan and W. Hirsch (eds), *Social Change. Explorations, diagnoses, and conjectures*, New York, Wiley, 370–83.

Logue, J., 1982, *Socialism and Abundance. Radical socialism in the Danish welfare state*, Minneapolis, University of Minnesota Press.

London Research Centre, 1991, 'Housing update No. 4', *Roof*, 16(6), November–December.

Low Income Housing Information Service, various dates, *Low Income Housing Round-up and Annual Budget Report*, Washington, DC, LIHS.

Lubove, R., 1974, *The Progressives and the Slums*, Westport, Conn., Greenwood Press.

Lukes, S., 1979, *Power. A radical view*, London and Basingstoke, Macmillan.

Lundgaard, B., 1981, 'High density/low rise housing', *Danish Journal*, (special issue), 15–21.

Lundqvist, L., 1992, *Dislodging the Welfare State? Housing and privatisation in four European states*, Delft, Delft University Press.

Lundqvist, L., Elander, I. and Danermark, B., 1990, 'Housing policy in Sweden. Still a success story?', *International Journal of Urban and Regional Research*, 14(3), 445–67.

McCoy, D., 1977, *Coming of Age. The United States during the 1920s and 1930s*, Harmondsworth, Penguin Books.

McDonnell, T., 1957, *The Wagner Housing Act: a case study of the legislative process*, Chicago, Loyola University Press.

Machin, H. and Wright, V., 1982, 'Why Mitterrand won: the French presidential elections of April–May 1981', *West European Politics*, 5(1), 5–35.

Madsen, O. and Devisscher, C., 1934, *Reports on Housing in Denmark*, New York, Columbia Housing Orientation Study (mimeo).

Magraw, R., 1983, *France 1815–1914: the bourgeois century*, London, Fontana.

Magri, S., 1977, *Logement et reproduction de l'exploitation. Les politiques étatiques du logement en France (1947–1972)*, Paris, CSU.

—— 1988, *La rationalisation urbaine dans les projets des reformateurs en France, 1900–1925*, Paris, CSU (mimeo).

Magri, S. and Topalov, C., 1987, 'De la cité-jardin à la ville rationalisée. Un tournant du projet réformateur, 1905–1925', *Revue Française Sociologique*, XXVIII, 417–51.

—— 1988, ' "Reconstruire": l'habitat populaire au lendemain de la première guerre mondiale', *Archives Européenes Sociologiques*, XXIX, 319–70.

Maier, C., 1975, *Recasting Bourgeois Europe: stabilisation in France, Germany and Italy in the decade after world war I*, Princeton, Princeton University Press.

Malpass, P., 1986, 'The development of public housing policy in Britain', Ph.D. thesis, University of Bristol.

—— 1990, *Reshaping Housing Policy. Subsidies, rents and residualisation*, London and New York, Routledge.

Malpass, P. and Murie, A., 1987, *Housing Policy and Practice*, 2nd edition, Basingstoke, Macmillan.

Manpower Demonstration Research Corporation, 1981, *Tenant Management: findings from a three-year experiment in public housing*, Cambridge, Mass., Ballinger.

Marcuse, P., 1980, 'Housing policy and city planning: the puzzling split in the United States, 1893–1931', in G. Cherry (ed.), *Shaping an Urban World*, London, Mansell, 23–58.

—— 1982, 'Determinants of state housing policies: West Germany and the United States', in N. Fainstein and S. Fainstein (eds), *Urban Policy under Capitalism*, Beverly Hills and London, Sage Publications, 83–118.

—— 1986a, 'Housing policy and the myth of the benevolent state', in R. Bratt (ed.), *Critical Perspectives on Housing*, Philadelphia, Temple University Press, 248–63.

—— 1986b, 'The beginnings of public housing in New York', *Journal of Urban History*, 12(4), 353–90.

—— 1988, 'Divide and siphon: New York City builds on division', *City Limits*, 13(3), 8–11, 29.

—— 1990, 'United States of America', in W. van Vliet (ed.), *International Handbook of Housing Policies and Practices*, New York, Greenwood Press, 327–76.

—— 1991, *Missing Marx*, New York, Monthly Review Press.

Marklund, S. 1988, *Paradise Lost? The Nordic welfare states and the recession 1975–1985*, Lund, Archiv forlag.

Marshall, A., 1884, 'The housing of the London poor', *Contemporary Review*, XLV, 224–31.

Marshall, T., 1963, *Class, Citizenship and Social Development*, Chicago, University of Chicago Press.

Martens, M., 1990, 'Ways of owning. A study of homeownership in Europe and the USA', Ph.D. thesis, University of Essex.

Marwick, A., 1970, *Britain in the Century of Total War*, Harmondsworth, Penguin Books.

—— 1974, *War and Social Change in the Twentieth Century: a comparative study of Britain, France, Germany, Russia*, London, Macmillan.

—— 1982, *British Society since 1945*, Harmondsworth, Penguin Books.

—— 1991, *The Deluge. British society and the first world war*, 2nd edition, Basingstoke, Macmillan.

Mathias, P. and Pollard, S. (eds), 1989, *The Cambridge Economic History of Europe, Volume VIII*, Cambridge, Cambridge University Press.

Mathias, P. and Postan, M. (eds), 1978, *The Cambridge Economic History of Europe, Volume VII, Part 1*, Cambridge, Cambridge University Press.

Meehan, E., 1975, *Public Housing Policy: myth versus reality*, New Brunswick NJ, Center for Urban Policy Research.

—— 1979, *The Quality of Federal Policy Making: programmed failure in public housing*, Columbia, University of Missouri Press.

Merrett, S., 1979, *State Housing in Britain*, London, Routledge and Kegan Paul.

—— 1982, *Owner Occupation in Britain*, London, Routledge and Kegan Paul.

Meyerson, M. and Banfield, E., 1955, *Politics, Planning and the Public Interest*, Glencoe, Ill., Free Press.

Michels, R., 1911 (reissued 1962), *Political Parties*, New York, Free Press.

Middendorp, C., 1991, *Ideology in Dutch Politics*, Assen/Maastricht, Van Gorcum.

Miller, K., 1968, *Government and Politics in Denmark*, Boston, Houghton Mifflin.

Milward, A., 1987, *War, Economy and Society 1939–45*, Harmondsworth, Penguin Books.

Mingione, E., 1991, *Fragmented Societies. A sociology of economic life beyond the market paradigm*, Oxford and Cambridge, Mass., Basil Blackwell.

Ministerie van Volkshuisvesting en Ruimteligke Ordening en Milienbeheer (MVROM), 1991, *Volkshuisvesting in cijfers 1991*, 's-Gravenhage,
MVROM.

Ministry of Health, 1938, *The Management of Municipal Housing Estates*,
London, HMSO.

—— 1939, *The Operation of Housing Associations*, London, HMSO.

Ministry of Housing, 1968, *Housing in the Nordic Countries*, Copenhagen,
Ministry of Housing.

—— 1974, *Housing in Denmark*, Copenhagen, Ministry of Housing.

—— 1975, *Current Trends and Policies in the Fields of Housing, Building and
Planning*, Copenhagen, Ministry of Housing.

—— 1983, *Rent Policy in Denmark*, Copenhagen, Ministry of Housing.

—— 1984, *Financing of Housing in Denmark*, Copenhagen, Ministry of
Housing.

—— 1988, *Cooperative Housing in Denmark*, Copenhagen, Ministry of
Housing.

Ministry of Housing and Building, 1988, *The Human Settlements Situation
and Related Trends and Policies*, Copenhagen, Ministry of Housing and
Building.

—— 1990, *Non-profit Housing in Denmark*, Copenhagen, Ministry of Housing
and Building.

Ministry of Housing and Ministry of the Environment, 1979, *Current
Trends and Policies in the Fields of Housing, Building and Planning 1979*,
Copenhagen, Ministry of Housing and Ministry of the Environment.

—— 1982, *Human Settlements Situation and Related Trends and Policies*, Copenhagen, Ministry of Housing and Ministry of the Environment.

Ministry of Housing, Physical Planning and the Environment, 1991,
Statistics of Housing in the European Community, The Hague, Ministry of
Housing, Physical Planning and the Environment.

Ministry of Reconstruction and Housing, 1948, *Housing in the Netherlands: the
relevant acts and regulations from 1900 onwards*, The Hague, Ministry of
Housing and Reconstruction.

Ministry of Housing and Reconstruction, 1950, *Housing Associations in the
Netherlands*, The Hague, Netherlands Government Information Office.

Minkenberg, M., 1992, 'The New Right in Germany', *European Journal of
Political Research*, 22, 55–81.

Mishra, R., 1977, *Society and Social Policy*, London and Basingstoke,
Macmillan.

—— 1984, *The Welfare State in Crisis*, Brighton, Wheatsheaf.

Mitchell, B., 1978, *European Historical Statistics 1750–1970*, New York,
Columbia University Press.

Mitchell, J. (ed.), 1985, *Federal Housing Policy and Programmes*, Rutgers,
NJ, Center for Urban Policy Research.

Mommsen, W. (ed.), 1981, *The Emergence of the Welfare States in Britain and
Germany 1850–1950*, London, Croom Helm.

Monti, D., 1989, 'The organisational strengths and weaknesses of resident-managed public housing in the United States', *Journal of Urban Affairs*, 11(1), 39–52.

Morgan, K., 1984, *Labour in Power 1945–51*, Oxford, Clarendon Press.
—— 1990, *The People's Peace. British history 1945–1989*, Oxford, Oxford University Press.

Morison, S., Commager, H. and Leuchtenberg, G., 1980, *The Growth of the American Republic. Volume Two*, New York and Oxford, Oxford University Press.

Murie, A., 1983, *Housing and Deprivation*, London, Heinemann.

Murie, A. and Lindberg, G., 1991, *ENHR Working Group on Public and Social Rented Housing. Report of workshop held in Gothenburg February 22–25 1991* (mimeo).

Murphy, J., 1929, 'Is government aid necessary in housing financing?' (comment on paper by E. Wood), in *Housing Problems in America*, New York, National Housing Association, 301–3.

Murphy, M. and Sullivan, O., 1986, 'Unemployment, housing and household structures among young adults', *Journal of Social Policy*, 15(2), 205–22.

Nagel, A.-H., 1992, 'Communalism or cooperativism? The postwar organization of housing provision in Bergen, Norway', in L. Lundqvist (ed.), *Policy, Organization, Tenure. A comparative history of housing in small welfare states*, Oslo, Scandinavian University Press, 71–86.

Nationale Woningraad, 1990, *Social Housing: the experience of the Netherlands*, Almere, NWR.

Neue Heimat, 1972, *Unternehmensgruppe 'Neue Heimat'*, Hamburg, Neue Heimat.

Neumann, F., 1942, *Behemoth. The structure and practice of National Socialism*, London, Gollancz.

Niethammer, L., 1981, 'Some elements of the housing reform debate in nineteenth-century Europe', in B. Struve (ed.), *Modern Industrial Societies. History, policy and survival*, Beverly Hills and London, Sage Publications, 129–64.

Nora, S. and Eveno, B., 1975, *L'amélioration de l'habitat ancien*, 2 volumes, Paris, La Documentation Française.

Novy, K., 1991, 'Housing policy in West Germany: winners and losers in the deregulation battle', in A. Norton and K. Novy (eds), *Low Income Housing in Britain and Germany*, London, Anglo-German Foundation, 17–40.

O'Connor, J., 1973, *The Fiscal Crisis of the State*, New York, St Martin's Press.

Offe, C., 1984, 'Ungovernability: the renaissance of conservative theories of crisis', in C. Offe, *Contradictions of the Welfare State*, London, Hutchinson, 65–87.

Offer, A., 1981, *Property and Politics 1870–1914*, Cambridge, Cambridge University Press.

OPAC des Vosges, 1992, *Evaluation sociale. Exercise 1991*, Epinal, Office Public d'Aménagement et de Construction des Vosges.

Organization for Economic Cooperation and Development (OECD), 1981, *The Welfare State in Crisis*, Paris, OECD.

—— 1992, *OECD Economic Outlook 52*, Paris, OECD.

Padgett, S., 1987, 'The West German Social Democrats in opposition 1982–6', *West European Politics*, 10(3), 333–56.

Padgett, S. and Paterson, W., 1991, *A History of Social Democracy in Postwar Europe*, London and New York, Longman.

Papa, O., 1992, *Housing Systems in Europe. Part II. A comparative study of housing finance*, Delft, Delft University Press.

Pappi, F., 1984, 'The West German party system', *West European Politics*, 7(4), 7–26.

Parkin, F., 1975, *Class Inequality and Political Order*, London, Paladin.

—— 1979, *Marxism and Class Theory*, London, Tavistock.

Parson, D., n.d., *Seeing Red: public housing, planning and McCarthyism*, Los Angeles, UCLA School of Architecture and Urban Planning (mimeo).

—— 1982, 'The development of redevelopment: public housing and urban renewal in Los Angeles', *International Journal of Urban and Regional Research*, 6(3), 393–413.

—— 1983, 'Los Angeles' "headline-happy public housing war"', *Southern California Quarterly*, LXV(3), 251–85.

—— 1984, 'Organized labor and the housing question: public housing, suburbanization, and urban renewal', *Environment and Planning D*, 2(1), 75–86.

Paterson, W., 1981, 'The Chancellor and his party: political leadership in the Federal Republic', *West European Politics*, 4(2), 3–34.

—— 1986, 'The German Social Democratic Party', in W. Paterson and A. Thomas (eds), *The Future of Social Democracy*, Oxford, Clarendon Press, 127–52.

Pearsall, J., 1984, 'France', in M. Wynn (ed.), *Housing in Europe*, Beckenham, Croom Helm, 9–54.

Perry, D. and Watkins, A. (eds), 1977, *The Rise of the Sunbelt Cities*, Beverly Hills and London, Sage Publications.

Perry, R., 1986, 'United Kingdom', in P. Flora (ed.), *Growth to Limits. The Western European welfare states since world war II*, Berlin and London, de Gruyter, 155–240.

Peterman, W., 1989, 'Options to conventional public housing management', *Journal of Urban Affairs*, 11(1), 53–68.

Peters, B., 1993, 'Britain', in M. Hancock, D. Conradt, B. Peters, W. Safran and R. Zariski, *Politics in Western Europe*, Basingstoke, Macmillan, 5–94.

Piven, F. and Cloward, R., 1971, *Regulating the Poor*, New York, Pantheon Books.

—— 1977, *Poor People's Movements*, New York, Pantheon Books.

Polikoff, A., 1978, *Housing the Poor. The case for heroism*, Cambridge, Mass., Ballinger.

Power, A., 1987, *Property Before People – the management of twentieth century council housing*, London, Allen and Unwin.

—— 1993, *Hovels to High Rise. Social housing in Europe since 1850*, London, Routledge.

Prak, N. and Priemus, H. (eds), 1985, *Post-war Public Housing in Trouble*, Delft, Delft University Press.

—— 1992, 'The Netherlands', in C. Pooley (ed.), *Housing Strategies in Europe, 1880–1930*, Leicester, Leicester University Press, 164–89.

Pridham, G., 1981, 'The 1980 Bundestag elections: a case of "normality"', *West European Politics*, 4(2), 112–23.

Priemus, H., 1981, 'Rent and subsidy policy in the Netherlands during the seventies', *Urban Law and Policy*, 4, 299–355.

—— 1987a, 'Economic and demographic stagnation, housing and housing policy', *Housing Studies*, 2(1), 17–27.

—— 1987b, 'Housing subsidies in the Netherlands: origins of a Parliamentary enquiry', *International Journal of Urban and Regional Research*, 11(3), 417–20.

—— 1988, 'Housing and urban management in the Netherlands', *Netherlands Journal of Housing and Environmental Research*, 3(1), 61–77.

—— 1989, 'Upgrading of large-scale housing estates in the Netherlands', *Netherlands Journal of Housing and Environmental Research*, 4(2), 145–60.

—— 1990a, 'Housing policy in the Netherlands: changing priorities', *International Journal of Urban and Regional Research*, 14(4), 687–96.

—— 1990b, 'The (un)controllability of the housing allowance', *Netherlands Journal of Housing and Environmental Research*, 5(2), 69–80.

—— 1991, 'Decentralisation of housing policy: harmful and successful; the case of the Netherlands', paper presented to the Conference on Housing Policy as a Strategy for Change, Oslo, 24–7 June (mimeo).

—— 1992, 'Social rented housing in the Netherlands: recent policy changes, financial "independence" and the relations between tenants and housing associations', in A. Murie and G. Lindberg (eds), *ENHR Working Group on Public and Social Rented Housing. Report of workshop held in The Hague, April 12* (mimeo), 25–53.

Przeworski, A., 1985, *Capitalism and Social Democracy*, Cambridge, Cambridge University Press.

Rainwater, L., 1970, *Behind Ghetto Walls*, Chicago, Aldine.

Rasmussen, K., 1981, 'High-rise housing', *Danish Journal* (special issue), 22–8.

Read, J., 1976, 'Housing and social reform in France', *Transactions of the Martin Centre for Architectural and Urban Studies, University of Cambridge*, Volume 1, 297–316.

Renouvin, P., 1927, *The Forms of War Government in France*, New Haven, Yale University Press.

—— 1969, *La crise européene et la première guerre mondiale*, Paris, Presses Universitaires de France.

Revue de l'Habitat Sociale, 1978, special issue on the Barre Report, February.

Rimlinger, G., 1971, *Welfare Policy and Industrialization in Europe, America and Russia*, London and New York, Wiley.

—— 1989, 'Labour and the state on the Continent, 1800–1939', in P. Mathias and M. Postan (eds), *The Cambridge Economic History of Europe, Volume VIII*, Cambridge, Cambridge University Press, 549–606.

Ritter, G., 1986, *Social Welfare in Germany and Britain*, Leamington Spa, Berg.

Robbins, L., 1966, 'Housing achievements', in W. Wheaton, G. Milgram and M. Meyerson (eds), *Urban Housing*, New York, Free Press, 9–13.

Roberts, G., 1987, 'Weiter so, Deutschland!": the 1987 Bundestag election in West Germany', *West European Politics*, 10(3), 449–54.

Roberts, J., 1978, *Europe 1880–1945*, London and New York, Longman.

Rohe, W. and Stegman, M., 1990, *Public Housing Ownership Demonstration Assessment*, Washington, DC, US Government Printing Office.

Rosenbaum, J., 1991, 'Black pioneers – do their moves to suburbs increase economic opportunity for mothers and children?', *Housing Policy Debate*, 2(4), 1179–1214.

Rusch, A., 1931, 'The financing of buildings. Germany', in *The Social Importance of Housing Now and in the Future*, Stuttgart, Verlag Julius Hoffmann, 147.

Rying, B. (ed.), 1988, *Danish in the South and the North II*, Copenhagen, Royal Danish Ministry of Foreign Affairs.

Safran, W., 1993, 'France', in M. Hancock, D. Conradt, B. Peters, W. Safran and R. Zariski, *Politics in Western Europe*, Basingstoke, Macmillan, 95–182.

Salicath, N., 1987, *Danish Social Housing Corporations. Volume 1*, Copenhagen, KBI.

Saunders, P., 1990, *A Nation of Home Owners*, London, Unwin Hyman.

Sayer, A., 1989, 'Postfordism in question', *International Journal of Urban and Regional Research*, 13(4), 666–95.

Sayer, A. and Walker, R., 1992, *The New Social Economy*, London and Cambridge, Mass., Basil Blackwell.

Schmidt, V., 1990, 'Engineering a critical realignment of the electorate: the case of the Socialists in France', *West European Politics*, 13(2), 192–215.

Schuler-Wallner, G. and Wullkopf, U., 1991, *Housing Shortage and Homelessness in the Federal Republic of Germany*, Darmstadt, Institut Wohnen und Umwelt.

Schwan, B., 1935, *Town Planning and Housing Throughout the World*, Berlin, Verlag Ernst Wasmuth GmbH.

Scott, A., 1988, *New Industrial Spaces*, London, Pion.

Searing, H., 1971, 'Housing in Holland and the Amsterdam School', Ph.D. thesis, Yale University.

Secretaries of State for the Environment and Wales, 1987, *Housing: the government's proposals*, London, HMSO.

Semmel, B., 1960, *Imperialism and Social Reform*, London, Allen and Unwin.

Shapiro, A.-L., 1985, *Housing the Poor of Paris, 1850–1902*, Madison, University of Wisconsin Press.

Shonfield, A., 1974, *Modern Capitalism*, London and New York, Oxford University Press.

Silver, H., McDonald, J. and Ortiz, R., 1985, 'Selling public housing: the methods and motivation', *Journal of Housing*, November/December, 213–23.

Sklair, L, 1975, 'The struggle against the Housing Finance Act', in R. Miliband and J. Savile (eds), *The Socialist Register 1975*, London, Merlin Press, 250–92.

Skocpol, T. and Amenta, E., 1986, 'States and social policies', *Annual Review of Sociology*, 12, 131–57.

Skriver, P., 1981, 'The single-family house', *Danish Journal* (special issue), 8–14.

Smith, D., 1989, *North and South*, Harmondsworth, Penguin Books.

Socialt Tidsskrift (ed.), 1947, *Social Denmark*, Copenhagen, Socialt Tidsskrift.

Sontheimer, K., 1972, *The Government and Politics of West Germany*, London, Hutchinson.

Stébé, J.-M., 1993, 'L'opération H. V. S. de Woippy-Saint-Eloy dans l'agglomération de Metz', *Espaces et Sociétés*, 72, 49–64.

Stedman Jones, G., 1971, *Outcast London*, Oxford, Clarendon Press.

Stegman, M., 1988, *The Role of Public Housing in a Revitalized National Housing Policy*, Cambridge, Mass., MIT.

—— 1990, 'A Bush/Kemp report card', *Journal of Housing*, September/October, 237–46.

Sternlieb, G. and Listokin, D., 1987, 'A review of national housing policy', in P. Salins (ed.), *Housing America's Poor*, Chapel Hill and London, University of North Carolina Press, 14–44.

Stewart, J. and Stoker, G. (eds), 1989, *The Future of Local Government*, Basingstoke, Macmillan.

Straus, N., 1944, *The Seven Myths of Housing*, New York, Alfred A. Knopf.

Struyk, R., 1980, *A New System for Public Housing*, Washington, DC, The Urban Institute.

Struyk, R. and Bendick, M. (eds), 1981, *Housing Vouchers for the Poor: lessons from a national experiment*, Washington, DC, The Urban Institute.

Struyk, R., Mayer, N. and Tuccillo, J., 1983, *Federal Housing Policy at President Reagan's Midterm*, Washington, DC, The Urban Institute.

Sutcliffe, A., 1981, *Towards the Planned City*, Oxford, Basil Blackwell.

Svensson, O., 1988, *Planning of Low-rise Urban Housing Areas*, Horsholm, SBI.

Svensson, P., 1974, 'Support for the Danish Social Democratic Party 1924–39 – growth and response', in *Scandinavian Political Studies Volume 9*, Beverly Hills and London, Sage Publications.

Swenarton, M., 1981, *Homes Fit for Heroes*, London, Heinemann.

Szelenyi, I., 1983, *Urban Inequalities under State Socialism*, Oxford, Oxford University Press.

—— 1987, 'Housing inequalities and occupational segregation in state socialist cities', *International Journal of Urban and Regional Research*, 11(1), 1-8.

Szelenyi, I. and Manchin, R., 1987, 'Social policy under state socialism: market redistribution and social inequalities in East European socialist societies', in M. Rein, G. Esping-Andersen and L. Rainwater (eds), *Stagnation and Renewal in Social Policy*, Armonk and London, M. E. Sharpe, 102-39.

Tarn, J., 1973, *Five Percent Philanthropy*, London, Cambridge University Press.

Taylor, A., 1965, *English History 1914-1945*, Oxford, Clarendon Press.

Taylor-Gooby, P. and Dale, A., 1981, *Social Theory and Social Welfare*, London, Edward Arnold.

Teuteberg, H. and Wischermann, C., 1992, 'Germany', in C. Pooley (ed.), *Housing Strategies in Europe 1880-1930*, Leicester, Leicester University Press, 240-67.

The Building Centre Committee, 1936, *Housing. A European survey*, London, Rolls House Publishing Co.

The Labour Party, 1934, *Up With the Houses! Down With the Slums!*, London, The Labour Party.

The President's Commission on Housing, 1982, *Report*, Washington, DC, US Government Printing Office.

Thomas, A., 1986, 'Social democracy in Scandinavia: can dominance be regained?', in W. Paterson and A. Thomas (eds), *The Future of Social Democracy*, Oxford, Clarendon Press, 172-222.

Thomas, A. D., 1986, *Housing and Urban Renewal*, London, Allen and Unwin.

Tilton, T., 1990, *The Political Theory of Swedish Social Democracy*, Oxford, Clarendon Press.

Titmuss, R., 1958, 'The social division of welfare', in R. Titmuss, *Essays on 'the Welfare State'*, London, Allen and Unwin, 34-55.

Tommel, I., 1992, 'Decentralisation of regional development policy in the Netherlands – a new type of state intervention?', *West European Politics*, 15(2), 107-25.

Topalov, C., 1985, 'Social policies from below. A call for comparative historical studies', *International Journal of Urban and Regional Research*, 9(2), 254-71.

—— 1987, *Le logement en France. Histoire d'une marchandise impossible*, Paris, Presses de la Fédération Nationale des Sciences Politiques.

—— 1988, *Naissance de l'urbanisme moderne et réforme de l'habitat populaire aux Etats-Unis 1900-1940*, Paris, CSU.

—— 1990a, 'Scientific urban planning and the ordering of daily life. The first "war housing" experiments in the United States, 1917-1919', *Journal of Urban History*, 17(1), 14-45.

—— 1990b, 'From the "social question" to "urban problems": reformers and the working classes at the turn of the twentieth century', *International Social Science Journal*, 125, 319-36.

Torgerson, U., 1987, 'Housing: the wobbly pillar under the welfare state', in B. Turner, J. Kemeny and L. Lundqvist (eds), *Between State and Market: housing in the post-industrial era*, Stockholm, Almqvist and Wiksell, 116–26.

Tosics, I., 1987, 'Privatization in housing policy: the case of the western countries and that of Hungary', *International Journal of Urban and Regional Research*, 11(1), 61–78.

—— 1988, 'Inequalities in east European cities', *International Journal of Urban and Regional Research*, 12(1), 133–6.

Ulbrich, R. and Wullkopf, n.d., *Housing in the Federal Republic of Germany*, Darmstadt, Institut Wohnen und Umwelt (mimeo).

Umrath, H., 1950, *European Labour Movement and Housing*, Brussels, International Confederation of Trade Unions.

UN Economic Commission for Europe, 1949, *The European Housing Problem. A preliminary review*, Geneva, United Nations (mimeo).

—— 1952, *Methods and Techniques of Financing Housing in Europe*, Geneva, United Nations (mimeo).

—— 1954, *European Housing Progress and Policies in 1953*, Geneva, United Nations.

—— 1958, *Financing of Housing in Europe*, Geneva, United Nations.

—— 1973, *Financing of Housing*, proceedings of the seminar organized by the Committee on Housing, Building and Planning of the ECE, Geneva, 20–4 August, Geneva, United Nations (mimeo).

—— 1976a, *Human Settlements in Europe. Post-war trends and policies*, New York, United Nations.

—— 1976b, *Economic Survey of Europe in 1975*, New York, United Nations.

—— 1980, *Major Trends in Housing Policy in ECE Countries*, New York, United Nations.

—— 1981, *Economic Survey of Europe in 1980*, New York, United Nations.

—— 1983, *Economic Survey of Europe in 1982*, New York, United Nations.

—— 1985, *Economic Survey of Europe in 1984–5*, New York, United Nations.

—— 1990, *Economic Survey of Europe in 1989–90*, New York, United Nations.

US Bureau of Labor Statistics, 1914, *Bulletin 158*, Washington, DC, US Government Printing Office.

US Bureau of the Census, 1991, *Statistical Abstract of the United States: 1991*, Washington, DC, US Government Printing Office.

US Commissioner for Labor, 1895, *The Housing of Working People*, Washington, DC, US Government Printing Office.

US Department of Commerce, Bureau of the Census, 1965, *Housing Construction Statistics 1889 to 1964*, Washington, DC, US Government Printing Office.

US Department of Housing and Urban Development, 1976, *Housing in the Seventies. Working papers volume 1*, Washington, DC, US Government Printing Office.

—— 1992a, *Characteristics of HUD-assisted Renters and their Units in 1989*, Washington, DC, US Government Printing Office.

—— 1992b, *Family Self-sufficiency*, Washington, DC, US Government Printing Office.

—— 1992c, *Opportunity and Empowerment Act of 1992*, Washington, DC, HUD.

van der Flier, M., 1923, *War Finances in the Netherlands up to 1918*, Oxford, Clarendon Press.

van der Kaa, H., 1935, *La question de l'habitation urbaine aux Pays-Bas*, Geneva, Société des Nations.

van der Schaar, J., 1979, *Sektorindeling en woningmarktprocessen*, The Hague, NIROV.

—— 1982, *Social and Owner Occupied Housing in the Netherlands. Consultant's report*, Delft, University of Delft (mimeo).

van der Wee, H., 1987, *Prosperity and Upheaval. The world economy 1945–1980*, Harmondsworth, Penguin Books.

van Ellemeet, M., 1935, 'The Netherlands. Housing', in B. Schwan (ed.), *Town Planning and Housing Throughout the World*, Berlin, Verlag Ernst Wasmuth GmbH, 267–71.

van Harten, T., 1991, 'Financing council housing', paper presented to the Prague symposium, 21–6 October (mimeo).

van Kempen, E., 1986, 'High-rise housing estates and the concentration of poverty', *Netherlands Journal of Housing and Environmental Research*, 1(1), 5–26.

van Kersbergen, K. and Becker, U., 1988, 'The Netherlands: a passive social democratic welfare state in a Christian Democratic ruled society', *Journal of Social Policy*, 17(4), 477–99.

van Mierlo, H., 1986, 'Depillarisation and the decline of consociationalism in the Netherlands, 1970–85', *West European Politics*, 9(1), 97–119.

van Weesep, J., 1981, 'Dutch housing policies – problems and prospects', paper presented to the European workshop 'Crisis of Housing Policy', Hamburg, 30 October–1 November (mimeo).

—— 1982, *Production and Allocation of Housing: the case of the Netherlands*, Amsterdam, Vrije Universiteit.

van Weesep, J. and van Kempen, R., 1992, *Low Income and Housing in the Dutch Welfare State*, Utrecht, University of Utrecht (mimeo).

Veiller, L., 1914, 'Housing reform through legislation', in C. Aronovici (ed.), *Housing and Town Planning*, Philadelphia, American Academy of Political and Social Science, 68–77.

—— 1920, 'Government housing: the example of England', *Proceedings of the Eighth National Conference on Housing*, 119–40.

Vergara, C., 1989, 'Hell in a very tall place', *Atlantic Monthly*, September, 72–8.

Vestergaard, H., 1982, *Social and Owner Occupied Housing in Denmark. Consultant's report*, Horsholm, Danish Building Research Institute (mimeo).

—— 1990, *Upgrading of Large Housing Estates: an evaluation of the results*, Horsholm, Danish Building Research Institute (mimeo).

—— 1991, *Revitalization of Danish Post-war Public Housing in Crisis – background, programme scope and evaluation of effects*, Horsholm, Danish Building Research Institute (mimeo).

—— 1992, 'The changing fate of social housing in a small welfare state: the Danish Case', in L. Lundqvist (ed.), *Policy, Organization, Tenure. A comparative history of housing in small welfare states*, Oslo, Scandinavian University Press, 36–46.

von Einem, E., 1981, *National Urban Policy: the case of West Germany*, Berlin, Institut für Stadtforschung (mimeo).

Wacquant, L., 1992, 'Redrawing the urban color line: the state of the ghetto in the 1980s', in C. Calhoun and G. Ritzer (eds), *Social Problems*, New York, McGraw-Hill.

Walsh, A., 1970, 'Is public housing heading for a fiscal crisis?', in M. Stegman (ed.), *Housing and Economics. The American dilemma*, Cambridge, Mass., MIT Press, 279–89.

Warner, S., 1972, *The Urban Wilderness*, New York, Harper and Row.

Weber, A., 1969, *The Growth of Cities in the Nineteenth Century*, New York, Greenwood Press.

Weir, M., Orloff, A. and Skocpol, T., 1988, *The Politics of Social Policy in the United States*, Princeton, Princeton University Press.

Westergaard, H. (ed.), 1930, *Sweden, Norway, Denmark and Iceland in the World War*, New Haven, Yale University Press.

Westle, B. and Niedermayer, O., 1992, 'Contemporary right-wing extremism in Germany', *European Journal of Political Research*, 22, 83–100.

Wilding, P., 1972, 'Towards exchequer subsidies for housing 1906–1914', *Social and Economic Administration*, 6(1), 3–18.

Wilensky, H., 1975, *The Welfare State and Equality*, Berkeley, University of California Press.

—— 1991, 'Leftism, Catholicism, and democratic corporatism: the role of political parties in recent welfare state developments', in P. Flora and A. Heidenheimer (eds), *The Development of Welfare States in Europe and America*, New Brunswick and London, Transaction Books, 345–82.

Wilensky, H. and Lebeaux, C., 1958, *Industrial Society and Social Welfare*, New York, Russell Sage Foundation.

Willmott, P. and Murie, A., 1988, *Polarization and Social Housing. The British and French experience*, London, Policy Studies Institute.

Wilson, J. (ed.), 1966, *Urban Renewal: the record and the controversy*, Cambridge, Mass., MIT Press.

Winter, G., 1979, 'Housing in West Germany: legal instruments and economic structure', in M. Partington and J. Jowell (eds), *Welfare Law and Policy*, London, Francis Pinter, 195–222.

Winter, J., 1986, *The Great War and the British People*, Cambridge, Mass., Harvard University Press.

Wohl, A., 1977, *The Eternal Slum*, London, Edward Arnold.

Wolinetz, S., 1989, 'Socio-economic bargaining in the Netherlands: redefining the post-war policy coalition', *West European Politics*, 12(1), 79–98.

—— 1990, 'The Dutch election of 1989: return to the centre–left', *West European Politics*, 13(2), 280–6.

Wollmann, H., 1986, 'Housing policy in West Germany – between state intervention and the market', in K. von Beyme (ed.), *Policy and Politics in the Federal Republic of Germany*, Aldershot, Gower, 132–55.

Wood, E., 1919, *The Housing of the Unskilled Wage Earner: America's next problem*, New York, Macmillan.

—— 1934, 'A century of the housing problem', *Law and Contemporary Problems*, 1(1), 137–47.

Wright, G., 1981, *Building the American Dream*, New York, Pantheon.

Wright, V., 1989, *The Government and Politics of France*, 3rd edition, London, Hutchinson.

Young, K. and Kramer, J., 1978, *Strategy and Conflict in Metropolitan Housing*, London, Heinemann.

Young, S., 1986, 'The nature of privatization in Britain, 1979–85', *West European Politics*, 9(2), 235–52.

Zeldin, T., 1975, *France, 1848–1945. Volume I. Ambition, love and politics*, Oxford, Clarendon Press.

Index